The Journals of the Lewis and Clark Expedition, Volume 2

August 30, 1803–August 24, 1804

Sponsored by the Center for
Great Plains Studies,
University of Nebraska–Lincoln,
and the American
Philosophical Society, Philadelphia

A Project of the Center for

Great Plains Studies,

University of Nebraska–Lincoln

Gary E. Moulton, Editor

Thomas W. Dunlay, Assistant Editor

The Journals of the Lewis & Clark Expedition

August 30, 1803–August 24, 1804

University of Nebraska Press

Lincoln and London

The preparation and publication of this volume
were assisted by grants from
the National Endowment for the Humanities.

The paper in this book meets the minimum
requirements of American National Standard for
Information Sciences—Permanence of Paper for
Printed Library Materials, ANSI Z39.48-1984.

Library of Congress Cataloging in Publication Data

(Revised for vol.2)   Main entry under title:
The Journals of the Lewis and Clark expedition.

Includes bibliographical references and index.
Contents: v.1. Atlas of the Lewis & Clark
expedition—v.2. August 30, 1803-August 24, 1804.
1. Lewis and Clark expedition (1804-1806)—Collected
works.   2. West (U.S.)—Description and travel —
To 1848—Collected works.   3. United States—Exploring
expeditions—Collected works.   4. Lewis, Meriwether,
1774-1809.   5. Clark, William, 1770-1838.   I. Lewis,
Meriwether, 1774-1809.   II. Clark, William, 1770-1838.
F592.4   1983   917.8'42   82-8510
ISBN 0-8032-2861-9 (v.1)   ISBN 0-8032-2869-4 (v.2)

Contents

Preface

An entirely new and complete edition of the journals of the Lewis and Clark expedition has been a hope of scholars and enthusiasts for many years. Realizing the deficiencies and incompleteness of the volumes done by Reuben Gold Thwaites in 1904–5, Donald Jackson may have been the first to formally declare the need. In an address to the Centennial Conference of the Missouri Historical Society in March 1967, he pointed out what had been apparent for some time: using the multiple published editions of the journals was becoming increasingly difficult, and "some kind of standard edition" was needed. But, his clarion call for action went unheeded for nearly a decade.

In 1977, an article recommending reissuing several important historical travel accounts in a modern format, among them Lewis and Clark's epic work, came to the attention of the University of Nebraska Press. Excited about the possibilities for a new edition, members of the press set out to determine if a wider level of interest for such a project existed. They turned first to an organization newly formed at the University of Nebraska, the Center for Great Plains Studies. The center was developed in 1976 out of a desire of several university professors to take an interdisciplinary approach to studying the Great Plains region of North America. The activities of the center are directed toward exploring all aspects of the Great Plains environment: the land, the people, the wildlife, the institutions, the economy, and the cultures of the Great Plains. The board of directors for the center were attracted from the start to the idea of sponsoring a new edition of the journals. Lewis and Clark were the first Americans to cross and describe the Great Plains, and much of the territory that the Corps of Discovery were assigned to examine lies within the region. Moreover, through the center a large number of scholars would be available for consultation with the proposed project. The board of directors were ready to accept sponsorship of the project, and members of the press were encouraging about the prospects of publication.

The Center for Great Plains Studies then moved to discover the scope and dimensions of such a project. Donald Jackson, serving as a consultant sought the cooperation of institutions that hold original Lewis and Clark materials and ascertained available financial support. His work was a success throughout. Not only did all the institutions with Lewis and Clark materials agree to share their journals and manuscripts with the anticipated project, but the principal holding institution, the American Philosophical Society, agreed to cosponsor the project should it materialize. In addition, Jackson wrote the first draft of a proposal to be submitted to the National Endowment for the Humanities, which became the basis for the final and successful proposal granted by NEH in July 1980.

By mid-1979, the project to publish a completely reedited version of the journals was under way under the present editor. The edition is cosponsored by the Center for Great Plains Studies of the University of Nebraska and by the American Philosophical Society, with the encouragement and cooperation of all repositories of Lewis and Clark manuscripts. The National Endowment for the Humanities, a principal funding agency for editorial projects, has continued its financial support, and the National Historical Publications and Records Commission has also endorsed the project.

The new edition will number eleven volumes, which will include an atlas of maps from the expedition; the journals of Lewis, Clark, Charles Floyd, John Ordway, Patrick Gass, and Joseph Whitehouse (all the extant journals associated with the expedition); and a volume of the expedition's natural history materials, including reproductions of the herbarium sheets that Lewis gathered on the trip, now at the Academy of Natural Sciences, Philadelphia. The first volume of the new edition, *Atlas of the Lewis and Clark Expedition*, was published in 1983. The maps were published first so that they could be used as a resource and reference tool for succeeding volumes. The present volume is the first of the nine journal volumes to follow.

It is a pleasure to acknowledge the numerous people who have been so helpful during the work on the journals of Lewis and Clark. First, recognition should go to the able and considerate workers at the institutions that hold the Lewis and Clark manuscripts.

> Academy of Natural Sciences, Philadelphia
>   A. E. Schuyler
> American Philosophical Society, Philadelphia
>   Whitfield J. Bell, Jr., Beth Carroll-Horrocks, Stephen Catlett, Murphy D. Smith
> Beinecke Rare Book Library, Yale University, New Haven, Connecticut
>   Archibald Hanna, George A. Miles
> Missouri Historical Society, St. Louis
>   Beverly D. Bishop, Anthony R. Crawford, Frances H. Stadler
> Newberry Library, Chicago
>   John Aubrey, Herbert T. Hoover

State Historical Society of Missouri, Columbia
    Lynn Wolf Gentzler
State Historical Society of Wisconsin, Madison
    Josephine L. Harper

Numerous scholars in diverse fields have helped clarify the variety of scientific endeavors in which the captains were engaged. Those experts gave much in time and advice, most with little hope of reward other than the advancement of scholarship to which they are so dedicated. Not listed are persons whose published works were so important. Those debts are acknowledged in the bibliography.

Anthropology, ethnology, linguistics:
    Warren Caldwell, University of Nebraska-Lincoln
    Raymond J. DeMallie, Indiana University
    Ives Goddard III, Smithsonian Institution
    James B. Griffin, University of Michigan
    John E. Koontz, University of Colorado
    John Ludwickson, Nebraska State Historical Society
    Kenneth Miner, University of Kansas
    Douglas R. Parks, Indiana University
    Robert L. Rankin, University of Kansas
    Mildred Mott Wedel, Smithsonian Institution
    Waldo R. Wedel, Smithsonian Institution
Archaeology:
    Donald L. Johnson, University of Illinois, Champaign-Urbana
    Thomas D. Thiessen, Midwest Archeological Center, Lincoln
    W. Raymond Wood, University of Missouri-Columbia
Astronomical instruments:
    Silvio A. Bedini, Smithsonian Institution
Botany:
    A. T. Harrison, University of Nebraska-Lincoln
    Curtis M. Twedt, Nebraska Game and Parks Commission
    Kathleen Young, Nebraska State Museum, Lincoln
Geology:
    T. Mylan Stout, University of Nebraska-Lincoln
    Michael R. Voorhis, University of Nebraska-Lincoln
    William Wayne, University of Nebraska-Lincoln
Miscellaneous subjects:
    John L. Allen, University of Connecticut (geography, cartography)
    Patrice Berger, University of Nebraska-Lincoln (French)
    Paul R. Cutright, Jenkintown, Pennsylvania (history, natural history)

William E. Foley, Central Missouri State University (history)
Donald Jackson, Colorado Springs (history, editing)
Joseph Porter, Joslyn Art Museum, Omaha (history, ethnology)
James P. Ronda, Youngstown State University (history, ethnology)
Zoology:
James Ducy, Omaha (birds)
Patricia Freeman, University of Nebraska-Lincoln (mammals)
Virginia C. Holmgren, Portland, Oregon (birds)
Paul A. Johnsgard, University of Nebraska-Lincoln (birds)
John D. Lynch, University of Nebraska-Lincoln (fishes)

Persons who have supported the project out of devotion to the expedition are legion. Words of encouragement, financial help, and constant good will from them have made this project more pleasant and its success more sure. One organization, the Lewis and Clark Trail Heritage Foundation, has been exemplary in its encouragement, but space does not allow naming its nearly eight hundred members.

Irving W. Anderson
Hazel Bain
Robert B. Betts
Chanler C. Biggs
Harold B. and Jane Billian
Robert C. Carriker
Marilyn Clark
E. G. Chuinard
Dale Davidson
Clarence H. Decker
V. Strode and Beverly Hinds
Helen Hetrick
Paul L. Hedren
Mildred R. Goosman

Robert E. and Ruth Lange
Arlen J. Large
Robert L. and Gladys Levis
Margaret Norris
Bob Saindon
William P. Sherman
Bob and Idena Singer
Everett L. Sparks
Gail M. and Ellie Stensland
Bunky Sullivan
Robert Taylor
Ralph S. Thompson
Edrie L. Vinson
L. Edwin Wang
Wilbur and Marty Werner

Also helpful were members of the Center for Great Plains Studies and those associated with the project more directly:

Rosemary Bergstrom, Brian W. Blouet, Rosalind Carr,
Frederick C. Luebke, Virginia J. Maca

Introduction

The Journals of the Lewis and Clark Expedition

History of the Expedition

The roots of the expedition of Meriwether Lewis and William Clark were already lengthy by the time of the Louisiana Purchase in April 1803. Thomas Jefferson's curiosity about the West was lifelong, sustained by his broad scientific interests and his hopes and dreams for the future of the United States. For at least twenty years before he launched Lewis and Clark across two thousand miles into immortality, Jefferson had planned for a transcontinental expedition starting up the Missouri River. In 1783, while serving in Congress, he asked the frontier Revolutionary War hero George Rogers Clark (the older brother of William) to consider leading a privately sponsored expedition to explore the West. Then, as later, he feared that Britain might secure a foothold west of the Mississippi (then the western boundary of the United States) and forestall American expansion. George Rogers Clark declined the offer.[1]

A few years later, while minister to France, Jefferson encouraged the hopes of John Ledyard, an American veteran of Captain James Cook's third voyage to the Pacific. Ledyard planned to travel eastward across Siberia, secure passage on a ship to some point on the western coast of North America, and then strike out alone across the continent. It was a far-fetched project at best, and the suspicious Russians frustrated it by expelling Ledyard from their country.[2]

In 1792 Jefferson, then secretary of state under Washington, and various friends and associates in the American Philosophical Society in Philadelphia tried to interest Dr. Moses Marshall, a physician and botanist from Philadelphia, in undertaking an expedition up the Missouri. They offered a reward of a thousand guineas to Marshall if he could provide proof of having reached the "South Sea," but apparently nothing came of the suggestion.[3]

The following year, Jefferson sponsored a more promising effort by André Michaux, a French botanist. Acting for the American Philosophical Society, Jefferson sent Michaux west to "find the shortest & most convenient route of communication between the U. S. & the Pacific ocean, within the temperate latitudes, & to learn such particulars as can be obtained of the country through which it passes, it's productions, inhabitants & other interesting circumstances." Avoiding Spanish authorities who might try to stop him, Michaux was to ascend the Missouri and, from its headwaters, locate the easiest route to some major stream flowing into the Pacific. Here already was the basic outline of the Lewis and Clark exploration. To appreciate how ambitious the scheme was it must be remembered that most of the territory Michaux was to traverse and the people who inhabited it were either little known or wholly unknown to Europeans. Moreover, Jefferson had every reason to believe that the Spanish government, which claimed jurisdiction over Louisiana, would be hostile to the project. Only ten years later Jefferson could provide Lewis and Clark with far more information about the lower Missouri and the Pacific Coast than he was able to give Michaux. In any event, Michaux became involved in international intrigues and never crossed the Mississippi.[4]

Jefferson made no further serious attempt to promote the exploration of the trans-Mississippi West until he became president in 1801; then, circumstances made the project seem not only feasible but also vitally necessary. As president, Jefferson was in a better position to launch such an expedition and to insure adequate financing; in the same year, world political conditions seemed, more than ever, to threaten the preemption of the West by some other nation.

By the time Jefferson entered the White House, there had been several significant advances in knowledge of the country beyond the Mississippi. In 1792, the American sea-going trader Captain Robert Gray had discovered and named the Columbia River. In the same year, Captain George Vancouver of the British Navy had made a thorough survey of the northwest coast, sending one of his officers about one hundred miles up the great river. In the same decade, fur traders from St. Louis, acting under the authority of the Spanish government, moved up the Missouri as far as the villages of the Mandans in present North Dakota. John Thomas Evans, who reached the Mandans in 1796, received instructions from his employer, James Mackay, that seem to anticipate Jefferson's instructions to Lewis and Clark. Evans was asked to ascend the Missouri to its headwaters, inquire of the Indians about a river flowing "toward the setting sun," and descend this stream to the Pacific. Along the way he was to collect specimens of animals and plants and to be "very accurate in his observations concerning the nations." Evans in fact got no farther than the Mandans, where he found British traders extending their commercial network from Canada. Evans's detailed maps of the Missouri from present northeast Nebraska to the Mandan villages were eventually of great assistance to Lewis and Clark.[5]

The catalyst, however, of Jefferson's decision to launch the expedition was apparently the publication of Alexander Mackenzie's *Voyages from Montreal . . . through the Continent of North America, to the Frozen and Pacific Oceans* (London, 1801); therein Mackenzie, a partner in the North West Company of Canada, described his 1789 trip to the Arctic Ocean and his 1792–93 journey across the Rockies to the coast of present British Columbia. He had made the first crossing of the continent north of Mexico and had discovered what he took to be the upper reaches of the Columbia. Having proved that such a crossing was possible, he urged in his book that Britain develop the transcontinental route, in order to secure the fur trade and open commerce with Asia. Here again was the danger that Jefferson had long feared—British preemption of the far West.[6]

Many historians have seen Jefferson's appointment of Meriwether Lewis as his private secretary in 1801 as evidence that he intended from the first to send the young man on a western expedition, especially since Lewis's knowledge of the "western country" was a factor in Jefferson's choice. Historian Donald Jackson argues that there is no proof of such an intention and suggests that Jefferson may have wished to make use of Lewis's knowledge of the army to weed out officers with Federalist leanings. Although Jefferson had stated the contrary, Lewis's frontier experience, especially with Indians, was meager. One should not forget, however, that Lewis had volunteered in 1793 for the expedition for which Michaux was actually chosen and that in 1805 he would write of the transcontinental exploration as "a darling project of mine for the last ten years."[7]

In any case, it was Lewis that Jefferson now selected to lead the enterprise on which he had definitely determined by the end of 1802. Born in Virginia in 1774, Lewis had served as an army officer in the Northwest Territory for several years and had some experience with wilderness travel. His formal education was slight by present standards, but he was well read and had the scientific interests that characterized so many of Jefferson's friends. What Jefferson really wanted was "a person who to courage, prudence, habits & health adapted to the woods, & some familiarity with the Indian character, joins a perfect knoledge of botany, natural history, mineralogy & astronomy." His knowledge of Lewis and his acquaintance with the American scientific community told him that Lewis was as close to such a paragon as he could realistically hope to find.[8]

The Louisiana Purchase did not prompt the expedition to explore west of the Mississippi; Lewis was already on his way across the Appalachians in the summer of 1803 when Jefferson sent him definite word of the diplomatic windfall that had occurred in Paris the previous April. Jefferson's hopes had always pointed toward eventual American penetration of the lands beyond the Mississippi, but the French decision to sell this vast territory presented the United States with an opportunity of which the president could only have dreamed for the distant future. Now an expedition became all the more important as an inspection and an assertion of sovereignty over the new empire.[9]

Jefferson and Lewis agreed that there must be a second-in-command competent to carry on if something were to happen to the commander; Lewis's choice was his old army friend William Clark. Four years older than Lewis, he had also served several years in the army on the frontier and had been Lewis's immediate superior for a time. After resigning his captain's commission in 1796, he had engaged in family business in Kentucky and Indiana. Clark had visited Lewis in Washington and had made Jefferson's acquaintance. In accepting Lewis's offer, Clark wrote, "The enterprise &c. is Such as I have long anticipated"; his words suggest that the two friends had discussed the possibility of such an expedition, and that Jefferson may have earlier given them both some hint of his plans.[10]

Lewis and Clark have become inseparable in history, and some historians, in order to distinguish them, have emphasized the contrasts in their personalities. Lewis is stereotyped as the moody, sensitive intellectual, Clark as the tough, pragmatic, barely literate frontiersman. The differences existed, but they may have been exaggerated. Lewis quite adequately demonstrated his mastery of wilderness craft on his great journey, and the expedition did not suffer as a result of Lewis's "hypochondriac affections," which even Jefferson noted in his protégé. If Clark's spelling was versatile and his grammar rough hewn—in a day when the rules were less firmly established than today—Lewis was not altogether a model in those respects, in spite of his more elegant literary style. Both were largely self-educated by today's standards. Clark lacked polish, but neither his vocabulary nor his ideas were those of a backwoodsman.[11]

Jefferson's conception of the expedition encompassed far more than geographic discovery, important as that was. It would be arbitrary to distinguish between his "practical" and "scientific" goals, for Jefferson, a true son of the Enlightenment, believed all knowledge to be of some benefit. He characterized the enterprise as "purely literary"—devoted to gathering and disseminating scientific knowledge—in sounding out the Spanish minister on his government's possible reaction to the expedition; the minister was understandably skeptical. After the Louisiana Purchase, of course, the practical aspect of the expedition became more immediately relevant.[12]

Jefferson's final instructions of June 1803, formidable in their scope even to the modern reader, reflect the broad range of interests of the third president. In a day of less rigid academic specialization when the distinction between professional and amateur was not fixed, Jefferson could be not only a political leader but president of the American Philosophical Society, then the principal group promoting scientific endeavor in the United States. Jefferson himself was per-

4

haps the nation's leading expert on the geography of the trans-Mississippi West, and geographic discovery was, of course, one of his principal purposes for the expedition. Lewis and Clark made the last search up the Missouri for the fabled Northwest Passage; they would find that previous conceptions of a single ridge of mountains or a "pyramidal height of land," offering an easy portage from the headwaters of the Missouri to those of the Columbia, were illusions. It remained for Lewis and Clark to discover that the Rockies were a complex series of ranges hundreds of miles wide. Clark's great map of the West, published in 1814, would in itself have justified the expedition.[13]

Jefferson had much more in mind, however. The captains were to open a highway for the American fur trade, to win over the Indians from Spanish or British influence, and to lay the foundation for what Jefferson hoped would be a carefully regulated trade and intercourse with the Indians that would avoid some of the evils of unrestrained competition and interracial conflict so common in American experience. Further, they were to observe and record the whole range of natural history and ethnology of the area and the possible resources for future settlers. Jefferson expected a great deal of two infantry officers, but they met the challenge.[14]

Lewis, a student of plants and animals since boyhood, made significant additions to zoological and botanical knowledge, providing the first scientific descriptions of many new species. Only in recent decades have his contributions been fully appreciated. The captains also made the first attempt at a systematic record of the meteorology of the West and less successfully attempted to determine the latitude and longitude of significant geographical points.[15]

Jefferson's instructions also reflected his lifelong interest in ethnology, and in carrying them out Lewis and Clark displayed an objectivity and tolerance rare in their generation. Lacking the conceptual tools of the modern anthropologist, they nonetheless provided the first general survey of the life and material culture of the village Indians of the Missouri, the Rocky Mountain tribes, and those of the Northwest Coast. They also achieved, on the whole, a record for peaceful cooperation with the Indians that few of their predecessors or successors could equal.[16]

In the spring of 1803 Lewis traveled to Philadelphia to purchase supplies for the expedition and to complete training in astronomy, natural history, health, and ethnology by consulting with the leading lights of the American Philosophical Society, all friends of Jefferson. At Lancaster, Pennsylvania, he spent three weeks with Andrew Ellicott, mathematician and astronomer, who instructed him in the technique of determining latitude and longitude and advised him on the purchase of navigational instruments. After his arrival in Philadelphia in early May, Lewis received further instruction and advice in the same subjects from Robert Patterson, Irish-born professor of mathematics at the University of Pennsylvania. Benjamin Rush, the most eminent American physician of the day, advised him on the purchase of medicines and on general health care, besides providing him with a questionnaire for use in his ethnological inquiries. Benjamin Smith Barton, professor of natural history and botany and author of the first textbook on botany written in the United States, advised Lewis in a field in which the young Virginian was already much interested, as did Caspar Wistar, professor of anatomy and the leading American authority on fossils.[17]

In addition to his studies, Lewis roamed the business establishments of the city, purchasing the extensive and varied collection of items needed for the expedition. Mosquito netting, ink powder, thermometers, Indian trade beads, waterproof lead canisters for gunpowder, cooking utensils, and clothing all went to make up the 3,500 pounds of equipment to be carried across the continent.[18]

Having prepared himself intellectually and having secured as much equipment as he could in the East, Lewis crossed the Appalachians in the summer of 1803, supervised the construction of his keelboat in Pittsburgh, and started down the Ohio on August 31. He picked up Clark at Clarksville, Indiana, and gathered the first of their recruits. Both leaders were commissioned officers in the army, and most of their men were enlisted in the army, some signed up especially for the trip, others already in the service and detailed for the expedition by their commanding officers. Lewis expected that Clark would hold the same captain's rank as he, but red tape in the Department of War resulted in Clark's receiving only a second lieutenant's commission. They concealed this embarrassing fact from the men, and Clark is always "Capt. C." in Lewis's journals. There was no disturbance in their remarkably harmonious relationship, and Lewis apparently treated Clark as "equal in every point of view," a partner whose abilities were complementary to his own. Nonetheless the situation irked Clark, who had been a captain in his earlier period of service and Lewis's superior officer. After the expedition's return he sent the commission back to the secretary of war as soon as possible, remarking that it had served its purpose, and in later years he concealed his lower official status from all but a few.[19]

A long winter's stay across from St. Louis, at River Dubois in Illinois, waiting for spring and for the transfer of Louisiana to the United States, enabled the captains to gather their men, evaluate and discipline them, and collect some additional information—notably the personal advice of James Mackay and the Missouri River maps of John Evans (*Atlas* maps 7–12). By the spring of 1804 they had eliminated a few less desirable recruits, had given the rest some idea of what was expected of them, and were ready to begin the great adventure.

Any government enterprise of comparable importance in the twentieth century would have a planning staff bigger than the Corps of Discovery of forty-odd men who set out from River Dubois on May 14, 1804. The planning staff for the expedition had consisted essentially of Jefferson and Lewis, with advice from

Jefferson's friends in the American scientific community. Up to the date of setting out, it was essentially Jefferson's expedition; after that date, the captains were on their own. They faithfully carried out Jefferson's program, but success or failure now depended on them.

For the first stage of the journey, as far as the Mandan villages, they followed the footsteps of others. There were maps of the route, however sketchy, and the Indians had had some acquaintance with traders. In this period the captains devoted much time to informing the Indians of the change of sovereignty, to insuring as much as possible that the Indians transferred their nominal allegiance, and to alleviating intertribal conflicts. The journey was marred in this period by some disciplinary problems, by the death of Sergeant Charles Floyd—the only man of the Corps who died on the trip—near present Sioux City, Iowa, and by their nearly violent encounter with the Teton Sioux near present Pierre, South Dakota.

They passed the winter of 1804–5 at Fort Mandan, near the Mandan and Hidatsa villages in North Dakota; the wait for the Missouri to thaw allowed them to gather much information from the Indians on the geography as far as the Missouri headwaters. In April 1805, they sent back their heavy keelboat and some enlisted men and "proceeded on" up the Missouri in canoes and pirogues. With them now was the Shoshone woman Sacagawea, with her husband Toussaint Charbonneau and their infant son Jean Baptiste. More than four months of travel, including a month-long portage of the Great Falls of the Missouri, ended at the Continental Divide on the Montana-Idaho border, with the dawning realization that the portage to the waters of the Columbia would not be the simple matter they had hoped.[20]

Promises of guns and trade maintained the expedition's friendly relations with the Shoshones; in exchange, the captains secured horses and guides for the trip across the mountains. They could not have known it beforehand, but they had come to one of the most difficult places for crossing the Rockies, and they had barely enough time to make the trip before winter closed the trails. After a cold, hungry trek across what Sergeant Patrick Gass called "this horrible mountainous desert," they reached the country of the Nez Perces on the Clearwater River in Idaho; there they built canoes and hurried on down the Clearwater, the Snake, and the Columbia to the Pacific.[21] All the way from Fort Mandan they had journeyed through country known only to the native inhabitants, until they neared the mouth of the Columbia and reentered the world of known geography. Clark's note of November 7, 1805: "Ocian in view! O! the joy," though premature, expressed the emotions of them all.

They passed a dreary, damp winter at Fort Clatsop, on the Oregon side of the Columbia estuary, knowing that snow would delay their returning earlier. Nonetheless, they accomplished considerable scientific work there, and the journals are rich with ethnographic and natural history materials. Jefferson had considered the possibility of at least part of the party returning by sea, if they should meet any trading vessels on the coast. The captains had apparently abandoned this idea, and in any case they met no ships, though evidence of white contact with the local people was abundant.

On March 23, 1806, they began their return by canoe and horseback, delaying a month among the Nez Perces in Idaho waiting for the snow to melt in the Bitterroot Mountains. Having crossed the Bitterroots, they split the party. So confident were they now of their ability to survive that they separated in order to add to their geographical knowledge. Lewis crossed the Continental Divide to the northeast to find a shorter passage over the mountains and to explore the Marias River in present Montana, while Clark went southeast to travel down the Yellowstone. Lewis's trip led him to a tragic encounter on the Marias in which he and his men killed two Blackfeet, the only real violence of the trip. Clark's journey was relatively uneventful.

Reunited in North Dakota, Lewis and Clark again visited the Mandan and Hidatsa villages, left Sacagawea, Charbonneau, and young Jean Baptiste there, and hurried on down the Missouri to St. Louis. Traders along the way told them that virtually everyone had given them up as lost, rumor asserting that they were dead at the hands of Indians or that "the Spanyards had us in the mines &C.," in Sergeant John Ordway's words.[22] Only the president still retained some hope. They arrived at St. Louis on September 23, 1806; three days later Clark closed his journal on an anticlimactic note: "a fine morning we commenced wrighting &c."

The Journal-keeping Methods of Lewis and Clark

Clark's last entry is a reminder that "wrighting &c." was one of the principal tasks of the captains, and one that they thoroughly fulfilled. As Donald Jackson has observed, Lewis and Clark were "the writingest explorers of their time. They wrote constantly and abundantly, afloat and ashore, legibly and illegibly, and always with an urgent sense of purpose."[23] They left us a remarkably full record of their enterprise, but questions about that record remain unanswered. One of the most vexing problems of the journals, as such, concerns a question whose answer might appear quite obvious: when and how were the journals written? The immediate and natural supposition of any reader is that the entries were written day by day on the dates placed at their heads by the authors. Examination of the journals now available, however, discredits that expectation. The existence of duplicate journals, mainly by Clark, for certain periods of the expedition, and internal evidence indicating that many entries cannot have been written on the days they cover, require greater consideration of the journal-keeping methods of the captains.

Nicholas Biddle, as a result of his collaboration with Clark in 1810 on the published history of the expedition, probably had more information about the two captains' methods of keeping a journal than anyone else who was not with the expedition, but he did not reveal it to his readers. By the time anyone again examined the journals at length, the authors were no longer available to provide what were no doubt simple explanations of many mysteries and apparent inconsistencies. When Elliott Coues examined the notebooks in the American Philosophical Society archives in 1892–93, he was struck by their good condition and concluded that the predominant red morocco-bound books, at least, could not have crossed the continent: "The covers are too fresh and bright, the paper too clean and sound. . . . The handwritings are too good, and too uniform. . . . The red books were certainly written after the return of the Expedition, and before Lewis's death in October, 1809—that is, in 1806–9."[24]

In opposition to Coues's belief that the journals might have been written, in part, as late as 1809 is Jefferson's statement that Lewis turned the notebooks over to him "on his return"—that is, on or soon after Lewis's arrival in Washington on December 28, 1806. Jefferson's understanding was that they had been written day by day, and that each notebook was sealed in a tin box when finished to protect it from the elements. Even assuming that Jefferson learned the exact procedure the captains followed, his description, written from memory nine years later, might not be precisely correct. However, he was hardly likely to have gained the impression that the volumes he specifically called "travelling pocket journals" were written on the trip if they were blank when he first saw them on Lewis's return. Nothing could have kept the president from poring over them, as he apparently did those sent back from Fort Mandan in 1805. His words strongly imply that the notebook journals were more or less complete by the time of Lewis's arrival in Washington.[25]

Of course, Coues never imagined that the captains wrote their journals from memory in the years after their homecoming. The red books he viewed at the American Philosophical Society did not include some other notebooks there that have different bindings; their condition convinced him that those could have been on the expedition, and he thought that true of some but not all the small, fragmentary items of a few sheets each that he examined. Those last he thought likely to be the remains of field journals made on the spot, day by day, their information later being transferred into the notebooks.[26]

When Reuben Gold Thwaites examined additional materials that he discovered a few years later, he found among them Clark's Elkskin-bound Journal, as he called it, covering the same period as some of the red books. This new volume, written on letter paper later sewn together and bound, undoubtedly in the field, seemed to fit exactly the description of field notes, later copied and expanded in the notebook journals. The Elkskin-bound Journal and some other new fragments made Thwaites confident that he understood the captains' basic procedures:

> It was the daily custom of the captains to make rough notes, with rude outline maps, plans, and miscellaneous sketches, in field-books which they doubtless carried in their pockets. When encamped for a protracted period, these were developed into more formal records. In this development, each often borrowed freely from the other's notes—Lewis, the better scholar of the two generally rewriting in his own manner the material obtained from Clark; while the latter not infrequently copied Lewis practically verbatim, but with his own phonetic spelling. Upon returning to St. Louis, these individual journals were for the most part transcribed into neat blank books—bound in red morocco and gilt-edged—with the thought of preparing them for early publication. After this process, the original field-books must have been cast aside and in large measure destroyed; for but one of these [*the Elkskin-bound Journal*] is now known to exist. There have come down to us, however, several note-books which apparently were written up in the camps.[27]

Thwaites did not attempt to say just when the field books were made, nor why some field notes and journals, notably the Elkskin-bound Journal, were preserved when so many others were "in large measure destroyed."

Thwaites's explanation is broadly plausible, but again we confront Jefferson's statement that the red books turned over to him at the beginning of 1807 were written on the trip. If Jefferson was mistaken on this point, then Thwaites's theory requires the captains to have written the entire body of red notebook journals—fourteen notebooks containing several hundred thousand words—between the arrival in St. Louis on September 23, 1806, and late December 1806. Clark's last journal entry (September 26, 1806), apparently written in St. Louis, says that "we commenced wrighting &c," but as noted, there is no indication of what they were writing.

Following Thwaites's theory, the red books had to have been written in the course of some three months or a little more, during which the captains were traveling; visiting relatives; seeing to other business; and attending public ceremonies, welcoming celebrations, and banquets. During that period Lewis was also escorting the Mandan chief Big White (Sheheke) to the capital. Moreover, substantial parts of Clark's journals for the last part of the expedition are evidently copied from Lewis. On the journey to Washington the captains separated in mid-November and did not reunite until January 21, 1807, when Clark reached Washington. Unless Lewis left a great part of his journals with Clark, which seems most unlikely, the period during which the journal writing could have been done narrows to a period of less than two months after the expedition's arrival in St. Louis. If we add the fact that Clark's next to last notebook journal has a lengthy passage in Lewis's hand, inserted in the middle with no apparent gaps in the writing, the theory that the red books were wholly the product of the period after the return to St. Louis seems questionable.

There are other good reasons for doubting the postexpedition theory of composition. Eighteen red books are known, all having some connection with the expedition, though it is not known when the captains obtained them. One of them is Codex O, as labeled by Coues, which contains Lewis's astronomical observations for the first year of the expedition and his summary of creeks and rivers. It is generally believed that this book was among the materials sent back from Fort Mandan in April 1805; it has no data collected after that time. If so, then the captains had it with them from the start, and in all probability they had all eighteen identical books from the beginning, wherever they were purchased. No one can possibly imagine that they carried eighteen notebooks to the Pacific and back without having intended from the first to write in them along the way.

There is no specific reference to the red books in any of the preexpedition lists of supplies. Lewis listed "Books" and "Writing paper" among his requirements for the trip, and since he did not specify titles, the books may well mean notebooks. He drew "8 Rect. books" from the U.S. arsenal in Philadelphia and purchased six packing boxes for "Stationary &c." there, in the spring of 1803. An undated memorandum in Codex C, in an unknown hand, lists goods packed for the expedition at some point. The list includes four bales of goods, each containing "2 tin Boxes, with 2 mem. Books in Ea."; a recapitulation of the same goods in the memorandum gives "8 tin Boxes with memm. Books". This gives sixteen books. Among Lewis's personal effects inventoried after his death in 1809 were "Sixteen Note books bound in red morocco with clasps." The coincidence in number is striking; it would indeed be conclusive, except that there are eighteen red books extant, all having some connection with the expedition. There is no really satisfactory way to account for the two extra books. Since there is no certainty when the memorandum in Codex C was written, we cannot say which red books might have been in use and so not listed among those packed. For instance, Lewis used Codex O for his astronomical observations from the beginning of the expedition. If the Codex C list was made up just before setting out from Wood River, Codex O might not have been packed away in a relatively inaccessible box in a bale but could have been with Lewis or easily available.

It is, of course, entirely possible that the captains purchased two more identical books after the expedition, and it would be exceedingly difficult to say which of those now known would be the extra two, since all eighteen red notebooks contain or apparently did once contain material that could have been written during the expedition. Neither is there any clear indication of which two red books Lewis would not have included among the expeditionary materials he had with him on his last journey in 1809. The captains' practice of taking pages from one notebook and inserting them in another makes it impossible to be certain what material (particularly the fragmentary Lewis items) may have been in what book at the time of Lewis's death, or at any other time before the Clark-Biddle collaboration in 1810.[28]

Jefferson says the books were "cemented" up in tin boxes for protection when completed, but that they had been removed from the boxes before Lewis delivered them to him. Lewis or Clark must therefore have told him those details, which implies that they gave him some information about their methods of journal keeping. The captains could have kept the notebooks in boxes sealed in some manner to keep out moisture, taking them out for writing in relatively sheltered camps or when the weather was good, while rough field notes served for daily entries under less favorable conditions.

Writing in 1807, David McKeehan, Patrick Gass's editor, sought to establish the reliability of Gass's work by stating, "At the different resting places during the expedition, the several journals were brought together, compared, corrected, and the blanks which had been unavoidably left, filled up."[29] This information, vague and unspecific as it is, could only have come from Gass; the journals referred to could be field notes or notebook journals, or both. Certainly such resting places would have been the points at which the notebook journals were brought up to date, if they were not, in fact, the journals in which the entries were kept day by day.

The discovery in 1953 of rough, unbound notes by Clark, covering, besides the period at Camp Dubois, the first eleven months of the expedition—the same period as Clark's first three notebooks—complicates as much as it clarifies. One can easily believe that these scribbled, interlined entries, written on miscellaneous sizes of loose paper, often over sketch maps, arithmetical calculations, and addresses on used envelopes, were first-draft notes taken in the field on the journey up the Missouri. It is then easy to imagine Clark copying and expanding on them in the notebooks whenever time allowed, even as late as the winter at Fort Mandan. Once they reached Fort Mandan, however, the Field Notes become increasingly skimpy, with gaps sometimes weeks in length. For this period we must either imagine another full set of field notes, whose existence is both unproven and unnecessary, or suppose that in this period Clark wrote his entries daily into a bound journal.[30]

There is, however, material in the notebooks that is not in the Field Notes, indicating that Clark wrote into them when events were fairly fresh in his mind. In his Codex A entry for July 4, 1804, we find reflections on the Kansa Indians not in the Field Notes. On the other hand, in the Codex A entry for July 23, 1804, he names Camp White Catfish, although the fish for which the camp was named was not caught until the next day. Thus we must assume that the codex entry was written on or after July 24, or that he wrote the entry on the twenty-third, inserting the name of the camp later—which from the appearance of the page is entirely possible.

In the Field Notes for August 20, 1804, Clark records in the present tense that Sergeant Charles Floyd was seriously ill, then writes of Floyd's death. In Codex B for the same day, Clark repeats the description of Floyd's illness and death. One must suppose either that Clark wrote both the Field Notes and Codex B simultaneously, with considerable difference in wording, or that he wrote the codex entry later, without taking into account his knowledge that Floyd had died. This journalistic convention persists throughout the journals and, of course, complicates the problem of determining the time of writing of particular entries. In any case, in the notebook entry of August 20, Clark refers to Floyd as "our Decesed brother," a phrase not found in the Field Notes—perhaps evidence that he wrote the notebook entry when the emotion was still fairly fresh.

On October 13, 1804, a court-martial of party members tried Private John Newman for "mutinous expression." Clark's brief record of the episode in his Codex C entry for October 13 says that Newman was tried "last night." Apparently he wrote the codex entry the day after the trial. The paragraph on the trial comes at the very end of the entry, so it is likely that the whole entry was composed on October 14, the day after its ostensible date. This is at a time when the Field Notes entries are still continuous and fairly extensive; the Codex C entry, however, includes much information not found in the Field Notes, apparently taken down by Clark at the time he received it. At this time he was obviously copying and expanding his first notes into the notebook journal quite promptly.

During the Fort Mandan winter, when Clark's notebook entries are quite full, entries in the Field Notes for widely separated dates follow one another without any evidence of missing pages. In fact, a single sheet, document 64 of Ernest Osgood's arrangement of the Field Notes, contains the entries for the period from November 19, 1804, to April 3, 1805; the entries follow one another with no indication of spaces for later insertion of material. Sheets in the Field Notes may have been lost, but it seems more likely that Clark wrote directly into his notebook journal. As further evidence, note that Lewis kept the bound book up to date when Clark was absent for ten days in February on a hunting trip; Clark then wrote a short summary of his excursion in the book on his return. From the appearance of the journal, Clark wrote this account immediately after his return, rather than inserting it later.

It does not seem wise to postulate the writing of field notes by either captain in cases where none have been found and there is no strong evidence of their having existed. Theories involving the existence of such notes are to be avoided unless the evidence clearly requires them. The sheer amount of labor involved in composing multiple sets of notes and journals argues against such suppositions. Considering the history of journal discoveries to date, however, no one would wish to assert positively that there are no lost notes or journals, or that none will ever be found. Certainly there are cases where notebook journal entries were clearly written weeks or months after the given date, and then it does not seem unreasonable to suppose that the writer kept notes of some sort.

The discovery of Clark's Field Notes consisting of the Dubois and River Journals, and other discoveries at various times and places, may seem to support the possibility of other such field journals. But the Dubois Journals relate to the period before the expedition proper and were not the basis, as far as we know, for a duplicate set of notebook journals. Obviously Clark kept both field notes and notebook journals for the journey up the Missouri to Fort Mandan, but it does not necessarily follow that he used the same procedure throughout the expedition, especially since he apparently did not follow this method at Fort Mandan and his field notes fall off sharply after his arrival there.

On April 7, 1805, the permanent party set out upriver from Fort Mandan; at the same time, the keelboat carrying the discharged members of the party headed downriver with a load of dispatches, papers, and specimens for delivery to Jefferson. At this point we encounter more complex problems of journal-keeping procedures and missing notes.

The first question concerns just what journal materials were sent to Jefferson on the keelboat. At several points in the summer and fall the captains indicated that they intended to send back a pirogue with some of the soldiers and boatmen under Corporal Richard Warfington. Clark indicates more than once that they were preparing materials to be sent back with that party. As it happened, they did not dispatch the return party until the following spring, for reasons never stated. Both Clark and Lewis wrote letters to Jefferson indicating what they were sending, but neither was specific enough to spare us some puzzlement. Clark wrote on April 3, 1805, that he was sending the "notes which I have taken in the form of a journal in their original state," apologizing because "many parts are incorrect." Lewis wrote that they were sending the president "a part of Capt. Clark's private journal, the other part you will find inclosed in a separate tin box. The journal is in it's original state, and of course incorrect, but it will give you the daily detales of our progress, and transactions." A great deal hinges on the meaning of the expressions "private journal" and "original state," and on how we interpret the two parts of Clark's journal.[31]

Various interpretations are possible. We could take Clark's Field Notes to be a "private" journal, and the notebook journals to be "public" or official; thus the Field Notes constitute one part and the notebook journals—Codices A, B, and C—the other. We might take the Dubois Journal and the River Journal, the two parts of the Field Notes, as the two parts meant, but there is no evidence that the Dubois Journal ever went to Jefferson, and the division into the Dubois Journal and the River Journal is merely a modern convenience. The argument can be made that the two parts were parts of the River Journal itself, on the basis of a notation by Clark on document 56 of the Field Notes. One side contains journal entries for September 20–23, 1804. The other side bears an address:

Sept 20 &
Genl. Jona. Clark of Kentucky
To the 22nd of Septr. 1804
To the care of Genl. Jona. Clark near Louisville Kty
To be opened by Capt. W. Clark or Capt. Meriwether Lewis.[32]

On the same document under the September 23 entry Clark wrote, "I must seal up all those scripts & draw from my Journal at some other time."

The address and the conclusion of entries on the same sheet seem to indicate that the captains still hoped to send a party back before winter, and that Clark intended to send the Field Notes to his oldest brother Jonathan, to be kept until his return. They had kept Warfington with them past the end of his enlistment in August so that he could head the return party. We might suppose that Clark made sure that his notebook journals were up-to-date at this point, since he could not use the Field Notes for this purpose after sending them back, and he may have brought the notebooks up-to-date similarly when they considered sending materials back from Camp White Catfish in July. On the other hand, if the notebooks were not up-to-date, this could be the reason why the return party did not set out before winter. This might even be the reason why Clark neglected the Field Notes at Fort Mandan and apparently wrote directly into his notebook journal, the earlier procedure having proved too time-consuming.

On document 58 of the Field Notes is a notation by Clark: "A Continuation of notes taken assending the Missourie in 1804—by W. Clark." It may be, then, that the two parts of Clark's "private journal" are the two parts of the Field Notes— the part sealed up to be sent to Jonathan Clark in September 1804, but not sent, and the notes taken after that time. The note about "A Continuation" could indicate that Clark thought of the Field Notes as being in two parts.[33]

Against the above interpretation, however, is another notation by Clark, written April 2, 1805, on document 64 in the Field Notes, during preparations to send off the keelboat and its cargo from Fort Mandan:

I conclude to Send my journal to the President of the United States in its original State for his own perusal, untill I Call for it or Some friend if I Should not return, an this journal is from the 13th of May 1804 untill the 3rd of April 1805.

Here again is the phrase "in its original state," suggesting that the journal referred to is the same as mentioned in the captains' letters to Jefferson as Clark's "private journal." What journal was it?

Clark says the journal began on May 13, 1804, which cannot apply to the Field Notes, unless he was in error. The last document of the Dubois Journal ends on May 14, and the River Journal's first sheet begins with the same date. The first notebook journal, Codex A, however, does begin on May 13. The journal to be sent back, Clark says, ends on April 3, 1805; that is true of the Field Notes and, in a sense, of the notebook journals. The April 3 entry in Codex C is followed by a list of items to be sent back on the keelboat, then the entries for April 4–7. Since the entry for April 3 in Clark's Field Notes shows that they expected to leave the next day, Clark could well have thought of the April 3 entry in Codex C as the last, adding a list of materials to be sent back for Jefferson's information. Thus, when he wrote in the Field Notes on April 2 that the journal went to April 3, that could also have been the case with the notebook journals. Since they did not, in fact, leave until April 7—due presumably to last-minute delays—it was natural for Clark to add entries for the extra days in Codex C.

With such an indication that Clark considered his notebook journals to be in their "original state," it seems reasonable that the two parts of his journal were the Field Notes and the notebook journals—Codices A, B, and C. That the notebook journals went to Jefferson is clear from Jefferson's letter to Benjamin Smith Barton in December 1805, referring to the feeding of cottonwood bark to horses by the Indians in terms very similar to those in Codex C but not in the Field Notes.[34] It seems most likely that the Field Notes also went to Jefferson, though there is no specific evidence proving this. Clark did note in a letter from Fort Mandan that he was sending "papers of considerable consequence" to his brother in Louisville, and the Field Notes would meet this description. It is likely, however, that those "papers" consisted of the Dubois Journal, not the River Journal. Document 65 bears the address of Jonathan Clark and the notation "notes at Wood River in 1803–4." Clark certainly did not send those notes—which surely must be the Dubois Journal—to Jonathan before the departure from St. Louis in 1804, for the other side of document 65 bears an entry for November 30, 1804, after they had reached Fort Mandan. From its appearance, document 65 could have been the wrapper in which the Wood River notes (Dubois Journal) were sealed for shipment to Jonathan Clark. If those notes were in a separate packet, it may have been because they were going to a different destination than the River Journal, sent to Jefferson. That Clark wrote a full entry for November 30 on document 65 may only mean that he thought of taking up regular keeping of the Field Notes after they had settled in at Fort Mandan, then abandoned the idea in favor of the notebook journals.[35]

Clark's journal-writing procedure, up to the departure from Fort Mandan, then, seems reasonably clear. On the upriver journey he kept daily field notes and copied and expanded them into his notebook journals as convenient, sometimes neglecting the Field Notes at Fort Mandan in favor of writing directly into

Codex C. The daily continuity of the Field Notes ends with November 13, 1804, the entries becoming increasingly irregular; document 64 covers the entire period from that date to April 3, 1805, and appears to be the last sheet of the Field Notes. During the building of Fort Mandan in early November, the keeping of two journals may have seemed too much of a burden in the midst of other demanding work. If so, then Codex C was presumably up-to-date at that time, and perhaps Codices A and B were also. Codices B and C, however, overlap on October 1, 2, and 3, and the entries in Codex C for the first and second are skimpy in comparison to those in Codex B. Possibly Clark began writing in Codex C when Codex B was not yet up to date, on the first of October. The fuller entry for October 3 is in Codex C, and conceivably he had caught up and filled in Codex B by then.

More difficult to explain is Lewis's journal-keeping procedure and particularly the large gaps in his writing, which raise the possibility of missing manuscripts. The largest gap, and the one most curious to historians, is the long hiatus from the start of the expedition in May 1804, until the group set out from Fort Mandan in April 1805. That gap is particularly bewildering because we would expect Lewis to be more conscientious at the outset of the expedition, especially in light of Jefferson's explicit instructions about the keeping of multiple journals.[36] So incredulous have some observers been at this gap that they have speculated that Lewis was probably keeping either field drafts or standard journals of the party's activities that have since been lost.[37]

To say that Lewis was keeping no journal from the outset is not precisely correct. There exist two small fragments, called Codices Aa and Ba by Coues, for the dates May 15 and 20, and September 16–17, 1804. Those sheets, apparently torn from one of the red books, suggest to some that Lewis was keeping a journal for the initial period, and that the remaining pages were so soiled, ruined, or unnecessary that they were discarded. Or perhaps the remaining pages are simply lost. Another explanation seems plausible and is presented here as part of a larger conception of Lewis's journal-keeping activities throughout the trip.

In Codex Aa it is noteworthy that the order of days is reversed; the entry for May 20 precedes the entry for May 15, with no break between the two. The entry for May 20 recounts Lewis's activities for that day as he set out by land from St. Louis for St. Charles where he was to rendezvous with Clark, who was leading the party upriver. The entry also reports the activities of Clark's party. Perhaps Lewis saw this entry as the beginning of his journal keeping since the captains had determined to set out the next day (May 21). Then why the addition of notes for May 15? That is a more detailed report of Clark's trip upriver, written as if Lewis had been present. Information in that entry exceeds the notes taken by Clark for that day in either of his two accounts (Field Notes and Codex A) and probably came directly from Clark. Perhaps Lewis thought he ought to add an entry for May 15 after his May 20 entry to give a more detailed account of the actual start of the expedition. Although Clark set out from River Dubois on May 14, the captains had earlier established May 15 as the date to begin, and perhaps Lewis still had that date in mind.

Codex Ba presents a different situation. On September 16 and 17, 1804, the group was encamped at "Corvus" Creek just above today's White River in South Dakota (see *Atlas* map 21). There the captains made the decision not to send back the pirogue with artifacts and other items representing their journey thus far. Perhaps Lewis had thought that their notes to that point would return to St. Louis with the other materials and eventually reach President Jefferson; thus, he may have considered that he was now beginning a journal, in a sense the first for him since he had apparently quit writing after his May 15 entry. Having made the decision not to send a boat and crew back, he may have ceased his journalizing (indeed, he stopped at midpage in midsentence) and perhaps delayed writing again until after the winter at Fort Mandan.

Even before those dates Lewis may have established a pattern of laxness in journal writing. He began a diary (here called the Eastern Journal) when he left Pittsburgh in August 1803, as he descended the Ohio River enroute to St. Louis, but from September 19 to November 11, he made no entries. He left thirty-nine pages blank in the notebook between those separated entries, however, perhaps with the intention of supplying the missing information later, but that hiatus was never filled. About October 26, Clark joined Lewis at Louisville, but Lewis did not turn over journal-keeping chores to his friend at that time. Had he done so, today we might have a more complete record of the remainder of the trip to Camp Dubois, for Clark was a more consistent recorder than his companion. Lewis returned to journalizing on November 11 and gave the journal to Clark on November 28, near Kaskaskia, as they separated while Lewis went ahead by land to St. Louis and Clark brought the boat party forward to establish Camp Dubois. From that point we have a nearly consistent record because of Clark's faithful journal keeping.[38]

Those writing gaps of Lewis's may be instances of a larger pattern of negligence. The gaps as a whole include the missing days from the Eastern Journal (September 19 to November 11, 1803); the lapse from May 14, 1804, to April 7, 1805 (with the exceptions noted); only spotty entries from August 26, 1805, to January 1, 1806; and the final hiatus from August 12, 1806, to the completion of the expedition. The last gap can be explained by Lewis's being partially disabled from a wound; in contrast to other stoppages, he noted that he was laying down his pen at that point. In all from May 1804, to September 1806, Lewis missed over four hundred days of journal entries.[39]

Some authorities have supposed that Lewis was keeping field notes during the period from Camp Dubois to Fort Mandan and intending to use that material to fill regular notebooks later, or that the fragments from a red book (the entries for May and September) were part of a complete set of notes that are now lost. Jackson has made the strongest case for Lewis having kept notes during the first leg of the journey, but he emphasizes the speculative nature of his conclusions. Briefly, Jackson believes that a mishap on May 14, 1805, may indicate a loss of journals. On that day one of the pirogues turned on its side and filled with water, and some of the papers and notebooks got wet. Jackson discovered that within a few days of the accident Clark began conscientiously to copy into his own journal Lewis's natural history notes, something he had not previously done. Jackson argues that the spoilages may have been greater than expected, convincing the captains that duplicating all records was necessary, not just keeping multiple diaries. He also conjectures that "perhaps Lewis's notes for the entire first leg of the expedition were either badly water-soaked or entirely lost." Thus, Jackson believes that the entries by Lewis for May and September 1804 may be fragments of a larger journal from that early period. Thwaites also thought that Lewis was a regular journal-keeper, but his reasoning is less plausible than Jackson's. He supposed that the journals may have been lost after Lewis's death in Tennessee. However, we would expect that Clark or Jefferson would have bemoaned such a loss at some time, but neither ever made reference to so serious a loss in any known source. Jackson's answer for a reason that there is no mention of the supposed loss of journals in May 1805 is that Lewis would tell Jefferson about the accident after his return but that there was no need to announce it to the world in his diary.[40]

Jackson and others who think Lewis kept a journal or field notes during the trip to Fort Mandan have found strong evidence in letters of Lewis and Clark to Jefferson just before the party set out from that post. The opening phrase of Clark's letter has been struck out and other words substituted by Lewis. Clark wrote, "As Capt. Lewis has not Leasure to Send ⟨write⟩ a correct Coppy journal of our proceedings &c." and Lewis substituted, "It being the wish of Capt. Lewis." There are several ways to read the excised parts: does Lewis not have time to send his journal, has he not had time to write it, or has he not had time to make a correct copy? Lewis's letter stated that he would send a canoe with some men back from the extreme navigable point of the Missouri River (a scheme later rejected) and with that boat "I shal send you my journal." Again, one can read the phrase variously: is Lewis to send a journal he has been keeping or one he intends to write? Rather than speculate on the hidden meaning of the letters, it is better to examine the totality of Lewis's journal keeping and to interpret from that perspective.[41]

Although extant daily entries by Lewis from St. Charles to Fort Mandan are lacking, there exists quite a bit of Lewis's writing from that period, and additional material is known to be missing. As the expedition's naturalist he kept fairly extensive notes on the flora and fauna of the region through which the party passed. In Codex R, he made a list of herbarium specimens that he was collecting. The descriptive writing is occasionally lengthy and shows not only Lewis's powers of observation but also his record-keeping activities. Observations of animals are almost as extensive and cover over fifty pages of Codex Q. The captain was also noting mineral deposits and geologic features along the Missouri and taking astronomical observations—both time-consuming tasks that included record-keeping. And, although Lewis cannot be credited directly, it is known that the captains were keeping lists of Indian vocabularies during this period, work that may have amounted to extensive note taking. The vocabularies are the missing material that might exhibit additional record keeping by Lewis.

From January to May 1804, Lewis was keeping a weather diary. Those observations are repeated in Clark's Codex C, and it seems probable that Lewis was copying Clark's entries. After May 14 there is a gap of weather data in both captains' books until September 19; the notations are then resumed with hardly an interruption until April 3, 1805, when Lewis began placing weather data with the daily entries. The weather notes indicate a substantial amount of writing because they consist of two temperature readings for each day, the general state of the weather, the wind direction, and the rise and fall of the river. There are also comments on natural history including sightings of animals and the budding and fading of flora. It is uncertain whether Lewis made the notes along the way or at Fort Mandan, but it was a collaborative effort of the captains.[42]

Evidence that Lewis may have done more extensive writing exists in the form of a single loose sheet from Clark's Field Notes (Osgood's document 35). The sheet is entirely in Lewis's hand and contains on one side a draft for Lewis's description of the Platte River, which he later transferred into Codex O as his survey of rivers and creeks. Although there is a date of July 21 (1804) on the document, the reverse contains lunar observations (also in Lewis's hand) for February 23, 1805, while the party was at Fort Mandan. It could be that the draft describing the Platte was also written at Fort Mandan and there copied into Codex O. Because the draft from the Field Notes is an incomplete portion, it is certain that other pages are missing; whether they describe only the Platte or are a full draft of his summary may never be known. If Lewis was keeping thorough topographical notes throughout the first portion of the trip, it helps explain why no daily entry material has been found. It may simply have amounted to too much writing.

Taken together, Lewis's recording activities up to Fort Mandan add up to a large amount of writing and may represent a proportional share of the writing duties of the captains. What emerges is a picture of the two men sharing journal-keeping chores, though not following Jefferson's prescription to the letter. It is difficult to believe that all of Lewis's daily-entry journals (except for a few pages of writing for May and September 1804), from St. Charles to Fort Mandan and during the winter of 1804–5, could be lost. Clark during that period filled three notebooks of writing, and Lewis, the more verbose, would have written even more. Unless actual journals by Lewis or definite references to such writing are discovered, it seems likely that he kept no record of daily events for this period.

One incident on the way to Fort Mandan may corroborate the notion that Lewis kept no journal of daily events during that period. On July 14, 1804, a sudden storm hit the river, and great gusts of wind turned one boat on its side so that it began to fill with water. Cool heads and quick action saved the vessel from destruction, but Clark reported that his notes of the previous day had blown overboard during the accident. Clark mentioned that the loss "obliges me to refur to the ⟨notes⟩ Journals of Serjeants, and my own recollection [of] the accurences Courses Distance &. of that day." If Lewis had been keeping a journal of events during this time, why would Clark go to the journals of the sergeants or depend on his own recollection for the "accurences?" Certainly he would have trusted Lewis's notes over his memory or the notes of enlisted men if Lewis's journal had been available.[43]

From the April 7, 1805, departure from Fort Mandan to late August 1805, complete notebook journals for both captains exist, with no fragmentary or parallel journals until August, although some copying was being done between the two men. There is no indication that either followed Clark's earlier practice of writing field notes and transferring them, with revisions, into notebook journals. Indeed, there is no reason to assume that the captains consistently followed any one plan or procedure throughout the expedition. Their responsibility was to keep as complete a record as possible of the many kinds of information that Jefferson wanted and to preserve that record from harm or loss. They could follow any procedure that suited their convenience and the conditions of the moment, in keeping with that mission. External conditions varied so much throughout the trip that there was every reason to change journal-keeping procedures to conform to the needs of the moment. When they were inconsistent in so much else, there is no reason to expect them to be consistent in this.

It is not necessary to believe, then, that for every finished journal there was a preliminary set of field notes nearly duplicating it, as in the case of the River Journal and Codices A and B. Without the known existence of field notes, or strong evidence requiring them, there is no need to assume that they were made. Duplication of journals would serve as insurance against loss or damage, but with both captains definitely keeping journals after April 7, 1805, there would be less need for keeping both field notes and notebook journals, which amounted to a time-consuming task.[44]

Field notes, however, would be of value in situations where there was an increased risk of damage or loss from weather or difficult travel conditions, when it seemed wise to seal up the notebooks in tin boxes (described by Jefferson) and keep field notes easily accessible or carried on the person. Such precautions could also be taken when one of the captains was scouting ahead on foot, accompanied by only a few men; he might leave his notebook journals with the main body, for convenience or in case something happened to him and he did not return. After such separations, one might copy the experiences of the other into his own journal, to insure the preservation of a complete record.

As they moved up the Missouri around the Great Falls, the captains were separated at various times in June, July, and August 1805, as one or the other was ahead, portaging the falls or later looking for the Shoshone Indians. In these intervals, Lewis sometimes copied Clark's journal for the days of separation under the date of their reunion, suggesting that he was keeping the notebook journal day by day. At other times, Lewis gave an account of Clark's activities in his own entries for each day, indicating that those entries must have been written after they were reunited. Clark in this period did not ordinarily copy Lewis's record of daily events while they were separated.[45]

In some of Clark's red notebooks are extra pages he apparently inserted, sometimes torn from other red books but at least once cut to fit from letter paper. The handwriting on the inserted sheets is neater and more legible than Clark's usual bold but rather careless hand, but it is definitely Clark's, and the need for legibility is the likely reason for many of the insertions. This circumstance strengthens the likelihood that the ordinary handwriting represents daily entries written on the trail, during the day or in camp. A notable example is Clark's insertion of pages to recopy his survey notes of the Great Falls portage, already written in his rougher hand in the middle of his June 17, 1805, entry, probably during the course of the day. He decided to copy the notes over for greater legibility and in fact inserted more sheets than he needed. The inserted sheets are in the middle of the original rough notes.[46]

There are four fragmentary journals by Lewis from August and September 1805, designated Codices Fa, Fb, Fc, and Fd by Coues. Each consists of a few loose sheets covering periods of two to five days. Codex Fa describes events also related in more detail in Lewis's Codex F; the others are all from periods after the end of Codex F, during a hiatus of over four months for which there are no other known Lewis journals, except for a later fragment, Codex Ia.[47] It is tempting to regard them as being literally "fragments," that is, portions of a lost body of field notes by Lewis covering perhaps the entire gap in his journal from late August 1805, to January 1, 1806. But the fragments themselves provide no evidence for this hypothesis. If they had portions of a previous day's entry at the beginning, or of the next day's entry at the end, there would be good reason to regard them as portions of a larger body of notes now lost. On the contrary, however, they appear to be complete in themselves. Codex Fa has a dated heading for an entry at the end that was never written, since only a blank space follows the date on the last sheet of the codex. Moreover, all of the fragments except Fc relate to periods when the captains were separated; Fa chronicles a scouting excursion ahead of the main body when Lewis might have preferred not to risk his notebook journal, and the other two describe periods when Clark scouted ahead and Lewis had to keep a record of the movements of the main party. Codex Fc derives from two days of relative leisure at Travelers' Rest in western Montana when Lewis may have intended to resume journal keeping after a lapse of about two weeks.[48] Lewis's later Codex Ia (November 29-December 1, 1805) also covers part of a period of separation and gives no indication of being part of a larger whole.[49]

In Codex G, Clark sometimes groups courses and distances for several days in one place, suggesting that he may have kept this information in separate notes and transferred it to his notebooks when time allowed. It may be that he kept course and distance notes on the same sheets with sketch maps, as he did with *Atlas* maps 33–42, although no such maps have been found for the route from the Great Falls to Travelers' Rest in western Montana, traversed during the period covered in Codex G.

On September 11 the Corps left Travelers' Rest on the Lolo Trail; this is the day on which Clark's Elkskin-bound Journal begins, continuing until December 31, 1805. It thus overlaps his red notebook journals Codex G (to October 10), Codex H (October 11–November 19), and Codex I (to December 31). This journal consists of sheets of letter paper sewn together and crudely bound in elkskin, presumably in the field. While we cannot be certain whether it was bound before or after writing, the fact that it ends precisely on the last day of 1805, the day before Lewis's known journal-writing again resumes, strongly suggests the latter.

From September 11 to 20, the Elkskin-bound Journal consists of courses and distances, with sketch maps of the Lolo Trail route. The courses and distances become progressively more detailed, briefly mentioning daily incidents; by September 13 they are in effect short journal entries in themselves. After September 21, the book becomes a regular journal of daily events. Here some speculation seems warranted. The Lolo Trail was one of the roughest parts of the trip, the trail hazardous and the weather terrible; the horse carrying Clark's writing desk slipped down a mountainside on the fifteenth, smashing the desk. These were conditions under which it would be prudent to seal up the notebook journals in tin boxes for protection and keep rough field notes along the trail. The sketch maps and courses and distances suggest that the elkskin book started out as the sort of route notes Clark kept at other times, such as those with *Atlas* maps 33–42. Their becoming progressively more extensive from September 11 to 20 suggests that Clark did indeed seal up Codex G at some point during this period, the Elkskin-bound Journal becoming the preliminary journal, the first draft for the notebooks. Clark went ahead with a few men, looking for game, on September 18, and the courses and distances in the elkskin book become particularly extensive from that date. There can be no certainty, however, that was the date when Codex G was sealed up.

From September 21, the elkskin book consists of regular daily entries in the conventional form, not in the form of courses and distances. September 20 was the day Clark met the Nez Perces at Weippe Prairie, Idaho, a meeting described in some detail in the elkskin notebook courses and distances. Lewis and the main party did not catch up until September 22. If Codex G was in a tin box on a packhorse with Lewis's group, we can understand why Clark wrote his regular September 21 entry in the elkskin book. He traveled a few miles that day but gave no courses and distances until the next day, September 22, when he wrote, "our first course of yesterday was nearly . . . ," as if he had not written it down anywhere else and was going by memory. There may have been no notes other than those in the elkskin book.

Clark's courses and distances for September 11–21 and September 25 are together in Codex G after the September 30 entry; he may have taken the notebook out on that day and brought it up to date, or he may have been keeping entries in it and simply have delayed copying the courses and distances because he was busy. In any case, he continued to keep journal entries in the elkskin book until December 31, paralleling notebook journal entries in Codices G, H, and I. That the Elkskin-bound Journal entries were the first draft and the codices the second seems probable. For much of the period from early October to early December the expedition was going downriver in small dugout canoes, and when they neared the Pacific Coast they entered an area of almost constant rain and storms. It may have seemed wise to keep the red books in their waterproof boxes much of the time and continue to use the sheets that became the Elkskin-bound Journal.

The elkskin book begins on the exact date of starting on the Lolo Trail, which may indicate that Clark had not kept detailed field notes for some time before that but had written daily information directly into his notebook journals. He could well have been keeping course and distance notes, with sketch maps of the route, as he had earlier, notes such as the pages in the elkskin book apparently started out to be. But why were those bound notes preserved if similar ones for an earlier period (the summer and fall of 1805) were not saved also? We must, of course, allow something for sheer chance, but the special care taken to bind the notes suggests a particular need to preserve material covering that period. One reason for preserving them might be the exceptionally large number of maps (nineteen) along with the journal material; none of the maps of the Elkskin-bound Journal are repeated in the codices for the same period. Again note that there are, to our present knowledge, no notebook journals by Lewis from late August 1805, to January 1, 1806; only fragmentary loose sheets are known, and all except one (Codex Fc) cover periods when the captains were separated.

The Elkskin-bound Journal ends the day before Lewis is known to have resumed his journal-keeping, the first day of 1806. It would be a remarkable coincidence if Clark just happened to run out of paper in the book on that day. Internal evidence indicates that large portions of Clark's notebook journals after early November 1805 were probably written months later. If the sheets in the elkskin book were the only continuous record by either captain for a period of over three and one-half months, then we can readily understand why they took special care to preserve them. If Clark's red books were sealed up and packed away for much of that time, we can also understand why what started out as rough notes and sketch maps became a journal of events as well.[50]

What was Clark doing with his notebook journals during the period (September 11–December 31, 1805) covered by the Elkskin-bound Journal? Entries in late September and early October 1805 in Codex G are generally more extensive than those in the Elkskin-bound Journal; both are brief during periods when Clark was ill or particularly busy. After the party set out down the Clearwater River in canoes on October 7, the Elkskin-bound Journal again becomes primarily expanded courses and distances. Codex H, however, begins on October 11, and from this point the elkskin book entries again become progressively more detailed and lengthy, as if it were again the record actually kept on the given dates. On November 7, 1805, the day the party arrived, or so they thought, in sight of the Pacific, Clark records the event in both journals in terms suggesting immediate emotion.

The Codex H entry for November 7, however, also contains a passage in quotes describing the dress of the local Indian women, noting that it was so skimpy that the "battery of venus is not altogether impervious to the penetrating eye of the amorite." Not only is the language most unlike Clark's, but the whole paragraph is placed in quotation marks to indicate that it was not Clark's. In fact, the whole paragraph occurs verbatim in Lewis's Codex J entry for March 19, 1806—over four months after the ostensible date of Clark's entry. This forces us to conclude that Clark wrote the November 7, 1805, entry in Codex H on or after March 19, 1806. Lacking any indication that the page with the quoted paragraph was inserted later, we must assume that the remainder of Codex H after that date—and Clark's subsequent notebook journals, largely copied from Lewis—were written on or after March 19, 1806—an assumption that creates some intriguing problems.[51]

There is some evidence, moreover, that much of Codex H before November 7, 1805, was not written until months after the given dates. In the entry in that journal for October 18, Clark notes how "the Great Chief and one of the *Chim-nâ-pum* nation" on the Columbia drew for him a sketch of the upper Columbia and its inhabitants and tributaries. Clark's copy of the sketch appears in the middle of the journal entry as if done at the same time as the entry itself. Yet the map labels as "Clark's River" the Pend Oreille River where it enters the Columbia. There is good reason to believe that the captains did not decide to give the name Clark's River to the combined Bitterroot-Clark Fork-Pend Oreille rivers until between April 17 and May 6, 1806 (see *Atlas*, pp. 10–11). An almost exact duplicate of the map in another notebook not containing daily entries shows the same stream as the "Flathead River," the name they used earlier. It may be, then, that Clark did not write the October 18 entry until late April or early May of 1806, inserting the sketch the Indians had given him under the appropriate date by copying from an earlier version. Codex H begins only a few days before that date, on October 11, 1805, so it might well be that, on finishing Codex G on October 10, Clark decided that since they were traveling downstream in canoes, it would be wise to use the Elkskin-bound Journal for daily journal keeping and keep his notebooks safely sealed away in boxes. As noted, the elkskin book's entries become increasingly extensive about this time.

Codex H ends on November 19 with a brief entry and Clark's words "See another book for perticulars." Codex I takes up with a longer entry for the same date, but only after thirty-four pages of introductory miscellaneous material— courses and distances from Fort Mandan to the Pacific, including some for a trip down the coast that Clark made in January 1806. That Codex I then takes up the narrative on November 19, 1805, immediately after this collection of data, suggests that Codex H was finished and the daily entries in Codex I begun in sequence. If so, then Clark also wrote Codex I after March 19, 1806, when Lewis wrote the "battery of venus" passage, which Clark copied under the date of November 7, 1805, in Codex H.

Why, then, did Clark wait so long to write this material in the red books? Up to December 31, 1805, he was writing in the sheets bound in elkskin and may not have seen any reason to start another journal, or he may not have gotten around to it. There is no clear evidence of such notes continuing after the first day of 1806. But Clark's Codex I has three short entries for January 1, 2, and 3 at one end of the book, upside down to all the rest of the writing in that book, which starts at the other end. It would seem that Clark began Codex I as a continuation of the Elkskin-bound Journal (ending December 31), then decided to do something else. It appears that he again took up Codex H, filled it up with entries paralleling the elkskin book through November 19, then continued in sequence in Codex I; if so, then he evidently did so after March 19, the date of Lewis's observations about the visibility of the "battery of venus." Apparently Clark wrote no journals of which we have knowledge for nearly three months, and this at Fort Clatsop, where he would have had relative leisure for writing. Codex I does contain a detailed record of Clark's trip down the Oregon coast on January 6–10, taken from notes (here called First Draft, January 6–10, 1806) of the kind the captains kept on other occasions when separated. Lewis's synopsis of Clark's trip is in his Codex J for January 10, the day of Clark's return, and was likely written at that time from Clark's verbal account and First Draft notes.

Lewis began a new journal (Codex J) on January 1, 1806, and continued a consistent writing until August 12 when he laid his pen down, ending his record of the expedition. That is the first journal writing by him, as far as we know, since August 1805, except for scattered fragments. Perhaps the new journal is another point of beginning as has been conjectured with Codices Aa, Ba, and Fc, and here his good intentions of journal keeping (combined perhaps with a New Year's resolution) were fulfilled. Codex J is a detailed record, to March 20, of life at Fort Clatsop, and contains extensive descriptions of local flora and fauna and the life of the nearby Indians, with numerous illustrations. Nowhere else did Lewis devote more time to fulfilling the scientific objectives of the expedition by recording so much. All of the observations are incorporated in the daily entries, generally after the record of the day's events. In what was evidently an additional measure to insure the preservation of this material, Clark copied most of it into his journals almost verbatim. For some reason Clark did not always copy material under the same date as Lewis and sometimes placed it under an entry several days earlier than that of Lewis. Clearly he was not copying Lewis day by day.

Clark's copying of Lewis for the period after January 1, 1806, is in a more careful, neater hand. There is no way of knowing whether Clark's neater hand was something he could do at any time he chose to make the effort, or whether it represents writing at leisure and in comfort after the return from the voyage. But if the reason for copying from Lewis was insurance against loss, it would make more sense to complete it as soon as possible during the journey.

Lewis's Codex J also includes natural history material appropriate to the Rocky Mountains and Interior Basin, notes additional to the few fragments extant for that period. If Lewis had kept a journal for that period (August–December 1805), why did he copy it into daily entries for the time at Fort Clatsop? Why not copy it into a separate journal covering the actual dates? That question must remain a mystery. There must have been some sort of natural history field notes or other journals for that period that are now lost. If Lewis did have notes in daily journal form covering the August-December gap, why did he not copy them into his own journal at Fort Clatsop when he would have had time? One answer might be that the notes he had were mainly natural history and ethnographic material, and that he did copy them into Codex J, under current dates. If both Lewis and Clark were copying from supposed notes made by Lewis before arriving at Fort Clatsop, then it might be clear why Clark's version of the scientific material comes under different dates than in Lewis's journals, while his daily record of events follows Lewis verbatim on the same dates. But Clark's duplication of Lewis's natural history notes in the codices (particularly Codex J) is so exact that the hypothetical notes must themselves have been as elaborate as those in Lewis's notebooks.[52]

As noted, Clark apparently did not write his November 7, 1805 entry in Codex H until on or after March 19, 1806, when he copied the "battery of venus" passage into that entry. March 19, when Lewis evidently wrote the paragraph, was just four days before the expedition left Fort Clatsop on the return trip. We can hardly imagine Clark writing over four months' worth of notebook journals, including extensive natural history notes, in that period of time, which surely was crowded with preparations for leaving. If he was copying from Lewis after the departure from Fort Clatsop, when did he do it—along the trail, during the lengthy stopover at Camp Chopunnish in Idaho, or after the arrival in St. Louis? And what did he do about his own daily journalizing during the homeward journey?

Clark's copying of Lewis continues during the first few days of the party's journey up the Columbia; he was still writing in the same book (Voorhis No. 2 in Thwaites's numbering system) and the entries could have been written some time later. The last two days of Voorhis No. 2, April 2 and 3, describe Clark's trip up the Willamette River on those days and could easily have been taken from field notes.[53] Lewis copied that narrative under his April 6 entry, with some changes in wording. Clark's Voorhis No. 3 begins on April 4 and is more a record of daily events without the extended descriptions copied from Lewis.

Since Voorhis No. 3 takes up immediately where No. 2 leaves off, however, it is logical to think that Clark did not start No. 3 until the other was finished—perhaps some time after the given date. Under April 6, Clark again has some natural history data copied from Lewis's entry of April 7. Clark may have been keeping some sort of field notes at this time. There are such notes made by him for the period of April 16–21, but for most of that time the captains were separated, with Clark trading for food at various Indian villages near the Great Falls of the Columbia. He might well have not wanted to be troubled with carrying a notebook journal at that time, but perhaps he was not keeping a journal at all in the period of the journey upriver. We have no idea when the two decided that Clark should copy Lewis's Fort Clatsop journals, perhaps doing no journalizing himself in the meantime, although the short entries for January 1–3 in his Codex I suggest the decision was taken in early January 1806. Nor is it clear how long after March 19 Clark waited to begin his copying.

From May 14 to June 10, 1806, the expedition was at rest at Camp Chopunnish, on the north bank of the Clearwater River in the Nez Perce country of Idaho, waiting for the snow to melt sufficiently on the Lolo Trail for their passage east. In this extended period of relative leisure Clark might have done some of the extensive copying from Lewis's journals. As noted, the use of the name "Clark's Fork" in a map placed with the October 18, 1805, entry in Codex H suggests that much of that notebook journal was not written until late April or early May of 1806, or later. That possibility would fit well with the hypothesis that much of Clark's catching up in his notebook journals and his copying from Lewis took place at Camp Chopunnish in May and June of 1806. Voorhis No. 3 has on its flyleaf a list of Chopunnish (Nez Perce) names for rivers; that fact suggests that the book, covering April 4-June 6, 1806, was out of its box and readily available during the period to record the information. Perhaps Clark finished his copying at Camp Chopunnish, although it would have been a substantial task. Clark records events of the period in words very similar to Lewis's, but daily events could obviously have been copied the day they happened. It is notable, however, that after the end of May we no longer have passages in Clark's journal that are clearly copied from Lewis, placed by Clark under dates earlier than in Lewis's journal.[54]

At the beginning of Codex M is a map of the Rockies based on a sketch given by "Sundary Indians of the Chopunnish Nation on the 29th 30th and 31st of May 1806." Clark may not have copied the sketch until several days later, but its presence in Codex M, which begins on June 6, near the end of the Camp Chopunnish sojourn, suggests that the book was unpacked and available at that time. It is therefore possible that Clark's copying from Lewis was complete to June 6 and he was able to start Codex M on the actual date.

Having returned to Travelers' Rest, the captains split the party on July 3, Lewis going northeast to seek a shorter route to the Missouri, Clark southeast to explore the Yellowstone. By all previous experience they should each have kept a journal during the period of separation, especially since they would be covering territory they had not previously explored.[55] Did they keep field notes on the trail or write in their notebook journals?

Lewis's Codex L runs to July 4, then resumes after eighteen blank pages with an entry for July 15; that is the only such unfilled gap in time in a notebook journal. The fragmentary Codex La (July 3–15) covers that period, and Lewis probably intended it as the first draft. He probably packed away the notebook Codex L for safekeeping while traveling through the mountains, then resumed writing in it on July 15, leaving the blank pages to fill in later from the material in Codex La. In fact he never got around to that, probably because he quit writing entirely on August 12, by which date all the writing in Codex L was probably complete. He probably wrote his account of the violent encounter with the Blackfeet on July 27–28 at least a few days later, after rejoining his party following a hurried ride across country. He continued Codex L to August 8, after which the fragmentary Codex Lb covers August 9–12; on the twelfth Lewis stopped writing entirely because of discomfort from the accidental gunshot wound inflicted by Pierre Cruzatte on August 11. He had rejoined Clark on August 12, and the latter could now keep a record for the whole party.

The loose pages constituting Codex Lb were evidently once part of a red notebook found among Clark's papers, which bears on its cover the notation "9 to 12

Augt. 1806"; it now contains no expeditionary material. Lewis evidently began writing in the book after finishing Codex L, then stopped after a few days because of the pain of his wound. In later years Clark removed those few pages to use the book for other purposes. Considering the unfilled gap in Codex L, it appears that Lewis's journal keeping ceased entirely on August 12, 1806, and was then complete as it now stands.

Clark's travels after leaving Lewis involved several shifts from horseback to canoes and back to horses, but there is little indication that he did not write entries directly into his notebook journal (Codex M) for much of the period. A fragment for this period, covering the days July 13–19 and July 24–August 3, consists of courses and distances for his Yellowstone exploration—July 13 was the day he left the Three Forks of the Missouri headed for the Yellowstone. The Codex M entries for those days are much more extensive than the material in the fragment. The gap in the fragment represents the period when Clark's party stopped to build canoes, when there were no courses and distances to be recorded. Codex M has fairly extensive entries for those days. The Codex M entries through July 23 are in sequence, with no large gaps or crowding; as far as we can tell, Clark could either have been keeping that journal day by day, or he could have brought it up to date to the twenty-third while encamped.

Clark reached the Missouri, at the mouth of the Yellowstone, on August 3. At the end of his August 3 entry in Codex M is a passage, over two pages in Lewis's hand, describing the Yellowstone, which obviously Lewis could not have written before the captains' reunion on August 12. Clark's August 4 entry then follows on the next page without any gap. Unless Lewis managed to fit his passage neatly into a gap left by Clark, then the subsequent entries by Clark must also have been written after August 12. Lewis may have written the passage on August 12 before he stopped writing, but he could also have written it weeks later, after he had largely recovered from his gunshot wound, even after the arrival in St. Louis.

In his August 10 entry in Codex M, Clark gives a description of a cherry in Lewis's characteristic technical vocabulary, which is in fact copied from Lewis's description in Codex Lb for August 12; Clark could not have copied it before August 12, the date of their reunion.[56] Clark has a lengthy description of Lewis's experiences after their parting, with courses and distances, in his August 12 entry. The day of their reunion was the logical place for that information, but there is no proof that he actually wrote it on the twelfth. After that narration, however, Clark finishes the entry with the remaining events of August 12, the natural sequence if he had written the entry on that date.

The last daily entry in Codex M is that of August 14; it breaks off in the middle and is taken up in Codex N, an unusual procedure for Lewis and Clark. The entry in Codex M runs into the bottom of a weather table for the month of August 1806, which is complete to the end of the month. It is not clear which was written first, since Clark might have broken off the August 14 entry to leave space for finishing the weather table already started. Otherwise, we would have to assume he wrote the August 14 entry after the end of August. Codex N takes up under the heading of August 15, yet it clearly describes the same Indian council as that of August 14, in Codex M; the transition from one day to the next is never clear. Hurried copying at a later date might be the explanation of the unusual confusion of dates.

At the end of Codex M, Clark wrote an undated "Memorandom" to himself about some things that needed to be done; among them was to "Copy a Sketch of the rochjhone [Yellowstone]." Under the date of August 10, Clark notes that he "finished a copy of my Sketches of the River Rochejhone," which may mean the memorandum was written before that date. He also notes that he must make "a copy of the courses and distances," perhaps meaning to copy the fragment giving courses and distances for July 13–19 and July 24-August 3. The last item is "to fill up [vacinces?] in my book." Those "vacancies" could be merely the various blanks left in the journals for names of streams decided on later; they could be portions of pages left blank for insertion of material; or they could be more extensive blank spaces in the notebooks. At any rate, the note emphasizes the uncertainty for scholars of determining when any particular entry or portion of one was written.

Clark's Codex N has several blank spaces at the end of entries, perhaps left for insertion of extra information in case of need; that provides no satisfactory indication of when the writing was done. Codex N also contains miscellaneous notes that could have been made at various dates. The first two pages (including one side of the front flyleaf) are lists of goods shipped from St. Louis after the expedition's return, written in the same direction as the journal entries that follow. It is possible, then, that Clark wrote the whole of the daily entries in the book (August 15–September 26) after the latter date. The use of the flyleaf, however, might be taken as an indication that the list was written after the journal entries. The confusion of dates at the beginning of Codex N, the gaps perhaps left for later insertions, and one instance (August 16–17) where one day's entry runs over into the beginning of the next, could all be taken as indications of haste. Such haste, however, could belong either to the period of the final rush downriver by the homesick explorers, or to the period after the return, when Clark was trying to finish his task. Codex N ends on September 26, three days after the arrival in St. Louis; the entries are progressively shorter the last few days, the last two notably so. There is no discernible reason why Clark chose to end at this particular point rather than on the day of arrival; that would be especially odd if he were copying the material from notes later.

There is still doubt, then, as to when Clark finished his writing. Jefferson's statement that "ten or twelve" red books were turned over to him on Lewis's return is too vague to support any precise conclusions. If Lewis showed the president all his own and Clark's daily notebook journals—Codices D through N and Voorhis Nos. 1, 2, and 3, there would be fourteen red books.[57] That leaves room for some unfinished journal keeping by Clark, consisting most probably of Codex N and part of Codex M if there was any such unfinished work. If Clark had delivered the remaining material on or soon after his own arrival in Washington on January 21, 1807, Jefferson might not have considered the circumstance memorable or worth mentioning years later, especially since he always tended to think and write of the expedition and the journals as essentially Lewis's.

The reader may not think the above a substantial advance beyond David McKeehan's statement of 1807 that "the several journals were brought together . . . and the blanks . . . filled up . . . at the different resting places." That is the procedure common sense would suggest, and it accords with the evidence available. In all probability, the bulk of the journals were complete when Jefferson saw them, some three months after the end of the expedition. Neither Jefferson nor McKeehan made any specific mention of field notes, but they were certainly made because some still exist. The possibility remains that the captains made other field notes and that some of those may yet be found. The evidence, however, does not require us to assume extensive sets of field notes amounting to duplicate journals covering the whole journey and copied into notebooks during or after the expedition.

Neither does the evidence indicate a uniform journal-keeping procedure followed consistently throughout the expedition. The captains followed their own convenience so far as consistent with making a complete record and with the safety of the documents themselves. If they had any fixed procedure in mind when they started out, they were certainly flexible enough to change it in the light of experience. Clark's full and extensive Field Notes for the journey up to Fort Mandan do not prove the existence of such notes for periods when none have been found. There are good reasons for believing that both captains wrote parts of their notebook journals later than their given dates, in the case of some of Clark's journals months later. At other times the evidence suggests that they kept the notebook journals day by day or soon after the given dates. They may have written in the notebook journals daily when the going was fairly smooth and the books were easily transported and protected. Under bad conditions they probably sealed up the notebooks in tin boxes for safety, using more or less extensive rough notes to keep a daily record.

The most significant criterion for the use of field notes would be the risk factor. In the beginning, when they were still gaining experience and testing procedures (on the journey to Fort Mandan), when travel and weather conditions were particularly bad (on the Lolo Trail), or during separations (the trip to the whale site on the Oregon coast), we can expect to find field notes with the finished journals.

The presence of several fragmentary, unbound codices naturally suggests a comparison with Clark's Field Notes of the first year; could they be the remains of a similar comprehensive set of preliminary journals, the basis of the notebook journals? The majority of them represent periods when the captains were separated; does this mean that the authors wrote them only because of that circumstance, or was that the reason those notes were preserved while many others were discarded? None of the fragments gives a clear indication of being part of a more extensive body of notes. There are no parts of a previous day's entry at the beginning, nor the beginning of another entry cut off at the bottom of the last page. In one or two cases the author may have intended to continue but left blank space indicating he never got around to it. The same appears to be the case with the Elkskin-bound Journal. The "fragments," as far as the evidence goes, are complete in themselves and not the remains of something larger. There was nothing, after all, to prevent the author of each fragment from copying it into his notebook and then discarding it with the rest of his hypothetical field notes. The preservation of these scattered pieces is more likely to have been the result of the captains' desire to preserve everything that could possibly be useful and relevant. Because so many of the fragments are Lewis's, they are part of the mysteries surrounding his journal keeping.

Nine of Lewis's fragmentary codices (Aa, Ba, Fa, Fb, Fc, Fd, Fe, Ia, and Lb) are apparently pages taken from notebooks, all but one (Ia) from red books. It is possible that Lewis removed the pages before writing on them, but it is equally possible that the writing was done in the books and the pages removed at some later period. Codex Fc, for instance, came from Codex P, and there is some reason to believe that those pages were not removed until 1810, when the book was used to copy natural history notes for Benjamin Smith Barton. As noted, many of the fragments represent periods when the captains were separated or when weather and travel conditions posed a special risk to the journals. On such occasions Lewis may have used a book that was largely blank, containing perhaps some relatively unimportant or duplicated data. Thus if the book he was carrying with him was damaged by weather or a dip in a river, or if he failed to return from a scouting mission, important material would not be lost, as would be the case if a regular daily journal suffered. This possibility may strengthen the likelihood that the so-called fragments are complete in themselves and not part of a body of lost field notes. Jefferson's reference to the red books as "travelling pocket journals," although he was not present when they were written, at least suggests that some of them were at some times carried on the person. Their size renders this quite possible. The "fragment" pages could have been removed from the books during the expedition, after the return, or when Clark and Biddle were working on the journals in 1810. If Lewis did have daily field notes and did not get them copied, what happened to them? When they saved so much else—so many fragments, scraps, and sketches—why not save material by the expedition leader covering periods when there is no other writing by him? Once again we have hypothetical lost journals, for whose existence there is no real evidence.

When Clark gave Nicholas Biddle custody of the notebook journals in 1810, Clark retained some of his own notebooks, which became part of Thwaites's discovery of material from the Voorhis family. The ones he retained covered periods for which there are known Lewis journals. The ones turned over to Biddle cover the periods where no Lewis journals are known to exist and the long separation in the summer of 1806. It certainly appears that the basis of Clark's choice of which of his own books to give Biddle was the existence or nonexistence of journals by Lewis covering the same period. If so, then the present gaps in Lewis's journals apparently existed by 1810 at the latest, and as noted no letters are known that lament the loss of daily journals by Lewis, either at the time of his death or earlier.

Clark's Elkskin-bound Journal represents a special case where extra care was taken to preserve a lengthy body of what evidently started out as rough course and distance notes with sketch maps made on the spot. But for most of the period covered by that journal there is no known writing by Lewis, and it seems that Clark did not write his notebook journals for at least half the period until months later. Moreover, conditions during the period were often such that the notebooks would have been safer in their sealed boxes. The Elkskin-bound Journal ends at the very point where Lewis's known journalizing resumes.

From the evidence it appears that Clark kept no regular journal for almost three months at Fort Clatsop (January, February, and March 1806), while Lewis was keeping his journal with its extensive notes on natural history and ethnology. Either they planned all along for Clark to copy those notes or decided on this precaution at some later point for safety's sake. It is unclear when Clark completed the copying of Lewis's Fort Clatsop journals or when he wrote the remainder of his notebook journals—how much he completed on the trail or how much, if any, after reaching St. Louis. We can only guess how long it took him to copy from Lewis or to compose his own entries. He introduced many of his own characteristic spellings into copied material, indicating that he was not trying to achieve literal faithfulness, and he sometimes changed the wording and included material from his own experiences where it seemed relevant.

At points where a notebook journal appears from good evidence to have been written weeks or months after the given date, it is not unreasonable to suppose the existence of some sort of field notes to assist memory. The clearest and most extreme case of the sort, Clark's notebook journals of fall 1805 to spring 1806

(Codices H and I and Voorhis No. 2), is explained by the existing Elkskin-bound Journal (from November 1805 to December 31, 1805), and after January 1, Clark copied from Lewis's journals. In cases where the interval between the given date and the actual writing of the entry was shorter, the notes could have been as extensive as the existing field notes of Clark's from the first year, or they might have been in the nature of expanded course and distance notes with sketch maps, of which various examples remain.

There is little reason to accept the theory that the red notebook journals were all written after the return from subsequently discarded field notes. Considering the great amount of extant material and the labor involved in writing it, we need not imagine extensive sets of field notes paralleling the notebooks when the existence of such notes is neither known nor required by the evidence. Whatever Clark's "we commenced wrighting" in his last journal entry refers to, it was probably not the task of writing all the red books covering a year and a half of travel. Most of the material we now have was written by the captains in the course of the expedition. In reading it, we are in a sense traveling with them and sharing their day-by-day experiences and uncertainties.

The Editing and Publishing of the Journals

Whatever the nature of the "wrighting" mentioned in Clark's last journal entry, the captains were in no doubt about the importance of their written record. Much of Jefferson's instructions to Lewis consisted of either detailed lists of the sort of information they were to record or admonitions about the importance of making duplicates and preserving their notes against loss. If they could make contact with some American ship on the Pacific coast, even if they did not choose to return by sea, they were to send some trustworthy member of the Corps of Discovery home by that route with a copy of their journals to date. Jefferson wanted a full record of their findings to present to the world as soon as possible in a multivolume work, including a narrative of the journey and a full exposition of their scientific and geographic discoveries, with appropriate maps and illustrations. The published accounts of Captain Cook's voyages and the journals of American naturalist William Bartram probably provided models of what Jefferson had in mind. Certainly he did not intend to have the journals published in their original, rough form; the convention of the time demanded that someone should produce a polished, literary version. Jefferson intended that Lewis, who had the sort of literary style admired at the time, should do the writing.[58]

Jefferson and everyone else associated with the work would meet repeated delays and frustrations; indeed, no one alive at the time would see the full record presented to the world. For all his good intentions, Jefferson himself was responsible for many of the initial delays, for he promptly appointed Lewis and Clark to official positions that prevented their devoting their time to preparing the journals for publication. Lewis he nominated as governor of the upper portion of Louisiana, with its capital at St. Louis, and Clark was to be superintendent of Indian affairs for the same region. The country needed men of knowledge and ability in those positions, and on the face of it no two were better qualified. Yet Lewis's appointment would prove disastrous for him.

Before leaving for St. Louis, Lewis made arrangements for publication with a Philadelphia publisher, John Conrad, and published a prospectus for a three-volume work to be financed, like many books of the time, by the subscriptions of prospective readers. According to the prospectus issued in April 1807, the first volume would be a narrative of the journey, the second would present the geography and "a view of the Indian Nations," and the third would give the scientific results. "Lewis & Clark's map of North America" was to be published separately "on a large scale." Jefferson and Lewis hoped to have the first volume out by the end of 1807.[59]

Not only did Lewis's duties as governor prevent his working on the narrative but the frustrations and pressures he met also tragically disrupted his personal life. Financial difficulties, political opposition, and probably alcoholism brought him to despair. In October 1809, on a journey to Washington to straighten out his tangled official accounts, he died of gunshot wounds by his own hand in a lonely cabin in Tennessee. Jefferson and Clark, who must have known him as well as anyone, seem to have had no doubt that he committed suicide, but various later historians have sought to prove that he was murdered. At the time of his death he had done nothing to prepare the narrative of the expedition for publication, but fortunately, the journals were found in his personal belongings. The task now fell to Clark, who was only too conscious of his deficiencies as a literary man.[60]

In the meantime, Sergeant Gass had published a heavily revised version of his journal in 1807. To supplement their own records, the captains had required the sergeants to keep journals, and others kept records as well; those journals will be discussed in another part of this volume, and existing journals will appear in this edition. Gass had no permission to publish, and Lewis was somewhat vexed at the sergeant's enterprise. Lacking any literary pretensions, Gass had his journal worked over by David McKeehan, who produced a heavily edited volume, probably quite unlike the original. Gass could add little to the scientific results, and the McKeehan text scrupulously avoids mentioning personal names and many other matters that would have added to the history of the journey. Gass does give a few pieces of information not found elsewhere, such as the dimensions of Fort Mandan (November 3, 1804); because he was a carpenter, he may have supervised the building.[61]

Jefferson had always thought of the journey as essentially Lewis's; Clark's function was to second the commander and take over if anything happened to Lewis. No such necessity arose during the expedition, but after Lewis's personal disaster, Clark did indeed have to take over and finish their joint task, now in a phase for which he considered himself little qualified. We might have expected that Jefferson, having left the presidency in 1809, would have had the time, as he certainly had the qualifications, to prepare the work for publication himself, but there is no evidence that he ever considered it, although he maintained his interest in its progress.

With Lewis's death, Clark became custodian of the captains' journals, and to him fell the duty of preparing the narrative account of the expedition. Unsure of his own literary abilities, he turned to Nicholas Biddle, a literary figure of Philadelphia. Reluctant at first to accept the task, Biddle eventually acquiesced and agreed to visit Clark at Fincastle, Virginia, the family home of Julia Hancock Clark, the captain's first wife. There Biddle spent about three weeks in the spring of 1810, learning about the expedition and poring over the journals. Biddle took copious notes in partially filled and unused notebooks from the expedition. His task was to write an account of the trip while leaving scientific matters to others. Biddle had full use of the captains' journals at that time and Sergeant John Ordway's journal as well, and took most of them with him. Later in Philadelphia he had the personal assistance of George Shannon, a private in the party.[62]

After Clark's return to the West, he and Biddle corresponded about the problems of publication and further questions that occurred to Biddle. The failure of John Conrad's publishing business in 1812 further delayed publication. In 1813, Biddle made arrangements with another Philadelphia firm, Bradford and Inskeep, and also turned the work over to Paul Allen for final revision. Although Allen's contribution was secondary, his name was the only one to appear on the title page as author. Biddle probably followed a literary convention of the time that a gentleman did not publish under his own name, if he did not earn a living by writing. Indeed, Biddle received not a cent for his work; neither did Clark, for Bradford and Inskeep also went into bankruptcy in 1814, the year of publication of *History of the Expedition under the Command of Captains Lewis and Clark*. Only 2,000 sets were printed. Two years after publication, Clark himself was still trying to obtain a copy.[63]

For nearly eighty years Biddle's work, except for the Gass volume, would stand as the sole literary product of the Lewis and Clark expedition. Many readers believed that in it they were reading the actual journals of the captains. Biddle was scrupulous about accuracy, taking care to question Clark on innumerable points. He had not traveled in the West, and he could not have known the country as the captains did. Because of a personal interest in ethnology, he included much of the wealth of information to be gleaned from the journals about native peoples.

Certainly his care, together with Clark's map of the West published with it (*Atlas* map 126), helped make the work a valuable source of information on the country and its people.

Very few of Lewis's impressive notes on natural history appear in Biddle's work, for the planned scientific portion of the *History* was left in the hands of Benjamin Smith Barton, a leading naturalist of Philadelphia. Before his death, Lewis had discussed his intended publication with Barton and had perhaps asked him to write the scientific volume—chiefly those parts concerned with natural history. Clark made a similar arrangement with Barton in 1810 and had the natural history notes in the daily-entry journals copied into other notebooks for the naturalist. Because of Barton's age and failing health, and perhaps his procrastination, no volume on the scientific achievements of the expedition ever appeared.[64]

After Jefferson and Biddle had deposited the journals with the American Philosophical Society in 1817 and 1818, the volumes rested virtually untouched for some seventy-five years, and Biddle's history remained their only representation to the world. Yet the Biddle paraphrase was by no means all that Jefferson had hoped; in particular, the omission of the scientific findings helped establish a view of the expedition, common to this day, as primarily a romantic adventure. That conception was altered largely through the work of one man of large scientific achievements and with an unassailable conviction of the correctness of his own views. Elliott Coues became the next editor of the Lewis and Clark documents and in his work illuminated the numerous scientific discoveries of the captains. Moreover, he codified the society's expedition documents under a reference system that is in use to this day. Although Coues was to become one of the most notable editors of western historical documents, his professional training was in quite different fields. He had served for eighteen years as an army surgeon, but his great interest was in birds, and he had become the leading American ornithologist of his day. His military duties took him to various regions traversed by Lewis and Clark, so that, unlike Biddle, he had firsthand knowledge of the West. He came to the editing task in 1891 when publisher Francis P. Harper sought someone to prepare a new edition of Biddle's history.[65]

In a sense, Coues rediscovered the Lewis and Clark manuscripts that had been deposited by Biddle and Jefferson with the American Philosophical Society in 1817 and 1818. Since that time the journals had hardly been touched, and although they were not lost, they were certainly little known. Society records demonstrate that while the journals rested securely in the archives between Biddle's and Coues's time there were a number of applications for their use. In 1837, Secretary of War Joel Poinsett asked the society to loan the journals to John James Audubon, who wished to prepare a natural history of the expedition. Audubon was then in Europe, and it was decided not to risk the journals to an ocean voyage, but the society offered full use of them at Philadelphia. In 1884, the society published its minutes up to 1838, which revealed to readers that the journals were in its keeping. During the next few years, ethnologists Daniel G. Brinton and Henry Henshaw and geographer Alfred J. Hill inquired about the manuscripts. But it was Coues who rekindled the nation's interest in Lewis and Clark.[66]

During the Christmas season of 1892, Coues began to examine the manuscript journals in the study of his home at 1726 N Street, Washington, D.C., having been loaned the documents to prepare his edition of Biddle's work. Coues was unawed by these original notebooks, for he quickly began to set them in order for easy reference and to tamper with them in a shameless fashion. He removed their brass holding clasps; he reordered and covered loose pages and set them in chronological sequence; and he labeled each notebook and paginated the lot. He even made a secret copy of the whole without the knowledge or consent of the society. Moreover, he added numerous and sometimes long interlinear notations and trimmed several ragged pages. For those reasons, despite their admiration for Coues's edition (his annotation was a magnificent addition to Biddle's work), scholars have been critical of the doctor.[67]

Not all that Coues did to the journals, however, should be considered detrimental. His labeling, reordering, and paging of the notebooks and loose papers provide a practical way of cataloging and referring to the journals. Besides designating the notebooks as codices and setting them in chronological order, Coues wrote out a lengthy description of the journals' contents—noting maps, drawings, figures, and tables—and discussed the authorship and disposition of each journal. All that work is very helpful, although it does not excuse his defacing of the manuscripts.[68]

Coues's 1893 edition of Biddle's *History* was in many ways a masterly work. He was able to identify many of the plants and animals mentioned and to locate many geographical points. With the aid of the journals, he elucidated many of Biddle's obscure passages, adding extensive supplementary quotes from the journals. Coues was a champion of the footnote, undaunted by problems of space; his notes come close to outrunning Biddle's text, and he was willing to alter Lewis's and Clark's language when quoting from the journals. He seldom hesitated to interject his own opinions or information, whether or not it was relevant to the subject; in particular, he could not refrain from mentioning if he had visited points passed by Lewis and Clark, and he seldom admitted doubt on any point if he could possibly avoid it. Nonetheless, his editorial work was a major contribution to the knowledge of the expedition.[69]

Coues evidently made his secret copy of the journals in anticipation of editing them for publication himself, but other work and his early death in 1899 prevented this.[70] Instead, the job fell to Reuben Gold Thwaites, who undertook the task for the publishing firm of Dodd, Mead and Company in 1901. Thwaites, head of the State Historical Society of Wisconsin, was already an experienced editor of several western historical documents. In the course of his Lewis and Clark research he discovered a number of new documents that greatly enhanced his edition. He included everything from the expedition that had been deposited at the American Philosophical Society by Jefferson and Biddle but decided against including Gass's journal because he considered it easily available elsewhere. Among his discoveries were the journals of Sergeant Charles Floyd and Private Joseph Whitehouse and, even more important, a number of daily journals and other documents by Clark that the latter had retained instead of giving them to Biddle in 1810. Those were in the possession of Clark's granddaughter and great-granddaughter, Julia Clark Voorhis and Eleanor Glasgow Voorhis, and now constitute the Voorhis Collection at the Missouri Historical Society, St. Louis. (See Appendixes B and C.)[71]

Thwaites's work would surely have satisfied Jefferson. All scientific material was included as well as the maps found in the Voorhis Collection. He also printed a number of the letters from the collection in an appendix. Yet Thwaites labored under certain handicaps of space and time and lacked the broad geographic and scientific knowledge that Coues brought to his work. Errors of transcription slipped by, and his organization of materials is open to criticism in some respects. By the standards of a later generation, his annotation was meager and somewhat erratic; he borrowed from Coues's footnotes and supplemented them with help from other scientists and his own knowledge of western history. The deficiencies of his work demonstrate both the increasing intellectual specialization and the amount of scholarship that remained to be done on the expedition. Nonetheless, Thwaites made available to the world for the first time the bulk of the captains' and their subordinates' journals, more or less as the authors had prepared them. It was his work that made possible the subsequent generations of Lewis and Clark scholarship that have finally rendered a new edition necessary.[72]

Thwaites thought he had probably uncovered all the Lewis and Clark material still in existence, but within a decade of his edition, new documents became available. Among expedition papers discovered by Biddle's grandsons in their grandfather's papers in 1913 were the three-volume journal of Sergeant John Ordway and a journal kept by Lewis and later Clark of the preliminary trip from Pittsburgh to Camp Dubois, from August 30 to December 12, 1803. Thwaites had known that Ordway had kept a journal and had been searching for it when he discovered the Voorhis journals, but the Lewis and Clark document—here called the Eastern Journal—was a totally unexpected discovery, for no one had suspected that any notes were kept on this initial phase of the trip. The editorial work on Ordway's journal and the Eastern Journal went to Milo Milton Quaife, Thwaites's successor at the State Historical Society of Wisconsin. Quaife was a professional historian, though at the time he took the job he lacked the editorial experience of both Coues and Thwaites, and the scientific and geographic knowledge of Coues. He carefully compared Ordway's account with those of Lewis, Clark, Floyd, and Whitehouse. He restrained himself in annotation, unlike Coues, and most of his notes relate to geography; however, he has been criticized for his dearth of annotation.[73]

The rediscoveries of Lewis and Clark documents described thus far, while pleasant surprises to scholars, were in places where such materials might reasonably have been expected, if they were in existence. In 1953, however, a major find came to light under totally unexpected circumstances. In St. Paul, Minnesota, Lucile M. Kane, curator of manuscripts for the Minnesota Historical Society, inspected the papers stored in an old desk of General John Henry Hammond, who had died in 1890. One bundle of papers, wrapped in a Washington, D.C. newspaper, proved to be sixty-seven sheets of field notes written by William Clark in 1804 and 1805, with some interpolations by Lewis. Portions of them cover the winter at River Dubois, about which little was previously known. The rest consist of preliminary notes for the period May 14, 1804–April 3, 1805, though entries are less frequent after November 1804. The first group of papers has been called the Dubois Journal while the second set has been labeled the River Journal. Thwaites had suspected that such notes were made, then copied and expanded in the regular notebooks at some subsequent time that he could not determine, and the new find confirmed his surmise, at least for the period of the River Journal.[74]

Ernest Staples Osgood, an experienced historian of the West, became editor of the Field Notes, but litigation over the ownership of the documents interrupted his work. The heirs of Hammond's estate eventually regained control of the papers from the Minnesota Historical Society and sold them. The final private owners, Frederick W. Beinecke and family, ultimately donated them to Yale University where they remain today. Osgood then concluded his editing of the papers and his book was published in 1964 by Yale University Press. Osgood's work is in many ways the best in the Lewis and Clark story to date. In annotating the Dubois Journal, he was able to illuminate a period hitherto largely obscure; the portions dealing with the actual journey to Fort Mandan, though covering more familiar events, provided much useful supplementary knowledge. Osgood devoted a lengthy introduction to the many problems of the origin and history of the documents and provided facsimiles so that readers could make their own comparisons.[75]

The need for a new edition of the journals has been apparent for some time. The number of discoveries of new journals and the nature of modern editorial techniques have made Thwaites's edition somewhat obsolete. In fact, Thwaites did not publish everything that was available in his day, for he omitted some miscellaneous material in the Voorhis Collection, and he did not include Gass's journal in his volumes since it was accessible at the time. Quaife also neglected to publish everything that came in with the Biddle family deposit but concentrated instead on the two outstanding finds, the Eastern Journal and Ordway's Journal. Those items and other overlooked material will be in this edition. More recently discovered material is also available here for the first time, most important, Joseph Whitehouse's paraphrased journal, discovered in 1966, which extends the available portion of the original. Moreover, the difficulty of obtaining some published material today (especially Quaife's and Osgood's works) has increased the need for this edition. Considering Thwaites's gaps, slight as they are, we can say that this is the first comprehensive, collated edition of all known journals.

The principal goal of the new edition is to present users with a reliable, definitive text. The aim is to approach Coues's unfulfilled ambition of creating a text that is "verbatim et literatim et punctuatim." Earlier editors, pressed for time and working virtually alone, were not so fortunate as to have several reviews by different persons of their transcriptions. Every effort is being made here to present a transcript that is nearly identical to the original.

The new edition will also give readers a thorough, uniform annotation of the journals. Previous editors, at least until Osgood, have relied largely on the work of Coues in his annotation of Biddle's paraphrased edition of 1814 or have not annotated as thoroughly as present users wish. Scholars have been particularly struck by the paucity of notes in Thwaites's edition. With the publication of Osgood's work in 1964, it became clear how antiquated previous editions were. Osgood had considerable editing skills, but he also benefited from the great amount of twentieth-century scholarship on Lewis and Clark. He was especially aided by the publication in 1962 of Jackson's edition of expeditionary correspondence, which had actually created a surge of new scholarship. Since Osgood's work covers only a portion of the trip (through the winter of 1804–5) and only a small part of the writing for that time (Clark's Field Notes), the additional writing and the long, interesting segment from April 1805 to September 1806 is largely fallow ground, to be worked here for the first time with modern annotation. A full discussion of the transcribing policies and the annotating guidelines adopted for this edition is given in the following section, Editorial Procedures. We hope that the new edition will foster a broader knowledge and spark a new enthusiasm for the expedition, its courageous members, and its accomplishments.

Notes

1. For the full history of Jefferson's involvement with the West, see Jackson (TJ); refer to pp. 42–43 for the proposed 1783 expedition. For the history of Western exploration leading up to Lewis and Clark, see DeVoto.

2. Augur is the standard biography of Ledyard; see also Watrous. DeVoto, 596–98, viewed Ledyard's chances as poor. See also Jackson (TJ), 45–56. Ledyard originally in-

tended to sail to the Northwest Coast in his own ship, captained by John Paul Jones, but could not raise the money.

3. Caspar Wistar to Moses Marshall [June 20, 1792], Jackson (LLC), 2:675; Cutright (LCPN), 11–12.

4. Jefferson to Michaux, April 30, 1793, in Jackson (TJ), 74–78.

5. DeVoto, 323–30, 359–79; Anderson; Nasatir (BLC), especially 1:75–115, and Mackay's instructions to Evans, 2:410–14. The Mackay-Evans expedition and Evans's maps are discussed in *Atlas*, 6–7.

6. Jackson (TJ), 94–96; DeVoto, 348–55.

7. Jackson (TJ), 117–24; Lewis's entry, April 7, 1805; Ronda, 15–16.

8. Coues (HLC), 1:xv–xliii; Dillon; Cutright (LCPN), 14–15. Jefferson's list of qualifications for the ideal expedition leader is in Jefferson to Caspar Wistar, February 28, 1803, Jackson (LLC), 1:17–18. For a view of Lewis as less than prudent, see Levi Lincoln to Jefferson, April 17, 1803, ibid., 34–36.

9. Jefferson to Lewis, July 15, 1803, Jackson (LLC), 1:109–10; see DeConde for the history of the Louisiana Purchase.

10. At this writing there is no full published biography of Clark; Loos's unpublished work is unique. See Bakeless (LCPD); Steffen. Clark to Lewis, July 18, 1803, Jackson (LLC), 1:110–11.

11. Steffen, 14–15, 31, 43–51; Coues (HLC), 1:xxxix.

12. Jackson (TJ); Steffen, 3–5, 31–40; Carlos Martinez de Yrujo to Pedro Ceballos, December 2, 1802, Jackson (LLC), 1:4–6.

13. For Jefferson's instructions, see Jefferson to Lewis, June 20, 1803, Jackson (LLC), 1:61–66; Cutright (LCPN), 2–9, analyzes them in some detail; see also Steffen, 37–40; Jackson (TJ), 78–80, 86–113; Allen, 109–16, passim.

14. Jackson (TJ), 112–13, 280–84; Steffen, 55–61, 62.

15. Cutright (LCPN), 2–3, 56–57; Burroughs; Criswell; Jackson (SBLC), 5–8; Jackson (TJ), 32–33, 173–76; Allen, 50, 224–25; for other American naturalists of the period, see Kastner.

16. Jackson (TJ), 128–29; Benjamin Rush to Lewis, May 17, 1803, Jackson (LLC), 1:50–51; Ray & Lurie, 358–70. For differing views of the expedition's Indian relations, see Nichols, 94–101, and Ronda, 252–55.

17. For Lewis's preparations in this period, see Cutright (ML), 3–20. For Rush's advice, see Rush to Lewis [May 17, 1803], Rush's Rules of Health, June 11, 1803, Jackson (LLC), 1:50–51, 54–55.

18. Cutright (ML); Lewis's purchases are itemized in Jackson (LLC), 1:76–99.

19. Lewis to Clark, May 6, 1804, Clark to Henry Dearborn, October 10, 1806, Clark to Nicholas Biddle, August 15, 1811, Jackson (LLC), 1:179–80, 347, 2:571–72.

20. They would have received some hint of this possibility from Evans's conjectural map of the area west of the Mandan villages (*Atlas* map 30), based on Indian information, which showed at least four ranges in the Rockies.

21. Gass's entry, September 19, 1805.

22. Ordway's entry, September 12, 1806. Spanish authorities did indeed send out expeditions from New Mexico as far as Nebraska in 1804, 1805, and 1806, in order to catch the

Americans either westbound or returning, but they came nowhere near the expedition. Jackson (TJ), 153–54; Cook, 446–83. The Spanish assumed that at some point the expedition would penetrate Spanish soil, and that this would be the prelude to the entry of American fur traders and settlers. The imprisonment of Zebulon Montgomery Pike and his men in 1806 indicates what the Spanish authorities had in mind for Lewis and Clark. See Nasatir (BR), 136–42, for the tension between the two countries at this time.

23. Jackson (LLC), 1:vii.

24. Coues (DOMJ), 31. The journals, editors, and editions will be taken up in more detail in the following section of the Introduction and additional information may be found in the appendixes of this volume. References to "codices" follow Coues's arrangement of the journals at the American Philosophical Society, Philadelphia, which will be explained in the next section of the Introduction.

25. Jefferson to Corrèa da Serra, April 26, 1816, Jefferson to Clark, September 8, 1816, Jackson (LLC), 2:611, 619.

26. Coues (DOMJ), 31.

27. Thwaites (LC), 1:xxxiv–xxxv.

28. Coues (DOMJ), 28–29 and Thwaites (LC), 6:263, agree that Codex O was sent back from Fort Mandan. Besides the red books, there were also "Nine memorandum books" in Lewis's effects, taken by Clark and therefore relating to the expedition. If we assume them to be bound books, we may tentatively (and very speculatively) identify them as Codices A, B, C, Q, and R, the Eastern Journal, the Weather Diary, Floyd's Journal, and Ordway's notebook No. 2. See Appendix C. "Six note books unbound" are nearly impossible to identify from the description, and there were numerous bundles of loose papers and maps. Jackson (LLC), 1:70, 92, 96, 98, 2:471. At the time of Lewis's death, Codex O was probably in the possession of Ferdinand Hassler, who was checking the astronomical observations. Clark to William D. Meriwether, January 26, 1810, Clark to Hassler, January 26, 1810, ibid., 2:490–92.

29. Gass's Prospectus, March 23, 1807, Jackson (LLC), 2:390–91.

30. Osgood (FN), xix, xxv, argues that Clark made a clean copy of his Field Notes, at least the latter part, at Fort Mandan. Why he would do so, when the notes were also copied in the notebooks, is not clear.

31. Clark to Jefferson, April 3, 1805, Lewis to Jefferson, April 7, 1805, Jackson (LLC), 1:230–32.

32. Osgood (FN), 302. The notation "Sept 20 &" may be the handwriting of Biddle.

33. Ibid., 305.

34. Jefferson to Barton, December 22, 1805, Jackson (LLC), 1:272; Osgood (FN), xxii–xxiii.

35. Osgood (FN), 321–22.

36. Jefferson to Lewis, June 20, 1803, Jackson (LLC), 1:61–66.

37. Jackson presents the strongest case for Lewis having kept a journal during the first leg of the journey, from Camp Dubois to Fort Mandan. His thesis will be considered in more detail in the paragraphs that follow. Jackson (TJ), 193–95.

38. The blank pages of the Eastern Journal were later filled by Biddle. See Appendix B.

39. Thwaites (LC), 1:xxxv n. 2; Cutright (HLCJ), 9–10.

40. It is interesting that Clark's entry for May 14, 1805, in Voorhis No. 1, consists of half a page by Clark and half a page by Lewis describing the boat incident, the latter in nearly the same language as in Lewis's journal, Codex D. (Voorhis No. 1 is a designation by Thwaites for the family who had the items when he discovered them. See Appendixes B and C.) The last line of Lewis's material is crowded onto the top of the page where Clark resumes; almost certainly Clark left the blank space for some lines about the mishap, which Lewis could have written the same day or much later. Jackson may consider the lost notes to be field notes; at one point he uses the term "unrevised notes." Jackson (TJ), 192–95; Thwaites (LC), 1:xxxv n. 2.

41. Clark to Jefferson, April 1, 1805, Lewis to Jefferson, April 7, 1805, Jackson (LLC), 1:226, 231–32. Jackson presumes that Lewis's substitutions mean that he wanted "Clark's statement to Jefferson to be completely noncommittal." Ibid., 226, headnote. Cutright thinks that the words imply that Lewis had not completed converting his field notes into a regular journal. His interpretation of Lewis's letter is that it cannot be taken as "*prima facie* evidence that he had a journal in form to send to Jefferson." Cutright's wording ("journal in form") leaves an opening for supposing field notes, as he does with Clark's letter. Cutright (LCPN), 120. Only one historian has concluded that Lewis kept no journal, "I do not think there is enough available evidence to support a conclusion that Lewis was keeping a journal on the first leg of the journey." But even he hesitates over a full commitment and in another instance writes, "Field notes . . . must have been taken by both Lewis and Clark during the whole journey." Osgood (FN), xxii, xv.

42. It may be significant that September 19 is the date of again taking up the weather notations, since it is so near the start of Codex Ba and the time of the decision not to send back pirogues to St. Louis. If Lewis was keeping the weather diary independent of Clark, and Clark was copying the weather data into his Codex C, then there may be a case of missing field notes, at least weather remarks, for Lewis during this period. Because Lewis's weather diary has so much of Clark's handwriting, it is here supposed that Clark was the weather recorder and Lewis the copier. However, one can as easily suppose missing weather notes of Clark as of Lewis.

43. Clark does not report the loss in Codex A but only in his Field Notes. Clark's entry (Field Notes), July 13, 1804. Ordway reported that Clark's notes for two days had blown overboard. Ordway's entry, July 14, 1804.

44. On many occasions the captains copied from each other's journals; judging from vocabulary and phrasing, Clark most often copied from Lewis, who was more literate and better versed in scientific terminology. Because Clark did not always copy the material under the same date as it is found in Lewis's journal, we can say with some confidence that Clark's notebook journal entries in 1805 and 1806 were not always written on the days given. Jackson has shown that after Fort Mandan there was a definite break in journalizing techniques, so that not only multiple journals but also duplicate records of important observations were being kept. Jackson (TJ), 192–95.

45. Initial times of separation and journal copying include the following: April 25–26, 1805, when Lewis added some notes about Clark's activities, which information he re-

ceived after the men reunited; June 4–8, 11–16, 1805, when Lewis copied from Clark's journal (Voorhis No. 1) into his own (Codex E) under entries on the day they rejoined, suggesting that Lewis was writing day by day in his notebook journal; and during the portage around the Great Falls of the Missouri and afterwards when Lewis included the "Occurrences with Capt. Clark and Party" as part of each day's entry (in Codices E and F), indicating that he wrote those individual entries after the two reunited. Lewis explained his procedure in the latter instance, for on June 23 he wrote, "I shall on each day give the occurences of both camps during our seperation as I afterwards learnt those of the lower camp from Capt. Clark." He continued this practice until they reunited on July 1. Without saying so, Lewis apparently continued the practice while separated from Clark, July 10–13, 15–16, 18–22, and 23–27, 1805. For periods when he was scouting ahead in July 1805, Clark gives the courses and distances of the main party in Codex G, presumably copying from Lewis at some time after their reunion. Courses and distances are given in blocks of several days, interspersed with several days' narrative entries, in a way that suggests Clark went ahead in Codex G to write them, leaving space to fill in the narrative material. The latter narrates only his own movements, and he may have written them within a few days of their occurrence.

46. Clark's entry for May 31, 1805, is another example of such an insertion.

47. For example, Lewis describes the pinyon jay on August 1, 1805, in Codex F, but it is not noted in Codex Fa, the supposed field notes. Other descriptions are also found in Codex F but not in Codex Fa.

48. Perhaps Lewis started Codex Fc in the middle of a blank book (Codex P) because he intended to fill in the space left with his journalizing for the two weeks from the end of Codex Fb (August 26). If so, he surely had notes of some kind on which to base the entries. Apparently he never got around to it, and there is no sign that he continued after September 10, 1805, at least not in Codex P.

49. A final fragment, Codex Fe, consists of ten pages torn from Codex D recording weather data for April 1–June 30, 1805, and six pages taken from another red book recording weather data for July 1–September 30, 1805. Lewis was the principal author, but Clark shared some of the writing.

50. The Elkskin-bound Journal contains some miscellaneous material of uncertain date, between the December 7 and 8 entries, including distances on the lower Columbia and a list of local tribes. Here also is an entry dated January 1, 1806, having no daily material but consisting of a list of sea captains who traded with the nearby Indians, from Indian information. Lewis has a similar list in Codex J under March 17. We cannot say which list was written first; Clark's list in the elkskin book has more details, and material of any date could have been included in the book.

51. Dunlay.

52. Cutright (LCPN), 263; Jackson (TJ), 192–93. Most of the material Clark copied from Lewis into Voorhis No. 2 is from the Lewis journals covering the Fort Clatsop winter. A notable exception is a description of the mule deer in Clark's entry for March 11, 1806; that he copied from Lewis's Codex D entry for May 10, 1805, ten months before the ostensible date of Clark's entry. Whenever Clark wrote Voorhis No. 2, he evidently had other

Lewis journals out, combing them for important material to duplicate. In addition, in his own May 10, 1805 entry in Voorhis No. 1, he inserted a note: "The Mule Deer Described in No. 8." Today's Voorhis No. 2 was apparently Number 8 in Clark's original numbering system, so he must have inserted the note before his collaboration with Biddle in 1810, when he adopted Biddle's numbering system for cross-references. See Appendix B.

53. Voorhis No. 2 contains a map of the area around the confluence of the Columbia and Multnomah (Willamette) rivers in the midst of the April 3 entry. It is quite similar to the one Clark apparently drew in Lewis's Codex K at the end of the April 3 entry, and there is no certainty which came first. It does suggest that the book (Voorhis No. 2) was available for sketching at the time or soon after.

54. As noted, Clark's Elkskin-bound Journal contains a number of sketch maps, some of them made going down the Columbia in October 1805. Obviously the journal was out and in use during the return up the Columbia. But the Lolo Trail maps in the same book do not have return campsites marked. That may indicate that Clark finished his copying of the Elkskin-bound Journal (to December 31, 1805) by the time he left Camp Chopunnish, having been engaged in copying from it there or during the upriver journey.

55. François-Antoine Larocque, a North West Company trader the captains had met at Fort Mandan, explored a considerable portion of the Yellowstone in 1805. Clark, of course, was unaware of this when he went down the river in 1806 and would have kept a detailed journal in any case. See Larocque.

56. Cutright (LCPN), 325; Jackson (TJ), 192–93.

57. Codex P would have been largely blank at this time, containing the pages now in Codex Fc, some of Lewis's weather notes, and miscellaneous memoranda. Some of the other fragmentary codices may also have been torn out of it. There is no certainty that Jefferson saw Codex P, therefore, but his vagueness about the number of books reduces the relevance of the matter in any case. The same uncertainty applies in the case of Voorhis No. 4.

58. Jefferson to Lewis [June 20, 1803], Jackson (LLC), 1:61–66. The full history of the publishing vicissitudes of the journals is in Cutright (HLCJ).

59. For the prospectus, see Jackson (LLC), 2:394–97; Cutright (HLCJ), 18.

60. Statement of Gilbert C. Russell, November 26, 1811, Clark to Jonathan Clark, October 28, 1809, Jefferson to Russell, April 18, 1810, Jackson (LLC), 2:573–74, 574–75 headnote, 726–27, 728, 747–49 n.; Dillon, 335–50.

61. Cutright (HLCJ), 19–32; Gass.

62. Cutright (HLCJ), 56–60; Clark to Biddle, February 20 and March 25, 1810, Biddle to Clark, March 3 and 17, 1810, Clark to Henry Dearborn, April 15, 1810, Jackson (LLC), 2:494–97, 546. Charles Willson Peale refers to Clark's diffidence about his writing abilities in Peale to Rembrandt Peale, February 3, 1810, ibid., 493.

63. Cutright (HLCJ), 59–66; Biddle to Jefferson, September 28, 1813, Jackson (LLC), 2:595, explains Allen's role.

64. Charles Willson Peale to Rembrandt Peale, February 3, 1810, Clark to Barton, May 22, 1810, Jackson (LLC), 2:493, 548–49. Biddle's prospectus for the work names Barton as the scientific editor, ibid., 548. On Barton's procrastination see Jackson's headnote, ibid.,

562. Biddle to William Tilghman, April 6, 1818, ibid., 636. Cutright (HLCJ), 62, 64–65, 67. Among Biddle's papers delivered to Barton would also be the Indian vocabularies collected by Lewis, which are now lost. See Saindon, 4–6.

65. Cutright & Brodhead, 339–63. Similar material is found in Cutright (HLCJ), 73–103.

66. Poinsett to Vaughan, July 28, 1837, and Vaughan to Poinsett, August 16, 1837, APS (CS) and APS (JCS); APS (EP), 475; Brinton to Henry Phillips, September [26?], 1888, Henshaw to Phillips, November 23, 1889, Hill to Phillips, December 26, 1891 and January 13, 1892 (given as 1891), APS (Arch). Stephen Catlett, manuscripts librarian at the society, called this material to my attention.

67. Cutright & Brodhead, 240, 345–46, 352–53.

68. Coues (DOMJ), 17–33. Besides the published description Coues also wrote a brief synopsis of each journal's contents and pasted it inside the front cover of each notebook.

69. Cutright & Brodhead, 353–58; Cutright (HLCJ), 97–102.

70. Coues tried to persuade Harper to publish a one-volume edition of the journals, but the publisher was not interested. Cutright & Brodhead, 345, 352.

71. Thwaites also discovered a "Donation Book" at the American Philosophical Society, which had not previously been identified as a Lewis and Clark item. It is a list by John Vaughan and Adam Seybert of Lewis's botanical and mineralogical specimens. Thwaites (LC), 6:151–64; Jackson (LLC), 1:220–21; Cutright (HLCJ), 104–27. Thwaites's discoveries and additions to the journal literature will be discussed in more detail in Appendix B.

72. Cutright, (HLCJ) 122–24.

73. Ibid., 128–44; Thwaites (LC), 1:lvi; Quaife (MLJO), 26.

74. Cutright (HLCJ), 145–52.

75. Ibid., 147–76; Osgood (FN); Tomkins, 105–6, passim.

Editorial

Procedures

The primary goal of this edition of the journals of the Lewis and Clark expedition is to present users with a reliable text that is largely uncluttered with editorial interference. The editorial procedures designed to provide such an authentic text have necessitated certain modifications in the original text due to the demands of modern typography and the inconsistent usage of the journalists, but every effort has been made to furnish a transcription that is true to the original. Difficulties that have worked against producing a printed transcript that nearly duplicates handwritten words have also prevented establishing foolproof and unchanging principles of editing. Readers have been advised when deviations from the following procedures occur.

There are usually two parts to each journal entry by Lewis or Clark. One is a narrative text describing the day's events; the other gives the course of travel and distance covered for the day, which the captains usually called "courses, distances, and references." These two sections are here called "text" and "course." The format for the text and course has been somewhat normalized. The course has been set in smaller type than the text in keeping with Lewis's and Clark's practice of writing in a smaller hand for this portion of the journal. The course has been printed in closely aligned columns, one for courses, one for distances, and one for references, after Clark's usual ordering. Lewis's style is somewhat different at the beginning so adjustments have been made in those instances. When the course material is run as a continuous line, as Clark occasionally wrote it in his Field Notes, it has been converted to columns for clarity. In the captains' entries the text sometimes precedes the course and sometimes follows it. Here the order of the text and course follows the journalists' changing arrangement. Where confusion might exist, a date has been given in brackets. The dateline has been set to the right margin whenever it appears on the line above the entry to allow the name of the journalist to be placed consistently on the left margin above the entry. Repeated dates above sections within an entry are placed as they appear on the original.

Grammatical consistency is a vexing problem to any historical editor but particularly to an editor of Lewis and Clark materials. The men's erratic, but delightful and ingenious, manner of spelling and capitalizing creates the most perplexing difficulties of all. "This is expecially true of Clark," one investigator noted, "who was not only the master misspeller of them all, but also displayed dazzling virtuosity in his approach to punctuation, capitalization, and simple sentence structure."[1] In this edition the spelling and capitalization have been retained as nearly as possible, but some conventionalizing has been necessary. Uncrossed *t*'s and undotted *i*'s and the like have been silently corrected. Misspelled words have been corrected in brackets when necessary for clarity. When letters or words defy comprehension, conjectural readings have been given in brackets with a question mark signifying the editor's uncertainty. With ambiguous spelling, the journalist's typical spelling has been taken as a guide, or the modern spelling has been adopted in disputed cases. With Clark that is nearly impossible. One researcher discovered that Clark spelled the word Sioux "no less than *twenty-seven* different ways."[2] Little can be promised in the way of consistency, for no rule can stand against Clark's inimitable style.

For capitalization some consistencies of the writers have been discovered; otherwise, individual letters have been judged against their rise along the line of writing and compared to the writer's normal usage. This procedure has generated a great number of capital letters. Clark again has confounded any system. One historian who struggled with his handwriting wrote: "In the matter of capitalization, one man has utterly bested me. William Clark, a creative speller, is also a versatile capitalizer—especially in handling words beginning with *s*. After many attempts to work out a sane norm I have retired in confusion. Clark uses four kinds of initial *s* and each can be interpreted as a capital."[3]

Several alterations from the original punctuation occur in the text. Periods have been retained mostly in their currently accepted context. Incidental and random periods, which may be pen rests, have been dropped. Spaced periods (leaders), used frequently in the course material, have also been discarded. Periods at the end of lines have been retained. When periods have not been supplied by the writer at the end of a sentence, none have been added. Rather, extra spacing has been used at the end of a sentence where no punctuation appears. If some other punctuation occurs at the end of a sentence (such as a comma or a semicolon), it has been retained and normal spacing follows. Random lines and dashes, occasionally used to separate entries, have been omitted. Multiple or lengthy dashes have been shown as a single dash. Underscoring has been retained, but occasional pen marks that are questionable underlining have been dropped. Multiple underscoring has been dropped except where double underlining has been used

1. Betts (WCW), 10.   2. Ibid.   3. Jackson (LLC) 1:ix.

with a figure that represents a total from a column of figures, such as in the mileage column of a day's course. Quotation marks have been discarded when they appear before every line; only beginning and ending marks have been used. When beginning or ending quotation marks are missing, they have been supplied in brackets at the most logical place.

Paragraphing follows the writer's usage, except that when a paragraph ends and a new one begins without indentation, the new line has been silently indented. When words and phrases are scattered across a page with no apparent order (as in Clark's Field Notes), the text has been printed in the most logical fashion. Otherwise, items have been printed as they appear from left to right and from top to bottom on the page. Signs, symbols, and abbreviations have been handled in this fashion. Signs and symbols found on a modern typewriter have been retained, and unidentified symbols have been dropped. Superscript letters have been brought down to the line of type. Lewis and Clark used a variety of marks under the superscript letters *st*, *th*, and *nd* of their ordinal numbers. Those have been lowered, marks beneath the letters have been discarded, and no punctuation has been added. Abbreviated and contracted words have been spelled out within brackets only if it seems that the word might not be understood. Most often they are unaltered. Scored-out, torn, and blotted passages have been handled in this way. Where words have been crossed out by the author for the apparent purpose of word choice, with no significant change in the text, the words have been silently omitted. Where words scored out by the author add new meaning, or convey a different sense to the passage, the deleted words have been placed between angle brackets. If it appears that someone other than the author has crossed out words, the affected passage has been restored and the action noted in the annotation. When a passage is unclear due to the condition of the paper, or because the writer has disfigured the page, a conjectural reading followed by a question mark has been given in brackets; otherwise, a note on the condition of the paper appears between brackets with the words italicized, such as [*torn*], [*blotted*], [*erased*], or [*unable to read*].

Over the years, persons besides the original authors have written on the pages of the journals. Nicholas Biddle was the first, about 1810, as he prepared a paraphrase of the journals. Some of Biddle's emendations were made for his own purposes and some perhaps were made on the advice of Clark, with whom Biddle occasionally collaborated during his labors. During the collaboration, Clark may have added his own postexpeditionary interlineations. Elliott Coues worked with the manuscripts at his Washington home in December 1892 and made numerous and long interlinear notations upon the pages. Perhaps one other, unknown person has also added words here and there in the journals. Those emendations and interlineations have been retained and have been handled in this way. Interlineations by the original author have been added to the line of type without editorial comment. Writings by Lewis or Clark that are interjections in one another's journals or perhaps later writings (usually in ink of a different shade), by Biddle (usually in red ink), by Coues, and by the unknown person have been placed in the text between brackets, with the emended words italicized and with the author's initials placed ahead of the words, such as: [*WC:*], [*ML:*], [*NB:*], [*EC:*], and [*X:*]. The letter *X* stands for the unknown or any unidentified person. Extremely complex or lengthy emendations have been explained in the annotation. Bracketed material without identifying initials and in italics is that of the editor. Where confusion might exist the following scheme has been used to identify the editor's remarks: [*Ed:*].

The format follows the plan adopted by Thwaites in the first edition of the journals. Thwaites printed Lewis's and Clark's entries together but separated the remaining diaries. When the writing of the enlisted men significantly alters or adds to information provided by Lewis and Clark, it has been abstracted and placed in footnotes to the captains' entries. This procedure should reduce annotation in later volumes by combining editorial work under a single entry or two rather than across several volumes. Under this plan the subordinates' journals will not be as heavily annotated and some comparison of volumes may be necessary. Readers have traditionally turned to the words of Lewis and Clark first and used the enlisted men's diaries as supplements—this plan will facilitate such practice. A comprehensive, synoptic index that coordinates all journal entries will be placed in the final journal volume. In the footnotes, subordinates' journals have been noted by dates of entry rather than by their published sources, thus anticipating their eventual publication in this series.

The chapter divisions used in Biddle's edition and maintained by Thwaites and Osgood have also been employed with only minor changes. Thwaites's remarks for this decision are appropriate: "They are convenient chronological and geographical divisions; they are familiar to scholars, and thus have acquired a certain historical and bibliographical standing; moreover, comparisons between the Biddle paraphrase and the Original Journals will be facilitated by their retention."[4] Comparisons between the new edition and Thwaites's volumes will also be facilitated by the retention of the chapter divisions.

Annotation in the new edition will be full but not discursive. Although footnotes will be kept within bounds, it is not the intention to produce a barebones transcription with little or no analysis. The explication of the journals is basic to the purpose of this edition, but the work is primarily the preparation of source material, meant to be borrowed from and enlarged upon by other scholars; there is no mandate to compose essays as footnotes. In general, the amount of

4. Thwaites (LC), 1:lviii.

information included in the annotations depends upon the importance placed on the subject by Lewis and Clark, or upon the significance of the subject to the expedition. In some cases where the information is controversial, conjectural, or confusing, the length of annotation may be disproportionate to the item's relevance to the expedition.

The design for annotation in this edition is similar to the method used in editions of letters, where footnotes are placed at the end of each letter rather than at the bottom of a page. Here the annotation follows each dated entry, and the numbers run consecutively within an entry. Since Lewis's and Clark's entries have been placed together, the annotation comes after the final entry for a day, regardless of the number of journal versions for that day. Lewis's entries, when available, always precede Clark's, and the author's name is given in brackets at the head of each entry. The text material takes priority over the course material for annotation, whatever its order in an entry. If items have been annotated in the text, similar matter has been ignored for annotation in the course. If items have been annotated from Lewis's entry and Clark has much the same material in his entry for that day, Clark's points have not been noted. The same is true if either writer has more than one version for a day's entry. The versions have been placed in the apparent order of their preparation. Annotation is to the first mention of a point and usually only to that mention. References to previous or later notes in this edition are to dated journal entries rather than volume, chapter, and note numbers.

Words defined in modern standard college dictionaries are not annotated, although archaic, regional, unusual, and misleading usages are noted. Variant or incorrect spellings that could mislead the reader sometimes need annotation. I have supplied definitions from the *Oxford English Dictionary* in such cases, but I have not cited it in the notes. Common or well-known places or things are not annotated unless their status in Lewis and Clark's time is significant.

Geographic features mentioned by the explorers are annotated in the journals, except in cases where such notations are too obscure to allow proper identification. Their trail, still doubtful in some areas, has been laid out as accurately as possible and campsites have been identified. The status and signficance of places and the state of geographical knowledge in Lewis and Clark's time are important considerations in the annotations.

Scientific information gained by the expedition—in botany, zoology, geology, medicine, and ethnology—all receive fuller treatment in this edition. Plants and animals are identified by their popular labels and scientific names, with questionable species so noted. Sources cited are primarily the most up-to-date scientific references available; earlier historical sources such as Coues, Gilmore, Criswell, or Cutright are also cited secondarily in some instances.

American Indian groups are identified by tribal names and linguistic affiliations; the latter can demonstrate patterns of historical connections between groups that sometimes cannot be learned either from tribal traditions or from historical records. Information on the location of tribes at the time of Lewis and Clark's visit, the basis of their economy, archaeological sites, other relevant points, and further references are provided in the notes. Significant Indian personalities are portrayed as fully as possible.

Members of the expedition have received the fullest biographical treatment possible within the limits of available information in the notes and in Appendix A. General biographical dictionaries have not been cited in the annotations. Although scholars and enthusiasts will be disappointed to learn that some persons such as "Blaze Cenas" still remain unidentified, persons, places, or things for which research has failed to provide an identification have not been annotated. Exceptions involve cases where the lack of information is itself significant or creates problems, such as the identity of the expedition member La Liberté.

The most important considerations in the annotations have been to substantiate statements in the text and to provide additional information immediately relevant to the expedition. In many areas the editorial staff has turned to the vast literature on the expedition and to numerous scholars and lay people who have graciously offered their assistance in their respective areas of expertise. Our hope is that the new edition will offer the same service to future students of the Lewis and Clark expedition.

EDITORIAL SYMBOLS AND ABBREVIATIONS

[roman]	Word or phrase supplied or corrected.
[roman?]	Conjectural reading of the original.
[*italics*]	Editor's remarks within a document.
[*Ed: italics*]	Editor's remarks that might be confused with *EC, ML, NB, WC,* or *X.*
[*EC: italics*]	Elliott Coues's emendations or interlineations.
[*ML: italics*]	Meriwether Lewis's emendations or interlineations.
[*NB: italics*]	Nicholas Biddle's emendations or interlineations.
[*WC: italics*]	William Clark's emendations or interlineations.
[*X: italics*]	Emendations or interlineations of the unknown or an unidentified person.
⟨roman⟩	Word or phrase deleted by the writer and restored by the editor.

SPECIAL SYMBOLS OF LEWIS AND CLARK

α	Alpha
∠	Angle
☽	Moon symbol
☞	Pointing hand
★	Star
☉	Sun symbol
♍	Virgo

COMMON ABBREVIATIONS OF LEWIS AND CLARK

Altd., alds.	altitude, altitudes
Apt. T.	apparent time
d.	degree
do.	ditto
h.	hour
id., isd.	island
L. L.	lower limb
L., Larb., Lard., Ld., or Lbd. S.	larboard (or left) side
Latd., Lad.	latitude
Longtd.	longitude
m., mts.	minute, minutes
M. T.	mean time
mes., mls., ms.	miles
obstn.	observation
opsd.	opposite
pd., psd.	passed
pt.	point
qde., quadt., qudt.	quadrant
qtr., qutr.	quarter
s.	second
S., St., Star., Starbd. S., Stb., or Stbd.	starboard (or right) side
sext., sextn., sextt.	sextant
U. L.	upper limb

Note: abbreviations in weather entries are explained with the first weather data, following the entry of January 31, 1804.

Meriwether Lewis. Portrait by Charles Willson Peale, 1807, courtesy of
Independence National Historical Park Collection, Philadelphia.

William Clark. Portrait by Charles Willson Peale, 1810, courtesy of Independence National Historical Park Collection, Philadelphia.

Introduction to Volume 2

Pittsburgh, Pennsylvania, to Vermillion River, South Dakota

August 30, 1803–August 24, 1804

On August 31, 1803, Meriwether Lewis left Pittsburgh in his newly completed keelboat, heading down the Ohio with perhaps eleven men. Impeded by low water, he took nearly a month to reach Cincinnati. About October 15 he reached Clarksville, Indiana Territory, just below the Falls of the Ohio, where William Clark awaited him. There they gained several recruits, chiefly young Kentucky woodsmen gathered in by Clark, and York, Clark's black slave. Leaving Clarksville on October 26, they recruited two or three men at Fort Massac (present Illinois) on November 11 and 12, including hunter and interpreter George Drouillard and Private Joseph Whitehouse, one of the expedition's journalists.

At the mouth of the Ohio, which they reached on November 14, they spent a week mapping and measuring and taking celestial observations, then started up the Mississippi on November 20. On their left hand now was present-day Missouri, part of the Louisiana Purchase, still under the rule of Spanish officials pending the transfer to the United States the following spring. On November 28, Lewis left Clark in charge of the boat and the men at the mouth of the Kaskaskia River and proceeded by land to St. Louis to confer with the Spanish authorities. He found them by no means pleased by the expedition; they requested that he make his winter camp on the American side of the river, pending the transfer of Louisiana. Clark proceeded upriver, met and conferred with Lewis on December 9, then left his partner at St. Louis and moved to the American side near the mouth of the River Dubois in modern Illinois. There on December 13 he established the camp where the Corps of Discovery awaited the coming of spring to begin the trip up the Missouri.

During the five months at Camp Dubois the captains gathered further recruits, some of them frontiersmen who enlisted especially for the expedition, others army enlisted men from various western garrisons who were assigned to the expedition by their commanding officers. The long and inevitably tedious winter enabled the captains to evaluate their men, to weed out a few undesirables, and to introduce the more undisciplined to the rigors of army regimen. During the wait they were also able to gather much knowledge about the Missouri River and its native peoples from the fur traders and river men of the region, in particular James Mackay, and to acquire copies of John Thomas Evans's maps of the river. The transfer of Louisiana to the United States was formally accomplished in March 1804, and spring soon brought weather suited for travel.

Lewis was in St. Louis when Clark left Camp Dubois on May 14, 1804, with the keelboat and two pirogues, manned by perhaps 42 men. The party arrived at St. Charles on the Missouri on May 16, and Lewis joined them on the twentieth. At St. Charles they added a few more boatmen and set out on the afternoon of May 21.

The journey up the Missouri, against the current, was slow and laborious; occasionally they could sail with a favorable wind, but more often they poled upstream or the men pulled the boats with a tow rope, walking on the shore. They soon left the last white settlements behind and began to exercise more caution as they entered Indian country. Several times they met fur traders headed down river with their pelts, having wintered among one tribe or another. One of them, Pierre Dorion, Sr., the captains hired to return upstream with them as an interpreter.

Toiling along in the increasing summer heat, plagued by boils, diarrhea, mosquitoes, and sandbars, the Corps of Discovery reached the mouth of the Kansas River, the future site of Kansas City, on June 26. Almost another month was required to reach the mouth of the Platte, on July 21. Just above the Platte they established Camp White Catfish, on the present Iowa shore, and rested a few days (July 22–26). On July 30 they reached a high bluff near the river in modern Nebraska, which they would call Council Bluff, for there they had their first council with the chiefs of the Otos and Missouris, informing them of the change in sovereignty in Louisiana; they remained at the bluffs until August 2.

Some disciplinary problems marred their progress; unauthorized tapping of the whiskey supply earned Private John Collins one hundred lashes. More serious was the desertion of Private Moses B. Reed and the boatman La Liberté in early August; Reed was captured, forced to run the gauntlet, and officially expelled from the party, though he remained with them for the time being because he could not be abandoned in the wilderness. La Liberté made good his escape.

A loss of a different sort soon followed. Just after a second council with the chiefs of the Otos in northeast Nebraska, Sergeant Charles Floyd died, probably of a ruptured appendix, at the present site of Sioux City, Iowa. His comrades buried him on a bluff on the Iowa shore, naming a nearby stream Floyd's River. He would, in fact, be the only man to die on the expedition, but this must have seemed too much to hope for at the time. Four days later they reached the Vermillion River, in present South Dakota, 112 days and about 860 miles out from Camp Dubois.

The Journals of the Lewis and Clark Expedition, Volume 2

August 30, 1803 – August 24, 1804

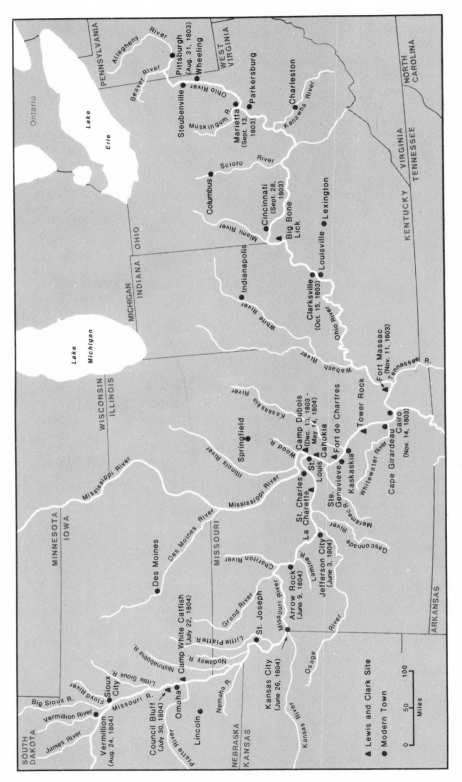

The Expedition's Route, August 30, 1803–August 24, 1804

Chapter One

Down the Ohio

August 30–November 19, 1803

[Lewis]   August 30th 1803.[1]

Left Pittsburgh[2] this day at 11 ock with a party of 11 hands 7 of which
are soldiers, a pilot and three young men on trial they having proposed to
go with me throughout the voyage.[3] Arrived at Bruno's Island[4] 3 miles
below   halted a few minutes.   went on shore and being invited on by
some of the gentlemen present to try my *airgun*[5] which I had purchased
brought it on shore charged it and fired myself seven times fifty five yards
with pretty good success; after which a Mr. Blaze Cenas being unac-
quainted with the management of the gun suffered her to discharge herself accedentaly   the ball passed through the hat of a woman about 40
yards distanc cuting her temple about the fourth of the diameter of the
ball; shee feel instantly and the blood gusing from her temple   we were
all in the greatest consternation   supposed she was dead by [but] in a
minute she revived to our enespressable satisfaction, and by examination
we found the wound by no means mortal or even dangerous; called the
hands aboard and proceeded to a ripple of *McKee's rock**[6] where we were
obleged to get out all hands and lift the boat[7] over about thirty yards; the
river is extreemly low; said to be more so than it has been known for four
years; about [*blank*] we passed another ripple near [*erasure*]   Past another
bear or ripple with more dificulty than either of the others   halted for
the night much fatiegued after labouring with my men all day—[8]   the

water being sufficiently temperate was much in our favor; gave my men some whiskey and retired to rest at 8 OClock—

*a discription of this place to [follow?]

1. Probably misdated. There is no August 31 entry, and in a letter to Jefferson of September 8, Lewis says he left on the thirty-first. Jackson (LLC), 1 : 121.

2. Pittsburgh, Allegheny County, Pennsylvania, is located at the point where the Monongahela and Allegheny rivers join to form the Ohio. It became the "Gateway to the West" and in 1800 had a population of 2,400, growing to nearly 5,000 by 1810. Buck & Buck, 75, 94–95, 217.

3. It is impossible to be certain who was with Lewis at this time. Of those who made the entire journey to the Pacific, George Shannon and John Colter may already have joined. The soldiers were probably detached by Lieutenant William A. Murray. The pilot was T. Moore, who was paid seventy dollars to conduct Lewis to the Falls of the Ohio. For expedition members, see Appendix A at the end of this volume. Ibid., 107 n. 1, 125–26 n. 1; Cutright (HLCJ), 8 n. 11.

4. Named for Felix Brunot, a French physician who settled in Pittsburgh about 1797, it stands where Chartiers Creek empties into the Ohio from the south. Brunot was reportedly a friend of Lewis, which would explain why he stopped at the island in spite of his hurry. Thwaites (EWT), 4 : 93 and n. 50; Buck & Buck, 374; Russell (FTT), 44.

5. This weapon, which much impressed the Indians along the expedition's route, was probably manufactured by Isaiah Lukens, horologist and gunsmith of Philadelphia; it was returned to him after Lewis's death in 1809, sold at auction on Lukens's death in 1847, and discovered and identified in 1976. Probably more useful for impressing the natives than for hunting, it had a butt reservoir and was much like a Kentucky rifle in appearance. Stewart (AAGS); Chatters; Halsey; Wolff, 131–32.

6. McKees Rocks is situated in Allegheny County, just north of the mouth of Chartiers Creek; the formation takes its name from Alexander McKee, who owned land in the area before the Revolution. The cutting action of the river left huge overhanging rocks. Espenshade, 224–25.

7. Much of our information on this vessel comes from drawings and measurements in Clark's Field Notes (see below, fig. 7 and accompanying notes). The craft was built in Pittsburgh in July and August of 1803, presumably to Lewis's specifications, and was somewhat modified at the River Dubois, Illinois, camp during the winter of 1803–4. It was fifty-five feet in length, with an eight-foot beam, a thirty-two-foot mast, a shallow draft, and a hold thirty-one feet long. At the stern was a cabin with a deck on top, and there was a ten-foot deck at the bow. As Clark's drawings show, it was basically a galley, little resembling the classic keelboat of the "Western Waters." It does strongly resemble a Spanish river galley of the 1790s illustrated in Nasatir (SWV), frontispiece—apparently a drawing by Clark. This seems to have been a standard type of vessel for use on inland waters, especially for military purposes. See Baldwin (KA), 16–19, 42–45, 162–64, and illustrations opposite 32, 42, 64; Appleman (LC), 49; Lewis to Jefferson, July 15 and 22, September 8, 1803,

Lewis to Clark, August 3, 1803, Jackson (LLC), 1:110–17, 121–22; Nicholas Biddle Notes, ca. April 1810, ibid., 2:534.

8. In Allegheny County the information does not allow precise location.

[Lewis]   September lst—

The Pilott informed me that we were not far from a ripple which was much worse than any we had yet passed, and as there was so thick a fogg on the face of the water that no object was visible 40 paces he advised remaining untill the sun should acquire a greater altitude when the fogg would asscend and disappear; I conscented; we remained untill eight Oclock this morning when we again set out— these Foggs are very common on the Ohio at this season of the year as also in the spring but do not think them as freequent or thick in the spring.   perhaps this may in some measure assist us to account for the heavy dues which are mor remarkable for their freequency and quantity than in any country I was ever in—   they are so heavy the drops falling from the trees from about midknight untill sunrise gives you the eydea of a constant gentle rain, this continues untill the sun has acquired sufficient altitude to dessipate the fogg by it's influence, and it then ceases.   the dues are likewise more heavy during summer than elsewhere but not so much so as at this season.—   the Fog appears to owe it's orrigin to the difference of temperature between the *air* and *water* the latter at this seson being much warmer than the former; the water being heated by the summer's sun dose not undergo so rapid a change from the absence of the sun as the air dose consiquently when the air becomes most cool which is about sunrise the fogg is thickest and appears to rise from the face of the water like the steem from boiling water—[1]   we passed the *little horsetale* ripple or riffle with much deficulty, all hands laboured in the water about two hours before we effected a passage; the next obstruction we met was the *big-horse tale* riffle,[2] here we wer obliged to unload all our goods and lift the emty Boat over, about 5 OCock we reach the riffle called Woollery's trap,[3] here after unloading again and exerting all our force we found it impracticable to get over, I therefore employed a man with a team of oxen with the assistance of which we at length got off   we put in and remained all night having made only ten miles this day.—[4]

1. Lewis's reflections on fog and dew and their determinants over the next several days bring him to posit a theory for the occurrence and to test his hypothesis by taking temperature readings of air and river during the time. Apparently cold air is moving down the valley sides and passing across the warm water of the Ohio River in a situation known as cold air drainage. Since the air is heated from below as well as moistened, the fog takes the form of rising streamers, and the phenomenon is generally called steam fog. Neiburger, Edinger, & Bonner, 123–24.

2. Zadoc Cramer's guide to the Ohio River refers to the first ripple and the second, which he calls Horsetail ripple; he places them along today's Neville Island, in Allegheny County, Pennsylvania. Cramer (5th), 29–30.

3. Cramer calls this Woolery's ripple. Ibid., 30; Baily, 55.

4. Apparently just downstream from Woollery's Trap, in Allegheny County.

[Lewis]   Septr. 2ed

Set out at sunrise 2 miles ½ to a riffle   got out and pulled the boat over it with some dificulty—   9 Oclock reched Logtown riffle[1] unloaded and with much difficulty got over   detain 4 hours.—   The hills on either side of the ohio are from 3 to 400 feet which runing parrallel to each other keep the general course of the river, at the distance of about two miles while the river pursuing a serpentine course between them alternately washes their bases.—   thus leaving fine bottom land between itself and the hills in large boddys, and freequently in the form of a simecicles or the larger segment of a circle or horseshoe form   The weather is extreemly dry but there was some appearance of rain this morning which seems now to have blown over—   supposed I had gotten over Logtown riffle but find ourselvs stranded again   suppose it best to send out two or three men to engage some oxen or horses to assist us   obtain one horse and an ox, which enabled us very readily to get over   payd the man his charge which was one dollar; the inhabitants who live near these riffles live much by the distresed situation of traveller   are generally lazy   charge extravegantly when they are called on for assistance and have no filantrophy or contience; passed the mouth of two little creeks to the north, called allfores[2] & [blank]   a riffle a head; the boat rubbed for some distance but by geting out and pulling her on by the thwarts we got her over;—   on each side of the river there are three banks, or suddon rises from the summets of which the land generally brake off for a certain distance pretty level untill arrives at the high hills before mentioned which appear to give a direction to the river— the fist bank or that which the river washes is generally from twenty to twentyfive feet, and the bottom lying on a level with this is ⟨usually⟩ only overflown in remarkable high floods, the consequence is that there is no drowneded or marsh lands on this river; this bottom which is certainly the richest land from it's being liable some times to be overflowed is not esteemed so valuable as the second bottom— The second bottum usually rises from twentyfive to thirty feet above the first and is allways safe or secure from inundation; usually good when wide from the 3d bank and contrary when the bottom is narrow or the river brakes against the 2d near the 3rd bank which it sometimes dose what is called the third bottom is more properly the high benches of the large range of hills before noticed and is of a more varied discription as well as it respects the fertility of it's soil as shape and perpendicular hight, the river sometimes but very seldom brakes against this bank— the second and third of these banks allways run parrallel with the high hills and that bordering on the river is of course shaped by it.[3] passed Waller's riffle[4] with but little dificulty— Thermometer[5] stood at seventy six in the cabbin the temperature of the water in the river when emersed about the same— observed today the leaves of the *buckeye*, Gum, and sausafras[6] begin to fade, or become red—

1. Logtown Riffle was named for Logstown, a village of Shawnee, Delaware, Iroquois, and other Indians established before 1748. It was an important trading and conference site before the French and Indian War. It was near the site of present Ambridge, Beaver County, Pennsylvania. Hodge, 1:773; Swetnam & Smith, 41–42.

2. Quaife locates an "Allfour's Run" in Beaver County; it is not on present maps. Quaife (MLJO), 33 n. 3.

3. The third bottom or "high benches" is upper level aggradation established during the Wisconsin glaciation and is generally underlaid by sand and gravel. Ray, 10, 35–38.

4. Cramer says this ripple was caused by a sandbar between Crow's Island (probably the present Hog Island) and the right shore. Cramer (6th), 41.

5. Lewis apparently purchased thermometers in Philadelphia, perhaps the type mentioned by Jefferson elsewhere (as noted by Jackson), mounted in a mahogany case. The last of them was broken crossing the Rockies. Lewis's List [June 30, 1803], Jackson (LLC), 1:69, 75 n. 1.

6. The buckeye is either *Aesculus octandra* Marsh., yellow buckeye, or *A. glabra* Willd., Ohio buckeye, horse chestnut; the gum is *Nyssa sylvatica* Marsh., black gum, sour gum, black tupelo; the "sausafras" is *Sassafras albidum* (Nutt.) Nees. Little, 103-E, 102-E, 144-E, 191-E; Fernald, 989; Gleason & Cronquist, 520; Cutright (HLCJ), 140.

[Lewis]   Sept. 3rd

Verry foggy this morning. Thermometer 63° Ferrenheit, immersed the Thermometer in the river, and the murcury arose immediately to 75° or summer heat so that there is 12° difference is sufficient to shew the vapor which arrises from the water; the fogg this prodused is impenetrably thick at this moment; we were in consequence obliged to ly by untill 9 this morning   Mr. Gui Briant[1] arrived with two boats loaded with firrs, he informs me that if I can reach, and get over the George-town barr 24 miles I can get on; this is some consolation.   we set out at 9 this morning and passed a riffle just below us called Atkins's   got over with tolerable ease passed the mouth of big bever creek[2] and came to ancor off Mackin-tosh[3] being 2½ miles—   discharge one of my hands.—   passed the riffle below Mackintosh.—   about three miles from this we stuck on another riffle the worst I think we have yet passed   were obliged to unload and drag over with horses.—   staid all night having made only six miles.—[4]

1. Guy Bryan, a wealthy merchant of Philadelphia, supplied goods to fur traders at Kaskaskia, Illinois. Jackson (LLC), 1 : 44 n. 4, 157 n. 9, 189, 2 : 680.

2. Now Beaver River, formed by the confluence of the Shenango and Mahoning rivers, and meeting the Ohio in central Beaver County, Pennsylvania. Espenshade, 142–43.

3. Named for General Lachlan McIntosh, who built it in 1778. The modern town of Beaver, Beaver County, is on the approximate site. Swetnam & Smith, 42–43.

4. About three miles down the Ohio from modern Beaver, Pennsylvania.

[Lewis]   Sept. 4th 1803.

Morning foggy, obliged to wait. Thermometer at 63°— temperature of the river-water 73° being a difference of ten degrees, but yesterday there was a difference of twelve degrees, so that the water must have changed it's temperature 2d in twenty four hours, *coalder*; at ¼ past 8 the murcury rose in the open air to 68°   the fogg dispeared and we set out; the dif-ference therefore of 5° in temperature between the warter and air is not sufficient to produce the appearance of fogg—   from the watermark we fixed last evening it appeared that the river during the night had fallen an inch perpendicularly.—   the Perogue[1] was loaded as his been my practice since I left Pittsburgh, in order as much as posseble to lighten the boat, the [man or men] who conducted her called as in distress about an hour after we had got under way, we came too and waaited her coming up   found she had sprung a leek and had nearly filled; this accedent was truly distressing, as her load consisting of articles of hard-ware, intended as presents to the Indians got wet and I fear are much damaged; proceeded about three miles further   got fast on a bar below georgetown, and with the assistance of some of the neighboring people got overe it with much difficulty; at Georgetown[2] purchased a canoe compleat with two paddles and two poles for which I gave 11$, found that my new purchase leaked so much that she was unsafe woithout some repairs; came too about a mile below the riffle on the east shore[3] pretty early in the evening where we stayed all night having made ⟨only⟩ about thirteen miles this day.   opened the articles which had got wet and exposed them to the sun; set some of my hands to repareing the canoes which I effected before night   had the articles well oiled and put up in oilcloth baggs and returned to the casks in which they were previously were, hired another hand to go with me as far as Wheeling—   the articles were not as much injured as I had supposed—[4]

about two miles above my camp passed the line, which divides the States of Virginia[5] and Pensylvania on the east side of the river and on the West that of Pensylvania from the State of Ohio; this line is made vi[si]ble from the timber having been felled about sixty feet in width, the young timber has spring up but has not yet attained the hight of the other that it can with ease be traced with the eye a considirable distance—   it passes the Ohio River at the mouth of mill Creek[6]   The water is so low and clear that we see a great number of Fish of different kinds, the Stergeon, Bass, Cat fish, pike,[7] &c.   we fixed some spears after the indian method but have had too much to attend to of more importance than gigging fish.—

1. The French word *pirogue* was used in the fur trade for a large dugout canoe or open boat. McDermott (GMVF), 118–19; Russell (FTT), 47. It is not clear if this vessel was actually a pirogue, as Lewis seems to have used the terms *pirogue* and *canoe* interchangeably. If it actually was a pirogue, it may have been either the red or the white pirogue so-called that figured prominently during the expedition. In this entry Lewis also mentions purchasing a canoe at Georgetown and then speaks of two canoes (as he does the next day, September 5), but this is probably two vessels in addition to the keelboat and not two canoes in addition to the keelboat and pirogue. Again the confusion of terminology. One more vessel was purchased at Wheeling on September 8, and Lewis calls it a pirogue.

Lewis's correspondence during this period is of little help in sorting this out.

2. Georgetown, in western Beaver County, Pennsylvania, near the state line, was founded in 1793 by Benoni Dawson. Thwaites (EWT), 4:101 and n. 59.

3. In Hancock County, West Virginia, about two miles below the state line.

4. Lewis may have intended a new entry on the next line; "September" is crossed out.

5. Present West Virginia was part of Virginia until 1863.

6. Mill Creek flows into the Ohio from the south on the Pennsylvania-West Virginia border, opposite Little Beaver Creek. Cramer (6th), 44.

7. The first fish is perhaps the shovelnose sturgeon, *Scaphirhynchus platorynchus*; the bass could be the smallmouth, *Micropterus dolomieui*, or the largemouth, *M. salmoides*; the northern pike is *Esox lucius*; the catfish could be the channel cat, *Ictalurus punctatus*, or the blue, *I. furcatus*. Lee et al., 44, 605, 608, 133, 446, 439.

[Lewis]   September 5th

Again foggey, loaded both my canoes and waited till the fogg disappeared   set out at 8 OCl.   had some difficulty in passing several riffles today but surmounted it without having recorse to horses or oxen— rained at six this evening and continued with some intervals through the night to rain pretty heard; took up at the head of Brown's Island;[1] it grew very dark and my canoes which had on board the most valuable part of my stores had not come up, ordered the trumpet[2] to be sound and they answered.—   they came up in a few minutes after; the stores in the canoes being well secured with oil cloth I concluded to let them remain on board and directed that the water which they maid should be bailed out of them occasionally through the night, which was done—   they still leaked considerably notwithstanding the repairs which I had made on them; we came 16 miles this day;

1. Present-day Brown's Island, where Lewis apparently camped for the night, is located opposite the town of Weirton, Hancock County, West Virginia. The name is from a nearby landowner of the period. Thwaites (EWT), 4:105–6.

2. Probably one of the "4 Tin blowing Trumpets" purchased in Philadelphia, which would be more convenient for signaling on this expedition than the drums and fifes used by the military at this period. Lewis's List [June 30, 1803], Jackson (LLC), 1:71, 95.

[Lewis]   September 6th 1803.

The fogg was as thick as usual this morning   detained us untill ½ past 7 O'C. when we set out—   observed the Thermometer in the air to stand at 71° water 73°—   the fogg continued even with small difference between the temperature of the air and water [s]truck on a riffle which we got over with some difficulty and in the distance of two miles and a half passed 4 others three of which we were obliged to drag over with horses; the man charged me the exorbitant price of two dollars for his trouble.— got on pretty well to Steuwbenville,[1] which we past at 2 Oc. being 6 M. from encam[pment] hoisted our fore sale found great relief from it we run two miles in a few minutes when the wind becoming so strong we were obliged to hall it in lest it should carry away the mast, but the wind abating in some measure we again spread it; a sudan squal broke the sprete [sprit] and had very nearly carried away the mast, after which we firled an[d] secured it tho' the wind was so strong as to carry us pretty good speed by means of the arning and firled sails.— struck on a riffle about two miles below the town hoisted our mainsail to assist in driving us over the riffle the wind blew so heard as to break the spreat of it, and now having no assistance but by manual exertion and my men woarn down by perpetual lifting I was obliged again to have recourse to my usual resort and sent out in serch of horses or oxen— Stewbenville a small town situated on the Ohio in the state of Ohio about six miles above Charlestown in Virginia and 24 above Wheeling—is small well built thriving place has several respectable families residing in it, five years since it was a wilderness— the oxen arrived got off with difficulty the oxen drew badly however with their assistance we got over two other riffles which lyed just below; we preceeded about a mile and a half further and encamped on the west bank having made *ten miles* this day.—[2]

1. Steubenville, Jefferson County, Ohio, was founded by Bezaleel Wells in 1797 on the site of Fort Steuben (established 1787); it was named for Baron Friedrich Wilhelm von Steuben, Prussian drillmaster of the American Revolution. Thwaites (EWT), 4:107–8 and n. 67; *Ohio Guide*, 319–23; Cramer (6th), 45.

2. In Jefferson County, about four miles below Steubenville. Quaife (MLJO), 37 n. 2.

[Lewis]   *September the 7th*

Foggy this morning according to custom; set out at half past seven, and in about two hundred paces stuck on a riffle all hands obliged to get out. observed the Thermometer at sun rise in the air to stand at 47° the tem[pe]rature of the river water being 68°—difference = 21°— got over the riffle, at 45 mts. after 8. passed Charles town[1] on the E. shore above the mouth of Buffaloe over which there is built a handsom wooden bridge, this has the appearance of a handsome little Village, containing about forty houses— this village is three miles below our encampment of last evening— reached Wheeling[2] 16 miles distant at 5 in the evening this is a pretty considerable Village contains about fifty houses and is the county town of Ohio (State of Virginia) it is situated on the east side of the river on an elivated bank; the landing is good, just below the town and on the same side big Wheeling creek emtys itself into the Ohio, on the point formed by this creek and the river stands an old stoccade fort,[3] now gone to decay; this town is remarkable for being the point of embarkation for merchants and Emegrants who are about to descend the river, particularly if they are late in geting on and the water gets low as it most commonly is from the begining of July to the last of September; the water from hence being much deeper and the navigation better than it is from Pittsburgh or any point above it— I went on shore waited on a Mr. Caldwell a merchant of that place to whome I had consigned a part of my goods which I had sent by land from Pittsburgh; found the articles in good order; her[e] met with Colo. Rodney[4] one of the commissioners appointed by the government to adjust the landed claims in the Mississippi Territory. in his suit was Majr Claiborne[5] and a young gentleman who was going on to the Territory with a view to commence the practice of the law. he is a pupil of Czar Rodney[6] of Deleware remained all night

1. Now Wellsburg, Brooke County, West Virginia. "Buffaloe" is present Buffalo Creek. Patrick Gass, one of the sergeants and journalists of the expedition, lived in Wellsburg for some years, died in 1870, and was buried there. Thwaites (EWT), 4:108–9 and nn. 68, 69; *West Virginia Guide*, 485–86; Callahan, 37, 80.

2. First settled about 1770 by Ebenezer Zane and relatives, it remains the county seat of Ohio County, West Virginia. Callahan, 25, 37, 78–79; *West Virginia Guide*, 281–86; Rice, 67.

3. Probably Fort Fincastle, established in 1774, later renamed Fort Henry in 1776 after Governor Patrick Henry of Virginia. See sources cited in previous note and Quaife (MLJO), 38 n. 2.

4. Thomas Rodney of Delaware, Revolutionary War soldier and judge, was appointed judge for Mississippi Territory by President Jefferson. His brother was the Revolutionary patriot Caesar Rodney. Hamilton.

5. Major Richard Claiborne of Virginia accompanied Rodney to Mississippi and served as clerk of the board of commissioners to settle land claims in the territory, a board headed by Rodney. Ibid., 62–64, 67.

6. The young gentleman was William Bayard Shields, who had studied law under Thomas Rodney's son, Caesar Augustus Rodney; Lewis would have known C. A. Rodney as a member of the House of Representatives and a staunch Jeffersonian. Shields became a lawyer and judge in Mississippi and was counsel for Aaron Burr at his first trial in Mississippi. Ibid., 62–64, 216 n. 2, 260.

[Lewis]

8th   this day wrote to the President,[1] purchased a perogue and hired a man to work her, my men were much fatiegued and I concluded it would be better to give them a days rest and let them wash their cloths and exchange their flour for bread or bake their bread in a better manner than they had the means of baking it while traveling; dined with Colo. Rodney and his suit, in the evening they walked down to my boat and partook of some watermellons. I here also met with Dr. Patterson[2] the son of the professor of mathematicks in the University of Philada.   he expressed a great desire to go with me   I consented provided he could get ready by three the next evening   he thought he could and instantly set about it; I told the Dr. that I had a letter of appointment for a second Lieut. which I could give him but did not feel myself altogether at liberty to use it as it was given me by the President to be used in the event of Mr. Clark's not consenting to go with me but as he had I could not use it without the previous consent of the President; however if he thought proper to go on with me to the Illinois[3] where I expected to winter I could obtain an answer from the President by the spring of the year or before the Missourie would be sufficiently open to admitt of my asscending it; and that in the event of the President's not consenting to our wishes, I concieved that the situation of that country was a much more elligible one for a phisician than that of Wheeling particularly as he stated the practice which he had acquired at Wheeling was not an object: the Dr. was to have taken his medicine with him which was a small assortment of about 100 L value. remained here all night—   The people began to top their corn and collect ther fodder—

1. Lewis to Jefferson, September 8, 1803, Jackson (LLC), 1:121–23.

2. William Ewing Patterson was the son of Robert Patterson, a friend of Jefferson, and one of those consulted by Lewis on his trip to Philadelphia the previous spring. The younger Patterson was apparently a chronic alcoholic, which would probably have offset

the advantage of having a trained physician with the expedition. Quaife (MLJO), 39 n. 3; Chuinard, 171–74 and n. 8.

3. At this time "the Illinois" was a broad term for both sides of the Mississippi north of the Ohio River; the settlements in Missouri were thus in "the western part of the Illinois." Evidently Lewis had already decided to winter in that area before starting up the Missouri. McDermott (GMVF), 90.

[Lewis]   9th Sept.

The Dr. could not get ready   I waited untill thre this evening and then set out   had some difficulty in geting over a riffle one mile below the town, got on six miles and brought too,[1] I was now informed that by some mistake in the contract between the Corporal[2] and the woman who had engaged to bake the bread for the men at Wheeling that the woman would not agree to give up the bread being 90 lbs. and that the bread was left   I instantly dispatched the Corpol. and two men for the bread and gave him a dollar to pay the woman for her trouble; about the time we landed it began to rain very heard and continued to rain most powerfully all night with small intervals: had my perogues covered with oil-cloth, but the rain came down in such torrents that I found it necessary to have them bailed out freequently in the course of the night; in attending to the security of my goods I was exposed to the rain and got wet to the skin as I remained untill about twelve at night, when I wrung out my saturated clothes, put on a dry shirt turned into my birth; the rain was excessively could for the season of the year—

1. About three miles below Bellaire, Ohio. Since Lewis does not indicate the side of the river, it may have been in Belmont County, Ohio, or Marshall County, West Virginia. Quaife (MLJO), 40 n. 1.

2. The only corporals associated with the expedition proper seem to have joined after this date.

[Lewis]   10th

The rain ceased about day, the clouds had not dispersed, and looked very much like giving us a repetition of the last evening's frallic, there was but little fogg and I should have been able to have set out at sunrise, but the Corporal had not yet returned with the bread—   I began to fear that he was ⟨miffed⟩ piqued with the sharp reprimand I gave him the evening before for his negligence & inattention with respect to the bread and had deserted; in this however I was agreeably disappointed, about 8 in the morning he came up bring with him the two men and the bread, they instantly embarked and we set out   we passed several very bad riffles this morning and at 11 Oclock six miles below our encampment of last evening I landed on the east side of R. and went on shore to view a remarkable artificial mound of earth called by the people in this neighbourhood the Indian grave.—[1]

This remarkable mound of earth stands on the east bank of the Ohio 12 miles below Wheeling and about 700 paces from the river, as the land is not cleard the mound is not visible from the river—this mound gives name to two small creeks called little and big grave creek[2] which passing about a half a mile on each side of it & fall into ohio about a mile distant from each other   the small creek is above, the mound stands on the most elivated ground of a large bottom containing about 4000 acres of land   the bottom is bounded from N. E. to S. W. by a high range of hills which seem to discribe a simecircle around it of which the river is the dimater, the hills being more distant from the mound than the river, near the mound to the N. stands a small town lately laid out called Elizabethtown[3]   there are but about six or seven dwelling houses in it as yet, in this town there are several mounds of the same kind of the large one but not near as large, in various parts of this bottom the traces of old intrenchments are to be seen tho' they are so imperfect that they cannot be traced in such manner as to make any complete figure; for this enquire I had not leasure. I shall therefore content myself by giving a discription of the large mound and offering some conjectures with regard to the probable purposes for which they were intended by their founders; who ever they may have been.—

the mound is nearly a regular cone 310 yards in circumpherence at it's base & 65 feet high terminating in a blont point whose diameter is 30 feet, this point is concave being depresed about five feet in the center, arround the base runs a ditch 60 feet in width which is broken or intesected by a ledge of earth raised as high as the outer bank of the ditch on the N. W. side, this bank is about 30 feet wide and appers to have formed the enterence to fortifyed mound—   near the summet of this mound grows a white oak tree whose girth is 13½ feet, from the aged appeance of this tree I think it's age might resonably calculated at 300 years, the whole mound is covered with large timber, sugar tree, hickory, poplar, red and white oak &c—[4]   I was informed that in removing the earth of a part of one of those lesser mounds that stands in the town the skeletons of two men were found and some brass beads were found among the earth near these bones, my informant told me the beads were sent to Mr. Peals museum[5] in Philadelphia where he believed they now were.—[6]

we got on twenty four miles this day.   we passed some bad riffles but got over them without the assistance of cattle   came too on the E. side in deep water and a bold shore   staid all night a little above sunfish creek[7]

1. Now Grave Creek Mound, at Moundsville, Marshall County, West Virginia, the largest conical tumulus in the Ohio valley, similar to those of the Adena culture of the area. Descriptions vary, but it is over seventy feet in height, some nine hundred feet in circumference at the base, and approximately fifty feet across at the top. One excavation found it to contain two large timbered burial vaults. *West Virginia Guide*, 513; Hodge, 1:506–7. The mound is pre-Hopewellian and is estimated to date from 100 B.C. James B. Griffin, professor emeritus of anthropology, University of Michigan, personal communication.

2. Now Little Grave Creek and Grave Creek, flowing into the Ohio north and south of Moundsville, respectively.

3. Joseph Tomlinson, Jr., laid out the town in 1798 and named it for his wife. It was consolidated with nearby Mound City in 1865 as Moundsville, county seat of Marshall County *West Virginia Guide*, 513; Thwaites (EWT), 3:360 n. 40.

4. The "sugar tree" is probably *Acer saccharum* Marsh., sugar, rock, or hard maple, but possibly *A. saccaharinum* L., silver, white, or soft maple; the hickory can be one of five species of *Carya*; the poplar is *Liriodendron tulipifera* L., tulip tree, tulip-poplar, poplar, whitewood; the red oak is *Quercus borealis* Michx. var. *maxima* (Marsh.) Ashe, northern red oak; the white oak is *Q. alba* L. Fernald, 986–88, 676, 543; Gleason & Cronquist, 453–54, 252; Little, 112-E, 113-E, 115-E, 117-E, 118-E. These species are more or less typical of the upland deciduous mixed mesophytic forests of the Cumberland Plateau region as described by Braun, 52.

5. Charles Willson Peale, noted portrait painter and father of a family of artists, was also the proprietor of Peale's Museum in Philadelphia, at the time the only natural history museum in the country. He began it in 1786 with fossils from Big Bone Lick in Kentucky; by 1802 he had 1,800 different birds, 250 "quadrupeds," and innumerable other species. At the time of the expedition the museum was housed in present Independence Hall. Peale was a friend of Jefferson and probably acquainted with Lewis, who would send back specimens eventually housed in his institution. Sellers; Kastner, 143–58.

6. The remaining one-half page and the next five pages are blank. Perhaps Lewis had in mind writing further descriptions.

7. In Marshall County, nearly opposite Clarington, Ohio. There may be some confu-

sion about Sunfish Creek, which is identified by Cramer (5th), as another stream higher up the Ohio. Quaife (MLJO), 42 n. 2.

[Lewis]   11th September

Set out about sunrise, passed Sunfish creek 1 mile &c &c   entered the long reach, so called from the Ohio runing in strait direction for 18 miles   in this reach there are 5 Islands from three to 2 miles in length each—[1]   observed a number of squirrels[2] swiming the Ohio and universally passing from the W. to the East shore   they appear to be making to the south; perhaps it may be mast or food which they are in serch of but I should reather suppose that it is climate which is their object as I find no difference in the quantity of mast on both sides of this river it being abundant on both except the beach nut which appears extreemly scarce this season, the walnuts and Hickory nuts the usual food of the squirrell appears in great abundance on either side of the river—[3]   I made my dog[4] take as many each day as I had occation for, they wer fat and I thought them when fryed a pleasent food—   many of these squirrils wer black,[5] they swim very light on the water and make pretty good speed—   my dog was of the newfoundland breed very active strong and docile, he would take the squirel in the water kill them and swiming bring them in his mouth to the boat. we lay this night below the fifth Island in the long reach on the E. side of the river having come 26 miles[6]

1. The islands today along the Long Reach are Paden, Williamson, Wells, Mill Creek, and Grand View islands.

2. These would be gray squirrels, *Sciurus carolinensis*; such migrations are rare today, the squirrel population having been much reduced. Hall, 1:417; Cutright (HLCJ), 140. Apart from two brief lists of trees and fish, this is the first of the many natural history observations in Lewis's journals. His interest in plants and animals, which he shared with Jefferson, dated from childhood. His command of technical terms, especially in his botanical descriptions, was impressive, but he seldom used the Linnaean system of Latin names for species, nor did he attempt to bestow such names on the many new species observed during the expedition. He carried several reference works with him that assisted him in writing his descriptions. These included Benjamin Smith Barton's *Elements of Botany; or, Outlines of the Natural History of Vegetables* (Philadelphia, 1803); John Miller, *An Illustration of the Sexual System of Linnaeus*, Vol. 1 (London, 1779); and Miller's *An Illustration of the Termini Botanici of Linnaeus*, Vol. 2 (London, 1789). Jackson (SBLC), 5–8; Cutright (LCPN), 1–25, 31.

3. The "beach" nut is *Fagus grandifolia* Ehrh., beech nut; the walnuts could be *Juglans nigra* L., black walnut, and/or *J. cinerea* L., butternut, white walnut, found on river terraces; the hickory nuts can be several species of *Carya*. Fernald, 540, 526; Braun, 95–97.

4. The first mention of Seaman, or Scannon, whose name appears infrequently in the journals. Lewis may have purchased him before reaching Pittsburgh and he served as hunter, watchdog, and companion. Though not mentioned after July 1806, it has been supposed that he was still with the party on its return in September 1806. A stream in Montana was apparently named for him, leading Don Jackson to conjecture the latest spelling of his name. Jackson (DS); Osgood (ODS).

5. A melanistic color phase. Cutright (HLCJ), 141 n. 48; Hall, 1:417.

6. This camp, from Lewis's description, would be below present Grand View Island, opposite Grand View, Ohio, in Tyler County, West Virginia. But see below, September 12, n. 1. Thwaites (EWT), 4:121.

[Lewis]

12th Septr.   set out at sunrise   it began to rain and continued with some intervals untill three in the evening   passed several bad riffles and one particularly at the lower end of the long reach called Willson's riffle[1] here we were obliged to cut a channel through the gravel with our spade and canoe paddles and then drag the boat through[2]   we were detained about 4 hours before we accomplished this task and again continued our rout and took up on the N. W. shore near a yankey farmer from whom I perchased some corn and pittatoes for my men and gave him in exchange a few lbs. of lead, we came 20 miles this day—[3]

1. Across from "Wilson's" Island—perhaps present Mill Creek Island—Cramer noted a "run." But this would put Lewis above his previous night's encampment, as he described it. He may not have spent the night just below the fifth island of the Long Reach as he supposed. Cramer (6th), 50.

2. Lewis described this process at length to Jefferson, September 13, 1803, Jackson (LLC), 1:124.

3. In Washington County, Ohio, about nine miles above Marietta. Quaife (MLJO), 43 n. 3.

[Lewis]

13th This morning being clare we persued our journey at sunrise and after passing a few riffles over which we had to lift the boat we arrived at Marietta,[1] the mouth of the Muskingum river, at 7 OClock in the evening   observid many pigeons[2] passing over us pursuing a south East course. The squirrels still continue to cross the river from N. W. to S. E—

Marietta is one hundred miles from Wheeling; lay here all night   wrote to the President of U S.[3]   dismissed two of my hands, one of whome by the name of Wilkinson I had engaged at Georgetown, the other Saml. Mongomery, I engaged at Wheeling, my party from Pittsburgh to Mackintosh was 11 [*written over 10*] strong from thence to georgetown 10 [*written over 11*], from thence to Wheeling 11 [*written over 10*], from thence to Muskingum 13 [*perhaps written over 12*], from thence to Limestone 12,[4] at Wheeling I engaged Mongomery and a young man come on board and agreed to work his passage, on the same terms I engaged another at Marietta or the mouth of Muskingum—[5]   This evening was visited by Colo. Green[6] the Postmaster at this place, he appears to be much of a gentleman and an excelant republican.—

1. Marietta, in Washington County, Ohio, the oldest settlement in the state, was founded in April 1788, at the mouth of the Muskingum River. The town became a base for white expansion north of the Ohio. Walker, 84–88; Wittke, 1:279–90; Roseboom & Weisenburger, 84–85; Thwaites (EWT), 4:123–26.

2. Passenger pigeons, *Ectopistes migratorius* [AOU, 315], which in Lewis and Clark's time flew in such great flocks as to obscure the sun. The last one died on September 1, 1914, in the Cincinnati Zoo. Cutright (HLCJ), 141.

3. September 13, 1803, Jackson (LLC), 1:124.

4. Present Maysville, Kentucky, was once called Limestone, but it would certainly be out of place here. From its appearance, the word may have been added later. Ibid., 1:125 n. 1.

5. Unable to identify the various personnel here counted by Lewis and their number is uncertain as well.

6. Griffin Greene was one of the founders of Marietta and a director of the Ohio Company. Quaife (MLJO), 44 n. 2.

[Lewis]   14th September—

Set out this morning at 11 oClock   was prevented seting out earlyer in consequence of two of my men geting drunk and absenting themselves. I f[i]nally found them and had them brought on board, so drunk that they were unable to help themselves   passed several riffles and lay all night on the N. W. shore—[1]   was here informed that there were some instances of the *goitre* in the neighbourhood   two women who lived on the bank of the river just below   they had emegrated to that place from the lower part of pensylvania and had contracted the disorder since there residence on the Ohio—   The *fever* and *ague* and bilious fevers[2] here commence their banefull oppression and continue through the whole course of the river with increasing violence as you approach it's mouth— saw many squirrels this day swiming the river from N. W. to S. E. caught several by means of my dog—

1. In Washington County, Ohio, just above Parkersburg, West Virginia. Quaife (MLJO), 44 n. 3.

2. The *fever, ague,* and *bilious fevers* are all contemporary names for malaria, referring presumably to various symptoms of the disease, which was endemic in the Ohio, Mississippi, and lower Missouri valleys. On November 13 Lewis notes his own attack of the disease. Chuinard, 174–75 and n. 19.

[Lewis]   *15 September*

Set out this morning at sunrise, passed the mouth of the little Kanaway[1] one mile below our encampment of last evening on the Virginia shore   it is about 60 yards wide at it's mouth   there is a considerable settlement on this river   it heads with the Monongahela,[2] passed the mouths of the little and big Hockhockin[3] and the settlement of Bellpray—a *yanke settlement*[4]   passed several bad riffles over which we were obliged to lift the boat, saw and caught by means of my dog several squirrels, attempting to swim the river, one of these, the only instance I have observed, was swiming from the S. E. to the N. W. shore—   one of the canoes fell a considerable distance behind, we were obliged to ly too for her coming up which detained us several hours; it rained very hard on us from 7 this morning untill about three when it broke away and evening was clear with a few flying clouds.   took up on the Virginia shore having mad 18 miles this day.—[5]

1. The Little Kanawha River joins the Ohio just south of Parkersburg, Wood County, West Virginia. The settlement may well have been Parkersburg's predecessor, Stokleyville. The name Kanawha may come from Conoy, the designation of a local Algonquian tribe related to the Delawares. Hodge 1:339–41; Swanton, 57–58.

2. Lewis was not quite correct here, but the West Fork of the Monongahela and the Little Kanawha run within a few miles of one another in southern Lewis County, West Virginia.

3. The Little Hocking River flows into the Ohio a few miles below Belpre, Washington County, Ohio; the Hocking River enters the Ohio at Hocking Port on the border of Athens and Meigs counties, Ohio. "Hockhocking" was the spelling in Lewis's day, and may mean "above-there-is (arable)-land" in the Algonquian language. Stewart (APN), 207.

4. One of two settlements here: Belpre, Ohio, just across from the Little Kanawha

River, or Belleville, in Wood County, West Virginia, a few miles below the Hocking River. Belleville was called Bellepre about the time Lewis passed down the Ohio, and since he names the town after mentioning the Little Hocking and Hocking rivers, it seems more likely he means Belleville, as Belpre is above those two streams. Thwaites (EWT), 4:127, 131; Quaife (MLJO), 44–45 n. 5.

5. In the vicinity of Belleville, about seventeen miles below the Little Kanawha. Quaife (MLJO), 45 n. 1.

[Lewis]   16th September:

Thermometer this morning in the air 54° in the water 72° a thick fogg which continued so thick that we did not set out untill 8 oClock in the morning the day was fair, passed severale very bad riffles and among the rest Emberson's Island,[1] while they were geting the boat through this long riffle I went on shore and shot some squirrels; my men were very much fatigued with this days labour however I continued untill nearly dark when we came too on the Virginia shore having made only 19 miles this day.—[2]

1. Cramer gives this as "Amberson's, or, Buffentin's Island." It is present Buffington's Island, opposite the mouth of Little Sandy Creek, Jackson County, West Virginia. Cramer (6th), 54.

2. In Jackson County.

[Lewis]   September 17th

The morning was foggy but bing informed by my pilot that we had good water for several miles I ventured to set out before the fog disappeared; came on seven miles to the old Town *Bar*,[1] which being a handsome clean place for the purpose I determined to spend the day and to open & dry my goods which I had found were wet by the rain on the 15th notwithstanding I had them secured with my oilcloths and a common tent which I had as well as it was possible and the canoes frequently bailed in the course of the day and night I found on opening the goods that many of the articles were much Injured; particularly the articles of iron, which wer rusted very much my guns, tomehawks, & knives were of this class; I caused them to be oiled and exposed to the sun the clothing of every discription also was opened and aired, we busily employed in this business all hands, from ten in the morning untill sun seting, when I caused the canoes to be reloaded, having taken the precaution to put up all the articles that would addmitt of that mode of packing to be put in baggs of oil-cloth which I had provided for that purpose and again returned to their severale casks, trunks, and boxes—

my bisquit was much injurd   I had it picked and put up in these baggs—this work kept so busy that I ate not any thing untill after dark, being determined to have every thing in readiness for an early start in the morning; the evening was calm tho' the wind had blown extreemly hard up the river all day—   It is somewhat remarkable that the wind on this river, from much observation of my own, and the concurrent observation of those who inhabit it's banks, blows or sets up agains it's courent four days out of five during the course of the whole year; it will readily be concieved how much this circumstance will aid the navigation of the river—   when the Ohio is in it's present low state, betwen the riffles and in many places for several miles together there is no preseptable courent, the whole surface being perfectly dead or taking the direction only which the wind may chance to give it, this makes the passage down this stream more difficult than would at first view be immageoned, when it is remembered also that the wind so frequently sets up the river the way the traveler makes in descending therefore is by the dint of hard rowing—or force of the oar or pole.

1. Cramer locates a large sand bar just across from Oldtown Creek, which empties into the Ohio River in Meigs County, Ohio. Cramer (6th), 54.

[Lewis]   18th September

The morning was clear and having had every thing in readiness the over night we set out before sunrise and at nine in the morning passed Letart's falls;[1] this being nine miles distant from our encampment of the last evening—   this rappid is the most considerable in the whole course of the Ohio, except the rappids as they ar called opposite to Louisville in Kentuckey—   the descent at Letart's falls is a little more than 4 four feet in two hundred fifty yards.

1. Described in 1807 as more a rapids than a falls, and something under one-half mile long. The rock formation that caused the falls has since been removed. The name may

derive from James LeTort, an early West Virginia Indian trader. Opposite is the small community of Letart Falls, Meigs County, Ohio. Thwaites (EWT), 4:139; *Ohio Guide*, 450; Stewart (APN), 255.

[*Ed: Here Lewis's writing breaks off until November 11. In the Eastern Journal there follow seven blank pages, a one-page note by Edward Biddle, and thirty-one pages of notes by Nicholas Biddle, probably written in 1810. In the interval of nearly two months, Lewis spent nearly a week in Cincinnati, visited the fossil beds at Big Bone Lick, Kentucky, and reached Clarksville, Indiana Territory, where he picked up Clark and several "young men from Kentucky" (see Appendix A). After nearly two weeks in Clarksville, the party left on October 26 and on November 11 reached Massac in southern Illinois. Appleman (LC), 51–57; Lewis to Clark, September 28, 1803, Lewis to Jefferson, October 3, 1803, Jackson (LLC), 1:124–31.*]

[Lewis]   11th November—[1]

Arived at Massac[2] engaged George Drewyer[3] in the public service as an Indian Interpretter, contracted to pay him 25 dollards pr. month for his services.— Mr Swan[4] Assistant Millitary agent at that place advanced him *thirty* dollars on account of his pay.—

1. Lewis has written 11 over 12 for the date and continued to make corrections through November 17. He must have discovered his error about November 18. There is a blank half page at the end of this entry and a considerable amount of unused space on the pages during the next week or so of journalizing.

2. The fort site, on a promontory just above Metropolis, Massac County, Illinois, commands a strategic view of the Ohio River. Established by the French in 1757, ceded to the British in 1763, and abandoned the next year, it was soon destroyed by Chickasaw Indians. The ruins were not restored until 1794 by Americans under orders from General Anthony Wayne. It was again abandoned as a military post after the War of 1812. Thwaites (EWT), 4:276–77; *Illinois Guide*, 433–34; Fortier, 57–71.

3. George Drouillard, whose name neither Lewis nor Clark ever managed to spell right, became one of the most valuable members of the expedition. See Appendix A.

4. William Swan of Massachusetts, stationed at Fort Massac from 1802 to 1804, was in charge of financial affairs at the post. Quaife (MLJO), 47 n. 4.

[Lewis]

12th Novr.   remained, took equal altitudes A. M. but was prevented from compleating the observation by taking an observation in the evening by the clouds—

[Lewis] 13th Novr.

left Massac this evening about five oclock— descended about three miles and encamped on the S. E. shore[1]   raind very hard in the eving and I was siezed with a violent ague which continued about four hours and as is usual was succeeded by a feever which however fortunately abated in some measure by sunrise the next morning,[2] ⟨I then took a⟩

[Clark]

Left Fort Masacre [Massac] the 13th of Novr 1803 at 4 oClock with an at[3]

1. In present McCracken County, Kentucky.

2. Perhaps an attack of malaria. Chuinard, 174–75.

3. This line is found on the first document of Clark's Field Notes, written crosswise to the rest of the material. The remaining material on the sheet is dated December 13–18, 1803, and will be found under those dates in this volume.

[Lewis]

14th Novr.   set out by light at sunrise   I took a doze of Rush's pills[1] which operated extremly well and I found myself much to my satisfaction intirely clear of fever by the evening.   passed Wilkinson ville[2] about 12 Oclock oposite to which is the first or great chain of rocks streching in an oblique manner across the Oho   this evening landed on the point at which the Ohio and Mississippi form there junchon[3]   felt myself much better but extreemly weak—

1. The pills (provided by Benjamin Rush) were a strong laxative. They consisted generally of ten grains of calomel, or mercurous chloride, and fifteen grains of jalap, or pulvis jalap, from the roots of the *Exogonium jalapa* of Mexico. They were used extensively on the expedition for treating gastrointestinal disturbances. Chuinard, 121–44, 155–56; Cutright (IGHB), 98.

2. Cantonment Wilkinson-Ville was established about 1787 as an outpost of Fort Massac in what is now Pulaski County, Illinois, and was named for General James Wilkinson. It was probably abandoned by 1804. *Illinois Guide*, 432–33; Thwaites (EWT), 4:278; Cramer (6th), 81.

3. The site of present Cairo, Alexander County, Illinois.

[Lewis]

Novr. 15th took equal altitudes[1] A. M. 8 59 6— lost the afternon from clouds which interveened and prevented them Capt [*written over Novr*] Clark made a partial survey of the point and asscertained by the Circumferenter[2] and projection that the width of the Ohio from

	Yards
the point was—	1274
The Missippi—	1435
and the width of them both from those observed points on their respective banks was—	2002

1. Here the captains made their first efforts to determine latitude and longitude, a task that would occupy considerable time during the expedition. Establishing longitude required the use of a chronometer, an instrument that was still in limited production and extremely costly. Malfunctioning of the chronometer or, more often, neglecting to wind it affected the men's calculations, since they could not reset it with the necessary accuracy in the field. Lewis had received three weeks of instruction in the use of the chronometer and in surveying from Andrew Ellicott, an astronomer and mathematician, and additional training from Robert Patterson, a mathematician. Even so, the accuracy of his and Clark's observations is open to question. Patterson provided Lewis with a handwritten manual for taking astronomical observations (see Astronomy Notebook, Appendix C), and he and Ellicott recommended some published works that were carried with the expedition. Those included Patrick Kelly, *A Practical Introduction to Spherics and Nautical Astronomy . . .* (London, 1796); *The Nautical Almanac and Astronomical Ephemeris . . .* (London, 1781–1804), which gave the daily locations of heavenly bodies, perhaps in an American edition; and Nevil Maskelyn, *Tables Requisite to be Used with the Nautical Ephemeris for Finding the Latitude and Longitude at Sea* (London, 1781). Brown, 208–40; Taylor, 245–63; Wilford, 128–37; Jackson (SBLC), 4–5; Bakeless (LCBE), 336; Cutright (LCPN), 20–21; Jackson (TJ), 176; Bedini (TT), 330–31; Bedini (SILC).

2. The circumferentor, with a "circle of 6 inches diameter," was a plain surveying compass. Lewis and Clark employed it to determine bearings and courses in mapping and to find "the magnetic azimuth of the sun and pole star." See Lewis's description of astronomical instruments, July 22, 1804. Wilford, 174–75; Bedini (TT), 464. The circumferentor may not have been a part of the regular Philadelphia purchase, but it was included in a summary list. Jackson (LLC), 1:96; Bedini (SILC), 63.

[Lewis]

Novr. 16th—

Passed the Missippi this day and went down on the other side after landing at the upper habitation on the oposite side.[1] we found here som

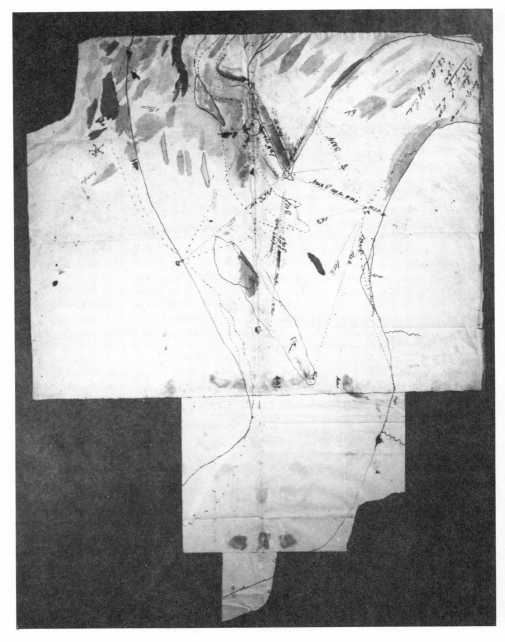

1. Confluence of Ohio and Mississippi Rivers,
ca. November 15, 1803, Field Notes, document 3

Shawnees and Delewars incamped;[2] one of the Shawnees a respectable looking Indian offered me three beverskins for my dog with which he appeared much pleased, the dog was of the newfoundland breed one that I prised much for his docility and qualifications generally for my journey and of course there was no bargan, I had given 20$ for this dogg myself— Capt Clark and myself passed own [down or over] to the lowist point in view on this the W. [*written over N*] side of the river from the point of junction of the rivers—[3] found below it a sand bar, and a willow point forming which in low water will prevent any vessels coming too within two or three hundred yards of the main sore or bank, tho' this is the place at which a fort must be erected if one is built on that side of the mississippi within many miles of the mouth of Ohio, from this place to the uper habitation (or the point which we maid from our place of observation in measuring the river) was 28 hundred and 50 yards; from the place of observation this place bore[4]   On our return which was at 5 m after 1 Oclock we were a little surprised at the apparent size of a Catfish[5] which the men had caught in our absence altho we had been previously accustomed to see those of from thirty to sixty pounds weight   we ditermined to asscertain the weight of this fish after taking the following dementions of it—

	F	Inches
Length—	4	3¼
width betwen the eyes—	1	1
Circumpherence arond the head just above the first fins and lower extremity of the gills *being the large part of the* fish—	3	9
The dementions of the mouth when opened to the ordinary, or easy practicable width was From the center of the lower to the upper jaw—	0	8
Width from side to side—	0	10
Weight—		
Head—		44
Enterals [entrails]—very emty—		14
other parts of the carcase		65

The loss of blood, its lying out of the water six hours in the sun, & the waistage from the circumstance of being obliged to weigh it in small draughts not having any method of weighing entire may be estimated at, at least	—5
Total weight—	128

I have been informed that these fish have been taken in various parts of the Ohio & mississippi weighing from 175 to 200 lbs. weight which from the evidince of the subject above mentioned I have no doubt is authentic—

saw a *heath hen* or *grows*[6] which flew of[f] and having no gun with me did not persue it—

1. This sentence is far from clear, but it appears they crossed to the western, or Missouri, side of the Mississippi and made observations there. See fig. 1. This would be in Mississippi County, Missouri.

2. The Delawares Lewis encountered here were a splinter group that had left the main body in Ohio in 1789 to follow some Shawnees across the Mississippi to the Cape Girardeau region. Lewis's Shawnees were probably part of the Absentee Shawnee. The Absentee group supported peace during the American Revolution and began moving in small groups to the Cape Girardeau region in the 1780s; many more followed after the tribe's defeat by Anthony Wayne in 1794. Both tribes received land grants from the Spanish administration in 1793, but the rapid influx of white settlers after the Louisiana Purchase pushed them south and west into Arkansas, Texas, and Indian Territory (Oklahoma). Weslager; Goddard; Callender (Shaw); Houck, 1:208–20.

3. See fig. 1.

4. Lewis may have intended to enter here the rest of the observations taken at the mouth of the Ohio but for some reason changed his mind. There is a small amount of space at the bottom of this page in the Eastern Journal, and the next sentence starts at the top of the next page. See the undated material following this entry.

5. Perhaps a blue catfish, which may weigh 150 pounds or more. Cutright (HLCJ), 142; Lee et al., 439.

6. Lewis was no doubt familiar with the eastern variety of heath hen, *Tympanuchus cupido cupido*, now extinct. Here he probably saw the western subspecies, *T. c. pinnatus*, called the greater prairie chicken. Both are now grouped as *T. cupido* [AOU, 305]. Cutright (HLCJ), 142.

[Lewis] [*undated, ca. November 15–19*][1]

Took equal alitudes of the sun

	h	m	s			h	m	s
A. M.	8	33	32	P. M	2	36	38.5
	8	35	35.5			2	38	27.5
	8	37	30.5			2	40	30.5

Altitude given by sextant[2] ☉'s center 39° 50′ 00″

Equal altitudes corrected

	h	m	s			h	m	s
A. M.	8	35	35.5	P. M.	2	38	27.5

	m	s
Chronometer[3] too slow M. T.	22	56.1
do. do. Apt. T.	22	55.1

[Clark] [*undated, ca. November 15–19*][4]

From the Point of the Mississippi & Ohio 25 poles from the highest Land on the Sand point— From thence to A Signal[5] on the Opposit Side of the Ohio is N. 30½ d E[6] 149 poles[7] & 32 po: & 7/10 to the bank— From the Said beginning up the Ohio N 52½° W 115 po: to a— Thence to the aforesaid Signal on the opposit Side of the Ohio is N 68° E—

From the Said Beginning Cross the Mississippi to a Signal is S 33° E— From Said point up the Mississippi is S 74° W 117 po: (to a Bluff of Sand opposit the Lower point of an Island) From thence to the Said Signal is S 56° E— (To the upper point of Island is S 53 W, to Lower point is S 15 E)

From the Said point or begn: to the point on the West Side of the Mississippi is S 75° E— From Said Point to a forked Tree on the East Side of the Mississippi Standing on the banke is S 77° E 700 poles (from thence to the high Land about 500 poles—

From the Signal on the East Side of the Ohio to a forked Tree on the bank below is S 66° E— To the Point on the W Side of the Miss: below is S 55° E— To the upper (house) or Signal is S 16° E° Passing the lower point of the Sand Bar makeing from the Island above

From the highest part of the point along the high land up the Miss: is S 48° W 4 po: 14 Links, S 72 W. 144 po: S 13 W. 8 po: to the river where the bank Caves in. N 85 E 46 poles to the Willows, where the Bank Sease to Cave in in the Course of the 3d Observation

(The Course of the bank on the Spa: [Spanish] Side of the Miss: from the upper house Down is nearly S 85° E. abt. 2½ miles, & S 80 E about 450 yards to the lower point—Capt L)

1. This material is separated from the November 16 entry by a blank half page. It may not have been written on the sixteenth but surely was completed during the time the party was at the juncture of the Ohio and Mississippi rivers. It and the next entry are placed here because of this entry's position in the Eastern Journal.

2. The sextant used by the expedition was purchased from Thomas Whitney of Philadelphia, as were many of the other scientific instruments. It was "a brass sextant of 10 Inches radius." Lewis's List and Supplies [June 30, 1803], Jackson (LLC), 1:69, 82, 96; Lewis's description of astronomical instruments, July 22, 1804; Bedini (TT), 337–39, 483; Bedini (SILC), 55, 62–63.

3. Lewis purchased the "Arnold's" chronometer, of "the most improved construction," from Philadelphia watchmaker Thomas Parker, and carried it in a special case. It was of English construction; the maker is not known, but it was commonly referred to as "Arnold's" because John Arnold of London was then one of the best-known makers of chronometers. See November 15, n. 1, above, and Lewis's description of astronomical instruments, July 22, 1804. Andrew Ellicott to Jefferson, March 6, 1803, Lewis to Jefferson, May 14, 1803, Jefferson to Lewis, May 16, 1803, Lewis to Ellicott, May 27, 1803, Lewis's Supplies [June 30, 1803], Jackson (LLC), 1:23, 48–49, 51, 91; Wilford, 128–37; Bedini (TT), 330–31; Bedini (SILC), 60–61.

4. This material comes from the Field Notes (document 2, incorrectly placed as document 3 in Osgood) and is the reverse of a map (see fig. 1) apparently made by Clark while the party was at the junction of the Ohio and Mississippi rivers.

5. Apparently some sort of marker or beacon.

6. Here begins the practice that the captains followed throughout the expedition of giving their courses by the compass, with the estimated distance on each course; this assisted Clark in mapping and might have been intended to assist future travelers. Courses other than due north, south, east, or west were expressed by the number of degrees the course varied from either due north or due south. Thus, "N. 30½ d E" would be thirty and one-half degrees east of due north, fifty-nine and one-half degrees short of due east. The bearing may have been taken with a pocket compass, such as one of three purchased by Lewis from Whitney, or with the plain surveying compass. It is not clear whether Lewis and Clark took a bearing at the beginning of a particular course, sighting on the point for which they were headed, or whether they sighted back at the end of a course toward the point at which it began. Distances were apparently estimates. Greenwood, 57–59, 66–67.

7. The pole, or rod, is a unit of measurement commonly given as 16½ feet. The link, mentioned below, is the standardized link, 7.92 inches, of the surveyor's chain made of wrought iron or steel. One chain of one hundred links measures 66 feet, or four poles, and eighty chains measures a mile. Lewis purchased a "two pole Chain" (33 feet) in Phila-

delphia in May 1803. Clark had some basic knowledge of surveying, and Lewis had been instructed by Ellicott and Patterson. Ibid., 53, 272; Lewis's List and Supplies [June 30, 1803], Jackson (LLC), 1:69, 82, 96.

[Lewis]   Novr. 17th

the [wind] blew very heard last night from N. and continued without intermission throughout the day   it became could about twelve oclock— the canoes were driven by the violence of the waves against the shore and filled with water   I therefore thought myself fortunate in having had them unladen on my arrival,—   measured the hight of the bank in the point and found it 36 F[eet] 8 I[nches] above the level of the water at thime [the time?] which may with much propriety be deemed *low water mark* as neither the Ohio or Missippi wer ever known to be lower—

I yesterday measured the bank on the W. side of the Mississipi and found it 52 feet 8 Inches and the bank at this hight is sometimes over-flown so that allowing the water to be on a level a dike in the point to be on a level with the opposite bank must be raised 16 feet and to render it completely safe a few feet higher—   the bank of the Mississippi side is from two to 4 feet higher than the extreem point and is about the same number of feet higher than the bank of the Ohio,—

[Lewis]   Novr. 18th

Set out early this morning with a canoe and eight men in company with Capt. Clark to visit and view the ground on which Oald Fort Jefferson stood;[1] the river run from the point of junction S. 80 E. to the point of an island about 4 miles distant; at this or oposite to it found six Shawano [Shawnee] hunting camps; the Island is formed by a *byo* [bayou] which makes out nearly in the direction observed course of the river, the river turning more to the S., this *byo* runs about 2¾ approaching the highland very nearly in *one point*, and [after] receieving the waters of Mayfield creek emptys itself again into the missippi, the lower mouth of this byo affords much the best navigation to the mouth of the creek, it is at the junction of this creek & byo that fort Jefferson stands on a rising ground, North of a Byo & West of the creek—   on our return landed on the span-ish side[2] ⟨most fortunately⟩ in order to take the course of the bank of the river on that side, in accomplishing this object we reached the huts of some persons who had established themselves for the purpose of trading with the Indians; found a number of our men who had left camp contrary to instructions & drunk, had much dificulty in geten

1. George Rogers Clark, older brother of William, established Fort Jefferson in 1780, naming it for Thomas Jefferson, then governor of Virginia; it was abandoned the next year. It stood a few miles below present Wickliffe, Ballard County, Kentucky, just above Mayfield Creek, the dividing line between Ballard and Carlisle counties. Quaife (MLJO), 50 n. 1; Thwaites (EWT), 4:280 and n. 184. *Atlas* map 6 appears to show the fort, but a tear on the sheet makes this uncertain.

2. Since Lewis's entry for November 18 seems to end abruptly and the only material for November 19 consists of astronomical observations, it is difficult to determine the camp-site locations for those days. The party remained in the vicinity of the Ohio-Mississippi junction, but there is no indication of what movements they made in the interim. Since the mooring they left on the twentieth was on the Ohio River side of the point between the two rivers, it is probable that the camp of the previous night (November 19–20) was in Alexander County, Illinois, in the vicinity of Cairo. Whether the camp of November 18–19 was in the same place, or on the "Spanish side" in Mississippi County, Missouri, or elsewhere, is not at all clear. Clark's map of the area in his Field Notes (fig. 1) shows a symbol on the Missouri shore which might be intended as a drawing of a tent; however, since it is also the point from which bearings were taken, it may signify no more than that.

[Lewis]   Novr. 19th

Took equal altitudes

	h	m	s				
A. M.	8	42	18	P. M.	2	25	21.5
	8	44	12		2	27	24
	8	46	10		2	29	26

Altitude Art. Horzn.[1] & Sectns. 41° 26′ 37″ Sextant Error 8′ 45″—

1. The artificial horizon was a device that provided a reflecting surface that was always parallel to the natural horizon and was used when the latter was obscured. It was employed primarily to measure the angle of elevation of heavenly bodies. The expedition had three, one using water, another a glass pane mounted on a wooden ball, and the third a mirror attached to a panel. A tripod stand was provided, and a spirit level was essential for adjusting the device. Bedini (TT), 339–40, 461–62; Lewis's List and Supplies [June 30, 1803], Jackson (LLC), 1:69, 82, 96; Lewis's description of astronomical instruments, July 22, 1804; Bedini (SILC), 55, 58–59, 63.

Chapter Two

Ascending the Mississippi

November 20–December 12, 1803

[Lewis]   Novr. 20th

Left our mouring on the Ohio side of the point at 10 OC. and after geting out well into the stream our course, time, and estimated distances were as follow

Course	Time	Estd. dist	Remark or refferences
	h	mils	miles
S. 70° W	1 50	3	*Isld.* Star. 1 ¼ long (1)
N. 20 W.	3 50	4 ½	2 *Isd.* 3 m long (2)
N. 53 W	2 00	3	to point Starbd (3)

21st[1]

Remarks—Novr. 20th

(1) There is a sand bar that extends about ¾ of a mile from the lower extremity of this Island, and reaches below the junction of the Ohio & Mississippi.   the Island lys in this form—[*here a sketch of the island, see fig. 2*]   it's greater diameter with the course of the stream; and from the present appeance of the land on the Starbord wif [will?] soon form a part of the main land of that shore tho' at this moment it is devided from it more than a quarter of a mile by a sand beach which has a small chanel of about 30 yards wide at the lower point of Isld. passing through it—

Remarks – (Nov.r 20th)

(1) There is a sand bar that extends about 3/4 of a mile from the lower extre=mity of this Island, and reaches below the junction of the Ohio & Mississippi. the Island lys in this form ———— with it's greater diameter with the course of the stream; and from the present appearance of the land on the starbord will soon form a part of the main land of that shore tho' at this moment it is devided from it more than a quarter of a mile by a sand beach which has a small chanel of about 30 yards wide at the lower point of Isd. passing through it — the course last marked was that of the lower extremity of the Island the uper point bearing a little to the N. of W. — Came too at 11.45 A.M. on a small sand bar 300 paces from the uper point of this Island, where I made the men take some refresh= -ment and observed the Meridian Altd. of the ☉'s upher Limb to be 67° 29' 53".

2. Sand Bar, November 20, 1803, Eastern Journal

the couse last marked was that of the lower extremity of the Island the uper point bearing a little to the N. of W.— Came too at 11.45 A. M. on a small sand barr 300 paces from the uper point of this Island, where I made the men take some refreshment and observed the Meridian Altd. of the ☉'s Upper ⟨lower⟩ Limb to be 67° 29′ 53″ with my sextant; the Error of which had been previously asscertained to be 8′ 45″—. *Latd   pr. this* obs— 36° 50′ 14.9″— (2) This Island lys close to the main land, and is devided from it by a small channel, the lower point distant 1½ miles from the upper point of the last Island; it is in this form [*here a sketch of the island, see fig. 3*] with a small island as laid down above it the whole extending 3 miles— a small distance above the second Iisland there is another lying as above laid down; above which a small distance and two hundred yards from the (3) point which formed the termination of the last course   we came too on the Starbd side and stayed all night: oposite our landing is the lower pt. of an Island on the Larbd.   we came by my estimate 10½ miles today.[2]

1. Only the date with no additional writing. The remaining one-half of this page is blank, as if Lewis intended to fill it in later but instead entered "remarks" for the twen-tieth. With these entries Lewis began shifting course and distance writing from preceding to following the remarks for the day. This edition follows the changing pattern.

2. Camped in Alexander County, Illinois, now started up the Mississippi.

[Lewis]   Novr. 21st

(1) This is inconsiderable, being ½ m. in length & distant ½ m. from the lower point of (2) another which commences with the last course on the Lad. side, makes a considerable bend to the S. E. and presents a large sand bar along it's border, on the center of the bend of this bar I made the following observation in order to obtain the variation of the nedle— A. M. 9 h 2 m 0 s by Chronometer; Altd. ☉'s L. L. 45° 42′ 15″ by Sextant; bearing S. 46° 30 E.— Chronometer too slow as deduced from observa-tion on 16th inst. 24 m 8¹/₁₀ s— Error of Sextat. 8′ 45″—. this Island continues & after geting above it find it had concealed another about the same magnitude of itself; these Islands lye in this form [*here a sketch of the island, see fig. 4*] (3) Obsered Meridian altd. of ☉'s U. L. 66° 56′ 15″ with Sext   Error 8′ 45—. having come by estimate 7 miles; from this place observed a large quantity of Misseltoe[1] on the trees bordering on the

with my sextant; the Error of which
had been Previously ascertained to
be 8'.45". ~~Said fr. this~~ obs. 36° 50'.14".9
(2) This Island lys close to the main land,
and is devided from it by a small chan-
:nel, the lower point distant 1½ ~~miles~~
~~from the last Island the miles~~ from the
upper point of the last Island; it
is in this form with a small
island as laid down above it the whole
extending 3 – miles - a small distance
above the second Island there is another lying as above laid down; above
which a small distance and two
hundred yards from the (3) point which
formed the termination of the last
course we came too on the Starbd
side and stayed all night: oposite
our landing is the lower pt. of an
Island on the Larbd. we came by
my estimate 10½ miles today.

3. Island, November 20, 1803, Eastern Journal

river, on the main shore Lard. side: in dscending the Ohio I furst observed this plant about the mouth of the Muskingum river; which is the
point at which I date the commencement of the *fever and Ague & bilious
fever*, to commence, or become common among the inhabitants of it's borders; it [mistletoe] continued increasing untill I arrived at the mouth of
the Ohio and sill continues in larger quantities on this than on the Ohio,
insomuch that the trees at this place were perfectly loaded with it— saw
a number of *black & white pided* ducks,[2] shot at them with my rifle and
crippled one but could not obtain it, I cannot therefore discribe them so
manutely as [I?] could wish   they are about the size of the *wood duck*,—
we shot at two deer[3] today that had come to the river to drink, but got
neither of them tho' one was badly wounded— just below the place of
observation the grand bend[4] as it is stiled by the french watermen, commences on the Lard. quarter and continues bearing from S. E. to N. W.
about 6 miles; about the center of the hollow of this bend on lard. quarter
a byo makes out, and dose not return to the chanel of the river again untill it reaches below Tanslagrass,[5] which is 50 miles below the mouth of the
Ohio: from the commencement of this ⟨last⟩ cours four Islands make
their appearance, which compleatly fill the river on the Stard. qutr. as
they also do that side of the great bend.— passed a small Island on the
Lad. qtr   came too on an *Isd* Lad. qtr. about the upr extremity of the
grand bend, staid all night.—[6]

Courses of this day Novr. 21st 1803.

	Time	Est. dist	Remarks & reffers
N. 50 W.	" 40	1 ¼	passed *Is* Lad. ¼ long (1)
Do. Do.—	3 0	3 ¾	do. *Is.* Lard. 3 miles long (2)
S. 20 E.—	2 30	1 ¼	To sand bar Stad. (3)
	2 30	2	small Is. Lard. qtr.
S. 72 W.	1 "	" ½	*Islds.* continues on stad.
N. 62 W.	" 30	½	still in the grand bend.
N. 52	2 25	1 ¾	To an Isld. on Lard. side where
Total dist		11	we halted for the night.

Set out at 7 OC. this morning 21st.

① This is inconsiderable, being ½ m. in length & distant ½ M. from the lower point of ② another which commences with the last course on the La. side, makes a considerable bend to the S.E. and presents a large sand bar along it's border, on the center of the bend of this bar I made the following observation in order to obtain the variation of the nedle — A.M. 9ʰ. 2ᵐ. 0ˢ. by Chronometer; Alt. ☉ L.L. 45° 42′ 15″ by Sextant; ☉ bearing S. 46° 30 E. — Chronometer too slow by observation as noticed from on 16ᵗ. inst. 24ᵐ. 8 5/10ˢ — Error of Sexta. 8′. 45″ —. This Island continues & after geting above it find it had concealed another about the same magnitude of itself; these Islands lye in this form ⬭ ⬭ — ② Observed Meridian alt⁰. of ☉'U.L. 66°. 56′. 15″ with Sext Error 8′. 45 —. having come by estimate 7 Miles;

4. Island, November 21, 1803, Eastern Journal

1. The "Misseltoe" is *Phoradendron flavescens* (Pursh) Nutt., mistletoe, American or false mistletoe. Fernald, 562; Gleason & Cronquist, 258.

2. Perhaps the bufflehead duck, *Bucephala albeola* [AOU, 153], one of the smallest ducks. Lewis compares it to the wood duck, *Aix sponsa* [AOU, 144].

3. The white-tailed deer, *Odocoileus virginianus*, with which Lewis was already familiar, since it was found over most of the eastern United States. Hall, 2 : 1091–97.

4. This bend lies between Alexander County, Illinois, and Mississippi County, Missouri, a few miles upstream from Cairo.

5. The first letter of this word is smudged and nearly illegible. Possibly it refers to the St. Francis River in southeast Missouri and northeast Arkansas. The word itself is of unknown origin.

6. Apparently this island was near the upstream end of the bend, between Alexander County, Illinois, and Mississippi County, Missouri, near the Scott County, Missouri, line.

[Lewis]   *Novr. 22ed 1803.*

Missilanious remarks &ec. Set out at ½ after 6 A M. the current very rapid and difficult.   (1) the iner part of every bend of this river where it makes any considerable turn is always filled with Island of different shapes and sizes; this remark applys to every part of this river so far as we have yet asscended.—   at the expiration of this course saw some *Heth hens* or grows—   one of my men went on shore and killed one of them, of which we made soome soup for my friend Capt. Clark who has been much indisposed since the 16th inst. this bird shall hereafter be more particularly discribed.—   (2) arrived oposite three new habitation of some Americans who had settled under the spanish government, this settlement is on a bottom called, *Tywappety*,[1] the bank is high: called at the uper habitation—   from the center of the river oposite this settlement a large Island[2] appears a head dist 1½ and gives much the appearance to the river of it's forking or reather resieving a very considerable river on the Lard. side—   was informed by a Mr. Findley[3] the owener of this habitation that there were fifteen families in this settlement—   I took the hight of this bank above the present state of the water which was considered as very low and found it's elivation 32 feet 6 inches; this bottom seldom overflows at least not since the present settlement has been formed which has been about 4 years—   overtook two keels[4] from Lousville bound to Kaskaskias loaded with dry goods and whiskey, belonging to Mr. Bullet[5] of Louisville: this place by the computation of the inhabitants is 25 miles above the mouth of the Ohio but by my estimate is only 22 miles. (3) one [island] of which on Lard. qutr. is about three miles in length and nearly the same in bredth oposite to the upper end of this Isld. met two Keeled boats loaded with firs for New-Orleans; at the same place on the Stard. the land appears not usually to be overflowed being covered with a considerable portion of poplar and white-oak timber, tho' the bank is several feet lower than that I measured this forenoon; this is the first poplar or white oak I have seen since we began to asscend the river; I have seen but little *cain*[6] since we left the Ohio, and my pilot informed me that from hence up the river there is not any in the neighbourhood of it; the banks appear every where to abound with the *sand* or *scrubing Rush*,[7] it grows much thicker, and arrises to a much greater hight in the bottoms of this river than I ever observed it elsewhere, I measured a stalk of it which was 8 feet 2 inches in length & 3⅛ inches in circumpherence; it grows as thick comparitively as the stalks of luxurient wheat; It rises in a single steem without branch or leaf being jointed at the distance of 1½ to 2 inches; it retains it's colour which is a deep green through the winter and affords an agreeable and healthy food for both cattle and horses; these I am informed will keep in fine order on them through the winter which, however is never very inte[n]se in this climate. the favorite soil for this plant is a rich loam intermixed with a considerable portion of sand.— the oak and poplar land before noticed continues on the Stad. side for several miles, and finally joins the highland which there puts in to the river— (4) we here kept close to the main shore on Stard qtr.— from the best estimate I could make the river appears to be in breadth including Islands from 1½ to 3 miles and the main chanel of it usually ½ mile wide— this character of the river will apply to it from the mouth of Ohio to this place. (5) the upper point of this Island is oposite to the uper point of Tywoppety bottom, there appears to be a hadsome farm at this point, and here the highland or main shore puts in with a much greater hight of land than we have seen since we began to asscend it appears to be a ridg pointing obliquely don the river the hight of it from it's appearance is most probably 100 feet above the level of the bottom.— from the water's edge to the top of the first rise or level of the bottom wass pretty well covered with large rock of many tons weight lying in a loose manner on the serface or but partially bedded in the earth— on the stard. side I went on shore and soon arrived at some highland, it being not more than 200 paces to the base of the rising ground which rises pretty suddonly to the hight of 100 Feet. the land is of an inferior quality on these hills being a stiff white clay soil.— observed a very fine quarry of white freestone on the Eastern bank of a small run which made into the river, from which the quarry is about half a mile. also observed some large mass of loose rocks nearly at the summits of these hills, these rocks appeared very heard, being formed of such pebbles as common to the river, united together by a strong scement of fine sand; with a small pro-portion of earth.— this quality so remarkable and observable in the waters of Ohio of scementing masses of pebble earth and sand, as also pretrefying vegitable and animal substances exposed to it for a length of time; this quality seems to be possessed equally by this river; of this I have had many evidences; beside those large masses of conjealed or scemented pebble, I met with several pieces of wood that had been petrefyed and afterwards woarn away by the gravel and the agetatition of the water un-till they had become smothe and had the appearance of stone common to runing streams; tho' the grain of the wood was quite distinct.[8] we came too for the night on the Stard. quat.[9] and lay upon a slate rock which here formed the beech; this slate appeared to ly in a vain of not more than 2 feet thick and seemed to be of an indifferent quality. one of my men [Nathaniel Pryor] who went out to hunt this morning has not yet come up, had several guns fired to bring him too, and the horn freequently blown but without effect— I have frequently observed among the sand and pebble of the river a substance that resembled *pit-coal* but which evedently is wood that has remained a great length of time berried in the mud of the mois[t] banks of the river, & when these banks are again washed away becomes exposed to view the gain of the wood is easily per-sieved as ⟨is⟩ was also the bark of some spesimines I met with which had not so perfectly assumed the coal state; I burnt some of this coal but found it indifferent, nor could I discover while it was berning that it emit-ted any sulphurious smell.[10]

Courses of this day. Novr. 22ed 1803

Course	Time	dist.	References &c
	h		
N. 20 W.	1 —	— ¾	Passd. an Ild. 1 ¼ Long Lard. (1), also another Isd. ¼ Long Lard.—
N. 30 W.	2 15	3 ¼	passd. several *Iisds*. Lard & Stad. (2)
" " "	2 45	3 —	continued to pass Islds. (3)
" " "	2 15	2 ½	passd. Isld. on Lard. ¾ (4)
N. 40 W.	" 50	1 —	upr. pt. of Isld. Lard. (5)
N. 35 W.	1 30	2 ½	to a slate rock on Stad. quarter where we lay all
Total	10 35	13 0	night here comes in the first highland we have yet met with; and here it may be said that the drowned land seases on this side the river from whence to the mouth it is of unequal widths from 1 ½ to 10 miles.

1. Tywappity Bottom straddles Scott and Mississippi counties, Missouri. The earliest American settlers arrived about 1797. Quaife (MLJO), 55 n. 1; Houck, 2 : 162–63.

2. Either Powers or Burnham Island, in Scott County.

3. Probably Charles Findley, who operated a ferry in the area. Houck, 3 : 61.

4. Keelboats, which had hulls with keels on the bottom, were able to move upstream, unlike flatboats, which were flat bottomed. See Baldwin (KA).

5. Probably either Thomas or Cuthbert Bullitt, "distinguished merchants" of Louisville, Kentucky. Quaife (MLJO), 55 n. 2.

6. The "cain" is *Arundinaria gigantea* (Walt) Chapm., large, or giant, cane. Fernald, 96.

7. The "sand or scrubing Rush" is probably *Equisetum hyemale* L. var. *robustum* (A. Br) A. A. Eat., stout scouring rush. Ibid., 8–9.

8. Lewis's "stiff white clay soil" is probably Quaternary valley fill and terrace deposits that were left in ponded tributaries of the Mississippi River during glaciations, although they reach generally only 50 to 60 feet above the river. "White freestone" refers to a poorly cemented rock, probably sandstone. The McNairy Sand of Cretaceous age fits this description and has been mapped in this area. The Lafayette Formation (Lewis's "loose rocks") consists of weakly to strongly cemented siliceous gravel and sand that caps most of the upland in this area. The petrified wood is probably pebbles of Cretaceous wood fragments from the McNairy Formation. Pryor & Ross.

9. In northwest Alexander County, Illinois.

10. The old forest bed of the Ohio River is a lens of peaty material that contains a large amount of partly coalified wood that retains its bark. It was buried in muds along the river during one of the interglacial ages prior to the Wisconsin glaciation. The Mississippi

should have had a similar alluvial history, so it would be reasonable that such a bed would be encountered here also. Billups.

[Lewis]   *Novr. 23rd 1803*

N. Pryor, the man who was hunting yesterday has not yet arrived, had several guns fired again and the horn wlown [blown]; waited untill half after 7 OC. and then set out without him   (1) about a mile from the commencement of this course a small creek puts in on the Lard. quatr. and abot ¾ of a mile another about the same size puts in on the same side.—[1] (2) this creek puts in on the Stard. qutr. nearly oposite the mouth of the last on the Lard. qutr. on the commencement of this course—   these creeks appear to be about the same size and may be recconed from 10 to 15 miles long—   1¼ miles from the last creek a large creek puts in on Stad. qtr. oposite to the mouth of this creek a small *Isld.* called *rock Island.*[2]   so called from the base of it being formed of a slate rock, there are some willows growing on it—   I know no names for these creeks—except the last which is called East Lacrush,[3] this creek appeared to be about 40 yards wide at it's mouth and may recconed at 30 miles in length; passing by land from Massac to Cape *Jeradeau*[4] you cross the waters of this creek; the distance between these two places is about 35 miles through a low lagoon country   (3) about ¾ of a mile from the commencement of this course, and just above a bold point which juts in, to the river, on the Lard. quarter, a large Creek puts in called Cape *La'crush*[5] from the rocky point just mentioned which has obtained that name—   this creek is about 25 yards wide at the mouth and may be recconed 30 m. long.   we have passed but three Islds. including Rock Island which was the first, a small one on the Lard. & one 3½ miles from Cape Jeradeau which we left on the Stard.   this last is reather a sandbar than & Island   some small parts of it are covered with *willows* & small *cottonwood.*—   This sand-bar discribed was a continuation of an Island about ¾ of a mile long commencing just below Cape Jeradeau and which was hid from my view when I made the foregoing remark with respect to it—   (4) landed at the cape and called on the Commandt.[6] and delivered the letters of introduction which I had for him, from Capt. Danl. Bisselle,[7] and a Mr. Drewyer[8] a nephew of the Commandt's. sent the boat on with orders to come too for the night at Old Cape Jeradeau which is a point of land on the Lard. about 2 miles distant from the Commandt's. tho' this was the first place of his residence on his settleing himself in this country which he told me was about eight years since. On my arrival at the Comds. dwelling I was informed that he had gone out with his family to attend a Horse rase he himself being as I afterwards understood a party to the rase— I persued him to the rase grown found him and delivered him my credentials, he treated me with much politeness in his way; the rase was just over before I reached the grown & the Comdt. was busied for some time in settling the disputes which had arrisen in consequence of odds being given among the by betters; the Comdts. horse lost the main rase, but won by six inches the by betts, the odds generally given against him in the by betts was 12 feet; the Comdt. lost four horses on the rase which had been valued at $200.— this seane reminded me very much of their small raises in Kentucky among the uncivilized backwoodsmen, nor did the subsequent disorder which took place in consequence of the descision of the judges of the rase at all lessen the resembleance; one fellow contrary to the descision of the judges swore he had won & was carrying off not only his own horse but that also of his competitor; but the other being the stoutest of the two dismounted him and took both horses in turn; it is not extrawdinary that these people should be disorderly they are almost entirely emegrant from the fronteers of Kentuckey & Tennessee, and are the most dessolute and abandoned even among these people; they are men of desperate fortunes, but little to loose either character or property— they bett very high on these raises in proportion to their wealth; it is not uncommon for them to risk the half or even the whole of their personal property on a single wager; their property consists principally in Horses and black Cattle; the Comdt. seemed to bear his loss with much cheerfullness. a son of his immediately made another rase for $600. these people have some specia[9] among them, but their circulating medium is principally Horses, Cattle, Cotton & lead—Horses from 50 to 200$. Cattle from 8 to 10$, Cotton & lead are less fluctuating in their price, the former is estimated a $100 a Ton and the latter at $80 pr. Ton— this settlement was commenced by the present Comdt. eight years since, with one other family, about 2 years after it began to form prety rapidly from the encouragement given these setlers by the Spanish government   it has now increased to the number of 1,111 persons, they are allowed a bounty in lands proportioned to the number of their respective familys which are called head rights; this land is entered, surveyed and recorded by the clerk of the Comdt.[10] which may or may not be confirmed by the Crown of Spain wich however is necessary to complete the title.—

The Comdt. is Canadian by birth of French extraction; he was on[c]e a very considerable trader among the Shawnees & Delewares; About the year 1781 a party under the command of Genl. George Rogers Clark of Kentuckey burnt the Store of this man—which stood at the mouth of a small creek a branch of the East branch of the Great Miami of the Ohio which still beares the name of Lorimier, which has since become more remarkable as it forms one point in the boundary line between the N. Western tribes and the U. S. made with them at Geenevile by Genl. Wayne in the year 1795—   the value of the property Lorimier lost on this occasion is estimated at 20 thousand dollars, this broke him as a mercht. but he seems to have entirely recovered his losses, and is now a man of very considerable property; he is a man about 5 F 8 I high, dark skin hair and [e]yes; he is remarkable for having once had a remarkable suit of hair; he was very cheerfull & I took occasion to mention this to him   he informed me that it was on[c]e so long that it touched the grond when he stood errect—nor was it much less remarkable for it's thickness; this I could readily believe from it's present appearance, he is about 60 years of age, and yet scarcely a grey hair in his head; which reaches now when cewed (the manner in which he dresses it) nearly as low as his knees, and it is proportionally thick; he appears yet quite active—   this uncommon cue falls dow his back to which it is kept close by means of a leather gerdle confined around his waist—   this man agreeably to the custom of many of the Canadian Traders has taken to himself a wife from among the aborigines of the country   his wife is a Shawnee woman,[11] from her complexion is half blooded only.   she is a very desent woman and if we may judge from her present appearance has been very handsome when young, she dresses after the Shawnee manner with a stroud leggings and mockinsons, differing however from them in her linin which seemed to be drawn beneath her girdle of her stroud, as also a short Jacket with long sleeves over her linin with long sleeves more in the stile of the French Canadian women; by this woman Lorimier has a large family of very handsome Children three of which have attained the age of puberty; the daughter is remarkably handsome & dresses in a plain yet fashonable stile or such as is now Common in the Atlantic States among the respectable people of the middle class.   she is an agreeable affible girl, & much the most descent looking feemale I have seen since I left the settlement in Kentuckey a little below Louisville.—[12]   The Comdt. pressed me to stay to supper which I did, the lady of the family presided, and with much circumspection performed the honours of the table: supper being over which was really a comfortable and desent one I bid the family an afectionate adieeu—;   the Comdt. had a Couple of horses paraded, and one of his sons conducted me to Old Cape Jeradeau, the distance by the rout we went was 3 miles   here I found my boat and people   landed for the night.[13]   found Capt. Clark very unwell.

The district of Commandant Lorimiere estends from the grand bend of the Mississippi to Apple River[14] without limitation back   this settlement extends the distance of sixty miles W. from the river as far as the river St. Francis. West from Cape Jeredeau about 16 miles is a large settlement of duch descendants who have emigrated from the Atlantic States;[15] these people here preserve their uniform charracter, of ⟨sober,⟩ temperate, laborious and honest people, they have erected two grist mills and a saw-mill—   The estimated distance by the french watermen to New Cape Jerd: is 42 miles from the mouth of Ohio.—   the old cape is 2 miles dist. bearing N. 10 E.

Novr. 23d

Course	Time	dist.	References
	h m	mils	
N. 30 W.	— 50	2 —	Creek Lard. 1 mil. Creek Lard. ¾ (1)
N. 3 W.	— 45	1 ¼	Crk. Stad. oposite last 1 ¼ Crk. (2)
N. 50 W.	2 30	2 ½	¾ large creek (3)
N. 43 W.	3 15	5 ¼	New Cape Jeradeau (4)
N. 10 E	1 15	2	Old Cape Do.— staid all night on Lard qutr.
	8 35	13 —	

1. These creeks are difficult to identify; Lewis is in the general area above Commerce, Scott County, Missouri, some 40 miles above the mouth of the Ohio.

2. Cumings shows Rock Island directly across from Cape Le Croix. Cumings, map 3.

3. Apparently modern Sexton Creek, in Alexander County, Illinois.

4. Cape Girardeau, Cape Girardeau County, Missouri, may have received its name from a French ensign. The earliest settlement (Lewis's Old Cape Girardeau) was on the rock promontory above the present site of the city. Louis Lorimier may have settled there with a band of Shawnee and Delaware Indians as early as 1786, but he was certainly established there by 1793. He developed a thriving trading post and encouraged Anglo-American emigration into the area. The town remained the local seat of government after the Louisiana Purchase but declined somewhat after the War of 1812. *Missouri Guide*, 199–202; Houck, 2:167–92.

5. Cumings refers to Cape Le Croix, also called La Bruche. Cumings, 67. Present Cape La Croix Creek divides Scott and Cape Girardeau counties.

6. Louis Lorimier was born near Montreal. He and his father established "Laramie's Station" to trade with the Indians in Ohio. As a Loyalist during the Revolutionary War, Lorimier led raiding parties of Indians into Kentucky; George Rogers Clark burned Lorimier's establishment as an enemy base in 1782. Within a few years he had moved to Spanish Louisiana and received a large land grant to establish a settlement for Indians, partly as a defense against possible American invasion. In spite of these indications of anti-American attitudes, he became an Indian agent for the United States after the Louisiana Purchase. As Lewis notes, "Laramie's Store" was specifically named as a location point in the Greenville Treaty of 1795, and the name is still perpetuated by the modern Lake Loramie, Shelby County, Ohio. Quaife (MLJO), 59 n. 1; Osgood (FN), 42 n. 4; Houck, 2:169–81; Nasatir (BLC), 2:771; Nasatir (SWV), 71–72 n. 27, 297–98 n. 22; *Ohio Guide*, 558.

7. Daniel Bissell joined the army in 1791; at this time he was in command at Fort Massac. He became a brigadier general in the War of 1812. Heitman, 221.

8. Perhaps George Drouillard, engaged by Lewis at Fort Massac on November 11, but the style of the reference suggests that it may be some relative of George's. It appears that George Drouillard may have been related to Louis Lorimier, especially since George considered himself a resident of the Cape Girardeau district. Peter Droullard and Jean Baptiste Droulliez were early Missouri settlers of the late eighteenth century. Allowing for the flexible spelling of the era, either might have been related to George and possibly was the "Mr. Drewyer" who wrote the letter. Skarsten (GDLC), 20–21; Houck, 2:150, 166.

9. Coins (specie) were usually in short supply on the frontier at this time.

10. The clerk was Barthelemi Cousin. Houck, 2:180–81.

11. Charlotte Pemanpieh Bougainville. Ibid., 2:170 and n. 9, 179 n. 21.

12. Among these children were Louis, Junior, a trader like his father, Auguste Bougainville and William, who received appointments to West Point, and Agatha, perhaps the attractive daughter Lewis noticed. Ibid., 1:231, 2:182, 190, 381.

13. Near the promontory where the settlement was first located, north of the later town, in Cape Girardeau County.

14. The District of Cape Girardeau extended from Apple Creek to Tywappity Bottom. Ibid., 2:167.

15. These "duch" were German-Swiss and North Carolinians of German descent who settled along Whitewater River. Ibid., 2 : 187–89.

[Lewis]   *Novr. 24th*

Set out this morning at 7 OCl.   as we were bearing off, Pryor the man who had been absent and lost for the last two days hailed, we passed the river and took him in   he was much fatiequed with his wandering and somewhat indisposed—   (1) The highland which sets in at Cape Jeredeau continues with small intervals of low Land. on that side of the river, the other appearing low and subject to be overflowed for a considirable distance say 2 or three miles—   (2) this Isld. is not considerable,—   came too on the sand bar at the upper point of it and took Meridian Altitude of ⊙'s L. L. with Sext.   found it 64° 50′ 30″   Error of sext. as usual—   (4) the main shore has been generally bold on the Lard. quart. all day but here putts in some high clifts the summits of which are crowned with pitch-pine & seader,[1] these rocks are nearly perpendicular in many places sixty feet, and the hight of the hills apear to be about 120 feet above the bank which forms their base of perhaps 15 or 18 feet tho from appearance they never over flow.   the rock which compose these clifts is a singular one tho' not uncommon to this country   it is a Limestone principally, but imbeded in this stone there are detached pieces of a stone resembleing flint of yellowish brown colour which appear at some former period to have been woarn smothe and assume different shapes and sizes as the pebbles of runing streams usually do tho' now firmly united and forming a portion of the solid mass of this rock—   many parts of the rock has also a considerable portion of grit or sand in it's composition tho' I was informed at Cape Jeradeau where the same rock appears, that it makes very good lime—[2] *I am not confident with respect to the accuracy of the observation* of this day, in consequence of some flying clouds which frequently interveened and obscured his [sun's] disk about noon and obliged me frequently to change the coloured glasses of the Sextant in order to make the observation as complete as possible.

Courses	Time	dist.	references &c *24th*
N. 50 E.	3 30	4 —	¼ to lower pt. of Isld. 2 M. Long Std. (1)
N. Due	— 45	1 ¾	1 mil. to Sand bar Lard. qtr. (2)

N. 22 W.	2 5	2 ½	passd. Isld. ¾ Long Lard. (3)
N. 20 W.	2 15	1 ¾	To rockey barr (4) staid all night [3]
Total	8 35	10 —	

1. Clark's identification of the pitch-pine (*Pinus rigida* Mill.) is in error. The only pine known to occur in Cape Girardeau County, Missouri, or Union County, Illinois, is the yellow, or shortleaf pine, *Pinus echinata* Mill. Little, 71-E, 52-E. The two pine species are similar in appearance and ecology, and the error is understandable. The expedition is passing through the very northeast edge of the oak-hickory region of the Ozark plateau. Braun, 104. The "seader" is the ubiquitous *Juniperus virginiana* L., eastern red cedar. Little, 31-E; Fernald, 59–60.

2. Limestone with embedded yellowish brown flint or chert is probably Sexton Creek Limestone, early Silurian in age. The rocks at Cape Girardeau mentioned here may be of the same unit, but they could also be Girardeau Limestone, which contains black chert or flint nodules and is slightly older, though still early Silurian in age. Cote, Reinertsen, & Killey; Willman et al., 99.

3. By Lewis's calculation, ten miles above Cape Girardeau, in either Cape Girardeau County, Missouri, or Union County, Illinois. Lewis does not indicate which side of the river was closest, but from his description of the country, the "rockey barr" on which they camped was perhaps nearer the Missouri shore.

[Lewis]   *25th Novr.—*

Set out this morning half after 6 O.Clk.   the coast on the Lard. qut. was higher than yesterday, the rock rising perpendicularly from the water's edge in many places & in others reather projecting than otherwise, it is the same rock discribed yesterday with a larger portion of flint: the flint appears to ly in stratas yet reather divided by the *limestone* even in those stratas, they appear to be from six inches to a foot asunder. all the stone of whatever discription which I have observed in this country appere to lye in horizontal stratas except where they have been evedently been forced or removed from their origional beds by the courant of the river on which they border.—[1]   (1) several small streams put in but not sufficenly large to deserve any particular notice   the country still appears high with small intervals of low land on the Lard. quarter, that on the Stard. is low and appears to overflow in high water but how far I had not an opertunity to inform myself—   (2) passed a small creek[2] on Lard. qtr. just above which were some Shawnee huts and tents—   (3) 1¾ from hence Apple river[3] puts in on Lard. qtr.   here we came too and *I took the meridian altd* of Sun's L. L. which was 64° 12' 30" the Error of sextt. as usual— this is the most considerable stream I have yet met with; it falls in just above a large flat rock now visible but conscealed in high water; it is about 40 yards in width at it's mouth from bank to bank, but vends very little water at this moment, tho' navigable in high water several miles; this as well as most of the creeks and rivers of inferior magnitude which put into the Mississippi appear much more inconsiderable than they really are; the cause is *this*— The Mississippi when full throws large quantitys of mud into the mouths of these rivers whose courents not being equal to contend with it's power become still or eddy for many miles up them the mud is thus deposited and as they are but comparitively short their courents subside before that of the Mississippi which when it dose subside and leave them free to act they have so small a quantity of water to discharge that it finds it's way to the river in a very small channel which it cuts through this mud; thus in a manner conscealing their magnitude from the passanger along the main river— The Apple River extends a considerable distance back in the country say 40 or 50 miles & heads with the waters of the St. Francis's River.[4] on this stream about 7 miles from it's mouth, is a settlement of *Shawnees*, which more than any other in this quarter deserves the name of a *villiage*[5] I could not ascertain their number. Oposite the mouth of this river [Apple Creek] and conscealed by a small Island on the Stard. qtr. muddy River falls in— this is also called *Cow River*, or River *Avaise*,[6] it is navigable thirty or forty mils in high water; and heads in extensive plains with the Saline of the Ohio and the Little Wabash a branch of the Great Wabash— there are many fine mines of *pitt* Coal on this stream, and one not far from its mouth whence boats asscend in common and high tide are loaded with and transport it the Saline on W. of mississippi and to Kaskaskias & elsewhere for the use of the blacksmiths and other artizans—[7] above the Island at the mouth of this river and on the same side there is another small Island close in to the main land which still continues low on that hand— the shore and land on the Lard. is still high with clifts of the limestone rock covered with scattering pine & seeader, some oak Hickory &c— Arrived at the *Grand Tower* a little before sunset, passed above it and came too on the Lard. shore for the night.[8] A discription of this place will be given in my journal tomorrow This seems among the watermen of the mississippi to be what the tropics or Equanoxial line is with regard to the Sailors; those who have never passed it before are always compelled to pay or furnish some sperits to drink or be ducked

Course	Time	dist.	References &c.
N. 52 W.	1 —	1 ¾	To mouth of Crk. Lard. qtr. (1)
N. 20 W.	3 —	3 ½	Creek Lard. 10 m. Long (2)
N. 11 E	1 15	1 ¾	To Apple river Lard. (3)
N. 10 W	2 —	2 —	To the *grand tower* (4)
Total	7 15	9 —	

The Country from Cape Jeradeau has been pretty generally high and bold on the Lard. and the reverse on the Stard quatr. at this place the high land approaches the river equally on both sides.— a mile and ¼ below the G. Tower on the lard. qutr. is a large bank of white clay that appears to be excellent *Spanis whiting*,[9] tho' it has a considerable portion of grit in it.—

1. Sexton Creek and Girardeau Limestone are difficult to distinguish in this area because both contain beds and nodules of black chert or flint. Pryor & Ross.

2. Any of several small creeks in the area.

3. Apple Creek serves as the boundary between Cape Girardeau and Perry counties, Missouri, as it enters the Mississippi.

4. Apple Creek is a shorter stream than Lewis apparently thought, and the White Water River lies between it and the St. Francis. Quaife (MLJO), 64 n. 1.

5. A settlement of the Absentee Shawnee, apparently located near the later village of Old Appleton, on Apple Creek in Cape Girardeau County. It may have contained as many as four hundred persons at the time. See above, November 16. Houck, 1:213–14; *Missouri Guide*, 35–37, 524–25.

6. The present Big Muddy River, which divides Union and Jackson counties, Illinois, where it enters the Mississippi. Lewis is correct about its headwaters only in the broadest sense. Lewis's reference to "Cow River" results from a confusion of the French words *vase* (mud) and *vache* (cow). It is "Riviere au Vase" on most early maps, and "R. aux Vaches" on only one. Clark showed it as "Pit Cole [Coal] R or R a Vayse" on *Atlas* map 3*a* and "pit Coal or Muddy River" on map 3*b*. Quaife (MLJO), 65 n. 1; McDermott (WCS), 143–44. To add to the confusion, there is a river that Lewis does not notice on the opposite side of the Mississippi several miles upstream from the Big Muddy. That river is today also called River aux Vases.

7. The Carbondale Formation, mid-Pennsylvanian in age, which contains some of the richest and most economically important coal beds of Illinois, crops out in the region described here. Willman et al., 187.

8. Tower Rock, as it is now called, is in Perry County, Missouri, opposite the Jackson County, Illinois, community of Grand Tower. From Jacques Marquette (1673) on, travelers have noted this landmark. Clark sketched the area, including Tower Rock, the Sugar Loaf, and their keelboat anchored near the shore, on *Atlas* maps 3*a* and 3*b*. Thwaites (JR), 59:143–45; Thwaites (EWT), 14:96–98, 26:89–90. The day's camp was just above the rock, as shown on the maps.

9. Whiting is a pigment made from powdered chalk or limestone. The Grand Tower Limestone of Middle Devonian age contains beds of very pure lithographic limestone that could readily have been ground to make whiting; it also contains scattered quartz sand grains. The area is shown as "Silica Mines" on the Altenburg quadrangle (Missouri-Illinois), U.S. Geological Survey, 1925. Willman et al., 117.

[Lewis]   *Novr. 26th*

Set out this morning at half after six. (1) throughout the whole of this course the land lys high on the Stad. qtr. and soon becomes low on the Lard. and continues so to the end of the course, on the Stard. the land rises into a fine bold looking range of hills 250 feet high which run parallel with the river— (2) Oposite to this stone quarry, is the upper point of *hat* [hot?] *Island,*[1] a small Island, of an oval form about the center of the river, the chanel being near lard. shore; came too at a stone bar a little above the rock and took Meridian Altd. of ☉'s L. L. found it 63° 34′ —″ Error of sextant as usual this observation may be depended on for it's accuracy to a single secd. the hills now are near the river on the Lard. and the land is low on the Stard. qutr.— there is a range of hills which run near, and prallel to the river on Lard. qutr. quite to Cape St. Combs—[2] The river from the Grand Tower upwards bears N. 5 W. below it bears—S 20 E. the extreem of the bason S. 30 W. The sugarloaf point or nobb—[3] S. 25 E. Hight of rock which forms the grand Tower is—92 Ft.— On the W. side and about 25 feet up this rock is a small cavern— the rock is limestone & the same quality of the clifts heretofore discribed (i e) intermixed with a considerable portion of *Flint stone*. When the river is high the courent setts in with great violence on the W. side of this rock and being confined on that by a range of high hills is drven with much impetuosity through a narrow channel fromed by the rock which composes this rock, and one which forms the base of the *Sugar-loaf* point, this courent meets the other portion of the river which runs E. of the Tower and on the Tower side in an obtuse angle; these strong courants thus meeting each other form an immence and dangerous whirlpool which no boat dare approach in that state of the water; the counter courent driving with great force against the E. side of the rock would instandly dash them to attoms and the whirlpool would as quickly take them to the botom. In the present state of the water there no danger in approaching it   I asscend it yesterday evening & measured the hight of it by a cord on the S. E. point, from whence I also took the bearings of the river bason &c. as above noticed.   the passage through this difficult pass of the Mississippi in high water is on the E. side of the river to the point which it forms on that side with the high-land where stands a large rock, thence across the river above the Tower to the Lard. shoar; but in low water the nearest and most convenient passage is the rout we took arond the E. side of the G. Tower.—   A ridge of Hills 200 feet high make across the river at this place; and the Gd. Tower as well as the *sugarloaf* point, as also a *rock* detached from both these and likewise the hills, another side of the bason all appear once to have formed a part of the range of hills which cross the Mississippi at this place, and which in the course of time have been broken down by the river—   the last mentioned *rock* is detached from the hills about 400 yards, and about 300 from the Sugar loaf point; the rock thus detatched measures 120 yards in circumpherence at it's base, and is 40 feet in hight perpendicular; it's sides show the water marks, and is so steep there is no possibility of asscending it without artificial aid.— There is a most beautifull and commanding view from the summit of the *sugarloaf point*; it commands the top of the grand Tower about 60 feet and overlooks the low surrounding country: the view of the river above is particularly beautifull; as well as the rang of hills which appear to the E. & streching from the river below; from S. to N.—   (1) this Creek is not very considerable but may be recconed 10 or 12 miles in length, *no name*.—

continuation of Note (2) this stone appears to possess excellent grit for *grind stones*; tho' the rock on the upper part of the hill is a *lime stone* such as appears common to those hills which border on the river, the country is high on the Lard qtr.

Novr. 26th

Couse	Time	distance	references &
	h m	miles	
N. 5 W.	2 40	4 ½	To Creek Stard. (1)

N. 70 W	1 20	1 ½	To grindstone quarry Lard (2)—
" " "	5 10	3 ¾	To uper point of small Inld. Lard qtr.—
" " "	— 20	— ¼	To Lard. shore where we staid all night[4]
Total	9 30	10 —	

[Lewis and Clark]   Louisville November 26th 1803[5]

  Sir,

    Pr

    Thos Lisbet   Blacksmith

Kaskaskies

Sext	42°	27	0″
qde	⟨43	45⟩	
	58°	33	00″

1. Cumings, 66, map 3, locates "Hot Island" a few miles north of the Grand Tower. Lewis's "a's" and "o's" are often indistinguishable.

2. Cape Cinque Hommes, in Perry County, Missouri, near Cross Town. Quaife (MLJO), 66 n. 1.

3. Shown on *Atlas* maps 3*a* and 3*b*.

4. In Perry County, Missouri, less than ten miles above the Grand Tower.

5. This material in Lewis's and Clark's hands is scattered over a small sheet in the Field Notes attached to the larger portion of document 2 (incorrectly shown as document 3 in Osgood). On the reverse of the document is Clark's map of the confluence of the Ohio and Mississippi rivers. Included is the date under which it is placed here, although the party had left Louisville some time before November 26.

[Lewis]   *Novr. 27th*

Set out this morning before sunrise— (1) ¾ of a mile to the mouth of this river[1] it is about 18 yards wide at it's mouth and affords but little water at this moment, tho' I am informed that there is a handsome settlement on it & that in high water it navigable many miles, it heads with the waters of the Saline of Mississippi & the St. Francis rivers—

(2) This is a bold point of rocks forming the extremity of a range of hills which have continued on our Lard quarter for a considerable distance the Creek of the same name[2] which puts in just above it is 20 miles in length and has a considerable number of inhabitants on it, and as many as three gristmills.—

(3) at the lower point of this Ild.[3] I came too and took Meridian Altitudes of ☉'s L. L.; found it 62° 54′ 30″ Error of Sextant 8′ 45″—.

Course	Time	dist.	
N. 70 W.	1 —	— ¾	To river Ameat Lard. qtr (1)
" " "	1 —	— ¾	To Cape St. Comes Lard. (2)
N. 21 E.	— 10	— ¼	To mouth of creek Lard. of the same name—
" " "	1 15	1 ¼	To large Isld. Lard
N. 50 W.	2 20	2 ½	To Isld. Lard. (3)
" "	2 —	3 —	wind served us here—
N. 44 W.	— 10	— ¼	Isld. Stard qtr.
" " "	1 40	3 —	To upper pt. of parrarie Lard.
N. 50 W.	— 45	1 ¼	Come too for the night at Lower pt. of Isld. Lard. qutr[4]
	10 20	13	

1. Lewis's "river Ameat" (see course and distance table of this entry); presumably it is Omete Creek (also "amite"), but that stream enters Cinque Hommes Creek just before the latter falls into the Mississippi. Perhaps Lewis refers to Brazeau Creek.

2. See above, November 26, n. 2. Cinque Hommes Creek is just above the cape.

3. Shown as "I. a la Merde" on Collot's 1796 map of the Mississippi. Collot's map, Tucker, 522–23.

4. Probably Horse Island, in Perry County, Missouri, opposite present Chester, Randolph County, Illinois; the state line crosses the river in various places in this area.

[Lewis]   *Novr. 28th.*

This morning left Capt Clark in charge of the Boat[1]

[Clark]   November 28th

Set out this morning of 8 oClock from the lower point of the horse Island, which Island is Situated opposit the mouth of Kaskaskies River Commonly Called *Aucau* Creek—[2] passed the mouth said River at half passed 8 oClock— the high lands make near the Mississippi below the mouth of said River, a bold and rockey shore

This morning being verry Smokey[3] prevents my being as acurate as I Could wish— passed a Small Creek[4] on the Larbd. Side near the point of a ridge of high Land makeing to the river. This Creek heads but a feew miles from the river, at 1 oClock passed *Donohoes* Landing on the Larbd.

side, this landing is the place that Boats receive Salt from the Saline Licks which is one mile and 2½ miles S W from the River, and is worked at present to great advantage, passed the mouth of the Saline Creek[5] at three oClock, this Creek mouthes behind an Island   This Creek has a thick settlement [sediment] on its waters, at the time I passed this Creek the horozon became darkened that I could not see across the River, which appeared to widened, and the Current much Swifter than usial   Passed an Island on the Larbd. side, also one on the Starbd side abov that on the Larbd. and after passing some verry swift water which was comfd [confined?] between Sand bars, I arrived at the Landing opposit old St. Genevie, (or Misar)[6]

Novr. 28th

Course	Time	Distance	Reference
	h	ms.	
S 50° W—	1 30	3 ¼	Pass the upper point of the Island, high banks above Lbd side
S 63 W—	0 50	1 ¾	high banks Lbd Side or Small Isld Stbd Side
N 52 W—	2 27	3 0	Donohoos ferry, a high pt. on Lbd side (2)
N 24 W	2 45	3 ¾	To pot. on Stbd side an Island, opt. an Island (3)
North	3 0	3 "	To the Landing above the Isl'd opposit Missar & Kasskaskies[7]
	10 32	14 ¾	

1. Here Lewis's known daily journal-keeping, except for scattered fragments, ceases until April 1805. In preparation for traveling to St. Louis, he left the boat in charge of Clark. Lewis apparently remained at Kaskaskia until December 5, entering astronomical observations on the second and third. Clark and the party remained at Kaskaskia until December 3. In the Eastern Journal, Lewis's November 28 entry is followed by several blank pages, then his astronomical observations (arranged in chronological order in this volume), then Clark's entry for November 28. Lewis left Kaskaskia on December 5 on horseback, arriving at Cahokia on December 7; the next day he visited the Spanish commandant at St. Louis, and on the ninth rejoined Clark and the party at Cahokia. Quaife (MLJO), 68 n. 1. Quaife thought Clark was the author of the astronomical observations. Lewis to Jefferson, December 19, 1803, Jackson (LLC), 1:145–47.

2. Clark's attempt at the French "Au Kas." Changes in the course of the Mississippi have altered the geography of the area considerably since 1803; the Mississippi now follows the former course of the lower Kaskaskia River.

3. Smoky here means misty.

4. Perhaps St. Laurent Creek.

5. Shown as "R. au Salines" on Collot's 1796 map, in Missouri just north of the dividing line between Perry and Ste. Genevieve counties, behind Kaskaskia Island. French inhabitants of Kaskaskia were working the salt springs of the area in the early 1700s, resulting in one of the first European settlements in Missouri. Collot's map, Tucker, 522–23.

6. Old Ste. Genevieve lay about three miles below the present site of the town in Ste. Genevieve County. It was known in early years as "Miserre," presumably because of hard times in its early years. In 1785 flooding on the Mississippi necessitated moving the town to its present location. Anglo-American settlers came in considerable numbers in the late 1700s, and by Lewis and Clark's time the population was nearly 1,000 persons. Clark's camp was on the opposite shore, in Randolph County, Illinois, near Kaskaskia. Houck, 1:337–62, 2:208–9, 3:140; *Missouri Guide*, 269–73.

7. Relatively unpopulated modern Kaskaskia sits in the middle of Kaskaskia Island, Randolph County, the original site having been submerged by the Mississippi in the late nineteenth century. George Rogers Clark captured the area from the British in 1778, but that occupation was brief. By 1800 some 467 persons lived in the town. Kaskaskia was the capital of Illinois Territory from 1809 to 1818, then the state capital for two years. *Illinois Guide*, 496–97; Belting; Alvord, 407, 324–28, 332, 359–74.

[*Ed: Here occurs a gap in the journal from November 28 to December 3, except for some astronomical observations on December 2. Clark left off his daily journalizing until he resumed the upriver journey. Apparently he remained in the Kaskaskia-Ste. Genevieve area during this time. Evidently he did not consider it necessary to keep a journal for the time he was not traveling. See also November 28, n. 1.*]

[Lewis]   December 2ed

On the Mississippi 3 miles W. of Kasskasskais made the following observations— *By Circumpherenter*— Azamuth of pole Star 7° 47′ 00″ at 8 h 11 m 45 s P. M. Pr. Chronometer

Moon & Aldeberan ★ W.

Time			*Distance*		
h	m	s			
10	51	8	60°	57′	45″
11	4	52	61	1	0
11	15	5	61	5	0
11	20	50	61	5	15
11	24	4	61	10	0
11	27	7	61	10	45

Distance Moon & Regulus ★ Eeast—

Time			Distance		
h	m	s			
12	11	12	17°	47'	15"
12	21	59	17	45	15
12	23	58	17	45	0
12	29	49	17°	44'	00"
12	35	4	17	37	15
12	39	56	17	37	0

Distance Moon & Aldebran ★ West—

Time			Distance		
h	m	s			
1	1	29	61°	37'	30"
1	7	10	61	41	00
1	10	37	61	39	30
1	14	53	61	39	15
1	17	0	61	40	30
1	19	45	61	40	15

[Lewis]   Decr. 3rd Continued my observations

Sextant Error 8' 45"

The distance between ☉ ☽ was too great to admit of taking the angle at A M. 8 h 30 m—therefore must for the longitude depend on the observation of last night made with Aldeberan and Regulus.—together with my Chronometer, as with her I took the time in my observation for equal Altitudes at the mouth of the Ohio, this peace has been going regularly since and I now took Eequal Altd.—

Equal Atds. of the ☉ Decr. 3d 1803
Sext Error 8' 45"—

	h	m	s.		h	m	s.
A. M.	9	9	59	P. M.	1	56	20
	9	11	18		1	58	45.5
	9	14	44		2	1	10

∠ given by the sextant for the double Altd. of the ☉ at the times of observation 42° 27' 0"—

☉'s Magnettic Azamuth by Circumpherentor—at 9 h 9 m 59 s A. M. S. 43° 45' East—

observed meridian Altd. of ☉'s Lower Limb, with my Octant[1] & artificial hor-
rizan, found it 58° 38′ Error of Octant 2° additive.—

Latd. from the preceeding observation with Octant—38° 20′ 57″

[Clark]   at Kaskaskais the 3d Decr[2]

⟨Sexion not⟩ right

```
 ⌐42°   27′    0″
  21    13    30
         2    37        − refraction T: 1,—              6
  21    10    53                                       1—42
         16   17        Semideameter p 2 +             F—30
              8         + Parallax T. 3 +
  21    27    18        Suns Center
  90
  67    32    42
  22     2     7        Decklination
  45    30    35
```

                                                    Kaskaskia 3d Decr

```
2  58°   33′   00″
   29    16    30
          1    43       − refraction Ta: (1)
   29    14    47
          16   17       + Diameter p: 2
               8        + Parallax Ta 3
   29    31    12
Deduct 90
   60    28    48
   22     2     7       Decklination
   38    26    41
    1    20
   39    46    41
```

at Kohokia Lattitude as worked by my Self is Degrees 38 6′ 58″ N—   The
Mouth Platt crek above Fort Charters[3] is Degrees 37° 55′ 36″ N

```
                              38    25    24
            4    32           38     6    58
            2    16                 18    26
                                     3
                                    15    26
```

Decr. 3d

Set out from the landing at half passed 4 oClock   passed an Island near the middle of the River the lower point within three quaters of a mile, came to on the Larbd side after Dark[4]

Course	Distance
N 70 d W.	3 miles

1. A predecessor of the sextant, the octant, or "Hadley's quadrant," as it was also known, was part of Lewis's pre-expedition purchases at Philadelphia. Jackson (LLC), 1:69, 82, 96; Lewis's description of astronomical instruments, July 22, 1804; Wilford, 96–97; Bedini (TT), 476, fig. 34.

2. The following calculations (largely crossed out) are found on document 2 in Clark's Field Notes (Osgood incorrectly prints the facsimile as document 3). The calculations are inserted here under the date given. They probably represent the preliminary calculations for the observations by Lewis entered in the Eastern Journal. Little is known of Clark's formal education, but like many army frontiersmen he knew the rudiments of basic surveying. There was virtually no formal training for army officers in the United States in his time—the West Point military academy was established in 1802—and it is doubtful if he acquired any such knowledge during his army career. Lewis received his instruction in taking celestial observations from Jefferson, Andrew Ellicott, and Robert Patterson, who drew up a handbook of instructions for Lewis's use, the Astronomy Notebook. As far as we know, Lewis was Clark's only instructor. While the subject is too technical for discussion here some terms used in the calculations may be clarified. Refraction, the bending of light rays by the atmosphere, causes a heavenly body to appear to be higher in altitude than it actually is and must be corrected for in calculation. Semidiameter must be allowed for in observations of the sun or moon; if the observation is based on the upper limb (top) or lower limb (bottom) of the body's disk, half the angular diameter of the body must be added or subtracted to obtain the position of the body's center. Parallax error is caused by the fact that the observer is standing on the earth's surface instead of its center, on which all navigational tables are based. Declination is the distance in degrees of the heavenly body north or south of the equinoctial, the celestial equator. Loos, 6; Steffen, 14–15, 45–46; Bedini (TT), 364–65; Wylie, 111–13, 156–57.

3. In Randolph County, Illinois, a few miles below the Monroe County line, and now within Fort de Chartres State Park. The settlement at the fort was the French capital of Upper Louisiana until the territory east of the Mississippi was ceded to Britain in 1763. The British occupied the post in 1765, but when the river began to encroach on it, they abandoned and destroyed the structure in 1772. Those were the ruins Clark saw and noted on December 4. *Illinois Guide*, 495–96; Alvord, passim.; Saucier & Seineke, 199–227.

4. In Ste. Genevieve County, Missouri, just below the town of that name.

[Clark]   December 4td

Set out this morning before Sunrise, at ¾ of a mile passed the mouth of a Small Creek Called Gabia,[1] at the mouth of this Creek is the landing place for the Tradeing Boats of St Genevieve, a Small town Situated on the Spurs of the high land at ¾ of a mile distant nearly South   This Village contains (as I am informed) about 120 families, principally French,— above the mouth of this Creek the high lands approach the river, Several French families are Setled near the bank, above the Creek, opposit this settlement and above the upper Point of the Island a Creek mouths on the Starbd. side[2]   (2) at ¾ of a mile above Gabia Creek the high lands juts to the river and form a most tremendious Clift of rocks   near the Commencement of this Clift I saw a Cave,[3] the mouth of which appeared to be about 12 feet Diameeter, and about 70 foot above the water.   (3) at 2 miles passed the mouth of a Small Creek[4] on the Larbd. side, opposit the upper point of a small Island; and lower point of a large Isld. situated opposit Old *fort Charters*   (4) came to on the lower point of a Small Isld. Lbd. side imediately opposit the Old Fort and took (tho not as accurate as I could wish) meridian altitude of ☉' L. L. found it 59° 58 m o   opposit this Island close on the Larbd. side is an Island abt. ¾ of a mile long, at 1 oClock passed the upper Point of Ft. Chartes Isle.   from this point I had a view of two sides of the Fort, which at the distance of about 2 miles and a half

The chanel which forms the Island next to the fort is intirely dry, and appears to be filling up with Sand and mud, the River at this place is wide, and remarkably Streight washing the base of the clifts of the high land of about 250 feet above the surfice of the River,—   Pass Several Small Creeks on the Larbd Side, came to on the lower point of an Island near the Larbd. Side and opposit a large Creek on the Starbd Side[5]

December 4th

Course	Time	Distance	Remaks. & refurncs.
	h m	h [miles]	
N. 60° W.	o 42	1 ¾	To pt. on Lbd. side psd. upr. pt. Isl. of 3 mil: long (1)

N. 50° W.	0 57	1 ½	To the pt. on Stbd. Side a Clift of Rock, on Lbd. Side (2)
N. 43° W.	5 54	13 ¼	To pt. of an Isld Lbd Side, pd. cave Lbd. 2 Isl: Lbd. Side (3); psd. Isl: Stbd, *Ft Charters*
N. 38° W.	1 38	2 ¾	(4)—To pt. of Isl Lbd. Side a Creek on Stbd Side near opposit
	9 11	19 ¼	

1. North and South Gabourie creeks run just above and below Ste. Genevieve. The name is perhaps taken from Laurent Gabourie, an early French settler. Houck, 1:339.

2. Perhaps Turkey Island and Prairie du Rocher Creek, in Randolph County, Illinois.

3. Perhaps what is shown as Gray's Cave on Raynolds & Simpson, map 5.

4. This may be Frenchman Creek.

5. This camp was in Jefferson County, Missouri. The island may be Lee Island, and the creek Marystown Creek, in Monroe County, Illinois. Ibid., map 4.

[Clark]   December the 5th

Set out this morning before sun rise, passed the upper point the Island at two miles, In this Course I observed (1), Several caves, also a number of Indented Arches of deferent sises in the Clifts on the Larbd. Side, which gave it a verry romanteck appearance, we passed Several Small Creeks on the Larbd. side in this Course.— I came to at the lower point of a large Sand bar, forming an Island on the Starbd Side, and took Meredien altitude of ☉'s L. L. and found it 59° 37′ 30″— Error of Sextn. as usial. (2) passed between two Islands,[1] of about one mile in length, one near the Center of the River and the other close to the Larbd. Side hideing the mouth of a large Creek called Platea;[2] (3) which is a Streen suficient large to aford water for mills (several of which are now established on the Creek) at all Seasons. The Emigrent amercains are Settled verry thick up this Creek, as also, on one we pass'd about four miles above called Swacken [or Swachen] Creek,[3] those Creeks head with the waters of the River St. Francies at the mouths of those Creeks is the first Settlements on the River above St. Geniesviur, (4) I came to on Lbd. side for the men to eate Dinner above a rock forming a worft [wharf] into the river 200 feet, as the Current of the river sets imedeately against this rock, we had some difecualty in passing it— this Rock appears to be Composed of Grit well calculated for Grind Stones— about half a mile above Swachen Crk on the Starboad Side is the mouth of the Leagle,[4] a Creek running from Bell fontain[5] 12 miles distant from its mouth, passing thro a thick Settlement of Americans in all its Course— at the mouth of this Creek I intended to land and take in Some Provisions which was to be delivered to me at this place— by enquriey I was Informed (by Mr. Blear [or Blean][6] the owner of the place) that no provisions had arrived. he "expected it every minete," the water being Shole, I proceeded on half a mile above the landing, and came to for the night—[7] The distance from Kaskaskies to this place is Called 37 miles by water— The high Lands which sets in opposit St. Genesvieve, Continues with Small intervales of Low Land on that Side of the Mississippi, the other appearing low and Subject to be overflowed

The Courses &c. December 5th

Course	Time	Dist.	refurrences & rmks.
	h m	miles	
N 44° W	3 40	7 ½	To mo. of Plate Creek on Lbd Side passing a pt. on the Stbd Side. pasd the upr. pt. of Isd. on which we camped at 2 miles psd. 3 Sml. creeks in this course (1)
N 26° W.	4 0	5 ¾	To pt. on Stbd. Side at the Mouth of Leagle. psd Sand bar on Stbd. side (2) pd. betwn. 2 Is: & Plate creek Lbd. Side (3) psd. Swachen [or Swacken] creek Lbd. Side (4) pd. Leagle Cr:
Ṅ. 12° W.	0 22	" ½	To a Sand bar about ½ a mile below an Isld. on Stbd. Side
	8 2	13 ¾	

1. Probably Cornice Island (larboard) and Calico Island (starboard). Raynolds & Simpson, map 4.

2. Platten Creek, at present Crystal City, Jefferson County, Missouri.

3. Anglo-Americans had considerable trouble with the name of Joachim Creek, which enters the Mississippi at Herculaneum, Jefferson County. "Swashon" was another version. Quaife (MLJO), 71 n. 2; Houck, 1:355 n. 44.

4. From the French "L'Aigle"; a later name was the English translation, Eagle Creek. Now Fountain Creek in Monroe County, Illinois. Quaife (MLJO), 72 n. 1.

5. Bellefontaine has been absorbed by the present town of Waterloo, Monroe County. The original settlement, founded in 1779, was on the trail between Fort de Chartres and Cahokia and was one of the first American communities north of the Ohio River. Ibid.; Howard, 57–58, 70; *Illinois Guide*, 494–95; Alvord, 359, 407.

6. Daniel Blouin was a merchant in Kaskaskia in the 1760s, and Louis Blouin was also active in the Illinois region in the same period. "Blean" may be one of these, or a relative. Houck, 1:342–43.

7. In Monroe County, a little above Fountain (Eagle) Creek.

[Clark]

December 6th   at the mo. of the Leagle—.   A Dark wet morning   I was informed this morning that Capt Lewis passd by this place yesterday on his way to St Louis accompanied by an Officer.[1]   I set out this morning ⟨about⟩ at 11 oClock, after receiving a Small Supply of Provisions on Board; (1) passed a Bieaue [bayou] which Comunicates with Leagle Creek   (2) passed the Lower Point of the first Island at ½ a mile also the upper point at 2½ miles, a Small creek of runing water opposite on the Larbd. Side.[2]   Passed a Small Isld. near the middle of the river nearly opposite the upper point of the last on the Larbd. Side of this Island the current is verry Swift, Seting imediately against the high lands, which terminates in a Bluff at the river   (3) pass'd a Small Creek of running water on the Larbd. Side above the last Island   (4) passd. the mouth of a Small Creek Lbd Side Called little Rock Creek,[3] Several Settlements are formed on this Creek also on the River above its mouth   (5) passed two Islands[4] on the Larbd. Side, one of those Islands large and lies near the main Shore   the other verry Small with a large Sand bar—; the head of those two Ilds. are imedeately below the Meremeck River[5]   (6) passed the mouth of the Merrenek and came to at a farm ¾ of a mile above,[6] this River is about 110 yards wide at its mouth.

Courses of the river &c. December 6th—

Course	Time	Distance	Remks & Refferenes
	h m	m	
N. 12° W.	1 42	3 ¼	To the upr. pt. of a Sm: Isl: in the mid: River, psd a Bio: Stbd Side. (1) psd. an Isd. 2 m: long. (2) psd a Sm Isd. in mid: river & creek Lbd. Side
N. 10° E.	1 12	3 ¾	To a pt. on Lbd. Side (3) psd. a smal Creek Lbd. Side abv. the last Island.
N. 33° E.	1 42	2 ¾	To a pt. on Stbd Side nl'y opposit the mo. of the Meremeck River (4) psd Sm: Cr: on Lbd Side & 2 farms above (5) psd. 2 Isd. Lbd side.

N. 31° E.	0 47	1 ″	To a pt. on Lbd. Side (6) Psd. the Meremick and
	5 23	10 ¾	come to at a farm for the night

1. Lewis was accompanied to St. Louis by John Hay, trader and postmaster of Cahokia, and Nicholas Jarrot, another Cahokia fur trader. Lewis to Jefferson, December 19, 1803, Jackson (LLC), 1 : 135 n. 2, 145–47 and n. 1.

2. Perhaps Glaize Creek.

3. Rock Creek enters the Mississippi at Kimmswick, Jefferson County, Missouri.

4. Chesley Island and First Island appear on Raynolds & Simpson, map 3. Only Chesley Island appears today.

5. Meramec River at its mouth divides Jefferson and St. Louis counties, Missouri. The name is from an Algonquian word for "catfish," used as the name of a tribe or band. *Missouri Guide*, 406, 449.

6. A little above the Meramec River in St. Louis County.

[Clark]   December the 7th

A Dark rainey morning with hard wind at N, E, upon which point it blew all the last night accompanyd. with rain— Set out a quarter past 7 oClock, the wing [wind] much against us   (1) passed a Small Island near the middle of the river; about 10 oClock the wind changed to the S, E, and gave us an oppertunity to Sailing   (2) passd an Island on the Starbd Side, at 12 oClock the wind was So violent as to take off one of the Mast's (3) passed a Small Village above the mouth of a large Creek,   This Village is Called Viele Pauchr[1] and Contains [*blank*] families of French, Situated about 4 miles below St. Louis on the Same Side, The high land continue to day on the Larbd. Side, I came to at 3 oClock at the Kohokia Landing,[2] which is at the mouth of Kohokia Creek ¾ of a mile from the Town, and in view of St Louis which is about 2½ miles distant.

Decr. 7th Course Distance &c. of the River

Course	Time	Distance	Remks. & referncs.
	h m		
N. 31° E.	1 45	2 0	To a pt. on Lbd. Side, passd several Sand bars.
N. 20° E.	2 40	3 ½	To a pt. on Lbd. Side passg. a Small Isle: (1) passd an Is. on Stbd. Side (2) wind & rain continue.
N. 12° E.	1 20	4 ¾	To a pt. on Stbd Sd. passd. a Creek Lbd. Sd. mast broke.

N. 32° E.　　1 46　　3 ¼　　To pt. at mo: Kohokia Creek Stbd side　(3) passd.

　　　　　　　7 31　　13 ½　　a small village above a creek on Lbd side.

1. The creek is River des Peres, which enters the Mississippi in St. Louis County, Missouri, a few miles above the Meramec River. "Viele Pauchr" is Clark's version of the French "Vide Poche" (empty pocket), a derisive name for the town of Carondelet, perhaps descriptive of its declining fortunes in comparison to neighboring St. Louis. Carondelet (after bearing various earlier names) was named for François Luis Hector, Baron de Carondelet, Spanish governor of Louisiana from 1791 to 1797. By Clark's time it may have numbered 250 residents. The town has now been absorbed by St. Louis. Houck, 2:63–64; Thwaites (EWT), 22:215 and n. 124.

2. Cahokia, in St. Clair County, is the oldest town in Illinois (although Fort Crèvecoeur has also been claimed to be the first permament village. See Alvord, 100). Today it has been virtually absorbed by East St. Louis. The name comes from a small band of the Illinois confederacy. By 1800 the population was over 700, but with the rise of St. Louis, and East St. Louis, the town declined. McDermott (OC); Hodge, 1:185–86; *Illinois Guide*, 492–93.

[Clark]　　　　　　　　　　　　　　　　　　　　　　December the 8th—[1]

1. The date is all Clark has written for this entry. His party remained at Cahokia until December 10. His only journal entries after the seventh until the trip was resumed are astronomical observations recorded on the tenth. He left the remainder of this page blank and also the next page, perhaps intending to cover the missing days later. Lewis rejoined the party on the ninth, having visited the Spanish "commandant" in St. Louis, Carlos Dehault Delassus, lieutenant governor of Upper Louisiana, who would not grant permission to ascend the Missouri without permission from his superiors. Having already decided to winter at Wood River, and knowing that the region would be transferred to the United States in a few months, Lewis was not particularly distressed. Dehault Delassus to Juan Manuel de Salcedo and the Marques de Casa Calvo, December 9, 1803, Lewis to Jefferson, December 19, 1803, Jackson (LLC), 1:142–47.

[Clark]　　　　　　　　　　　　　　　　　　*Saterday 10th December* 1803.

At the landing opposite the town of Cahokia, and a little above its mouth took Meridian Altd. of ☉'s U. Limb.— found it 57° 46′ 30″— the sun was reather dim, therefore it possible that this obsevation may have been liable to a small error—

Latd. pr. this obstn.— 38° 38′ 9″[1]

Course	h m		
N. 32 E	1 27	2 ½	to St. Louis on the Larbd Side, passed the mouth of a Creek or Beyou on the Stbd & a Creek on Lbd.[2]

1. This line appears to be Lewis's handwriting.

2. This entry is not very informative, but apparently the expedition moved upstream from Cahokia to a point in present St. Clair County, Illinois, directly opposite St. Louis. This would be in the area of modern East St. Louis.

[Clark]   December the 11th—

a Verry rainey morning   the wind from the N, E, crossed the river to St. Louis,[1] Capt Lewis detain for to acquire information of the Countrey[2] and to prepare Despatchs to the Government by the next mail.   at 11 oClock I proceeded on, at about one mile (1) passed two Creeks[3] on the Larbd Side, the upper Creek, which at the Commencement of a willow point is Suffiently large to admite a Boat in its mouth—.   the wind changed to N. W. about 3 oClock, passed several large Sand bars in the middle of the river, and Camped on the Side of a large Island,[4] Situated on the Starboad Side, the rain Continud until 3 oClock to day, The banks of the River on each Side is Subject to over flow, from the last mentioned Creek, The Current of the water is against the Westerley Shore, and the banks are falling, where there is no Rock

Decr. 11th

Course Destanc &c.

Course	Time	Diste.	Remks. & refrs
	h m	m	
North	0 50	1 ¼	along the Town of St Louis to a pt. on Same side of the river.
N. 10° W	2 25	1 ¾	To a pt. on Lbd. Side psd 2 creeks on Lbd Side verry swift water.
N 2° W	2 15	3 ¼	To the Side of an Isd. Stbd. Side passed Some
	5 30	6 ¼	verry strong water; & sevl large Sand bars in the river on th Stbd. [*apparently written over Lbd.*] of Cent. [center?]

1. St. Louis, capital of Spanish Upper Louisiana, not quite forty years old when Lewis and Clark arrived, was already the center of the fur trade for a huge region drained by the Missouri River; with the expedition began the city's long role as the "Gateway to the West" for the United States. Although not founded until France had lost control of Louisiana to Spain, the town was essentially French in language and culture until after the American takeover, and the French fur magnates continued to dominate St. Louis for some decades. In 1763, the French authorities in New Orleans granted Maxent, Laclede, and Company exclusive rights to the fur trade on the Missouri. Pierre Laclede Liguest, the junior partner, immediately sailed north with supplies and some thirty persons to Fort de Chartres, where the party spent the winter. With him were his consort, Marie Therese (Bourgeois) Chouteau, and René Auguste Chouteau, her son by her estranged husband. On February 14, 1764, Laclede sent young René Auguste Chouteau, whom he regarded as a foster son, across the river with a party of workers to begin construction of the post, named for Louis IX, king of France, who had been canonized for his part in the Crusades.

By the end of the year some forty families had settled in the new village, including many French people from east of the river unwilling to live under British rule. The settlers called the place "Pain Court" (short of bread), perhaps indicating early hardships or simply the lack of agriculture in this trading community. Later, under the Spanish government the officials were commonly local residents, ethnically French, and the French fur trade dominated the economy. The Spanish withdrew Laclede's monopoly and competitors rushed in, but the founder still prospered. In May 1780, the Spanish garrison and the townspeople beat off a British-directed Indian attack, part of the western operations of the American Revolution. In 1799, the town had a population of 925; when incorporated as a village in 1808, with somewhat expanded boundaries, it had 1,400 residents. Houck, 2 : 1–78; *Missouri Guide*, 298–301; McDermott (MIG).

2. For the results of Lewis's inquiries, see Dehault Delassus to Juan Manuel de Salcedo, December 9, 1803, and Lewis to Jefferson, December 28, 1803, Jackson (LLC), 1 : 142–43, 148–55.

3. The upper creek could be Gingras Creek.

4. Perhaps Cabaret Island, also called Wood Island, opposite Granite City, Madison County, Illinois. Collot's map, Tucker, map 28; Cumings, map 1.

[Clark]   Monday the 12th of December

A hard N W wind all last night   Set out this morning at 7 oClock, passed the head of the Isd on which we Camped last night at one mile— nearly opposit the head of this Island is a Settlement[1] in a Small Preree on the Larbd. Side, and the lower point of a large (1) Island[2] close to the Sterbd. Side   (2) opposit the middle of this Island on the Larbd. Side, the high Lands is within two or 300 yards of the River; above the high Lands on the Same Side is an (3) Island[3] in the bend of the river above the mouth of a Creek   (4) passed the upper point of the Island on the Stbd. ⟨left⟩

which is about 4 miles long with a verry narrow Chanl. seperateing it from the Stbd. Shore— Large banks of Sand is thrown up from the last mentioned Island on the Lbd Side to the mouth of Musoures (5) a Small Island lies close to the Stbd. Side at the lower point is a Settlement on land which does not appear to have been over flown latterly; (6) about [*blank*] miles higher up and above the upper pt. of the last mentioned Island, & nearly opposit the Missouries I came to in the mouth of a little River called Wood River,⁴ about 2 oClock and imediately after I had landed the N W wind which had been blowing all day increased to a *Storm* which was accompanied by Hail & Snow, & the wind Continued to blow from the Same point with violence.

not soon after I had landed two Canoos of Potowautomi Indians⁵ Came up on the other Side and landed formed their Camp and three of them in a Small Canoo Came across when the waves was so high & wind blowing with violence that I expected their Canoo would Certounly fill with water or turn over, but to my astonishment found on their landing that they were all Drunk and their Canoo had not received any water.

The hunders which I had sent out to examine the Countrey in Deferent derections, returned with Turkeys & opossoms⁶ and informed me the Countrey was butifull and had great appearance of Gaim.

December 12th

Course	Time	Dists.	Remks. & References (1)
	h m	mils	
N. 13° E.	2 15	2 ¼	To pt. on Lbd. Side above a Settlemt.— psd. the upr. pt. of the Isd. (1) opst. is the Lowr. pt. on Isd. Stbd. side
N. 22 E.	2 20	6 ¼	To pt. on Lbd Side— psd. Creek (2) above the high Land. (3) psd. an Island abe. on Lbd. Side (4) psd. the upr. pt. of the Isld. on Stbd.—
N. 3° E.	1 40	2 ¾	To the mouth of Wood Creek on Stbd Side (5)
Total	6 15	11 ¼	passd. Sm Isd. on Stbd. Sd. and Landed in the mo: of Wood Creek (6) a violent wind &c.

1. Probably the village of St. Ferdinand, or San Fernando, de Florissant, apparently established on Cold Water Creek by French settlers from east of the Mississippi about the time of the founding of St. Louis (1764). At the time of the Louisiana Purchase it con-

tained sixty houses. On Collot's 1796 map it appears simply as Florissant, and Clark's sketch map of the area (see fig. 6) shows "Florisan." It is now Florissant, St. Louis County, Missouri, a suburb of St. Louis. Houck, 2 : 198; Collot's map, Tucker, map 28; *Missouri Guide*, 340–43.

2. Perhaps Chouteau Island, "Great Island" on Collot's 1796 map. Collot's map, Tucker, map 28.

3. This also might be Chouteau Island, and the creek Watkins Creek.

4. Apparently named Rivière à Dubois after a long forgotten Frenchman rather than because of trees, so the literal translation "Wood River" originally had no validity; Wood's River would be more accurate, but long usage has now established the former as the river's name. It was on the south side of the river that Clark established the winter quarters later variously called Camp Wood, Camp Wood River, and Camp Dubois (none of which names were actually used by the captains) on a site selected earlier by Lewis on the basis of local information. Although Clark describes the mouth as being nearly opposite the mouth of the Missouri, his sketch map of the area (fig. 6) shows the mouth of Wood River well to the south of that of the Missouri. Various nearly contemporary maps, as well as Lewis and Clark's 1804 map (*Atlas* map 6), show the two mouths directly opposite. Today both rivers have shifted their courses considerably, and Wood River enters the Mississippi well above the Missouri, in Madison County, Illinois. Because of these shifts, the approximate site of the camp is now in St. Charles County, Missouri, on the western side of the Mississippi. Osgood (FN), 3 n. 1; Appleman (LC), 287–90; Lewis to Jefferson, December 19, 1803, Jackson (LLC), 1 : 147; McDermott (WCS), 144–46; Collot's map, Tucker, map 28.

5. The name Potawatomi comes both from a self-designation and a Chippewa name for these people. The Potawatomis, together with the Ottawas and Chippewas, descended from a common ancestral group, but by the time of Lewis and Clark they had had at least two centuries of cultural independence. Their domain included parts of modern Illinois, southern Wisconsin, northern Indiana, and southwestern Michigan. Within fifty years the Potawatomi would be divested of their extensive land holdings and survive as small, scattered remnants in Oklahoma, Kansas, Michigan, and Canada. Clifton, 725, 728–29, 731, 736–42; Edmunds, 3–4, 240–75.

6. The wild turkey, *Meleagris gallopavo* [AOU, 310], and the opossum, *Didelphis virginiana*. Hall, 1 : 5.

Chapter Three

Wintering
at Camp Dubois

December 13, 1803–May 14, 1804

[Clark] [1]

Tuesday—on the 13th   fixed on a place to build huts   Set the men to
Clearing land & Cutting Logs—   a hard wind all day—   flying Clouds,
Sent to the neghbourhood, Some Indians pass.

1. Here begin the Field Notes, kept by Clark during the five months spent at the Wood
River winter camp. The Dubois Journal consists of twelve loose sheets of different sizes,
on which are found not only dated entries but other miscellaneous, undated material; the
thrifty captains used the same sheets for a variety of purposes. In Osgood's edition of the
Field Notes, each sheet was given a document number, and the material was arranged
largely according to the document on which it occurs. The same document numbers are
used here in reference to the sheets. In this edition, chronological order is followed wherever possible; thus, entries that bear a date before December 13, 1803, have been placed
with the Eastern Journal material in chapters 1 and 2. Material that cannot be dated is
placed according to the sheet on which it occurs. In determining order, the sheets are
read from left to right and top to bottom insofar as possible, allowing for the fact that on
many sheets the writing runs in several different directions. Obverse and reverse of each
sheet are determined by the dates of the entries. Apparently the captains did not regard
this journal as an official document because they were not traveling and the expedition
had not actually begun; hence it is extremely sketchy and disorganized. On both sides of
this first sheet are drawings of squares and rectangles, apparently representing plans for
the River Dubois camp (see fig. 5). It is not clear which plan was eventually adopted.
There are also many jottings on this sheet that are illegible or that seem unworthy of
adding to this text, words like "Perogues" or "take off the Deed [dead?]." Doodles are also
present. Facsimiles of these documents are accessible in Osgood's edition.

[Clark]

Wednesday—14th   Contined to Cut logs, Sent out into the neghbr-
hood yesterday, Som Indians passed, wind Continu to blow hard   river
riseing—

[Clark]

Thursday—15th   I cut a road to the prairey 2490 yards East   Com-
minc the Cabins   one Indian Came with meat, 2 [men?] Pass to dy   hunters [k]illed Some grouse[1]   Snow

   1. Perhaps the ruffed grouse, *Bonasa umbellus* [AOU, 300]. Johnsgard, 253–73.

[Clark]

Friday—16th   Continu to raise Cabins, Sent off C Floyd to Koho
[Cahokia] with Letters for Capt Lewis to put in the post office &.   Several
boats pass down to day   a Pierogue Came to, a Mr Saml Griffeth[1] good
farmer who Lives 9 miles up the Misouris & a Mr. [Martin? Charles?]
Gilbert[2] a Trader in Salt   the winds high to day—   Cloudy—   rais one
Cabin at night   I write a Speech &c &c.

   1. Samuel Griffith came from New York and settled in Missouri by 1795. His farm,
situated in the neck of land separating the Mississippi and the Missouri rivers, is shown on
a map by Clark in the Field Notes (see fig. 6). Osgood (FN), 4 n. 3.
   2. This man's given name is difficult to read both here and at another place on this
sheet, where it could be "Warle" or "Warler."

[Clark]

S[aturday] 17th   a Cold fine morning   Towok [Took] equal altitudes

	m				m		
A. M.	[38]	38	45	P. M	[3]2	20	41
do	[3]8	41	59	"	[3]2	21	46 = 32° 47′ 45″
do	[3]8	43	1	"	[3]2	23	45

Missed the altidude at 12 oClock with the quadrent[1]

   1. Lewis purchased a "Hadleys Quadrant with Tang[en]t Screw" in Philadelphia before
the expedition. It is the octant mentioned by Clark on December 3, 1803. Jackson (LLC),
1:69, 82, 96.

[Clark]

Sunday 18th   Clear morning   Took the me[ridian?] altitude of the Suns Lowr Limb with the Sextent   found it to be 56° 15′ 22″, The Chronomter too Slow about 24′ 20″—   I also took the median altitude of the Suns Lowr limb with the quadt and foun 52° 57m o   the errour of the instrument is 1° 20′ 00″ + ad +

Lat = 38° 21′ 36$\frac{1}{10}$″
Qudt = 38 31 57$\frac{1}{10}$

Sexton[1]

2		56	15	22		
		28	7	41		
			4	38		− refraction—
		28	7	3[2]		
			16	18	9	Sun Diamtr +
		28	23	21	9	
				8		
		28	23	29	9	Suns Center
			8	49	0	Err of [enstr? = instrument?]
		28	14	40	9	True altitude
		90				
		61	45	19	1	N, reasonabl Distanc
		23	28	43		S, Suns Declination
		38	21	36	$\frac{1}{10}$	

	52°	57′	0″	
	26	28	30	
			38	−
	26	27	52	
		16	18	9
	1	20	8	
	28	4	18	9
	90			
	61	55	41	1
	23	23	[44?]	
	48	31	57	$\frac{1}{10}$

decntl.

	52	57	
		38	−
	52	19	

	16	18	9	
52	35	19	9	
6	20	8		
58	55	27	9	
90				
2	37	4	32	1

52	57	0³	
26	28	30	
	16	18	+
26	44	48	
		38	−
1	20	10	
28	4	18	

	12	37
	12	19
		18
		6
		24

I took the altitude of the ⊙ L L with the Sext: the 18 Decr. and Calculated the Lattidude of River Dubois i. e.—

	38°	21'	36"	$\frac{1}{10}$	
	38	21	36	$\frac{1}{10}$	
also 19th and made it	38	23	8		[Decl?] day
also 3d January 1804 do	38	21	35		
also 4 do do do	38	21	6	$\frac{2}{10}$	
	76	44	14	$\frac{2}{10}$	
	76	43	11	$\frac{1}{10}$	
Diffn	2	1	3	$\frac{1}{10}$	
	38	22	31	$\frac{5}{10}$	+
	38	21	35	$\frac{7}{10}$	
	38	22	7	$\frac{2}{10}$	True Lattidud[4]

1. The following undated material is found with the December 18 entry and apparently represents calculations of latitude and longitude. Some of the arithmetic may be incorrect; smears and overwriting make parts difficult to transcribe.

2. There may be a number before "28" (perhaps 6), but it does not figure in the calculations.

3. These last two sets of figures are difficult to decipher because of overwriting. The arithmetic does not come out correctly as given here.

4. The material from "I took" to "True Lattidud" is upside down on the obverse of document 1 of the Dubois Journal, and is placed here by the first given date.

[Clark]   Monday 19th Der 1803

Took the altitude of S L Limb with the Sextt   found it 56° 15′ 22″   also with the quaderant found it 52° 57′ 0″   the er[ror] of quadt is [*blank*]

The Waggons Came with provisions this evening   Floyd returned with a Letter from Cap Lewis[1]   one from S S[2] and Sundery papers—   an ax & a Flat Saw to be returned

At M: [Mouth?] Missouries   the 19th Decr[3]

Sexton

2	56°	9	7″	
	28	4	33	1/10
		1	47	0 —
	28	2	46	1/10
		16	18	9/10 +
			8	+
	28	19	13	
		8	49	—
	28	10	24	
	90			
	61	49	36	
	23	25	28	
	38	23	8	

Differ with yesterday   54 seconds

1′32″
 38
54 Seconds

Latidude qde.

54°	10′	00″	
27	5	0	
	1	47	—
27	3	13	
	16	18	9
26	46	54	1
		8	+
26	47	2	1/10
1	20		+
28	7	2	1/10

Differ 4′ 21 9/10″

90
61	52	57	9/10
23	25	28	
38	27	29	9/10

Differ from yesterday 3' 18" less

55	32"	8/10			4	27	2/10
11	27	2			1	9	
	1	9			3	18	2/10
		8					

1.9

1. See Lewis to Clark, December 17, 1803, Jackson (LLC), 1 : 144.

2. This may be S. L (St. Louis), Z. Z, or Z. T (perhaps for Zenon Trudeau).

3. The following material on the reverse of document 2 of the Field Notes (misplaced as document 3 in Osgood's facsimiles) was marked off by Clark as a unit; it is placed under the date given at the head.

[Lewis]   [*undated*][1]

Blaize Cenas. H. Baker 95—[12th ?] Mr Wharton, Lawler.

[Mr] Andrew McFarlane [hav]ing informed me that he was about to make application to the general government ⟨for⟩ to be remunerated for certain losses he sustained on his farm by the troops which were ⟨stationed⟩ cantoned on it under the comd of Genl Mor[gan] during the fall and winter 1794 and spring 1795 and being myself present during the whole of that period— I am induced to give the following statment ⟨of facts which fell within the perview of my own observation⟩ to be used by him as he may think most expedient[2]

1. Undated material in Lewis's hand at a right angle to the material directly above, placed here by location.

2. Apparently a rough draft for a letter in response to MacFarlane's request. Lewis served with the army under General Daniel Morgan that was engaged in putting down the Whiskey Rebellion of 1794 in western Pennsylvania. This letter was presumably to help MacFarlane recover his losses from the government. Baldwin (WR).

[Clark]   Tuesday ⟨19⟩ 20th Decr

I Detain the waggon to haul logs for my building & Took the altitude of the Sun by both enstruments   found ☉ L L by Sextt. was 56° 9' 7" by quaterent ☉ U L 54° 10′ 0″   the eror of qudt is 1° 20′ 0″   hauled Logs to day with the Comosaries Teem   men move into ther huts this eveninge. Chronometer has ⟨Slow⟩ Stoped last night   I wound her up at 12 to day as usial and She now goes   a hard frosty morning.

[Clark]

Wednesday 21st Decr.   Cloudy Day   the waggoner charged me three Dollars for his Services yesterday, Send out Shields & Floyd to hunt to day, they Kill 7 Turkeys verry fat, I commence puting up the Logs for my huts to day—   water fall verry fast

[Clark]   Thursday 22nd Decr. 1803

a verry great Sleat this morning, the river Coverd with running Ice, and falls verry fast   15 Inches last night   the boat a ground in the Creek, I had pries[1] fixed along to Support the boat, and all the heavy articles taken out in front & Center and Sto[r]ed under a guard on the bank—   mist of rain, which prevents our doeing much to our huts to day, at 3 oClock Drewyer & 8 men 2 horses arrive from Tennessee,[2] those men are not such I was told was in readiness at Tennessee for this Comd & &.   recvd a Letter from Cap Lewis[3] also one from Mr. Gratiot[4] offering a horse and his Services to Cap L; & my self in any way

1. Evidently wedges or props of some sort.
2. Men detailed to the expedition from Captain John Campbell's company of the Second Infantry Regiment, stationed at South West Point, Tennessee. Among them were Corporal Richard Warfington and Privates Hugh Hall, Thomas P. Howard, and John Potts. The other four, whose names are unknown, were rejected. Clark's comment suggests that Campbell had sent some of his less desirable men. See Appendix A, this volume. Appleman (LC), 62, 366 n. 54.
3. See Lewis to Clark, December 17, 1803, Jackson (LLC), 1:144.
4. Born in Switzerland, Charles Gratiot came to Montreal in 1769 and engaged in the fur trade, establishing a store at Cahokia in 1777. During the Revolution he was of assistance to George Rogers Clark, and so was probably known to William Clark. In 1781 he moved to St. Louis, married into the prominent Chouteau family, and became himself a leading fur trader and citizen. The formal transfer of Upper Louisiana on March 10, 1804, took place on the portico of his home. He helped Lewis and Clark considerably in the months before the start of the expedition.

[Clark]   Friday 23rd December 1803

a raney Day   continue to put up my huts   the men much fatigued ⟨puting up⟩ Carrying logs, I Send to Mr. Morrisons[1] farm for a Teem & Corn, which arivd about 3 oClock, a raney Desagreeable day   Mr. Griffeth Came down from his farm with a Load of Turnips &c. as a present to me, Drewyear Came home to day after a ⟨long⟩ hunt, he Killed three Deer, & left them in the woods, the Ice run to day   Several Deleaway pass, a chief whome I saw at Greenville Treaty,[2] I gave him a bottle of whiskey, the water falls fast, the boat Supt. by Skids. Set the Detachment latterly arrived to build them a hut

1. William Morrison was a prominent Kaskaskia merchant and landowner who owned a farm in the vicinity of Camp Dubois. Jackson (LLC), 1:144–45 n. 4; Osgood (FN), 9 n. 1.

2. At the Treaty of Fort Greenville, August 3, 1795, General Anthony Wayne forced the Indians of the Northwest Territory to surrender much of present Ohio and parts of Indiana and Illinois.

[Clark]

Satturday 24th Decr.   Cloudy morning, I purchase a Cargo of Turnips for 3/—a bushel of Mr. Gririffeth, men Continue to put up & Cover the necessary huts, Drewyear returned with 3 Deer & 5 Turkeys   I send Shields with Mr. Griffeth to purchase me some butter on the other Side of the river is [in? *i.e., from*] the folks, finish Covering our huts this evening— two French Perogues pass up the river to day, and peregoue with black guard Americans, passed down the river, The Indian Come in with a Deer this evening   a French man who passed up to day told me that a man of abt. 30 years of age well acquainted with the Missoures for 8 years, wished to go with me, but was afraid that the Comdt. Should Know of it   his name is *Lackduer* [*Besernnet?*][1]

1. Ladouceur and Bissonette were common French surnames in St. Louis; nothing else is known of this man. Osgood (FN), 10 n. 4.

[Clark]

Christmas 25th Decr: I was wakened by a Christmas discharge ⟨of⟩

found that Some of the party had got Drunk ⟨2 fought,⟩ [1] the men frolicked and hunted all day, Snow this morning, Ice run all day, Several Turkey Killed Shields returned with a cheese & 4 lb butter, Three Indians Come to day to take Christmas with us, I gave them a bottle of whiskey and they went off after informing me that a great talk had been held and that all the nations were going to war against the Ozous [Osage?] in 3 months, one informed me that a English man 16 ms. from here told him that the Americans had the Countrey and no one was allowed to trade &c. I explained the ⟨thing⟩ Intention of Govmt to him, and the Caus of the possession, Drewyear Says he will go with us, at the rate ofd [offered?] [2] and will go to Massac to Settle his matters. [3]

1. There were apparently several instances of fighting among the men during the winter at Camp Dubois; see below, January 3, January 6, and April 13, 1804. It is not clear how many such incidents occurred or who was involved in the fight mentioned here.

2. Twenty-five dollars per month was the amount agreed on at the first meeting of Drouillard and Lewis at Fort Massac; see above, November 11, 1803.

3. Beside this entry in the left margin is written the word "Dog" in a box with apparently decorative doodles and an undetermined word in an oval. The word "Day" is written interlinearly several times.

[Clark] [1]

⟨January⟩ December 26th Monday— a Cloudy day one of my party Killed 7 Turkeys last night at roost— Continue working at the huts— The Ice run, This day is moderate, two men Willard & Corpl. Roberson Came home to day at about 11 oClock, Corpl White house & York Comce [commenced] sawing with the whip Saws— [2] nothing material—

1. Several doodles at the left side of this entry and next.

2. "Roberson" or Robertson is a mysterious figure; he may be the Corporal John Robinson listed on the rolls of Amos Stoddard's artillery company, from which the expedition drew several men about this time. Later on he was disciplined and apparently demoted to private (see below, Detachment Orders, March 3 and April 1, 1804); he may be the man from Stoddard's company who was sent back down the Missouri on June 12, 1804. Joseph Whitehouse is always referred to as a private hereafter; perhaps he too was reduced in rank, or possibly Clark confused him with Corporal Richard Warfington, since both men were relatively new additions to the group at this time. The reference to York is the first mention in the journals of Clark's slave. See Appendix A, this volume. Jackson (LLC), 1:373 n. 29.

[Clark]

December 27th Tuesday— a fair day   I put out Blankets goods &c. &c to dry and Stored them in the Store room apparently in good order ⟨I⟩ nearly finish my Chimney to day   missed my observation—   at abt. 3 oClock to day three frenchmen in a Pierogue Came down pursuing a Swan[1] which they had wounded Some distance above, the Swan swan [swam] as fast as they Could row thier Pierogue and I thought reather gained on the pieroge as they passed—   they Cought it 2 m below. I send home the Cart & oxen, Sent out Drewyer to hunt to day, early—   he returned Late with a Buck, he Saw three Bar[2] on the other Side of the Prarie

1. Likely the trumpeter swan, *Cygnus buccinator* [AOU, 181], but perhaps the tundra swan (formerly whistling swan, after Lewis and Clark), *C. columbianus* [AOU, 180].
2. The only bear in the area would be the black bear, *Ursus americanus.* Hall, 2:947–51.

[Clark]

28 Decr.   a Cloudy day   no Ice in the river, nothing remarkable to day—   Drewyer Kill a Deer & the Indn Kill another

[Clark]

29th   Snow this morning   Cloudey & wet all day, finish my hut and write 2 Letters one to G. H.[1] & one to Col Anderson[2]   rain at night

1. Perhaps George Hancock of Fincastle, Virginia, whose daughter Julia married Clark in 1808. Osgood (FN), 10 n. 6.
2. Richard Clough Anderson, a Virginian, was a soldier in the American Revolution. Moving to Kentucky in 1783, he married a sister of Clark's.

[Clark]

30th Decr.   Snow in the morning   I move into my hut, Cloudy morning   Colter Kill a Deer & a turkey, Drewyer & Serjt. Odway set out for Kohokia, I arrange the guards on a new plan, wrote to Cap Lewis

[Clark]

Saty. 31st of Decr   I Issued certain [orders?] & prohibited a Certain [*blank*] Ramey[1] from Selling Liquor to the Party, Several things Killed to

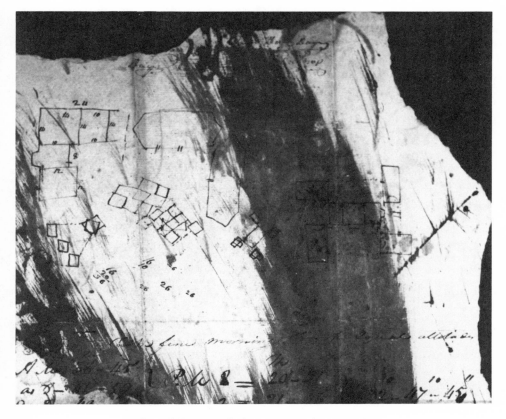

5. Plan of Camp Dubois, ca. December 29, 1803,
Field Notes, reverse of document 1

day. Colter [Oddawey?][2] Willard Leakens[3] Hall & Collins Drunk.   began
to snow at Dark and Continued untill 9 oClock   Cloudy to day[4]

1. Matthew Ramey took up residence in the St. Louis district in 1803; William Ramy
signed a memorial to the president from the St. Charles district in 1806. Osgood (FN),
11 n. 8.

2. Osgood interprets this illegible word as "Oddawey," but Sergeant Ordway was absent
from camp from December 30 to January 2. The word may be "souber" written over another word, in which case Willard, Leakens, Hall and Collins were the only drunken men.
Ibid., 11.

3. For Leakens (possibly "Seakens"), see below, February 4, 1804, concerning his discharge. Nothing else is known of him.

4. Below this entry and written crossways are the following figures:

$$12$$

$$\frac{3}{70/480/7}$$

[Clark]

January 1st 1804   Snow about an inch deep   Cloudy to day, a woman Come forward wishing to wash and doe Such things as may be necessary for the Detachmt   Several men Come from the Countrey to See us & Shoot with the men, they bring Sugare &c. to trade, I purchase Sugar 6 lb at ⅙ per pound, I put up a Dollar to be Shot for, the two best Shots to win   Gibson best   the Countrey people won the dollar—   (R [Reed?] & Ws. [Wiser, Windsor?] Drunk)   a Perogue Passed Loaded with Salt & Dry goods. Jos: Vaun[1] offers to let the Contrator have Beef at 4$ pd. [pound or produce?] or 3$ 50 Cents in money, Pokers hake, the Nut is Sheshake, a plant growing in the ponds with a large broad leaf, stem in the middle of the leaf   in french Volies[2]   Three men Mr. Lisbet[3] Blacksmith &c, one Man offers to sell pork at [blank]   apply to Hannerberry,[4] the blacksmith has traveled far to the north, & Visited the Mandols [Mandans] on Missouris, a quiet people 6 Day fr[om] [Ossini?][5] or Red river & that the M: [Missouri River] is about 150 yds. over at this nation

1. Perhaps Joseph, Joshua, or Josiah Vaughn, who all lived near the camp. Madison, 72, 82–83.

2. *Nelumbo lutea* (Willd.) Pers., American lotus, yellow nelumbo, yellow lotus, water chinquapin, pond-nuts, is an aquatic plant that Lewis describes more elaborately in an undated entry at the end of this chapter. "Pokers hake" may be Clark's attempt at the Kickapoo name, which Lewis wrote as *Po-kish'-a-co-mah*. "Volies" is the French term for the plant, *graine de volaille*. It is commonly found in oxbow lakes along the Mississippi and Missouri rivers. Fernald, 641; Steyermark, 668. Its importance to Indians is described by Gilmore, 27, in terms very similar to Lewis's.

3. The lack of punctuation makes it uncertain whether "Lisbet" was the blacksmith. The word itself is unclear. He might be the "Thos. Lisbet Blacksmith" on document 2 of the Field Notes (placed under November 26, 1803, entry). Nothing is known of this person. Osgood read it as "Leebice" (which it may well be) and related that to François Labiche, a member of the party. Osgood (FN), 11 n. 3.

4. Probably Patrick Heneberry, an early settler in this part of Illinois, and at the time an employee of William Morrison. Jackson (LLC), 1 : 144–45 n. 4.

5. If this word is read as "Ossini" or something similar, it may be a reference to the Assiniboine River of Saskatchewan and Manitoba, a tributary of the Red River of the North. There were British fur-trading posts on both rivers, from which traders sometimes traveled to the Mandan villages.

[Clark]

January 2nd   Snow last night, ⟨rain⟩ a mist to day   Cap Whitesides[1]

Came to See me & his Son, and some country people, Serjt. Odderway return & bring me Some papers from Capt Lewis, who is [in] Kohokia on business of importance to the enterprise, the party verry merry this evening. Mr. Whitesides says a no. of young men in his neghborhood wishes to accompany Capt. Lewis & myself on the Expdts   Cap L. allso sent me a Letter from Capt. Amos Stoddard[2] which mentions his aptnt. to the Comd. of upper Louisiane, & to take possession of St Louis &c.

1. William Whiteside, a veteran of the Battle of King's Mountain (1780), came to Illinois from Kentucky in 1793 and settled at New Design, between Kaskaskia and Cahokia. Osgood (FN), 11–12 n. 5.

2. Amos Stoddard was born in Connecticut but grew up in Massachusetts. At seventeen, in 1779, he enlisted in the Continental army and served to the end of the Revolutionary War. He was a lawyer and political figure in Massachusetts until 1798, when he rejoined the army as captain of artillery. After the Louisiana Purchase he was civil and military commandant of Upper Louisiana until civil government could be established. In March 1804, in St. Louis, he carried out the official transfer of Upper Louisiana from Spain to France, and from France to the United States. He assisted the preparations for the Lewis and Clark expedition in various ways, and several men from his company were detailed to accompany the captains. He was promoted to major in 1807 and died of wounds received fighting the British at Fort Meigs, Ohio, in 1813. He was the author of *Sketches, Historical and Descriptive, of Louisiana* (Philadelphia, 1812). Heitman, 619; Osgood (FN), xxiv–xxvii.

[Clark]

Tuesday Jany 3rd 1804   a Verry Cold blustering day ⟨the Merkery?⟩ in Doneyan[1] Co: Thermometer one oClock in the open air the ⟨quicksilver⟩ mercuria fell to 21 D. below the freezing point [*11° F*], I took the altitude of the suns L. L. and made it 57° 16 0 N by the Sexton, all the after part of the Day the wind so high that the View up the Missouris appeared Dredfull, as the wind blew off the Sand with fury as to Almost darken that part of the atmespear   this added to agutation of the water apd. truly gloomy   Comy [commissary] Kiled a Beef &

at 3 oClock the q s or murcy. fell to 22 D. below feesing [*10° F.*]

at 4	do—	do—	do	27½ ditto [*4½° F.*]
at 5	do—	do—	do	30 or (O)

⎫ in the air ⎬ ⎭

the wind violent all Day from N. N W. & N W.[2]

3d Jany 1804   Excessive Cold after Sunset

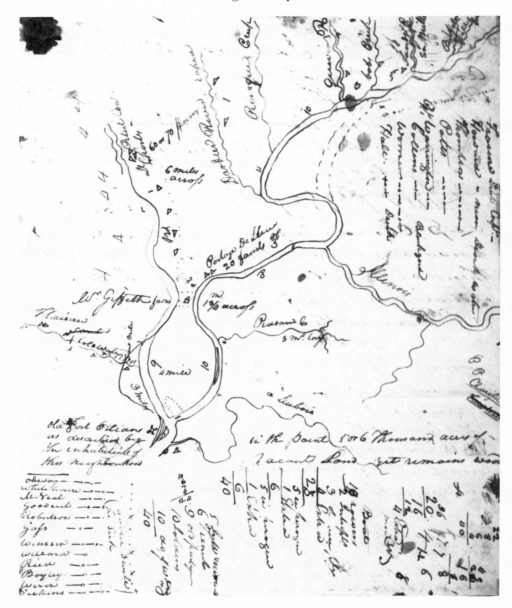

6. Confluence of Missouri and Mississippi Rivers,
ca. January 3, 1804, Field Notes, reverse of document 4

1. John Donegan (or Denegan) and Joseph Donegany (Donegani) were making thermometers in Philadelphia in 1785. Although thermometers are among Lewis's list of requirements for the trip, there is no direct evidence that any were purchased. Lewis kept temperature readings on the Ohio and Mississippi rivers, and Clark continued the practice at Camp Dubois, thus providing strong indirect evidence that thermometers were purchased in Philadelphia. This reference helps to confirm that supposition and to dispel

the idea that the St. Louis physician Antoine Saugrain made thermometers for Lewis and Clark. Bedini (TT), 302–3; Jackson (LLC), 69, 75 n. 1.

2. The phrase "Say (10)" at the bottom of the obverse of document 4 is repeated at the top of document 5; it was apparently a device for keeping the loose pages in order. This is the first sheet to use such a device, and it does not appear to be part of a larger system. On later sheets Clark used "O, ancore" and "say on." Because there is no indication of missing material, we should not suppose that nine sheets preceded this one, leaving us to discover six missing sheets to add to the three that we now have in advance of this one.

[Clark]   [*undated*][1]

The Americans are Settled up the Mississippi for 56 miles as high up a[s] the Sandy river[2] from thence across to the Missouries river   a Salt works is establish[ed] on a Small river 30 miles up the river 10 miles from the mississippi   I am told that an old french fort was once built on the opsd Side of the river from me, and that Some remains of the clearing is yet to be seen, this must be the fort which was built in the year 1724 by M. de Bourgmot the Comdt[3]

The first Settlement made in this quarter was made 1679.   de la Salle at [*blank*] then Called Crevecoeur[4]

arkansas was settled by 10 F. men in 1685[5]

a fort was built by the F. at Prud-homme, or Chick: Bluffs in the year 1722 Assumption[6]

a Settlement was on an Island above the Ohio with an armed schooner in 1742

D. [Drouillard?] Says that about 7 m from the mouth of the Tennessee up the first Creek opposit the Island, and at the edge of the [Canons?], more S. of [Nalla?]—⟨and⟩ is a Lead mine   he also says that about 15 m N. is a mine of ore white and Deep [?] Black,[7]

Flag the word of the [*perhaps one word illegible*]

but one heart

Explain the Pond & fishing place above Waubash

> Floyd—[8]
> Shields—
> Bratten—
> Newmon—
> R. Fields—

147

J. Fields—
G Shannon—
Pryor—
+ Gibson
√ Colter—
Odderway—
Whitehouse—
√ Robertson—
McNeal—
Goodrich—
o Windser—
Reed—
√ Wiser—
Gess—
+ Willard
+ Boyley
+ Leakens
Worrington
Worner
Thompson
Howard
√ Potts
√ Collins
+ Frasure
+ Hall

+ Frasure [struk?] Corpl.—
Howard—never Drink water
Thompson—
Potts—
Cpl. Warrington—
Collins—Blackgard
Worner—
Hall + — + Drink

Odway—   .
. Whitehouse—   .
. M Neal—   .
. Goodrich—   .
. Robertson—   x
Gass—   .
. Winser—   .

	Willard—	x
✓	Reed—	.
	Boyley—	x
	Wiser—	.
	Leekins—	x

22	40	36	7	7		6
8	24	20				8
6	16	16	4	1	+	
4	8	12				
40	8	4 Extra Men [*one word illegible*]				

Boat

19 rowers
2 Interpts
3 of our pty.
4 Extra
28
5 in perogue
1 Extra
6
5 in perogue
1 Extra
6
40

10
6
7
1
24

5 Intp [& ourselves?]
6 French
9 old party
10 Soldiers
10 do, if [wtng = wintering?]
40

(about 3 will be sick)

1. This undated material is on the reverse of document 4 of the Field Notes on which the December 31–January 3 entries are written. On half of this side is a map by Clark (see fig. 6).

2. "Sandy C" on fig. 6, the map on the reverse of document 4 of the Field Notes. Present Sandy Creek enters the Mississippi in Lincoln County, Missouri.

3. Fort Don Carlos, erected by the Spanish in 1768. Clark has apparently confused it with Fort Orleans, established in 1723 in Carroll County, Missouri, by Etienne de Bourgmont (see below, July 5, 1804). The sources for Clark's information on these places is not known. Osgood (FN), 12 n. 7.

4. Robert Cavelier, Sieur de La Salle, founded Fort Crèvecoeur in January 1680 on the Illinois River near the village of the Peoria Indians. It was near present East Peoria, Tazewell County, Illinois. *Illinois Guide*, 23, 273.

5. Perhaps referring to six men left at the Arkansas (Quapaw) Indian villages a few miles up the Arkansas River from the Mississippi by La Salle's lieutenant Henri de Tonti in 1686. Osgood (FN), 12 n. 9.

6. Fort Prudhomme was established at the third Chickasaw Bluff, near modern Natchez, Mississippi, in 1682. Osgood (FN), 12 n. 1.

7. There are lead and zinc deposits near the mouths of the Tennessee and Cumberland rivers in Kentucky. Cumberland Island, a large island about ten miles up the Ohio from the mouth of the Tennessee is opposite the mouth of present Caney Creek, on which galena ore was discovered. Fifteen miles northeast is the Sheridan mining area. Osgood (FN), 12–13 n. 3. The primary lead ore is galena, which is dark gray, but secondary ores near the surface include the white minerals cerussite and anglesite, which are products of weathering. The principal primary ore of zinc is sphalerite, sometimes also called blackjack, but an important secondary (weathering) ore is smithsonite ($ZnCO_3$), known also as white ore or bone ore. Brobst & Pratt, 317–18, 701–2.

8. These lists, scattered in various places, apparently represent an attempt by Clark to evaluate the men and determine who should be retained. The numbers following may be calculations of how many men would be needed and how they should be placed on the different vessels. The dots, dashes, zeros, checks, and plus signs beside the names may have had some relevance that is not understood now.

[Clark]

Wed: Jany. 4th   a Cold Clear morning, the river Covered with Ice from the Missouri, the Massissipi above frosed across, the Wind from the West, The Thermometer this morning at 19° below freesing [*13° F.*], Continue Cold & Clear all day, I took the altd. of S. [sun's] L. L and found it to be 57° 27′ 15″ N, purchase 12 lb Tallow for 6/—of Whitesides, who Sold the Beef to the Com: [commissary] at 3$ pr. Hw [hundredweight]   Several Countrey people here to day—   at 4 oClock the murcuria of the Thmtr. in a corner of a warm room was 20 D. above (o)—

Worner & Potts fight after Dark without my Knowledge & the Corpl.[1] head of the mess left the hut & Suffered them to bruse themselves much, he has no authority, the other Part of the detachment verry merry at night the 4th Jany. 1804

2	⌊57°	27′	15″		
	28	43	37	⁵⁄₁₀	T.
		1	44		− refraction (1)
	28	41	53	⁵⁄₁₀	P
		16	19	³⁄₁₀	+ Sim: Damt [diameter?] (3)
			8		+
	28	58	20	⁸⁄₁₀	
		8	49		− E Ensmt. [error of instrument?]
	28	49	31	⁸⁄₁₀	
	90				−
	61	10	28	²⁄₁₀	
	22	49	22		Declena.
Dgt.	38	21	6	²⁄₁₀	

1. If this was Corporal John Robinson (Robertson), we may have the reason for his reduction to private. See above, December 26, 1803. Corporal Warfington seems to have retained the confidence of his superiors, suggesting that he was not the corporal concerned here.

[Clark]

Thursday 5th Jany   the Creek rose Considerably last night   the river full of Ice, and the wind which blows from the West blows it to this Shore, a madderate day, I suffer some men to assist Higgins to raise his hut. Two men [1] whome I sent to hunt grouse returned with a part of a hog which they found hung up in the woods & brought it in a[s] Bear meat. I took the altitude of ☉ U. L. with the quaderent and made it 55° 40′ 30″ N. Errer of instrmt. 1° 13′ 0″ + quadt

5th Jany 1804

2	⌊55°	40′	30″	☉ L L
	27	50	15	altitude of ☉ up limb
		1	48	− refraction (T. 1)
		48	27	
		16	19	− ☉ demeter (P 3)
		32	8	
			8	+ Parallax (T. 3)
	*27	32	16	The Suns Center

Declination

	*(27	32	16	
	1	17	0	+ E. E [error of instrument?]
	28	49	16	
	90			
	61	10	44	
	22	43	31	Declination
The Latd. with Qudt =	38	27	13	on the 5th Jany 1804.[2]

I visited the boat frequently this day under apprehenion of the Creek which is now riseing washing the earth from the foot of the pries which is fixed under.

1. One was John Collins. See below, January 9, 1804.
2. Two other sets of calculations for this day are crossed out and are not printed here. They vary slightly from figures above.

[Clark]

Jany. 6th   I was up last night at 12 to right the Boat   the banks were Caveing in, which made it necessary to fix the pries frequently, this morning early I fixed the pries, and large Pees of the bank sliped in, which obliged all hands to, go Down & make all secure   I ordered those men who had fought got Drunk & neglected Duty to go and build a hut for a Wo[man] who promises to wash & Sow &c. I Spoke to the men on the Subject of my order, ⊙ U L with quade. to day was is 1° 1′ 1″ ad +   a hog found in the Prairie by some men & they Skined [it]   I send out Shields to enquire in the neighbourhood whoes hog it was & inform me. Thermometer at, 12 oClock 31 above o   at 4 oCk at 30° abov (o)[1]

6th Jany   The banks about the Boat Continue to Cave in, which causes great attention in me to prevent the Boats getting injered by any one part falling more than another—   the Sawyears, come on to day better than usial, Whitehouse & Reed, agree better than they did last week—or in other Words Re[ed] Saws better from practice.

1. Two astronomical calculations are crossed out in the lower right-hand corner of the page at this point. They are not printed here. "Say (11)" is used at the end of this paragraph (bottom of document 5) and at the beginning of the next (top of document 6), perhaps to keeping the papers in order.

[Clark]

7th Satdy Jany— Some rain last night, a thow [thaw] and Some rain to day. the boat give me much trouble, [as?] the banks are Continuly Slipping in on each Side which looses the pries, up last night and frequent thro the rain to day attending the boat, I drew a map for the purpose of Correcting from the information which I may get of the Countrey to the N W[1]

1. See *Atlas*, 7 and map 6.

[Clark]

Sunday 8th Janry Rained moderately all last night, a butifull morning a few large sheets of thin Ice running this morning, Send out Colter & George [Drouillard?][1] to the head of the Debouis [Dubois] R. to hunt— The Wind rise from the S W at 10 oClock, Took the meridian altitude of ☉ L L with Sext. made it 58° 22′ 52″ N,— a French man & his famly Came to see me to day I trade with them for Onions, & gave Tin &c. This man made Complaint that he had lost a Hogg— Some Hog meat had been brought in as before mentioned, as the men whome brought it in are absent, I pospone the inquirey untill tomorrow I Lay down to sleep, to make up for the want of rest, Clouded up at ½ past 2 oClock the wind chifted to the N W, moderate. R Field Killed a Deer to day, this is the first of his turning out—

1. George Gibson or George Shannon might be meant, but Drouillard was one of the party's outstanding hunters. Subsequent references to "George" are probably also to him.

[Clark]

Mon. 9th Jany— Some Snow last night, a hard wind this morning from W, N W, river Rises with large Sheets of Ice out of Mississippi, the morning is fair (the man *Ramey* gives me much trouble) I took Collins & went to the place he found a Hog Skined & Hung up, the Crows[1] had devoured the meet, Killed Prary fowl[2] and went across a Prary to a 2nd Bank where I discovered an Indian Fortification,[3] near the Second bank I attempted to cross a Bond [pond] of about 400 yds wide on the Ice & Broke in this fortress is 9 mouns forming a Circle two of them is about

7 foot above the leavel of the plain on the edge of the first bank and 2 m from the woods & about the Same distance from the main high land, about this place I found great quantities of Earthen ware & flints— about ½ m. N. is a Grave on an Emenince   I returned before Sun Set, and found that my feet, which were wet had frozed to my Shoes, which rendered precaution necessary to prevent a *frost bite*, the Wind from the W, across the Sand Islands in the Mouth of the Missouries, raised Such a dust that I could not See in that derection, the Ice Continue to run & river rise Slowly— exceeding Cold day

1. The common, or American, crow is *Corvus brachyrhynchos* [AOU, 488].

2. Probably the greater prairie chicken, first noticed November 16, 1803.

3. Clark had reached the northwest edge of the Cahokia Mounds, at present Mitchell, Madison County, Illinois, about eight miles north of Cahokia. The mounds apparently served as foundations for ceremonial structures and were built between 900 and 1300 A.D. All except one of this northern group of mounds have been obliterated, but those farther south are now within Cahokia Mounds State Park. Bareis & Porter; *Illinois Guide*, 15–16, 610, 612.

[Clark]

Tuesday 10th   a fine day, the river rose 6 Inches last night, the Creek also rises & Boat nearly afloat   I am verry unwell all day, owing I believe to the Ducking & excessive Cold which I underwent yesterday, at 1 oClock Joseph Fields returned, & crossed the River between the Sheets of floating Ice with Some risque, his excuse for Staying so long on the Mississippi[1] were that the Ice run so thick in the Missourie where he was 30 miles up that there was no crossing, he Says that the people is greatly in favour of the Americans, Cap. Mackey[2] has Just returned from Surveying of some lands up the Missouries, which has been laterly granted   he says "a boutifull Countrey presents its Self on the route he went & returned." Three miles to the first settlements from this place in a [West][3] direction. I feel unwell to day

1. "J. Fields" is written on the upper left corner of the reverse of this document, just above "Mississippi."

2. James Mackay was born in Scotland and came to America in about 1776; he engaged in the fur trade in Canada and from there made a trip to the Mandan villages on the Missouri in 1787. He came to Louisiana about 1794 and, having sworn allegiance to the

Spanish government, became manager of the Spanish-controlled Missouri Fur Company's affairs on the upper Missouri. He set out up the Missouri in 1795 and established a post in present northeastern Nebraska. From there he sent up the river John Thomas Evans, who he hoped would reach the Pacific. In fact, Evans got no farther than the Mandan villages. Mackay himself explored the Niobrara, Loup, and Elkhorn rivers in northern and western Nebraska and returned to St. Louis in 1797. Subsequently he became a landowner, a surveyor, and an official for the local Spanish government. His advice and information on the Missouri River country were of great value to Lewis and Clark. He also seems to have furnished them copies of Evans's maps of the Upper Missouri (*Atlas* maps 7–12, 30). For additional information, see *Atlas*, 16–17. Nasatir (JM), 185–206; Williams; Nasatir (BLC), 1:351–65, 371; 2:485–99, 514–26, passim.; Diller (JMJ).

3. There is a hole in the paper here. The original word may have been "N West," referring perhaps to the settlement at the junction of Coldwater Creek and the Missouri, shown in fig. 6.

[Clark]

Wednesday 11th Jany.   I was unwell last night   Slept but little, a fine morning, the river Still riseing, the Missouries run with fine Ice, the Boat is afloat, one man *McNeal* ⟨lost⟩ out last night, he Sepperated from the hunting party about 7 miles from this place, he returnd this evening   Sgt. Ordday was also lost all night   at 1 oClock the wind blew strong from the west and turned Couled & Cloudy this afternoon, I am a good deel indisposed.[1]

1. Clark jotted several *R*'s and *S*'s after this entry.

[Clark]

Thursday 12th Jany: 1804   my Chimney got on fire last night, a fair morning, the wind from the S West, the river Continue to rise moderatly, I took maridinal altitude of Suns Lower Limb with Sextent and made it 59° 31′ 52″ N   th[e] Error of Enstrument as usial   river Continue to rise with large Sheets of ice running against the Ice atached to the bank with great force, the Boat is a float, and in perfect order

[Clark]

Friday 13th January   Sent N Pryor with Letters &c. to Cap Lewis a[t] Kohokia   the river rise, a fall of Snow last night, the Missouris is riseing and runs with Ice   a Cloudy & warm day, I am better &c.   a fine rain in the evening.

[Clark]

Saturday 14th January   a Snow fall last night of about an Inch [and one] half   The river ⟨Still riseing⟩ falling and running with Ice, a fair Sun shineing morning—   the party Caught 14 Rabits[1] to day & 7 yesterday.   a Cold afternoon. The Mississippi, is Closed with Ice.

    1. Probably eastern cottontails, *Sylvilagus floridanus*. Hall, 1 : 300.

[Clark]

Sunday 15th Jany: river falling & runs still with Ice, I took the M—altitude of ☉ L L. & made it 60° 33′ 50″ N, at Sun Set Maj Rumsey[1] the Comsy arrived with Some provisions in a waggon of Mr. Todd,[2] Seven or Eight men followd the waggon Intoxicated from the whiskey they receced [received] of R—[Ramey, Rumsey?] on the way out of the barrel which was for the Party, I ordered a Gill to each man   a Cold night   the Wag: in passing the Lowr Prarie which was Covrd. with Ice Suft [sufficiently] Strong to bear the teem but not the waggon which caused it to be dift [difficult] to pass

    1. Nathan Rumsey was agent for Elijah G. Galusha, contractor for army rations in the area. Jackson (LLC), 1 : 168 n. 1. In the margin at this point are some illegible jottings.
    2. Several farmers named Todd lived in the American Bottom north of the river Dubois camp. Osgood (FN), 17–18 n. 3.

[Clark]

Monday 16th Jany: this Morning Maj. R [Rumsey] observed that he brought 2 trunks of Goods, and asked pirmition to Sell them to the Citizen for Provisions, and the mens Coon Skins, I accented to the plan, and agreed he might untill other arrangements, after the arrival of Capt Lewis—   I settled with the Contractor for what has been furnished to this day and find him Due the Party 30 gills of whiskey which he payd,— and 750 rats. [rations] of Soap Candles & vinager, for which he gave his Due bills, the Party made up a Shooting match, with the Country people for a pr. [pair of] Leagens, Reuben Fields made the best Shot, next one Wist [Windsor or Wiser?] & the 3 & 4 was Shields R, F[razer?][1] Colter Gibson &, Mr. Prior returned at 8 oClock in the evening with a letter from Capt. Lewis[2] (Lent Colter 3/—lent George 3/—) and one from Louisville & 3 newspapers which Capt. Lewis had Sent me— also a file & 3 plain bits[3]

1. Probably Robert Frazer, since Reubin Field was already mentioned. Near this part of the sheet are some numbers, which appear to be the following:

$$
\begin{array}{r}
47 \\
\underline{47} \\
1040 \\
\underline{588} \\
6920
\end{array}
$$

2. The cover for this letter may have been document 29 in the Field Notes. See July 8, 1804.

3. This entry and part of the next are much overwritten with lists and figures in the lower right-hand corner of the sheet. They appear to be the following words, written in a column: Provision, Whiskey M[an?], my St [*letters unclear*], my Helth, The Mens [cmpt.?], whip saw file, R Fields, Hays Papers, maps, 2 3, [Bits?]. Cf. Osgood (FN), 18 n. 5.

[Clark]

Tuesday 17th Jany   a verry Cold morning, at 7 oClock the Thermometer in the air fell 8° below, o, the wind from the N W, a Stiff Breeze   Ice run greatly out of Missouries— at 9 oClock the Thermometer 6d below o— at 10 oClock 3d below o at 12 oClock at o, at 1 oClock 1° above o, at 2 oClock 1½° above o, 3 oClock at o,[1] at 4 oClock the Thermometer was 1½° below o at 5 the Ther: was at 3° below o,— at 9 oClock 6° below o, a verry Cold night; the Missouris has fallen to day about 6 Inches, runs with Ice— Ice from Shore 20 yds in the river is 5½ Inches Thick—

1. Here, at the bottom of document 6, is the word "over," which recurs at the top of document 7 where the entry continues.

[Clark]

Wednesday 18th Jany.   a Cloudy morning with moderate breaze from the N W. b[y] W   The river run with Ice, at 8 oClock the Thromtr. Stood at 1° below 0,— 9 oClock 1° ab[ove] 0, at 10 oClock 2° abov 0, at 11 oClock rose to 4° above 0, and beg[an] to Snow, at 12 oClock The Thermt. at 2 above 0. Snow above 1 Inch at 1 oClock 2 abov 0, at 2 oClock 1 abov 0, and left off Snowing—

[Clark]

Thursday 19th Jany Som Snow fell last night, a Cloudy morning, the river continues to fall, & Some Ice running, at 8 oClock this morning the Thermormeter Stood at 13° above 0, the wind moderate from the N W, at 9 oClock 15° abov 0, at 10 oClock 16° above 0, at 11 oClock 16° above 0, at 12 oClock 19° above 0, at 1 oClock 17° abo 0, at 2 oClock at 15½°—abov 0, at 3 oClock at 13° abov 0, at 4 oClock 11° abov 0, at [5?] oClock 10½ abov 0,— Gibson Killed 3 Deer & Colter 3 Turkey, Shields 4 Turkey, Worne[r] & Thompson 14 rabits—

[Clark]

Friday 20th 1804 Jany— a verry Cold night, river Still falling ⟨some⟩ no Ice running out of the Missouries, the wind this morning from N W— The Thermometer at 7 oClock stood at 5° below 0, at 8 oClock 7° below 0, at 9 oClock 4° below 0, at 10 oClock 2° below 0, at 11 oClock 2° above 0, at 12 oClock 4° abov 0,— Took the M Altitude of ☉ L. L with Sext: & made it 62° 30′ 45″ N (cromtr. too fast 1 h 26′ 10″) at 1 oClock the Thmtr. Stood at 6° above 0, at 2 oClock the Them at 8° above 0, The river Mississipi raised & some [of] the Ice formed above the Missouris broke Loose & floted down, this Ice is 9 Inches Thick, ⟨no ice flotes down the⟩ at 3 oClock 11 abov 0, (Cloudy) at 4 oClock at 8° abov 0, at 5 oClock 7½° abov 0,— a Cloudy, many Grous Caught to Day & Hall Caught 14 Rabits—

[Clark]   Satturday 21[1]

1. Only the date with no additional writing here. The entry for the twenty-first is continued on the next document after some miscellaneous intervening material.

[Clark]   [*undated, ca. January 21, 1804*][1]

1804	mes	months	days
From *Dubois* to the Manden Nation 1500 miles at 10 mes. pr Day will be 150 days Viz: May June, July Augt. & Sept.—	1500 in	5	0
From Do. at 12 mes. pr. day—125 days Viz: May June July Augt. & 5 days in Septr		4	5

1st Winter

	mes	months	days
From Mandens to the rock mountains is 12° W. at 41 mes. [*to a degree of longitude*] Say 900 miles at 10 pr Day is 90 Days, Viz: Septr. Octr. Novr. & 4 Ds	900 in	3	0
From Same at 12 miles pr Day 65 Days Septr. Octr & 19 of Novr		2	15
From the mountains to the Ocean in Longtd. 123° W say 10° at 41 miles to a degree of Longtd. add the windings 650 miles at 10 miles will take May June and July, [85?] Days	650 in	3	0
From the Same place at 12 ms. 54 days, May & June		2	[5?]
The time to the Ocean @ 10 ms per Day		11	0 Days
The Time @ 12 ms. pr day		8	20 days

1805

(Delay 15 days)

	mes	months	days
Returning from the Ocean to the river 650 miles @ 10 ms. pr Day is 65 days Viz: 15 in August, Septr. 20 in Octr.	650 m	2	5
do— Viz ⟨to Mandens 900 m⟩ in 65 Days m at 12 m pr Day 54 Day, 15 July Augt. 9 in Septr		1	24
ditto to the Mandens @ 20 ms pr. Day 45 Days Septr. Octr—	900	1	21
ditto @ to the mouth Nov. & Dec @ [*blank*]		2	0
Returning to the Mandan @ 10 pr		3	26
do do at 12 do		3	15

	Months to Mandens	Months to mountains	Months to ocean	Time [*word illegible*] lost winter &c.		Total Time	
	Ds	D				month	Day
at 10	5 0	3 0	2 0	5 28	=	15	28 } Total going
at 12	4 5	2 15	2 0	5 12	=	14	2 } out[2]
10 or 12 miles return	2 0	1 15	2 5	0 0	=	5	25 Total returning (say to Decr 1805[)]
				Total		19	27 at 12 miles pr. Day progression
				Total		21	23 at 10 miles pr. Day progression

⟨If 36 men including Drewyer⟩[3]
⟨Big boat 24⟩   ⟨12⟩
                                 ⟨25⟩

2 of us
1 Sevt.
2 Intprs =   5

If we take 37 men
The Boat of   25 men
1 Pierogue   6
1   do—   6
                    37

If the party to consist of 30 men
Boat of   24 men
1 Periogue of   6
                    30

If the Party to Consist of 25 men all in the Boat of 20 ores

If 40 men

Boat of	26
1 Perogue—	8
1 do—	6
	40

If 50 men

Boat	26 men
1 Perog.	10
1 do	7
1 do—	7
	50

⟨Those Numbers will Depend on the probability of an oppisition from roving Parties of Bad Indians which it is probable may be on the [R.? *blot*]⟩

Defined the word Sense[4]

It is a faculty of the Soul, whereby it perceived external Objects, by means of the impressions they make on certain organs of the body. These organs are Commonly reconed 5, Viz: the Eyes, whereby we See objects; the ear, which enables us to hear sounds; the nose, by which we receive the Ideas of different smells; the Palate, by which we judge of tastes; and the Skin, which enables us to feel—the different, forms, hardness, or Softness of bodies.[5]

2 men takes up 3 feet {
Boat 31 feet in Hol[d]
do 14 do on Cabn.
do 8—4 wide
} Inches
32 Long
22 wide
} a [Bench or Bank?]

	foot	In	
Lockers, must be	2	6 wide	
do—&—	31 feet Long		} 156 foot of Plank @ [*word illegible, per-*
do. about—	1 — 6 Deep		*haps a space and abbreviation for weight*]

pr. foot is [*perhaps a space and abbrevia-tion for weight*]

Lockers on the Cabin	14—0—long	
do wide	3—0—wide	} 84 feet
do	3—0—Deep	

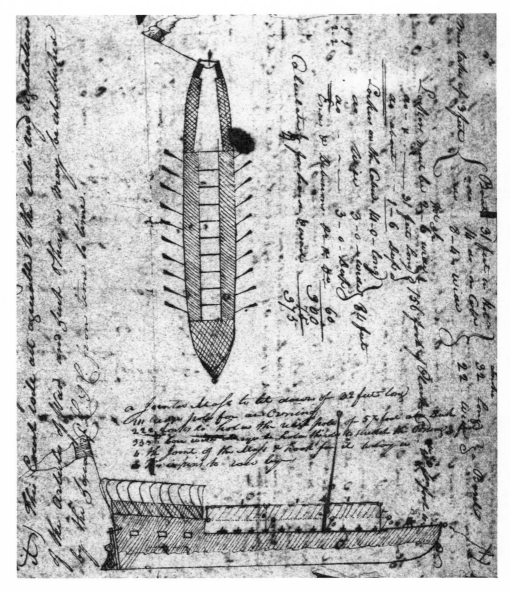

7. Sketches of the Keelboat, ca. January 21, 1804,
Field Notes, reverse of document 7

Ends & Divisions &c. &c. &c.	60
	300

Calculate ¼
  for Season[ing] & wast   75
                                    375

a Jointed Mast to let down of 32 feet long[6]
1 1 1   [ridge] poles for an Orning
2 2 2   [for]ks to hold the ridge pole of 5½ foot abv Deck
3 3 3   [Base with an eye?] to hold the poles to stretch the Orning 3 foot
      4   the Joint of the Mast & hook for it to Lay in
           T[his?] is pins to row by

    as examples are necessary[7]

   Supposeing the party to Consist of 2 Intptrs 4 Non Comd. officers and 21 men and the rules to be observed is Strictly such as Cap. L & C shall from time establish, and a violiation or Disobediance shall be Subject to Such punishment as derected by the articles of War, in like Cases and Such other punishments, as Shall be inflicted by the Sentence of a Court Martial which ⟨Shall⟩ are to be formed in the following manner, Viz; one Intptr or Sergt. to act as president and at least 1 n Comd. officers & 5 privates members   The Court to Consist of not less then 7 members, ⟨in Capital offenses and⟩ at other times when Convenient one of the Capts. will preside at the Court   in that Case the Court will have an addition to their number of a presdt. ⟨who will have 2 votes⟩ (but in all Cases Capt L. & C doe reserve to themselves the right rudcing N C officers at will of inflicting such punishment as they may thing [think] right agreeable to Law at any time which from the nature of the offence & the good of the Service require it)   This Court will act agreeable to the rules and regulations of the Articles of War and Such others as may be established by the Said Cpt L. & C. from time to time.

   1. The following material, at right angles to the main body of writing on the page, represents Clark's attempt to figure the amount of time necessary for the expedition. In hoping for a return by the end of 1805, he seriously underestimated the actual length of the voyage.

   2. On these "totals going out" there is quite a bit of overwriting and alteration of figures.

3. In this material, upside down to the main body of writing on the page, Clark again tries to figure the number of men needed and their assignments to the different boats. The "Big boat" is the keelboat.

4. The following paragraph begins the reverse of document 7 (printed upside down in Osgood). It appears to have been copied from some other source, perhaps as an exercise in writing by Clark.

5. Here follow two sketches of the keelboat, which are the most important sources of information about that vessel (see fig. 7). The accompanying numbers are Clark's calculation of the amount of lumber necessary to build lockers on the boat. Other modifications may have been carried out at Camp Dubois during the winter. For further information, see above, August 30, 1803, and sources cited there.

6. A key to the keelboat diagram. Clark drew a figure of the "pins to row by" in place of numbers on the last line.

7. These words and the following paragraph are upside down on this page. In the right-hand corner written diagonally in Clark's hand in different-colored ink from the other writing are two apparently irrelevant jottings: [17°?] 27′ 15″ [*and*] Puberty.

[Clark]

Satturday 21st 1804   The Snow this morning is about 2 ½ Inches Deep, & Snowing fast, The Thermometer Stood at 7d abov 0, at 8 oClock, & wind from the N E, The river running with Ice and falling a little, at 9 oClock the Thermtr. at 7° abv 0,—   at 10 oClk The Thmtr. 7d abov 0, at 11 oClock 10° abov 0, & Snow's—   at 12 oClock 10° abov 0, ⟨Snow⟩ or fine Haile increas, at 1 oClock 10° abov 0, at 5 oClock 17° abov 0, [*letters illegible*] haileing fine hail,

[Clark]

Sunday 22nd Jany: 1804   Snow all the last night, and Snows this morning, the debth is 5¾ Inches, The Thermometer Stands at 9 oClock this morning in the Open Air at 11° abov 0,—, at 12 oClock rose to 14° abov 0, and Stoped Snowing   wind Easterly   at 3 oClock 13d abv 0, riv nearly Clear of Ice,

[Clark]

Smunday [Monday] 23rd Jany 1804   a Cloudy morning but little Ice runig to day   The Thermtr. at 8 oClock 11° abo 0, at 12 oClock Stood at 10° abov 0, (I pen an Ordr to Corpl.)   at 3 oClock 17° abo 0, in the evening the wind raised [receed?] and Shifted to the North   Cought 14 rabits & Killed 2 Deer—

[Clark]

Tuesday 24th   a Butifull morning   Clear Sunshine   the wi[n]ds ligh[t] from the N W, the Thermometer at 9 oClock Stood at 4° abo o, (I take fesick),[1] at 10 oClock 8° abov o, wind West, at 12 oClock—14° abo o, at 3 oClock 11° abov o, Smone [some] Small pieces of Ice running   Sick, [games?] to day

1. "Physic," probably a laxative, the standard remedy for nearly every ailment at the time.

[Clark]

Wednesday 25th Jany   a verry Clear mon [moon?]   Shiney night   a fair morning, last night was a verry Cold one   (I was Sick all night[)]   The branch[es] of Trees and the Small groth ar gilded with Ice from the frost of last night which affords one of the most magnificent appearances in nature, the river began to Smoke[1] at 8 oClock and the Thermometer Stood at 2° below o, at 9 oClock at o, at 10 oClock at 5° abov o, at 11 oClock 12° abv o, at 12 oClock 16d abov o, at 1 oClock 16° abov o, at 2 oClock 19° abv o, at 3 oClock 16 abov o, wind from W N W—   Sick—   2 Deer Killed to day &

1. A mist caused by the difference between air and water temperatures. See above, September 1, 1803.

[Clark]

Thursday 26th Jany 1804   a Cloudy warm Day   I am verry unwell all day, Gibson Killed two Deer, R. *field* one, the men Kill Racoons[1] [ten? hen?] Rabits &. in great quantity, verry little Ice running to day   the fessic I took yesterday work to day. The men make a Sled to haul wood   one man Stay out to night (Winser)   I direct a Slay to be built to haul things from the Countrey & Fdy. 26th[2]

To Stow away in the *Boat*[3]

Kegs		In		I	
45	for pok	18	long	10	Thick
50	for flour	24	"	15	"
18	whisky	15		12	"
7	Corn				
120					

1. *Procyon lotor.* Hall, 2:967–72.

2. The words "Fdy. 26th" are apparently directions to the next entry, showing Clark's confusion of dates.

3. This material, in the lower left-hand corner of the obverse of document 8, is apparently a plan for stowing supplies on the keelboat.

[Clark]

Friday 27th Jany: 1804.[1]   a Cloudy morning   Some Snow, this morning I am verry unwell, to day at 1 oClock 28 abov 0, (I send off Howrd express to day to Cap Lewis at Koho: [Cahokia] with a Letter[2] ⟨I am some better,⟩   Winser who was out Last night returned   he Killed a Deer & Turkey—   Gibson Killed 1 Deer to day, Collons one near Camp

1. Under the beginning of this entry is the following calculation, apparently from an astronomical observation:

11	10	
1	22	27
9	47	33

2. Document 28 of the Field Notes may originally have been the envelope for Lewis's reply to this message. See below, July 6, 1804.

[Clark]

Saty: 28th Jany: 1804   a Cloudy morning   verry cold wind from the N W   Some floating Ice in the River   at 9 oClock 5° above 0, Snows at 10 oClock 8° abov 0, at 11 oClock 10° abov 0, Sun Shines, 3 french men from Parare De Soue[1] called, at 12 oClock 12° abov 0, at 1 oClock 14° abov 0, Mr. *Bagley*[2] Came with Potatos fowls &—   I trade him   Mr. *Cummins*[3] Came with meel & Brandy from Contractor   at 2 oClock 18° abov 0, Mr. Anty Coxe called toDay to inqure after his horses, at 3 oClock 20° above 0, 4 oClock 18° abov 0, Some womin came to day   at 6 oClock 14° abov 0, Porter[4] all frosed & several bottles broke, I Deliver out 12 flints & Some Canstr. Pow[d]er to hunters.

1. Perhaps Portage des Sioux, in St. Charles County, Missouri, a village founded in 1799 on the neck of land between the Missouri and the Mississippi, where Indians apparently portaged between the two rivers. Osgood (FN), 25 n. 4; *Missouri Guide*, 343–44. See also May 15, 1804.

2. The Reverend David Badgley from Virginia settled in American Bottom, Illinois, in 1797. Osgood (FN), 25 n. 5.

3. A Cummings lived below the camp, at Six Mile Prairie. Ibid., 25 n. 6.

4. A bitter, dark brown beer brewed from malt partly charred or browned by drying at a high temperature. It contained about 4 percent alcohol.

[Clark]

Sunday 29th Jany   a butifull morning   the river rise a little   no Ice The Thermometer at 9 oClock Stood at 16° above 0, at 11 oClock 22d abov 0, at 12 oClock 24° abov 0, Took the alltiude of Suns Lowr Limb 66° 50′ 30″—   E. E. [instrument error?] 5′ [*minute symbol written over degree symbol*]—   at 3 oClock 28° abov 0, at 4 oClock 26° abov 0, at 5 oClock 23° abov 0,—   Shields Killed a Deer to day, Express returned from Koho: brought a Letter from Capt. Lewis, & 4 other from Kenty. 8 bottles of wine Some Durant[1] & files

1. Durant, or durance, was a strong, felted cloth of woolen or worsted, usually made in imitation of buff leather.

[Clark]

Monday 30th Jany 1804   a Cloudy morning, Some Snow   send out 10 hunters to day in three parties, at 9 oClock The Thermotr. Stood at 22d abov 0, a little wind from N.   at 10 oClock 24° abov 0, cleared up & Sun Shown   Stoped Snowing, but little Ice running this morng—   at 11 oClock 25° abov 0, at 12 oClock 25° abov 0, Took M alt. of Suns L. L. 67° 22′ 52″—   Er[ror] of Entrement [instrument] 6′—, at 1 oClock 25° abov 0, at 2 oClock 26° abov 0, Reed Killed a Deer & wild Cat,[1] Cloudy. 3 men Cross the river to day, at 3 oClock 28° abov 0, at 4 oClock 27° abov 0, at 8 oClock 16° abv 0, about Sun Set Capt: Lewis arrived accompanied by Mr. J. Hay[2] & Mr. Jo Hays[3] of Kohokia—   The hunter killed 5 Deer to day—

1. Presumably a bobcat, *Lynx rufus.* Hall, 2:1051–55.

2. John Hay, fur trader, merchant, and postmaster of Cahokia, was born in Detroit. He worked for the North West Company in the country of the Assiniboin Indians in present-day Canada, then settled in Cahokia before 1799, engaging in the Indian trade from that place. Lewis met Hay at Cahokia on December 7, 1803, and the trader accompanied him on his first visit to St. Louis. Hay gave Lewis a copy of the Mackay-Evans journal of the Missouri River venture of 1795–97 and considerable other information on the Northwest and the fur trade. William Henry Harrison to Clark, November 13, 1803, Lewis to Jeffer-

son, December 19, 1803, Lewis to Jefferson, December 28, 1803, Jackson (LLC), 1:135 and n. 2, 145–47, 148–56 and nn. 8, 9; *Atlas*, 5.

3. John Hays should not be confused with John Hay. Hays, born in New York City, worked for the Hudson's Bay Company on the upper Mississippi and the Red River of the North. He settled in Cahokia in 1793, worked for Hay for a time, and was sheriff at the time of meeting Lewis and Clark. Osgood (FN), 25–26 n. 9.

[Clark]

Tuesday 31rd Jany: a fair morning the Trees guilded with ice at 7 oClock the Thermometer Stood at 7 oClock 10° below 0, (fowd, 0,)[1]

Jany 31st at 9 oClock some Ice running this morning, my head akes much, I went up the river with Cap Lewis & Gentlem[en] at 12 oClock 24° ab 0, at 2 oClock 28° abv 0, at 4 oClock 28° abv 0, Mr. Whitesides & Chittele[2] crossed from the opposit Side of the Mississippi— at 9 oClock P M 15° abov 0, wind S W. by W— took Latts

1. The entry continues on the next sheet (document 9), and the words in parentheses are repeated, apparently to help match the two documents. Osgood's facsimile of document 9 is reversed.

2. Perhaps Hanson Catlett, of Eddyville, Kentucky, surgeon's mate for Amos Stoddard's company in St. Louis in 1804, or else Warren Cottle, at that time residing in the Cuivre River district of Upper Louisiana. Jackson (LLC), 1:168 n. 1, 2:739–40 n. 1; Osgood (FN), 27 n. 1.

[Lewis and Clark]   [*Weather, January 1804*][1]

Thermometrical observation shewing also the rise and fall of the Mississippi,[2] appearances of weather winds &c at the mouth of the river Dubois commencing 1st Jany 1804. in Longitude 89° 57′ 45″ W. Latitude 38° 55′ 19.6″ N. Thermometer on the N. Side of a large tree in the woods

Explanations.

In the miscellanious column or column of remarks are noted, the appearance quantity and thickness of the floating or stationary ice, the appearance and quantity of drift-wood, ⟨the rapidity of the courent of the river below the mouth of the missouri, the falling of the banks—⟩ the appearance of birds, reptiles and insects, in the spring disappearance in the fall, leafing flowering and seeding of plants, fall of leaf, access and recess of frost, debth of snows, their duration or disappearance. ⟨Longitude and Latd.⟩³

Notations of *the weather*
- f. means fair
- c. —Cloudy
- r. —Rain
- s. —Snow
- h. —Hail
- t. —Thunder
- l. —Lightning
- a. —after—as *f. a. r.* means that it is *fair after rain* which has interveened since the last observation— *c. a. s.*—*Cloudy after snow* intervening *c. a. r. s.*—cloudy after rain & snow—

Notation of *the river*
- R. means *risen* in the last 24 Hours ending at ☉ rise
- F. —*fallen* in the same period—

Notations of Thermometer a. o means *above naught,* & *b. o*—*visa versa*

Remarks on the Thermometer[4]

1—By two experiments made with Ferenheit's Thermometer which I used in these observations, I asscertained it's error to be 11°⁵ too low or additive +— I tested it with water and snow mixed for the friezing point, and boiling water for—the point marked boiling water.—

Note[6] when there is not room in the column for the necessary remarks it is transferred by the refference of Numbers to an adjoining part of this book—

day of month 1804	Therm. at ☉ rise	weather	wind	Therm. at 4 oClock	weather	Wind	River rise or fall	F I.
Jany 1		Cloudy			Cloudy			
" 2		C a S			C			
" 3				2½ a o	f	N W. W		
4	11 a o	f	W			W		
5		f	W		f	W		
6		f	W N W	30 a o	f	W N W		
7[7]		h	S W		c & r	S W		
8		f	S W		f	N W		
9		f	W N W	1 b. o	c	W N W		
10		f			f			6

11								
12								
13		c & s	S W	o	r & s	S W		
14		f a s			f			
15								
16								
17[8]	8 b. o	f	N W	1½ b. o	f	N W	f	6
18	1 b o	c	N W W	1 a o	s & f	N N W	f	
19	13 a o	c	N W	11 a o	c	N W	f	
20	5 b o	f	N W	8 a o	C	N W	f	
21	7 a o	c & s	N E	17 a o	s & h	N E	f	
22[9]	11 a o	S	shfty.	13 a o	s	N W	f	
23	11 a o	c	N E	17 a o	c	N	f	
24	4 a o	c	N W	11 a o	c	W	f	
25[10]	2 b o	f	W N W	16 a o	f	W	f	
26		c	S W		c	S W	f	
27		f			f			
28	5 a o	C. s	N W	18 a o	c a s	N W	r	
29	16 a. o	f	W	23 a o	f		r	
30	22 a o	c & s	N	16 a o	f a s		r	
31	10 a o	f	S W by W	15 a o	f	w	r	

[*Remarks*][11]

Jany 1 Snow 1 Inch Deep

"   2 Snow last night inconsiderable

"   3 wind blew hard

     4 river Covered with ice out of the Missouries

     5 the River a Dubois rise a little

     6   ditto   do

     7   do   do

     8 Ice run down the little river [Dubois]

     9 Snow last night

   10 Missouri rise

   11 W C very sick[12]

   12   do

   13 Snow'd last night

   14   do   do

   15 W C Sick

   16   do

17 river falls & full of Ice 5 ½ In. thick

18   do

19. no ice running

20 Ice running out of the Missippi 9 In thick [13]

21 Snow 2 ½ In Deep [14]

22 do 5 ¾ In Deep   Ice runing down the Missouri, [15]

23 Ice Stoped

24 The Trees covered with ice to day

25 Some ice [16]

26 warm Day

27 do   do

28 cold & Ice runing

29 no Ice running

30 Capt. Lewis arrive [17]

31 Ice run a little

1. Here begin the captains' systematic weather observations, kept independently of regular journal entries. In this edition the data are placed at the end of the appropriate month. Included here are tables and observations from Lewis's Weather Diary and Clark's Codex C (see Introduction and Appendix C, this volume). The two sets of tables and remarks are combined to provide complete information without repetition. In this edition I have followed the Weather Diary as far as it goes and compared Codex C or other miscellaneous weather notes with it. It is uncertain which was the original source and which the copy, but internal evidence points to the Weather Diary as being the principal document. Insignificant changes between sources, such as word choice and sentence structure, are ignored; substantive differences are noted. The "remarks" include some events unrelated to weather, such as natural phenomena or daily events; they are retained with the weather data. Sometimes the remarks form a column of the table, sometimes they are placed separately. This edition follows the latter practice. In the Weather Diary, Lewis wrote the introductory material, the column headings, and the January 1 observations; the rest of the observations for the month seem to be in Clark's hand. Lewis was in St. Louis most of the time. There is also a copy of this January 1804 table in the notebook Voorhis No. 4, in Clark's hand, made at an unknown date. It appears to follow the Weather Diary more closely than it does Codex C, but some ten days (January 2, 5, 7, 8, 10, 11, 12, 14, 15, and 16) are missing and there are various discrepancies, chiefly in the remarks; some of those appear to be the result of writing remarks on the wrong line. In general, the Voorhis No. 4 table appears to be a hasty copy made later for some unknown purpose and does not seem worthy of detailed notice here.

2. Clark, in Codex C, adds "(Missouri)" here.

3. Clark, in Codex C, does not have this paragraph.

4. These remarks are from Lewis's Weather Diary, in his hand, under the heading "*Notes of refference for Jany 1804.*" Clark repeats them in Codex C under the title given here.

5. Clark has 8° in Codex C.

6. In his Weather Diary, Lewis placed a column for remarks within the table of observations; Clark, in Codex C, placed his remarks on separate pages—the style followed here. The preliminary note was at the head of Lewis's column of remarks.

7. In Codex C, under the second column of weather for this date, Clark has "c. a. r. h." rather than "c & r."

8. The "f" in first weather column is written over "N W."

9. The "S" in the first weather column is written over "shfty."

10. The "f" in the first weather column is written over "W N W."

11. The remarks in the Weather Diary are by Clark from January 2 on.

12. In Codex C, Clark entered no remarks for January 11, 12, 14, 15, 16, and 18, probably because of the illness he noted in the Weather Diary.

13. Clark, in Codex C, says, "No ice passing to day."

14. Clark, in Codex C, has "Ice running out of the Missoury, 9 In thick   Snow 2½ In Deep."

15. Clark, in Codex C, writes, "Ice running out of the Missouri, Snow 5¾ In Deep."

16. There are no remarks in Codex C for January 25, 26, and 27.

17. Clark, in Codex C, adds "from Kahokia."

[Clark]

Widnesday 1st Feby 1804   a Cloudy morning & warm wind from the S W, I rode out 6 miles on Mr Hays horse   am verry Sick, wind was verry high at 1 oClock, a warm Day, all the good put out & aired   I am very unwell

[Clark]

Thurday 2nd Feby   Mr's. Hays & Hay Set out for Kohokia, Cap Lewis & my Self accompanyed them one mile, & then went to Mr. [*blank*] & Kanes[1] and returned to Dinner, verry Sick   wind high from S W

1. Perhaps Francis Koehn, who had a cabin a mile or so southeast of the camp. Original survey of Chouteau and Wood River townships, 1808, courtesy of Everett L. Sparks.

[Clark]

Friday 3d   I am verry unwell all day; take medisone without[1]   fair Thawing Day

1. Clark may have written another word (perhaps "effect") on the next line, which was then overwritten by the next entry. The final words, "fair Thawing Day," are squeezed between the two lines.

[Clark]

Satturday [*written over another word, perhaps "effect"*] 4   Discharge Leakens for theift with a Small Correction   a warm Day   Some rain last night, in the Evening the River Covered with large Sheetes of Ice from both rivers, the River & Creek[1] rised Suffecent to take the boat up the Creek some distance   moderate day   I am verry Sick   wild fowl pass

1. The river was the Mississippi and the creek River Dubois; see below, February 7, 1804.

[Clark]

Sonday 5th Feby   Still Sick, The french man Wife &c Came to See us to day   Mes. Cane als[o]. Hanley[1] Sent us Some Butter & milk, river riseing & Covered with Small Ice. Cp L send out Shields to get walnut Bark for pills,[2] fowl pass

1. Samuel Hanley lived in Randolph County, Kaskaskia Land District, Indiana Territory, having settled there before 1788. Osgood (FN), 27 n. 3.
2. Walnut bark is strongly emetic and was probably used as a mild purgative. Lewis, whose mother was an herb doctor, was fond of such remedies. Ibid., 27 n. 4; Chuinard, 189–90 and n. 18.

[Clark]

Monday 6th Feby   a fair day   Snow nearly gone, Some Ice Still runing   Sick take Walnut pills, Winser killed a Badger.[1] My P[ills]—work &c.   great numbers of wild fowl flying Notherly. Swans in great number, river began to fall   Thompson return from Kohokia

1. *Taxidea taxus*. See entries and note at July 30, 1804. Cutright (LCPN), 70; Hall, 2 : 1009–13.

[Clark]

Tuesday 7th   Some rain last night, Rain this morning, the [river] falling 8 Inches. Sergt. Odway returned from Kohokia @ 2 oClock   rain

Incres a little, The Creek or River a Dubois rasin fast, Swept off a Canoo belonging to a Maumies Indian[1] from out its mouth. if the present fresh continus a fiew days, the water passing down this Small river [the Dubois] will Wash off all that immence quantity of mud which has filled up its mouth for 300 yards by the Missouris ooze or mud 8th

1. On the upper Maumee River, near present Fort Wayne, Indiana, were seven Indian villages that were destroyed by whites in 1790. Two were Miami, three Delaware, and two Shawnee. Perhaps the Indian Clark refers to was a member of the Miami tribe. Hodge, 1:823, 852–54; Anson.

[Clark]

Wednesday 8th Feby: 1804   a Cloudy morning   Some rain, and Snow a Great raft of Ice Come Down the Creek to day, the river rises & some running Ice, a Man arrives from Mr. Hay at Koho; with Letters & an Invitation to 2 balls at St Louis

[Clark]

Thursday 9th   a fine morning   river Still rise & Ice pass down the greater part out of the Missouries

[Ed: There are no further dated entries in the Field Notes until March 21, when Clark resumes immediately below the February 9 entry on this same sheet (document 9). The remarks from the weather data provide some knowledge of events for this period. Both captains left Camp Dubois for St. Louis on February 10, and Clark apparently remained there for some time. Lewis had returned to camp by February 13 but kept no known journal. Clark was back at the camp by February 29 but did no known writing, and he apparently left within a few days. The captains probably witnessed the ceremony in St. Louis by which France transferred Upper Louisiana to the United States on March 10, 1804. Thereafter both were occupied in St. Louis and on a journey up the Missouri to stop a Kickapoo war party from attacking the Osages. During the captains' absence Sergeant John Ordway was in charge of the camp and apparently had some problems with the restless enlisted men. See below, March 3 and April 13, 1804. Osgood (FN), 27 n. 5; Lewis to Clark, February 18, 1804, Jackson (LLC), 1:167–68.]

Detatchment Orders

[Lewis]   Camp River Dubois, Febr. 20th 1804.[1]

The Commanding officer directs that during the absence of himself and Capt. Clark from Camp, that the party shall consider themselves under the immediate command of Sergt. Ordway, who will be held accountable for the good poliece and order of the camp during that period, and will also see the susequent parts of this order carried into effect—

The sawyers will continue their work untill they have cut the necessary quantity of plank, the quantity wanting will be determined by Pryor; during the days they labour they shall recieve each an extra gill of whiskey pr. day, and be exempt from guard duty; when the work is accomplished, they will join the party and do duty in common with the other men.—

The Blacksmiths[2] will also continue their work untill they have completed the [articles?] contained in the memorandam with which I have furnished them, and during the time they are at work will recieve each an extra gill of whiskey pr. day and be exempt from guard duty; when the work is completed they will return to camp and do duty in common with the detatcment.—

The four men who are engaged in making sugar will continue in that employment untill further orders, and will recieve each a half a gill of extra whiskey pr. day and be exempt from guard duty.—

The practicing party will in futer discharge only one round each per. day, which will be done under the direction of Sergt. Ordway, all at the same target and at the distance of fifty yards off hand. The prize of a gill of extra whiskey will be recieved by the person who makes the best show at each time of practice.—

Floyd will take charge of our quartes and store and be exempt from guard duty untill our return, the commanding Officer hopes that this proof of his confidence will be justifyed by the rigid performance of the orders given him on that subject.—

No man shal absent himself from camp without the knowlege and permission of Sergt. Ordway, other than those who have obtained permission from me to be absent on hunting excurtions, and those will not extend their absence to a term by which they may avoid a tour of guard duty, on their return they will report themselves to Sergt. Ordway and recieve his instructions—

No whiskey shall in future be delivered from the Contractor's store except for the legal ration, and as appropriated by this order, unless otherwise directed by Capt. Clark or myself—

Meriwether Lewis Capt.
1st U. S. Regt. Infty.

Sergt. Ordway will have the men peraded this evening and read the inclosed orders to them—[3]

M. Lewis

1. The first of the Detachment Orders (see Appendix C). Sergeant Ordway was left in charge because no other sergeants had yet been appointed, and Ordway, who had been serving in the regular army, already held the rank and was an experienced soldier.

2. John Shields and Alexander Willard were the expedition's blacksmiths, Shields being particularly versatile. Lewis to Henry Dearborn, January 15, 1807, Jackson (LLC), 1:367, 372 n. 26; Russell (FTT), 39, 41, 358–61.

3. These lines were placed on the back of the sheet after it was folded. The orders are endorsed "To Floyd" in Lewis's hand and "1804 Merryweather Lewis" in an unknown hand.

[Lewis and Clark]   [*Weather, February 1804*][1]

day of month 1804	Therm at ☉ rise	weather	wind	Therm at 4 Oclk	weather	wind	r. & f.	River feet	inchs
Feb. 1st	10 a 0	f.	S. W.	20 a 0	f.	S. W. S	r.	"	1½
" 2[2]	12 a 0	f.	N. W.	10 a 0	f.	N. W.	r.	"	½
" 3	12 a 0	f	S. W.	19 a 0	f	W.	"	"	"
" 4	17 a. 0	f	S. W.	28 a 0	f	S.	r	"	½
" 5	18 a 0	f.	S. E.	31 a. 0	c. a. f.	S. E. S.	r	2	6½
" 6	19 a 0	f.	N. W.	15 a 0	c.	S.	"	"	"
" 7	29 a. 0	r. a. c	S. E.	30 a 0	r. & c.	S. E	f	"	8
" 8	22 a 0	c. a. r	N. W.	20 a 0	c. a. s.	N.	r	1	"
" 9	10 a 0	f. a. s	N. N. E	12 a 0	c	N. E	r	2	"
" 10	3 a 0	f.	N. E	17 a. 0	f	S. W	r	1	4
" 11	18 a 0	h. a. c.	S E.	31 a 0	s. a. h f.	S. E	r	1	"
" 12	15 a 0	f	S S E	25 a 0	f	S. W.	f.	"	2
13	12 a 0	f	N W	20 a 0	f	W.	r & f	"	1
14	15 a 0	f	S. W.	32 a 0	f	S. W.	⟨f⟩	"	"
15	18 a 0	f	S. W.	32 a 0	f	W.	⟨f⟩	"	"
16	28 a 0	c	S E.	30 a 0	r. a. c	S S E.	r	"	2½
17	15 a 0	c. a. r.	S W.	32 a 0	f.	W.	r		2
18[3]	10 a 0	f	N. W.				r	"	7½
19	10	f	N W						
20	10 a.0	f	N W	28 a 0		S. S. W	f		2½
21[4]	20 a 0	f	N W	34 a 0		N W	f		½

22	14 a o	f	N. E	26 a o		N, E	r	1½
23	6 a o	f	N W	24 a o		N W	r	1
24	6 a o	f	N E	26 a o		N E	f	2
25[5]	20 a o	f	N E	38 a o		S. S. W.		
26	16 a o	f	N E	30 a o		N E	f	½
27[6]	21 a o	c—	N. E	24 a o	r. & f. s	N W	f	1
28	4 a o	c & s	N W	6 a o	c a s	N W	f	2
29	8 a o	h & s	N W	12 a o	c. a. s	N W	f	2½

[Remarks][7]

Feb. 1st the wind blew very hard, no frost, snow disapearing fast

" 2 frost this morning   the snow has disapeared in spots

" 3 frost this morning, the snow thawed considerably, raisd boat[8]

" 4 frost, considerable number of swan & Geese from N & S.

5 emmence quantities of ice runing some of which 11 Inches

" 6 a small white frost, the snow disappeared   a small snow storm[9]

" 7 a small quantity of soft ice runing, Swans passing

" 8 many swans from N. W.   creek rose & took off my water mark,

" 9 the river raised 2 feet, large quantity of drift ice from Misso[uri]

" 10 ice still drifting in considerable quantities, some geese passed fr S.

" 11 Swans from the N. The sugar maple runs freely,

" 12 Pigeons, ducks of varis kinds, and gese have returned

13 the fist appearance of the blue crain,[10] sugar trees run

14 but little drift ice, the Misipi is not broken up.[11]

15 immence quantities of Swan, in the marra—.[12]

21 in the evening the river began to rise ½ Inch

23 [river] fall in the evening ½ Inch

25 River on a Stand

27 River rose 3 Inches & fell imediately

28 began to Snow and Continued all day

29 Snow all night & untill 11 oClock a. m. & Cleared away   the weather had been Clear since ⟨Capt Lewis⟩ lef Camp untill this.[13]

1. The table of observations follows Lewis's Weather Diary, wherein the observations from the first through the eighteenth are in Lewis's hand; from February 19 they are in

Clark's hand. Significant variations from Clark's Codex C are noted. Lewis's ditto marks in the river column do not seem to mean a repeat of the item above; they appear to be spacers.

2. Clark, in Codex C, has river rise 1 ½ inches for February 2.

3. In the first column of weather "f" is written over "N W."

4. Codex C gives the river rise as 1 ½ inches for February 21.

5. The second column of thermometer readings gives 28 in Codex C.

6. The first column of thermometer reading in Lewis's Weather Diary could be either 21 or 4. It is clearly 4 in Codex C.

7. These remarks follow Lewis's Weather Diary, kept by Clark from February 19. Variations from Codex C are noted below.

8. Numbers (1, 4, 2, 3) whose purpose is unclear were inserted at the end of remarks for February 3, 4, 5, and 8.

9. Clark, in Codex C, also says, "a quantity of Soft ice running" and "Swans passing."

10. Probably the great blue heron, *Ardea herodias* [AOU, 194], which is still often called a crane.

11. Clark, in Codex C, adds here "Sugar trees run."

12. In Clark's Codex C the last word appears to be "mars," presumably meaning "marsh."

13. There are no remarks for February 28 and 29 in the Weather Diary. Those given are from Codex C. On the flyleaf of Codex P are remarks on the weather by Lewis for February 28 and 29 and the month of March, in Lewis's hand. Those for February are substantially the same as those given here; in the February 29 entry, "I" is substituted for "Cap Lewis," which is struck out. Lewis left River Dubois sometime after February 20 and before February 29.

[Lewis]   *Detachment Orders March 3rd 1804.*

The Commanding officer feels himself mortifyed and disappointed at the disorderly conduct of Reubin Fields, in refusing to mount guard when in the due roteen of duty he was regularly warned; nor is he less suprised at the want of discretion in those who urged his oposition to the faithfull discharge of his duty, particularly Shields, whose sense of propryety he had every reason to beleive would have induced him reather to have promoted good order, than to have excited disorder and faction among the party, particularly in the absence of Capt. Clark and himself: The Commanding officer is also sorry to find any man, who has been engaged by himself and Capt. Clark for the expedition on which they have entered, so destitute of understanding, as not to be able to draw the distinction between being placed under the command of another officer, whose will in such case would be their law, and that of obeying the orders of Capt. Clark and himself communicated to them through Sergt. Ordway, who, as one of the party, has during their necessary absence been charged with the execution of their orders; acting from those orders expressly, and not from his own capriece, and who, is in all respects accountable to us for the faithfull observance of the same.

A moments reflection must convince every man of our party, that were we to neglect the more important and necessry arrangements in relation to the voyage we are now entering in, for the purpose merely of remaing at camp in order to communicate our orders in person to the individuals of the party on mear points of poliece, they would have too much reason to complain; nay, even to fear the ultimate success of the enterprise in which we are all embarked. The abuse of some of the party with respect to the prevelege heretofore granted them of going into the country, is not less displeasing; to such as have made hunting or other business a pretext to cover their design of visiting a neighbouring whiskey shop, he cannot for the present extend this prevelige; and dose therefore most positively direct, that Colter, Bolye, Wiser, and Robinson do not recieve permission to leave camp under any pretext whatever for *ten days*, after this order is read on the parade, unless otherwise directed hereafter by Capt. Clark or himself. The Commanding officers highly approve of the conduct of Sergt. Ordway.—

The Carpenters Blacksmiths, and in short the whole party (except Floid who has been specially directed to perform other duties) are to obey implicitly the orders of Sergt. Ordway, who has recieved our instructions on these subjects, and is held accountable to us for their due execution.—

Meriwether Lewis

Capt. 1st U S. Regt. Infty comdg Detatchment

Sergt. Ordway will read the within order to the men on the parade the morning after the reciept of the same.—[1]

M. Lewis Capt.

1. Endorsed: "1804 Merrywethe Lewis" in an unknown hand.

[Clark]   Wednesday 21st March 1804

I returned to Camp at Wood river down the Missouris from St Charles in a Boat from the Platte river,[1] Cap Lewis & my self Mr. Chotieu[2] &

Gratiot & went to stop 110 Kickpo[3] from going to war against the Osarges & [*perhaps words missing*]   good W[eather?]   river rise

1. Probably the Platte River in northwest Missouri, meeting the Missouri River in Platte County, rather than the stream of that name in Nebraska. It is not clear from the passage whether the captains had gone as far as the Platte on this trip, but it seems unlikely, and they probably went no farther than the vicinity of St. Charles. If it was a trading vessel that Clark caught to return to River Dubois, it could have been coming down from either the Nebraska or the Missouri stream. Appleman (LC), 73.

2. This could be either René Auguste or Jean Pierre Chouteau, but perhaps the latter since Lewis was writing of visiting his garden within the next week. Lewis to Jefferson, March 26, 1804, Jackson (LLC), 1 : 170. On the Chouteaus, see Foley & Rice.

3. By the time of the Lewis and Clark expedition some Kickapoos were moving west from Illinois, across the Mississippi River, to escape advancing European settlement. Some eventually moved as far as northern Mexico, where they still remain; most of the tribe are now located in Kansas and Oklahoma. Gibson; Callender, Pope, & Pope. For the Osages, see May 31, 1804.

[Clark]

Thursday 22d   Set the workmen to work about the Boat, Sent a man to examine if the Indians had recrossed home.   butifull weath   river Missories rise

[Clark]

Friday 23rd   the man returned, with a Lette[r] from Mr. [Souier?][1] the Comdr. of Passage Desous [Portage des Sioux], informing me that the Kickapoos has gone home, good weath th [river?] continu to rise—10 Inchs to day & 8 last night

1. François Saucier was born near Fort de Chartres, in French Illinois, and moved across the Mississippi after the British occupation in 1765. In 1799 the Spanish authorities asked him to undertake the founding of a settlement at Portage des Sioux, of which he was appointed commandant—chief civil and military officer—serving until the United States took possession. Houck, 2 : 88–89.

[Clark]

Saty. 24   I sent Newman with Letters to Koho. & to Cap Lewis at St. Louis, fair weather   river rise fast

[Clark]

Sunday 25th   a fair morning   river rose 14 Inch last night, the men find numbers of Bee Trees, & take great quantities of honey, at 11 oClock 24 Sauckees[1] Came pass from St Louis, and asked for Provisions   I ordered them 75 lb Beef, 25 lb flour, & 50 lb meal— Guterge [Goodrich] returned with Eggs & [Toe?],[2] Willard brought in 10 pr. Hinges   George Shannon Caught 3 large Cat fish— The musquetors are verry bad this evening. Newman return with Letters & Papers from St Louis. (ancore)[3]

1. The Sauk (or Sac) and Fox Indians, so closely allied by this time that they appeared to outsiders to be virtually one tribe, lived on both sides of the Mississippi in Iowa, Wisconsin, and Illinois. Callender (Fox); Callender (Sauk); Hagan.

2. The first letter of this word could be "L." Possibly Clark means "tow," short fibers of flax, hemp, or jute; also known as oakum, it was often used for caulking seams or leaks in wooden boats and sometimes in treating wounds, all possible uses on the expedition. Both captains use "toe" for the verb "tow." However, "low" or "lowe" is an old Scottish or northern English word for a flame or candle.

3. This word—presumably intended for "encore"—refers the reader to the next sheet of the Field Notes (document 10), where it is repeated before the March 26 entry.

[Clark][1]

Monday the 26th of March 1804, a verry Smokey day   I had Corn parched to make parched meal, workmen all at work prepareing the Boat, I visit the Indian Camps, In one Camp found 3 Squars & 3 young ones, another 1 girl & a boy   in a 3rd Simon Girtey[2] & two other familey— Girtey has the Rhumertism verry bad   those Indians visit me in their turn, & as usial ask for Something   I give them flour &c. Several fish Cought to day, the Mississippi R Continu to rise & discharge great quantity of form [foam?] &.

1. Under this entry, at right angles, Clark has written "Ne Angua Ne unguh," probably an attempt at spelling the Osage name of present Niangua River, a tributary of the Osage River in central Missouri. It may mean "many springs." It appears with its present spelling on Clark's 1804 map prepared at Camp Dubois and on subsequent maps (*Atlas* maps 6, 32*a*, 32*b*, 32*c*, 125). The attempts at phonetic spelling suggest that the source of information was oral, from traders or Indians. Lewis and Clark did not visit the stream on the expedition. Under the entries on this sheet (document 10) is an apparently conjectural sketch map of the Missouri River and its junction with the Kansas River. See fig. 15. Wood; *Missouri Guide*, 567.

2. Simon Girty was one of the most hated Americans of his day. As a Loyalist in the Revolution, he led Indian war parties against the settlements of the Ohio Valley and apparently continued the same activity for many years after as a British Indian agent. He may not have been any more active than other British agents, but he acquired among the Americans a special reputation (perhaps greatly exaggerated) for malice and cruelty. From the 1790s on, Girty made his home in Canada, and he believed, probably correctly, that his life would not be safe in the United States. There is no other record of his having crossed the border, except with the British forces in the War of 1812. Apparently he judged that a visit to the sparsely settled region along the Mississippi, in company with a party of peaceful Indians, would be safe enough. Clark is remarkably matter-of-fact about this encounter with a man who must have been one of the prime villains of his boyhood. Osgood (FN), 29 n. 7; Butterfield.

[Clark]

Tuesday 27th   rain last night verry hard with thunder, a Cloudy morning.   one man Sick to Day   all hands parching Corn &c   Som Delaways pass down to St. Louis   (Simon Girty)   river continue to rise,   beating at two morters parched Corn.   "I am unwell"

[Clark]

Wednesday 28th   a Cloudy morning, all hands at work prepareing for the voyage up the Missourie. Cap Louis arrived at 4 oClock from St Louis

[Clark]

Thursday 29th   Rained last night   a violent wind from the N this morng with rain, Some hail   we have a trial of John Shields. John Colter & R Frasure which take up the greater part of the day, in the evening we [*we written over I*] walk to Higgens   a blustering day all day, the blacksmiths return with part of their work finished, river Continue to rise, Cloudy Day

[Lewis]   [*various dates, December 4, 1803–March 29, 1804*][1]

Decr. 4th [1803]   this day drew in favour of William Morrison or the Secretary of War draught dated Jany 1st 1804 payable 3 days after sight for $136—

No. 2—on the Setr. of War for 33$ forwarded Gover harrison[2] in favor of it being for flagg stuf sent me by the govn. and was drawn payable 3 days after sight.—   dated 25th Febr—

No. 3 4 & 5. for 500$ each and left blank as to the name of the person in whos favour they wer drawn, and sent to Mr. Pike[3] for negociation   were dated on the 28th of March 1804.   *these draughts* wer not negocitated but were returned me and distroyed—[4]

No. 6. drawn in favor of Mr. John Hay dated March 29th 1804 Cahokia—for the sum of 159$ 81½ Cents.—on Secty. of war.

No. 3[5] of which duplicates were signed for 1,500$ fifteen hundred dollars on the War Department, in favor of Charles Gregoire[6] or order, dated St. Louis March 28th 1804.—

1. These accounts, from Codex P, p. 137, are placed according to the last date. The page is crossed out.

2. William Henry Harrison, the future president, was at this time governor of Indiana Territory.

3. Possibly Zebulon Montgomery Pike, the future explorer, then an army lieutenant. The name appears in other financial records of the expedition, always without a first name; Pike may have been acting as a paymaster. Clark to Lewis [April 1804], Charles Gratiot to William Morrison, May 12, 1804, Jackson (LLC), 1:175, 176 n. 4, 189.

4. The last sentence is crowded in and the ink is a different shade, perhaps indicating a later addition.

5. This final paragraph also appears to be a later addition.

6. Charles Gregoire was a resident of Ste. Genevieve. Financial Records of the Expedition [August 5, 1804], ibid., 2:420, 429 n. 3.

[Clark]

⟨Wedny⟩ Friday 30th of March 1804.   a fair Day   I write engagements & Capt. Lewis write   ⟨I [loaded?] a small pr Pistols to [prevent?] the [consignments?] which may arrive this evenging in inforcing our regulation &. not to do Injury⟩[1]   Priors is verry Sick   I sent out R Fields to kill a squirel to make him Suip,   I red the orders on Parade this evening J. Sh: [Shields] & J. Co. [Colter] asked the forgivness & & promised to doe better in future.   the other [prisoners?] were dismissed &c

1. This passage is exceptionally hard to read, for it not only is crossed out but lies in a crease in the page. Apparently the captains anticipated some trouble with the men, either over the announcement of the verdict of the court-martial or over the stealing of goods from the supplies due to be delivered that evening. Clark may have crossed the passage out after the trouble failed to materialize. Osgood (FN), 29 n. 9

[Clark]

Satturday 31st of March   a fine morning   Sent over two men to the Island to See about a horse which was Seen in distress there, Majr. Runsey arrived

[Lewis and Clark]   [*Weather, March 1804*][1]

Day of month 1804	Therm at ☉ rise	weather	wind	Therm at 4 Oclk	weather	wind	r. & f.	River feet	inchs
March 1st	12 b o	f	N W	4 a o	·		N W	f		9
2	11 b o	f	N W	22 a o		E	f		3
3	10 a o	f	E	18 a o		S W	f		6½
4	4 a o	f	N E	20 a o		E	f		5
5	10 a o	f	N W	20 a o		N W	f		3
6	4 a o	f	N W	10 a o		N W	f		3
7	8 b o	c & s.	N W	18 a o	s	N W			
8[2]	6 a o	c & s	N W	20 a o	s	N W	f		½
9[3]	18 a o	c	N W	28 a o	c	N W	R		2
10	14 a o	c & f.	N W	32 a o	f	N W	r		2½
11[4]	20 a o	f	E	38 a o	f o	S W	f		2½
12	22 a o	f	N E	24 a o	f	N E	R		1½
13	16 a o	f	N W	20 a o	f	N W	f		1½
14	12 a o	f	N E	18 a o	f	N E	f		4½
15	2 a o	c & s	N W	48 a o	r. a. s	N E	r		5
16	6 a o	f	E	48 a o	f	S S W	r		11
17	20 a o	f	N E	46 a o	f	N E	r		7
18	10 a o	f	E	52 a o	f	N E	f		3
19	10 a o	f	N E	60 a o	f	S S W	f		2½
20	12 a o	f	E	68 a o	f	S S W	f		1½
21[5]	34 a o	f	S S W	54 a o	f	N W	f		2
22	30 a o	f	N W	48 a o	f	N W	f		2
23	22 a o	f	N E	52 a o	f	N E	r		4
24	14 a o	f	E	60 a o	f	S S W	r	1	5½
25	24 a o	f	S S W	54 a o	f	E	r	2	
26[6]	36 a o	f	E	52 a o	f	E	r		10
27	42 a o	r & t	E	50 a o	f a r	N E	r		7
28	42 a o	˙c	N E	52 a o	c	E	r		5½
29	28 a o	r a t	N E	38 a o	h & r	N E	r		1
30		c a r	N W		f	N W	r		2
31[7]		f	N W		f	N W W	r		2

[*Remarks*][8]

March 7th   Saw the first Brant return.[9]

    8th   Rain Suceeded by Snow & hail

    9th   Cloudy in the morning

  19th   The weather has been generally fair but verry Cold, the ice run for Several days in Such quantities that it was impossible to pass the River [Mississippi]   Visited St. Charles[10] Saw the 1st *Snake* which was the kind usially termed the *Garter* Snake, Saw also a *Beatle* of black Colour with two red Stripes on his back passing each other Crosswise, from the but of the wing towards the extremity of the Same.[11]

  20th   Heard the 1st frogs on my return from St Charles after haveing arrested the progress of a Kickapoo war party[12]

  21st   I arrived at River Dubois from St Charles

  25th   Saw the 1st White *Crain* return[13]

  26th   the weather worm and fair

  27th   The buds of the Spicewood[14] appeared, and the tausels of the mail Cotton wood were larger than a large Mulberry, and which the Shape and Colour of that froot, Some of them had fallen from the trees.   the grass begins to Spring. The weather has been warm, and no falling weather untill this time tho the atmispere has been verry Smokey and thick, a heavy fall of rain commenced which continued untill 12 at night, attended with thunder, and lightning— Saw large insects which resembled Musquitors, but doubt whether they are really those insects or the fly which produces them, they attempted to bite my horse, but I could not observe that they made any impression with their Beaks.[15]

  28th   Capt. Lewis returned to Camp[16]

  29th   Tried Several men for missconduct

  31st   Windey

1. This table follows Lewis's Weather Diary, kept by Clark this month; its temperature readings are eight degrees higher than those in Codex C, with exceptions noted within the table. In Codex C, Clark indicated that the thermometer registered eight degrees too low (see above, Weather Diary, January 1804, n. 5); Lewis gave the error as eleven degrees, but in April and May Lewis applies the eight-degree correction. Since Clark compensated for the error for March in the Weather Diary but not in Codex C, he apparently did not keep the two tables simultaneously. In the Weather Diary over the March 1, 2, and 3 entries in the first column of temperature readings are plus signs, perhaps an indication that the eight-degree correction had been added.

2. In Codex C the river fall for March 8 is 1½ inches.

3. In Codex C the 4 p.m. temperature for March 9 is 10° above zero.

4. In Codex C the 4 p.m. temperature for March 11 is 20° above zero.

5. In Codex C the 4 p.m. temperature for March 21 is 36° above zero.

6. In Codex C there is a blot in the "feet" column for the river rise for March 26, which may be an illegible number or a dash to indicate a blank.

7. In Codex C the 4 p.m. wind direction for March 31 is N W.

8. The remarks follow those in Clark's Codex C. There are almost no remarks in Lewis's Weather Diary, which Clark kept for March. Remarks similar to Clark's appear in Lewis's hand for March on the flyleaf of Codex P; differences are noted below. The gaps in the remarks presumably reflect Clark's absence from River Dubois for much of the month. Possibly he made some of the observations at St. Louis or elsewhere.

9. The captains' references to "brant" are often obscure, especially here where color is not noted. The snow goose, *Chen caerulescens* [AOU, 169], they later called the "white brant," but apparently they were not familiar with the species before seeing it on April 9, 1805. This might be the Canada goose, *Branta canadensis* [AOU, 172], since brant is often a common name for dark geese. Kortright, 82.

10. Lewis's note in Codex P ends "this day visited St. Charles.—" The material about the snake and the beetle he placed under his March 21 remarks.

11. The common garter snake, *Thamnophis sirtalis*. Benson, 90. The "Beatle" may be a box-elder bug.

12. Substantially this same entry is in Lewis's Codex P remarks for March 21. The frog is probably the striped chorus frog, *Pseudacris triseriata*. Ibid., 88.

13. Apparently the now rare and endangered whooping crane, *Grus americana* [AOU, 204], which could be found in Illinois in the 1800s. Burroughs, 184–85. But perhaps the great egret, *Casmerodius albus* [AOU, 196], described by Lewis on August 2, 1804. Holmgren.

14. *Lindera benzoin* (L.) Blume, spice bush. Fernald, 678.

15. Perhaps crane flies (*Tipulidae*) or midges (*Chironmidae*).

16. Lewis's Codex P remarks for March 28 read, "day cloudy & warm, left Cahokia to which I had passed over from St. Louis last evening, for my camp."

[Clark]   [*April 1, 1804*]

Sunday   a fair morning   Mr: Dr Catlates[1] Boat arrived with provisions, & we Sent down a Cannoo for the Docr. who intended to Come [*written over go*] by Land, The French Man & his Wife Came on a visit to day, a Draft for Squads, &c. &. the [Comosary?] bo[at] Dr. Catlates Boat arrived with provisions, Capt Lewis went to St. Louis with Dr. Catlate on business, a northern Light[2] Seen [commenc?] at about 10 oClock, &. frequently Changeing Coler, appearing as [various?] in the atmusfier &.

Detachment Order

[Clark]   Camp River Dubois april 1st 1804[3]

The Commanding officers did yesterday proceed to take the necessary inlistments and select the Detachment destined for the Expedition through the interior of the *Continent* of North America; and have accordingly seelected the persons herein after mentioned, as those which are to Constitute their Perminent Detachment. (Viz).

William Bratten	+
John Colter	+
John Collins	+
Reubin Fields	+
Joseph Fields	
Charles Floyd	
Peter[4]	
Ct Mll [court-martial?][5]	
Patric Gass	+
George Gibson	
Silas Goodrech	+
Thomas P. Howard	
Hugh Hall	+
Hugh McNeel	
John Newmon[6]	+
John Ordway	+
Nathaniel Pryor	+
John Potts	+
Moses B Reed[7]	
George Shannon	+
John Shields	+
John B Thompson	+
Richard Winser	
William Werner	

Peter Wiser ⟨+⟩
Joseph Whitehouse + &
Alexander Willard

The Commanding officers do also retain in their service untill further orders—: The following Persons, Richard Warvington, Robert Frasure, John Robertson, & John Boyley.[8] [*NB: Moses B. Read*] who whilst they remain with the Detachment Shall be incorpereted with the Second, and third Squads of the Same, and are to be treated in all respects as those men who form the Permonant detachment, except with reguard to an advance of Pay, and the distribution of Arms and Accoutrements intended for the expedition.

The following Persons (Viz *Charles Floyd, John Ordway,* and *Nathaniel Pryor* are this day *appointed Sergeants.* with equal *Power* (unless when otherwise specially ordered). The authority, Pay, and emouliments, attached to the Said rank of Sergeants in the Military Service of the United States, and to hold the Said appointments, and be respected Accordingly, dureing their good behaviour or the Will and pleasure of the sd. Commanding officers.

To insure order among the party, as well as to promote a regular Police in Camp, The Commanding officers, have thought to devide the detachment into three *Squads,* and to place a Sergeant in Command of each, who are held imediately responsible to the Commanding officers, for the regular and orderly deportment of the individuls Composeing their respective Squads.—

The following individuals after being duly balloted for, have fallen in the Several *Squads* as hereafter stated, and are Accordingly placed under the derection of the Sergeants whose names preceeds those of his Squad.

(Viz:) 1st *Squad*
Sergeant Nathaniel Pryor
Privates
George Gibson
Thomas P. Howard
George Shannon
John Shields
John Collins
Joseph Whitehouse

Peter Wiser
Hugh Hall

2nd Squad
Sergt. Charles Floyd
Privates
Hugh McNeel
Patric Gass
Reeubin Fields
Joseph Fields
John B. Thompson
⟨John Newmon⟩[9]
Richard Winser
x Richard Worthington
Robert Frasure

3rd Squad
Sergt. John Ordeway
Privates
William Bratten
John Colter
⟨Moses B. Reed⟩
Alexander Willard
William Warner
Silas Goodrich
John Potts
John Robertson
John Boleye

The Camp Kittles, and other Public utensels for Cooking Shall be produced this evening after the parade is Dismissed; and an equal division shall take place of the Same, among the non commissioned officers Commanding the Squads. Those non-commissioned officers Shall make an equal Division of the proportion of those utensils between their own messes of their respective Squads,— each squad shall be devided into two messes, at the head of one of which the Commanding Serjeant Shall Preside. the Serjeants messes will Consist of four privates only to be admited under his discrission, the ballance of each Squad Shall form the Second mess of each Squad.

Dureing the indisposition of Sergeant Pryor, George Shannon is appointed (protempor) to discharge his the Said Pryor's duty in his Squad—

The party for the Convenience of being more imediately under the eye of the Several Sergeants haveing Charge of them, will make the necessary exchange of their *Bunks* and rooms for that Purpose as Shall be verbally directed by us.—

Untill otherwise derected, Sergeant John Ordway will Continue to Keep the *Rouster* and detaile the men of the detachment for the Several duties which it may be necessary, they should perform, as also to transcribe in a book furnished *Him* for that purpose, those or Such other orders as the Commanding officers Shall think proper to publish from time, to time for the government of the Party—.

Signed[10]

Merrwether Lewis

Wm. Clark

1. Probably Hanson Catlett. See above, January 31, 1804, n. 2.

2. Aurora borealis.

3. The first of the Detachment Orders in the Orderly Book (see Appendix C). The captains selected the men for their "Permanent Detachment," which would go with them to the Pacific, and Corporal Warfington's detachment, which would be sent back with dispatches from some yet undetermined point on the Missouri. Changes were made in these assignments over the next year. It is uncertain what the marks next to the names represent.

4. Peter Wiser (Weiser) is mentioned later in the list. Possibly the name refers to Pierre (Peter) Cruzatte, the French boatman who may have joined at St. Charles in May and who went to the Pacific; his name could have been inserted later.

5. These letters are in the upper right-hand corner of the second page and may have no relevance to this entry.

6. Newman was tried and convicted of "mutinous expression" and expelled from the party. See below, October 13, 1804.

7. Reed deserted and, after apprehension and trial, was expelled from the party. See below, August 18, 1804.

8. These are the persons selected to be the returning party (see Appendix A, this volume). Warfington was in charge of that group, but changes were made from this list. Frazure (Frazer) was added to the permanent party, apparently in place of Reed (see below, October 8, 1804). April 1 is the last time Robertson's name appears. When he left the party is uncertain, but he may have been the man of Captain Stoddard's company mentioned by Whitehouse as being sent back on June 12, 1804. Biddle apparently added Reed's name here because Reed, after his expulsion, was sent with the return party. He did not add Newman, who also went back with that party.

9. Someone crossed out the names of Newman and Reed on this list, no doubt after their expulsion from the party. The mark by the name of Richard Worthington (Warfington) may refer to his being a corporal, not a private.

10. Clark evidently signed for Lewis here.

[Clark]

Monday 2nd of April   Mr. Hays & Amdol arrive from Koho: by Land in the evening Majr Garroes[1] Boat come up on his way to Prarie de chaine [Prairie du Chien] loaded with Provisions &, for Sale at that place, a cleaning to Day   three men Sick   all mess arranged, & men makeing Parched meal, those Gentlemen Stay w[it]h me all night, I send down willard to St. Louis—

1. Nicholas Jarrot, born in France, settled in Cahokia in 1794 and engaged in the fur trade on the upper Mississippi. Lewis met him at Kaskaskia in December 1803, and he accompanied the captain to St. Louis. Here he was bound for Prairie du Chien, Wisconsin, an important trading location. Jackson (LLC), 1:147 n. 1; Osgood (FN), 29–30 n. 2.

[Clark]

Tuesday 3rd   I wrote a letter to Mr. John Campbell,[1] of Prarie De chaine by Mr. Hay & the Gentlemen bound to [*tear, perhaps one word missing*] [t]hat place, those Gentlemen Set out at Sun rise, I have meal mad & the flour Packed & repacked, also Some porkie packed in barrels, a Windey Day   Capt Lewis return with Dr. Catlate   wind blew verry hard all night. Some rain

1. Campbell, a Scotch-Irish trader, had been dealing with the Indians at Prairie du Chien since about 1790. He was appointed U.S. Indian agent in 1807 and killed in a duel the following year. Jackson (LLC), 1:124 n. 1; Osgood (FN), 30 n. 3.

[Clark]

Wednesday 4th   all day Packing Provision   Setled account with the Contractor for all the Issues to the first of the month &. what Provisions he had furnished   hard wind and rain last night, Mr Crawford[1] sent his Canoo by to a [*tear, perhaps word missing*]   speach to the Sioux & Iowoy Indians[2]

1. Lewis Crawford, later a member of the North West Company in Canada, was a trader at Prairie du Chien from about 1790. Lewis entrusted him with a message to Indians on the Des Moines River about the change of sovereignty in Louisiana. He was also to collect vocabularies for the captains. Lewis to Amos Stoddard, May 16, 1804, Amos Stoddard to Henry Dearborn, June 3, 1804, Amos Stoddard to Jefferson, October 29, 1804, Jackson (LLC), 1:189–91 and n. 1, 196–97, 212–13; Osgood (FN), 30 n. 4.

2. At this time the Iowas (Ioways) lived in present northern Missouri and Iowa, and gave their name to the latter state. They spoke a Siouan language of the Chiwere group, closely related to Oto and Missouri. Their economy was based on hunting and horticulture. For the Sioux, see August 31, 1804. Hodge, 1:612–14; Blaine.

[Clark]

Thursday 5th   Thunder & lightning last night   wrote the Speaches, to the Aiyous & [Sioux?][1] & Ioways, Several Country people came to Day to pay a visit, men and wimin, the wind is violintly hard from the W, N, W. all day   river Still rise, Send by Mr. Crawford Some queries reletive to the Indians, and Vocabulary also some instructions &c.   the Contractors Boat return to St. Louis.   the [wind] Shift to the North at Sun Set & Cold, Banks fall in

1. This word is written over and nearly illegible, but "Sioux" is presumably meant.

[Clark]

Friday 6th   a Cloudy Day   river fall 10 Inches, the Bark Canoo set out for Mackenaeck,[1] give out Knives Tomahawkes &c. &c. to the men, Sgt. Pryor Still Sick, Several Countrey people Came to Camp to day   at one oClock the wind bley [blew] hard from the N W, in this Countrey the windy points for rain & Snow is from S E, to, N E, the fair weather winds S W & West, Clear and Cold from the N W & North, wind Seldom blows from the South—   at about 9 oClock P M began to Snow and Continued a Short time, wind blew hard from the N West   I write to S G & F T, give order &c. &c

1. The island of Mackinac, or Mackinaw, now part of Michigan and situated in the strait of the same name between Lakes Michigan and Huron, was long a center of the fur trade, and a French, British, and finally American military post. The original form of the name, Michilimackinac, meaning "place of the big wounded person," was derived from "Mishinimaki" (or "Mishinimakinagog"), the name of a supposed extinct Algonquian tribe. Hodge, 1:857.

[Clark]

Satturday 7th   Set out at 7 oClock in a Canoo with Cap Lewis my servant york & one man   at ½ past 10 arrived at St Louis, Dressed & Dined with Capt Stoddard, & about 50 Gentlemen, a Ball Succeeded, which lasted untill 9 oClock on Sunday   no business to day—

Detachment Orders

[Ordway]

River a Dubois April 7th 1804.[1]

During the absence of the Commanding officers' at St. Louis, the Party are to Consider themselves under the immediate command of Sergt. John Ordway, who will be held accountable for the Poliece; and good order of the Camp, dureing that period. Every individual of the party will Strictly attend to all the necessary duties required for the benefit of the party; and to the regulations heretofore made which is now in force. Sergt. Floyd will stay in our quarters, attend to them, and the Store; and to the other duties requred of him; he will also assist Sergt. Ordway as much as possable.—

Signed[2]
Wm. Clark
Meriwiether Lewis

1. A portion of this order in Clark's hand is also on a fragment of letter paper. Of the legible words on that sheet, no substantial differences have been noted. See Appendix C.
2. The signatures are also in Ordway's hand.

[*Ed: There is no entry for April 8.*]

[Clark]

Monday 9th & Tuesday 10th, Wednesday 11, attending to Sunderey Stores &c

[Clark]

Thursday 12th   Set out from St. Louis at 6 oClock a m in Majr Rumseys boat &c

[Lewis, Clark, and Unknown] [*undated, ca. April 1804*][1]

S. [Shields?][2] opposeds order & has threttened Od [Ordway's]—Life wishes to return

Wa[rner]—& P. [Potts] fought   [*see above, January 4*]

F. [Fields? Frazer? Floyd?] & W H. [Whitehouse?] do

N. [Newman] & Co [Colter? Collins?]—do

Co [Colter? Collins?]—Lo[aded] his gun to Shute S. O. [Sergeant Ordway?] & Disobyed Orders

R. F[ield] was in an a mistake & repents

Gib. [Gibson] Lost his Tomahawk

Wh[itehouse]—wishes to return

Fr[azer]   do   do   has don bad

		5
		18 men
		1
		1
		1
		1
		1
		25
15	Howard 13[3]	1
2	of us & york	1
1	Interpeter	1
	G Drewyer	1
	C. Floyd	4
	N Pryor	
	R. Fields	
	Jo Fields	
	J. Shields	
	J Shannon	
	J. Gibson	
	J Colter	
	J Bratten	
5	Newmon	1
4	St Odderway	2
3	Gass	3
8	Robertson	

— Goodrich
6 McNeel — 4
11 —Wiser — 5
9 Boleeye — 6
— Willard
10 Reed — 7
— Whitehouse   8 French
1 Wenser — 8
— Woverington
2 Thompson — 9
7 Worner — 10
12 —Potts — 11
13 —Collens — 12
— Frasure
14 Hall

Kansas[4]			Sous [Sioux]—	4
Otoes			Loup [Skiri]	
Parnees [Pawnees]	} 1		Chayon [Chawi?]	} 5
republican			Mandans &c	6
Mahar [Omaha]—	2			
Poncaras [Ponca]	} 3			
Rickerie [Arikara]				

$$22—6$$
$$\frac{7—1}{29\quad 7}\,^{5}$$

Cp L[ewis][6]   32
    C[lark]   2
    D[rouillard?]   40
    I.[nterpreter?]
    y[ork]   5
    22
    $\frac{4}{8}$ 26

    $\frac{1}{1}$ $\frac{9}{40}$

           26
             3

8. Sketch of the White Pirogue, ca. April 12, 1804,
Field Notes, reverse of document 10

No man is to absent himself from Camp on any pretence whatever
without permission from the Comdgn. offecer present, under the pain of
punishment agreeable to the rules & articles of War for Disobedience of
Orders; the guard shall Strictly attend to former Orders without the
Smallest Variation [7]

> Whitehouse
> Willard
> Potts
> Colter

210
65

145

[Unknown]

Leave Cahoke 8 o'c—

Arrive at Kaskas[kia]— [fine?] dy—

Leave Caho. 8 O'C Thursday moring—and arive at Kas. ⟨by way of the American bottom⟩ 6 O'C Friday evening— leave Kas. Saturd—8 O'C—arrive St Ginevieve 12 O'C same day— leave St Genevieve 1 O'C P M. same Day, arrive Cape Girardeau—monday 12 O'C— Leave Cape Girardeau 2 O'C—arrive at New Madrid 12 O'C Widnesday—

[Lewis]

on their return leave New Madrid Thursday 6 O Clock A. M Friday 6 Oclock P. M. leave Cape Girardeau 6 oclk. A M. Saturday arrive at St. Genevie Sunday 6 oC P. M leave it, at 7. same day and arive at Kaskaskias at 9 P. M. on the same day— leave Kaskaskias at 6 A. M. on Monday and arrive on Tuesday 5 Oclock P. M. at Cahokia— [*some illegible letters crossed out*]

	Floyd[8]	✓
	Pryor	
	Fields	✓
	Bratten	✓
	Shields	
	Shannon	
	Colter	✓
	Gibson	9
x	Odeway	1
x	Wnser	2
x	Gass	3
x	Newmon	4
x	Thompson	5
x	Warner	6
x	Howard	7
x	McNeel	8
	Robertson	9

Boleye 10
x Reed 11
x Willard 12
x Wiser 13
x Collins 14
x Hall
Potts
Goodrich
√ Worthington
√ Whitehouse
√ Frasure

R Worthington ⎫
Robertson ⎬ to return
Boleye ⎪
Frasure ⎭

Newmon
Robertson
Willard
Hall

Hall +
Potts
Goodrich
* Frasure
x Worthyton
x Boley

11
  70
770
  70
 70
  7
[980?]

11 Kegs of Porke at 70 w
21 flour
[hw? *could be abbreviation for hundredweight*] 14 flour Kegs
& 5, 10 Gal Kegs Empty

Hall
Potts
Goodrich

Wortheyton
Whitehouse
Frasure
Boley

Bratton
Colter
Collins
Floyd
Fields
Fields
Goodrich
Gass
Gibson
Howard
Hall
Newmon
McNeil
Odeway
Reed
Pryor
Potts
Shields
Shannon
Thompson
Whitehouse
Willard
Warner
Wesir
Winser

740 lbs Pork bone extracted
603 lbs of Bone
137 Difference

50 Kegs in the Boat
21 of which is filled with flour
11   do of Poark

4   do by Mr. [E.?] of flour

35 ready by tuesday morning

[on?] the; 3d of April

(55 flour Keggs in)

   Pork Kegs they will way about 80

<u>14</u> [*one word illegible*]

94

4175 Complete rations @ 14½ Cents [9]	605 37 ½
5555 Ration of flour at 4½ cents	231 97 ½ [*should be 249.97½*]
25 Cask Corn @ 50 Cents	12 50
12 do Salt 3$—	36 —
100 G. Whiskey 128 Cents	128 00
10 bus Corn fo I. [Indians?]—	50 00
20 G Whiskey Do—	25 00
58 Keggs—50 cents—	29 0
4000 rats. pork @ 4½ cents—	180 0
45 Keggs @ 1$—	45 0
15 do— @ 75 Cts.—	11 0
5 Ditto @ 1$—	<u>5 0</u>
	1304 45 [*should be 1376.85*]

1. The following is a mass of undated miscellaneous material, written in every direction, which takes up the reverse of document 10 of the Field Notes. A few random scribblings (some illegible) are not printed here. Clark is the author where not specified otherwise.

2. Here Clark summarizes a number of disciplinary problems during the winter at Camp Dubois. Apparently some men were expelled and allowed to return on a promise to do better. S. was probably John Shields, because Lewis expresses particular shock at his conduct in the Detachment Order of March 3, and Shields was one of those tried by court-martial on March 29. F. might be Reubin or Joseph Field. Charles Floyd is probably not meant, since he was made a sergeant soon after. Colter may have been the one who loaded his gun, since he was one of those tried on March 29. R. F is probably Reubin Field, since Frazer is mentioned below as in error wishing to return.

3. This list must be another attempt to determine the composition of the expedition party. Howard's name probably goes at the end of the list, since the numbers to either side of his name coordinate with those below and since Clark had come to the bottom of the page. The numbers at either side of some names may have relevance beyond a simple count, but the meaning is not now known. Tick marks (not printed) may have been a means of evaluation, but this is conjecture.

4. In this list of Indian tribes "republican" refers to the Republican, or Kitkahahki, division of the Pawnees; "Loup" to the Loup, or Skiri, division of that tribe. "Chayon," may be Cheyenne, but being joined with "Loup," it must refer to the Chawi, or Grand, division

of the Pawnees. The numbers by the names may refer to the number of villages or divisions of each, based on information from traders or Indians. Hodge, 1:238; Parks.

5. Following these numbers is a drawing of a "Perogue of 8 Tuns" (fig. 8), the so-called white pirogue. This is the only contemporary illustration of one of the two boats taken as far as the Great Falls of the Missouri River. It may have been drawn as an aid in determining how to store goods.

6. The names and perhaps the figures seem to represent further attempts by Clark to determine how many men should compose the expedition and to assign them to various boats. Part of this material runs into the paragraph beginning "No man is to absent himself. . . ."

7. This is probably a first draft for a detachment order and is similar to the order of February 20.

8. Unidentified symbols drawn to the right or left of some of these names are here represented as a check mark.

9. The word "Soap" is placed near this list of supplies and perhaps is a part of it.

[Clark]

Friday 13th   arrived at Camp at 10 oClock A. M.   all is well[1]

The 13th of April 1804   at 10 oClock I arrived in Majr. Rumseys boat from St Louis, with Sundery articles for our voyage, a Cloudy day   I hoist a Flag Staff, After part of the day fair, river falling   I give out to the men Lead, Powder, & an extra gill of Whiskey—   *5$ of Cap Lew at St Louis*

1. This much of the April 13 entry is at the bottom of document 10 of the Field Notes, immediately after the April 12 daily entry. This rest is on document 11. At the head of that document is the word "*Journal*," apparently in Clark's hand.

[Clark]

Satturday 14th 1804   a fair Day   wind high from the [*blank*]   I sent Reed to St Louis with a letter & Some [Scerlet?] &c. Locks to be mended, lent Majr Runsey 12$—   paid Reed 10$ took out of bag 8$ in all 30$ out of bag to day—   a Gentleman from winchester[1] by the name of McLain Came to Camp bound on land hunting, I had finished off and packed up to day in part of my Store of Provisions—

> 13 Bags of Parched meal of 2 bus: each
> 9 do—   Common Meal of N C—[2]   do
> 11 do & 3 barrels of N: Corn Huled do

3 do: & 30 —½³ do—of Flour— do

7 Barrels of Salt of 2½ bushels each— do

Received of Majr Runsey

14 flour Kegs ⎫
19 Pork Kegs ⎬ 14th apl.
537 [lb?] Salt ⎭

in 44 in Pork Kegs 3115 [w?]⁴

do 6 &c. do— 590

in [all?] 3705

1. Of the many Winchesters in the United States, this was most likely the town in either Virginia or Kentucky. McLain, a prospective settler or a land speculator, is unidentified. Stewart (APN), 536.

2. The "N C" may mean Natchez corn here and elsewhere. This is apparently what Clark has written on an undated list of articles for the trip. The list is on the reverse of *Atlas* map 3*a* and is printed here after the May 14 entry in this chapter.

3. From the list on reverse of *Atlas* map 3*a* it appears that Clark here means thirty half barrels rather than thirty and one-half barrels.

4. These figures were inserted sideways in a blank space of this entry and go with a list of April 16. The number 3115 was written over what appears to be 3366 in order to match some calculations that Clark did the next day. The "w" given here and elsewhere may stand for weight, but the letter or letters are very uncertain. Osgood interpreted it to be "lb." Osgood (FN), 36.

[Clark]

Sunday 15th of April, a fair morning Sent out Shields with Mr. McLaine to the head of Wood River. Settled with Mrs. Cane for all to this day & paid 12/c. Clouded up at 12 oClock the wind from the S. W blew verey hard a Boat pass up the ⟨Missouris⟩ Mississippi under Sail at 1 oClock— Several men out to day Hunting & visiting. Mr. Wolpards¹ Boat came up to day at 2 oClock under Sail, Left St Louis at 8 oClock a. m. Some Shooting at a mark

1. Probably Adam Woolford, or Woodford, who operated a boat between St. Louis and Louisville, Kentucky. Jackson (LLC), 1 : 176 n. 5; Osgood (FN), 34 n. 1.

[Clark]¹

Monday 16th a fair morning Some rain last night & hard wind from the S, W. by W. Packed away

1 Keg of Hogs Lard
1 bag of Coffee 50 w
2 do Sugar—
1 do Beens—
7 bags of Biscuit
4 Barrels of Biscuit
1 Bag Candle wick
2 Boxes of candles
″ one part Soap
44 Kegs of Pork packed w. 3115 [*3115 written over 3366*]
6 Half barrels of pork do w 590

Several men confined for Drunkness to day, wind verry hard.

1. The words "(31 candles)" are above the first line of this entry and may be a part of the entry.

[Clark]   [*undated, ca. April 16, 1804*][1]

	Pork	
No.	1.	68
	2.	68
	3.	94
	4.	68
	5.	73
	6.	69
	7.	68
	8.	68
	9.	68
	10.	69
	11.	68
	12.	[*blank*]
	13.	68
	14.	68
	15.	68
	16.	68
	17.	68
	18.	68
	19.	68
	20.	68
	21.	68

22.	68
23.	68
24.	68
25.	68
26.	68
27.	68
28.	68
29.	68
30.	68
31.	68
32.	68
33.	90
34.	90
35.	90
36.	90
37.	68
38.	68
39.	68
40.	68
41.	68
42.	68
43.	68
44.	68
45.	68
46.	90
47.	100
48.	100
49.	100
50.	100
	3605^2
No. 12.	100
	3,705

1. These figures are written crossways at the bottom of the obverse and the top of the reverse of document 11 and are inserted here because Clark appears to have made corrections in his April 15 entry based on these calculations. I have deleted the subtotal at the end of side one.

2. If this is a correct reading of Clark's figures, this subtotal should be 3,603.

[Clark][1]

Tuesday 17th   Reed came from St. Louis at 45 m after 10 oClock with Letters for me from Col. Anderson   I sent out 4 men to hunt a horse to Send to Cap. Lewis, out all day without finding him   makeing a Mast fixing orning & packing Pork to day   The after part of this day Cool

Completed packing fifty Kegs of Pork, & roled & filled them with brine, also packed one Bar: Meal, & one bu Parched [corn] of an inferior quality. (out of the bag 10$[)]

1. There are a few scattered numbers to the side of this entry: 33, 24, and 25.

[Clark]

Wednesday 18th April 1804.   a fair morning.   Newmon Killed a Black Lune [Loone?].[1] Vegetation appears to be Suppriseingly rapid for a fiew days past, R F [Reubin Field? Robert Frazer?] Killed a muskrat.[2] Several of the inhabitents Came to Camp to day. Majr runseys boat fall down one mile to river   Com to Carry to the Salt works. I send Sergt. Floyd & G Shannon with two horses to Capt. Lewis at St. Louis, at 3 oClock Capt Lewis arrive.   the wind from the S. E.   rained the greater Part of this night.

1. There is no American loon that is predominantly black. Probably it is the double-crested cormorant, *Phalacrocorax auritus* [AOU, 120], although the common loon, *Gavia immer* [AOU, 7], is dark gray on its head and back in winter. Less likely this could be the widely distributed American coot, *Fulica americana* [AOU, 221], although the captains later refer to that species as a "black duck" (November 30, 1805, and March 10, 1806). Burroughs, 224–25.
2. *Ondatra zibethicus*. Hall, 2:824–28.

[Clark]

Thursday 19th   a rainy morning   Slept late, Thunder and lightning at 1 oClock, men Shoot at a mark, rain at 2   Setled with Majr. Rumsey &c   rain Continue

[Clark]

Friday 20th   rain last night & this morning.   the river fall Sloly   I have my Sword, Durk [dirk] &c. fixed   rain all day, assort Papers &c.   dark Sultrey weather (took out of the Bag 32$ &[)]   Some Thunder

[Clark]

Satturday 21St   rain all last night Slowley   a Cloudy morning   some rain   river raised last night 12 Inches   at three oClock a Cannon was herd up the Missouris, Soon after Mr. Choteau arrived with 22 Indians, we Saluted them and after Staying one [h]Our, Cap Lewis & myself Set out with them to St Louis, where we arrived before night.[1]

Detachment Orders

[Ordway]   April 21st 1804.

Dureing the absence of the Commanding officers at St. Louis the Party are to be under the immediate Command of Sergeant John Ordway agreeable to the Orders of the 7th Instant

Signed[2]

Wm. Clark Capt

1. Under the April 21–25, 1804, entries on document 11 of the Field Notes, are drawn six numbered boxes, in two rows of three. "Choteau" is probably Jean Pierre Chouteau.
2. Ordway also signed for Clark.

[Clark]   [*April 22, 23, 24, 1804*]

Sundy, mon: & Tuesday, at St Louis

[Clark]

Wednesday 25   at ½ past 12 Set out for Camp, and arrved at night in a Perogue

[Clark]

Thursday 26.   Mr. Hay arrived, river falls,

[Clark]

Friday 27.   prepareing to pack up Indians goods

[Clark]

Saturday 28   Mr. Hay packing up   all hands at work prepareing. Several Country men Came to win my mens money, in doing So lost all they had, with them.   river fall   Say on[1]

1. These last two words appear at the bottom of document 11 and at the top of document 12 of the Field Notes, apparently as a guide to continuity.

[Clark]

Sunday 29th of April 1804, Mr. Hay Still packing up goods, Some Kikapoo Chiefs come down, Wolpards Boat arrive from St Charles.   river Still fall

[Clark]

Monday 30th   a fair day   all hands at work   mr. Hay nearly finish packing up goods [*undetermined word, perhaps* "kunish"]   Mr McClain arrive.   river Still fall

[Lewis and Clark]   [*Weather, April 1804*][1]

Day of the month	Ther-mometr. at ☉· rise	Weather	Wind at Sunrise	Ther-momtr. at 4 oClock	Weather	Wind at 4 oClock	[rise] & fall	River feet	Inchs.
April 1		f	N E		f	N E.	r		2½
2	16 a o	f			f	N E	r		3½
3	50 a o	f	N E		r	N E	r		3½
4	52 a o	c. a. r.	N W				r		11
5	32 a o	c. a. r.	N E		t r		r		2
6	26 a o	c. r.	N W		s a r		f		4½
7	18 a o	f a c	N W		c		f		2
8[2]	18 a o	c	N E		c r		f		2½
9	26 a o	f a c	N E		c		f		2
10	18 a o	f	N W		f		f		6½
11	18 a o	f	N E		f		f		7½
12	24 a o	c	N W		f a c		f		7
13	34 a o	c	N E		c		f		6½
14	30 a o	f	S W		f		f		5
15	30 a o	f	N W				f		6½
16	44 a o	c	N W		f. a. c.		f		5½
17	34 a o	f a c	N W		f		f		5
18[3]	26 a o	f a c	N W W		c		f		3
19	42 a o	r	S S E				f		4
20[4]	42 a o	⟨C⟩ r	S. E	45 a o	r	S E	f		3½
21	39 a o	r	S. W.	50 a o	f a r	W.	r	1	2

22	36 a o	⟨c⟩	N. W.	42 a o	C	N. W.	r	1	6
23	30 a	f.	N. W.	72 a	f	W	f		1
24	44 a	f.	N. W.	52 a	f	N W.	r		8
25	34 a	f.	N W.	46 a	c	N W	r		2½
26	24 a	f.	N W.	66 a	f.	N. W	f		6
27[5]	36 a	t L. r	W.	70 a	f	S W.	f		8
28	38 a	f.	N. W	72 a	f	N. W.	f		7
29	40 a	f	N W	60 a	f	S. E.	f		7
30	26 a	f	S E	64 a	f	N. E.	f		6

[*Remarks*][6]

April 1st The Spicewood is in full bloe, the dogs tooth violet, and may apple[7] appeared above ground, a northern light appeared at 10 0 C P. M. verry red.

2d Capt Lewis went to St Louis. Mr. Hay[s] arrive[8]

3d Mr. Garrous Boat loaded with provisions pass up for Prarie de chien, to trade   a cloudy day[9]

5th the buds of the peaches, apples & Cherrys appear—   wind high[10]

6th a large flock of Pellicans[11] appear.

7th the leaves of Some of the Apple trees have burst their coverts and put foth, the lieves of the green wood bushes have put foth—.   maney of the wild plants have Sprung up and appear above ground.   cold air[12]

9 windey[13]

10th no appearance of the buds of the Osage Apple, the Osage Plumb has put forth their leaves and flower buds.   tho it is not completely in bloe.[14]

13th The peach trees are partly in blume   the brant, Geese, Duck, Swan, Crain and other aquatic birds have disappeared verry much, within a fiew days and have gorn further North I prosume. the Summer duck raise their young in this neighborhood and are now here in great numbers[15]

17th wind verry high every day Since the 3rd instant   Some frost to day[16]   Peach trees in full Bloome, the Weaping Willow has put forth its leaves and are ⅕ of their Sise, the *Violet* the *doves* foot, & *cowslip* are in bloe,[17] the dogs tooth violet is not yet in blume. The trees of the forest particularly the Cotton wood begin to obtain from their Size of their buds a Greenish Cast at a distance— the Gooseberry which is also in this countrey and lilak have put forth their leaves—[18] frost

18   Windey Day   at St Louis[19]

26th   The white frost Killed much froot near Kahokia, while that at St Louis escaped with little injurey—

30th   white frost, Slight did but little injurey—.

1. The table is from Lewis's Weather Diary, kept by Clark until April 20, when Lewis took up the observations and remarks. The temperature readings in Codex C are generally eight degrees below those in the Weather Diary, as in March, but some discrepancies are noted within the table.

2. In Codex C, the sunrise temperature on April 8 is 10° above zero.

3. In Codex C, the sunrise temperature on April 18 is 16° above zero; the sunrise wind direction is north-northwest.

4. In Codex C, under the sunrise weather for April 20, the "C" has not been crossed out.

5. In Codex C, under the sunrise weather for April 27, the middle letter between "t" and "r" is illegible but does not appear to be "L."

6. These remarks are from Codex C, by Clark. There are only a few brief remarks in the Weather Diary for April, and significant variations are noted below.

7. The white dog's-tooth violet, *Erythronium albidum* Nutt., and the mayapple, *Podophyllum peltatum* L., are among the earliest forest floor wildflowers to begin spring growth. Fernald, 436, 673.

8. Codex C says "Hay" and the Weather Diary, "Hays." The entry for this date in the Field Notes confirms the latter.

9. The note about the cloudy day appears only in the Weather Diary.

10. The peaches, apples, and cherries are *Prunus persica* (L.) Patsch, *Pyrus malus* L., and *Prunus avium* L., respectively, and are introduced species that were apparently cultivated in the St. Louis area at the time and viewed there by the captains. In addition to the sweet cherry (*Prunus avium*), *P. mahaleb* L., mahaleb cherry, and *P. cerasus* L., sour cherry, may also have been cultivated. Gleason & Cronquist, 385–87. The note about the wind appears only in the Weather Diary.

11. The American white pelican, *Pelecanus erythrorhynchos* [AOU, 125]. See Lewis's detailed description of this bird on August 8, 1804.

12. The note about cold air appears only in the Weather Diary.

13. This note appears only in the Weather Diary and is repeated or indicated by "do" (ditto) through April 16.

14. The "Osage Apple" (more commonly Osage orange) is *Maclura pomifera* (Raf.) Schneid., bois d'arc, bodark, bowwood, hedge apple, and is thought to be native to Arkansas, Oklahoma, and Texas. The wood is hard, strong, and durable and was valued by Indians for bows and apparently arrows. It was extensively cultivated by early settlers for fencerows and windbreaks. Fernald, 555; Stephens, 152; Gilmore, 24; Steyermark, 563. The "Osage Plumb" is *Prunus angustifolia* Marsh., Chickasaw plum, sandhill plum. Stephens, 282. In March 1804, Lewis sent some cuttings from these plants to Jefferson and described them in some detail after discussions with Jean Pierre Chouteau. It was Chouteau who first introduced the Osage orange to St. Louis. Lewis's excellent descriptions allowed accurate identification of these plants. Lewis to Jefferson, March 26, 1804, Jackson (LLC), 1 : 170–72. It is believed that a row of Osage oranges in the cemetery of St. Peter's Church, Philadelphia (formerly the garden of Bernard McMahon), originated with these cuttings or seeds brought back by Lewis after the expedition. Importantly, these may be the first items Jefferson received that were later combined with other specimens from the expedition and eventually deposited in the Academy of Natural Sciences, Philadelphia. This edition will include a separate volume in which the academy's collection will be discussed and the specimens photographed and identified as closely as possible. Thwaites (LC), 6 : 153; Cutright (LCPN), 61, 373–74.

15. The "Summer duck" is the wood duck.

16. In Codex C, Clark wrote remarks for April 17 and 18 immediately after those for April 3, then crossed them out and wrote a fuller entry for the seventeenth in the proper place. The first part of the entry here (as far as this note) is the first one, the remainder is the second.

17. The weeping willow, *Salix babylonica* L., was apparently cultivated in the St. Louis area as a landscape tree. The violet cannot be identified. The dove's foot is probably *Geranium carolinianum* L., cranesbill. Cowslip is probably *Mertensia virginica* (L.) Pers., Virginia cowslip, taking into consideration its early flowering, the rich soil, and bottomland habitat, as well as its more common eastern distribution. *Dodecatheon meadia* L., American cowslip, is known to the St. Louis area but is much more limited in its eastern distribution and different in habitat requirements. Fernald, 506, 1139; Steyermark, 1254, 1165, 962–63.

18. The cultivated gooseberry is *Ribes grossularia* L. and the lilac is *Syringa vulgaris* L. Since Clark noted them together, they were probably being cultivated in the St. Louis area. The native gooseberry, *Ribes missouriense* Nutt., Missouri gooseberry, however, is also commonly found in the thickets and woodland borders of the area. Fernald, 750, 1150, 749. Steyermark, 785–86.

19. Clark wrote this entry for April 18 after the one for the third (see above, n. 12) and then crossed it out, writing no other in Codex C. The Weather Diary entry says only "windey." On April 18, Clark was not in St. Louis, but at River Dubois, according to his Field Notes. Nor can "at St Louis" belong to the entry for April 5 directly under the words, for Clark was also at River Dubois that day.

[Clark]   [*May 1, 1804*]

Tuesday 31st Some fog this morning   Several Country people arive   I
attempt to ⟨Heel the boat⟩[1]

1. Apparently Clark intended to tilt the boat to one side to work on the bottom.

[Clark]

Wednesday 2nd May   Mr. Hay, Wolpard, & leave Camp to St Louis at
12 oClock   Several *Drunk*   Heel the boat.

[Clark]

Thursday 3rd   I write letters to Sundy Gentlemen by Mr. Choteau[1]
Some wind, rive[r] falling   worked at Boat   hauled her up & examined
the bottom, Mr Lousa [Lisa][2] & other arrive   also Sergt. Floyd from St
Louis with Letters to me.[3] Majr. Rumsey was polite enough to examine all
my provisions   Several Kegs of Pork he Condemed.

1. Probably Jean Pierre Chouteau. One of the letters was probably a letter of introduction for Chouteau dated May 2; internal evidence suggests that Clark wrote from a draft
by Lewis. Clark to William Croghan, May 2, 1804, Jackson (LLC), 1 : 178–79 and headnote.
2. Manuel Lisa, of Spanish descent, was already a fur trader on the Missouri; within a
few years after the return of Lewis and Clark he became the most famous and enterpris-
ing of the pioneers of the trade on the upper Missouri before the War of 1812. By 1807
his Missouri Fur Company had a post on the Yellowstone, and by 1810 his men were
established at the Three Forks of the Missouri. Several former members of the expedition, including George Drouillard, John Potts, Peter Weiser, and John Colter, worked for
him; the first two lost their lives in his service. Lewis apparently had difficulties with Lisa
in St. Louis during this winter of 1803–4 and disliked him intensely, as did many others.
Nonetheless, within a few years, Clark and Lewis's brother Reuben became Lisa's partners in the Missouri Fur Company. During the War of 1812 he rendered valuable service
to the United States by keeping the upper Missouri Indians at peace with the Americans.
Oglesby; Lewis to Clark, May 6, 1804, Jackson (LLC), 1 : 179–80 and n. 2.
3. See Lewis to Clark, May 2, 1804, Jackson (LLC), l:177–78.

[Clark]

Friday 4th   a rainey Day, much Shooting   Several Boats pass down to
day—   the river riseing a little   I send two men to St. Louis with letters
Maps   Salt & [Linen?][1]

[Ordway]   Camp at River a Dubois May the 4th 1804

Orders, Corporal Wareington, Frasier, Boley, & the Detachment late from Captain Stoddards Company will form a mess under the direction of the Corporal, who shall be held accountable for their conduct in Camp.—

Orders. The Sergeants are to mount as officers of the Day During the time we Delay at this place, and whilst on Duty to Command the Detachment in the absence of the Commanding officer— he is to see that the Guard doe their Duty, and that the Detachment attend to the regulations heretofore made and those which may be made from time to time. No man of the Detachment Shall leave Camp without permission from the Commanding officer present, except the French Hands who have families maybe allowed to Stay with their families whilst at this Island

Sergt. Ordway for Duty to Day.   Sergt. Floyd tomorrow & Sergt. Pryor the next day—

Signed[2] Wm. Clark
Capt. Commdg.

1. Conceivably, salt and linen were items the two men were to obtain in St. Louis. The last word might be "Lewis," but if so, the meaning is hard to discern.
2. Ordway also signed for Clark.

[Clark]

Satturday 5th   a Cloudy day   rains at different times   a Sauckee Chief with 8 or 10 arrive & Stay all night   2 Perogus of Kickapoos return from St Louis. I gave 4½ gals whisky & some Tobacco.

[Clark]

Sunday 6th   Several of the Countrey people In Camp Shooting with the party   all git beet and Lose their money   a fair Day

[Clark]

Monday 7th   I Load the Boat all day, a fair Day   Mr. Rumsey ride a public horse[1] to St Louis   a fair day   Sent Sjt. Ordway with a perogue to St Louis after Colter arrived express,[2] & [reed][3] with a Hors & Tallow.

1. Evidently the horse was government property, perhaps one being used by the expedition.

2. Colter came from St. Louis bearing Clark's commission as a second lieutenant and Lewis's letter, which expressed regret that this was not the captain's rank Clark had been led to expect and assured Clark that his authority and pay would be the same as Lewis's. They concealed Clark's rank from the rest of the expedition party. Lewis to Clark, May 6, 1804, Jackson (LLC), 1 : 179–80.

3. The word is nearly illegible, but Moses Reed had accompanied Colter on this trip. Ibid.

[Clark]

Tuesday 8th of May   Load the Boat & one perogue to Day. Verry hot day, after Loading the Boat maned her with 20 oares & went the middle of the river & up the Mississippi a fiew miles, took the different Courses of the rivrs in the point,[1] returned & found Doct. Catlet at Camp.

1. Evidently Clark took practice compass bearings up the Mississippi and Missouri from the point of their junction.

[Clark]

Wednesday 9th   a fair Day   warm. I move the party into tents   Mr. Rumsey & Several other men arrive, Dr. Catlet Set out late for St: Louis. the others Soon after, I send to the Missouries water for drinking water, it being much Cooler than the Mississippi which Keeps possession of about ¼ of the bead [bed] or Channel

[Clark]

Thursday 10th   Some rain last night   Cloudy morning verry hot, in the after part of the day, I continued to fix Tents Covering, adjuust the Load &c. order every man to have 100 Balls for ther Rifles[1] & 2 lb. of Buck Shot for those with mussquets &. F[2]

1. The Corps of Discovery had at least fifteen of the new Model 1803 rifles, the first ones issued; this weapon, the first rifle specifically designed for the U.S. Army, was about .54 caliber with a thirty-three-inch barrel, but the expedition version may have been a predecessor or prototype differing in some respects from the standard issue. The captains sometimes referred to them as short rifles, because they were considerably shorter than the civilian Kentucky long rifles of the period. The captains apparently had their

own Kentucky long rifles, and some of the enlisted men who were already in the army may have brought with them long rifles of the Kentucky type issued to them in their original units. Other enlisted men apparently carried Model 1795 muskets, .69-caliber weapons based on an earlier French design, which were the standard infantry arms. The muskets, which were smoothbores, could be used as shotguns by substituting shot for the single ball. All of these guns were flintlocks. Olson identifies what may possibly be a surviving Model 1803. Russell (GEF), 151–57, 176–82; Russell (FTT), 34–43; Olson; Hult; Lewis's List [June 30, 1803], Jackson (LLC), 1:70.

2. This letter may be simply a doodle.

[Clark]

Friday 11th   a warm morning   I write all day   in the evengn. about 4 oClock a violent gust from the N W by W, [rasd?] the [vestles?] up the Creek Some distance, Seven french arrive with Drewyer—[1]   I send Drewyer and the horse's to St Louis

1. These "french" may have been boatmen recruited by Drouillard in the river settlements.

[Clark]

Sat: 12th   Docr. Catlet Set out at 11 oClock   rain all the evening, I Still arrangeing the Stores &c.

[Clark]

Sunday 13   a rainey Day   a frenchman arrive, Soon after *Hall* from St. Louis with Letters from Capt Lewis   I Send out to enquire for Rumsey &

River a Dubois
opposit the mouth of the Missourie River

[Clark]   *Sunday* May the 13th 1804—[1]

I despatched an express this morning to Capt Lewis at St. Louis, all our provisions goods and equipage on Board of a Boat of 22 oars, [*NB: Party*] a large Perogue of 7 oares [*NB: in which 8 French*] a Second Perogue of 6 oars, [*NB: Soldiers*][2] Complete with Sails &c. &c. men Compe. with Powder Cartragies and 100 Balls each, all in health and readiness to Set out. Boats and every thing Complete, with the necessary Stores of provisions & such articles of merchendize as we thought ourselves autherised to precure—tho' not as much as I think necssy for the multitud of Inds. tho which we must pass on our road across the Continent &. &.

Latd. 38 d 55 19⁶⁄₁₀   North of equator[3]

Longtd. 89   57 45—   West of Greenwich

1. This is the first dated entry in Clark's notebook journal Codex A.

2. The Detachment Orders of May 26, 1804 (see below), indicate substantially the same arrangement of men in the boats, although one or two shifts may have taken place. As Biddle's interlineations indicate, the crew of the keelboat consisted primarily of those intended at the time for the permanent party to the Pacific, in the squads of Sergeants Floyd, Ordway, and Pryor. The larger pirogue, manned by Patroon (foreman) Baptiste Deschamps and seven of his hired French boatmen, is later referred to as the red pirogue. The smaller, or white, pirogue carried Corporal Warfington and his squad of five soldiers, who were then intended to return from somewhere up the Missouri before winter.

3. This latitude and longitude is at the bottom of a page in Codex A; the May 13 entry, apparently written later, had to be interlined with it. The position is probably that of the River Dubois camp, but if so the Captains have placed it too far east. The approximate location is just west of 90° W.

[Clark]

Monday 14th[1]   a Cloudy morning   fixing for a Start   Some provisions on examination is found to be wet   rain at 9 oClock   many of the neighbours Came from the Countrey mail and feemail   rained the greater part of the day, I set out at 4 oClock to the head of the first Island[2] in the Missourie 6 Miles and incamped, on the Island   rained.   I refur to the Comsmt. [commencement] of my Journal No 1.[3]

1. There are two entries for May 14, 1804, in the Field Notes. The first is at the end of document 12 and is considered the end of the Dubois Journal; the second begins document 13 at the beginning of the River Journal. Chapter 4 of this volume will begin with the latter entry for May 14, 1804.

2. Near the mouth of Coldwater Creek, St. Charles County, Missouri, a little above the present town of Fort Bellefontaine and below the crossing of U.S. Highway 67. Osgood (FN), 41 n. 2; MRM map 1.

3. Clark's "Journal No. 1" is now designated Codex A, following Coues. See the Introduction to this volume.

[Lewis and Clark]   [*Weather, May 1804*][1]

day of the month	Ther-mometer at ☉ rise	Weather	Wind at ☉ Rise	Ther-mometer at 4 oCk. P M	Weather	Wind at 4 oCk. P. M	raise or fall	River Feet	Inches
May 1s	28 a	f.	S E	62 a	f	N. E.	f		4½
2	27 a	f.	S E	76 a	f	S S E	f		6
3	32 a	f	S S E	80 a	f	S S W	f		4½
4	48 a	t. l. c. r	S.	64 a	C a r	S	r		2
5	50 a	t l. r	W	66 a	c a r	W	r		2½
6	42 a	f	S. W	78 a	f	S W	f		2½
7	46 a	f	S E	60 a	f	S S W	f		4½
8	52 a	f	N. E	70 a	f	S W	f		4
9	50 a	f	E.	84 a	f	S W	f		2
10	54 a	C	N. E	75 a	f	N. W	f.		3½
11	48 a	f	E	78 a	f	S. W	f.		2½
12	44 a	f	E	80 a	f	W	f		3
13	50	C. a. r.	W	48 a	C a r	N W	f		2
14	42 a	C	S E	64	f	N.	⟨f⟩		o

[*Remarks*][2]

5 The thunder and lightning excessively heard this morning

10 distant thunder, sutery this evening.

12 the wind at 4 was uncomly hard.

14 end of observations at the river Dubois[3]   Set out from the River Dubois up the Missouri

16th arrived at St. Charles[4]

20th rained the after part of the Day   Capt. and Several gentlemen arrive from St. Louis.

21st leave St. Charles   heavy rain in the evening with wind.   great number of Muscators

25h strawbury in the praries ripe and abundant[5]

27h servisburries or wild Courants, ripe and abundant[6]

30th Mulburies begin to ripen, very abundant in the bottom[7]

1. This table for May is based on Lewis's Weather Diary, kept by Lewis. Its temperature readings are consistently eight degrees above those in Clark's Codex C. No observations

were tabulated by either captain after May 14 until September 1804, or at least no such tables have been found.

2. Both captains' remarks for the month of May are substantially the same; here I have followed Lewis's Weather Diary, noting substantive differences. Although tabled observations ceased after May 14, both men continued intermittent remarks on the weather and natural phenomena in the Weather Diary and Codex C weather tables into July. Those are found with the appropriate months.

3. The first part of this remark, as far as the note, is Lewis's, in his Weather Diary; the latter part is Clark's, in Codex C.

4. Clark wrote remarks for May 16, 20, and 21 in his Codex C weather table, then later crossed them out. There are no remarks for those dates in Lewis's Weather Diary.

5. *Fragaria virginiana* var. *illinoensis* (Prince) Gray, wild strawberry. Steyermark, 824.

6. *Amelanchier arborea* (Michx.) Fern., serviceberry, shadbush, sarviceberry, juneberry. Ibid., 800.

7. The common native red mulberry, *Morus rubra* L. It is often confused with *Morus alba* L., white mulberry, a native species of eastern Asia, which is now common in northern and central Missouri. Ibid., 562.

[Clark]   [*undated, ca. May 14, 1804*]

A Memorandum of Articles in readiness for the Voyage[1]

			w
Viz:	14	Bags of Parchmeal of 2 bus: each about	1200
	9	do Common Do do do	800
	11	do Corn Hulled do do	1000
	30	half Barrels of flour ⎱ (Gross 3900 w) do	3400
	3	Bags of do ⎰	
	7	do of Biscuit ⎱ (Gross 650) do	560
	4	Barrels do ⎰	
	7	Barrels of Salt of 2 bus: each " (870) do	750
	50	Kegs of Pork (gross 4500) do	3705
	2	Boxes of Candles 70 lb and about 50 lb (one of which has 50 lb of soap [)] do	170
	1	Bag of Candle-wick do	8
	1	do Coffee	50
	1	do Beens & 1 of Pees	100
	2	do Sugar do	112

1	Keg of Hogs Lard do	100
4	Barrels of Corn hulled (650) do	600
1	do of meal (170) do	150
600	lb Grees	
50	bushels meal	
24	do Natchies Corn Huled	
21	Bales of Indian goods	
	Tools of every Description & &.	

our party

2 Capts. 4 Sergeants, 3 Intptrs., 22 Amns. 9 or 10 French, & York also 1 Corpl. & Six in a perogue with 40 Days provisions for the party as far as the provisions last

1. This list is on the reverse of *Atlas* map 3*a*. On the map side is the endorsement in Clark's hand: "A List of Articles for Missouri voyage." The list is a compilation of other lists scattered throughout earlier entries, but it may also be partial or incomplete. See in particular entries of April 14 and 16 above. Clark's listing four sergeants is probably an error as there were only three, Ordway, Pryor, and Floyd, the latter replaced by Gass at his death on August 20, 1804.

[Clark]   [*undated, ca. May 1804*][1]

Capts. Lewis & Clark wintered at the enterance of a Small river opposit the Mouth of Missouri Called Wood River, where they formed their party, Composed of robust ⟨Young Backwoodsmen of Character⟩ helthy hardy young men, recomended.

The Country about the Mouth of Missouri is pleasent rich and partially Settled. On the East Side of the Mississippi a leavel rich bottom extends back about 3 miles, and rises by Several elevations to the high Country, which is thinly timbered with Oake &. On the lower Side of the Missouri, at about 2 miles back the Country rises graduilly, to a high plesent thinly timberd Country, the lands are generally fine on the River bottoms and well Calculating for farming on the upper Country.

in the point the Bottom is extensive and emencly rich for 15 or 20 miles up each river, and about ⅔ of which is open leavel plains in which the inhabtents of St. Charles & potage de Scioux had ther crops of corn &

wheat. on the upland is a fine farming country partially timbered for Some distance back.

1. This material is at the beginning of Clark's notebook journal Codex A. Since it appears to relate to the period at River Dubois it is placed here. The last paragraph is crowded in above the heading of the first dated entry, for May 13, 1804, and may have been written after that entry.

[Lewis]   [*undated*][1]

Information of Mr. John Hay—commencing at the discharge of the Ottertail Lake, which forms the source of the Red River, to his winter station on the Assinneboin River—

	Leagues
From Ottertail Lake	
To the Shugar rappid	18 —
Buffaloe River—N. Side	10 —
Commencement of shaved prarie	9 —
Expiration of Do. do.	18 —
(Tho' on a streight line not thought more than *6 leagues*)	
Stinking bird river, South side	60 —
(heads with river St. Peters)	
Shayen or Shaha South side	14 —[2]
River au Bouf North side	4 —
Tree River South side	10 —
Wild oates river N. Side	2 —
Goose river South side	7 —
Pond River S. side	1/3
Sand Hill river—not certain but b[e]lieved to be on the South side	5[3]
To the grand fork or *Red Lake River* N. Side	20 —
Turtle river S. Side	3 —
Dirty water river S. side	3 —
Salt water river N. side at the head of this river is a salt spring	18 —
Pierced wood river N. S.	12 —

Pembenar river N. S.	3
To a wintering establishment of the N. W. Company on the S. side	8 —
Paemicon river S. side	3 —
Mr. Reaum⟨e⟩'s Fort S. side 1792	⅓
Pond river S side	14 —
Kuckould burr river S. side	3 ½
Rat river N side	7
Assinniboin N side	16 ½ [4]
Dead river S. side	8
Lake Winnepique	10
From the mouth of the Assinaboin up the same to the mouth of Mouse River S side	139 ½

Notes— [(]1) the general course of the red River from Leaf river to the mouth of the assinnaboin is due West

(2ed) the River Pembenar heads in three large lakes bearing as it proceds upwards towards the Assinnaboin— the first lake three leagues in length and 1 in width— the turtle mountain bearing S W. distnt. 7 leagues— the second smaller lying N N W. not very distant from the former   the third and last [lake] large and extending within a few miles of the mouth of Mouse river branch of the Assinnaboin—

(3) Salt is made in sundry places on the Red river (to [w]it) just below the mouth of river Pembenar on the S. side. head of salt river, also on the South side of the red river a little way below the dirty water river—

1. This undated information on a loose sheet in the Voorhis Collection, Missouri Historical Society, St. Louis, could have been given Lewis at any time during the winter of 1803–4, because Hay visited the camp numerous times and doubtless met with the captain frequently in St. Louis. Hay was describing a journey down the Red River of the North, that is, northward, between Minnesota and North Dakota and into southern Manitoba. The streams mentioned are chiefly tributaries of the Red, many bearing the same names today. References to their being on the north or south side are confusing since the general course of the Red is northward. The geographic features are not identified here because they are outside the expedition's travels. J. Reaume ("Mr. Reaum⟨e⟩'s Fort") was an early fur trader in Minnesota and in 1792 had a post on Leaf River. Innis, 254–55 n. 297. See also Tyrrell; Wallace; MacKay; Davidson; and Coues (NLEH). Additional notes by Clark on this same sheet were made at Fort Mandan, probably from information given to

him by Canadian traders. Those notes and a small map will be placed in the appropriate place in volume 3 of this edition.

2. Here a subtotal of 129.

3. Here a subtotal of 157, after which a new page with the subtotal carried over but not repeated here.

4. Here to the side another subtotal:

$$
\begin{array}{r}
269 \\
\underline{3} \\
707
\end{array}
$$

Lewis was apparently trying to calculate the distance in miles by estimating three miles to a league. His calculation is in error.

[Lewis]   [*undated*]

Memorandoms Misscellanious [1]

Mr. Labaum[2] informs that a Mr. *Teboux* who is at present with Loua-sell[3] up the Missouri can give us much information in relation to that country.—

1. This note is from Codex P, p. 133. The information was probably acquired during the winter at River Dubois and is placed here before the departure from Camp Dubois.

2. Perhaps Louis Le Baume, who in 1801 was operating a salt works on Salt River in northeast Missouri. Houck, 1 : 343 n. 21.

3. For Pierre-Antoine Tabeau, see October 10, 1804. For Régis Loisel, see May 25, 1804.

[Lewis]   [*undated*][1]

The Kickapoo calls a certain water plant[2] with a large Circular floating leaf found in the ponds and marshes in the neighbourhood of Kaskaskias & Cahokia—*Po-kish'-a-co-mah*, of the root of this plant the Indians pre-pare an agreable dish, the root when taken in it's green state is from 8 to 14 inches in circumpherence   is dryed by being exposed to the sun and air or at other times with a slow fire or smoke of the chimnies, it shrinks much in drying—   The root of this plant grows in a horizontal direction near the surface of the rich loam or mud which forms the bottoms of their ponds or morasses, generall three, sometimes four or more of these roots are attatced together by a small root or string of hearder substance of a foot or six inches in length, the root of the plant thus annually pro-gresses shooting out a root from a bud at the extremity of the root of the presceeding years groath, this in the course of the Summer p[r]oduces a new root prepared with a bud for the progression of the next season, also one leaf and one seed stalk the stem of the former supporting or reather attatched to a large green circular leaf 18 inches to two feet in diameter which fl[o]ats while green usually on the serface of the water, the sta[l]k is propotioned to the debth of the water, and of a celindrical form, is an inch and a half in circumpherence at or near it's junction of the root thence regularly tapering to the leaf where it is perhaps not more than an inch, the large fibers of the leaf project from the extremity of the stalk in every direction at right angles from it to the circumpherence of the leaf like rays from the center, there are from twelve to eighteen of those fibers— the leaf is nearly a circle smoth on both sides and even and regular on it's edges— near the same part of the root from which the leaf stalk project the seed stalk dose also— it is about the same size and form of it but usually a foot longer standing erect and bearing it[s] blossum above the surface of the water which I am informed is of a white colour— The seed vessel or matrix is the form of a depressed cone the small extremity of which is attatced to the uper end of the stalk; before it has attained it's groath it resembles an inverted cone but when grown the base obtains a preponderancy and inclining downwards rests it's edge against the stalk— the base is a perfect circular plain from ⟨fifteen to⟩ eighteen to twenty inches in circumpherence in it's succulent state, and from two to three inches in hight— the surface of the cone when dryed by the sun and air after being exposed to the frost is purforated with two circular ranges of globular holes from twenty to 30 in number around one which forms the center placed at the distance of from an eighth to ¼ of an inch assunder, each of those cells contains an oval nut of a light brown colour much resembling a small white oak acorn smothe extreemly heard, and containing a white cernal of an agreeable flavor; these the native frequently eat either in this state or roasted; they frequently eat them also in their succulent state— the bear feed on the leaves of this plant in the spring and summer— in the autumn and winter the Swan, geese, brant, ducks and other acquatic fowls feed on the root— the cone is brown, pitty and extreemly light, and when seperated from the stalks flots on the suface of the water with its base down— the Indians procure it and prepare it for food in the following manner— they enter the bonds [ponds] where it grows, barefooted in autumn, and feel for it among the mud which being soft and the root large and near the surface they readily find it   they easily draw it up it having no fiborus, or colateral roots to attatch it firmly to the mud   they wash and scrape a thin bleack rind off it and cut it croswise into pieces of an inch in length   when it is prepared for the pot it is of a fine white colour boils to a pulp and makes an agreeable soupe in which way it is usually dressed by the natives   when they wish to preserve it for any length of time they cut it in pieces in the manner before discribed string it on bark or leather throngs of a convenient length and hang it to dry in the sun, or expose it to the smoke of their chimnies, when thus dryed it will keep for several years, it is esteemed as nutricius as the pumpkin or squash and is not very dissimilar in taste—   The Chipiways or sateaus call this plant *Wab-bis-sa-pin* or Swan-root—[3]   The ferench or Canadians know it by two names the Pois de Shicoriat or Graine de Volais—   the roots of this plant are from one foot to eighteen inches in length—

The common wild pittatoe[4] also form another article of food in savage life   this they boil untill the skin leaves the pulp easily which it will do in the course of a few minutes   the outer rind which is of a dark brown coulour is then scaped off   the pulp is of a white coulour, the pettatoe thus prepared is exposed on a scaffold to the sun or a slow fire untill it is thoroughly dryed, or at other times strung upon throngs of leather or bark and hung in the roofs of their lodges where by the influence of the fire and smoke it becomes throughly dryed, they are then prepared for use, and will keep perfectly sound many years, these they boil with meat or pound and make an agreeable bread   this pittaitoee may be used in it's green or undryed state without danger provided it be well roasted or boiled—   it produces a vine which runs too a considerable length usually intwining itself about the neighbouring bushes and weeds, the vine is somewhat branched, and in it[s] progress at the distance of $2\frac{1}{2}$ inches it puts forth one leaf stem at right angles with the vine, which is furnished with two par of ovate leaves and turminated by one of a similar shape, these are of a pale green colour not indented on their edges, reather a rough appearance, the vine is small and green except near the ground where it sometime assumes a redish hue—   the fruit is connected by a small liggament at both ends extending for many yards in length and attatching together in some instances six eight or more of these pittaitoes—   it's root is pereniel   the vine annual.

There is also another root[5] found in mashey lands or ponds which is much used by the Kickapoos Chipaways and any other nations as an article of food   it is called by the Chipeways *Moc-cup-pin*[6]   this in it's unprepared state is not only disagreeable to the taste but even dangerous to be taken even in a small quantity; in this state it acts as a powerfull aemetic.   a small quantity will kill a hog yet prepared by the Indians it makes not only an agreeable but a nutricious food—   I have not seen the plant and can therefore only discribe it from information—   the leaf is said to be broad and to float on the water—   the root is from 10 to 12 inches in length and about ⅔ds. as much in thickness—   it has a rough black skin, the pulp is white and of a mealy substance   when properly prepared the preparation is this—   having collected a parsel of these roots you cut and split a sufficient parsel of wood which is set on end as the coliers commence the base of their coal pitts, the [l]engths of these sticks of wood being as nearly the same as you can conveniently cut them and about 4 feet in length thus forming when put together an even surface at top   on this is thrown soft earth of from two to 3 Inches in debth the roots are laid on this and earth thrown over the whole forming the Colliers kiln complete   fire is then communicated to the wood beneath and it is suffered to burn slowly for several days untill the wood is exausted or they concieve their roots are sufficiently cooked—   they then take them out scrape them & cut them into slices crosswise of half an inch thick and laying them on a scaffold of small sticks build small fires under them and dry them untill they become perfectly firm   thus prepared they are fit for uce and will keep for years if not exposed to wet—   they are either boiled to a pulp in their soupe or less boiled eat them with bears oil or venison and bears flesh—   they sometimes pound it and make a bread of it.—

1. This material is found at the beginning of Lewis's Weather Diary and was probably based on information gathered during the winter at Camp Dubois. See Appendix C.

2. *Nelumbo lutea*, first mentioned on January 1, 1804.

3. Ives Goddard III gives the Chippewa word as *waabiziipin*, signifying "swan tuber." See also Smith (EOI), 396, who refers to a species other than *Nelumbo lutea*.

4. *Apios americana* Medic., Indian potato, ground nut, potato-bean. It grows on the banks of streams and floodplains and "is the true *pomme de terre* of the French and the modo or wild potato of the Sioux Indians, and is extensively used as an article of diet."

Report of Commissioner of Agriculture for 1870, quoted in Gilmore, 42–44. See also Fernald, 936; McDermott (GMVF), 125.

5. Probably *Nymphaea tuberosa* Paine, white water lily, tuberous water lily. Although it no longer occurs in Missouri, it is found in pond margins and slow streams along the Platte and Missouri rivers in eastern Nebraska, as well as in Illinois, Indiana, and Ohio. Steyermark, 667–68; Barkley, 16; Fernald, 641.

6. Goddard gives the Chippewa word as *makopin*, signifying "bear tuber." See also Smith (EOI), 399, who refers to a species other than *Nymphaea tuberosa*.

[Clark]   [*undated*][1]

The names of the Forts or British Trading Establishments on the Ossiniboin

		Legs		
1	St quens Fort (La prairie[)][2]	20 from red river		
2.	Mouse River fort[3]	58	do	38
3.	Hump Mountain fort[4]	83	do	25
4.	Catapie River[5] (the rout to the Missouri) 150 miles.	99	do	16
5.	Swan River[6]	114	do	15
6.	Coude de l'homme (or Mans Elbow)[7]	129	do	15
7.	Sourse at Lake Manitou[8]	149	do	20

red river, of Lake Osnehuger[9] 285 Leagues long. (Hay) wooded & low on both Sides.

1. This list is in Clark's Codex C; although undated, it is clearly a condensed version of information received from John Hay during the winter at River Dubois, and so it is placed with other undated material the captains gathered during that time. During the winter of 1803–4, Mackay had provided Lewis and Clark with some extracts from his journals, covering both his activities on the Missouri in 1795–97 and his trading ventures in Canada. Hay, who had also worked for the North West Company in Canada, apparently translated Mackay's journal from French for the captains and added comments based on his own experience. The resulting document was among expedition papers found in Nicholas Biddle's collection that he had not turned over to the American Philosophical Society in 1818; the family later donated these documents to the society (see Appendixes B and C, this volume). Quaife (ECMJ).

This list gives the names or locations of various Hudson's Bay Company and North West Company trading posts in present Manitoba and Saskatchewan, on the Assiniboine

River or in adjacent regions, ca. 1794–95, when Hay was in the region. Clark may have copied the list both for use in mapping and because of the interest the captains took in the fur trade of the area and possible British competition for the trade and allegiance of the Missouri River tribes. Abstracting the information into Codex C may have made for handier reference. See Thompson's map as printed in Coues (NLEH), 3: unpaged.

2. "Quens Fort (La prairie[)]" refers to Fort de la Reine (Queen's Fort), founded by Pierre Gaultier de Varennes, Sieur de la Vérendrye, in 1738, at present Portage de la Prairie, Manitoba, on the Assiniboine. In 1796 the Hudson's Bay Company built a post near the site. The North West Company had a post in the same vicinity. Coues (NLEH), 1:290–91 n. 7; Masson, 1:270.

3. "Mouse River fort" was Assiniboine House, at the mouth of the Souris (Mouse) River where it meets the Assiniboine River in southwest Manitoba, established by the North West Company in 1795. The headquarters of the Hudson's Bay Company's in the same vicinity, Brandon House, was started in 1794. Innis, 154; Coues (NLEH), 1:207–8 n. 9; Masson, 1:272; Davidson, 90; Glover, 157–58 n. 3.

4. "Hump Mountain fort" was Montagne à la Bosse, a North West Company establishment built before 1794 on the Assiniboine about twenty miles west of present Brandon, Manitoba. Masson, 1:273–74; Larocque, 11, 82; Voorhis, 119.

5. "Catapie River" is the Qu'Appelle River of southern Saskatchewan, a tributary of the Assiniboine on which the North West Company established Fort Esperance about 1784, two days' journey by canoe from the mouth. Masson, 1:274–75; Innis, 233; Glover, 157 n. 2; Davidson, 46–47, 50.

6. "Swan River" was apparently the Hudson's Bay Company's Swan River (or Swan Lake) House, built in 1790 on the Swan River a few miles southwest of Swan Lake, in west-central Manitoba. The North West Company also had an establishment on Swan River. Glover, lxxx and n. 1; Coues (NLEH), 1:213, 299–300 n. 15; Innis, 245, 256; Davidson, 109; Voorhis, 168.

7. "Coude de l'homme (or Mans Elbow)" was apparently the North West Company's Fort Alexandria, or Upper House, built in 1780 on the Assiniboine River above a sharp bend called the Elbow, in eastern Saskatchewan. Or, the reference may be to the North West Company's Somerset House, also called Elbow Fort, on the Swan River about fifty miles upstream from Swan Lake, Manitoba. Hay's list, however, reflected the situation as of about 1794–95, and the latter post was not built until 1800. Glover, lxxxi and n. 1; Coues (NLEH), 2:494 and n. 58; Masson, 1:275; Davidson, 109; Voorhis, 165, 168.

8. "Sourse at Lake Manitou" is apparently the Portage of Lake Manitoba, which is the Meadow Portage between Lake Manitoba and Lake Winnipegosis. The post associated with this portage was Fort Dauphin, originally founded by Pierre de la Vérendrye in 1741. Several later North West and Hudson's Bay Company posts were constructed in the vicinity and were also called either Fort Dauphin or Dauphin Lake House. Glover, lxxix and n. 1; Coues (NLEH), 1:175 n. 40, 207 n. 7; Voorhis, 58.

9. "Red river, of Lake Osnehager" is the Red River of the North. The lake's name probably comes from Quinipagou, the Algonquian name of Lake Winnipeg, into which the Red River of the North flows. Thwaites (LC), 6:268–69 n. 1.

Chapter Four

From River Dubois to the Platte

May 14–July 22, 1804

[Clark]   May the 14th—Monday[1]

Set out from Camp River a Dubois at 4 oClock P. M. and proceded up the Missouris under Sail to the first Island in the Missouri and Camped on the upper point opposit a Creek on the South Side below a ledge of limestone rock Called Colewater,[2] made 4½ miles, the Party Consisted of 2, Self one frenchman and 22 Men in the Boat of 20 ores, 1 Serjt. & 7 french in a large Perogue, a Corp and 6 Soldiers in a large Perogue.[3]   a Cloudy rainey day. wind from the N E.   men in high Spirits

[Clark]   *Monday May 14th 1804*[4]

Rained the forepart of the day   I determined to go as far as St. Charles a french Village 7 Leags.[5] up the Missourie, and wait at that place untill Capt. Lewis Could finish the business in which he was obliged to attend to at St Louis and join me by Land from that place 24 miles; by this move-ment I calculated that if any alterations in the loading of the Vestles or other Changes necessary, that they might be made at St. Charles

I Set out at 4 oClock P. M. in the presence of many of the Neighbouring inhabitents, and proceeded on under a jentle brease up the Missourie to the upper Point of the 1st Island 4 Miles and Camped on the Island which is Situated Close on the right (or Starboard) Side, and opposit the mouth of a Small Creek called Cold water, a heavy rain this after-noon

The Course of this day nearly *West*   wind from N. E

[Lewis]   [*undated, ca. May 14, 1804*][6]

The mouth of the River Dubois opposite to the mouth of the Missouri River is situated in—

Longitude West from Grenwh.	89°	57′	45″
Latitude N.	38°	55′	19.6″

Note—The *Longitude* of the mouth of the River Dubois was calculated from four sets of observations of the ☉ & ☽, in which the ☉ was twice West, and twice East; two sets with Aldebaran, ☆ East in one, and W. in the other; and one set with Spica, ☆, ☆ East. the Longtd. above stated is the mean result of those observations, and I think may with safety be depended on to two or three minutes of a degree. The Chronometer's error on M. T. was found at the mouth of the Ohio by 3 sets of Equal Altitudes, and the Longtd. of the mouth of the River Dubois as given by this instrument from Equal altitudes of the ☉ on the 17th of December 1803 was 90° 00′ 20″. West from Grenwh. making a difference from the Longitude calculated from observation of 2′ 35″—

The *Latitude* is deduced from a number of Meridian altitudes of the ☉, taken with the sextant and artificial horizon, the results of which observations seldom differed more than from 15 to 20″; I therefore believe that the Latitude above stated may be depended on as true to 100 hundred paces.—

The mouth of the River Dubois is to be considered as the point of *departure*.

1. The first entry of the Field Notes (River Journal), written at the head of document 13. At the top of the sheet is the notation, apparently by Nicholas Biddle, "May 14 to 25th"; Biddle probably added those notations to most of the documents of the River Journal to make it readily apparent the dates each sheet covered. He did not do that with the Dubois Journal sheets, although he probably did examine them, because his narrative dealt only with the expedition proper, beginning May 14, 1804. Osgood (FN), 41.

2. Probably the St. Louis limestone of middle Mississippian age. See also the first entry for May 14 in Chapter 3.

3. Because of discrepancies in the records and journals, especially concerning the French boatmen, it is difficult to determine exactly the number of men who left River Dubois with Clark. George Drouillard was absent on an errand and may not be the Frenchman singled out by Clark; possibly he was Baptiste Deschamps, the patroon (fore-

man) of the hired French boatmen, although later he seems to have been in charge of a pirogue (see May 26, 1804, Detachment Order, below). The exact number and names of the French boatmen remain unclear throughout (see Apendix A, this volume). Clark may not have counted York, his personal servant, in his total. Among those leaving Wood River, besides Clark and York, were twenty-five members of the permanent party, as then planned, who were to make the full trip to the Pacific: Sergeants Floyd, Ordway, and Pryor, and Privates Bratton, Collins, Colter, Reubin and Joseph Field, Gass, Gibson, Goodrich, Hall, Howard, McNeal, Newman, Potts, Reed, Shannon, Shields, Thompson, Werner, Whitehouse, Willard, Windsor, and Weiser. Corporal Richard Warfington's detachment, who were to return from some point up the Missouri with dispatches, then included Privates Boley, Dame, Frazer, Tuttle, and White. Private John Robertson (Robinson) may also have been present at this time; perhaps he was one of the six soldiers in a pirogue—probably Warfington's squad. (See sketch of Robertson, Appendix A, this volume.) The enlisted men's journals all state that there were three sergeants and thirty-eight "working hands"; whether York counted as a working hand is not clear. If one counts twenty-five in the permanent party and seven men in Warfington's detachment, nine French boatmen are necessary for the three sergeants and thirty-eight hands. Adding York, one has forty-two men leaving River Dubois with Clark. Other Frenchmen may have been hired at St. Charles, notably Pierre Cruzatte and François Labiche, who became members of the permanent party. Appleman (LC), 367 n. 64.

4. This May 14 entry is in Clark's notebook Codex A. Clark's entries from the Field Notes will uniformly come first and notebook journal entries second for each date, reflecting the probable order of composition.

5. A league is a variable measure of about three miles. That must have been Clark's usage since his mileage tables show St. Charles as being twenty-one miles above St. Louis.

6. Undated astronomical note in Codex O. See Appendix C, Lewis's description of astronomical instruments, July 22, 1804, and notes with the November 15, 1803, entry. It is placed in this chapter because here began the leaders' regular astronomical observations at their "point of departure." Observations from Codex O are normally placed after the regular daily entries.

[Lewis]   *Tuesday May 15th*[1]

It rained during the greater part of last night and continued untill 7 OCk. A. M. after which the Prarty proceeded, passed two Islands[2] and incamped on the Stard. shore at Mr. Fifer's landing[3] opposite an Island, the evening was fair. some wild gees[4] with their young brudes were seen today. the barge run foul three several times ⟨today⟩—on logs, and in one instance it was with much difficulty they could get her off; happily no injury was sustained, tho' the barge was several minutes in eminent danger; this was cased by her being too heavily laden in the stern. Persons accustomed to the navigation of the Missouri and the Mississippi also be-low the mouth of this river, uniformly take the precaution to load their vessels heavyest in the bow when they ascend the stream in order to avoid the danger incedent to runing foul of the concealed timber which lyes in great quantities in the beds of these rivers

[Clark]

Tuesday 15— rained all last night and this morning untill 7 oClock, all our fire extinguished, Some Provisions on the top of the Perogus wet, I sent two men to the Countrey to hunt, & proceed on at 9 oClock, and proceeded on 9 miles and Camped at a Mr Pip:[er's] Landing just below a Coal Bank[5] on the South Side   the prarie Comes with ¼ of a mile of the river on the N. Side   I sent to the Setlements in the Pairie & purchased fowls &.   one of the Perogue are not Sufficently maned to Keep up.

*Course Distance and time ascending the Missouri River[6]

Tuesday May the 15th 1804

Course	Distance	Time	Remarks & refurences*
	mes	h m	
West	1 0	0 25	to point on Stbd Side, passed the bend of the Is-land High Lands on the Larbord Side
N. 18° W	2 0	1 5	to a pt. on Stb: Side opposit an Island (2) a Sand Bar in the Midlle
N. 11 W	2 ½	20	a Pot [point] Stbd. Side
N. 20 W	1 ½	1 40	Point on the Larboard Side passed an Island (3)—[7]
S 10 W	1 ½	0 50	Point on the Starboard (4)
S 22 W	1 0	1 0	to Point on Stbd Side passed an Island[8] near the
	9 ½	6 20	middle of the River (5)

Refurences from the 15th of May   (2) a large Island to the Starboard; (3) passed a Small Island in the bend to the Starbord, opposit *Passage De*

Soux[9] and with[in] 1 ½ miles of the mississippi, observed a number of Gos-selins on the edge of the river   many passing down, Strong water & wind from the N E—(4) Passed a Place Lbord Called the Plattes, a flat rock projecting from the foot of a hill, where there is a farm,[10] (5) pass an Small Isld near the Center of the river, run on Several logs this after noon, Camped at Mr. Pipers Landing.

[Clark]   *May* 15th *Tuesday*

Rained the greater part of the last night, and this morning untile 7 oClock—   at 9 oClock Set out and proceeded on 9 miles   passed two Islands & incamped on the Starbd. Side at a Mr. Pipers Landing opposit an Island, the Boat run on Logs three times to day, owing her being too heavyly loaded a Sturn, a fair after noon, I Saw a number of Goslings to day on the Shore, the water excessively rapid, & Banks falling in—.

Course & Distance assending the Missourie Tuesday 15th May—

Course	mes	
West	1 0	To a pt. on St. Side
N. 80° W	2 0	To a pt. on St. Side
N. 11° W	2 ½	To a pt. on Stbd Side
N. 20° W	1 ½	To a pt. on Lbd. Side
S. 10° W	1 ½	To a pt. on Stbd. Side
S. 22° W	1 0	To a pt. on Stbd. Side
	9 ½	(See *Suplemt. in* No. 3)[11]

1. This entry is in Lewis's fragmentary Codex Aa (see Appendix C, this volume). It comes after the more extensive entry for May 20—these are the only two entries in the codex—and apparently was written after that entry, since Lewis would not have had the information on which to base it until he joined the party on the twentieth. Perhaps he considered the fifteenth to be the actual date of starting out and thought his journal should have an entry for that day. See the Introduction to this volume.

2. One of the two islands may be Pelican Island. See MRC map 1.

3. Probably James Piper, as Clark gives his name, who was in Missouri by 1798 and owned land in the St. Charles district on the Missouri River. The island may have been the Charbonnier Island of later times, and the camp was in St. Charles County, Missouri, some five miles downstream from the town of St. Charles. The continual changes of the

lower Missouri and the lack of any route maps by Clark for this part of the trip greatly complicate the location of points mentioned. The camp is on the starboard, or right-hand side of the boat, which is bound upstream. Houck, 2:101 n. 44; Osgood (FN), 41 n. 5; MRC map 2.

4. Probably the Canada goose, with which the captains were already familiar. Burroughs, 193.

5. Probably what was later called Charbonnier Point, in St. Charles County. MRC map 2.

6. This material is separated from the rest of the entry for May 15 on this sheet (document 13) of the Field Notes. At this point Clark apparently tried to keep his course entry separated from daily events; later he would place courses and distances and the daily narrative of events together. The asterisks in this section are probably keyed to one after the dateline for May 16, indicating that the course material should precede it.

7. Perhaps Pelican Island.

8. Perhaps Charbonnier Island; see above, n. 3.

9. The village of Portage des Sioux was established by Spanish authorities in 1799 in the mistaken belief that the Americans would build a fort on the east side of the Mississippi. François Saucier was the founder and served as commandant until the American occupation. The area east of the town, between the Mississippi and the Missouri rivers, was also the property of the town and is also called Portage des Sioux. The area served as a portage between the Mississippi and Missouri rivers and shortened a twenty-five-mile water trip to a two-mile crossing by foot. The present town is on the Mississippi River in St. Charles County. Houck, 2:91; *Missouri Guide*, 343–44; MRC map 1.

10. In the vicinity of what was later called Car of Commerce Point, in St. Charles County. MRC map 2.

11. This reference, undoubtedly inserted later, is to Lewis's Codex Aa, which was originally in Codex C (number 3 in Clark's numbering system—see Introduction and Appendix C, this volume).

[Clark]   Wednesday May 16th*

A fair morning, Set out at 5 oClock   passed the Coal hill (Call by the natives Carbonear [Charbonnier])   this hill appears to Contain great quantytes of Coal, and also ore of a rich appearance haveing greatly the resemblance of Silver[1]   Arrived Opposit St Charles[2] at 12 oClock, this Village is at the foot of a Hill from which it takes its real name *Peeteite Coete* [Petite Côte] or the *little hill*, it contains about 100 indefferent houses, and abot 450 Inhabetents principally frinch, those people appear pore and extreemly kind, the Countrey around I am told is butifull. interspursed with Praries & timber alturnetly and has a number of American Settlers Took equal altituds with Sextion M a [median altitude?] 68° 37° 30″   Dined with the Comdr.[3] & Mr. Ducetts family—[4]

					h	′	″
A M	7°	55′	6″	P M	4	4	35
	7	57	35		4	6	0
	7	58	49		4	4	19[5]

Course Distance and time assending the Missouris the 16th of May last 1804

Course	Distance	Time	remarks &c
South	2 0	1 5	to Pt L: Side opsd. a Cole bank[6] after passing the head of the Sd. Island, and a Drift wood abov
S 85 W	7 0	3 25	to the Center of St Charles. ⟨½⟩ (1)

(1) Passed an Island on the L Side[7] just above the bank one just above, two Small ones oposut under the St. Shore, one on Lb. Side below St Charles, arrived at this place at 12 oClock   a fine Day

[Clark]   May 16th *Wednesday*

a fair morning   Set out at 5 oClk   pass a remarkable Coal Hill on the Larboard Side Called by the French Carbonere, this hill appear to Contain great quantity of Coal & ore of a [*blank*] appearance[8]   from this hill the village of St Charles may be Seen at 7 miles distance—   we arrived at St. Charles at 12 oClock   a number Spectators french & Indians flocked to the bank to See the party. This Village is about one mile in length, Situated on the North Side of the Missourie at the foot of a hill from which it takes its name *Petiete Coete* [*NB: petite côte*] or the *Little hill*   This village Contns. about 100 [*NB: frame*] houses, the most of them Small and indefferent and about 450 inhabitents Chiefly French, those people appear pore, polite & harmonious—   I was invited to Dine with a Mr. Ducett [*NB: Duquet*]   this gentleman was once a merchant from Canadia, from misfortunes aded to the loss of a Cargo Sold to the late Judge Turner[9] he has become Somewhat reduced, he has a Charming wife an eligent Situation on the hill Serounded by orchards & a excellent gardain.

Course & Distance assending the Missourie the 16th of May—

Course	ms	
South.	2 0	to a pt. on Lbd Side
S. 85° W.	7 0	To the mid: of St. Charles passed much hard water & 3 Isds.
	9 0	

St. Charles

[Ordway]   *May 16th 1804*[10]

☞ Note the Commanding officer is full assured that every man of his detachment will have a true respect for their own Dignity and not make it necessary for him to leave St. Charles—for a more retired Situation—

W. C.

1. A coal bed above the base of the Pennsylvanian rocks was mined for a few years in the vicinity of Charbonnier. Abundant pyrite was reported from the shales associated with the coal bed. Some pyrite is very pale yellow, nearly silvery, as is marcasite, a second mineral with the same composition but with a different crystal form. Both pyrite and marcasite are often associated with coal-bearing rocks. See Osgood (FN), 41 n. 7.

2. St. Charles was the earliest white settlement west of the Mississippi and north of the Missouri. As Clark notes, the place was first called *Les Petites Côtes* (the Little Hills). In 1787, Auguste Chouteau surveyed the settlement, and soon after the district of St. Charles was established. The parish church, and hence the settlement, was named for St. Charles Borromeo. To the Spanish it was San Carlos del Misuri. By the time of the Louisiana Purchase, the French inhabitants of the town were surrounded by American settlers in the countryside, including Daniel Boone and his family who had settled in the area in the late 1790s. *Missouri Guide*, 260–64; Houck, 2:79–86; Osgood (FN), 41 n. 8.

3. The commandant at St. Charles was Charles, or Don Carlos, Tayon, of French-Canadian extraction and one of the original settlers of St. Louis. He entered the Spanish military service in 1770, fought the British and their Indian allies in the Revolutionary War, and as a reward was given a regular rank as a sublieutenant. He became commandant at St. Charles in 1793. Houck, 2:9, 42–44, 81–82.

4. François Duquette, a Canadian, after residing for a time at Ste. Genevieve, came to St. Charles in 1796. He set up a windmill for grinding grain and was one of the little community's most prosperous citizens before the misfortune Clark alludes to in the following entry for May 16. Ibid., 2:85–86, 257; *Missouri Guide*, 267.

5. A symbol here refers to the courses and distances for the day, on another portion of the same sheet (document 13).

6. At Charbonnier Point, just above Charbonnier Island. MRC map 2.

7. Perhaps Vingt-un, or Holmes, Island. Ibid.

8. Biddle has crossed out from the ampersand to "appearance," added a period there, and capitalized the *f* in "from."

9. George Turner was a federal judge in the Northwest Territory, his circuit including Kaskaskia, in the 1790s. Williams, 512–13; Nasatir (BLC), 1:316–17; Diller (NM), 178.

10. This Orderly Book order and Clark's initials are in Ordway's hand. The warning, as will be seen, was not heeded.

[Clark]

Thursday the 17th 1804   a fine Day   3 men Confined for misconduct, I had a Court martial & punishment   Several Indians, who informed me that the Saukees [Sauks] had lately Crossed to war against the Osage Nation   Som aplicasions,[1] I took equal altitudes   made the m a. to be 84° 39′ 15″

A M	8 H	35	40		P M	3	23	24
″	″	37	50		″	″	24	50
″	″	8	20		″	″	25	50

measured the Missouries at this place and made it 720 yards wide, in Banks.   a Boat came up this evening, I punished Hall[2] agreeable to his Sentence in part, a fine after noon; Suped with Mr. Ducett an agreeable man more agreeable Lady, this Gentleman has a Delightfull Situation & garden.

[Clark]   *May the 17th Thursday 1804*

a fair day   Compelled to punish for misconduct. Several Kickapoos Indians Visit me to day, George Drewyer arrive. Took equal altitudes of Suns L L made it 84° 39′ 15″ ap T.

	h	′	″			h	′	″
A. M.	8	35	40		P M	3	23	24
″	8	37	50		″	3	24	50
	8	38	20		″	3	25	50

Measured the river   found it to be 720 yards wide, a Keel Boat Came up to day—   Several of the inhabitents Came abord to day   receved Several Speces of Vegatables from the inhabitents to day

[Ordway]   *Orders* St. *Charles Thursdy* the 17th of May 1804—[3]

a Sergeant and four men of the Party destined for the Missourri Expidition will convene at 11 oClock to day on the quarter Deck of the Boat, and form themselves into a Court martial to hear and determine (in behalf of the Capt.) the evidences aduced against William Warner & Hugh Hall for being absent last night without leave; contrary to orders;—& John Collins 1st for being absent without leave—   2nd for behaveing in an unbecomeing manner at the Ball last night— 3rdly for Speaking in a language last night after his return tending to bring into disrespect the orders of the Commanding officer

Signd. W. Clark Comdg.
Detail for Court martial

Segt. John Ordway Prs.

members
R. Fields
R. Windsor
J. Whitehouse
Jo. Potts

The Court convened agreeable to orders on the 17th of May 1804 Sgt. John Ordway P. *members* Joseph Whitehouse Rueben Fields Potts Richard Windsor

after being duly Sworn the Court proceded to the trial of William Warner & Hugh Hall on the following Charges Viz: for being absent without leave last night contrary to orders, to this Charge the Prisoners plead *Guilty.* The Court one of oppinion that the Prisoners Warner & Hall are Both Guilty of being absent from camp without leave it being a breach of the Rules and articles of war and do Sentence them Each to receive twenty-five *lashes* on their naked back, but the Court recommend them from their former Good conduct, to the mercy of the commanding officer.— at the Same court was tried John Collins Charged 1st for being absent without leave— 2d. for behaveing in an unbecomming manner at the ball last night 3dly for Speaking in a languguage after his return to camp tending to bring into disrespect the orders of the Commanding officer— The Prisoner Pleads Guilty to the first Charge but not Guilty to the two last chrges.— after mature deliberation & agreeable to the evidence aduced. The Court are of oppinion that the Prisnair is Guilty of all the charges alledged against him it being a breach of the rules & articles of War and do Sentence him to receive fifty lashes on his naked back— The Commanding officer approves of the proceedings & Desicon of the Court *martial and orders* that the punishment of John Collins take place this evening at *Sun Set* in the Presence of the Party.— The punishment ordered to be inflicted on William Warner & Hugh Hall, is remitted under the assurance arriveing from a confidence which the Commanding officer has of the Sincerity of the recommendation from the Court.— after the punishment, Warner Hall & Collins will return to their squads and Duty—

The Court is Disolved.

Sign. Wm. Clark

1. Perhaps applications to join the expedition.

2. Probably a mistake; the court-martial record below says that Hall and Werner were to be granted leniency and only Collins was to be punished. None of the enlisted men's journals mention the affair.

3. The order and court-martial record in the Orderly Book, including the signatures, are in Ordway's hand.

[Clark]

Friday May the 18th 1804 a fine morning took equal altitude and made it 97° 42′ 37″ M. A—

A M.	9	9m	51″	P M.	2	49′	24″
	9	10	16		2	50	50
	9	11	34		2	51	0

I had the Boat & Pierogue reloded So as to Cause them to be heavyer in bow than asturn recved of Mr. Lyon[1] 136 lb. Tobacco on act. of Mr. Choteau[2] Gave out tin Cups & 3 Knives to the French hands, Mr. Lauriesme [Lorimier] returned from the Kickapoo Town to day[3] [He] delayed a Short time & Set out for St. Louis, I Sent George Drewyer with Mr. Lauriesmus to St Louis & wrote to Cap Lewis Mr. Ducett made me a present of rivr Catts[4] & Some *Herbs* our french hands bring me eggs milk &c. &. to day The wind hard from the S. W. Two Keel Boats came up to this place to day from Kentucky

[Clark] *May* the 18th *Friday* 1804

a fine morning, I had the loading in the Boat & perogue examined and changed So as the Bow of each may be heavyer laded than the Stern, Mr. Lauremus who had been Sent by Cap Lewis to the Kickapoo Town on public business return'd and after a Short delay proceeded on to St Louis, I Sent George Drewyer with a Letter to Capt Lewis Two Keel Boats arrive

from Kentucky to day loaded with whiskey Hats &c. &.   the wind from the
S W.   Took equal altitudes with Sexetn Made it 97° 42' 37" M T.

	h	'	"			h	'	"
A. M.	9	9	51		P M.	2	49	24
	9	10	16			2	50	50
	9	11	34			2	51	10

Error of Sextion 8' 45"—

(*Point of Observation No. 1*)

[Lewis]   St. Charles May 18th 1804[5]

Observed equal Altitudes of the ☉ with Sextant.

	h	m	s			h	m	s
A M.	9	9	51		P. M.	2	49	24
	"	10	16			"	50	50
	"	11	34			"	51	10

Altd. by Sextt. at the time of this Observt.   97° 42 37
Result.

		m	s
Chronometer too fast M. T.		4	18.7
Longtd. by Chrotr. W. from Grent.	90°	15'	7"
Latd. by Hor. ∠ P. M. Obstn. of ☉'s Cent.	38°	54'	39"

1. Probably Matthew Lyon, who at this period was a resident of Kentucky and had a contract for army supplies. An Irish immigrant, Lyon gained fame in the 1790s as a Republican congressman and journalist from Vermont who stoutly opposed the Federalists, President John Adams, and the Alien and Sedition Acts, even to the point of going to jail. Jackson (LLC), 1 : 168 n. 1; Osgood (FN), 42 n. 3; Austin.

2. Both Auguste and Pierre Chouteau were later reimbursed for expenditures of about this date. Lewis's Account [August 5, 1807], Jackson (LLC), 2 : 420.

3. Apparently Lorimier had been on a mission to the Kickapoos for the United States. The wandering Kickapoos had various settlements in Missouri about this time, and the location of this one is hard to determine. See March 21, 1804. There was a village near Ste. Genevieve, but Lorimier would not have passed by St. Charles in returning from there to his home in Cape Girardeau; nor would he have passed a settlement on the Gasconnade River southwest of St. Louis. A location north of the Missouri River seems more likely. See May 22, 1804. Gibson, 22–23, 32, 38, 46, 52; Houck, 1 : 362.

4. Perhaps the channel catfish, but later on (see July 24, 1804) this fish is treated as if it were previously unknown. Lee et al., 439; Cutright (LCPN), 425.

5. Since Lewis did not actually arrive at St. Charles until May 20, Clark probably made the observation, which Lewis later copied into this Codex O entry.

[Clark]

Satturday   May the 19th 1804   a Violent Wind last night from the W. S W, Succceeded by rain with [which] lasted Som hours, a Cloudy Morning, many persons Came to the boat to day   I took equal altitudes. mar time 76° 33′ 7″

A M—	8	12′	50″		P M—	3	45	59
″	8	14	9		″	3	46	22
″	8	15	30		″	3	47	41

I heard of my Brothers illness to day which has given me much Concurn,[1] I settle with the men and take receipts for Pay up to the 1st of Decr. next, I am invited to a ball in the Village, let Several of the men go,—[2]   R Fields Kill a Deer   George Drewyear returned with a hundred Dollars, he lost

[Clark][3]

We the Subscribes do acknowledge to have received of Capt. ⟨following⟩ Several Sums mentioned against our respective names, in Liew of Cloathing and rations not Drawn, and Due us for the respective periods herein expressed—for which we have Signed triplicate receipts this 19th of May 1804   St Charles—

		Term paid			amt.				
	Commencement	for	Day & Mo		reived				
Names	of Service	mon	Day	Dollars	Do	Cts.	Signer Names	Witness	

[Clark]   *May 19th Satturday 1804*

A Violent Wind last night from the W. S. W. accompanied with rain which lasted about three hours   Cleared away this morn'g at 8 oClock, I took receipt for the pay of the men up to the 1St. of Decr. next, R. Fields Kill a Deer to day, I recve an invitation to a Ball, it is not in my power to go. George Drewyer return from St Louis and brought 99 Dollars, he lost a letter from Cap Lewis to me, Seven Ladies visit me to day

Took equal altituds of ⊙ L. L & made it 76° 33′ 7″

	h				h		
A M	8	12	20	P M.	3	45	49
	8	14	9		3	46	22
	8	15	30		3	47	41

Error of Sexton as usial—

1. There is no record of any illness of either Jonathan or George Rogers Clark at this time. Clark refers to this brother's recovery in a letter of May 21, 1804, without giving his name. Osgood (FN), 43 n. 6; Clark to William Croghan, May 21, 1804, Jackson (LLC), 1 : 195–96.

2. Whitehouse was probably among them, although he has dated the entry May 18. He refers to "verry agreeable dancing with the french ladies, &c."

3. This paragraph and the form following it are found together on a separate part of the same sheet (document 13) as the May 19 entry; they are evidently a first draft for the pay receipts referred to above, May 19.

[Lewis]   *Sunday May 20th 1804*[1]

The morning was fair, and the weather pleasent; at 10 oCk A M. agreeably to an appointment of the preceeding day, I was joined by Capt. Stoddard, Lieuts. Milford[2] & Worrell[3] together with Messrs. A. Chouteau, C. Gratiot, and many other respectable inhabitants of St. Louis, who had engaged to accompany me to the Vilage of St. Charles; accordingly at 12 Oclk after bidding an affectionate adieu to my Hostis, that excellent woman the spouse of Mr. Peter Chouteau,[4] and some of my fair friends of St. Louis, we set forward to that village in order to join my friend companion and fellow labourer Capt. William Clark who had previously arrived at that place with the party destined for the discovery of the interior of the continent of North America   the first 5 miles of our rout laid through a beatifull high leavel and fertile prarie which incircles the town of St. Louis from N. W. to S. E.   the lands through which we then passed are somewhat broken up fertile   the plains and woodlands are here indiscriminately interspersed untill you arrive within three miles of the vilage when the woodland commences and continues to the Missouri the latter is extreamly fertile. At half after one P. M. our progress was interrupted [*hole*]   the near approach of a violent thunder storm from the N. W. and concluded to take shelter in a little cabbin hard by untill the rain should be over; accordingly we alighted and remained about an hour and a half and regailed ourselves with a could collation which we had taken the precaution to bring with us from St. Louis.

The clouds continued to follow each other in rapaid succession, insomuch that there was but little prospect of it's ceasing to rain this evening; as I had determined to reach St. Charles this evening and knowing that there was now no time to be lost I set forward in the rain, most of the gentlemen continued with me, we arrived at half after six and joined Capt Clark, found the party in good health and sperits. suped this evening with Monsr. Charles Tayong a Spanish Ensign & late Commandant of St. Charles at an early hour I retired to rest on board the barge— St. Charles is situated on the North bank of the Missouri 21 Miles above it's junction with the Mississippi, and about the same distance N. W. from St. Louis; it is bisected by one principal street about a mile in length runing nearly parrallel with the river, the plain on which it stands—is narrow tho' sufficiently elivated to secure it against the annual inundations of the river, which usually happen in the month of June, and in the rear it is terminated by a range of small hills, hence the appellation of *petit Cote*, a name by which this vilage is better known to the French inhabitants of the Illinois than that of St. Charles. The Vilage contains a Chappel, one hundred dwelling houses, and about 450 inhabitants; their houses are generally small and but illy constructed; a great majority of the inhabitants are miserably pour, illiterate and when at home excessively lazy, tho' they are polite hospitable and by no means deficient in point of natural genious, they live in a perfect state of harmony among each other; and plase as implicit confidence in the doctrines of their speritual pastor, the Roman Catholic priest, as they yeald passive obedience to the will of their temporal master the commandant. a small garden of vegetables is the usual extent of their cultivation, and this is commonly imposed on the old men and boys; the men in the vigor of life consider the cultivation of the earth a degrading occupation, and in order to gain the necessary subsistence for themselves and families, either undertake hunting voyages on their own account, or engage themselves as hirelings to such persons as possess sufficient capital to extend their traffic to the natives of the interior parts of the country; on those voyages in either case, they are frequently absent from their families or homes the term of six twelve or eighteen months and alwas subjected to severe and incessant labour, exposed to the ferosity of the lawless savages, the vicissitudes of weather and climate, and dependant on chance or accident alone for food, raiment or relief in the event of malady. These people are principally the decendants of the Canadian French, and it is not an inconsiderable proportian of them that can boast a small dash of the pure blood of the aboriginees of America. On consulting with my friend Capt. C. I found it necessary that we should pospone our departure untill 2 P M. the next day and accordingly gave orders to the party to hold themselves in readiness to depart at that hour.—

Captn. Clark now informed me that having gotten all the stores on board the Barge and perogues on the evening of the 13th of May he determined to leave our winter cantainment at the mouth of River Dubois the next day, and to ascend the Missouri as far as the Vilage of St. Charles, where as it had been previously concerted between us, he was to wait my arrival; this movement while it advanced us a small distance on our rout, would also enable him to determine whether the vessels had been judiciously loaded and if not timely to make the necessary alterations; accordingly at 4 P. M. on Monday the 14th of May 1804, he embarked with the party in the presence of a number of the neighbouring Citizens who had assembled to witness his departure. during the fore part of this day it rained excessively hard. In my last letter to the President dated at St. Louis I mentioned the departure of Capt. Clark from River Dubois on the 15th Inst,[5] which was the day that had been calculated on, but having completed the arrangements a day earlyer he departed on the 14th as before mentioned. On the evening of the 14th the party halted and encamped on the upper point of the first Island which lyes near the Larbord shore,[6] on the same side and nearly opposite the center of this Island a small Creek disimbogues called Couldwater.

The course and distance of this day was West 4 Miles   the Wind from N. E.

[Clark]   *Sunday 20th May*

a Cloudy morning   rained and a hard wind last night   I continue to write Rolls, Send 20 men to Church to day[7]   one man Sick   Capt Lewis and Several Gentlemen arrive from St Louis thro a violent Shoure of rain, the most of the party go to the Church.

[Clark]   *Sunday 20th May [NB: at St Charles]*

A Cloudy morning rained and hard wind from the [*blank*] last night, The letter George lost yesterday found by a Country man, I gave the party leave to go and hear a Sermon to day delivered by Mr. [*blank*] a romon Carthlick Priest   at 3 oClock Capt. Lewis Capt. Stoddard accompanied by the Officers & Several Gentlemen of St Louis arrived in a heavy Showr of Rain   Mssr. Lutenants Minford & Werness. Mr. Choteau Grattiot, Deloney, LaberDee Ranken[8] Dr. SoDrang[9]

rained the greater part of this evening. Suped with Mr. Charles Tayon, the late Comdt. of S: Charles a Spanish Ensign.

1. This entry occupies the major portion of Lewis's fragmentary Codex Aa. See Introduction and Appendix C, this volume.

2. "Milford" to Lewis and "Minford" to Clark, he was Clarence Mulford, first commissioned in 1800, from the state of New Jersey. In 1804 he was a lieutenant in Captain Amos Stoddard's artillery company; he resigned in 1811. Heitman, 482.

3. Stephen Worrell, of Pennsylvania, was another of Stoddard's junior officers. He was appointed in 1801 and resigned in 1806. Ibid., 713.

4. Lewis's hostess was Pierre Chouteau's second wife, Brigitte Saucier Chouteau.

5. Lewis's last known letter to Jefferson before leaving St. Louis does not mention the date of departure; it is simply a list of goods shipped to Jefferson and is largely in Clark's hand. Possibly the list was an enclosure with the letter referred to by Lewis. Lewis to Jefferson, May 18, 1804, Jackson (LLC), 1:192–94 and headnote.

6. The first letter of the word appears to be "*L*," but Clark's entries for May 14 clearly locate the island on the starboard side.

7. Ordway was one of them, and perhaps Whitehouse, although his journal is unclear on the point.

8. Sylvester Labbadie was related to the Chouteaus by marriage. David Delaunay became a judge under the new government. James Rankin, identified by Thwaites as "an early settler," was a surveyor and the first sheriff of St. Louis until removed from office in 1805. Thwaites (LC), 1:22 n. 1; Houck, 2:225, 383.

9. Dr. Antoine François Saugrain was born in Paris and educated in physics, chemistry, and mineralogy, as well as medicine. After an adventurous career that included travel in Mexico in the service of Spain and capture by Indians along the Ohio River, he brought a party of French immigrants to settle at Gallipolis, Ohio, in 1790. In 1800 he settled in St. Louis, where he was surgeon for the Spanish troops, and in 1805 he received a similar appointment in the U.S. Army from President Jefferson. He was known to Jefferson, who

as minister to France in 1787 had given Saugrain a letter of introduction to George Rogers Clark; hence, he was probably also known to William Clark, at least by reputation. He apparently gave help and advice to the captains before the expedition, although the story that he scraped the back off his wife's mirror to provide them with mercury for a thermometer is probably untrue. Saugrain has been called the "First Scientist in the Mississippi Valley." Chuinard, 195–212; Jackson (TJ), 45, 62 n. 7; Lewis to Jefferson, May 18, 1804, Jackson (LLC), 1:192.

[Clark]   Monday 21st May

Dine with Mr. Ducete & Set out from St. Charles at three oClock after getting every matter arranged, proceeded on under a jentle Breese, at one mile a Violent rain with Wind from the S. W.   we landed at the upper point of the first Island on the Stbd Side & Camped,[1] Soon after it commenced raining & continued the greater part of the night; 3 french men got leave to return to Town, and return early (refur to Fig:, 2.)

25st refured to fig: 2[2] Left St: Charles May 21st 1804. Steered N. 15° W 1¾ Ms   N 52° W to the upper point of the Island and Camped dureing a rain which had been falling half an hour, opposit this Isd. Coms in a Small creek on the St. Sd. and at the head one on the Ld. Side[3] rains powerfully.

[Clark]   *May 21st 1804 Monday—*

All the forepart of the Day Arranging our party and prcureing the different articles necessary for them at this place—   Dined with Mr. Ducett and *Set* out at half passed three oClock under three Cheers from the gentlemen on the bank and proceeded on to the head of the Island (which is Situated on the Stbd Side) 3 miles   Soon after we Set out to day a hard Wind from the W. S W accompanied with a hard rain, which lasted with Short intervales all night, opposit our Camp a Small creek coms in on the Lbd Side—

Course & Distanc 21st of May

S. 15° W	1 ¾	To belge of Isd.
N 52° W	1 ½	To upper Pt. of Isd. Std Sd.
	3 ¼	

1. In St. Charles County, Missouri, approximately three miles southwest of the town of St. Charles. The island, apparently called St. Charles Island, seems to have disappeared. Thwaites (LC), 1:26 n. 1; MRC map 2.

2. This paragraph is on a separate part of the same sheet (document 13). Why Clark uses the word "figure" is not clear.

3. This first creek is probably either Ducket or Little Ducket Creek, in St. Charles County, both probably named for François Duquette. The second is probably Creve Coeur Creek, on the opposite shore in St. Louis County. MRC map 2.

[Clark]   Tuesday May 22nd

delayed a Short time for the three french men who returned and we Set out at 6 oClock   a Cloudy morning   rained Violently hard last night   Saw Several people on the bank to day & passed ⟨many⟩ Several Small farms. Capt. Lewis walk on Shore a little & passed a Camp of Kickapoo Indians,[1] & incamped in the mouth of a Small Creek in a large Bend on the Stbd Side.[2]

The Courses & Distances of this day is as follows Viz.

S 60° W.	3	miles Passed the upper point of the Isd. on which we lay last night to a pt. L: Sd.
S: 43° W	4	miles— this Course passes a pt. on Lbd. Sd. and this an Island in the Mid: R: to a pt. St. Sd.
West	3 ½	miles psd. the Mo: of Bonom [Bonhomme] Creek[3] Lbd. Sd. at. 1 ½ ms an Isd. in mid: R: to pt on Sbd. Sd. abov
S. 75° W.	7 ½	Miles— psd. a pt. on Lbd. round an Isd. bend to the N: 2
Total	18	Sm: Isd. opsd. one nearest the Larboard Side to the pt. in the Cent. to Stb. opposit the lower pt. of Tavn. [Tavern] Isld:[4] and at the mouth of Osage Woman river[5]

[Clark]   *May* 22nd *Tuesday* 1804

a Cloudy morning   Delay one hour for 4 french men who got liberty to return to arrange Some business they had forgotten in Town, at 6 oClock we proceeded on, passed Several Small farms on the bank, and a large creek on the Lbd. Side Called *Bonom* [NB: *bon homme*]   a Camp of Kicka-poos [NB: *an Indian nation residing on the heads of Kaskaskia & Illinois river 90 miles N E of the mouth of the Missouri, & hunt occasionally on the Missouri*] on the St. Side   Those Indians told me Several days ago that they would Come on & hunt and by the time I got to their Camp they would have Some Provisions for us, we Camped in a Bend ⟨under⟩ at the Mo: of a Small creek, Soon after we came too the Indians arrived with 4 Deer as a Present, for which we gave them two qts. of whiskey—

Course & Distance th 22d May

S 60° W.	3	ms. to a pt. Lbd Side
S 43° W.	4	ms. to a pt. on Stbd. Side
West	3 ½	ms. to a pt. on Stbd Sd. psd *Bonon*
S 75° W.	7 ½	ms. to a pt. in Bend to Stbd Side at the mo. of Osage
	18	Womans R

This Day we passed Several Islands, and Some high lands on the Starboard Side, Verry hard water.

1. Possibly the Kickapoo town referred to on May 18, 1804, but "town" usually refers to a more permanent Indian settlement than the hunting camp this seems to have been.

2. Clark indicates that this stream was "Osage Woman's River," that is, Femme Osage River, or Creek. On May 23 he states that they had to go two miles to reach Femme Osage River. Perhaps the stream was one of several small watercourses downstream from Femme Osage River that are nameless on later maps. MRC map 3; MRM map 7.

3. Bonhomme Creek, in St. Louis County, Missouri. See fig. 9. MRC map 2.

4. Tavern Island seems to have disappeared, unless it was the later Howell Island. The name must have come from the cave nearby (see below, May 23, 1804, n. 2). See fig. 9. MRC map 3.

5. As indicated in n. 2, there is confusion about the identity of this stream.

[Clark]

Wednesday May 23rd   8 Indians Kick: [Kickapoo] Came to Camp with meat   we recved their pesents of 3 Deer & gave them Whisky:

Set out early   run on a log: under water and Detained one hour   proceeded on the Same Course of last night, (2 miles) passed the mouth of a creek on the Sbd. Side called Woman of Osage River[1] about 30 yds. over, abounding in fish, Stoped one hour where their was maney people assembled to See us, halted at an endented part of a Rock which juted over the water, Called by the french the tavern[2] which is a Cave 40 yds. long with the river 4 feet Deep & about 20 feet high, this is a place the India[ns; *hole in paper*] & french Pay omage to, many names are wrote up on the rock   Mine among others, at one mile above this rock coms in a small Creek called Tavern Creek,[3] abov one other Small Creek[4], camped at 6 oClock[5] (after expirencing great dificuselty in passing Some Drifts)[6]

9. Missouri River near Mouth of Little Femme Osage River,
ca. May 23, 1804, Field Notes, reverse of document 15

on the Stb Side, examined the mens arms   found all in good order except the Detachment of Solds [soldiers] in the Perogue—   R Field Killed a Deer.

[Clark][7]

May 23rd   Course of last night S: 75 W   Contined 2 miles to the Said point St. Side   passed the upper Point of the Island   Thence S 52° W. ⟨9⟩ 7 Miles to a pt. on St. Sd. passing Tavern Island   two Small Isd. in a bend to the St: side   the Mo: of Oge womans River at 1 m: the Cave Called the Tavern, Lbd Side at 5 [or 4?] m: Situated in the Clifts, opposit a Small Island on the Stbd Side (R. & Jo: Fields came in) with many people, passed the Tavern Cave, Capt Lewis' assended the hill which has peninsulis projecting in raged points to the river, and was near falling from a Peninsulia *hard water all Day*   Saved himself by the assistance of his Knife, passed a Creek 15 yds. wide at 1 mile called Creek of the Tavern on the Lbd. Side, Camped opposit the pt. which the Last Course was to.   one man Sick.

[Clark]   *May 23rd Wednesday 1804*

We Set out early   ran on a Log and detained one hour, proceeded the Course of Last night 2 Miles to the mouth of a Creek on the Stbd. Side Called Osage Womans ⟨Creek⟩ R, about 30 yds. wide, opposit a large Island and a [NB: (american)] Settlement.[8] (on this Creek 30 or 40 famlys are Settled,[)] Crossed to the Settlemt. and took in R & Jo: Fields who had been Sent to purchase Corn & Butter &c.   many people Came to See us, we passed a large *Cave* on the Lbd. Side ⟨Called by the french the *Tavern*⟩[9] about 120 feet wide 40 feet Deep & 20 feet high   many different immages are Painted on the Rock at this place.   the Inds & French pay omage.   many nams are wrote on the rock, Stoped about one mile above for Capt Lewis who had assended the Clifts which is ⟨about⟩ at the Said Cave 300 fee high, hanging over the Water, the water excessively Swift to day, we incamped below a Small Isld. in the Meadle of the river, Sent out two hunters, one Killed a Deer

Course & Distance 23rd May

S. 75° W	2	mils to Osage Womn. R the Course of last Night
S. 52 W	7	mils. to a pt. on St. Side
	9	

This evening we examined the arms and amunition   found those mens arms in the perogue in bad order   a fair evening   Capt. Lewis near falling from the Pencelia of rocks 300 feet, he caught at 20 foot.

1. Femme Osage River, in St. Charles County, Missouri. See fig. 9. MRC map 3.

2. Sergeant Ordway calls this cave the "Corn Tavern," suggesting its use as a cache by trappers and traders. Tavern Rock lies in present Franklin County, Missouri, and probably took its name from its use as a rest stop for river travelers. See fig. 9. MRC map 3; Thwaites (EWT), 6:35; Osgood (FN), 44 n. 6.

3. Tavern Creek is in Franklin County; it does not appear by name in fig. 9. MRC map 3.

4. Probably Little Tavern Creek, just above Tavern Creek in Franklin County. MRM map 8.

5. According to the journals, in St. Charles County. Fig. 9, however, appears to show this camp on the opposite side of the Missouri in Franklin County a mile or more upstream from Tavern Creek. MRC map 3.

6. Collections of driftwood. Criswell, 34.

7. This entry in the Field Notes for May 23 is on a sheet (document 14) different from the first (document 13). It is not clear which was composed first.

8. This community, which apparently never formally constituted a town, was Boone's Settlement, in the vicinity of Matson, St. Charles County. The colony of Kentuckians was named for Daniel Boone, who came there in 1799 and received a grant of 1,000 arpents of land from the Spanish government, having been preceded there by his son, Daniel Morgan Boone, in 1797. The old frontiersman was appointed judge and commandant of the Femme Osage district in 1800 and held the post until the American takeover. The site of his cabin is a few miles northwest of Matson, in southwest St. Charles County. Thwaites (LC), 1:27 n. 1; Houck, 2:93–94; *Missouri Guide*, 362–65; Bakeless (LCPD), 360–64.

9. The words in angle brackets were apparently crossed out by Biddle. Just before "Called" is what appears to be an *L*-shaped bracket, probably also intended to call attention to the deletion of the phrase.

[Clark]

Thursday May the 24th 1804   Set out early   passed a Small Isd in the Midlle of the river, opposit the on the Lbd. Side is projecting Rock of ½ a mile in extent against which the Current runs, this place is called the Devils race grounds,[1] above this Coms in a Small Creek called the little quiver,[2] a Sand Island on the Stbd Side, passed Several Islands & 2 creeks, on the Stbd Side[3] a Small Island on the Lbd Side above we wer verry near loseing our Boat in Toeing   She Struck the Sands (which is continerly roaling) ⟨& turned⟩ the Violence of the Current was so great that the Toe roap Broke, the Boat turned Broadside, as the Current Washed the Sand from under her She wheeled & lodged on the bank below as often as three times, before we got her in Deep water, nothing Saved her but [*sentence unfinished*]

[Clark][4]

May 24th   Set out early, Killed a Deer last night.   examined the mens arms, & Saw that all was prepared for action, passed an [sm? *i.e., small?*] Island in the M. R, [Missouri River? midriver?] opposit a hard place of water called the Devill race grown, S 63° W 4 miles to a point on the Sd: Starboard Side   N 68 W   to a point on Lbd Side 3 ms: Passd. a Small Willow Island on the Lbd. Side to the point of a Isd. L' Side—   S 75° W to a point on Stbd Side 3 Miles, Passed the upper point of the Island. Crossed and in a verry bad place we got our Boat a ground & She Bocke the Toe Roap & turned the Land, [bring?] [*one word illegible*] the in Wheeling three times, got off returned to the head of the aforesaid Island, and Came up under a falling Bank.   hard water   this place being the worst I ever Saw, I call it the retregrade bend.   Camped at an old house.[5]

[Clark]   *May* 24th Thursday 1804

Set out early   passed a Verry bad part of the River Called the Deavels race ground, this is where the Current Sets against Some projecting rocks for half a mile on the Labd. Side, above this place is the mouth of a Small Creek Called *queivere*, passed Several Islands, two Small Creeks on the Stbd. Side, and passed between a Isld. an the Lbd. Shore   a narrow pass above this Isld is a Verry bad part of the river, we attempted to pass up under the Lbd. Bank which was falling in So fast that the evident danger obliged us to Cross between the Starbd. Side and a Sand bar in the middle of the river, we *hove* up near the head of the Sand bar, the Sand moveing & banking caused us to run on the Sand. The Swiftness of the Current wheeled the boat, Broke our *Toe* rope, and was nearly over Setting the boat, all hand Jumped out on the upper Side and bore on that Side untill the Sand washed from under the boat and wheeled on the next bank   by the time She wheeled a 3rd Time got a rope fast to her Stern and by the means of Swimmers was Carred to Shore and when her Stern was down whilst in the act of Swinging a third time ⟨She was Drawn⟩ into Deep water near the Shore, we returned, to the Island where we Set out and assended under the Bank which I have just mentioned, as falling in, here George Drewyer & Willard, two of our men who left us at St. Charles to Come on by land joined us, we Camped about 1 mile above where we were So nearly being lost, on the Labd Side at a Plantation. all in Spirits. This place I call the *retragrade* bend as we were obliged to fall back 2 miles

Course & Distance of the 24th May

S. 63° W,	4	ms. to a pt. on Stbd. Side
S. 68° W,	3	ms. to a pt. on Lbd Side
S. 75° W,	_3_	ms. to a pt. on Stbd. Side ⟨Chereton 20 yds wide.⟩
	10	

1. Perhaps what was later called Liffecue Rocks, in Franklin County just above the May 23 camp. The river has changed its course considerably over the years. MRC map 3; MRM map 8.

2. Perhaps Fiddle Creek, just above Liffecue Rocks, in Franklin County. MRC map 3.

3. Probably Sehrt Creek and Bigelow Creek, just above present Augusta in St. Charles County, Missouri. MRM map 8.

4. This May 24 entry is on a sheet of the Field Notes (document 14) separate from the first (document 13).

5. In Franklin County, some four or five miles below present Washington. MRC map 3. Figures written under the second May 24 entry probably represent the day's mileage: 4, 3, 2, 3, and a total of 12. The two miles' difference from the Codex A entry is the distance lost falling back, as Clark relates.

[Clark]   25 *May*[1]

Set out early   Course West to a Point on Sbd. Side   at 2 Miles passd a Willow Isd. in a Bend to the Lbd: a creek called wood rivr[2] Lbd. Side N 57° W. to a pt. on the Sb. Side 3 Miles passed the Mouth of a Creek St. Side Called Le quever,[3] this Same course continued to a Point Ld. Side 2½ Miles further.   opposit a Isd. on Sd Side Passed a Creek Called R. La freeau[4] at the pt. N 20° W 2 miles To a Small french Village called La Charatt[5] of five families only, in the bend to the Starbord   This is the Last Settlement of Whites, an Island opposit[6]

[Clark]   *May 25th Friday 1804*

rain last night   river fall Several inches, Set out early psd. Several Islands   passed wood River on the Lbd Side at 2 miles   passed [*NB: again*][7] ⟨the⟩ Creek on the St. Side Called *La Querer* [*NB: quiver*] at 5 miles   passed a [*NB: small*] Creek ⟨called R la freeau⟩[8] at 8 mile, opsd. an Isd. on the Lbd Side, Camped at the mouth of a Creek called ⟨*River a Chauritte*⟩, [*NB: La Charrette*] above a Small french Village of 7 houses and as many families, Settled at this place to be convt. to hunt, & trade with the Indians, here we met with Mr. Louisell[9] imedeately down from the ⟨*Seeeder*⟩ [*NB: Cedar*] Isld. Situated in the Countrey of the *Suxex* [*NB: Sioux*] 400 Leagues up   he gave us a good Deel of information Some letters[10]   he informed us that he Saw no Indians on the river below the *Poncrars*—[*NB: Poncaras*] [Poncas]   Some hard rain this evening

Course & Distance 25th May

West—	3	ms. Stb Side passed Creek
N. 57° W	5	ms. pot. Lbd. Side psd Creek
N 20° W.	2	ms. to mo. Chaurette Creek on the St. Side & *Village*
	10	

The people at this Village is pore, houses Small, they Sent us milk & eggs to eat.

1. Biddle wrote a heading, "May 25th to May 29th," at the top of this sheet (document 15).

2. Dubois Creek in Franklin County, Missouri. As with River Dubois in Illinois, Clark has translated literally, though it may in fact be a personal name. MRC map 3.

3. Perhaps Lake Creek, in Warren County, Missouri. Quivre River was an alternate name for Rivière aux Boeufs, which enters the Missouri in Warren County, above Washington. The location of the mouths of streams may have shifted greatly since 1804. It is nearly impossible to reconcile this stream with the "queevere" creek of the previous day (see above, May 24, 1804). Moreover, Clark records passing Rivière aux Boeufs on May 26. Possibly Clark was misinformed about these streams. Houck, 2:95; MRC map 4; MRM map 9.

4. Perhaps later Tuque Creek, in Warren County, opposite the town of Washington, but see above, n. 3. It is not entirely clear from the text which side of the Missouri this creek was on. MRC map 4.

5. La Charette, on Charette Creek, in Warren County, in 1804 the westernmost white settlement on the Missouri. French and American settlers had come there before 1800,

and a small Spanish fort, San Juan del Misuri, was established about 1796. From the fort came the alternative name used by Patrick Gass, St. John. Daniel Boone moved there from Boone's Settlement sometime after 1804; he died and was buried there, but in 1845 his remains and those of his wife were moved to Kentucky. The village site, near present Marthasville, has been washed away by the Missouri. *Missouri Guide*, 364–65; Houck, 2:91–92, 94.

6. Probably St. John's Island. MRC map 4.

7. Biddle's interlineation suggests that this is the same stream as that of May 24, but see above, n. 3.

8. Biddle apparently crossed out these words.

9. Régis Loisel was apparently born in the Parish of L'Assomption, Montreal, and came to St. Louis in about 1793. By 1796 he had formed a partnership with Jacques Clamorgan, which in 1798 became the reorganized Missouri Company. After this combination broke up, he formed a new partnership with Hugh Heney on July 6, 1801. The date on which he founded his fort on Cedar Island is uncertain; it may have been in 1800, or perhaps two years later. For the post, in present Lyman County, South Dakota, see below, September 22, 1804. Loisel wintered there with his partner, Pierre-Antoine Tabeau, in 1803–4. After his meeting with Lewis and Clark, he carried to New Orleans a copy of his report on the Missouri River tribes, which he delivered to the Marquis of Casa Calvo, the former Spanish governor of Louisiana. The latter forwarded it to Madrid, with a recommendation that Loisel be made an Indian agent to secure the friendship of the tribes for Spain and forestall American ambitions in the West. Loisel, however, died in New Orleans in October 1804, at the age of thirty-one. Abel, 20–31; Nasatir (BLC), 1:114–15, 2:611–13, 735–40, 736 n. 3, 757 n. 8.

10. Perhaps letters of introduction to some of Loisel's trading associates, such as Heney and Tabeau, both of whom the captains would meet later up the Missouri.

[Clark][1]

May 26th 1804.   Set out at 7 oClock after a hard rain & Wind, & proceed on verry well under Sale.   Wind from the E N E

S 50° W.	3 ½	ms. to a point opposit the mouth of Beef Island & River[2] on the Lbd Side,
N 80° W	2 ½	miles to point on the Lbd, Side, passed Beef Isd. on Lbd Side Beef Creek on the Back of the Isd.
N 88 W.	3 ½	Ms. to pt. to St. Side above the upper point of Beef Island
N. 82° W	1 ½	miles to Pt. St. Side,
N 37° W	5 ½	miles to a Point on the Lbd. Side an Island on the Starbd. Side, passed a willow Island and a Creek called Sheppards R, on the Lbd Side about, passed 2 willow Islands on the Lbd. Side in a Bend

N 60 W.	2	M to a point on the St. Side passed an Isd. on the St. Sd.
⟨N 71° W.	3	m: to a pt. on Ld Side Passed a⟩ of the Said Isd

The wind favourable to day   we made 18 miles   a Cloud rais & wind & rain Closed the Day

[Clark]   May the 26th Sattarday 1804.

Set out at 7 oClock after a heavy Shour of rain   (George Drewyer & John Shields, Sent by Land with the two horses with directions to proceed on one day & hunt the next)   The wind favourable from the E N E passed [*NB: a large island called Buffaloe Island ⟨Creek back of Beef Isd⟩ separated from the land by a small channel into which Buffaloe creek empties itself*] ⟨Beef Island and river⟩ on Lbd Side at 3½ Ms   Passed a Creek on the Lbd. Side Called Shepperds Creek,[3] passed Several Islands to day   great Deal of Deer Sign on the Bank   one man out hunting, w[e] Camped on an Island on the Starboard Side near the Southern extrem of Luter Island [*NB: (Qu L'outre)*][4]

Course & Distance to day

S 50° W.	3 ½	ms. to a pt. St. Side opsd. pt. Beef Isd.
N 80° W	2 ½	Ms. to pt. Lbd. Sd.
N 88° W	3 ½	Ms to Pt. Std Sd. abov Beef Isd.
N 82° W	1 ½	Ms. to pt St. Side
N 37° W.	5	ms. to pt. Lbd Sd. passed 2 Is & Shepds R.
N 60° W.	2	ms. to pt. on St. Sd. pd. a Isd. L. S
	18	

Detatchment Orders.

[Lewis]   May 26th 1804.[5]

The Commanding Officers direct, that the three Squads under the command of Sergts. Floyd Ordway and Pryor heretofore forming two messes each, shall untill further orders constitute three messes only, the same being altered and organized as follows (viz)—

1 *Sergt. Charles Floyd.* (1)[6]

Privates:
2 Hugh McNeal

      3 Patric Gass
      4 Reubin Fields (2)
      5 John B Thompson
+   6 John Newman[7]
      7 Richard Winsor
     + Francis Rivet & [*NB: French*]
      8 Joseph Fields (3)

      9 *Sergt. John Ordway.*

      Privates.
    10 William Bratton (4)
    11 John Colter (5)
x 12 Moses B. Reed [*NB: + Soldier*]
    13 Alexander Willard
    14 William Warner
    15 Silas Goodrich
    16 John Potts &
    17 Hugh Hall

    18 *Sergt. Nathaniel Pryor.* (6)

    Privates.
    19 George Gibson (7)
    20 George Shannon (8)
    21 John Shields (9)
    22 John Collins
    23 Joseph Whitehouse
    24 Peter Wiser
F 25 Peter Crusat &[8]
F 26 Francis Labuche

The commanding officers further direct that the remainder of the detatchmen shall form two messes; and that the same be constituded as follows. (viz)—

Patroon, Baptist Dechamps

Engages
Etienne Mabbauf
Paul Primaut
Charles Hébert
Baptist La Jeunesse
Peter Pinaut

Peter Roi &
Joseph Collin

1 *Corpl. Richard Warvington.*

Privates.
2 Robert Frasier
3 John Boleye
4 John Dame
5 Ebinezer Tuttle &
6 Isaac White

The Commanding officers further direct that the messes of Sergts. Floyd, Ordway and Pryor shall untill further orders form the crew of the Batteaux; the Mess of the Patroon La Jeunesse will form the permanent crew of the red Perogue; Corpl. Warvington's mess forming that of the white perogue.—

Whenever by any casualty it becomes necessary to furnish additional men to assist in navigating the Perogues, the same shall be furnished by daily detale from the Privates who form the crew of Batteaux, exempting only from such detale, Thomas P. Howard[9] and the men who are assigned to the two bow and the two stern oars.— For the present one man will be furnished daily to assist the crew of the white perogue; this man must be an expert boatman.—

The posts and duties of the Sergts. shall be as follows (viz)— when the Batteaux is under way, one Sergt. shall be stationed at the helm, one in the center on the rear of the Starboard locker, and one at the bow. *The Sergt. at the helm,* shall steer the boat, and see that the baggage on the quarterdeck is properly arranged and stowed away in the most advantageous manner; to see that no cooking utensels or loos lumber of any kind is left on the deck to obstruct the passage between the burths— he will also attend to the compas when necessary.—

The Sergt at the center will command the guard, manage the sails, see that the men at the oars do their duty; that they come on board at a proper season in the morning, and that the boat gets under way in due time; he will keep a good lookout for the mouths of all rivers, creeks, Islands and other remarkable places and shall immediately report the same to the commanding officers; he will attend to the issues of sperituous liquors; he shall regulate the halting of the batteaux through the day to give the men refreshment, and will also regulate the time of her departure taking care that not more time than is necessary shall be expended at each halt— it shall be his duty also to post a centinel on the bank, near the boat whenever we come too and halt in the course of the day, at the same time he will (acompanied by two his guard) reconnoiter the forrest arround the place of landing to the distance of at least one hundred paces. when we come too for the purpose of encamping at night, the Sergt. of the guard shall post two centinels immediately on our landing; one of whom shal be posted near the boat, and the other at a convenient distance in rear of the encampment; at night the Sergt. must be always present with his guard, and he is positively forbidden to suffer any man of his guard to absent himself on any pretext whatever; he will at each relief through the night, accompanyed by the two men last off their posts, reconnoiter in every direction around the camp to the distance of at least one hundred and fifty paces, and also examine the situation of the boat and perogues, and see that they ly safe and free from the bank—

It shall be the duty of the *sergt. at the bow*, to keep a good look out for all danger which may approach, either of the enimy, or obstructions which may present themselves to ⟨the⟩ passage of the boat; of the first he will notify the Sergt. at the center, who will communicate the information to the commanding officers, and of the second or obstructions to the boat he will notify the Sergt. at the helm; he will also report to the commanding officers through the Sergt. at the center all perogues boats canoes or other craft which he may discover in the river, and all hunting camps or parties of Indians in view of which we may pass. he will at all times be provided with a seting pole and assist the bowsman in poling and managing the bow of the boat. it will be his duty also to give and answer all signals, which may hereafter be established for the government of the perogues and parties on shore.

The Sergts. will on each morning before our departure relieve each other in the following manner—(viz) The Sergt. at the helm will parade the new guard, relieve the Sergt. and the old guard, and occupy the middle station in the boat; the Sergt. of the old guard will occupy the station at the bow, and the Sergt. who had been stationed the preceeding day at the bow will place himself at the helm.— The sergts. in addition to those duties are directed each to keep a seperate journal from day today of all passing occurences, and such other observations on the country &c. as shall appear to them worthy of notice—

The Sergts. are relieved and exempt from all labour of making fires, pitching tents or cooking, and will direct and make the men of their several messes perform an equal propotion of those duties.—

The guard shall hereafter consist of one sergeant and six privates & engages.—

Patroon, Dechamp, Copl. Warvington, and *George Drewyer*, are exempt from guad duty; the two former will attend particularly to their perogues at all times, and see that their lading is in good order, and that the same is kept perfectly free from rain or other moisture; the latter will perform certain duties on shore which will be assigned him from time to time: all other soldiers and engaged men of whatever discription must perform their regular tour of guad duty.—

All detales for guard or other duty will be made in the evening when we encamp, and the duty to be performed will be entered on, by the individuals so warned, the next morning.— provision for one day will be issued to the party on each evening after we have encamped; the same will be cooked on that evening by the several messes, and a proportion of it reserved for the next day as no cooking will be allowed in the day while on the mach—

Sergt. John Ordway will continue to issue the provisions and make the detales for guard or other duty.— The day after tomorrow lyed corn and grece will be issued to the party, the next day Poark and flour, and the day following indian meal and poark; and in conformity to that ratiene provisions will continue to be issued to the party untill further orders.— should any of the messes prefer indian meal to flour they may recieve it accordingly— no poark is to be issued when we have fresh meat on hand.—

Labuche and Crusat will man the larboard bow oar alternately, and the one not engaged at the oar will attend as the Bows-man, and when the attention of both these persons is necessary at the bow, their oar is to be maned by any idle hand on board.—

Meriwether Lewis Capt.
Wm. Clark Cpt.

1. This entry and that of May 27 are written crossways to the previous entry on one side of document 15 of the Field Notes.

2. River au Boeuf (Rivière aux Boeufs, or Buffalo River) in Franklin County, Missouri. The island is Boeuf, Buffalo, or Shelton, Island. MRC map 4.

3. Rivière à Berger, later Big Berger Creek, in Franklin County; an island nearby was Isle à Berger. "Shepherd" is the literal translation of *berger* in French, but the river and island seems to have been named for Joseph Berger, a Canadian fur trader operating from St. Louis in the latter 1700s, or possibly for Pierre Berje, an early settler of St. Charles. McDermott (WCS), 147; MRC map 4.

4. Biddle's interlined "Qu" probably stands for "question." His "L'outre" (more correctly *la loutre*, "otter" in French) Island was in present Montgomery and Warren counties, Missouri, opposite the town of Hermann. The island on which they camped might be the later Bates Island, situated near the Gasconade-Franklin county line. MRC map 5.

5. From the Orderly Book in Lewis's hand, except for Clark's own signature.

6. Numbers and other additions beside the names (except "&") are apparently by Biddle.

7. The symbol by Newman's name may refer to his having been expelled from the permanent party later, especially since there is also an *x* by the name of Moses Reed, the other man expelled.

8. The *F*'s probably stand for "French."

9. Note that Howard is not mentioned in the above lists. The reason for his exemption is not clear; he may have been temporarily incapacitated or assigned to special duty.

[Clark][1]

Sunday May 27th   as we were Setting out this morning two Canoos loaded with Bever elk Deer Skins & Buffalow Robes, from the Mahars [Omaha] nation, they inform that they left that place 2 months, a gentle Breese from the S. E,

N: 71 W.	3	Miles to a point on the Labd Side opposit the lower point of [*blank*] Island, passed a willow Island on the L. Sd opposit the upper Point of the Isd we Camped on last night
S 82° W	6	ms to a pt: on Lbd Side passed the lower pt. of a Isd Passed 4 *Casiex* [cajeux][2] 3 from Grand Osage one form the Parnees [Pawnees], Passed two Isd. on the S Side a Creek of 20 yds Wide on the Lb. Side near the upper point,[3] this Creek is Called Ash Creek
N 74° W	1 ½	Miles to pt. on Lbd. Sd nearly opst. the upper pt. of the big Island called [*blank*] Isle, on the Stbd Side back of this Isd. Coms in Otter R & two other Creeks,

S 70° W.   5   M: to a Pt. on St Sd opposit Gasconnade River passing a pt. on Lbd Side

we camped on an Isd in the mouth of Gasconade R,[4] this river is 157 yards wide   a butifull stream of clear water.   19′ foot Deep   Hills on the lower Side

[Clark]   *May 27th Sunday* 1804

as we were pushing off this Morning two Canoos Loaded with fur &c. Came to from the Mahars [*NB: Mahar*] nation, [*NB: living 730 miles above on the Missouri*] which place they had left two months, at about 10 oClock 4 *Cajaux* or rafts loaded with furs and peltres came too one from the *Paunees*, [*NB: Paunees on the river Platt*] the other from Grand Osage,[5] they informed nothing of Consequence, passed a Creek on the Lbd Side Called *ash Creek*[6] 20 yds wide, passed the upper point of a large Island[7] on the Stbd Side back of which Comes in three Creeks one Called Orter Creek,[8] her[e] the men[9] we left hunting Came in   we camped on a Willow Island in the mouth of Gasconnade River. George Shannon Killed a Deer this evening

Course & Distance 27th May.

N 71° W.	3	ms to pt. Lbd. Sd. pd. an Isd.
S 82° W.	6	ms. to pt Lbd. Sd. pd. 2 Isd. a Creek
N 74° W.	1 ½	ms. to pt Lbd. Sd. pd. upr. pt by Isd. & 2 Creeks
S. 70° W.	5	ms. to pt. opsd. the Gasconnade R
	15 ½	

1. To the side of this entry and covered by it is a column of barely legible numbers that appear to be the previous day's distances, with a total of 18.

2. *Cajeu* (plural, *cajeux*) was a French-Canadian term for a small raft, especially one made by lashing together two canoes. McDermott (GMVF), 41.

3. At this point there is a small sketch under the entry, of document 15, showing a river bend and an island.

4. The Gasconade River enters the Missouri at present Gasconade, Gasconade County, Missouri. MRC map 5; MRM map 13.

5. These men had been trading with the Great (or Grand) Osages, probably on the Osage River in Missouri.

6. Probably later Frame, or Frene, Creek, entering the Missouri at present Hermann, Gasconade County. MRC map 5; MRM map 13.

7. Probably L'Outre (more properly *la loutre* in French) Island. MRC map 5.

8. The literal translation of its early name, Rivière à la Loutre, in Montgomery County, Missouri. Ibid.

9. George Drouillard and John Shields; see above, May 26.

[Clark]   Monday 28th May[1]

rained hard all the last night   Some wind from the S W, one Deer Killed to day, one Man fell in with Six Indians hunting, onloaded the perogue, & found Several articles Wet, Some Tobacco Spoiled.   river begin to rise

[Clark]   *May 28th Munday* 1804 *Gasconnade*[2]

Rained hard all last night   Some thunder & lightening hard wind in the forepart of the night from the S W.   Ruben Fields Killed a Deer   Several hunter out to day   I measured the river found the Gasconnade to be 157 yds. wide and 19 foot Deep   the Course of this R. is S 29° W,[3] one of the hunters fell in with 6 Inds. hunting, onloaded the large Perogue on board of which was 8 french hands   found many things wet by their cearleness-ness, put all the articles which was wet out to Dry—   this day So Cloudy that no observations could be taken, the river begin to rise, examine the mens arms and equapage, all in Order

1. Under this entry and running into the next is a small sketch on the reverse of docu-ment 15. There is also a column of figures under this entry: 3, 4, 1½, 1½, 9 and a total of 19.

2. Clark's interlineation, written under the date in Codex A.

3. Biddle apparently has crossed out this passage from "the Course" to here.

[Clark]

Tuesday 29th May   Sent out hunters, got a morning obsvtn and one at 12 oClock, rained last night, the river rises fast   The Musquetors are verry bad, Load the pierogue

[Clark][1]

May 29th 180[4]   Set out from the mouth of the gasconnade, where we took obsevn &c.   left a Perogue for a man lost in the woods,[2] Course

N. 54 W 2 m to a point Lb. Side. Passed the Isd. on which we Camped, river still rised, water verry muddey   N. 78° W 2 Ms. to a pt. on Lb Side   passed two willow Islands first Smaller and a Creek on Lbd. called Deer Creek[3] one oposit the point St. Side and incamped on the Lb Side[4]   rain all night

[Form?] the tents together [gro?] along the [Bank?] N; 76 W 25 Poles S 26 W, to the point above—   S 19° to the pot below the River[5]

from the pole on the Bank to the upper point is S [11?] E to the lower point [is?] S L L S 42½ East to the pole at the Lower Side

Gasconnade[6]

			28 ½ poles Wide 157 yds.
below the mouth of Gascond		35	do do 193
above	do	do	38 ½ do do 215

Course of the River gasconnade is S 20° W—   River up N 70° W   The River Down N 29° E

[Clark]   *May 29th Tuesday*

rained last night, Cloudy morning   4 hunters Sent out with Orders to return at 12 oClock   Took equal altitudes of Suns Lower limb   found it 105° 31′ 45″

	h	′	″			h	′	″
A M.	9	25	24		P M	2	35	31
	9	26	3			2	37	20
	9	27	27			2	38	52

Error of Sextion 8′ 45″—

⊙s Magnetic Azzamuth S 83° W.		h	m	s
Time at place of obsvn. by Cromtr. P. M.		4	4	44

Double altitude of ⊙ L Limb	71°	24′	oo″

Cap Lewis observed meridean altitude of ⊙ U L—back observation with the octant & artificeal horozen—   gave for altitude on the Limb 38° 44′ oo″   ⊙ octant Error 2 o o +

had the Perogues loaded and all perpared to Set out at 4 oClock after finishing the observations & all things necessary   found that one of the hunters had not returned, we deturmined to proceed on & leave one perogue to wate for him, accordingly at half past four we Set out and came on 4 miles & camped on the Lbd Side above a Small Creek Called Deer Creek, Soon after we came too we heard Several guns fire down the river, we answered them by a Discharge of a Swivile on the Bow[7]

Course to day & Distance *29 May*

N. 54° W,	2	ms. to pt. Lbd Sd.
N. 78° W	2	ms. to pt. Lbd. Sd. pd. Deer Creek
	4	

(Poi[n]t Obsn. No. 2)

[Lewis]   *Tuesday May 29th*[8]

On a small Island opposite to the mouth of the *Gasconade* made the following obsertns.

Equal Alds. of ☉, with Sextant.

	h	m	s			h	m	s
A. M.	9	25	24		P. M.	2	35	31
	"	26	3			"	37	20
	"	27	27			"	38	52

Altd. by Sextnt. at the time of this observt.   *105° 31' 45"*

Note.—The ☉ was so much obscured during the A. M. observation, that I cannot be positive as to it's accuracy, not could I obtain the A. M. obstn. at an earlyer hour fron the same cause.

observed ☉'s magnetic azimuth by Cercumftr.—   S. 83° W.

	h	m	s
Time by Chronometer P. M.	4	4	44
altd. by Sextant of ☉s L. L.	71°	24'	00"
Latitude of place of observation	N. 38°	44'	35.3"
Variation of nedle—[*blank*]			

Observed Meridian altd. of ☉'s L L. with Octant by the back observt.   39° 3' 00"

Latitude deduced from this observation   38° 44' 35.3

1. This second entry for May 29 is at right angles to the first on document 15. Under it is a sketch map of the Missouri River from Bonhomme Creek to above Tavern Creek, in St. Louis, Franklin, and St. Charles counties, Missouri. See fig. 9. Wood; MRC map 3.

2. Joseph Whitehouse, who had been exploring a cave. The red pirogue, manned by the French *engagés*, stayed behind for him.

3. Probably Bailey Creek, entering the Missouri in Gasconade County, Missouri, near the Osage County line. MRC map 5; MRM map 14.

4. Just above Bailey Creek, very near the Osage-Gasconade county line. MRC map 5; MRM map 14.

5. This and the following paragraph are in pencil, written in the angle between the two May 29 entries on document 15. They are nearly illegible. Apparently they belong to the period when the party camped at the mouth of the Gasconade.

6. These measurements, which Clark took at the mouth of the Gasconade on May 28, are written in ink below the previous penciled paragraphs.

7. The swivel gun was a small cannon widely used by armies, navies, and fur traders in this period. As the name implies, it was placed on a Y-shaped mount that swiveled, giving it great flexibility. It could fire a solid shot or a number of smaller projectiles and was therefore a useful antipersonnel weapon. During the expedition's tense encounter with the Teton Sioux (September 25, 1804), the swivel was loaded with sixteen musket balls, each of which would probably have gone through more than one victim. The gun probably had a bore of less than two inches and fired a ball weighing about one pound. The expedition also had two blunderbusses, likewise mounted on swivels; these were large, bell-mouthed shoulder arms, used with buckshot like heavy shotguns. All of these weapons were probably mounted on the walls of Fort Mandan during the winter of 1804–5. The Corps cached all three at the Great Falls of the Missouri in June 1805, and recovered them in August of the following year. They gave the little cannon as a gift to the Hidatsa chief Le Borgne (One Eye) during the return trip in order to win his good will; the blunderbusses were brought back to St. Louis. Russell (GEF), 251–65; Russell (FTT), 45–48, 77–84.

8. Lewis's observation from Codex O.

[Clark][1]

May 30th, Wednesday, Set out at 7 oClock after a heavy rain, rained all last night, a little after Dark last night Several guns were herd below, I expect the French men fireing for Whitehous who was lost in the woods.

Course

West	2	M. to a pt. Lbd Side opsd. an Isld. a Cave on the St Side Called Monbrains Tavern, a Creek above,
S. 80° W	2	ms. to pt. Lb. Side passed an Isd. on the St. Side, a Sand bar & Creek Called rest Creek on the Lbd Side— Rain hard,

S 78° W	3	mes to pt. on Lbd Side psd a willow Isd. in mid: R. a willow Island
S. 66° W,	4	ms. to a pt. Lbd. Side, opposit the mouth of a Small River called Miry River of about ⟨40⟩ 80 yds wide a Willow Isd. in the River, a large Isd. above
S 48° W	6	Ms. to a pt. on Lbd.[2] Side, passed a Isd. in the mid: Came to in the mouth of a Creek at Lbd Side [*blank*] yds wide Called [*blank*][3] one on St. Side of 60 yds wide called little Miry at 2 ms. Passed a Creek of 15 yd. wide on the Lbd Side at 14 Miles Called Grindstone Creek & incamped in the Mouth, Low land on both Sides of the river & Creek

[Clark]   *May 30th Wednesday* 1804

Rained all last night   Set out at 6 oClock after a heavy Shower, and proceeded on, passed a large Island a Creek opposit on the St. Side Just abov a *Cave* Called *Monbrun Tavern* [*NB: Montbrun's*] & River,[4] passed a Creek on the Lbd. Side Call *Rush* Creek[5] at 4 Miles   Several Showers of rain the Current Verry Swift river riseing fast   Passed Big ⟨Miry⟩ [*NB: Muddy*] River[6] at 11 Miles on the Starboard Side, at the lower point of a Island,[7] this River is about 50 yards Wide, Camped at the mouth of a Creek on Lbd Sd of abt 25 yds. Wide Called Grinestone Creek,[8] opposit the head of a Isd. and the mouth of Little ⟨Miry⟩ [*NB: Muddy*] River[9] on the St Side, a heavy wind accompanied with rain & hail   we Made 14 miles to day, the river Continue to rise, the County on each Side appear full of Water.

Course & Distance of May 30th

West	2	ms. to a pt. L. Sd. opsd. a Cave & pt. Isd.
S 80° W.	2	ms. to a pt. on L. Sd. psd. Isd. & rush Creek
S 78° W.	3	ms. to a pt. on L. Sd. psd. a wil: Isd.
S 66° W.	4	Ms. to a pt. on Lbd. Sd. opsd. Mery R: & Isd.
S 48° W.	6	ms. to a pt. on St. Sd. opsd. Som Sm. Isd. Psd.
	17	a creek 2 ms. Swift say 17 mile

1. Biddle's heading at the top of this sheet (document 16), reads "May 30 to June 1st." The columns of numbers next to this entry appear to be partial additions of the day's dis-

tance. Other numbers are at the bottom of the page under another entry but also seem to be distances for May 30.

2. This abbreviation appears to be "Lbd.," but in the courses and distances of the Codex A entry, below, it is "St." There was a point on the starboard, in Callaway County, Missouri, at approximately the right spot, visible through most of the century. Nicollet (MMR), 355; MRC map 6.

3. Apparently the same as Grindstone Creek, below; see n. 8.

4. Little Tavern Creek meets the Missouri in Callaway County, about two miles below the present town of Portland; just above it is Big Tavern Creek. The island may be later Portland Island. See fig. 10, a sketch map on document 17. MRC map 5.

5. Rest Creek in the Field Notes entry, probably later Greasy Creek, meeting the Missouri River at the town of Chamois, Osage County, Missouri. The mouth may have been farther down the Missouri in 1804. It appears without a name in fig. 10. Ibid.; MRM map 14.

6. "Big Miry R" on fig. 10, probably Auxvasse River, in present Callaway County. MRC map 6. Biddle probably crossed out Miry when he substituted Muddy.

7. Perhaps later St. Aubert Island. Ibid.

8. This creek, at whose mouth they camped, is probably later Deer Creek, in Osage County. See fig. 10. Ibid.

9. "Little Miry R" on fig. 10; evidently later Muddy Creek, in Callaway County. Ibid. Biddle probably crossed out Miry when he substituted Muddy.

[Clark]   *May 31st Thursday* 1804[1]

rained the greater part of last night, the wind from the West raised and blew with great force untile 5 oClock p. m. which obliged us to lay by   a *Cajaux* of Bear Skins and pelteries came down from the Grand Osarge,[2] one french man one ⟨half⟩ Indian, and a Squar, they had letters from the man Mr. Choteau Sent to that part of the Osarge Nation Settled on Arkansa River mentioning that his letter was Commited to the flaims,[3] the Inds. not believeing that the Americans had possession of the Countrey they disregard'ed St Louis & their Supplies &c.—   Several *rats* of Considerable Size was Cought in the woods to day—[4]   Capt Lewis went out to the woods & found many curious Plants & Srubs, one Deer killed this evening

1. There is no May 31, 1804, entry in the Field Notes. The one given is in Codex A.

2. When first mentioned by Europeans in 1673 the Osages were living on the upper Osage River in present western Missouri. During the early eighteenth century the group known as the Little Osages moved away and settled on the lower Missouri River, near the Missouri Indians. Those remaining on the Osage River were known as the Great (or Grand, or Big) Osages. Late in the eighteenth century the Little Osages rejoined their kinsmen. By

the time of Lewis and Clark about half of the Great Osages had moved to the Arkansas River in present-day Kansas. They speak a Siouan language of the Dhegiha group and had an economy based on hunting and horticulture. Hodge, 2:156–58; Mathews; Din & Nasatir; Chapman (IO).

3. The name of the emissary, apparently sent by Auguste or Pierre Chouteau on behalf of the new government, does not appear. The chief who burned the letter was probably Makes-Tracks-Far-Away, otherwise known as Big Track, or Big Foot, leader of the Osages on the Arkansas. Mathews, 300, 344, 354–55; Jackson (LLC), 1:203 n. 3.

4. Evidently the eastern wood rat, *Neotoma floridana*, then new to science; Clark mentions it again briefly on July 7, 1804. Lewis's description on February 27, 1806, was the first scientific account of the species. Cutright (LCPN), 58, 444; Coues (HLC), 1:40 n. 86; Hall, 2:748–50.

[Clark]

June 1st Friday 1804   Set out early, the Same Course S 48° W of Wednesday   contd. 4 ms   passed the Mouth of Little Miry on the Stb & ⟨Bear Creek on the Larbd. at 6 Ms   this Creek is about 25 yds wide,⟩ [A? &?] high rich Land on the Lb Side, S. 45° W to an Island[1] opposit a hill on the S. Sd. 6 Ms.   this Isd is on the Lbd.   passed the Mo. of Bear creek[2] 25 yds wide at 2 ms. & three Small Isd., Some Swift water and banks falling in, Wind a head from the West, S 39° W 3 ms. to the Pt. above the mouth of Osage River[3] Larb Side, Camped   fell a number of Trees in the Point to take observation   a fair after noon, Sit up untill 1 oClock to take Som observations &c.[4]

[Clark]   ⟨May⟩ *June 1st 1804 Friday*

Set out early   a fair morning   Passed the mouth Bear Creek 25 yds. Wide at 6 Miles, Several Small Islands in the river   the wind a head from the West   the Current exceedingly rapid   Came to on the point of the Osarges River on the Labd Side of Missouries   this osages river Verry high, [*NB: we*] felled[5] all the Trees in the point to Make observations   Sit up untill 12 oClock taken oservation this night

Course & Destance June 1St

S. 48° W	4	ms. to pt. Lbd. psd. Little Muddy on [Lbd.?] Sd. river 50 yds Wid
S 45° W	6	Ms. Isd psd. Bear Creek L. Sd. 20 yds. Wid
S. 39 W.	3	ms. to Pt. of Osge River
	13	

Passed a Small S⁰ on the S⁶ᵈ N. 25. W. 3 M.
h... or St P passes a... S⁰ a S S⁰ and
Leuser Creek on the Same Side 20 yd
Wide passes a Creek on L⁰ S⁰ 20 yd Wide, Call
Mast Creek, this is a Short Creek from...
above & below the Mouth gentle...
of about 50 foot, Delightfull Timber
of Oake ash walnut Hickory &c &
Wind from N.W. by W. N. 58. W. M. passed
a Creek Called Toucar on the L⁰ Side, N 75 W
3 Mⁱ to a Pt S P⁰ Called Batue a de charm,
a plain on the hill opposit I got out &
Walked on the L S⁰ thro a Charming Bottom
of rich Land about... May then I
assended a hill of about 170 foot on the
top of which is... and about 100 acrs
of Land which... Timber on this hill
one of the party Says he has found...
a very extensive Cave under this hill
the Land on the...
is... the is a very bad part
the River... Deer Killed to day
our hunters one of the horses is
... the other lost his Shows to day
the Bottom on the S Side to day
covered with... nor very good
Batue a deshoon... the hill land Comes to the bank...

10. Missouri River near Mouth of Osage River and East,
ca. June 1, 1804, Field Notes, reverse of document 17

[Lewis]   *Friday June 1st (Poi[n]t. Obstn. No. 3.)*[6]

On the point of land formed by the confluence of the Great Osage River and the Missouri made the following observations.

Pole ★'s magnetic Azimuth by Circumfetr.			N. 7° W.

		h	m	s.
Time by Chronometer at place of Obstn.	P. M.	10	29	20
Pole ★'s magnetic Azimuth by Circumfertr.			N. 6° 10′ E.	

		h	m	s
Time by Chronometer, June 2ed	A. M.	0	1	20
Latitude of place of observation		38°	31′	6.9″

1. Perhaps the later Bear Creek Island. MRC map 6.

2. Probably later Loose Creek, in Osage County, Missouri. See fig. 10. Ibid.

3. The Osage River meets the Missouri River at the Osage-Cole county line, just northeast of present Osage City. It is a large, unnamed stream on fig. 10. Ibid.

4. The following numbers are written in a column under the last line of this entry: 4, 3, 6—apparently the distances that day.

5. Biddle changed Clark's "fall" to "felled" after adding "we."

6. Lewis's observation from Codex O.

[Clark][1]

June 2nd— Took the Dirts. [directions] of Son & moon &c &c. I measured the Osage & Missouris at this place made ther width as follows, the Missoure 875 yd. wide The Osage R 397 yds. wide, the distance between the 2 rivers 80 poles up is 40 ps. [poles?] Took equal altitudes & Mredian altitude also—and made them [*blank*] I assended the hill in the point 80 ps. from the pt. found it about *100* foot high, on the top is 2 graves, or mouns,[2] a Delightfull prospect from this hill which Comds. both rivers

Drewyer & Shields came to the opposit Side to day at SunSet we sent across & brought them over, they had been absent 7 Days Swam many creeks, much worsted. They informed us that the Countrey on both Sides of muddy river's to the hill called by the french [*blank*] 3 ms. below this place, a Small Praries below the hill, 4 Deer Killed to day I assend a hill &. after measuring the river &c. &c. &c.

[Clark]

June 2nd Satturday   Cap Lewis Took the Time & Distance of ☉s & moons nearest limbs, the Sun East—   and Meridean altitude of Suns U. L. with Octant, back observation gave for altitude 37° 28″ 00″.

Error of Octant 2° 00′ 00″ +.   made Several other observations—   I made an angle for the Wedth of the two rivers. The Missourie from the Point to the N. Side is 875 yards wide   the Osage River from the point to the S. E Side is 397 ⟨337⟩ yards wide, the destance between the two rivers at the pt. of high Land (100 foot above the bottom) and 80 poles up the Missouries from the point is 40 poles, on the top of this high land ⟨of⟩ under which is a limestone rock two Mouns or graves are raised—   ⟨I took Meridine altitude of the Suns⟩   from this pt. which Comds [*NB: commands*] both rivers I had a delightfull prospect of the Missouries up & down, also the Osage R. up.   George Drewyer & John Shields who we had Sent with the horses by Land on the N Side joined us this evening much worsted, they being absent Seven Days depending on their gun, the greater part of the time rain, they were obliged to raft or Swim many Creeks, those men gave a flattering account of the Countrey Commencing below the first hill on the N Side and extendg Parrelal with the river for 30 or 40 Ms. The Two Muddey river passing Thro: & som fine Springs & Streams   our hunters kill Several Deer to day, Some Small licks on the S E of the Osage River.

[Lewis]   *Saturday, June 2ed*[3]
Observed time and distance of ☉'s and ☽'s nearest Limbs, ☉ East. with Sextant.

	Time				*Distance*	
	h	m	s			
A. M.	7	18	32.5	74°	47′	23.7″

Note—this is the mean of a set of 8.

	h	m	s			
A. M.	8	13	45	74°	23′	30″
	″	16	42	″	21	00
	″	22	27	″	20	30
	″	24	56	″	19	20
	″	26	21	″	17	15
	″	27	10	″	17	30

	Time			Distance		
	h	m	s			
A. M.	7	42	12	74°	36'	00"
"		43	52	"	35	00
"		45	39	"	34	45
"		47	22	"	32	00
"		49	34	"	32	45
"		51	12	"	32	00

Note—this set is probably a little inaccurate in consequence of the moon's being obscured in some measure by the clouds.—

	h	m	s			
A. M.	7	53	38	74°	32'	00"
"		56	19	"	29	15
"		58	32	"	29	00
	8	0	10	"	28	45
"		2	12	"	26	30
"		4	26	"	26	20
"		6	00	"	25	45
"		7	38	"	24	00

	h	m	s			
A. M.	8	35	58	74°	14'	7.5"
"		38	28	"	14	00
"		40	2	"	13	20
"		43	9	"	13	00
"		44	47	"	12	45
"		46	4	"	12	00

Equal altitudes of the ☉, with Sextant

	h	m	s					
A. M.	8	58	9	P. M.	3°	3'	49"
"		59	27		"	5	8
	9	00	53		"	6	37

Altitude by Sextant at time of Obstn.   95° 50' 45"

meridian Altd. of ☉'s L. L. by Back observation with Octant—	37°	28'	—"
Latitude deduced from this observation	38°	31'	6.9"

☉'s magnetic azimuth by Circumferenter.   Due West

	h	m	s
Time by Chronometer P. M.	4	59	14
Altitude by Sextant of ⊙'s L. L.	52	21	00
⊙'s magnetic azimuth by Circumfetr.		N. 88° W.	

	h	m	s
Time by Chronometer P. M.	5	11	30
Altitude of ⊙'s L. L. by Sextant	47°	16	—"
⊙'s magnetic azimuth by Circumftr.		N. 86° W.	

	h	m	s
Time by Chronometer P. M.	5	23	14
Altitude by Sextant of ⊙'s L. L.	42°	52'	—"

1. Beside the date are these figures in column: 7 and 6. Written under the entry at right angles are the words "Carsuex-Raft."

2. Five mounds are known on the high point of land north of modern Osage City, in two groups: one of three mounds, and one of two, the latter on the extreme eastern part of the point. Clark undoubtedly saw the group of two. Many prehistoric, Middle to Late Woodland earthen burial mounds dating to the first millennium A.D. and a little later are found along the Missouri River bluffs in central and western Missouri. Fowke; Chapman (AM), 2:21–137.

3. Lewis's observation from Codex O.

[Clark]   June Sunday 3rd 1804[1]

the fore part of the day fair   I attempted to take equal alltitudes, & M[eridian] Altitudes, but was disapointed, the Clouds obsured the Sun, took the D. of ⊙ & ☽ : Capt Lewis & George Drewyer went out & Killed a Deer, We Set out at 5 oClock P M   Cloudy & rain, *West* 5 Ms. to the mo. of Murrow Creek[2] Lb Sd.   a pt. St. Side   Keeping along the Lbd Side 1 Ms., passed the mouth of a Creek on Lbd Side 3 ms., I call Cupboard, Creek,[3] mouths behind a rock which projects into the river, Camped in the mouth of the Creek aforesaid [Moreau River], at the mouth of this Creek I saw much fresh Signs of Indians, haveing Crossed   2 Deer Killed to day. I have a verry Sore Throat, ⟨great⟩ & am Tormented with Musquetors & Small ticks.

[Clark]   *June* 3rd Sunday 1804

The forepart of the day fair   Took meridional altitude of ⊙s U: L with the Octant and Glass Horrison adjusted back observation.   the instrument gave 38° 2′ 00″—   it was Cloudy and the Suns disk much obsured, and Cannot be Depended on.

We made other Observations in the evening after the return of Capt Lewis from a walk of three or four ms. round—   We Set out at 5 oClock P. M. proceeded on five miles to the mouth of a Creek on the L. S. 20 yds. wide Called Murow, passed a Creek at 3 ms. which I call *Cupbord* Creek as it Mouths above a rock of that appearance. Several Deer Killed to day— at the mouth of the Murow Creek I Saw much Sign of war parties of Inds. haveing Crossed from the mouth of this Creek. I have a bad Cold with a Sore throat. Near *West 5 Miles*

[Lewis]   *Sunday June 3rd*[4]

Observed time and distance of ⊙'s and ☽'s nearest limbs, the East:—

	Time			Distance		
	h	m	s			
A. M.	6	22	21	61°	40′	—″
	″	24	5	″	40	—
	″	25	36	″	39	45
	″	26	44	″	39	30
	″	28	18	″	37	—
	″	29	51	″	37	30
A. M.	6	36	25	61	35	—
	″	41	27	″	34	45
	″	49	6	″	33	—
	″	54	36	″	30	15
	″	55	41	″	30	7·5
	″	57	—	″	30	—

	Time			Distance		
	h	m	s			
A. M.	7	—	7	61°	27′	30″
	″	3	57	″	27	30
	″	6	1	″	27	15
	″	7	53	″	26	52
	″	9	55	″	26	—
	″	11	5	″	25	15

		h	m	s				
A. M.		7	14	6		61°	23′	30″
		″	16	2		″	24	—
		″	17	53		″	23	15
		″	19	33		″	22	—
		″	23	28		″	20	45
		″	25	7		″	20	45

		h	m	s				
A. M.		7	29	16		61°	19′	—″
		″	31	17		″	16	15
		″	32	56		″	17	—
		″	33	56		″	15	30
		″	34	50		″	15	—
		″	35	59		″	15	—

		h	m	s				
A. M.		7	39	55		61°	14′	—″
		″	40	55		″	13	45
		″	42	39		″	13	15
		″	45	16		″	12	45
		″	46	38		″	11	30
		″	47	41		″	11	—

Equal altitudes of the ☉, with Sextant.

		h	m	s.
A. M.		8	26	1
		″	27	19
		″	28	41

P. M.—The ☉ was obscured by clouds and the observation consequently lost.—

meridian altd. of ☉'s L. L. by back observation with Octant 38° 2′ —″

The ☉'s disk was much obscured by clouds during this observation, not much confidence is therefore due it's accuracy.—

1. Biddle placed the heading "June 3 to 5th" at the top of document 17 in the Field Notes.

2. The Moreau River, the party's camp for the night, enters the Missouri in Cole County, Missouri, just east of Jefferson City, the present state capital. It is probably named for one of several Frenchmen named Moreau residing in Missouri. Fig. 14, a sketch map on the reverse of document 18 of the Field Notes, appears to show the Missouri upstream from the Osage River, without naming most of the streams. MRC map 6; McDermott (WCS), 147.

3. Apparently Rising Creek, in Cole County, some two miles east of the mouth of Moreau River. MRC map 6.

4. Lewis's observation from Codex O.

[Clark][1]

June 4th 1804 Monday, a fair Day   Sent out 3 hunters, our mast broke by the boat running under a tree   Passed an Islands on Stbd Side on which grow Seede[r][2] a Creek at [*blank*] miles on the Starbd Sd. *Course* N. 30° W 4 ms. to pt. on St. Side below 2d Isd.   passed a Creek on Lbd Side 15 yd. wide, I call *Nightingale* Creek.   this Bird Sang all last night and is the first of the kind I ever herd,[3] below this Creek and the last   Passed a Small Isd on the Stbd. N. 25 W. 3 ms. to a pt. on St. Sd.   passed a Sm. Isd. on St. Sd. and *Seeder* Creek[4] on the Same Side 20 yds wide   passed a Creek on Lbd Sd. 20 yd wide, I call Mast Creek,[5] this is a Short Creek, fine land above & below the mouth. Jentle rise of about 50 foot, Delightfull Timber of Oake ash walnut hickory &c. &c.   wind from N W. by W. N. 58° W. 7½ ms. passed a Creek Called *Zoncar*[6] on the Lbd Side, N 75 W 3 me. to a pt. S. Sd. called *Batue a De charm*,[7] a plain on the hill opposit. I got out & walked on the L Sd. thro a Charming Bottom of rich Land about one mile   then I assended a hill of about 170 foot on the top of which is a Moun[8] and about 100 acres of Land of Dead timber on this hill   one of the party says he has found Lead ore[9] a verry extensive Cave under this hill next the river, the Land on the top is fine, This is a very bad part of the river   Seven Deer Killed to day by our hunters—   one of the horses is Snaged, the other lost his Shous to day   the Bottom on the St. Side to day is covered with rushes, not verry good [*one word illegible*]   the high land Comes to the bank on the Labd Side and good 2d rate land.

[Clark]   *June* 4th *Monday* 1804

a fair day   three men out on the right flank   passed a large Island on the St. Side Called Seeder Island, this Isd. has a great Deel of Ceedar on it, passed a Small Creek at 1 ms. [*NB: 1 mile*] 15 yd. Wide which we named Nightingale Creek from a Bird of that discription which Sang for us all last night, and is the first of the Kind I ever heard.   passed the mouth of Seeder Creek at 7 ms. on the S. S. abt. 20 yds. Wide above Some Small Isds.   passed a Creek on the L. S. abt. 15 yds. wide. *Mast* [*NB: Mast*] *Creek*, here the Sergt. at the helm run under a bending Tree & broke the mast, Some delightfull Land, with a jentle assent about the Creek, well timbered, Oake, Ash, walnut &c. &c. passed, wind N W. by W.   passed a Small Creek Called Zan Cau C on the L. S: at this last point I got out and walked on the L. Sd. thro a rush [*NB: rush*] bottom for 1 Miles & a Short Distance thro: Nettles[10] as high as my brest   assended a hill of about 170 foot to a place where the french report that Lead ore has been found, I saw no mineral of that description, Capt Lewis Camped imediately under this hill,[11] to wate which gave me Some time to examine the hill, on the top is a moun of about 6 foot high and about 100 Acres of land which the large timber is Dead   in Decending about 50 foot a projecting lime Stone rock under which is a Cave   at one place in this projecting rocks I went on one which Spured up and hung over the Water   from the top of this rock I had a prospect of the river for 20 or 30 ms. up, from the Cave which incumposed [encompassed] the hill I decended by a Steep decent to the foot, a verry bad part of the river opposit this hill, the river Continu to fall Slowly, our hunters killed 7 Deer to day   The land our hunters passed thro: to day on the S. S. was Verry fine the latter part of to day.   the high land on the S. S: is about 2d rate

Course & Distance 4th June

N. 30° W.	4	ms. a pt. on S. Sd. psd. a C. & 2 Isd.
N. 25° W.	3	ms. to a pt. on S. Sd. psd. Seeder C.
N. 58° W.	7 ½	ms. to pt. on L. S. a Creek on L. S.
N. 75 W.	3	Ms. to a pt. on S. Sd. opsd. Mine Hill
	17 ½	

1. Under the lower portion of this entry on this sheet of the Field Notes (reverse of document 17) is a sketch map of the area between the Osage River and Little Tavern Creek (see fig. 10). In some instances it is difficult to distinguish between map and text. See Wood.

2. The island retained the name Cedar Island; it lay nearly opposite Jefferson City at present Cedar City. The "seeder" is eastern red cedar. Steyermark, 45; MRC map 6.

3. Either Wears Creek or Coon Creek, both at Jefferson City. MRC map 7; MRM map 17. There is no true nightingale (*Luscinia megarhynchos*) in America. The cardinal, *Cardinalis cardinalis* [AOU, 593], was sometimes called the Virginia nightingale, but this bird would have been familiar to the captains. The same objection applies to the mockingbird, *Mimus polyglottos* [AOU, 703], which has also been suggested. Paul Johnsgard (personal communication) suggests that it might be the whip-poor-will, *Caprimulgus vociferus* [AOU, 417]. But in the weather remarks on June 11, the "whiperwill" is named. Perhaps Lewis recognized the bird and made the weather observation, while Clark was unfamiliar with the species and used the term nightingale; or perhaps nightingale was a common name at

the time for the whip-poor-will. One final possibility is the hermit thrush, *Catharus guttatus* [AOU, 759]. Coues (HLC), 1 : 14 n. 27; Cutright (LCPN), 55 n. 13; Holmgren, 32.

4. Cedar Creek now flows into Turkey Creek, which reaches the Missouri at Cedar City, Callaway County, Missouri. See fig. 14. MRC map 7; MRM map 17.

5. Evidently later Grays Creek, in Cole County. See fig. 14. MRC map 7.

6. Perhaps later Meadow Creek, in Cole County, Missouri. MRC map 7.

7. A *bature* is a sandy beach built up inside a curve in a river. There may be some connection with Jean Marie Ducharme of Cahokia, who traded with the Little Osages and Missouris in 1772–73. On the other hand, *charme* was a French word for the hornbeam or yoke elm, *Carpinus caroliniana* Walt. Osgood (FN), 50 n. 4; McDermott (WCS), 148; McDermott (GMVF), 21; Steyermark, 524–26.

8. Probably the same group of mounds noted on June 2.

9. This area is within the central Missouri lead-zinc region, and galena (lead ore) has been reported not only from the Jefferson City (Ordovician) limestone and all lower formations, but even from some of the coal beds of the area. Hinds, 158–59.

10. *Urtica dioica* L. var. *procera* (Muhl.) Wedd., tall nettle. Steyermark, 567.

11. In northwestern Cole County, probably in the vicinity of the later Sugar Loaf Rock. Coues (HLC), 1 : 14 and n. 30; MRC map 7. Called "Mine Hill" in course and distance table of second entry for this day.

[Clark]

June 5th Tuesday, Jurked the Vennison Killed yesterday,[1] after Seting over the Scouting Party or hunder of 3 men Set out at 6 oClock   Course N 57° W to a pt. on S. Sd. 5 ms.   passed a Creek on L. Sd. I call Lead C[2] of 15 yds   passed one on the S. Called Lit: good-womans Creek[3] about 20 yds. wide   Passed a Willow Isd.   a Butifull Prarie approaching near the river above Lead C & extends to the Mine river[4] in a westerly Derection, passed the Mouth of the Creek of the Big Rock[5] 15 yds Wide at 4 ms. on the Lbd Sd.   at 11 oClock brought a *Caissie* [cajeu] in which was 2 men, from 80 League up the Kansias River, where they wintered and caught a great qty of Beever but unfortunatey lost it by the burning of the plains, the Kansas Nation[6] hunted on the Missourie last Winter and are now persueing the Buffalow in the Plains, passed a Projecting Rock called the *Manitou* a Painting[7]   from this Deavel to the Pt. on the Lbd Side N 23° W 7½ Ms. The Same course 2½ ms. Creek Cld. Manitou[8]   passed a ⟨large Isd.⟩ on the Lbd. Side about 40 yd. wide, a Sand bar in the middle of the River   passed up between the Sand & L. Shore one Mile to a Small Creek 10 yd. wide, (I call Sand C).[9] We run on the Sand and was obliged

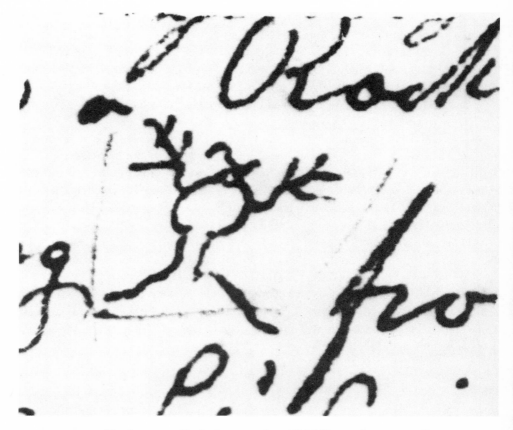

11. Manitou on a Rock, June 5, 1804, Field Notes, document 18

to return to the Starbd Side, I am verry unwell with a Slight feever from a bad cold caught three days ago at the *Grand' so'* [Osage?] R— passed a Small Willow Isd. on S. Side, a large one in the Middle of the river,[10] York Swam to the Isd. to pick greens, and Swam back with his greens, the Boat Drew too much water to cross the quick Sands which intervened, She draws 4 foot water, a fair wind our mast being broke by accidence provented our takeing the advantage of it passed the lower point of a large Island, opposit the Current devides between ⟨three⟩ 4 Small Isds on the St Side. we found the water excessively hard for 12 Miles as we were oblged to pass up the center of the Current between two of the Isds. & round the heads of the other 2 the Current Setting imediately against the points which was choked up with Drift for a mile— Above those Isd. on the St. Side we camped altogeth[er][11] our Hunter or Spis [spies][12] discovered the sign of a war party of abt. 10 Men[13]

[Clark]   *June 5th Tuesday 1804*

after Jurking the meet Killed yesterday and Crossing the hunting party we Set out at 6 oClock, from the last Course & distance, N 51° W. 5 ms. to a pt. on the St: Sd.   passed a Small Creek on the Ld. S: I call *Lead* C.   passed a Creek on the S. S. of 20 yds. wide Cald. Lit: [*NB: Little*] Good Womans C.   on the L. S. a Prarie extends from Lead C. parrelel with the river to Mine river, at 4 ms. Passed the Creek of the big rock about 15 yds. wide on the L. Sd.   at 11 oClock brought too a Small *Caissee* [*NB: raft made of two canoes tied together*] in which was two french men, from 80 Leagues up the Kansias [*NB: Kanzas*] R. where they wintered, and Cought a great quantity of Beaver, the greater part of which they lost by fire from the Praries, those men inform that the Kansas Nation are now out in the plains hunting Buffalow, they hunted last winter on this river   Passed a projecting rock on which was painted a figue [14] and a Creek at 2 ms. above Called Little Manitou Creek from the Painted rock   this Creek 20 yds. wide on the L. Sd.   passed a Small Creek on L. S. opposit a Verry bad Sand bar of Several ms. in extent, which we named *Sand* C   here my Servent York Swam to the Sand bar to geather greens for our Dinner and returnd with a Sufficent quantity wild *Creases* [*NB: Cresses*] or Teng [*NB: Tongue*] grass,[15] we passed up for 2 ms on the L. S. of this Sand and was obliged to return, the Watr. uncertain the quick Sand Moveing   we had a fine wind, but could not make use of it, our Mast being broke, we passed between 2 Small Islands in the Middle of the Current, & round the head of three   a rapid Current for one mile and Camped on the S. S. opsd. a large Island in the middle of the river; one Perogue did not get up for two hours, our Scout discovd. the fresh sign of about 10 Inds. I expect that those Indians are on their way to war against the Osages nation probably they are the Saukees

Course & Destance June 5th

N. 51° W.	5	ms. to a pt. on S. S: psd. 3 C. 1 S. 2 L. S.
N. 23° W	7 ½	ms. a pt. L S. psd. Mont. Creek
	12 ½	

1. Jerking was done by cutting meat into very thin strips and drying it in the sun. The finished product was commonly used as a travel ration by Indians, trappers, and fron-

Praries, those men inform that.
the Kansas Nation are now out in
the plains hunting Buffalow, they
hunted last winter on this river
Passed a projecting rock on which
was painted a figure and a Creek
at 2 m̃ above Called Little Manitou
Creek. from the Painted rock this
Creek 20 yd. wide on the L. S. passed
a Small Creek on L. S. oppost a
Very bad Sand bar of Several m̃.
in extent, which we named Sand
C here my Servent york Swam
to the Sand bar to geather greens,
greens for our Dinner and returnd
with a Suffecent quantity weld
<ins>Cresses</ins>   <ins>Tongue</ins>
Creases or teng grass, we passed
up for 2 m̃ on the L. S. of this Sand
and was oblieged to return, the water
uncertain the quick Sand moveing
we had a fine wind, but could
not make use of it, our Mast
being broke, we passed between

12. Manitou on a Rock, June 5, 1804, Codex A, p. 34

280

tiersmen in general. "Jerky" comes from the Spanish *charqui*, itself derived from a Quechua Indian word. Wentworth; Fletcher & La Flesche, 2:344–45.

2. Perhaps either Rock Creek or Mud Creek, in Cole County. MRC map 7.

3. Bonne Femme Creek, in Boone County, Missouri. Ibid.

4. Lamine River, in Cooper County, Missouri. See below, June 8, 1804.

5. Possibly either Rock Creek or Mud Creek, in Cole County, Missouri. MRC map 7.

6. The Kansa, or Kaw, people were a small tribe residing on the Kansas River when first known to Europeans in the late seventeenth century. They spoke a Siouan language of the Dhegiha group, closely related to Osage. Their economy was based on hunting and horticulture. In 1804 their village was on the Blue River near present Manhattan, Kansas. The tribe gave its name to both the state and the river. Hodge, 1:653–56; Swanton, 293–94; Wedel (KA), 50; Unrau.

7. See fig. 11. A more elaborate version (fig. 12) is in the Codex A entry for this day.

8. Moniteau Creek reaches the Missouri just east of the Moniteau-Cole county line, Missouri. "Manitou" is a French version of an Algonquian word designating a spirit, and here probably refers to the figure on the rock, as Clark indicates. Hodge, 1:800–801; MRC map 7.

9. Perhaps Factory Creek, near the Moniteau-Cole county line. MRC map 7.

10. Perhaps the later Ville Monteau Island. Ibid.

11. In Boone County, in the neighborhood of the later town of Sandy Hook on the opposite shore. "Altogether" may mean that they kept the camp compact because of the report of the war party. MRC maps 7, 8.

12. "Spy" on the frontier was virtually synonymous with "scout."

13. Under the latter part of this entry on this sheet of the Field Notes (reverse of document 18) is a sketch map (fig. 14) of the Missouri River from about the mouth of the Osage River to some distance above the mouth of the Grand River. See Wood.

14. See fig. 12.

15. Probably one of the native species of *Rorippa*, yellow, or marsh, cress. The habitat description fits that of either *Rorippa sinuata* (Nutt.) Hitchc., spreading yellow cress; *R. sessiliflora* (Nutt.) Hitchc., sessile-flowered cress; or *R. palustris* (L.) Bess., bog yellow cress. Probably the reference is to the last, the most common species in Missouri. Steyermark, 758–60; Barkley, 123.

[Clark]   Wednesday the 6th of June 1804.[1]

Mended our mast this morning and Set out at 7 oClock, under a Jentle Braise from the S, E by S   N 28° W 3½ miles to a hill on St Sd. pass:g the N: belge of the Island Called Split rock Island, the river rose last night a foot   the Countrey about this Isd. is delightfull   large rush bottom of rushes below on the St. Side   N 49° W, 1½ Ms. to the mouth of Split rock ⟨Creek⟩ River[2] [*blank*] yds. wide on the Starboard Side opod. the pt. of a Isd: passed a place in the projecting rock Called the *hole*   thro' the rock, a ⟨Small⟩ round Cave pass thro the Pt. of rock's   *West* 1½ ms. to a pt. on

Std. Sd. opposit a Clift of rocks abt 200 foot   N 31° W. 4 ms ½ to a pt. on L: Side   passed *Saline* Creek[3] on the L. Side   a large Salt Lick & Spring 9 me. up the Creek, one bushel of water will make 7 lb. of good Salt

(Information)   Took Meridian altitude of ☉ Limb. 37° 6' 0'' equat to [*blank*] of Lattidude.

on this Creek [Saline], So great a no of Salt Springs are on it that the water is brackish   N 51° W to a Belge of an Isd[4] on the S. Sd. at 3 ms. Passed a Willow Isd. in Middle, Some wind in the after part of to day from the S E, (the Banks are falling in greatly in this part of the river) as also is one Side or the other in all the Course, we assended on the North Side of the Isd. and finding that the perogues Could not Keep up Camped 2 hs. by Sun. on the Sd Sd[5]   the land below this is good.

[Clark]   *June 6th Wednesday 1804*

Mended our Mast this morning &, Set out at 7 oClock under a jentle breise from S. E. by S   passed the large Island, and a Creek Called Split rock Creek at 5 ms. on the S. S. psd. a place to the rock from which 20 yds. we.   this Creek takes its name, a projecting rock with a hole thro: a point of the rock, at 8 ms. passed the mouth of a Creek Called *Saline* or Salt ⟨Creek⟩ R on the L. Sd. this ⟨Creek⟩ River is about 30 yds. wide, and has So many Licks & Salt Springs on its banks that the Water of the Creek is Brackish, one Verry large Lick is 9 ms. up on the left Side   the water of the Spring in this Lick is Strong as one bushel of the water is said to make 7 lb. of good Salt   passed a large Isd. & Several Small ones, the water excessivly Strong, So much So that we Camped Sooner than the usial time to waite for the pirogue, The banks are falling in Verry much to day   river rose last night a foot.

Capt. Lewis took meridean altd. of Suns U. L. with the octant above Split Rock C. & made the altitude 37° 6' 00   error of octt. as useal 2° 0' 0'' + The Countrey for Several miles below is good, on the top of the high land back is also tolerable land   Some buffalow Sign to day[6]

I am Still verry unwell with a Sore throat & head ake

Course & Destance June 6th

N. 28° W	3 ½	ms. to a Hill on S. S. pd. N. Bilg: of Isd.
N 49° W	1 ½	Ms. to a Creek Split rock

West—	1 ½	Ms. to a pt. on S. S. opsd. a Clift
N 31° W	4 ½	ms. to a pt. on L. S. psd. Saline C. L. S.
N. 51° W	3	ms. to a bilg of an Isd. to left pd. Sm. Isd.
	14	

(Point of observation No. 4.)

[Lewis]   *Wednesday, June 6th* 1804.[7]

On the Starbord shore one & ½ miles above the mouth of the *split rock* creek.

observed meridian altd. of ☉'s L. L. with Octant by back observation 37° 6′ —″

1. Biddle's notation at the top of this sheet of the Field Notes (document 19), reads "June 6 to June 9th."

2. A literal translation of the French name, Roche Percée, now Perchee Creek, in Boone County, Missouri. Thwaites (LC), 1:41 n. 2; MRC map 8.

3. Petite Saline Creek, so called from salt deposits in the vicinity, enters the Missouri River in northwest Moniteau County, Missouri. Coues (HLC), 1:16 n. 35; MRC map 8.

4. Evidently the island later called Rocher Island and still later Terrapin Island; it is no longer on maps. Nicollet (MMR), 358; MRC map 8; MRM map 21.

5. In Boone County, probably a little downstream from where Interstate Highway 70 crosses the Missouri River. MRC map 8.

6. The first mention of the buffalo, *Bison bison*, in the journals. They did not actually shoot one until August 23, 1804. Hall, 2:1108–10.

7. Lewis's observation from Codex O.

[Clark]

Thursday 7th of June 1804   Set out early   passed the head of the Isd from the Isd. ⟨to a pt on Lbd Side⟩ N. 61° W. to the mouth of a Creek Called big monitu[1] on St. Sd. 4½ ms. psd. a Sand bar in the river, Som Buffalow Sign   Sent out George Drewyer & Newmon to hunt ⟨them⟩   Capt Lewis and 6 men went to a Lick up this Creek on the right Side over 2 mes. & 2 other not far above   the water runs out of the bank & not verry Strong.   3 to 500 G[allons] for a bushell.

S 88° W. 2 Miles to a pt. on Lbd. Side, high bluff on the Stbd. Side, Monitou Creek is 30 yds. Wide at the mouth, passed a painted part of a Projecting rock[2]   we found ther a Den of rattle Snakes,[3] Killed 3 pro-

13. Manitou, Buffalo, and Indian on a Rock,
June 7, 1804, Field Notes, reverse of document 19

ceeded   on   passed, S 81° W 4 ms. to a pt. on S. Side   passed an Island
in the Middle of the river,[4] S. 87° W. to a pt. of high Land on the L. S:
pass:'g over the Middle of a willow Island, ms. 3 ½   proceed on ½ a mile
on this Course a[nd] Camped at the mouth of Good womans river[5] on the
S. S. about 35 yds wide, & navagable Som D[istance].   our hunters brought
in 3 bear[6] this evening—& infd. that the Countrey between this R. & the
Monitou R is rich and well watered, Capt. Lewis went out an hour this
evening

[Clark]   *June 7th Thursday* 1804
   Set out early passed the head of the Island opposit which we Camped
last night, and brackfast at the Mouth of a large Creek on the S. S. of 30
yds wide Called big *Monetou*, from the pt. of the Isd. or Course of last
night to the mouth of this Creek is N 61° W 4½ ms. a Short distance
above the mouth of this Creek, is Several Courious Paintings and Carve-
ing in the projecting rock of Limestone inlade with white red & blue flint,
of a verry good quallity,[7] the Indians have taken of this flint great quantities. We landed at this Inscription and found it a Den of rattle Snakes,
we had not landed 3 minutes before three verry large Snakes wer ob-

served on the Crevises of the rocks & Killed— at ⟨whilst from⟩ the mouth of the last mentioned Creek Capt. Lewis took four or five men & went to Some ⟨Creeks⟩ Licks or Springs of Salt water from two to four miles up the Creek on Rt. Side the water of those Springs are not Strong, Say from 4 to 600 Gs. of water for a Bushel of Salt passed Some Small willow Islands and Camped at the Mouth of a Small river called *Good Womans River* this river is about 35 yards wide and Said to be navagable for Perogues Several Leagues Capt. Lewis with 2 men went up the Creek a Short distance. our Hunters brought in three *Bear* this evening, and informs that the Countrey thro: which they passed from the last Creek is fine rich land, & well watered.

Course & Destance June 7th

N 61° W	4 ½	ms. to Mo: of Manitou on S. S.
S 88° W	2	Ms. to pt. on Lbd Side
S 81° W	4	Ms. to pt. S. S. psd. an Island
S 87° W	3 ½	ms. to pt. of High Land on L. S. psd. W. Isd.
	14 ms.	Passed the Mo: of good womans R

1. Moniteau Creek meets the Missouri at Rocheport, on the Howard-Boone county line, Missouri. MRC map 8.

2. See fig. 13.

3. Probably the timber rattler, *Crotalus horridus*. Burroughs, 273.

4. Perhaps the later Diana Island. MRC map 8.

5. At the mouth of Bonne Femme Creek, in Howard County, some three to four miles below present Booneville, on the opposite shore. Ibid.

6. According to Whitehouse, they were a female and two cubs, killed by Drouillard.

7. The lower Mississippian rocks (Pierson, Fern Glen, Reeds Spring, Grand Falls, Burlington, and Keokuk formations) of central Missouri are noted for their chert (flint) content. Some are mottled and colorful. Pierson cherts are red to brown; those of Fern Glen are grayish green and Reeds Springs are black; most of the remainder are cream to light gray. Howe & Koenig, 59–66.

[Clark] *June 8*th Friday[1]

Set out at Daylight proceeded on the Course of last night S 87° W 3 ms passed a Willow Island, from the Point of last Course S 81° W. 3 ms. to a pt. on S. S: passd a [*blank*] Isd. in the middle of the river, passd a run[2] on the Ld S: above a pt. of rocks 3 ms. on which thir is a number of Deer

Licks, N 88° W. 3 Ms. to a pt L S: N. 83° W 2 ms. to the Mo of Mine River,[3] psd an Isd.— This river is 90 yards wide & navagable for Perogues about 90 Ms. I went out on the L S. about 4 ms. below this R. and found the Countrey for one mile back good Land and well watered the hills not high with a gentle assent from the river, well timbered with oake, walnit Hickory ash, &c. the land Still further back becoms thin and open, with Black & rasp Berries,[4] and Still further back the Plains Commence, The french inform that Lead ore is found on this river in Several places, it heads up between the Osagees & Kansas River the right hand folk [fork] passes in a Short distance of the Missourie at the antient Little Ozages Village[5] our hunter[6] Killed, 2 Deer, after Staying one hour at the mouth of this River, Cap Lewis went out & proceeded on one Mile & came in, he fount the land in the point high and fine Course N. 64° W 1 Ms. to a pt. on S. S. N. 80° W to the Lower pot a Id. on L. S. passed a ⟨large⟩ Small Isd. in the m: R. at (3 Ms.) met 3 men on a *Caussee* from R Dis Soux,[7] above *The Mahar* [Omaha] Nation loaded with fur. ⟨N 39 W 3½ Ms. to pt on S. S. opsd. a Prarie⟩ Camped on the Lower point of an Id. L. S. called the Mills,[8] here I found Kegs an Pummey [pumice] stone, and a place that fur or Skins had been burred [buried] by the hunters our Hunters Killed 5 Deer, Some rain, the Countrey on the S. S. is Verry fine

[Clark]   8th of *June, Friday 1804*

Set out this morning at Daylight proceeden on the Course of last night Passed two willow Islands & a Small Creek above a Rock point on the L. S. at 6 miles on which there is a number of Deer Licks, passed the *Mine* River at 9 ms. this river is about 70 yards wide at its mouth and is Said to be navagable for Perogues 80 or 90 ms. the ⟨main⟩ [NB: *West*][9] branch passes near the place where the Little osage Village formerly Stood on the Missouries, & heads between the Osarge & Kansias Rivers, the left hand fork[10] head with nearer Branches of the Osage River, The french inform that Lead Ore has been found in defferent parts of this river, I took Sjt. Floyd and went out 4 Ms. below this river, I found the land Verry good for a Mile or 1½ Ms. back and Sufficiently watered with Small Streams which lost themselves in the Missouries bottom, the Land rose gradeuelly from the river to the Summit of the high Countrey which is not more that 120 foot above High Water mark, we joined the Boat & Dined in the point above the mouth of this River, Capt. Lewis went out above the river & proceeded on one mile, finding the Countrey rich, the wedes & Vines So thick & high he came to the Boat— proceeded on passed an Island ⟨about⟩ and Camped at the lower point of an Island on the L. S. Called the Island of mills [*NB: mills*] about 4 ms. above Mine River at this place I found Kanteens, Axs, Pumey Stone & peltrey hid & buried (I suppose by some hunters) none of them (except the pumey Stone) was teched by one of our party, our hunters Killed 5 Deer to day, Commenced raining Soon after we Came too which prevented the party Cooking their provisions— our Spies inform that the Countrey they passed thro: on S. S. is a fine high bottom, no water.

Course & Distance 8th June

S 81° W.	3	ms. to a pt. on S. S. psd. Deer L. Creek L. S
N 88° W,	3	ms. to a pt. on L Side
N 83° W.	2	ms. to mouth of Mine Rivr. L. S.
N 64° W.	1	Ms. to a pt. on S. S.
N 80° W.	3	ms. to the Lower pt. of Isd. of Mills
	12	

This day we met 3 men on a Cajaux from the River of the Soux above the *Mahar nation* those men had been hunting 12 mo: & made about 900$ in pelts. & furs they were out of Provesions and out of Powder. rained this night

1. These figures are beside the June 8 date: 3, 3, 2. Other figures here are crossways on this sheet of the Field Notes (document 19):

$$3 \frac{1}{4}$$
$$18$$
$$9$$
$$10$$
$$10$$
$$18$$
$$\underline{15 \frac{1}{2}}$$
$$83 \frac{3}{4}$$

$$4$$
$$17$$
$$\underline{13}$$
$$117\ ^3/_4$$
$$5$$
$$17\ ^1/_2$$
$$12\ ^1/_2$$
$$14$$
$$14$$
$$\underline{12}$$
$$192\ ^3/_4$$
$$\underline{24}$$
$$216$$
$$\underline{5}$$
$$221$$

2. Perhaps Loupes Branch, at present Booneville, Cooper County, Missouri. MRC map 9.

3. The Lamine River reaches the Missouri River in Cooper County. The name is thought to derive from the report in 1714 by Sieur de Bourgmont that the Indians mined lead on its banks. See fig. 14. *Missouri Guide*, 359; MRC map 9.

4. Probably *Rubus occidentalis* L., black raspberry, one of the most common raspberries in Missouri. A number of other *Rubus* species, however, blackberry and raspberry, also occur along the Missouri River. Steyermark, 835–36.

5. The fork is the Blackwater River, which meets the Lamine in northwest Cooper County. The Little Osage village on the Missouri River is identified as the Plattner site, which is about three miles northeast of the town of Malta Bend, in Saline County. It was occupied in the mid-eighteenth century. Chapman (AM), 6–38.

6. Drouillard, according to Whitehouse.

7. Probably the Big Sioux River, which forms the boundary between Iowa and South Dakota.

8. Near the Saline-Cooper county line, probably east of the line and perhaps on the second of two islands later called Arrow Rock Island. MRC map 9.

9. Biddle apparently crossed out "main" when he substituted "West."

10. The Lamine River itself.

[Clark]

9th of *June* ⟨*Friday*⟩ *Satterday*   Set out early, water verry Swift   got fast on a log, detained us ¼ hour   Hard rain last night.   N 39° W 3 ½ Ms. to a pt. on the S. S. opposit the Commencement of the 1st Prarie, Called Prarie of the Arrows,[1] the river at this place about 300 yds. Wide   passed a Small Creek, Arrow Creek 8 yds. wide L. Sd.   the Current exceedingly Strong

N 34° E 2 ms. to the Belg of a Small Island Situated on the L. Sd. Passed
the mo: of Arrow Creek N 83° W 1½ ms. to a pt ⟨of High Land⟩ on L. S.
opposit Black bird C Small[2]   passed the head of the Isd. & a small Willow
one to the L. S. (☉s merdn. altd. back obsvn. 37 00′ 00[)]   N. 39° W 2 Ms.
to a pt. ⟨on S. S.⟩ of High Land on the L. Side opst. a pt. on St. S. River
about 350 yds. wide at this pt.   a Wind from the S at 4 oClock   (Handson
Sutn[)] [situation?]   on the High pt. a prarie & Small Lake below   N 32°
E 3½ Ms. to a pt. on L. S.   passed an Isld. in the mid R—   in passing up
on the S. S. opsd. the Isd. the Sturn of the boat Struck a log which was not
proceiveable   the Curt. Struck her bow and turn the boat against Some
drift & Snags which [were] below with great force; This was a disagreeable and Dangerous Situation, particularly as immense large trees were
Drifting down and we lay imediately in their Course,—   Some of our *men*
being prepared for all Situations leaped into the water Swam ashore with
a roap, and fixed themselves in Such Situations, that the boat was off in a
fiew minits, I can Say with Confidence that our party is not inferior to any
that was ever on the waters of the Missoppie   we Crossed to the Island
and Camped,[3] our hunters lay on the S. S.   ⟨*Gibson verry nearly*⟩   the
wind from the S. W.   the river continue to rise Slowly   Current excessive
rapid—   The Countrey on the S. S. high bottom & Delghtfull land   that
on the L. S. is up land or hills of from 50 to 100 foot higher than the
bottom & a thinly wooded, Countrey, Lands tolerably Good; Comminced
raining at 5 oClock and continued by intervales the greater part of the
night. We discovered that one of our French hands had a Conpt. [com-
plaint]—   We Commsd Doctering, I hope the Success in this case, usial to
an [*sentence incomplete*]

[Clark]   *9th of June 1804 Satturday*
    a fair morning, the River rise a little   we got fast on a Snag Soon after
we Set out which detained us a Short time   passed the upper Point of the
Island   Several Small Chanels running out of the River below a ⟨Bluff⟩
[*NB: cliff of rocks called the arrow rock*][4] & Prarie (Called the Prariee of
Arrows) where the river is confined within the width of ⟨300⟩ [*NB: 200*]
yds.   Passed a Creek of 8 yds. wide Called Creek of Arrows, this Creek is
Short and heads in the Praries on the L. S.   passed a Small Creek Called
Blackbird Creek S. S. and One Islands below & a Prarie above on the

L. S.   a Small Lake above the Prarie— opposit the Lower point of the 2d. Island on the S. S. we had like to have Stove our boat, in going round a Snag her Stern Struck a log under Water & She Swung round on the Snag, with her broad Side to the Current expd. to the Drifting timber, by the active exertions of our party we got her off in a fiew Mints. without engerey and Crossed to the Island where we Campd.   our hunters lay on the S. S.   the Perogue Crossed without Seeing them & the banks too un-certain to Send her over— Some wind from the S accompanied with rain this evening— The Lands on the S. S. is a high rich bottom   the L. S. appears oven [open?] and of a good quallity runing gradually to from fifty to 100 foot.

Course & Destance June 9th

N 39° W,	4	Ms. to a pt. on S. S. opsd. a Prarie
N 34° E.	2	ms. to pt. of an Isd. L. S.
N 83° W	1 ½	ms. to a pt. on L. S. opsd. B. Bs Cr.
N 39 W.	2	ms. to a pt. of High Ld. on L. S.
N 32 E	3 ½	ms. to a pt. on L. S. psd. an Isld
	13	

(Point of Observation No. 5.)

[Lewis]   *Saturday June 9th*[5]

On the N. W. side of a small island, two miles above the *prarie* of *the Arrows*.

Observed meridian Altd. of ☉'s L. L. with Octant by the back observatn.   37° —′ —″

1. In the vicinity of the present town of Arrow Rock and Arrow Rock State Park in Saline County, Missouri. Arrow Creek is probably Pierre Fresne Creek, in Saline County. MRC map 9; MRM map 24.

2. Evidently later Richland Creek, in Howard County, Missouri. Coues (HLC), 1:18; MRM map 24.

3. Somewhat above Richland Creek and probably below the later village of Bluff Port, Howard County. MRC map 9; MRM map 25.

4. The name of the bluff, called Pierre à Flèche as early as 1723, supposedly derives from an Indian tradition. The present town of Arrow Rock and Arrow Rock State Park,

both in Saline County, commemorate the name. After Fort Osage (see below, June 23, 1804) was abandoned in 1813, the post was moved to Arrow Rock. Coues (HLC), 1 : 18 n. 40; *Missouri Guide*, 357; MRC No. 9. Biddle apparently crossed out "Bluff" when he substituted "cliff of rocks."

5. Lewis's observation from Codex O.

[Clark][1]

June 10th Sunday 1804   Some rain last night   we set out early   Saw a number of Goslings this morning, Continued on the Course of last night, thence N. 8 E. 2½ ms. to a pt. on the L. S.   passed a part of the River that the banks are falling in takeing with them large trees of Cotton woods[2] which is the Common groth in the Bottoms Subject to the flud   North 1 Me along the L. Side ⟨N. 23° W to the Mo: of Chareton⟩ N. 40° W. 1 ms. along the L, S. opposit the two Charletons [Charitons],[3] on the N. Side, those rivers mouth together, the 1st 40 yds. wide the next 90 yds. Wide and navagable Some distance in the Countrey, the land below is high & not verry good. Came to and took Mdnl. altd. of Sons U. L. back obsvn. with the octant   Made it 37° 12′ oo″, delayed 1½ Hour. N. 70° W ½ of a me. along the L. Sd.—   S 60° W ½ m. on L. S. the Same Course to the Pt. S. S. 1½ Ms. We halted and Capt Lewis Killed a Buck   the Current is excessively Swift about this place N. 80° W. 3 ms to [*hole*] a pt. on S. S. passed a Isd. Called Sheeco Islan[4]   wind from the N W   Camped in a Prarie on the L. S.,[5] Capt Lewis & my Self Walked out 3 ms.   found the Country roleing open & rich, with plenty of water, great qts [quantities] of Deer   I discovered a *Plumb*[6] which grows on bushes the hight of Hasle [hazel], those plumbs are in great numbers, the bushes beare Verry full, about double the Sise of the wild plumb Called the Osage Plumb & am told they are finely flavoured.

[Clark]   *10th of June* 1804

A hard rain last night, we Set out this morning verry early   passed Some bad placies in the river   Saw a number of Goslings morning   pass near a Bank which was falling in at the time we passed, passed the two River of *Charletons* which mouth together, above Some high land which has a great quantity of Stone Calculated for whetstons[7]   the first of those rivers is about 30 yds. Wide & the other is 70 yds wd. and heads Close to the R:

⟨Dumoin⟩ [*NB: du Moines*][8] The ⟨Aieways⟩ [*NB: Ayauways*] ⟨Nation⟩ have a Village on the head of these River   they run through ⟨an even Countrey⟩ [*NB: a broken rich thickly timbered country*] and is navagable for Perogues Cap Lewis took Medn. altd. of ⊙ U. L with Octant, back obsvn. made it 37° 12′ 00″—   delayd 1½ hours.

Capt. Lewis Killed a large Buck, passed a large Isd. called Shecco and Camped in a Prarie on the L. S. I walked out three miles, found the prarie composed of good Land and plenty of water roleing & interspursed with points of timberd land, Those Praries are not ⟨open⟩ like those, or a number of those E. of the Mississippi Void of every thing except grass, they abound with Hasel Grapes[9] & a wild plumb of a Superior [*NB: size &*] quallity, called the Osages Plumb   Grows on a bush the hight of a Hasel ⟨⟨and is three times the sise of other Plumbs,⟩[10] and hang in great quantities on the bushes   I Saw great numbers of Deer in the Praries, the evening is Cloudy, our party in high Spirits.

Course & Distance June 10th

N. 8° E	2 ½	ms. to a pt. on L. S.
North.	1	Me. along the L. Side
N. 40° W.	1	ms do do do
N. 70° W.	0 ½	opsd. the mo. of Charltons R.
N 60° W	2	Ms. to a pt. on S. S.
N 80 W.	3	ms. to a pt. on S. S. opsd. a Pln.
	10	

(*Point of observation No. 6.*)

[Lewis]   *Sunday June 10th*[11]

On the Larbord shore ¾ of a mile below the mouth of the lesser Charitton river.

Observed Meridian Altd. of ⊙'s L. L. with Octant by the back observatn.   37° 12′ —″

1. Biddle's notation on the top of this sheet of the Field Notes (document 20), reads "June 10 to 14." A column of figures is also at the top of this sheet: 2½, 1, 2, 1, 1, 1, 2 [½], and a total of 12.

2. *Populus deltoides* Marsh. var. *deltoides*, cottonwood. Steyermark, 507.

3. The Little Chariton River meets the Chariton a little above the mouth of the latter in Chariton County, Missouri, a short distance upstream from the present town of Glasgow. The name apparently derives from that of Jean Chariton, an early trader. See fig. 14. Stewart (APN), 87; MRC map 10.

4. Chicot Island, later Harrison Island. Coues (HLC), 1:20 n. 45; Thwaites (LC), 1:45 n. 2; MRC map 10.

5. In northeast Saline County, Missouri, some five miles above the Chariton River by Clark's estimate. MRC map 10.

6. Possibly *Prunus hortulana* Bailey, wild goose plum, hortulan plum, or *P. munsoniana* Wight & Hedrick, wild goose plum, which have the appropriate description and are known to occur in the area. Steyermark, 860–61. However, the captains may have been thinking of the Chickasaw (Osage) plum, which they had seen in St. Louis. See weather remarks for April 10, 1804. The hazel, mentioned for comparison, is *Corylus americana* Walt., hazelnut. Steyermark, 524.

7. Natural whetstones are produced from very fine-grained sandstones that are extremely uniform in texture, firmly cemented, and medium bedded (beds of one to six inches thick). Beds of this kind are known from lower Pennsylvanian rocks, which crop out along the bluffs in this area.

8. The source of the Chariton River, in south-central Iowa, is near the South and Middle branches of the Des Moines River. The Indians referred to are the Iowas (see above, April 5, 1804). Petersen, 305–11. Biddle is apparently crossing out words in this paragraph to substitute his own.

9. *Vitis* sp.

10. Biddle apparently crossed out this passage.

11. Lewis's observation from Codex O.

[Clark][1]

11 June Monday—   as the wind blew all this day from the N, W. which was imedeately a head we Could not Stur, but took the advantage of the Delay and Dried our wet articles examined provisons and Cleaned arms, my Cold is yet verry bad—   the river begining to fall   our hunters killed two Deer, G Drewry killed 2 Bear in the Praraie to day, men verry lively Danceing & Singing &c.

[Clark]   *11*th *June* 1804 *Monday*

The N W. wind blew hard & Cold   as this wind was imediately a head, we Could not proceed   we took the advantage of this Delay and Dried our wet articles examin'd Provisions &c. &c.   the river begining to fall the hunters killed two Deer   G: Drewyer Killed two Bear in the Prarie, they were not fat. we had the meat Jurked and also the Venison, which is a Constant Practice to have all the fresh meat not used, Dried in this way.

1. Some figures (3½, 2½, 3) are immediately below the June 11 entry in the Field Notes.

[Lewis]   Grand River   June 12th 1804[1]

Sir,

I have purchased from Mr Louiselle's Pattroon *three hundred pounds* of voyager's grease for which I am to pay by my A [account?]

[Clark]

12th of June, Tuesday   We Set out early, passed thro: a verry bad bend N. 25° W. 3½ to a pt. L. S.   N. 70° W. 2½ ms to a pt. on S. S.   passed a Sand bar—N 60° W 3¹/ ms. to a pt. on S. S.   passed *Plumb. C*[2] at ½ a me. on L. S. and halted to Dine, and 2 Caussease [cajeux] Came Down from the Soux nation, we found in the party an old man who had been with the Soux 20 years & had great influence [*hole*] with them, we provld. [prevailed] on this old man Mr. [*hole*] *Duriaur*[3] to return with us, with a view to get Some of the Soux Chiefs to go to the U. S.   purchased 300 lb. of Voyagers Grece @ 5$ [pr?] Hd.[4]   made Some exchanges & purchuses of Mockersons & found it Late & concluded to incamp.[5]

Those people inform that no Indians are on the river, The Countrey on each Side of the river is good

[Clark]   12th *of June, Tuesday* 1804

Set out early   passed Some bad Placies, and a Small Creek on the L. S. Called *plumb Creek* at abt. 1 me.   at 1 oClock we brought too two *Chaussies* one Loaded with furs & Pelteries, the other with Greece buffalow grease & tallow   We purchased 300 lb. of Greese, and finding that old Mr. Durioun was of the party we questioned him untill it was too late to Go further and Concluded to Camp for the night, those people inform nothing of much information

Colcluded to take old Durioun [*X: (who went accg)*] back as fur as the Soux nation with a view to get some of their Chiefs to Visit the Presdt.

of the United S. (This man being a verry Confidential friend of those people, he having resided with the nation 20 odd years) and to accompany them on[6]

Course & Distance June 12th

N. 25° W.	3 ½	ms. to L. S. passed Plumb C
N 70 W.	2 ½	ms. to pt. on S. S.
N. 60° W.	3	ms. to pt. on S. S.
	9	

1. This passage in Lewis's hand, under the entries for June 25 and 26, 1804, is in the Field Notes (document 23).

2. Possibly later Bear Creek, Saline County, Missouri. MRM map 26.

3. Pierre Dorion, Sr., was born before 1750, probably in Quebec, and was in Cahokia, Illinois, in 1780. Clark perhaps had heard of Dorion before, for the trader had at least corresponded with George Rogers Clark in 1780. Within a few years of that date he had gone up the Missouri to the Yankton Sioux, where he married and settled down as a trader. He was employed by Régis Loisel as an interpreter at Loisel's post at Ile aux Cedres. He took a delegation of Yankton chiefs to St. Louis for the captains and was later involved in various negotiations with Indians, serving for a time as a government subagent under Clark. He died sometime after 1811. Munnick (PD); Speck, 150–86; Irving (Astor), 97–100; Osgood (FN), 55 n. 1.

4. In the Codex A entry of this date Clark or someone else has interlined "buffalow grease & tallow" over "Greece." Perhaps this was a base material for making pemmican. Nute, 54.

5. Clark is not entirely clear which side of the river the camp was on, but Ordway says they camped on the north side. This would place them in south-central Chariton County, Missouri, in the vicinity of where Missouri Highway J ends. MRC map 10.

6. On this day, according to Whitehouse, a man belonging to Captain Amos Stoddard's artillery company was sent back down the river, presumably with Dorion's boat. No other journalist mentions the event. This man may have been John Robertson, or Robinson, who was with the party at River Dubois but appears in no record or roll of the expedition proper. See Appendix A, this volume.

[Clark][1]

13th *June Wednesday* ⟨Papers for the Secretary *at War*⟩[2] we Set out early passed a verry round bend to L. S.[3] passed two Creeks 1 me. apt. Called Creeks of the round Bend,[4] between those Creeks Stbd S. is a butifull Prarie, in which the antient Missourie Indians had a Village,[5] at this place 300 of them were killed by the Saukees, a fair Day. Passed the antient Missouries villages on right   Course N 40° W 2½ pt. L S., S 29° W 3 ms. pt. S. S., this nation once the Most Noumerous is now almost extinct, about 30 of them, liveing with Otteaus on the R. Platt, the remainder all distroyed, took altd. of S. U L with qdt. which gave N 28 W. 1½ ms to a pt. S. S.   Passed some Charming land, I have not Seen any high hils above Charliton [Chariton River] and the hils below for Several days Cannot to turmed hills but high Land, not exceeding 100 abov the high water mark   N 30° W, to a pt. L. S. 2 ms.   passed a verry bad Sand bar, where the boat was nearly turning & fastening in the quick Sand and came too in the mouth of Grand R. S. S.[6]   this River is about 120 yards wide and navagable for Purogues a great distance, it heads with the River Dumoine [Des Moines][7] ⟨St. Peters⟩, passing the river ⟨Dumn.⟩ Carlton. [Chariton]   a Butifull open Prarie Coms to the river below its mouth, we landed and walked to the hills which is abt. ½ a mile.   the Lower prarie over flows.   the hunters Killd. a Bare & Dere, this is a butifull place   the Prarie rich & extinsive, Took Some Looner Observations which Kept Cap L. & my Self up untill half past 11 oClock.

[Clark]   13th *June Wednesday*, 1804

   We Set out early   passed a round bend to the S. S. and two Creeks Called the round bend Creeks   between those two Creeks and behind a Small willow Island in the bend is a Prarie in which the Missouries Indians once lived and the Spot where 300 [*NB: 200*] of them fell a Sacrifise to the fury of the *Saukees*   This nation (Missouries) once the most noumerous nation in this part of the Continent now reduced to about 80 fes.[8] and that fiew under the protection of the *Otteaus* [*NB: Ottoes*] on R Platt who themselves are declineing   passed Som willow Isds. and bad Sand bars, Twook Medn. altitude with Octent back observation   it gave for altd. on its Low L 36° 58' 0″ the E [error] Enstrement 2° 00' 00″ +.   the Hills or high land for Several days past or above the 2 Charletons does not exceed 100 foot   passed a Batteau[9] or Sand roleing where the Boat was nearly turning over by her Strikeing & turning on the Sand. We came too in the Mouth of Grand River on S. S. and Camped for the night, this River is ⟨about⟩ from 80 to 100 yards wide at its Mouth and navagable for Perogues a great distance   This river heads with the R. Dumoine   below its mouth is a butifull Plain of bottom land   the hills rise at ½ a mile back

14. Missouri River near Mouth of Osage River and West,
ca. June 13, 1804, Field Notes, reverse of document 18

The lands about this place is either Plain or over flown bottom   Capt Lewis and my Self walked to the hill from the top of which we had a butifull prospect of Serounding Countrey   in the open Prarie we Caught a racoon, our hunters brought in a Bear & Deer   we took Some Luner observation this evening.

Course & Distance 13th June 1804

N. 40° W	2 ½	Ms. to a pt. L. S.
S. 39° W.	3	ms. to a pt. S. S. psd. 2 Creeks
N. 28 W	1 ½	Ms. to a pt. Stbd. S.
N. 30 W	2	ms. to a pt. L. S. opsd. Gd. R
	9 ms.	

(Point of observation No. 7.)

[Lewis]   *June 13th*[10]

On the S. side of an Island near it's upper point two miles below the mouth of the *Grand river.*—

Observed meridian Altd. of ☉'s L. L. with Octant by the back observatn.   35° 58′ 00″

(Point of observation No. 8.)

Wednesday June 13th

At the mouth of the *Grand River.*
Observed time and distance of ☽ from Spica ♍ ★ East.

	Time			*Distance*		
	h	m	s			
P. M.	9	17	49.5	39°	36′	—″
	″	22	38	″	28	—
	″	32	40	″	24	—
	″	41	39	″	20	45
	″	47	8	″	17	32
	″	59	48.5	″	11	45
	h	m	s			
P. M.	10	14	19	39°	1′	30″
	″	18	47	″	—	30
	″	21	51	38	58	15
	″	27	12	″	56	30

"	39	34		"	53	00
"	45	41		"	48	—
	h	m	s			
P. M.	10	54	38	38°	41'	45"
"		59	49	"	39	—
	11	3	8	"	37	30
"		6	44	"	36	45
"		10	40	"	34	00
"		16	—	"	31	45

1. Some figures are written to the side of this entry: 2½, 3, 1½, 2, and a total of 9.

2. The words crossed out are immediately under the date. Possibly Clark intended to write here a list of papers to be sent back to Secretary Henry Dearborn with the intended return party.

3. It would appear that this bend in Chariton County, Missouri, was cut off by a change in the course of the Missouri River later in the nineteenth century. The curve and a remaining lake are quite evident on MRC map 10. It was later known as Bowling Green Bend. Coues (HLC), 1:22 n. 48.

4. One of those was probably later Palmer Creek. Ibid.; MRC map 10.

5. The Missouris, or Missourias, called after the river, when first noticed in 1673 were situated at the mouth of the Grand River (see below, n. 6) in Missouri, about where Clark places the village here. They are said to have been a large and important tribe before they were almost annihilated during the latter half of the eighteenth century by Mississippi River tribes, particularly the Sauks and the Fox. Their earliest known village was near Miami Landing, now called the Utz site. Eventually they moved to the southwestern tip of Saline County, to a spot known as the Gumbo Point site. See also notes for June 13. By about 1798 they were forced to move up the Missouri River into Nebraska, to join the culturally related Otos; both tribes spoke the Siouan language of the Chiwere group and had economies based on hunting and horticulture. Henceforward the two tribes acted together and were treated by the United States as one. The last full-blooded Missouri is said to have died in Oklahoma in 1907. Chapman (OM); Hodge 1:911–12; Irving (IS); Bray (MIT).

6. Grand River, one of the principal streams of northern Missouri, forms the boundary between Carroll and Chariton counties where it meets the Missouri River. It appears likely that the mouth of the Grand in 1804 was farther north above present Brunswick. It is not clear on which side of the Grand they camped. Nicollet (MMR), 361; MRC map 10.

7. The headwaters of the Grand and its principal tributary, the Thompson River, are near the heads of the South and Middle Des Moines in southern Iowa. Petersen, 301–5.

8. This may be an abbreviation for "fires," that is, families. Thwaites (LC), 1:47.

9. Clark probably refers again to a *bature*, a sandy beach on the inside curve in a river. See June 4, 1804.

10. This entry and the next are Lewis's observations from Codex O. Preceding this date is the symbol for the planet Mercury.

[Clark]

14th June, Thursday   We set out at 6 oClock after a thick fog   proceeded on verry well S. 33 W 2 Ms. to the lower pt of an Isld. S. S.   ⟨N⟩ S. 60° W. thro a narrow 1 me channel to a Small prarie S. S.   opposit this Isd. on L. L. is a Butifull high Plain.   from the Isd. S. 70° W. to a pt. L. S. 2½ ms. just below a piec of High Land on the S. S. Called the place of Snakes, passed the worst place I have Seen on L. S.   a Sand bar makeing out ⅔ Cross the river   Sand Collecting &c forming Bars and Bars washg a way, the boat Struck and turned, She was near oversetting   we saved her by Some extrodany exertions of our party (ever ready to inconture any fatigue for the premotion of the enterprise[)], I went out to walk on the Sand Beech, & Killed a Deer & Turky[1]   during the time I was from the boat a Caussee came too from the Pania [Pawnee] nation loaded with furs   We gave them Some whiskey and Tobacco & Settled Some desputes & parted   S. 5 E. 3 ms. to pt. on S. S. passed a Creek S. S. 25 yds. wd. Called Snake Creek[2] or ([*blank*])   passed a bad Sand bar S. S. in passing which we were obliged to run great Sesque [risk] of Loseing both Boat & men, Camped above,[3] G. Drewyer tels of a remarkable Snake inhabiting a Small lake 5 ms. below which gobbles like a Turkey & may be herd Several miles, This Snake is of [emence?] Size.[4]

[Clark]

14th, *June Thursday*   we Set out at 6 oClock, after a thick fog   passed thro: a narrow pass on the S. S. which forms a large Isd.   opposit the upper point of this Island on the L. S. is one of the worst quick or moveing Sand bars which I have Seen   not withstanding all our precaustons to Clear the Sands & pass between them (which was the way we were Compd. to pass from the immens Current & falling banks on the S. S.) the Boat Struck the point of one   from the active exertions of the men, prevented her turning, if She had turned She must have overset.   we met a *Causseu* from the Pania [*NB: Paunee*] on the River Platt, we detained 2 hours with a view of engageing one of the hands to go to the Pania nation with a View to get those people to meet us on the river.[5] I went out (Shot a Deer)   we passd a high land & clay bluff on the S. S. Called the Snake bluff from the number of Snakes about this place, we passd a Creek above the Bluff about 18 yds. wide, This Creek is Called Snake Creek, a bad Sand bar Just below which we found difficuelty in passing & Campd above, our Hunters Came in. George Drewyer, gives the following act. of a Pond, & at abt. 5 miles below the S. S. Passed a Small Lake in which there was many Deer feeding   he heard in this Pond a Snake makeing Goubleing Noises like a turkey.   he fired his gun & the noise was increased, he has heard the indians Mention This Species of Snake   one Frenchman give a Similar account

Course & Distance June *14th*

S. 33° W	2	ms. to Lowr. pt. on an Isd. S. S.
S. 60° W	1	Me. thro: a chanel on S S.
S. 70 W	2	Ms. to pt. L. S. passed a bad Sand
S. 5 E	3	ms. to a pt. on S. S. passed a Creek S. S.
	8	

1. "Killed a Deer & Turky" is written with a sharper quill and appears to have been inserted later in a space left for it.

2. Probably Wakenda Creek, in Carroll County, Missouri, whose old bed appears in MRC map 11. Osgood (FN), 56 n. 8.

3. Clark is not clear which side this camp was on, but Ordway places it on the north (starboard) side of the Missouri. It was in Carroll County, nearly opposite the present town of Miami, and near where Missouri Highway 41 crosses the river. MRC map 11.

4. This appears to be one of the marvelous snake stories common in American folk-lore, perhaps derived from an Indian belief. Coues (HLC), 1 : 25 n. 54.

5. It is nowhere indicated in the journals whether this man was in fact hired, and if so, what his name was. If he was hired, this complicates the roll of the French *engagés*. See May 26 and July 4, 1804. Biddle says they were unsuccessful in hiring him. Floyd says the four were "3 French men and one Negro [X: *Mallato*]" and that "2 of them is half preades of the poncas," by which he may mean Pawnees. Coues (HLC), 1 : 25.

[Clark][1]

15 June Friday 1804, we Set out early   proceeded on about 1 me. and the Boat turned on a Sawyer[2] which was near doeing her great damage, the river is riseing fast & the water exceedingly Swift,

S. 35° W	2	ms. alg. S. S.
S 50° W.	1 ½	Me. to a pt. on L. S. passed a Prarie & Creek on the L. S
S. 51° W	2 ½	me. to a pt. on S. S. psd. a Small Willow Island

S. 8. w		to pt. L. S. ¾ of a me. psd. the Lower pts. of 2 Isd.
S. 80° W.	2	Ms. to the upr. pt. of an Isd. on S. S. passed thro a verry bad part of the river, the wost moveing Sands I ever Saw, the Current So Strong that the Ours [oars] and Sales under a Stiff breese Cld. not Stem it, we wre oblged to use a toe rope, under a bank Constantly falling
S. 5° W.	2	Ms. to a pt. on S. S. psd. along a Isd. on the left, to the lowr. pt. of one Still on the left
S 12° W	1 ½	ms. to a pt. S. S. opsd. the Antient Village of the little Osage

passd. a bad Sand bar on which we Stuck for a Short time   this is Said to be the worst part of the river and Camped opsd. the bend in which the Antient Villages of the little Osarge & Missouries,[3] the lower or first of those villagies (L. Osages) is Situated in Butifull Plain at the foot of Some riseing land, in front of their Villges next the river is a butifull bottom Plain in which they raised their Corn &c.   back of the Village the high Prarie extends back to the Osarge River, about 3 Ms. above & in view the Missouries Nation resided under the protection of the *Osarges*, after their nation was riducd by the Saukees below,[4] thos built their Village in the Same low Prarie and lived there many years, the war was So hot & both nations becom So reduced that the Little Osage & a fiew of the Missoures moved & built a village 5 ms near the Grand Osage,[5] the rest of the Missoures went and took protection under the *Otteaus* [Otos] on Platt river

[Clark]

15th, *June, Friday* 1804   Set out early and had not proceeded far e'er we wheeled on a Sawyer which was near injuring us Verry much, passed a plain on the L. S.   a Small Isd. in the midle   the river riseing, water verry Swift   Passed a Creek on the L. S.   passed between two Islands, a verry bad place, Moveing Sands, we were nearly being Swallowed up by the roleing Sands over which the Current was So Strong that we Could not Stem it with our Sales under a Stiff breese in addition to our ores, we were Compelled to pass under a bank which was falling in, and use the Toe rope occasionally, Continued up pass two other Small Islands and Camped on the S. S. Nearly opposit the *Antient Village* of the *Little Osarges* and below the Antt. *Village* of the *Missoures*   both *Situations* in view an within three

Ms. of each other, the *Osage* were Settled at the foot a hill in a butifell Plain which extends back quite to the Osage River, in front of the Vilg: Next to the river is an ellegent bottom Plain which extends Several miles in length on the river in this low Prarie the *Missouries* lived after They were reduced by the *Saukees* [*NB: Saukees*] at Their Town Some Dists. below. The little osage finding themselves much oppressed by the Saukees & other nations, left this place & built a village 5 ms. from the Grand *Osarge Town* about [*blank*] years ago. a few of the Missoures accompanied them, the remainder of that nation went to the Otteaus on the River Platt. The River at this place is about ⟨3⟩ 1 [*NB: one*] ms. wide our hunters did not Come in this evening the river beginning to fall

Course & Distance June 15th

S. 35° W	2	Ms. along the S. S.
S. 50° W	1 ½	Ms. a pt. L. S. passed a pra: & Creek L. S.
S. 51° W	2 ½	Ms. a pt. S. S. psd. a willow Isd.
S. 8° W	¾	Ms. to a pt. L. S. passd. Low pt. 2 Isds.
S. 80° W	2	Ms. to upr. Pt. Isd. S. S. psd. bad plain
S. 5° W	2	Ms. to a pt. S. S. passed bad plain
S. 12° W	1 ½	Ms. to a pt. S. S. psd. a Isd. in Midl. opsd.
	12 ¼	Old Village Lit: Osage.

(*Point of Observation No. 9.*)

[Lewis]   *Friday June 15th*[6]

On the Starboard shore two miles below the Island of the Old village of the little Osages.—

Observed Meridian Altd. of ☉'s L. L. with Octant by the back observation   36° 42′ —″

1. Biddle's notation at the head of this sheet of the Field Notes (document 21) reads "15 to 16."

2. A submerged tree with one end stuck in the mud, the other bobbing up and down in the current with a sawing motion, one of the great menaces to river navigation. Criswell, 75.

3. The Missouri Indian village that is identified as the Gumbo Point site. See entries for June 8 and 13, 1804, and Chapman (LOM). Nicollet shows an "Old Village of Little Osages" in the vicinity, although he may have relied on Clark's information. Nicollet (MMR), 362; MRC map 11.

4. The area below where the Missouris resided may be a reference to the Utz site, where they lived from prehistoric to early historic times. Bray (ETG).

5. They would have moved near one of the villages on the Big, or Grand, Osage River in west-central Missouri. Chapman (OOIT), 146, 279 (fig. 2), 280 (fig. 3); MRC map 11.

6. Lewis's observation from Codex O.

[Clark]

16th *June Satterday*   Set out at 7 oClock   Proceed on N. 68° W. 2½ ms. passed a Isd. close on the S. S. at the lower point   Drewer & Willard had camped & had with them 2 bear & 2 Deer   we took in the meat & proceeded on. Some rain this morning   *West* 2 Ms. pass an Isd on S. S. & prarie, to a Belge of Snag Isd.[1] L. S.   a butifull extensive Prarie on S. S. Hills to about 9 ms. distant. Mr. Mackey has Laid down the rems. [remains] of an old fort in this Prarie, which I cannot find[2]   S 85° W. 1 me. along the Isd. L. S.—   S 61° W alg L. S. 1 me.   S 30° W, 3, ms. to pt. S. S. opsd. an Isd. & head of the last   S 40° W 1 me. S. S. Passed a verry bad place where the Sand was *moving* constantly, I walked on Shore obsd. fine high Bottom land on S. S.   Camped late this evening.[3]

[Clark]   16th, *June Satturday* 1804

Set out at 7 oClock   at about a mile ½ we Came to the Camp of our hunters, they had two Bear & two Deer   proceeded on pass a Island on the S. S.   a heavy rain came on & lasted a Short time, we came to on the S. S. in a Prarie at the place where Mr. Mackey lay down a old french fort, I could See no traces of a Settlement of any Kind, in this plain I discovered a Kind of Grass resembling Timothey[4] which appeared well calculated for Hay, this Plain is verry extensive   in the evening I walked on the S. S. to see if any timber was Convt. to make Oars, which we were much in want of, I found Som indifferent timber and Struck the river above the Boat at a bad Sand bar the worst I had Seen which the boat must pass or Drop back Several Miles & Stem a Swift Current on the opsd Side of an Isd.   the Boat however assended the middle of the Streem which was diffucult Dangerious   We Came to above this place at Dark and Camped in a bad place, the misquitoes and Ticks are noumerous & bad.[5]

Course & Destance June 16th

N. 68° W.   2 ½   Ms. to a pt. L. S.   pass Isd. S. S.

West.	2	ms. to a blg. in Snag Isd. L. S.
S. 85 W.	1	Me. on L. S. a bad Sand mid.
S. 61 W.	1	me. on L. S. do do
S. 30 W.	2 ½	Ms. to a pt. S. S. passed upr. Sd. Isd. and 2 Sm. Isds.
S. 40 W	1	me. alg S. S. an Isd. mdl. & bad ps.
	10	

1. Perhaps later Wakenda, or Cranberry, Island. MRC map 11.

2. Sieur Etienne Véniard de Bourgmont established Fort Orleans in 1723. The site was in Carroll County, Missouri, above the mouth of the Grand River and nearly opposite the Little Osage village on the opposite side of the Missouri. See entry for June 8. Mackay's map (*Atlas* map 5) shows a "vieux fort" some miles above the mouth of the Grand; Clark might have been using the map or Mackay's journal. Coues (HLC), 1:23–24 n. 51; Osgood (FN), 57–58 n. 2; *Missouri Guide*, 372; Chapman (OOIT), 279 (fig. 2); Bray (ETG); MRC map 11.

3. In Carroll County, near the present town of Waverly on the opposite shore and the crossing of U.S. Highway 65. MRC map 12.

4. *Phleum pratense* L., timothy, a native of Europe, was introduced as a hay crop about 1720 and is now widely naturalized, but it is not likely that this was the species seen by Lewis and Clark. It was probably reed canary grass, *Phalaris arundinacea* L., which is superficially similar to timothy and has the appropriate ecological habitat of moist floodplains. On August 17 Clark mentioned "a kind of Timothey, the Seed of which branches from the main Stalk & is more like a flax Seed than that of a Timothey." There are relatively few native grasses that have the flower structure of timothy, and the branching pattern noted here supports the tentative identification of reed canarygrass. Steyermark, 153, 188, 190; Weaver, 57–58.

5. The mosquitoes are *Aedes vexans*, and the ticks are either *Dermacentor variabilis*, American dog tick, or *Amblyomma americanum*, lone star tick.

[Clark]   June 17 1804 Rope walk Camp[1]

The Current of the River at this place is a Stick will float 48 poles 6 feet in the rapidest part in 23 Seconds,[2] further out is 34, Still further 65 — 74 — 78 & 82 are the Trials we have made.

[Clark][3]

June 17 Sunday 1804   Cloudy   Wind, S. E.   Set out early S. 65° W 1 Me.   Came too to Make ores, and a Cord for a Toe Rope   all this day imployed in getting out Ores, & makeing for the use of the Boat out of a large Cable rope which we have, G Drewyer Came up [with] a Bear & 2 Deer, also a fine horse which he found in the woods, Supposed to have been left by Some war party from the osages, The *Ticks* are numerous and large and have been trousom [troublesome] all the way and the Musquetors are beginning to be verry troublesome, my Cold Continues verry bad   the French higherlins Complain for the want of Provisions, Saying they are accustomed to eat 5 & 6 times a day,[4] they are roughly rebuked for their presumption, the Country about abounds in Bear Deer & Elk[5] and the S. S. the lands are well timbered and rich for 2 ms. to a butifull Prarie which risies into hills abt 8 or 9 ms. back—   on the L. S a Prarie coms. on the bank which is high and contines back rich & well watered as far [& Light?; as Sight?][6]

[Clark]   June 17th Sunday *1804* (S. 65° W. me. S. Side—)

Cloudy morning   wind from the S. E.   we Set out early and proceeded on one mile & came too to make oars, & repair our Cable & toe rope &c. &c. which was necessary for the Boat & Perogues, Sent out Sjt. Pryor and Some men to get ash timber for ores, and Set Some men to make a Toe Rope out of the Cords of a *Cable* which had been provided by Capt Lewis at Pitts burg for the Cable of the boat—   George Drewyer our hunter and one man came in with 2 Deer & a Bear, also a young Horse, they had found in the Prarie, this horse has been in the Prarie a long time and is fat, I suppose he has been left by Some war party against the *Osage*, This is a Crossing place for the war partis against that nation from the *Saukees*, *Aiaouez*, [NB: Ayauways] & Souix. The party is much aflicted with *Boils* and Several have the Decissentary, which I contribute to the water [NB: *(which is muddy.*][7]

The Countrey about this place is butifull   on the river rich & well timbered   on the S. S. about two miles back a Prarie coms. which is rich and interspursud with groves of timber, the County rises at 7 or 8 miles Still further back and is roleing—   on the L. S. the high lands & Prarie Coms. in the bank of the river and Continus back, well watered and abounds in De[e]r Elk & Bear   The Ticks & Musquetors are verry troublesom.

1. Biddle's notation at the head of this sheet of the Field Notes (document 22) reads, "June 18 to 22." It was Biddle who apparently changed the date on this entry from 18 to 17. A ropewalk was a place where rope was manufactured; since they were making a tow-

rope, the name seemed appropriate. The towline, or cordelle, was used where rowing or poling was difficult or impossible; most of the crew went ashore and pulled the boat upstream with the rope. The camp was in Carroll County, Missouri, about a mile above the June 16 camp. Baldwin (KA), 64; MRC map 12.

2. A pole was 16½ feet, so the speed of the current in the rapidest part would be approximately 2.36 miles per hour.

3. This entry is immediately below the previous one for June 17 on the same sheet of the Field Notes.

4. The "almost superhuman exertions" of river boatmen undoubtedly required a great deal of energy, leading to the custom of eating frequently, which the men saw as their right. Baldwin (KA), 86–87.

5. They did not actually see an elk, or wapiti (*Cervus elaphus*), until July 14, 1804. Hall, 2:1084–86.

6. The last three words are crowded onto the ragged bottom of the sheet and are nearly illegible.

7. The party was living on a high-protein diet. The jerked meat probably was contaminated with bacteria, of whose existence they were unaware; the germ theory of disease was half a century in the future. Although they had gathered "greens" on June 5, their diet in general probably lacked fresh fruit and vegetables. Unwashed clothing, infrequent bathing, and infected mosquito bites may also have contributed to their ailments. Chuinard, 222; Osgood (FN), 59 n. 7.

[Clark]

June 18th Monday   Some raind last night, Sent out 6 Hunters ⟨last⟩ to day across the R: they Killed 5 Deer & Colte[r][1] a Bear verry fat   we continue to repare our ropes & make oars all day, heavy rain all the fore pt. of the day, the party Drying meat & greesing themselves, Several men with the Disentary, and two thirds of them with ulsers or Boils, Some with 8 or 10 of those Tumers   Mesquetors verry bad   we finish our *Cords* & *oars* this evening   Men in Spirits[2]

[Clark]   *June* 18th *Monday*

Some rain last night, and Some hard Showers this morning which delay our work verry much, Send out Six hunters in the Prarie on the L S.   they kill 5 Deer & Coltr a Bear, which verry large & fat, the party to wok at the oars, make rope, & jurk their meat all Day   Dry our wet Sales &c. in the evening, The misquiter verry bad

1. This word and the Codex A version have been interpreted as "Cotte" and "Coht," that is, "caught," by Osgood and Thwaites, respectively, but it almost certainly means that John Colter killed a bear. Osgood (FN), 59; Thwaites (LC), 1:52.

2. This column of figures comes immediately after the June 18 entry on this sheet of the Field Notes (document 22): 3, 1 ½, 1 ½, 1 ½, 4 ½, and a total of 13 ½.

[Clark]

June 19th Tuesday   raind last night   Arranged everry thing and Set out 8 oCk   wind in favor from the S. E.

Course

N. 87° W	3	Ms. to up. pt of a Isd. on [S. S.? *blot*]
S. 80° W.	1 ½	pt. L. Sd. psd. up pt. Isd. on S. S.— hard water.
S. 70° W	1 ½	me. along the L. S., high rich Bottom
S. 58° W	4 ½	pt. S. S. Passed an Isd. Close on the L. S. & 3 Sand bars
S. 68 W.	3	Ms. pt S. S. pass *Tabbo* Creek 15 yds. wide on L S. opsd. a Small Isd. we passed thro between 2 Isds. by Clearing away Drift wood, passed the Lower pt. of the Isd. of Pant[h]ers S. S. formed by a narrow Channel
S. 83° W.	4	ms. Plenty of Goose & Rasp buries on the banks, passed a verry bad point of rocks of ½ a mile oblige to Draw the Boat up by a rope, Camped opposit a Lake at 2 ms. distant on the L. S. this lake is large and is a place of great resort for Deer and fowls of everry Kind the bottom low & covered with rushes[1]

[Clark]

June 19th Tuesday

rain last night   after fixing the new Oars and makeing all necessary arrangements, we Set out under a jentle breese from the S. E. and proceeded on   passed two large Islands on the S. S.[2] leaving J. Shields and one man[3] to go by land with the horses   Some verry hard water, passed Several Islands & Sand bars to day   at the head of one we were obliged to cleare away Driftwood to pass, passed a Creek on the L. Side Called ⟨Tabboe⟩ [*NB: Tabo*][4] 15 yds. wide   passed a large Creek at the head of an Island Called Tiger River[5] [*NB: 25 yds*] on the S. S. The Island below this ⟨river⟩ Isd. is large and Called the Isle Of Pant[h]ers, formed on the S. S. by a narrow Channel, I observed on the Shore *Goose & Rasp* berries[6] in abundance   in passing Some hard water round a Point of rocks on the L. S. we were obliged to take out the roape & Draw up the Boat for ½ a mile, we Came too on the L. S. near a Lake of the Sircumfrance of Several miles Situated on the L. S. about two miles from the river[7]   this Lake is Said to abound in all kinds of fowls, great quanties of Deer frequent this Lake dureing Summer Season, and feed on the hows [haws][8] &c. &c. they find on the edgers   the Lands on the North Side of the river is rich and Sufficiently high to afford Settlements, the Lds. on the South Side assends Gradually from the river   not So rich, but of a good quallity and appear well watered

Course & Distance June 19th

N. 87° W,	3	ms. to upr pt. of an Island
S. 80° W	1 ½	ms. to a pt. L. Side psd 4 wil. Isds.
S. 70° W	1 ½	ms. along the L. S.—
S. 58° W	4 ½	ms. to a pt. S. S. psd. a Isd. S. S.
S. 68 W	3	ms. to pt. S. S. psd. Tabbo Creek
S. 83 W	4	ms. to pt. L. S. Campd. 1 me.
	17 ½	

1. "Rushes" refers to *Equisetum* sp., scouring rush, horsetail. This is probably the common horsetail, *E. arvense* L. Steyermark, 11.

2. In the neighborhood of what was later called Baltimore Bar. MRC map 12.

3. Whitehouse reveals that the other man was John Collins.

4. Tabo Creek, in Lafayette County, Missouri, perhaps named for Pierre-Antoine Tabeau, a fur trader whom the captains would meet among the Arikaras on October 10, 1804. It is Nicollet's "Tabeau River." McDermott (WCS), 148; Nicollet (MMR), 364; MRC map 12.

5. The Tiger River and Island of Panthers are named for the cougar, or mountain lion, *Felis concolor*. The creek may be Crooked River in Ray County, Missouri. However, it appears that they did not actually pass it until the next day; see below, June 20, 1804. Hall, 2:1039–43; MRC map 12.

6. Gooseberries are a species of *Ribes*, here possibly Missouri gooseberries.

7. In Lafayette County, a few miles below present Lexington. The lake appears as Nicollet's "Marais de [Apakwa?]," a few miles east of present Lexington. The point passed just before they camped may have been what was later called Sheep Nose. Nicollet (MMR), 364; MRC map 12.

8. Probably one or more of the many species of *Crataegus*, hawthorn, red haw, known to occur in the area. These are *C. crus-galli* L., cockspur thorn; *C. mollis* (T. & G.) Scheele, summer haw, turkey apple; and *C. calpodendron* (Ehrh.) Medic., urn-tree. Less probably *Viburnum prunifolium* L., black haw, or *V. rufidulum* Raf., southern black haw. Steyermark, 810–22, 1414–15.

[Clark]

June 20th Wednesday 1804   Set out after a heavy Showr of rain and proceeded on the Same Course of yesterday S. 83° W 3 ms.   passed Some
Sand Isds. in the bend to L. S.   bad water   a large creek on the S. S.
called Tiger Creek,[1] a willow and a large Isd[2] above S. S.,

S 42° W.	1	m alg L. S. wind S. W. hard, Some high land on L. S.
S. 46° W	2	ms. to P: L. S. psd. the head of the Isd.
S. 50° W,	1 ½	me. pt. L. S. opsd. an Isd. and large Butifull Prarie called Sauke Prarie, pass hard water, Saw *Pilicans* on a Sand bar
S. 70 W		along L. S. passd. Isd. ¾ Me. Swift water, one remarkable circumstance in the water of this River is a free use of it will create prespreation, the Swet run off our men in a Stream when th[ey] row hard, York verry near loseing his Eyes by one of the men throwing Sand at him in fun & recved into his eyes— passed Some bad water.
S. 25° W	1 ½	me. pt. on the S. Side, we came to at ½ a me. on the lower point of a Willow Isd S. S. in View of a Sand bar on both sides of the Isd. over which the water riffleed and roered like a great fall, We took Some Luner observations of the moon & Stars Set up untill one oClock the Musquetors verry troublesome our flank Guard or Hunters [Shields and Collins] have not been with us for two nights, We saw them to day at the Mouth of the Tiger R, the lands on the L S. is very fine & well timbered near the river and appears equally good on the other side but not so high[3]

[Clark]

June 20th, Wednesday

Set out after a heavy Shower of rain and proceeded on the Same Course
of last night   passed a large butifull Prarie on the S. S. opposit a large
Island, Calld Saukee Prarie, a gentle breese from the S. W. Some butiful
high lands on the L. S.   passed Som verry Swift water to day, I saw *Pelicans*
to day on a Sand bar, my servant York nearly loseing an eye by a man
throwing Sand into it, we came too at the lower Point of a Small Island,[4]
the party on Shore we have not Seen Since we passed Tiger R—   The
Land appeard verry good on each Side of the River to day and well timbered, we took Some Loner [lunar] observations, which detained us untill

1 oClock   a butifull night but the air exceedingly Damp, & the mosquiters verry troublesom

Course and Deistances June 20th

S. 42° W.	1	me. along L. S.
S. 46° W	2	me. to pt. S. S. psd. an Isd.
S. 51° W	1 ½	ms. to pt. L. S. opsd. Isd & Sauckee Prairie on S. S.
S. 70° W	¾	me. along L. S. water bad
S. 25° W	1 ½	ms. to a pt. S. S. psd. Isd & bad Sand
	6 ¾	

(Point of Observation No. 10.)

[Lewis]   Wednesday June 20th[5]

On a small Island about one mile & ¾ below Euebaux's Creek.—   Observed time and distance of ☽ from Spica ♍ ★ West.—

Time			*Distance*
h	m	s	
P. M. 10	59	40.3	46° 17′ 25″

This is the mean of a set of six observations.

Magnetic azimuth of Pole star by Circumferenter well adjusted with spert. levl. [spirit level] N. 7° 55 W

	h	m	s
Time by Chronometer P. M.	12	49	46.6

T[h]is is the mean of a set of six observations suffering several minutes to elaps betwen each.—

1. Apparently Crooked River, in Ray County, Missouri. In Codex A Clark indicates that they passed this stream on June 19, though it is not in his courses and distances for that day. Gass and Ordway both say the expedition passed Tiger River on the twentieth, while Biddle's *History* places the event on the nineteenth, presumably following Codex A. Evidently the June 19 camp was near the mouth of that stream on the opposite side, either above or below, wherever the mouth was in 1804. MRC map 12, made about 1890, shows what may be an old channel of Crooked River, but the two mouths were not far apart. It seems most probable that they camped on the nineteenth just beyond Sheep Nose Point, with the mouth of Crooked River in sight, and passed the stream early the next morning. Coues (HLC), 1:27–28 and nn. 60, 61; Osgood (FN), 59 n. 8.

311

2. Clark interlined "and a large Isd." and indicated its insertion here. Obviously they passed a willow island and a large island, the latter perhaps the later Lexington Island. Osgood (FN), 234; MRC map 12.

3. Some figures written diagonally at the bottom of this entry appear to be "270 W."

4. Perhaps later Wolf Island, a few miles below present Wellington, Lafayette County, Missouri. MRC map 13.

5. Lewis's observation from Codex O. The creek is apparently present Sniabar River, near Wellington, Lafayette County, Missouri. See entry for June 21.

[Clark]

21st June Thursday 1804   river raised 3 Inches last night   after our bow man Peter Crousat a half Mahar Indian examined round this Small Isd. for the best water, we Set out determined to assd. [ascend] on the North Side, and Sometimes rowing Poleing & Drawing up with a Strong Rope we assended without wheeling or receiving any damige more than breakeing one of my S. [starboard?] Windows, and looseing Some oars which were Swong under the windows

The Course of last night[1]

S. 25 W	1	me. psd. the lower point of a large Island on the L. S. behind which is two Creeks this Isd & Creeks are Called *Eue-beux* after a french man, The water we Drink, or the Common water of the missourie at this time, contains half a Comn Wine Glass of ooze or mud to every pint—
S. 77° W,	2 ½	mes. alg: S. S. psd. the hd of the Isd. & Small one in midl.
N. 30° East	1 ½	ms. psd. a Counter Current on the L. S. Pass Lower pt. of a Isd. Close on the L. S.
North alg. L. S.	1	me. Some wind from the *S. S. E* at 3 oClock[2]
N. 18° W	½	me. L S.
N. 84° W	½	me
S 80° W	¾	me. along L. S. passed Several Small willow Isds. on L. S. High Land on the ⟨L⟩ S. S
S. 35° W.	¾	me. alg L. S, pass 2 Isd. Small on the right.
S. 14° W	2	ms. to pt. S. S. Came to at the last mentioned point

Two me[n] Sent out to hunt this afternoon Came in with a Deer,[3] at Sun Set The ellement had every appearance of wind, The hunters inform me that the high Countrey on the S. S. is of a good quallity, and well timbd. The High lands on the L. Side is equally good   The bottom land on this river is alike, 1st low and covd. with Cotton wood & willows Subject to over flow   the 2nd is higher groth Cotton Walnut ash Mulberry Linn [linden] & Sycomore[4]

[Clark]   21St *June Thursday*

The river rose 3 Inches last night   after the Bows man Peter Crousat viewed The water on each Side of the Island which presented a most unfavourable prospect of Swift water over roleing Sands which rored like an immence falls, we Concluded to assend on the right Side, and with much dificuilty, with the assistance of a long Cord or Tow rope, & the *anchor* we got the Boat up with out any furthr dang. [damage] than Bracking a Cabbin window & loseing Some *oars* which were Swong under the windows, passed four Isds to day two large & two Small, behind the first large Island two Creeks mouth Called (1) Eue-bert [*NB: Hubert*] Creek & River & Isd.[5]   the upper of those Creeks head against the Mine River & is large, passed a verry remarkable bend in the River to the S. forming an accute angle,[6] the high lands come to the river on the S. S. opposit the upper large Island, this Isd. is formed by a narrow chanel thro. the Pt. of the remarkable bend just mentiond below this Isd.   on the L. S. is a Couenter Current of about a mile—   passed between Several Small Islands Situated near the L. Side and camped above on the Same Side,[7]   Two men Sent out to hunt this evening   brought in a Buck & a pore[8] Turkey.

at Sun Set the atmespier presented every appearance of wind, Blue & white Streeks Centering at the Sun as She disappeared and the Clouds Situated to the S. W, Guilded in the most butifull manner. The Countery and Lands on each Side of the river is various as usial and may be classed as follows.   viz: the low or over flown points or bottom land, of the groth of Cotton & Willow, the 2nd or high bottom of rich furtile Soils of the groth of Cotton, Walnut, Som ash, Hack berry,[9] Mulberry, Lynn & Sycamore.   the third or high Lands risees gradually from the 2nd bottom (cauht whin it Coms to the river then from the river) about 80 or 100 foot roleing back Supplied with water the Small runs of (which losees themselves in the bottom land) and are covered with a variety of timber Such as Oake of different Kinds Blue ash,[10] walnut &c. &c. as far as the Praries, which I am informed lie back from the river at some places near & others a great Distance[11]

Course & Distance June 21st 1804

S. 77° W,	2 ½	ms. along S. S. psd. the hd. of a lg Isd. L. S.
N. 30° E,	1 ½	ms. pt. L. S. psd. a cl. Low pt. Isd. on L. S. (1)
North,	1	me. along the Larboard Side
N. 18° W,	½	me. do do do
N. 84° W.	½	me. do do do
S. 80° W,	¾	me. do do psd. Sevl. Sm Isds. L. S.
S. 35 W	¾	me. do do psd. do do do
	7[½?]	

1. This course differs from the Codex A material because it picks up the last course of the previous day and adds the first course of the next day.

2. The first four courses of the day are added up at the side of the entry: 1, 2 ½, 1 ½, 1, and a total of 6.

3. Ordway says that he and Drouillard were the hunters.

4. The ash is either *Fraxinus americana* L. var. *americana*, white ash, or *F. pennsylvanica* March. var. *subintegerrima* (Vahl) Fern., green ash; the "Linn" is *Tilia americana* L., basswood, linden; the "Sycomore" is *Platanus occidentalis* L., sycamore, plane tree, buttonwood. Steyermark, 1179–80, 1043, 789.

5. Apparently called *chenail-a-Hubert* (or *Hebert*), but an alternative reading is *chenail-a-barre* (*chenail* or *chenal* = channel). Hubert, or Hebert, is taken to be the "french man," but *chenail-a-barre* would be a *chenail* with a bar or blockage across it. From the latter form comes the present name, Sni, Sniabar, or Snibar River, applied apparently to the larger stream, near the present town of Wellington, Lafayette County, Missouri. Coues (HLC), 1 : 29, n. 62; Stewart (APN), 450; MRC map 13.

6. Later called Camden Bend, after the town on its banks in Ray County, Missouri. It was still there in about 1890, but in later years the river made a new channel and cut off the bend, leaving it as an oxbow lake, present Sunshine Lake. The Ray-Lafayette county line still follows the old course of the river. The June 21, 1804, campsite is therefore no longer on the Missouri River. MRC map 13; MRM map 36.

7. Here Clark seems to indicate that they camped on the larboard side, but in the Field Notes he indicates the starboard side; larboard is confirmed by Ordway and Floyd. They had been going round what was later called Camden Bend (see n. 6, above) and the camp was in Lafayette County. Nearby on the high ground on the opposite side of the river was the future site of the town of Camden. MRC map 13.

8. Someone has written over "pore" to make it "poor."

9. Clark accurately includes the hackberry, *Celtis occidentalis* L., in the list of upper floodplain tree species that occupy the higher, more stable river terraces. Bragg & Tatschl, 343, 347.

10. Clark describes the ravine and bluff vegetation above the river, which includes several species of oak, blue ash (*Fraxinus quadrangulata* Michx.), black walnut, and other species that follow the ravine back to the high prairies at some distance. Steyermark, 1180–82.

11. Clark's ecological description distinguishes between the cottonwood- and willow-dominated "low" floodplain vegetation, the more diverse "2nd or high bottom" vegetation, the "third or high lands" forests, and, finally, the treeless upland prairies. Those designations of forest types are accurate and typical of Missouri River topography and forest vegetation. Bragg & Tatschl, 343; Weaver, 49.

[Clark][1]

22nd *June Friday*   after a Violent gust of wind accompanied with rain from the West, which commenced at Day brake, and lasted about one hour, we Set out under a gentle Breeze from the N W. and proceeded on   S. 14° W. 2½ ms. to pt. on L. S.   Ord[way][2] Killed a goose, S 25° W 3 Ms. to a pt. on S. S.   psd. Snags and Swift water on the S. S.—   S. 66° W: ½ a me. on S pt.   N 60 W 4½ me. to pt. L. S.   passed ⟨the Lower pt. of⟩ a large Isd. on the S. S.—   (*Ferenthiers* Thermometr at 3 oClock P, M, 87 d which is 11 d above Summr heat)[3] and one [island] on the L. S. opposit against which there is a handsom Prarie of high Bottom & up Land, Capt Lewis went out in this Prarie & walked Several miles, Come to opposit the mouth of a large Creek on the S. S. Called River of the Fire Prarie[4]   at the mouth of this creek the party on Shore Shields & Collins was camped waiting for our arrival & inform that they Pass'd thro: Some fine Lands, and well watered   G D. [Drouillard] Killed a fine Bear to day

[Clark]

22nd *June Friday*   river rose 4 Inchs last night. I was waken'd ⟨at⟩ before day light this morning by the guard prepareing the boat to receive an apparent Storm which threttened violence from the West   at day light ⟨the⟩ a violent wind accompanied with rain cam from the W. and lasted about one hour, it Cleared away, and we Set out and proceeded on under a gentle breeze from the N. W.   passed Some verry Swift water Crouded with Snags, pass two large Island opposit each other, and immediately opposit a large & extensive Prarie on the Labd Side, This Prarie is butifull a high bottom for 1 ½ a mile back and risees to the Common leavel of the Countrey about 70 or 80 feet and extends back out of view. Capt. L walked on Shore a few miles this after noon   (at 3 oClock P M. *Ferents* Thermometer Stood at 87°: = to 11 d above Summer heat)   we came to on the L. Side opposit the mouth of a large Creek Called the River of the Fire Prarie, at the mouth of this Creek the Party on Shore were waiting our arrival, they informed that the Lands thro: which they passed was fine & well watered

Course & Distance June 22nd

S. 14° W.	2 ½	ms. to a pt. on the S. S.
S. 25° W	3	ms. to a pt. on the S. S. *bad wat*[er]
S 66° W	½	me. on S. Side
N. 60° W	4 ½	mes. to a pt. on the L. S. psd. 2 Isds: and a Prarie
	10 ½	

1. Biddle's note at the head of this sheet of the Field Notes (document 23) reads, "22d to 26."

2. Osgood interprets letters interlined above the word "Killed" as "Ord" for "Ordway." The sergeant himself says that "one of the men" killed the goose. Osgood (FN), 61.

3. "Summer heat" was an arbitrary average summer temperature commonly marked on thermometers at the time, in this case seventy-six degrees.

4. Near the Jackson-Lafayette county line, Missouri; the exact location is related to the River of the Fire Prairie, which is itself problematical. Both Clark's journals indicate that this stream was on the starboard, or north, side of the Missouri, with the camp on the opposite side. However, Fire Creek on later maps is on the south side of the river, in Jackson County, and is probably the Little Fire Creek referred to by Ordway and Floyd. The only sizable stream in the vicinity on the north side is Fishing River, a few miles upstream. Clark's 1810 map of the West (*Atlas* map 123) shows Fire Prairie River on the north side of the Missouri and Fire Prairie Creek on the south side, their mouths nearly opposite each other. In Clark's postexpedition list of rivers and creeks, he says that Fire Prairie Creek comes in from the southwest. Coues suggests that the mouth of Fishing River had moved upstream some time after 1804. This would also simplify matters, in that the island on which the expedition was forced by wind to spend most of June 23, 1804, could be Fishing River Island, which by the 1890s was downstream from the mouth of Fishing River, instead of upstream from it, as the expedition's island would have to be. It is possible, however, that this island, described by Biddle as separated from the north bank by a narrow, timber-choked channel, later became part of the mainland. To add to the confusion, Nicollet shows Fire Creek as "Clear water Creek" and indicates a "Fire Prairie River" on the south bank in present Jackson County, and mouthing above Fishing River, which is

not readily identifiable with a major stream in that vicinity today. Coues (HLC), 1:30 and n. 63; Nicollet (MMR), 365; MRC map 13.

[Clark]

23rd June Satturday   Some wind this morning from the N W.   Set out at 7 oC   Proceeded on N. 70 d. W 2 Ms. to an Isd. Close on the S. S.[1]   I went on Shore & walked up thro: a rich bottom for about Six miles, Killed a Deer & much fatigued   N. 75 E. to a point in a bend L. S. 1½[2]   the river fell 8 Inches last night.

[Clark]

23rd June Satturday   Some wind this morning from the N. W.   we Set out at 7 oClock, and proceeded on to the head of a Island on the S. S.   the wind blew hard and down the river which prevented the Pty moveing [*NB: proceding*] from this Island the whole day, Cap. Lewis had the arms examined &c.   at the lower end of this Island I got out of the boat to walk on Shore, & expected the party on Shore would overtake me at the head of the Island, they did not & I proceeded on round a round and extensive bend in the river,[3] I Killed a Deer & made a fire expecting the boat would Come up in the evening.   the wind continueing to blow prevented their moveing, as the distance by land was too great for me to return by night I concluded to Camp, Peeled Some bark to lay on, and geathered wood to make fires to Keep off the musquitor & Knats. Heard the party on Shore fire, at Dark Drewyer came to me with the horses, one fat *bear* & a Deer, river fell 8 Inches last night

Course & Distance June 23rd

N. 70° W   2   ms. to an Isd. on S. S. (I went out)
N. 75° E   1 ½   ms. psd. the head of the Isd. to pt. L. S.
3 ½

[Clark]   *Kansas* River June 23rd 1804[4]

Equal altitudes with Sexton   Es. 8' 45"—

	h	m	S
A. M.	8	9	42
"		10	59
"		12	26

[Lewis]   *Saturday June 23rd 1804.*[5]

On the upper point of a large island about four miles above the Fire prarie.

Observed Meridian altd. of ☉'s L. L. with the octant by the back obstn.   36° __' __"

1. Later Fishing River Island, assuming that Fishing River (Fire Prairie River) shifted its mouth upstream later. It may be, however, that the island they camped on later joined the mainland. (See above, June 22, 1804.) Biddle indicates that the island was directly opposite the high ground on which Clark established Fort Osage in 1808. This was near the later town of Sibley, Jackson County, Missouri, some miles upstream from Fishing River Island. Coues (HLC), 1:30 and nn. 63, 64.

2. The course appears to be in Lewis's hand.

3. Clark is not altogether clear about which side of the river he was on, but probably he was on the starboard side, in present Ray County, Missouri. He apparently walked around what was later called Jackass Bend. Evidently he camped near the upper end of the bend. MRC map 13; MRM map 39.

4. Clark's observation at the end of Codex A.

5. Lewis's observation from Codex O.

[Lewis and Clark]

Sunday June 24th   set out at ½ after six continuing the course on the Lard. side   N. 80 E ¼ of a mile to point Lard.   N. 55 ¼ of a mile to point Lard. Due west to a point Stard 3 miles   good water[1]

(I [Clark] joined the Boat theis morning with a fat Bear & two Deer, last evining I Struck the river about 6 miles (by land) abov the Boat, and finding it too late to get to the Boat, and the wind blowing So hard Down the river that She could not assend, I concluded to Camp, altho I had nothing but my hunting Dress, & the Musquitors Ticks & Knats verry troublesom, I concld to hunt on a Willow Isd. Situated close under the Shore, in Crossing from an Island, I got mired, and was obliged to Craul out, a disegreeable Situation & a Diverting one of any one who Could have Seen me after I got out, all Covered with mud, I went my Camp & [s]Craped off the Mud and washed my Clothes, and fired off my gun which was answered by George Drewyer who was in persute of me & came up at Dark   we feasted of meet & water   the latter we made great use of being much fatigued & thirsty—   The meet which hung up near the water ⟨attracted⟩ a large Snake   made Several attempts to get to it and was so Detirmined that I Killed him in his attempt, the Snake appeared to make to that part of the meet which Contained the milk of a Doe,[2] On this part of the River I observe great quantites of Bear Sign, they are after Mulbiries which are in great quantities)

N 85 d W. 4½ ms. to a pt. on L Side, Came to above the mouth of a Creek on the L. S. abt. 20 yds. Wide Called *Hay Cabbin* Creek[3]   Latd. of this place is 38° 37′ 5″ North— Capt. Lewis took Sergt. Floyd and walked on Shore, George Drewyer Killed 2 Deer   R Fields Killed a Deer dureing the time we wer Jurking the meet I brought in, West ½ ml. along the L. S.

S 21° W. 3 ms. to a pt. on the S. S.   pass 2 Creek on the S. S. just above Some rocks Some distance from Shore   1 of These Creek is Called *Sharriton-Cartie*,[4] a Prarie on the L. S. near the river. Capt Lewis Killed a Deer, & Collins 3. ⟨Drewer 2 to day⟩   emince number of Deer on both Sides of the river, we pass between two Sand bars at head of which we had to raise the boat 8 Inch to get her over, Camped at the Lower point of a Isd. on the L S.[5]   the Party in high Spirits.

[Clark]

24th, *June Sunday*   Set out at half after Six. I joined the boat this morng at 8 oClock   (I will only remark that dureing the time I lay on the band [bank] waiting for the boat, a large Snake Swam to the bank imediately under the Deer which was hanging over the water, and no great distance from it, I threw chunks and drove this Snake off Several times. I found that he was So determined on getting to the meet I was Compelld to Kill him, the part of the Deer which attracted this Snake I think was the milk from the bag of the Doe.) I observed great quts. of Bear Signs, where they had passed in all Directions thro the bottoms in Serch of Mulberries, which were in great numbers in all the bottoms thro which our party passed.)

Passed the mouth of a Creek 20 yds. wide name [*NB: named*] *Hay Cabbin Creek* from camps of Straw built on it

came to about ½ me. above this Creek & jurked, the meet killed yesterday and this morning ⟨took⟩ *Lattitude* of this place 38° 37′ 5″ N.   Capt. Lewis walked on Shore & Killed a Deer, pass a bad part of the river, on the S. S. the rocks projected into the river Some distance, a Creek above

Called *Shariston Carta*, in the evening we Passed thro: betwen two Sand bars   at the head we had to raise the Boat 8 Inches to get her over, Camped ⟨at⟩ near the lower point of an Island on the L. Side, party in high Spirrits. The Countrey on each Side of the river is fine interspersed with Praries, in which imence herds of Deer is Seen, on the banks of the river we observe numbers of Deer watering and feeding on the young willow, Several Killed to day

Course & Distance June 24th

N. 80° E	¼	me. on the Larboard Side
N. 55 E	¼	me. on [other?]
West	3	ms. to a point on S. S.
N 80° W.	4 ½	Ms. to a pt. on L. S. passd. Hay Cab. C
West	½	me. on L. Side
S. 21° W	3	ms. to a pt. on S. S. psd. a rock & Creek L. S.
	11 ½	

(*Point of observation No. 12.*)

[Lewis]   *Sunday June 24th* [6]

On the Starboard shore, about ½ a mile above the mouth of *hay-cabbin creek*.

Observed meridian altd. of ☉'s L. L. with octant by the back obsert.   36° 13′ —″

1. The first portion of this entry in the Field Notes is in Lewis's hand; Clark resumes thereafter.

2. Clark seems to allude here to the folk belief the "milk snake," which reportedly sucks the milk from cows' udders.

3. The Little Blue River, in Jackson County, Missouri. Nicollet gives it both the name Clark uses and the present one. Clark's name, as he notes in the Codex A entry, derives from some form of grass hut or shelter, built on the stream by Indians or others. Nicollet (MMR), 366; MRC map 13.

4. Apparently Clark's rendering of *Charretins écartés*, which can be interpreted to mean either a stream called Charretin that is some distance from another of the same name (Chariton River, passed on June 10), or two streams called Charretin that are joined at the mouth but separated just above. The latter description would fit Big Shoal Creek and Little Shoal Creek, in Clay County, Missouri, which join a little above where the former

meets the Missouri. The other of the two creeks mentioned might be Rush Creek, downstream from Big Shoal Creek. Coues (HLC), 1:31 n. 66; Osgood (FN), 61 n. 7; MRC map 14; MRM map 40.

5. In Jackson County, above Missouri City. There may have been various changes in the river since 1804, but a large nameless island appears in Nicollet (MMR), 366 (1839) and MRC map 14 (ca. 1892) in about the right place to be the one near whose lower point the camp was located.

6. Lewis's observation from Codex O.

[Clark][1]

Monday June 25th   a heavy fog Detaind us about an hour   Set out passed the Isd on a course from the last point S 49° W, 3 Ms to a point on the S. S.   S 55° W ½ Me. S. S.   a Coal-Bank on the opposit or L. S Side, this bank appears to Contain great quantity of excellente Coal,[2] the wind from the N: W   a Small Creek Called Coal or (Chabonea)[3] N 50° W to the Pt, L. S. 3½ Miles   Hard water & logs, Bank falling in, Passed a Small Creek L. S. Called *Labeenie*[4] ⟨Lat. 38 37′ 5″⟩   a Prarie is Situated on the S. S. a Short Distance from the river, which contains great quantities of wild apples of the Size of the Common apple,[5] the French Say is well flavered when ripe, which is the time the leaves begin to fall N 70° W ½ me. along the right Side of a Willow Isd. Situated on the L. Side S. 80° W ½ me. L. S.   S 55° W. ½ me. to Pt. of Smal Isd. L. S.   S 15° W ½ me. L. S.—   S. 2° E 2 me. pt on Lbd S. (here I will only remark that the Deer in the Morning & evening are feeding in great numbers on the banks of the River, they feed on young willow, and amuse themselves running on the open beeches or points[)]   We have hard water this afternoon round the heads of Small Islds. on the L. Side below a Small High Prarie S. 48° W. 2 Ms. pt. S. S.   passd. a small Isd. on which we Camped[6] The party on Shore did not join us to day, or have we Seen or her [heard] of them   river falling fast about 8 Inches in 24 hours, the Hills on the L. S. this evening higher than usial about 160 or 180 feet.   the lands appear of a Simalier to those passed

[Clark]

25th, *June Monday*   a thick fog detained us untile 8 oClock, passed a Island, at 3 miles passed a Coal-mine, or Bank of Stone Coal, on the South

Side, this bank appears to Contain great quantity of fine Coal, the river being high prevented our Seeeing that contained in the Cliffs of the best quallity, a Small Creek mouth's ⟨in⟩ below This bank Call'd after the bank ⟨*Chabonea*⟩ [*NB: Charbon*][7] Creek   the Wind from the N. W.   passed a Small Creek on the L. Side at 12 oClock, Called Bennet's Creek   The Praries Come within a Short distance of the river on each Side which Contains in addition to Plumbs[8] Raspberries & vast quantities of wild ⟨crab⟩ apples, ⟨which is of a [*blank*][9] and wild flowers⟩   great numbs. of Deer are seen feeding on the young willows & earbage in the Banks ⟨op⟩ and on the Sand bars in the river.   our party on Shores did not join us this evening   we Camped on an Island Situated on the S. Side, opposit some hills higher than Common, Say 160 or 180 feet above the Bottom. The river is Still falling   last night it fell 8 Inches

Course & Distance June 25th

S. 49° W.	3	ms. to a pt on S. S.
S. 55 W.	½	me. on the S. S. psd. a *Coal Mine*
N. 50° W	3 ½	ms. to Pt. on L. S. psd. a Creek L S
N. 70° W	½	me. on L. S. pass willow Isd.
S. 80° W	½	me. on L. S. ditto
S. 55° W	½	me. on L. S. ditto
S. 15° W	½	me. on L. S. ditto & round Pt.
S. 2° E	2	ms. to a pt. on S. S.
S, 48 W	2	ms. to a pt. on S. S. psd. a Isd.
	13	

1. The latter part of this entry and most of the next is written over a note by Lewis. See his entry for June 12, 1804, above.

2. Several coal beds, ranging from six inches to two and one-half feet thick, are known from the eastern part of Jackson County, Missouri. One, the Brush Creek mine east of Kansas City, produced coal for several years but was abandoned in 1904. Hinds, 211–14.

3. Perhaps later Sleepy Branch, Jackson County. MRM map 40.

4. The "Bennet's Creek" of the Codex A entry, perhaps named for François M. Benoit, later referred to by Clark as "Bennet" (see below, July 14, 1804), or a member of his family. Biddle gives it as "La Benite," the name it bears in Nicollet. La Benite Park perpetuates that name. It is evidently the later Sugar Creek in Jackson County. Coues (HLC), 1:32 and n. 69; Osgood (FN), 62 n. 8; Nicollet (MMR), 368; MRC map 14; MRM map 41.

5. Probably *Pyrus ioensis* (Wood) Bailey, wild crab, which is the most common crab apple in Missouri. *P. coronaria* L., wild crab, is also known in the area but is much less common. Steyermark, 799.

6. They evidently went around the later Liberty Bend, now cut off by the Missouri, and camped opposite the modern community of Sugar Creek, Jackson County, a suburb of Kansas City. MRC map 14.

7. Biddle apparently crossed out "Charbonea" when he substituted "Charbon."

8. Probably *Prunus americana* Marsh., wild plum. Steyermark, 860. The captains gave the word *plums*, like *currants*, a broad application.

9. A space of more than half a line was left here for a later insertion that was never made. The entire phrase, placed in brackets in the original, was later crossed out.

[Clark]

Tuesday June 26th   We Set out early   wind from the S. W.   on the Course of last night

S 62° W	½	me. on S. S. an Island on the L: Side
S 80° W	½	me. S. S, passed the mouth of a Small river called Blue Water river (in french *R. La Bléue*) this River heads with the Mine river in a divideing ridge between the Kancis & Osage Rivers[1]
N 87° W,	1	me. S. S.
N 85° W	3	Ms. to point on the L. Side Mdn. altd. *38° 32′ 15″ N.* high land on S. S. abt. 90 foot high jutting over the riv[er]
S 80 W.	½	me. L. S.
S. 37° W	2 ½	ms. to pt. S. S. psd. a large Danjerous Counter-Current on the S. S. above Some rocks a Small willow Isd. in the bend to the L. S. Killed a large rattle Snake emence number of Parrot-quetes
S 58° W	1	me. alg S. S. our Party on shor cam in Killed 7 Deer, & 3 from the boat
N 54 W.	½	me to a pt L. S at mouth of the Kansas River Camped

[Clark]

June 26th Tuesday 1804   we Set out early, the river falling a little, the wind from the S. W.   Passed the mouth of a Small river on the L. Side above the upper point of a Small Island, Called Blue water river, this river heads in Praries back with the Mine River about 30 yds. wide   Lattitude of a pt. 4 ms. above this river is *38° 32′ 15″* North, the high lands which is on the Northe Side does not exceed 80 feet high, at this Place the river appears to be Confd. in a verry narrow Channel, and the Current Still more So by Couenter Current or Whirl on one Side & high bank on the other, passed a Small Isd. in the bend to the L. Side we Killed a large rattle Snake, Sunning himself in the bank passed a bad Sand bar, where our tow rope broke twice, & with great exertions we rowed round it and Came to & Camped in the Point above the *Kansas* [WC: *zás*] *River*[2] I observed a great number of *Parrot queets*[3] this evening, our Party Killed Several 7 Deer to day

Course & Distance June 26th

S. 62° W.	½	me. on the S. S. Isd. on L. S.
S. 80° W.	½	me. on the S. S. psd. Blue Water R L. S.
N. 87° W.	1	me. on the S. S.
N. 85° W.	3	ms. to a pt. on the L. S. mdle [abt?]
S. 80° W.	½	me. on L. S.
S. 37° W.	2 ½	mes. to a pt. on S. S. psd Ltt. Crt.
S. 58° W.	1	me. on S. S. psd. a bad place
S. 78° W.	¾	me. to the upr. pt. of Kansas R
	9 ¾	= 366 & ⟨¾⟩ ms. to mouth of Missouris[4]

(*Point of observation No. 13.*)

[Lewis]   *Tuesday June 26th*[5]

On the Larboard shore about four mes. above the mouth of the *blue water* river.—

Observed meridian altd. of ☉'s L. L. with octant by the back observt. 36° 10′ —″

1. The Big Blue, or Blue, River enters the Missouri at Kansas City, Jackson County, Missouri. It heads in eastern Kansas, between the Kansas River and the Marais des Cygnes River, a major tributary of the Osage, a great distance from the Lamine River. It should not be confused with the better-known Big Blue River, which rises in Hamilton County, Nebraska, and enters the Kansas River at Manhattan, Kansas. MRC map 14.

2. This camp just above the mouth of the Kansas, or Kaw, River, would be in present Kansas City, Wyandotte County, Kansas. It was the first camp of the expedition in that state, assuming no major changes in the mouth of the river. Clark apparently interlined a

correction for the second syllable of "Kansas." He may have intended it as a guide to pronunciation rather than an amended spelling. Ibid.

3. The Carolina parakeet, or parroquet, *Conuropsis carolinensis* [AOU, 382], which is now extinct. This is apparently the first reference to the species west of the Mississippi. Cutright (LCPN), 58.

4. According to MRC map 14, made about 1892, the mouth of the Kansas was just over 390 miles above the mouth of the Missouri. Changes in the course of the Missouri River and the captains' tendency to underestimate river mileage account for the discrepancy.

5. Lewis's observation from Codex O.

[Clark][1]

June 27th, *Wednesday*   a fair warm morning, the river rose a little last night.   we determin to delay at this Place three or four Days to make observations & recruit the party   Several men out Hunting,[2] unloaded one Perogue, and turned her up to Dry with a view of repairing her after Completeing a Strong redoubt or brest work frome one river to the other, of logs & Bushes Six feet high, The Countrey about the mouth of this river is verry fine on each Side as well as the North of the Missouries   the bottom, in the Point is low, & overflown for 250 yards.   it rises a little above high water mark and Continus up that hight of good quallity back to the hills [*blank*] ⟨mile a⟩ A high Clift, on the upper Side of the Kansis ½ a mile up

below the Kanses the hills is about 1 ½ miles from the point on the North Side of the Missouries   the Hill or high lands is Several miles back, we compareed the instrmts   Took equal altitudes, and the Meridian altituade of the Suns L L to day *Lattitude 38° 31' 13" Longitude* [*blank*]   Measured The width of the Kansas River by an angle and made it 230 yds ¼ wide, it is wider above the mouth   the Missouries at this place is about 500 yards wide, The Course from the Point down the midle. of the Missourie is S. 32° E, & turns to the North. up Do: is N 21° W. & do   do—Do.   up the right side of the Kansas is S. 54° E, & the river turns to the left, Several Deer Killed to day.

(*Point of observation No. 14.*)

[Lewis]   *Wednesday June 27th*[3]

On the point formed by the confluence of the Kancez River and the Missouri, made the following observations.—

Equal altitudes of the Sun, with *Sextant*

	h	m	s		h	m	s
A. M.	8	22	33	3	49	19
"		23	53	"	50	39
"		25	17	"	52	3

Altd. by Sextant at the time of this observt. 81° 15′ 15″

⊙'s magnetic azimuth by Circumfetr. S. 81° E.

	h	m	s
Time by Chronometer A. M.	8	22	33
Alt of ⊙'s U. L. by Sextant	81°	15′	15″
Latitude of place of observation	39°	5′	25.7″
Variation of the nedle			[*blank*]

Observed Meridian altd. of ⊙'s L. L.
with Octant by the back observation. 36° 25′ —″

Latitude deduced from this obsert. 39° 5′ 38.5″

⊙'s magnetic azimuth by Circumferentr. S. 88° W.

	h	m	s
Time by Chronometer at p. Obs. P. M.	4	52	33
Altd. of ⊙'s L. L. by Sextant.	56°	51′	—″

⊙'s magnetic azimuth by Circumftr. S. 89° W.

	h	m	s
Time by Chronometer P. M.	5	2	6
Altd. of ⊙'s L. L. by Sextant	53	10	15

Observed magnetic azimuth of pole ★ with my Circumferenter, taking time by Chronotr. *Time by Chronomtr.—* ★'s *magt. Azimuth*

	h	m	s				
P. M.	9	54	—	N.	8°		W.
	9	58	4	N.	8°		W.
	10	—	40	N.	7	45	W.

1. There are no separate entries for June 27 and 28 in the Field Notes. The entries for the two days in Codex A are given here.

2. According to Ordway, one of the hunters, Cruzatte, killed a deer.

3. Lewis's observation from Codex O.

[Clark]

28 *June Thursday*   took equal altitudes &c. &c. &c. & varaitian of the Compass   repaired the Perogue   Cleaned out the Boat   Suned our Powder wollen articles   examined every thing   8 or 10 huntrs. out to day[1] in different direction, in examineing our private Store of Provisions we found Several articles Spoiled from the wet or dampness they had received, a verry warm Day, the wind from the South, The river Missourie has raised yesterday last night & to day about 2 foot.   this evening it is on a Stand, Capt. Lewis weighed the water of the Two rivers   The Missouris 78° The Kansais 72°[2]   ⟨The Weight is⟩   To Describe the most probable of the various accounts of this great river of the Kansas, would be too lengthy & uncertain to insert here, it heads with the river Del Norid in the black Mountain or ridge which Divides the waters of the Kansas *Del Nord*, & Callarado & oppsoitly from those of the Missoureis (and not well assertaind)[3]   This River recves its name from a nation which dwells at this time on its banks & 2 villages one about 20 Leagues & the other 40 Leagues up,[4] those Indians are not verry noumerous at this time, reduced by war with their neighbours, &c.   they formerly liveid on the South banks of the Missouries 24 Leagues above this river in a open & butifull plain and were verry noumerous at the time the french first Settled the Illinois, I am told they are a fierce & warlike people, being badly Supplied with fire arms, become easily conquered by the Aiauway & Saukees who are better furnished with those materials of war, This nation is now out in the plains hunting the Buffalow [*NB: They consist of about 300 men*]   our hunters Killed Several Deer and Saw Buffalow, men impd Dressing Skins & makeing themselves Comfortable, the high lands Coms to the river Kanses on the upper Side at about a mile, full in view, and a butifull place for a fort, good landing place, the waters of the Kansas is verry disigreeably tasted to me.

[Lewis]   *Thursday June 28th*[5]

Observed Equal Altitudes of ☉, with Sextant

	h	m	s			h	m	s
A. M.	8	9	42		P. M.	4	1	50
	"	10	59			"	3	9.5
	"	12	26			"	4	35.5

Altd. by Sextant at the time of Observtn.   76° 16′ 52″

Meridian alt of ☉'s L. L. with Octant by the back observation   36° 31′ —″

Latitude deduced from this obst.   39° 5′ 25.7″

1. According to Ordway, Reubin and Joseph Field were among them.

2. In his Field Notes, Clark gives these figures as the weights of the water of the two rivers (see below, the combined entry for June 26–29, 1804). Biddle gives the figures, in degrees, as the specific gravity of the two kinds of water. Specific gravity is usually expressed as the ratio of the weight of a substance to the weight of an equal volume of pure water at the same temperature. Coues (HLC), 1:33.

3. The captains applied the term "Black Mountain" or "Black Hills" to all the eastern outlying ranges of the Rockies, then known chiefly through Indian information. At this time, geographical theory postulated a pyramidal height of land in the west, from which the Missouri, Kansas, Colorado, Columbia and Rio Grande del Norte (Clark's "Del Nord") rose and went their several ways. Before Lewis and Clark, the Anglo-Americans had little conception of the extent and complexity of the Rocky Mountain region; as Clark observed, the features of this region were "not well assertaind." Allen, 190, 202–3, 240, 376, 382–83.

4. Although there are a number of known Kansa villages on the Kansas River in the area noted, the identity of the two villages has yet to be determined. Wedel (KA), 52.

5. Lewis's observation from Codex O.

[Clark][1]

29th of June 1804, Set out from the Kansas river ½ past 4 oClock, proceeded on passed a Small run on the L. S. at ½ Mile[2] a (1) *Island* on the S. S. at 1½ me.   Hills above the upr. pt of Isd. L. S.   a large Sand bar in the middle. Passed a verry bad place of water, the Sturn of the Boat Struck a moveing Sand & turned within 6 Inches of a large Sawyer, if the Boat had Struck the Sawyer, her Bow must have been Knocked off & in Course She must hav Sunk in the Deep water below   Came to & camped on the S. S. late in the eveninge.[3]

Course & Distance June 29: *refrunceis*

	N 21 d W.	3 ½	ms. to a pt. on L S: passed a Pt. on L. S. and the lower pt. of an Isd S. S.
(1)	N 18° W.	¾	on L S. opsd. head of Isd
	S. 79° W	3	ms. to a pt. on S. S.
		7 ¼	

[Clark]

29th June Friday   obsvd. the distance of ☉ & ☽, took Equal & maridinal altd. and after makeing Some arrangements, and inflicting a little punishment to two men we Set out at ½ past 4 oClock and proceeded on   (1) passed a large Island on the S. Side, opposit a large Sand bar, the Boat turned and was within Six Inches of Strikeing   the rapidity with which the Boat turned was so great that if her bow had Struck the Snag, She must have either turned over or the bow nocked off   S W wind

Course Distance and refferences June 29th

N. 21 W.	3 ½	Ms. to a pt. on L. S. psd: pt. Isd. S. S. (1)
N. 18° W.	¾	me. on the L. S. psd. Hd. of the Isd.
S. 79 W.	3	ms. to a pt. on the S. S.
	7 ¼	

[Clark]   Camp mouth of the *Kanseis June 29th 1804.*[4]

Ordered

a Court martial will Set this day at 11 oClock, to Consist of five members, for the trial of *John Collins* and *Hugh Hall*, Confined on Charges exhibited against them by Sergeant Floyd, agreeable to the articles of War.

Detail for the Court

Sergt Nat. Pryor presd.
2 John Colter ⎤
3 John Newmon ⎥ mbs.
4 Pat. Gass ⎥
1 J. B. Thompson ⎦
John Potts to act as Judge advocate.—

The Court Convened agreeable to order and proceeded to the trial of the Prisoners Viz John Collins Charged "with getting drunk on his post this morning out of whiskey put under his Charge as a Sentinal and for Suffering *Hugh Hall* to draw whiskey out of the Said Barrel intended for the party"

To this Charge the prisoner plead *not guilty*.

The Court after mature deliveration on the evidence abduced &c. are of oppinion that the prisoner is *Guilty* of the Charge exibited against him, and do therefore Sentence him to recive *one hundred Lashes on his bear Back.*

Hugh Hall was brought with ["]takeing whiskey out of a Keg this morning which whiskey was Stored on the Bank (and under the Charge of the guard) Contrary to all order, rule, or regulation"

To this Charge the prisoner "Pleades Guilty."

The Court find the prisoner guilty and Sentence him to receive *fifty* Lashes on his bear Back.

The Commanding Officers approve of the Sentence of the Court and orders that the Punishment take place at half past three this evening, at which time the party will Parrade for inspection—

[Lewis]   *Friday June 29th*[5]

Observed Equal altitudes of ☉, with Sextant

	h	m	s			h	m	s
A. M.	9	6	46		P. M.	3	4	29
"		9	3		"		5	51
"		9	29		"		7	15

Aldt. by Sextant at the time of Observt.   98° 18′ 45″

Observed time and distance of ☉'s and ☽'s nearest Limbs, with Chronometer and Sextant, the ☉ East.—

	Time				Distance		
	h	m	s				
A. M.	7	6	2		104°	13′	30″
"		9	7		"	12	15
"		11	23		"	11	30
"		15	38		"	10	—
"		17	5		"	9	45
"		18	33		"	8	15
"		20	2		"	8	—
"		22	—		"	7	30
	h	m	s				
A. M.	7	33	57		104°	3′	15″
"		35	11		"	3	—
"		36	33		"	3	—
"		37	37		"	2	—
"		39	18		"	1	15
"		40	26		"	1	—

	h	m	s				
	″	41	23		″	1	—
	″	43	1		103°	59	53
		h	m	s			
A. M.	7	51	21		103°	56′	15″
	″	56	49		″	55	15
	″	58	47		″	54	52
	8	—	45		″	54	—
	″	3	49		″	51	45
	″	6	57		″	51	—
	″	8	53		″	50	15
	″	10	44		″	49	30
		h	m	s			
A. M.	8	16	3		103°	48′	—″
	″	17	51		″	46	30
	″	20	6		″	45	—
	″	21	42		″	45	—
	″	23	5		″	44	—
	″	25	40		″	43	15
	″	28	3		″	42	45
	″	30	36		″	41	52
		h	m	s			
A. M.	8	37	25		103°	37′	15″
	″	39	15		″	37	—
	″	40	10		″	36	—
	″	43	3		″	35	—
	″	44	36		″	34	45
	8	46	7		103°	33	30
	″	47	34		″	33	00
	″	48	35		″	32	15
		h	m	s			
A. M.	8	49	55		103	32	—
	″	51	54		″	31	45
	″	52	57		″	31	15
	″	53	31		″	31	—
	″	54	16		″	30	45
	″	55	11		″	29	—
	″	56	45		″	28	45
	″	57	41		″	28	15

Meridian Alt of ☉'s L. L. with Octant by the back observation   36° 36′ —″

Latitude deduced from this obstn.   39° 5′ 21.2″

1. Biddle's notation at the head of this sheet of Field Notes (document 25) reads "29 June to July 1st."

2. Perhaps later Jersey Creek, in Wyandotte County, Kansas. MRC map 14.

3. A camp on the starboard side of the stream today would be in the vicinity of Riverside, Platte County, Missouri. Ibid.

4. From the Orderly Book.

5. Lewis's observation from Codex O.

at the Mouth of the River Kansies

[Clark]   June 26″ 27″ 28 & 29th—[1]

This river is 366 miles above the mouth of Missouri   it is in Lattitude 38° 31′ 13″ North

it is 230 yds. wide at its mouth & wider above   from the point up the Missourie for about 3 ms. N. 21° W, Down the Middle of the Missourie is S. 32° E, up the upper bank of the Kansais, is S. 54° E   the river turns to the East above a pt. of high land, well Situated for a fort & in view of the Missouris   one mile up & on the upper Side, the width of the Missouris at this place is about 500 yds.

Missourie Water weighs 78.   The Kanseis weghs 72   river Miss[ouri] raised in the time at the Kanseis 2 foot and begun to fail.

The wood land on each side of the Mouth of this river is extensive and of a good quallity as far as our hunters was back, but badly watered with Springs, only two being Seen by them

Some punishment of two men *Hall* & *Collins* for takeing whiskey out of the Barrel last night [*Ed: see Detachment Order of June 29*] agreeable to the Sentences of a Court Mtl of the party who we have always found verry ready to punish Such Crimes—

Many Deer Killed to day

Allarm post or order of Battle arms to be Situated & the Duty &c.[2]

Messes of men under a Serjiant who is to detail for every day one man of his Squad to Cook &c. who Shall have the management of the provisions dureing that day or issue, each Days rations must be divided &c. &c

Order of encampment, Tents, fires & Duty

Signals &c &c.

S 81 [W?] to pt   pased on [at?] S. S. 5 Ms.[3]

1. Biddle's notation at the top of this sheet of the Field Notes (document 24) reads "26 to 28." On document 24, Clark wrote a series of notes covering the entire period they were camped at the mouth of the Kansas River, making no separate Field Notes entries for June 27 and 28.

2. This outline for general orders (this paragraph and next) that may have been issued at the mouth of the Kansas was written under the main body of preceding material and at right angles to the rest.

3. Brief course and distance material under the main body of material above, written diagonally to the rest.

[Clark]

30th June, Set out verry early this Morng   Saw a verry large wolf[1] [*blank*] on the Sand bar this morning walking near a gange of Turkeys (1) at 10 miles above the Kansis passed the mouth of a Small River Call the (*Petite Plate*) or the little Shole river,[2] this river is about 70 yds. Wide and has Several rapids & falls, well Calculatd for mills, the land on this river is Said to be Roaling, Killed 2 Deer Bucks Swinging [swimming] the river   the wind from the S. W.   here we opened the Bag of Bread given us by [*blank*] which we found verry good, our Bacon which was given us by [*blank*] we examined and found Sound and good   Some of that purchased in the Illinois Spoiled, ⟨I found⟩ a relish of this old bacon this morning was verry agreeable, Deer to be Seen in every direction and their tracks ar as plenty as Hogs about a *farm*, our hunts. Killed 9 Deer to day   the land below the last river is good, that above, between the two rivers which is near together is Slaik'y[3] and bad on the N. Side, the other Side is good land, Landed on the L. S. below an Isd called Dimond Island[4]

Course Distance & refurrencees June 30th[5]

N. 20° W	2	Ms. to pt L. S. Boat wheeled
N. 30° W	½	Me. on the L. S.— High lands on the S. S.
S. 64° W.	2 ½	ms. to Pt. on S. S. psd. Little Rivr Platt. (1)
West	1	me. on S. S. a Small Creek on L. S.
N. 60° W	4	ms. to a pt. on the L. S.
	10	

[Clark]   30th *June* Satturday 1804

Set out verry early this morning, a verry large wolf Came to the bank
and looked at us this morning, passd the (1) mouth of a Small river 10 ms.
above the *Kanseis* Called by the french Petite River Platte (or Shoal river)
from the number of falls in it, this river is about 60 yards wide at its mouth
and runs Parrilel with the Missouries for ten or twelve miles, ⟨I am⟩ [*NB:
(Some of the party who went up*] told that the lands on this Small river is good,
and on its Several falls well Calculated for mills, the wind from S. W.   came
to at 12 oClock & rested three hours, the [sun or day?] being hot the men
becom verry feeble, Farnsts. Thermometer at 3 oClock Stood at 96° above
o, emence numbs. of Deer on the banks, Skipping in every derection, the
party Killed nine Bucks on the river & Bank to day, The Countrey on the
S. S. between the Shoal River & Missouris is indifferent Subject to overflow, that below and on the L. S. is high & appers well timbered, Camped
on the L. S. opsd. the Lower point of a Isd. Called diamond Island, Broke
our mast

Course Distance & reefrs. June 30th

N. 20° W.	2	Ms. to pt. L. S. Boat turned
N. 30° W.	½	me. on L. S. High Land S. S.
S. 64° W.	2 ½	ms. to pt. on S. S. psd. R Plate (1)
West—	1	Me. on S S. a Sm. Creek L. S.
N. 60° W	4	ms. to pt. on L. S.
	10	

(Pot. Obst. No. 15.)

[Lewis]   *Saturday June 30th*[6]

On the Larboard Shore ¾ of a mile below *the Little river Platte.*—

Observed time and distance of ☉'s and ☽'s nearest limbs; the ☉ East *with Sext.
& Chrontr.*

	Time				*Distance*	
	h	m	s			
A. M.	7	55	36	90°	58′	—″
	″	57	16	″	57	45
	″	58	49	″	57	45
	8	1	20	″	56	15

	h	m	s		°	′	″
"	2	52		"		55	—
"	4	16		"		55	—
"	5	26		"		54	45
"	6	11		"		54	45
"	7	10		"		54	30
"	8	9		"		54	30
	h	m	s				
A. M.	8	11	11		90°	50′	30″
"		12	39		"	50	15
"		13	57		"	50	—
"		14	57		"	49	45
"		15	54		"	49	15
"		16	53		"	49	—
"		17	30		"	48	45
"		18	53		"	48	—
"		19	45		"	48	—
"		20	24		"	47	45

1. Presumably a gray wolf, *Canis lupus*, which Lewis describes May 5, 1805. Hall 2:928–33.

2. The Platte, or Little Platte, River in Platte County, Missouri, not to be confused with the stream of that name in Nebraska. In 1804, its mouth was probably several miles down the Missouri from its present position. "Platte" in French implies that the stream is relatively level, wide, and shallow. Clark's "Shole" is, of course, "shoal." Stewart (APN), 376; MRC map 15.

3. Slaky means miry or muddy.

4. Diamond Island was still on maps about 1890 but no longer is. The camp was in northeast Wyandotte County, Kansas, in the vicinity of the present village of Wolcott. MRC map 15; MRM map 42.

5. The courses and distances for this Field Notes entry come on the same sheet (document 25) after a portion of the entry for July 1 and were later crossed out. Here they are placed under the correct date.

6. Lewis's observation from Codex O.

[Lewis and Clark]   [*Weather, June 1804*][1]

June

10h   rasberreis perple, ripe and abundant,

11h   many small bird are now setting   some have young, the whiper-
           will *setting*[2]

16 June   the wood duck now has it's young, this duck is abundant, and except one Solatary Pelican and a few gees these ducks were the only aquatic fowls we have yet seen

1. No tables of weather observations for June 1804 have been found, but both captains entered a few remarks, Clark in Codex C and Lewis in his Weather Diary. These are observations of natural phenomena related to seasonal change and climate, such as plant ripening and animal migrations, rather than weather data as such. Those given follow Lewis, but the comments of both men are virtually identical. They are placed at the end of the appropriate month, as before.

2. Whip-poor-will. See June 4, 1804.

[Clark]

July 1st 1804, last night one of the Sentinals Chang'd [challenged] either a man or Beast, which run off, all prepared for action, Set out early passed the Dimond Isd. pass a Small Creek on the L. S. as this Creek is without name we Call it Biscuit Creek[1] Brackfast on the upper point of a Sand beech, The river still falling a little a verry warm Day. I took Some medison last night which has worked me very much party all in helth except Boils—[2]

passed a Sand bar in the river above the Isd. Covered for a me. with Drift Wood, Came to Capt Lewis took Medn. altitude & we delayed three hours, the day being excessively hot, Turkeys are plenty on the Shore, ⟨Some of the men⟩ G. Drewyer inform that he Saw *PueCanns* [pecan] Trees[3] on S. S. yesterday great quantities of raspburies an Grapes, (2) pass a Creek on the L. S. called *remore* (Tree Frog) Creek,[4] an Isd above in the Mid: and ⟨a Pond on⟩ 2 Willow Isds on the S. S. all of the Same name;[5] The two Willow Isds. has been made within 3 years & the Main Chanl. runs now on the L S. of the large Island where there was no runing wate[r] at low water from this Island the range of Hills up the river to the N, W, pass a run on the L. S.[6] a Butifull extensive Prarie, Two Islands just above Called (Isles des Parques) or Field Islands,[7] those Islands are, one of our French hands tels me that the French intended to Settle here once & brought their Cows and put them on those Islands, Mr Mackey Says the first village of the Kanseis was a little above this Island & made use of as fields, no trace of anything of that Kind remains to be

15. Missouri River near Mouth of Grand River to Beyond Mouth
of Kansas River, ca. July 1, 1804, Field Notes, document 10

Seen on the Isds.   fine Land on the L. Side, Hills near the river all day, Camped on the lower pot. of 1st Isd.—[8]

July 1

N. 62° W.	1 ½	me. to S. S. Side of an Island (Dimond I[)]
N. 40° W.	¼	me. on S. S. of the Isd. 1 Sand Isd. on Left
N. 28° W.	¾	me. to Pt. on L. S. passed the upper point of Isd
N. 45 W.	3 ½	mils to a pt. on S. S. Cours Cond. to tree in ops.
	6	Prary on the Ld S.[9]

Course Distance and refurrences (by Ltte) July 1.

	6	Mes on the course's of this morning—
N. 32 d W	1 ½	ms. to a pt. on the L. Side.
N. 14 d W.		to the right Side of an Isd. passed a Creek on L. S. (2)[10]
N 58 W.	2 ½	ms. to pt. L S. passed the head of the Isd.
N. 42 W.	1 ½	ms. to a pt. on S. S.
N. 27 W	½	me. to North Side of a Island (3) Creek L. S. and a Butifull extensive [Prarie?] High and dry[11]
	13	

[Clark]   *July* 1st, *Sunday* 1804

a Small allarm last night   all prepared for action, Set out early this morning   passed on the North Side of Dimond Island, a Small Creek mouths opposit I call *Biscuit* Creek,—   a large Sand bar in the middle of the river 1 ½ ms. above the Isd. Covered with Drift wood.   river fall a little. The wind from S. W.   Came to above this Drift and delayed three hours to refresh the men who were verry much over powered with the heat, Great quantity of Grapes & raspberries, (2) passed a Small Creek on the L. S. below one large and two small Islands. This Creek and Isds. are Called *Remore* (or Tree Frog)   a large Pond on the S. S., the main Current of Water run'g on the L. S. of the Island, I am told that Three years ago the main Current run on the S. S. of the Island and no appearance of the two Smaller Islands, Camped on the lower point of one of the two large & 2 Small Isds. Called *Isles des Parques* or field Islds   a high butifull Prarie on the L. S.   one of the french hands Says "that the french Kept their

Cattle & horses on those Islands at the time they had in this quarter a fort & trading establishment.["]

Course Distance & refrs. July 1st

N. 62° W.	1 ½	ms. on the S. Side of the Isd.
N. 40° W	¼	me. do do do
N. 28° W	¾	me. to pt. on L. S. psd. the Isd.
N. 45° W	3 ½	ms. to a pt. on S. S. psd. Drift
N. 32° W	1 ½	Me. to a ⟨the lower⟩ creek ⟨pt. of a Isd⟩. L. S.
N. 58 W	2 ½	Ms. to pt. L. S. psd. the head of Isd.
N. 42 W.	1 ½	ms. to a pt. on ⟨L⟩ S. S.
N. 27 W.	½	me. to pt. of Field Isd. prarie L. S.
	12	

paecaun Trees Seen on the S. S.   Deer and turkeys in great quantities on the bank

(Point Obstn. No. 16.)

[Lewis]   *Sunday July 1st*[12]

On the Larboard shore one ½ miles above the upper point of the dimond Island.

Observed Meridian Altd. of ☉'s L. L. with Octant by the back obstn.   36° 59′ 30″

Latitude deduced from this obstn.   39° 9′ 38.6″

1. Probably Island Creek, which mouths above Diamond Island near the Wyandotte-Leavenworth county line, Kansas. MRC map 15; MRM map 42.

2. The first part of this day's entry in the Field Notes is on document 25; the remainder is on document 24. At the beginning of the second portion are drawn an asterisk and star; these Clark must have intended as a reference to other material, but the place they are repeated is at the head of the courses and distances for June 30. Since a portion of the courses and distances for July 1 is found under those for June 30, he may have misplaced his reference symbols.

3. *Carya illinoensis* (Wang.) K. Koch, pecan. This mention of pecan in Leavenworth County, is its northern limit on the Missouri River. Steyermark, 511, 514; Barkley, 37.

4. This might be either Ninemile Creek, or Fivemile Creek, Leavenworth County. McDermott (WCS), 148–49; MRC map 15.

5. These islands might be part of what was later called Delaware Bar, but the position

relative to Ninemile Creek (see n. 4, above) is not precisely that described by Clark. The possibility of changes in the river is always present, as indicated by Clark's own description. If Tree Frog Creek is Fivemile Creek, then the large island might be later Leavenworth Island. MRC map 15.

6. Perhaps Threemile Creek, at present Leavenworth, Leavenworth County. Ibid.; MRM map 44.

7. Opposite present Leavenworth and Fort Leavenworth. The river course has evidently changed considerably over the years. MRC map 15.

8. Opposite present Leavenworth, probably on later Leavenworth Island. Nicollet renders them as one long mass labeled "Old Cluster of Islands Called Isles des Parcs," in the position of later Leavenworth Island. Probable river changes over the years make it difficult to determine the exact locations in relation to the Missouri-Kansas state line. Nicollet (MMR), 371; MRC map 15.

9. The first part of the courses and distances for this entry in the Field Notes is at the bottom of document 25. A sunburst symbol, by Clark, directs the reader to the other portion, at the bottom of document 24.

10. This course is not found in Codex A.

11. Some figures are at right angles to the rest of the writing on the page: 13, 10, 7, and a total of 30. Apparently Clark was adding mileage for July 1 and the previous two days. Clark's total for July 1 should probably be 12. Additional notes at bottom of page: N. 22 d E, North, (16). "N. 22 d E" is the first course of the next day.

12. Lewis's observation from Codex O.

[Clark][1]

July the 2nd 1804   Set out verry early this morning   passd on the Left of the Isles des parques   High butifull Situation—   on the L S. the land indifferent lands   a Creek coms in on the S. S. Called *parques*,[2] all at once the river became Crowded with drift that it was dangerous to cross   this I Suppose was from the caveing in of the banks at [t]he head of Some Island above, (3) passed a Creek on the L. S. called *Turquie* or Turkey Creek[3]   passed a verry bad Sand bar on the L. S.   the 20 Oars & Poals could with much dificuelty Stem the Current, passed a large Island on the S. S. Called by the Inds. *Wau-car-ba war-con-da* or the *Bear Medison* Island,[4] at 12 oClock came to on the Island and put in a mast, detained four hours, exceedingly hot, wind in forepart of the day from the S. E, George Drewyer informs that the Lands he pass through yesterday & to day on the S. S. was generally Verry fine   he Saw two Springs of fresh water near the Island, Deer Sign has become So Common it is hardly necessary to mention them, we Camped after dark on the S. S. opposit the 1st old Village of the Kanzas which was Situated in a Valley between two points of high land,[5] on the river back of their village commenced an extensive Prarie ⟨the French⟩ a large Island in front which appears to have made on that Side and thrown the Current of the river against the place the Village formerly Stood, and washes away the bank in that part. The french formerly had a Fort at this place,[6] to protect the trade of this nation, the Situation appears to be a verry elligable one for a Town, the valley rich & extensive, with a Small Brook Meanding [meandering] through it and one part of the bank affording yet a good Landing for Boats   The High Lands above the Fere [Fire] river on each Side of the Missouries appear to approach each other much nearer than below that plaice, being from 3 to 6 miles between them, to the Kansas, above that place from 3 to 5 Ms. apart and higher Some places being 160 or 180 feet   the river not So wide   We made a Mast of Cotton wood, ⟨yesterday⟩ to day in the Course of the evening & night it turned of a butifull red Colour

N. 22° E W	1 ¼	ms to a pt on the L S. in a bend (1)
N. 10° W	2 ¼	Ms. to a pt. of a little Isd on the S. S. passed the head of the Isd. (2) a Creek L. S
N. 34° E	1 ½	to a pt on L. S. psd. passed Turkey Creek L. S. (3)
N. 10° W.	½	me. on the L. S. high land on the S. S.
N. 46 W.	1 ¼	me. on Lbd. S. ⟨opsd. Lower pt.⟩ of an Isd. (4) on S. S.
S 50 W.—[7]		To the old village of the Kansas on L. S. pass a Bulge of Isd.
S 78 W	½	of a me. to a Pt. on S. S. psd. 2 runs on S. S.
S. 81° W	2 ¼	mes. to a pt on the S. S. passed the head of the Island near opsd. pt.
N. 82° W	2	mes. to a pt. on the S. S. passed verry Swift water, & Camped.
	10 ¼	
N. 53 W[8]	1	me. alg. S. S.
N 50 W	¼	me. alg. S. S.
N. 18 E	1	me to pt. on L. S opsd. an Isd. N. 40° E to Low pt. of Island 1 ¼ ml.

[Clark]

July 2nd, 1804   Set out early and proceeed on the left of the Islands, two of which are large   a high bottom Situated on the L. S.   passed the mouth of a Creek on the S. S. Called ⟨Turquie⟩ [*NB: Parques*][9] Creike, at this place I observed that the river was Crouded with Drift wood, and dangerous to pass   as this dead timber Continued only about half an our, I concluded that Some Island of Drift had given way   (3) passed a Creek on the L. S. called Turky Creek, a bad Sand bar on the L. S.   we could with dificuelty Stem the Current with our 20 oars & and all the poles we had, passed a large Island on the S. S. Called by the Indians *Wau-car-ba war-cand-da* or the *Bear Medesin* Island, at 12 oClock landed on the Island & put up a mast which detained us four hours—   a verry hot day   winds from the S. E.—   George Drewyer inform's that the Lands he passed through yesterday and to day on the S. S. was verry fine, few Springs, we Camped after dark on the S. S. above the Island & opposit the 1st old village of the Kanzes which was Situated in a valley, between two points of high Land, and imediatly on the river bank, back of the village and on a riseing ground at about one mile   The French had a garrison for Some time and made use of water out of a Spring running into Turkey Creek. an extensive Prarie, as the Current of the river Sets against the banke and washes it away the landing place for Boats is indifferent—   The high lands above the Fire river, approaches nearer each than below, being from 3 to 6 miles distant and above Kansas from 3 to 5 miles distant and the Hills at Some places are from 160 to 180 feet above the bottom

Course and distance & reffersns. July 2d

N. 22° W.	1 ¼	ms. to a pt. on L. S. in a bend (1)
N. 10° W	2 ¼	ms. to a pt. of a Lit: Isd. on S. S. passd Isd. (2)
N. 34° E	1 ½	ms. to a pt. on L. S. psd. Turkey Cr: (3)
N. 10° W	½	on the L. S. High Lds. on S. S.
N. 46 W.	1 ¼	ms. on S. S. of an Isd. on S. S. (4)
S. 87 W,	½	Me. on S. S. a point psd. a run
S. 81° W	2 ¼	mes. on S. S. psd. head of Island
N. 82 W	2	ms. on the L. S. psd. Swift water
	11 ½	1st old village Kansas

1. Biddle's notation at the top of this sheet of the Field Notes (document 26) reads "July 2 to 5."

2. Probably Bee Creek, in Platte County, Missouri, whose mouth has perhaps shifted upstream over the years. Nicollet labels it both "Bee Creek" and "Parc Creek? (L. & C.)"; he was probably using Biddle's text as a reference. Nicollet (MMR), 371; MRC map 15.

3. Perhaps Corral Creek, in Leavenworth County, Kansas. MRC map 15.

4. Nicollet gives it as "Wasabe Wakandege Island," evidently later Kickapoo Island, north of Fort Leavenworth, Leavenworth County. Robert L. Rankin gives the Omaha name as *wasábe wakką́daki*, "the spirit black bear." Nicollet (MMR), 372; MRC map 15.

5. The "Village" in Nicollet is in the right location, in extreme northeast Leavenworth County, to be the old Kansa village. It is apparently where the Kansa Indians were living in the Salt Creek locale in the 1740s and 1750s. From here they moved west into the lower reaches of the Kansas River. Nicollet (MMR), 372; Wedel (KA), 51. The camp was near present Weston, Platte County, Missouri. MRC map 16.

6. Fort de Cavagnial, or Cavagnolle, named after the French governor of Louisiana, was founded in 1744 and abandoned in 1764, when Louisiana was transferred from France to Spain. It is the "fort & trading establishment" mentioned by Clark in his notebook journal on July 1. It was in Leavenworth County, perhaps three miles north of present Fort Leavenworth, and was built to control the trade with the Kansa and Osage Indians and perhaps to promote trade with the Spanish in New Mexico. Hoffhaus; Barry, 22–23; Mathews, 218–19.

7. This course does not appear in Codex A, and there are other discrepancies, including the final mileage total for the day.

8. These three courses and distances, immediately under those for July 2, were evidently the first ones for July 3. Clark repeats them in full in the appropriate place under that date, but there are discrepancies.

9. Clark made a mistake here and Biddle later interlined the correction. "Parques" Creek came first, then Turkey Creek. See nn. 2 and 3, above.

[Clark] [1]

July 3rd 1804   Set out verry early this morning and proceeded on under a gentle Breeze from the South   passed two Islands   one a Small Willow Island on the L. S. (1)   The other a large Island Called Cow I. (*Isle Vache*),[2] this Island is large, opposit to the head on the S. S. is a (2) large Pond, a Bad Sand bar on the S. S.   we attemptd without Success, & was oblige to Cross back, I Saw a White horse on the L. S. in view of the upper point of the Island, (3) passed a large Sand bar at the S. point, w[e] halted to day about a mile above the Island and found a horse, which had been lost by the Indians, verry fat and jentle, Sent him on to join the others which was ahead on the L S   at this place, the french had a tradeing house, for to trade with the Kanzes on a high bottom on the L. S. near the hills which is Prarie   proceeded on round a large Sand bar on the L. S. & Camped[3] (opposit a large Sand bar in the middle of the river).   on the L. S. a Butifull Small Stream passes back of the trading house, before mentioned[4]

July 3d 1804[5]

N 53° W.	1	miles along the S. Side
N 50 W.	¼	me. do do
N. 18° E	1	me. to a pt on the L. S. opsd two Islands, one Small near point (1)
N. 32° W	¾	to Pt. on left side of the Island
N. 10° W	½	me. to pt. on the L. S.
N. 60° W	¼	me. to Pt. on Isd. L. S.
N. 78 W.	½	ml to pt. on L. S. opposed the head of the Isld, a pond on S. S. (2)
S. 56° W	2 ¼	me. to Pt. on S. S. of the Missourie
N. 45 E	3	Ms. to a pt on L. S. passed Several Sand bars (3)
N. 12 E	½	me. on L. Side round a Sand bar & Camped

11

[Clark]   *July 3td, Tusday 1804*

Set out verry early this morning and proceeded on under a gentle Breeze from the S.   passed two Islands (1) one a Small willow Island on the L. S. the other large Called by the french *Isle ⟨la⟩ de Vache* or *Cow Island*, opposit the head on the S. S. is a large Pond Containg Beever, & fowl, a bad Sandbar on the S. S. above the Island, on the L. S. we halted at an old Tradeing house, [*NB: deserted*] here we found a verry fat horse, which appears to have been lost a long time   a butifull Small run passes back of the Tradeing house near the high land, we came to at a round bend on the L. S. and Camped

Course Distanc & refrs. July 3rd

N. 53° W.	1	me. on the S. S.
N. 50° W.	¼	me. do. do

344

N. 18° E	1	Me. to a pt. on L. S. opsd. 2 Ids (1)
N 30° W	¾	me. to pt. Left of an Isld.
N 10° W.	½	me. to pt. L. S.
N 60° W	½	me. to a pt. on the Island
N 78 W	½	me. to a pt. L. S. at Hd. of Isd. (2)
S 56° W	2 ¼	ms. to a pt. on S. S. of Missouri
N 50° W	1	Me. on the S. S.
N 45 E	3	Ms. to a pt. on L. S. pass a Bar
N 12 E	½	Me. on L. S. Camped
	11 ¼	

1. Some calculations are upside-down under this entry of document 26:

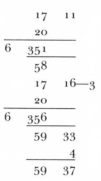

2. Cow Island was still on the map about 1890, a short distance above the Atchison-Leavenworth county line, Kansas, on the Platte County, Missouri side of the river. MRC map 16.

3. In Atchison County, Kansas, somewhat above the present town of Oak Mills. Ibid.; Barry, 49.

4. Possibly later Walnut Creek. MRC map 16. Clark inserts an asterisk here to indicate the place for the day's course material, found on another part of this sheet (document 26).

5. There are variations in the course material here and those found in Codex A, including the mileage total.

[Clark]¹

July 4th *Wednesday* 1804, Set out early   passed the mouth of a Beyeue [bayou] leading from a Lake on the S. S.   this Lake is large and was once the bend of the River, it reaches Parrelel for Several miles, Came to on the L. S. to Dine & rest a Short time, a Snake bit Jo: Fields on the Side of his foot which Swelled much, apply Barks to the wound,² pass a Creek on the L. S. about 15 yards wide cuming out of an extensive Prarie   as this Creek has no name, and this day is the 4th of July, we name this Independance us. [U.S.] Creek[3]   above this Creek the wood land is about 200 yards, back of those wood is an extensive Prarie open and high, which may be Seen six or seven [miles?] below—   Saw great Nos. of Goslins to day nearly Grown, the last mentioned prarie I call Jo Fields Snake Prarie, Capt Lewis walked on Shore & Saw a large moun[d] & 3 roads leading We Camped in the plain[4]   one of the most butifull Plains, I ever Saw, open & butifully diversified with hills & vallies all presenting themselves to the river covered with grass and a few scattering trees   a handsom Creek meandering thro   at this place the Kansaw Inds. formerly lived and had a verry large Town[5]   passed a Creek (4)[6]   I observed Spring braking out of the bank, a good Situation for a fort on a hill at the upper part

July 4th 1804

N. 70° W	1	me. on L. S. S, pd a Pond
S. 45 W	3	ms. Pt. L. S. ⟨L pond⟩ a Sm Isd L S
N. 75 W.	¼	me. on S. S.
N. 40° W	6	ms. to pt. S. S. opsd Pr [prairie]
N. 12° E	2 ¾	Mes. to L. S. psd. Sm. Isd. L S
N 10 E	2	to a pt S. S. opsd (3) Passed a Creek L. S. called Creek of Old Vilg of the Kansies of 30 yd. wide and camped (4) where the old village was on the L S

The Plains of this countrey are covered with a Leek Green Grass, well calculated for the sweetest and most norushing hay[7]—interspersed with Cops [copses] of trees, Spreding ther lofty branchs over Pools Springs or Brooks of fine water. Groops of Shrubs covered with the most delicious froot is to be seen in every direction, and nature appears to have exerted herself to butify the Senery by the variety of flours ⟨raiseing⟩ Delicately and highly flavered raised above the Grass, which Strikes & profumes the Sensation, and amuses the mind   throws it into Conjecterng the cause of So magnificent a Senerey [*several words illegible, crossed out*] in a Country thus Situated far removed from the Sivilised world to be enjoyed by noth-

ing but the Buffalo Elk Deer & Bear in which it abounds & [*page torn*]
Savage Indians[8]

The names of the french Ingishees [*engagés*], or Hirelens [hirelings]—[9]

1 Battist de Shone [Baptist Deschamps] *Patrn* ⟨Perogue⟩

*2 Joseph Le bartee [Liberte?][10]

3 Lasoness [Baptist La Jeunesse]

4 Paul Preemau [Paul Primeau]

5 Chalo ⎫ in Perogue

6 E. Cann

7 Roie

8 Charlo Cougee

*J: Le bartee [Liberte?] ⎱ in the large Boat
Rivee [Rivet] ⎰

Pieter Crousatt half Indian ⎱ bow men
William La Beice [Labiche] Mallat ⎰

3 Sergts. & 23 men for the Boat[11] ⟨Good⟩
George Drewyer. Hunter & 4 Horses ⟨Bowmen⟩
1 Corpl & 4 Privates in a Perogue to be Sent *back* from Plate river
Mr. Dueron [Dorion] inteptr for the Sues
Capt. Lewis my Self & York
in all 46 men July 4th   4 horses & a Dog

[Clark]

July 4th *Wednesday*   ussered in the day by a discharge of one ⟨discharge⟩
shot from our Bow piece,[12] proceeded on, passed the mouth of a (1) Bay-
eau lading from a large Lake on the S. S. which has the apperance of being
once the bed of the river[13] & reaches parrelel for Several Miles   Came to
on the L. S. to refresh ourselves &. Jos: Fields got bit by a Snake, which was
quickly doctered with Bark by Cap Lewis.   (2) Passed a Creek 12 yds. wide
on L. S. comeing out of an extensive Prarie reching within 200 yards of the
river, as this Creek has no name, and this being the   we Din[e] (on corn)
the 4th of July the day of the independance of the U. S. call it ⟨Creek In-
dependence⟩ 4th of July 1804 Creek, Capt. Lewis walked on Shore above
this Creek and discovered a high moun from the top of which he had an
extensive view, 3 paths Concentering at the moun   Saw great numbers of
Goslings to day which Were nearly grown, the before mentioned Lake is

clear and Contain great quantities of fish an Gees & Goslings,   The great quantity of those fowl in this Lake induce me to Call it the Gosling Lake, a Small Creek & Several Springs run in to the Lake on the East Side from the hills   the land on that Side verry good— (3) We came to and camped in the lower edge of a Plain where 2d old Kanzas village formerly Stood, above the mouth of a Creek 20 yds wide   this Creek we call *Creek Independence*[14]   as we approached this place the Praree had a most butifull appearance   Hills & Valies interspsd with Coops [copses] of Timber gave a pleasing deversity to the Senery.   the right fork of Creek Independence Meandering thro: the middle of the Plain   a point of high Land near the river givs an allivated Situation.   at this place the Kanzas Indians formerley lived.   this Town appears to have covd. a large Space, the nation must have been noumerous at the time they lived here, the Cause of their moveing to the Kanzas River, I have never heard, nor Can I learn; war with their neghbors must have reduced this nation and Compelled them to retire to a Situation in the plains better Calculated for their defence and one where they may make use of their horses with good effect, in persueing their enemey, we Closed the [day] by a Discharge from our bow piece, an extra Gill of whiskey.

Course & Distance refrs July 4th 1804

N. 70° W.	1	me. on L. S. passd. a Bayo: S. S. (1)
S. 45° W.	3	ms. to a pt. on S. S. a Sml. Isd. on L. S.
N. 75° W.	¼	me. on S. S.
N. 40° W.	6	mes. on S. S psd a prarie & Creek (2)
N. 12° E.	2 ¾	ms. to pt. on L. S. psd. a Sml Isd. L. S.
N. 10° E	2	ms. to pt. on S. S. opsd. old vilg (3) psd. Creek L. S.
	15	

(*Point Obstn. No. 17.*)

[Lewis]   *Wednesday July 4th*[15]

   On the Larboard Shore three miles below a high Prarie hill on same shore, near the 2nd old vilage of the Kancez.

   Observed Meridian altd. of ☉'s L. L. with Octant by the back observtn.   38° —′ —″

   Latitude deduced from this obsertn.   39° 25′ 42.5″

1. The following words at right angles to the rest of the entry are overwritten by the July 4 entry: "Lock, Moles, Vests, Seeds, [presen?] of [Twith?], 4 Cartrges Boxes, ring."

2. Possibly the bark of the slippery elm, *Ulmus rubra* Muhl., but more likely Peruvian bark, or *cinchona*. On later occasions Lewis used Peruvian bark in a poultice, as he presumably did here (see Codex A entry) in case the snake was a new poisonous species. Cutright (LCPN), 63–64; Fernald, 551.

3. Probably either later Whiskey or Clay Creek, in Atchison County, Kansas. They passed both a Fourth of July Creek and an Independence Creek on this day. This creek was called Fourth of July Creek in Codex A, where Clark has apparently reversed the names. MRC map 16.

4. If Independence Creek (the second creek) was that later bearing the same name (see n. 14, below), then this camp was near Doniphan. MRC map 17.

5. The archaeological sites of the Kansa Indians are identified as part of the Oneota culture, and this Oneota village (referred to by Clark, below, as "2d old Kanzas village") is the Doniphan site, in the present town of Doniphan, Doniphan County, Kansas. The earliest documented Kansa village, it was apparently occupied in the first half of the eighteenth century. Wedel (KA), 29–30, 51, 98–105, 109–12, 118–30.

6. Evidently the stream they called Independence Creek in Codex A (see n. 14, below).

7. The "Leek Green Grass" that covered the upland plains between the copses of trees is big bluestem, *Andropogon gerardi* Vitman. This entry describes the open, savanna-like aspect of the tall-grass prairie/oak-hickory vegetation border that is typical of this region. Braun, 177–79.

8. This paragraph of description is on a separate sheet of the Field Notes (document 27). It seems to be a longer version of Clark's description of the scenery in his Codex A entry for July 4, 1804, and so it is placed under that date. Osgood (FN), 69 n. 3.

9. This list is on the opposite side of document 27 from the paragraph above it, and the date July 4 occurs in the last line of this material. It supplements the list of *engagés* of May 26, 1804, but inconsistencies between the two lists add to the confusion about this group of party members. For further information, see Appendix A, this volume.

10. This name occurs twice and is especially marked both times. The same man's name may have been written twice or there may have been two men with the same family name or *dit* name. Either person might be the La Liberté who deserted later (see below, July 29–August 17, 1804). For further information, see Appendix A, this volume.

11. Clark crossed out two lines of course and distance material and added this short summary of the party as of July 4, 1804, below the list of *engagés*.

12. Probably the swivel cannon. See above, May 29, 1804.

13. Such oxbow lakes in portions of the old riverbed are characteristic of this part of the Missouri. The continual shifting of the river's course would make it difficult to identify this lake with one on later maps, but several examples in the immediate area in the late 1800s can be seen on MRC maps 15, 16.

14. Probably present Independence Creek, on the Atchison-Doniphan county line. Clark indicates that the creek has two forks, which is the case with Independence Creek, Rock Creek entering it from the north. MRC map 17.

15. Lewis's observation from Codex O.

[Clark][1]

July the 5th 1804   Set out verry early this morning, Swam the horse across the river, proceeded on for two miles under the bank where the old Kansas town formerly stood (Say in 1724)   The Cause of those people moveing from this place I cannot learn, but naterally conclude that War has reduced their nation & compelled them to retire further into the Plains with a view of defending themselves & opposeing their enemey (more effectually[)] on hors back (I neglected to mention yesterday that the Lake on the S. S. was large   Say ¾ me. wide & 7 or 8 long   one creek & Several brooks running into it from the hills, it contains Great quantities of Sun fish & *Gosling's* from which we gave it the name,) passed Some verry bad Sand bars Situated parrelel to each other, (1) the Boat turned three times once on the [Plat?] of a Drift wood. She recved no ⟨dammage⟩ proceiviable damage, we came to for Dinner at a Beever house, Cap Lewis's Dog *Seamon* [Scannon] went in & drove them out.   the high Lands on the L. S. is open, a few trees Scattering   (2) passed a Small Creek on the L. S. in the ls[1st] bend to the left I call ⟨Roses Creek⟩ yellow oaker [ochre] creek from ⟨the number of rose about &⟩ a bank of that *Mineral* just above.[2]   we camped on the L. S. under a high bank[3]   Latd. 39° 25′ 41″ North

Course & Distance July 5th 1804

N 35° E	1	me. on the S. S. opposit the old village of Kanzes
S. 56° E	2	Me. on the L. point a Large Eddey on the L. S. and a bad Sand bar
East—	1	me. on L. S. a Sand bar in middle & & (1) Boat turned 3.
N. 18° W.	2	mes. to a pt on S. S. opsd. a Prarie psd. a Creek L. S. (2)
North	1	me. on S. S.
S. 70 E	3	me. to a pt. of Willow on the L S. wind from S E
	10	

on the banks of this river I observe great quants of Grapes, berries & roses   Deer is not So plenty in this three days past as they were below that. Elks are plenty about those Praries. Some Buffalow Sign.

[Clark]   *July* 5th *Thursday* 1804

Set out verry early, proceeded on near the bank where the old village

Stood for two miles, (Swam the hors found a few days ago)   passed Some bad Sand bars, The Origan of this old village is uncertain   M. de Bourgmont[4] a French officer who Comdd. a fort near the Town of the Missouris in about the year 1724 and in July of the Same year he visited this Village   at that time the nation was noumerous & well desposed towards the french   Mr. Du Pratz must have been badly informed as to the Cane opposd this place   we have not Seen one Stalk of reed or cane on the Missouries, he States that the "Indians that accompanied M De Bourgmont Crossed to the Canzes Village on ⟨rafts⟩ floats of Cane"[5]

Those people must have been verry noumerous at that time as Mr. De B: was accompanied by 300 Warriers, 500 young people & 300 Dogs of burthen out of this Village

The Cause of Those Indians moveing over to the Kanzis river I have never lernt—   we passed Some bad Sand bars, Situated parrelel to each other (1)   The Boat turned twice on the quick Sand & once on ⟨the⟩ a raft of Drift, no procievable damage   Prarie Contine on the high land on the L. S.   passd a Small Creek (2)   on L. S. in the first bend to the L S. I call Yellow-Oaker Creek from a quantity of that Mineral in a bank a little above

The river Continue to fall a little—   I observe great quantities of Summer & fall Grapes, Berries & Wild roases on the banks—   Deer is not so plenty as usual, great Deel of Elk Sign.   (Wind from S E)

Course Distance & reffers. July 5

N. 35° E	1	me. on S. S. opsd. the pls. of Old Vilg.
S 56° E	2	me: to L. pt. a eddey on L. S.
East	1	me. on L. S. Sevl. Sand bars (1)
N 18° W	2	Ms. to a pt. on S. S. opsd a prarie pd. (2)
North	1	me. on the S. S.
S. 70° E	3	ms. to pt. of will. on L. S.
	10	

1. Biddle's notation at the top of this sheet of the Field Notes (document 28) reads, "July 5 to."

2. One of several small streams in Doniphan County, Kansas. Quaife identifies it as Brush Creek. Nicollet shows a "yellow ocher" creek at about the right spot. Quaife (MLJO),

92 n. 3; Nicollet (MMR), 374; MRC map 17; MRM map 47. Yellow ocher generally refers to the mineral limonite, used in pigments and, where found on the frontier in large masses, sometimes as a source of iron by blacksmiths.

3. In Doniphan County, some miles northeast of Doniphan. There are a number of high banks in the area. MRC map 17.

4. Etienne Véniard, Sieur de Bourgmont, a Frenchman of "an adventurous and undisciplined nature," was commandant of Detroit in 1705 and first visited the Missouri Indians in 1714. Having deserted, he lived for some time among the Missouris and Osages, marrying an Indian woman; eventually he received a pardon for desertion. He founded Fort Orleans, in Carroll County, Missouri, in 1723 (see above, June 16, 1804). At various times he explored up the Missouri River, possibly as far as the Arikara villages in South Dakota. After various ventures among the Plains tribes, he took a delegation of Indian chiefs to Paris in 1725 and apparently remained in France. Nasatir (BLC), 1:12–22; Houck, 1:31, 173, 223, 258–68; Barry, 13, 18–21, 27, 189.

5. Antoine Simon Le Page du Pratz was a French military engineer who came to Louisiana in 1718 and spent sixteen years there, chiefly on the lower Mississippi. Clark is referring to the 1774 English translation of his three-volume *Histoire de la Louisiane* . . . (Paris, 1758). The passage that puzzled Clark occurs in an account of Bourgmont's 1724 mission to the Indians on the Kansas River. The confusion arises from a faulty translation; the "canes" do not appear in the original, which states that the Indians crossed the river in *cajeux* (rafts) made of unstated materials. Lewis borrowed a copy of the work from Benjamin Smith Barton of Philadelphia in 1803 and returned it to the owner after the expedition. It is now in the custody of the Library Company, in Philadelphia. Nasatir (BLC), 1:13, 17, 21, 56; Jackson (SBLC), 9–10; Cutright (LCD); Allen, 91, 96, 156, 178.

[Clark][1]

6th July Friday. We Set out early this morning & Proceeded on   (the river falls Slowly)   wind S. W)   passed a Sand bar in 1st bend to the right   (1) passed a Small Island at the S. pt.   a verry warm day   (worthy of remark that the water of this river or Some other Cause, I think that the most Probable throws out a greater preposn. of Swet than I could Suppose Could pass thro: the humane body   Those men that do not work at all will wet a Shirt in a Few minits & those who work, the Swet will run off in Streams)   opposit the 3rd point passed a Prarie on the S. S. Called Reeveys Prarie (fro a man of that name being Killed in it[)][2]   opposit this Prarie the river is Confined in a verry narrow Space Crowded on S. S. by [emence?] Sands which were moveing and difficuelt to pass.   the Hunts. Sent in 3 Deer Jurked   on the 4th point of to day is a Small Island & a Sand bar 2 miles out in the river, this is Called the Grand Bend, or *Grande de Tour,*[3] I walked on this Sand bar   found it a light Sand intersperced with Small Pebbles of various Kinds, also *pit Coal* of an excellent quallity was lodged on the Sand,[4] We camped on the L. S. at a small creek[5]   a whiper will perched on the boat for a Short time, I gave his name to the Creek

Course Distance & refurenies July 6, 1804[6]

N. 58° E.	1	Me. on the L. Side opposit a Sand bar in the river
North	3	ms. to a pt. on S. S. an Isd: (1) (N 45 E. thro the Chanel)
N. 10° W	¼	on S. S. an Isd.
S. 76 E	½	me. on S. S. to the head of the Island, a Pad *Batteue*
S. 60° E	1 ¾	ms. to a pt. on the L. S. (Willows)
N. 70° E	1 ½	Me. along a Sand bar on the L. S. opposit a Prarie (2)
N 50° W	1	me. on the L. P. Passed a bad Sand
West	3	ms. to a pt. on the S. S. a Small Island (3) & Sand bar
	12	

(N 6 4 E)[7]

⟨N. 40° E	2	Me. on the S. S.⟩
⟨N. 76° E	2	me. to pt. on L. S.⟩
	12	

[Clark]

July 6th, *Friday*   We Set out early this morning, wind from the S. W. passed a large Sand bar in the 1st. bend to the right. (1) passed a Small Island at the S. point   opposit the 3rd point we passed a Prarie on the S. S. Called Reeveys Prarie   at this place the river is Confined in a verry narrow Channel Crouded by a Sand bar from the L. Point   This Sand bar from the L. Point, this Sand bar is verry bad, at the 4th Point from the S. S. is a verry extensive bar, at the Point of which is a Small willow Island   this is Called the *Grand Detour* ⟨of⟩ or *Great bend* [*NB: great band is higher up*][8]

I walked on this Sand bar and found the Sand was light, with Collection of Small pebble, & some Pit Coal   I observe that the men Swet more than is Common from Some Cause, I think the Missouries water is the principal Cause   our hunters Sent in 3 Bucks today   The river Still fall a little

Course Distance & refferns. July 6th

N. 58° E	1	me. on L. S. opsd. a Sand bar
North	3	ms. a pt. on S. S. on Isd. (1)
N. 10° W.	½	Me. on S. S. psd. hd. of Isld. a Sand bar
S. 60° E	1 ¾	me. to a willow pt. on L. S.
N. 70° E	1 ½	Me. over a Sand bar L. S. op Prarie (2)
N. 50 W	1	ms. on the L. S. pasd. a Sand bar
West	3	ms. to a pt. on S. S. a Sand & (3) Isd.
	12	

1. Biddle placed the notation "July 5 to July 6 to" at the head of the reverse of this sheet of the Field Notes (document 28), above the July 6 entry. This July 6 entry is written over the following address, indicating that the sheet was earlier used as an envelope. The hand may be Lewis's. "Captn. William Clark   River Dubois   [pr.?] Howard."

2. In present Buchanan County, Missouri. Clark may be referring to an incident in 1795 in which Benito and Quenache de Rouin, traders returning from the Kansa village, were robbed and beaten but apparently not killed by Iowas. The two were left at the mouth of the Kansas River, but the site of the robbery is not known. Clark does not repeat the explanation of the name in his Codex A entry. Since Ordway gives the explanation in his journal, it is likely that he was copying from the Field Notes. Nasatir (BLC), 1:316, 318; MRC map 17.

3. Perhaps the later St. Joseph Bend, at St. Joseph, Buchanan County. See below, n. 8, on the Grand Detour. MRC map 17.

4. Weathered outcroppings of coal are soft; unweathered (or pit) coal from the part of a pit below the weathered zone is solid and firm.

5. Coues identifies the stream as Peter's Creek, Doniphan County, Kansas. The extreme shifts in the Missouri over the years make it difficult to say whether the actual campsite was in present Kansas or Missouri, but the party was near present St. Joseph, Missouri. Coues (HLC), 1:40 n. 85; MRC map 17; MRM map 48.

6. There are discrepancies between this course material and that in Codex A.

7. These figures are written under the courses and distances for July 6. The courses and distances that are crossed out appear to be the first ones of the next day, July 7.

8. Clark or Biddle corrected the original statement, perhaps after Clark saw the bend in the Missouri commonly called the Grand Detour, in South Dakota. See below, September 19, 1804, and *Atlas* map 22. Neither feature should be confused with the Great Bend of the Missouri in North Dakota, where the river shifts from an easterly to a southeasterly direction.

[Clark][1]

7th of *July Satturday* 1804   Set out early   passed Some verry Swift water on the L. S. which Compelled us to Draw up by the Cord.   a verry warm morning, passed a butifull Prarie on the right Side which extends back, those Praries has much the appearance from the river of farms, Divided by narrow Strips of woods   those Strips of timber grows along the runs which rise on the hill & pass to the river   a Cleft above, one man sick (*Frasure*)   Struck with the Sun, Saw a large rat on the Side of the bank,[2] Killed a wolf on the Bank[3]   passed (2) a verry narrow part of the river, all confined within 200 yards, a yellow bank above, passed a Small willow Island on the S. point, (in Low water those Small Willow Islands are joined to the Sand bars makeing out from the Points)   a pond on the S. S near the prarie we passed yesterday in which G D. Saw Several young Swans   we Came to and Camped on the L. S.[4] and two men Sent out last evening with the horses did not Join us this evening agreeable to orders—   a hard wind with Some rain from the N, E at ⟨Dark⟩ 7 oClock which lasted half an hour, with thunder & lightning.   river fall a little

Course Distance & reffurrences July the 7th

N. 40° E	2	ms. on the L. point ⟨round⟩ over the Sand bar
N 76° E	3	Ms. to the pt. on the L. S. passed Sand bars
N 50° E	1 ¾	ms. to a Prarie in the bend to the S. S. (1) St. Mickles Pra: [St. Michael's Prarie]
N 30° W	1	me. on the L. S. a Bluff on S. S. Hunts. Sent in 2 Deer
N. 76° W	¼	me. on L. S.
S 66° E	2	me. to pt. on S. S. from which a Sand bar makes
N. 74° W	1 ½	on the S. Side opposite a yellow Clift river abt. 200 yds wide (2)
N. 45° E	½	me. on S. S. a pt of a Willow Island (3)
N. 70 E	2	ms. to a pt on L S.— a Sand bar puts out
	14	

[Clark]   *July* the 7th *Satturday* 1804

Set out early   passed Some Swift water, which obliged us to draw up by roapes, a Sand bare at the point opposit a butifull Prarie on the S. Side

Calld. (1) St. Michul,[5] those Praries on the river has verry much the appearence of ⟨old⟩ farms from the river Divided by narrow Strips of wood land, which wood land is Situatd. on the runs leading to the river.　passed a ⟨Clift⟩ Bluff of yellow Clay above the Prarie.[6]　Saw a large rat on the bank. Killed a Wolf.　at 4 oClock pass a Verry narrow part of the river　water Confd. in a bead not more than 200 yards wide at this place　the Current runs against the L. Side.　no Sand to Confine the Current on the S. S. passed a Small sand Island above the Small Islds. Situated at the points, in low water form a part of the Sand bars makeing out from those points

Incamped on the S. S.　at 7 oClock a Violent Ghust of wind from the N. E. with Some rain, which lasted half an hour (G D. informs me that he Saw in a Pond on the S. S. which we passed yesterday; a number of young Swans—,[)]　one man verry Sick, Struck with the Sun, Capt. Lewis bled him & gave Niter which has revived him much[7]

Course Distance & reffrs. July 7th

N. 46° E.	2	me. on the S. pt. over a Sand bar
N 76° E	3	ms. to a pt. on the L. S. a Sd. bar
N. 50° E	1 ¾	ms. to a prarie on S. S. (1)
N. 30° W	1	me. on the L. S.　a Bluff on S. S.
N. 76° W	¼	Me. on the L. S.
S. 66° E	2	me. to a pt. on S. S.　a Sand bar
N. 74° W	1 ½	mes. on the S. S. opsd. a yellow clif
N. 45° E	½	Me. on the S. S.
N. 70° E	2	Ms. to a pt. on L. S.　a Sand bar
	14	

1. Biddle's notation at the head of this sheet of the Field Notes (document 29) reads "July 7th to 9th."

2. Probably the eastern wood rat, first mentioned on May 31, 1804.

3. Whitehouse says Lewis wounded the animal and Colter killed it.

4. A camp on the larboard side today would place them in Doniphan County, Kansas. The various river shifts in the area may have placed the actual site in northwest Buchanan County, Missouri, a little upstream from St. Joseph. MRC map 18.

5. At the present site of St. Joseph, Missouri. MRC map 17.

6. Thick accumulations of loess—a pale, yellowish brown loam of sandy, claylike silt— were deposited by wind during the so-called Wisconsin glaciation in the Pleistocene Epoch

and stand in steep bluffs, sixty or more feet above the floodplain in some places, near this area.

7. Bleeding was the standard remedy of the times for nearly everything. The "niter" was potassium nitrate (saltpeter), used to increase the flow of perspiration and urine and to reduce fevers. Cutright (LCPN), 94; Chuinard, 154, 156.

[Clark][1]

8th of July Sunday   Set out early this morning, the Sick man [Frazer] much better, Serjt. Oddeway was waiting at a Creek[2] on the S. S. below an Island, passed (1) two Island on the S. S. and came to at the upper point, G Drewyer went out   R. Fields & Guterich [Goodrich], five men Sick to day with a violent Head ake &c. and Several with Boils, we appoint a Cook to each mess to take Charge of the Provisions.   in Serjt. Pryor's = *Collens* in Sjt. Ordway's *Werner* in Sergt. Floyd's *Thompson,* The french men Killed a young Deer on the Bank, (2) passed up a narrow Channel of about 80 or 100 yds wide about 5 miles to the mouth of Nadawa River[3] which coms in to this channel from the N W. and is abt. 70 yards wide at its mouth [*blank*] feet Deep and has a jentle Current, Perogues can navagate this river near its head, which is between the Missourie & the Grand River, passed up the gut ¾ of a mile to the river at the head of the ⟨river⟩ Island & camped[4]   opposit the head of this Island is another nearest the ⟨Larboard Shore,⟩ Middle R   this Island Nadawa is the largest I have Seen, formed by a Channel washing into the Nadawa river.— "8 or 10000 acrs"

Course Distance & Reffurcs. 8th July.

N. 28° E	1	me. on the L pt. a Sand bar
N. 10° W.	1 ½	to the Lower point of a Island on the S. S.
N 25° W.	3	Me. to a pt. on the L. S. passed the Isd. & one on the side (1)
N. 56 W.	1 ½	ms. to the Lower point of an Island (2) S 30 W. up the Chnl.
West—	¼	mile on Left of the Island
S 10° W.	¼	Me. to a pt. on S. Shore.
N. 25° W.	¼	me. to Pt on Isld
N. 40° W.	¼	me. to the bend on S. S.

N. 70 W	½	me. to a bend on the S. S.
S 70 W	¼	me. to a bend in the Island.
N 82 W	½	me. to a do in Isld.
N 42 W.	[¼?]	me. to a do do S. Side—
S 50 W	½	me. to do in do
	8 ¼ [5]	
	10 [6]	
N. 65 W	¼	me. to a bend on Isld
N. 18 W	¼	me. to a bend S. S.
N 38 W	½	me. to a bend S S
S. 20° W	½	me. to a pt a Isd. opsd. the Nadawa R
	11 ¼	
S 15° W	¼	to a bend of Isd.
S 80 W	¼	to the head of Isle
	½	
	12	

$$59 \quad 22^{7}$$
$$\underline{25 \quad 41}$$
$$13-41$$

[Clark]   *July the 8th Sunday* 1804

Set out early   passed a Small Creek on the S. S. and two (1) Small Islands on the S S.   five men Sick to day with a violent head ake &c.   we made Some arrangements as to provisions & Messes, came to for Dinner at the lower point of a very large Island Situated near the S. S.   after a delay of two hours we passed a narrow channel of 45 to 80 yds wide five miles to the mouth of (3) *Nádăwă River*,[8] This river Coms in from the North and is navagable for Perogues Some distance.   it is about 70 yards wide a little above the mouth, at the mouth not So wide, the mud of the Gut running out of the Missourie is thrown and Settles in the mouth half a mile higher up   this Channel or gut is the upper point of the Said Island, This Island is Called Nadawa, & is the largest I have Seen in the river, containing 7 or 8000 acres of Land Seldom over flowed   we Camped at the head of this Island on the S. S.   opposit the head or our Camp is a Small Island near the middle of the river, river Still falling.   our flank party did not join us this evening

Course Distance & Refrs. July 8th

N. 28° E	1	me. on L. pt.— a Sand bar
N 10 W	1 ½	ms. to Low: pt. of Little Nadawa Isd. S. S.
N. 25 W.	3	me. to a pt. on an L. S. passd. 2 Isds. (1)
N. 56 W.	1 ½	ms. to L. pts. of Big Nadawa Isd. (2)
West—	¼	me. on the left of the Island
S. 10° W	¼	me to pt. on the S. S.
N. 25 W	¼	mes. to pts. on the Island
N 40 W	¼	me. to a bend on the S. S.
N. 70 W	½	me. to do do do S. S.
S. 70 W	¼	me. to do do do Island
N 82 W	½	me. to do do do do
N. 42 W	½	ms. to do do do S. S.
S. 50 W	½	me. to do do do Island
N 60 W	¼	me. to do do do do
N 18 W	¼	me. to do do do S. S.
N 38 W	½	me. to do do do S. S.
S 20 W	½	me to do do at the Mo. of *Nadawa* (3)
S 15 W	¼	me. to do do do Island
S 80 W	¼	me. to do on S. S. opsd. the head of Isd.
	12 ¼	

Detachment Orders

[Lewis]   Nadawa Island July 8th 1804.—[9]

In order to insure a prudent and regular use of all provisions issued to the crew of the Batteaux in future, as also to provide for the equal distribution of the same among the individuals of the several messes, The Commanding Officers Do appoint the following persons to *recieve*, *cook*, and *take charges of* the provisions which may from time to time be issued to their respective messes, (viz) John B. Thompson to Sergt. Floyd's mess,

William Warner to Sergt. Ordway's mess, and John Collins to Sergt. Pryor's Mess.— These *Superintendants of Provision,* are held immediately responsible to the commanding Officers for a judicious consumption of the provision which they recieve; they are to cook the same for their several messes in due time, and in such manner as is most wholesome and best calculated to afford the greatest proportion of nutriment; in their mode of cooking they are to exercise their own judgment; they shall ⟨point⟩ allso point out what part, and what proportion of the mess provisions are to be consumed at each stated meal (i. e.) morning, noon and night; nor is any man at any time to take or consume any part of the mess provisions without the privity, knowledge and consent of the Superintendant. The superintendant is also held responsible for all the cooking eutensels of his mess.   in consideration of the duties imposed by this order on Thompson, Warner, and Collins, they will in future be exempt from guard duty, tho' they will still be held on the royster for that duty, and their regular tour—shall be performed by some one of their rispective messes; they are exempted also from pitching the tents of the mess, collecting firewood, and forks poles &c. for cooking and drying such fresh meat as may be furnished them; those duties are to be also performed by the other members of the mess.—

M. Lewis
Wm. Clark

(Point of observation No. 18.)

[Lewis]   *Sunday July the 8th* 1804.[10]

On the Starboard shore immediately below an high bluff situated ¼ of a mile below the lower point of Nadawa Island.

Observed Meridian altd. of ☉'s L. L. with Octant by the back observtn.   39° 18' —".

Latitide by this observation   39° 39' 22.7"

1. This July 8 entry is written over the following address, indicating that the sheet was earlier used as an envelope, probably by Lewis: Captn Wm Clark   River Dubois   Pryor.

2. If Nicollet's identification in 1839 is correct, this is apparently Mace Creek, reaching the Missouri near Amazonia, Andrew County, Missouri; Nicollet labels it "Ordway's Creek (L. & Cl.) or Nadoway [Set?] Creek." Ordway says that the captains named it after him, and Biddle also uses his name. No extant expedition map shows that name or the stream

itself, which may have appeared on one of the missing route maps of the lower Missouri. Coues (HLC), 1:41; Nicollet (MMR), 375; MRC map 18.

3. The Nodaway River today forms the boundary between Holt and Andrew counties, Missouri, on the lower part of its course. Nicollet remarks on the changes in the group of islands above Ordway's Creek, and the mouth of the Nodaway may also have shifted subsequently, altering the shape and location of Nodaway Island and rendering the smaller islands indistinguishable from the bottomlands. The name is apparently an Algonquian term applied to enemy tribes, metaphorically "snakes." Fenton, 320; Coues (HLC), 1:41 n. 88; Stewart (APN), 330; Nicollet (MMR), 375; MRC map 18.

4. Near the present mouth of the Nodaway and the town of Nodaway, in Andrew County. Nodaway Island was still on the map near the end of the century. MRC map 18.

5. Clark here reached the bottom of the page, added to get a subtotal of mileage, and continued the July 8 courses and distances in the right margin, at right angles to the rest of the writing. Here again he ran out of space and had to repeat the last two courses and the final mileage total above the rest of the marginal column.

6. This figure does not match the above subtotal because Clark, apparently to save space, had placed two courses on the same line for four lines, giving him another column of mileages totaling 1¾ miles, which he added to the 8¼ miles in the main column. There are discrepancies between this material and the figures in Codex A.

7. In this problem at the lower righthand corner of the page, Clark is apparently working with minutes and seconds. His subtraction appears to be wrong and the answer ought to be 33—41. Presumably he was trying to figure latitude or longitude.

8. Diacritical marks often appear over Indian words in the notebook journals from this point on. They may be Biddle's.

9. From the Orderly Book; in Lewis's hand except for Clark's signature.

10. Lewis's observation from Codex O.

[Clark]

July the 9th *Monday* 1804   Sent one man[1] back to the mouth of the River to mark a tree, to let the party on Shore See that the Boat had passed the river, Set out ⟨at Su⟩ early   passed (1) the head of the Island[2] Situated in the middle of the river a Sand bar at the head, (2) passed the mouth of a Creek or Bayou on the S. S. leading from a large Pond of about three miles in length,[3]   at 8 oClock it commenced raining, the wind changed from N E. to S. W.   (3) at 6 miles passed the mouth of a Small Creek on the L. S. called Monters Creek,[4]   the river at this place is wide with a Sand bar in the Middle, passed a place on the L. S. about 2 miles above the Creek, where Several french men camped two years to hunt—   (4) passed a Island on the S S. of the river in a bend, opsd. a high

Land on the L. S.[5]   wind Shifted to the N. W. in the evining, opsd. this Island, and on the L. S. *Loup* or *Wolf* River[6] Coms in, this river is about 60 yards Wide, but little water running at the mouth, this river heads with the waters of the Kanzas, and has a perogue navigation Some distance, it abounds with Beaver, Camped opposit the head of the Island on the L. S.[7]   Saw a fire on the S. S.   Supposedly the four flankers, to be theire, Sent a perogue for them, the Patroon & Bowman of the Perogue French,[8] they returned & informed, that when they approached the fire, it was put out, which caused them to return, this report causd. us to look out   Supposeing a pty. of Soux going to war, firierd the *bow piec* to allarm & put on their guard the men on Shore   everey thing in readiness for Defence.

Course Distance & Reffurencies for July the 9th—

S. 60° W.	1 ½	ms. to the upper point of an Island in the River (1) passed the mouth of a Gut from a pond (2) S. S.
S. 20° W.	3 ½	ms. to a point on the S. S. passed a Sand bar and point on L. S.— (rains).
N 82 W.	3 ½	ms. to a point on the ⟨L.⟩ S. Side, psd. a Sand bar, a Small Creek on the L. S. (3)
N. 68° W	5 ½ 14	ms. to a point on the L. S. (4) passed a Island on the S. S.— Just a below the pt. pass Wolf R (5)

[Clark]   *July* 9th *Monday* 1804

one man Sent back to the river we passed last night to Blase [*NB: notch*] a tree with a view to notify the party on Shore of our passing   Set out and passed the head of the (1) Island which was Situated opposit to our Camp last night   a Sand bar at the head (2) opsd. this Island a ⟨Gut⟩ Creek or Bayaue Coms in from a large Pond on the Starboard Side, as our flanking party Saw great numbers of Pike in this Pond, I have laid it down with that name anex'd,[9] at 8 oClock the wind Shifted from the N, E to S W and it commenced raining.   (3) at Six miles passed the mouth of Creek on the L. S. Called ⟨Monter's⟩ [*NB: Montain's*] Creek, about *two*[10] mile above is some Cabins where our Bowman & Several frenchmen Campd. two years [*NB: ago*][11]   (4) passed an Island on the S. S. in a Bend of the river opposit Some Clifts on the L. S.   the wind Shifted to the N W   opposit this

Island and on the L. Side (*Loup*) or *Wolf River* Coms in, this river is about 60 yards wide and heads with the waters of the Kansis, and is navagable for Perogues "Some destance up"   Camped at a point on the L. S. opposit the head of the Island, our party was incamped on the Opposit Side, their not answering our Signals Caused us to Suspect the persons Camped opposit to us was a war party of Soux, we fired the Bow piece to alarm the party on Shore, alled prepared to oppose if attacted

Course Distance & refrs. July 9th 1804

N. 60° W	1 ½	Ms. to up pt. of Isd. psd. a ⟨Gut⟩ Creek S S (1) (2)
S 20° W	3 ½	ms. to pt. S. S. psd. pt. of Sand bar S. S.
N 82° W	3 ½	ms. to pt. S. S. psd. Sand, & a Creek S. S. (3)
N 68° W	5 ½	Ms. to pt. L. S. psd. Wolf R L. S. opsd. Isd. (5)
	14	

1. According to Ordway the man was Bratton.

2. Evidently the head of Nodaway Island. Nicollet (MMR), 376; MRC map 18.

3. Probably Little Tarkio Creek, in Holt County, Missouri, which seems to have had various beds in this vicinity over the years. One of them passed through what is now a sizable oxbow lake in the Missouri bottom. Nicollet shows "Pike pond (L. & C.)" near the head of Nodaway Island and downstream from the mouth of the creek; either the creek had already shifted its course or Nicollet misread Biddle. Nicollet (MMR), 376; MRC maps 18, 19.

4. Either Charleston Creek or Mosquito Creek, in Doniphan County, Kansas, depending on the course of the Missouri River in 1804. MRC map 18.

5. This high bluff in Doniphan County, was later grandiosely called Lookout Mountain. Ibid.

6. Wolf Creek, in Doniphan County. *Loup* is French for "wolf." It should not be confused with the Loup River in Nebraska, which Lewis and Clark never saw although they heard of it. Ibid.; MRM map 51.

7. Precise location not possible because of shifts of the Missouri over the years; using the course of the river today, the camp would be near the present town of Iowa Point, Doniphan County. MRC map 18.

8. If the arrangements were still the same as those of May 26, 1804, this would be the red pirogue, with Patroon Baptiste Deschamps in charge.

9. The pike, strictly speaking, is northern pike, but various fishes resembling it are also loosely called pike. Lee et al., 133. The lake does not appear on Clark's maps; he may have "laid it down" on a lost map or in a list of streams.

10. The word could be read as either "ones" or "two," but the Field Notes entry confirms the latter.

11. The bowman would be either Cruzatte or Labiche. This site is in Doniphan County, a few miles down the Missouri from Iowa Point. MRC map 18.

[Clark]

July 10th *Tuesday*   Set out this morning with a view to Land near the *fire* Seen last night, & recornetre, but Soon discovered that our men were at the fire, they were a Sleep early last evening, and from the Course of the Wind which blew hard, their yells were not hea[r]d by party in the perogue, a mistake altogether—.   proceeded on, passed [*hole*] Prarie on the upper Side of Woolf River, at 4 miles passed (1) a Small Creek L. S. Called [*hole*] R. *Pape*[1]   this Creek is about 15 yds. Wide—and called after a Spanierd who killed himself at th[e] mouth.   (2) Dined on an Island Called *de Selamen*[2] and delayed 3 hours, and proceeded on, opposit this Isld. on the L. S. is a (3) butifull Bottom Prarie whuch will Contain about 2000 acres of Land covered with wild rye & wild Potatoes,[3] gread numbers of Goslings on the Banks & in the Ponds near the river, Capt Lewis Killed two this evening, we came to & Camped for the night. at a point on the S. S. opposit a yellow Clay Clift.—[4]   our men all getting well but much fatigued, the river is on a Stand nether rise nor fall, The bottom on the S. S. is verry extensive & thick.   the Hills or high land is near the river on the L. S. and but thinly timbered, back of those hills is open plains.

Course Distance & Reffrs. July 10th[5]

N. 80° W.	3 ¼	ms. to the Starboard Point passed a Sand Bar
N. 19 E	2	ms to a point on the L S. passed a Creek (1)
North	¾	Me. to Lower point of an Island (2)
S. 80° W.	¾	ms to a pt. on the Left side of the Island opsd. a prarie (3)
N. 50° W.	1 ¼	me to a pt on the P: L. S passed a bad Sand bar
N. 83° W.	2	me. to a pt. S. S.—
	10 Miles	

[Clark]   *July 10th Tuesday* 1804

Set out early this morning and Crossd the river with a view to See who the party was that Camped on the other Side, we Soon discovered them to be our men,—   proceeded on passed a Prarie on the L. S. at 4 miles passed a Creek L. S Called (1) ⟨*Pappie*⟩ [*NB: Pape's Creek*] after a man who Killed himself at its mouth, this Creek is 15 yds wide— (2) Dined on an Isld. Called ⟨*de Salamin*⟩ [*NB: Solomon's Island*]⁶ Delayed 3 hours on this Island to recruit the men opposit on the L. S. is a butifull bottom Plain of about 2000 acres (3) Covered with wild rye & Potatoes, [*NB: ground apple; pomme de terre*] intermix't with the grass, we camped on the S. S. opposit a yellow Clay Clift, Capt. Lewis Killed t[w]o young Gees or Goslings this evening— The men of the party getting better, but much fatigued— The river on a Stand— The bottom is verry extensive on the S. S. and thickly intersperced with Vines

The High Land approaches near the river on the L. S. and well timbered next to the river, back of those hills the Plains Commence.

Course Distance & refrs. July 10th

N. 80° W.	3 ¼	Ms. to pt. S. S. passd. a Sand bar
N 19° E.	2	ms. to pt. L. S. pasd. a Creek (1)
North	¾	me. to Low: pt. of an Isld. (2)
S. 80° W.	¾	me. to pt. on left of an Isd. opsd. Pra (3)
N 50 W.	1 ¼	ms. to pt. on L. S. passed Sd. bar
N 83 W.	2	ms. to a pt. on S. S. Isd (5)
	10	

1. Probably later Cedar Creek, Doniphan County, Kansas. MRC map 18.

2. Obviously a reference to Solomon's Island, which appears in Nicollet at the right place. MRC map 18 shows it near the mouth of Nodaway River. Clark could have been misinformed and led Nicollet into error through Biddle, but the captain indicates on July 9, 1804, that one of the bowmen had spent considerable time in the area. It is likely that the name itself shifted over the years, through mapmakers' errors or some other reason. The name might be from Salomin or Solomon Petit, who engaged in trade with the Poncas in the 1790s. McDermott (WCS), 149; Nicollet (MMR), 376; MRC maps 18, 19.

3. Wild rye is *Elymus canadensis* L., Canada wildrye, judging from the habitat description. Likewise, "potatoes" (*Apios americana*, Indian potato, ground nut), are found in similar habitat. Both are typical of moist, subirrigated soil that is subject to periodic flooding. See Lewis's description in an undated entry at the end of Chapter 3. Steyermark, 130, 947; Weaver, 34–35.

4. If the river's course remains the same, a camp on the starboard side would be in Holt County, Missouri. The site would be near the Nebraska-Kansas boundary on the opposite shore. MRC map 19.

5. The mileage figures are much altered and overwritten. At the end of the course material (the bottom of the page of document 30) is this course, apparently having no relationship to surrounding material: S. 66 W.

6. Biddle apparently crossed out phrases in this entry to substitute his own.

[Clark][1]

July 11th *Wednesday*, Set out early   proceeded on   passed a Willow (1) Island in a bend to the S. S.   Sent out Dreweyer & Jo: Fields to hunt, Back of this Island a creek coms in on the S. S. called by the Indians Little *Tarkio* Creek[2]   I went on Shore above this Island on the S. S. found the bottom Subject for overflow wet and verry thickly interwoven with grape Vines—   proceeded on at about ½ a miles from the river about 3 ms. and observed fresh Sign of a horse, I prosueed the track, with an expectation of finding a Camp of Indians on the river, when I got to the river, I saw a horse on the Beech, this horse as appears was left last winter by Some hunting party, probable the *Othouez* [Otos], I joined the Boat on the Sand Island Situated opposit the mouth of the Ne Ma har River,[3] this river Coms in on the L. S.   is about 80 yds Wide and navagable for Perogues Some Distance up   the praries Commnce above the mouth and Continus on both Sides of this R   Drewyer killed 6 Deer to day J. Field one   Several hunters Sent out up the Nemahar R

Course Distance & Reffurence July 11th 1804

N 30 W	3	mes. to ⟨a point on the L S above⟩ the head of a Small ⟨prarie, & opposit a⟩ willow (1) Island on the S. S. in a bend
⟨N. 86°⟩		
West	3	ms. pssg. a point on the S. S. to the South Side of a Sand Island
	6	opsd. a Ne-Mahar R (2)

[Clark]   July 11th, Wednesday 1804

Set out early   passed a Willow Island (1) in a bend on the S. S.   back of this Island a Creek Coms in Called by the Indians *Tar-ki-o*

I went on Shore above this Creek and walked up parrelel with the river at ab ut half a mile distant, the bottom I found low & Subject to overflow, Still further out, the under groth & vines wer So thick that I could not get thro: with ease   after walking about three or 4 miles I observed a fresh horse track where he had been feeding   I turned my course to the river

and prosud the track and found him on a Sand beach   This horse Probably had been left by Some party of Otteaus hunters who wintered or
hunted in this quarter last fall or Wintr. I joined the party on a large Sand
Island imediately opposit the mouth of ⟨Ne Ma haw⟩ [NB: Nĕmăhāw][4]
River, at which place they had Camped, this Island is Sand   about half of
it Covered with Small Willows of two different Kinds, one Narrow & the
other a Broad Leaf.[5]   Several hunters Sent out to day on both Sides of
the river, *Seven* Deer Killed to day. Drewyer Killd Six of them, made Some
Luner observations this evening.

Course Distance & refrs. July 11th

N. 30° W	3	ms: to the head of a willow Isd. (1) in a bend to S. S.
West—	2 ¾	Ms. to Lowr. pt. of a Sand Isld. on the S. S. psd. pt. S. S. (2)
North—	¼	me. on the N. Side of Isd. & camped
	6 miles	

(Point of observation No. 19.)

Wednesday July 11th[6]

[Lewis]

On *Newfound Island* opposite to the mouth of the great Ne-mi-Haw
made the following observations *with Sextant and Chronometer.*

Alt. by Sextant of time of observation

						h	m	s
☉'s L. L.	88°	26′	15″		P. M.	3	26	38
☉'s Center	"	"	"			"	27	59
☉'s U. L.	"	"	"			"	29	27
						h	m	s
☉'s L. L.	39°	3′	—″		P. M.	5	36	35
☉'s U. L.	"	"				"	39	31
☉'s magnetic azimuth by Circumfet.						N. 89° W.		
Altd. of ☉'s L. L. by Sextant						39°	3′	—″
						h	m	s
Time by Chronometer						5	36	35
Latitude of place of observation						39°	55′	56″

Observed time and distance of ☽ from Spica ♍ ★, East, with Cronomtr. & Sextant.

	Time			Distance	
P. M. 8	41	42	31	35	—
"	46	26	"	30	45
"	50	18	"	30	45
"	54	44	"	27	30
"	58	48	"	26	—
9	2	—	"	24	—
"	7	15	"	21	—
"	10	17	"	20	30
"	12	15	"	19	—
"	14	3	"	17	30
"	16	15	"	16	30
"	18	22	"	15	45
"	22	50	"	13	—
"	30	33	"	6	15

1. Biddle placed this notation at the top of this sheet of the Field Notes (document 30), above the July 11 entry: "July 9 to 13th."

2. Probably later Little Tarkio creek, in Holt County, Missouri. The routes of both Big and Little Tarkio creeks through the bottom to the Missouri seem to have shifted frequently. MRC maps 18, 19.

3. The Big Nemaha River, whose Oto Indian name, nímǫha, signifies "miry water," enters the Missouri in Richardson County, Nebraska, just above the Nebraska-Kansas line. The camp, opposite the river mouth on an island, may have been in present Holt County, Missouri. The island itself (Lewis's "Newfound" of July 11 "New" of the next day) appears unnamed on Nicollet's map and is missing on later maps. Fitzpatrick, 105; Nicollet (MMR), 377; MRC map 19.

4. Biddle apparently crossed out "Ne Ma how" to substitute his own word.

5. The small willows with narrow and broad leaves are probably *Salix exigua* Nutt. ssp. *interior* (Rowlee) Cronq., sandbar, or coyote, willow, and *S. amygdaloides* Anderss, peach-leaved willow, respectively, although seedlings of the larger willow tree *S. nigra* Marsh., black willow, could also be found on the sandbars described. Steyermark, 497, 494, 496; Barkley, 102–4.

6. Lewis's observation from Codex O.

[Clark]

*July 12*th *Thursday*   Som hunters out on the S. S.   those on the L. S. did not return last night, our object in delaying here is to tak Some Observations and rest the men who are much fatigued   made Sundery observations, after an early Brackfast I took five men and went up the River *Ne Ma har* about three miles, to an open leavel part of an emence prarie, at the Mouth of a Small Creek on the Lower Side,[1] I went on Shore, & passed thro the plain   passed Several noles to the top of a high artificial Noal   from the top of this noal I had an emence, extensive & pleaseing prospect, of the Countrey around, I could See the meandering of the Little River [Nemaha] for [*hole*] at least 10 miles winding thro a meadow of 15 or 20000 acres of high [*holes*] bottom land covered with Grass about 4½ feet high, the high lands which rose irregularly, & were toped with *Mounds* or antent Graves which is to me a Strong evidence of this Countrey haveing been thickly Settled—.[2]   This River is about 80 yards wide with a gentle Current and heads up near the Parnee [Pawnee] Village on River Blue a branch of Kansas,[3] a little timbered land near the mouth for 1 mile above, only a fiew Trees, and thickets of Plumbs Cheres &c are Seen on its banks   the Creeks & little reveens makeing into the river have also Some timber—   I got grapes on the banks nearly ripe, observed great quantities, of Grapes, plums Crab apls and a wild Cherry, Growing like a Comn. Wild Cherry only larger & grows on a Small bush,[4] on the side of a clift Sand Stone[5]   ½ me. up & on Lower Side I marked my name & day of the month near an Indian Mark or Image of animals & a boat   Tried Willard for Sleeping on his post, our hunters killed some Deer,[6] Saw Elk & Buffalow.

[Clark]   July 12th, Thursday 1804

Concluded to Delay here to day with a view of takeing equal altitudes & makeing observations as well as refreshing our men who are much fatigued—   after an early Brackfast I with five men in a Perogue assended the River *Ne-Ma-haw* about 2 ⟨three⟩ miles to the mouth of a Small Creek on the Lower Side, here I got out of the Perogue, after going to Several Small Mounds in a leavel plain, I assended a hill on the Lower Side, on this hill Several Artificial Mounds were raised, from the top of the highest of those Mounds I had an extensive view of the Serounding Plains, which afforded ⟨a⟩ one of the most pleasing prospects I ever beheld, under me a Butifull River of Clear water of about 80 yards wide Meandering thro: a leavel and extensive Meadow, as far as I could See, the ⟨view of the⟩ prospect Much enlivened by the fine Trees & Srubs which

⟨was⟩ is bordering the bank of the river, and the Creeks & runs falling into it,—. The bottom land is covered with Grass of about 4½ feet high, and appears as leavel as a Smoth Surfice, the ⟨2 bottom⟩ [*NB: the upper land*] is also covered with Grass and rich weeds[7] & flours, interspersed with Copses of the Osage Plumb. on the riseing lands, Small groves of trees are Seen, with a numbers of Grapes and a Wild Cherry resembling the Common Wild Cherry, only larger and grows on a Small bush on the tops of those hills in every derection. I observed artifical mounds (or as I may more Justly term Graves) which to me is a Strong indication[8] of this Country being once Thickly Settled. (The Indians of the Missouris Still Keep up the Custom of Burrying their dead on high ground) after a ramble of about two miles about I returned to the perogue and decended down the River, gathd. Som *grapes* nearly ripe, on a Sandstone Bluff about ¼ of a mile from its mouth on the Lower Side I observed Some Indian marks, went to the rock which jucted over the water and marked my name & the day of the month & year— This river heads near one [*NB: See note*][9] of the Villages of the Pania [*NB: Pawnee*] on the [*NB: Blue*] River Blue, a branch of the *Kansas* River.— above this river about half a mile the Prarie Comes to the *Missouri* after my return to Camp on the Island Completed Som observations, Tred [tried] a man [*WC: Wld.*][10] for sleeping on his Post & inspected the arms amunition &c. of the party found all complete, ⟨No⟩ Took Some Luner Obsevations. three Deer killed to day. *Latd. 39° 55′ 56″ N.*[11]

[Lewis and Clark] Camp New Island July 12th 1804.[12]

A Court matial consisting of the two commanding officers will convene this day at 1 OCk. P.M. for the trial of such prisoners as may be brought before them; one of the court will act as Judge Advocate.—

M. Lewis
Wm. Clark

The Commanding officers. Capt. M. Lewis & W. Clark constituted ⟨formed⟩ themselves ⟨into⟩ a Court martial for the trial of Such prisoners as are *Guilty* of *Capatol Crimes*, and under the rules and articles of *War* punishable by *Death,*[13]

Alexander Willard was brought foward Charged with "*Lying down and*

Sleeping on his post whilst a Sentinal, on the night of the 11th. Instant" (by John Ordway Sergeant of the Guard)—

To this Charge the prisoner pleads. *Guilty* of *Lying Down*, and *not Guilty, of Going to Sleep.* The Court after Duly Considering the evidence aduced, are of oppinion that the *Prisoner* Alexdn. Willard is guilty of every part of the Charge exhibited against him.   it being a breach of the *rules* and articles of *War* (as well as tending to the probable distruction ⟨the Sulution⟩ of the party) do *Sentence* him to receive *One hundred lashes on his bear back, at four different times in equal propation.*—   and order that the punishment Commence this evening at Sunset, and Continue to be inflicted, (by the Guard) every evening untill Completed

Wm Clark

M. Lewis

[Lewis] *Thursday July 12th*[14]

Observed Equal Altitudes of the ☉ with Sextant

A. M.	7	58	59	P. M.	4	12	29
	8	—	19	"	13	48
	"	1	45	"	15	14

Altitude by Sextant at the time of this obst.   70° 42′ 45″

Observed meridian Altd. of ☉'s L. L. with Octant by the back observatn.   40° 53′ —″

Latitude deduced from this observatn.   39° 55′ 56

Observed time and distance of ☉'s and ☽'s nearest limbs the ☉ West, with Sextant.

		Time			Distance	
	h	m	s			
P. M.	4	51	11	70°	31′	30″
	5	5	48	"	35	30
	"	11	52	"	37	30
	"	12	47	"	38	—″
	"	16	30	"	39	—″
	"	18	8	"	39	15
	"	19	51	"	39	30
	"	21	9	"	39	30

"	24	50	"	41	30
"	26	14	"	42	30

	h	m	s			
P. M.	5	32	40	70°	42′	—″
"		33	53	"	44	45
"		38	55	"	45	45
"		42	11	"	46	30
"		43	42	"	47	30
"		45	25	"	47	30

⊙'s magnetic azimuth by Circumftr.   N. 86° W.

	h	m	s
Time by Chronometer P. M.	5	59	20

Altd. of ⊙'s L. L. by Sextant   31° 26′ 30″

⊙'s Magnetic azimuth by Circumft.   N. 85° W.

	h	m	s
Time by Chronometer P. M.	6	5	10

Altd. of ⊙'s L. L. by Sextant   29° 19′ 30″

Observed time and distance of ☽ , and Spica ♍ ★, East, with Sextant.—

Time			*Distance*		
h	m	s			
P. M. 8	26	58	19°	18′	15″

Note—this is a mean of four observations which were not so perfect as I could have wished them, in consequence of the moon being obscured in some measure by the clouds, which soon became so general as to put an end to my observations during this evening.—

1. Evidently "Lower Side" means the south bank of the Big Nemaha River, the lower side in relation to the course of the Missouri; the creek is probably Roys Creek. Clark is in southeast Richardson County, Nebraska, more or less due south of the modern community of Rulo. MRC map 19; MRM map 53.

2. Clark is here describing a late prehistoric Oneota village, the Leary site. The mounds on the hills overlooking the village have not been investigated, principally because they have also been used by modern Iowa Indians for grave sites. The "Several noles" that Clark passed on the plain are believed to be refuse middens of a late prehistoric Oto village. Hill & Wedel.

3. The Big Blue River of Nebraska and Kansas, a tributary of the Kansas River, should not be confused with the Big Blue of Missouri, which flows into the Missouri River. See note for June 26, 1804. In the codex entry Clark mentions more than one Pawnee village

on the Big Blue. Two Pawnee villages nearly match this description, the Blue Springs site and the James site, both of which are just north of the town of Blue Springs, Gage County, Nebraska. The Blue Springs site was probably occupied by the Pitahawiratas (Tappage Pawnees), who abandoned it about 1825. Grange, 20, 26.

4. In this entry, Clark describes an extensive floodplain prairie (high bottomland) several miles upstream which was covered with tall grasses, probably *Spartina pectinata* Link, prairie cordgrass, slough grass, and others, such as big bluestem. Weaver, 189–90. The grapes are probably *Vitis riparia* Michx., river-bank grape, although a number of other grape species occur here. Barkley, 219–20. The wild cherry is *Prunus virginiana* L., choke cherry, which has a larger fruit than that of the "Comn. Wild Cherry," *P. serotina* Ehrh., black cherry. Clark is correct in noting the smaller stature and different habitat of the choke cherry. Steyermark, 862.

5. Rocks that crop out near the mouth of the Big Nemaha River are late Pennsylvanian in age, part of the Wabaunsee Group, which consists of about 350 feet of shale with a few thin limestone beds and fewer sandstones, which are unnamed. Burchett et al.; Condra & Reed.

6. Ordway notes that Drouillard, as one of the hunters as usual, killed two deer.

7. Probably *Pilea pumila* (L.) Gray, richweed, clearweed, but somewhat confusing since it normally occupies cool, moist, shaded places, not a drier, grassy area such as the upper floodplain terrace of the Nemaha River, which is being described. Fernald, 558. See entries of July 14 and 15.

8. The word "indication" appears to have been written over the word "evidence."

9. This interlineation may be a reference to Lewis's "Summary of Creeks and Rivers" in Codex O, where he elaborates slightly on this information, or to some similar compilation by one or both captains. See Appendix C, this volume. Red lines, probably Biddle's, cross out this sentence.

10. An interlined abbreviation for "Willard."

11. The camp was probably north of the Nebraska-Kansas state line, which is 40° N. MRC map 19.

12. Lewis wrote the first part of this order in the Orderly Book, to the first pair of signatures, where Clark signed for himself. Clark then wrote the rest of the order and may have signed for Lewis the second time.

13. Willard's offense, under the military regimen of the party, was punishable by death according to the regulations. Hence, the captains themselves constituted the court, instead of a panel of enlisted men as was the case with lesser offenses. It is doubtful that they had any intention of inflicting so severe a penalty, but they wished to impress on everyone the seriousness of such a lapse, which in the event of a surprise attack could mean the deaths of many or all of the party.

14. Lewis's observation from Codex O.

[Clark]¹

My notes of the 13th of July by a Most unfortunate accident blew over Board in a Storm in the morning of the 14th obliges me to refur to the

⟨notes⟩ Journals of Serjeants, and my own recollection [of] the accurrences Courses Distance &c. of that day—[2]   last night a violent Storm from the N. N, E.—   (1) passed *Tar-ki-o* River,[3] at 2 miles a chanl. running into this river 3 ms. abov forms St Josephs Isld.   Passed an elegt Prarie in the 1st bend to the left. Conta[in]ing a grass resmlg Timothy, with Seed like flax, (2) passed a Island in a bend to the S. S. at 12 ms. I walked on Shore S. S.   lands, low & overflows, Killed two Goslings nearly Grown, Sailed under a Wind from the South all day, Camped on a Sand Island on the L. Pt. opposit a high & extensiv Prarie,[4] on the S. S. the Hills about 4 or 5 me. off, this Plain appears extensive, great appearance of a Storm from the North W.   this evening verry agreeable   the wind Still from the South—

John Ordway FG[5]

Appere. from Camp

from the Osagies Nation with twenty odd of the Natives or chiefs of the Nation with him [sa]iled dowen the Mississippi bound to St Louis & 3 guns fired   [show]ers of rain   Showers of Rain all that night

Course Distance & reffurrence July 13 1804

N. 8° E	1	Me. to Pt. on S. S. passed the Sand Island
N. 28 E	3 ½	me. to pt. on L. S. psd. *Tar-ki o* R. St. Joseps Isd L. S. (1)[6]
S. 70° W	3	ms. to pt. on S. S. opsd. a Prarie (2)
N 46° W.	1 ½	ms. on the S. point opsd. the Prarie & a Hill L. S.
N. 30° W	1 ½	Ms. to a pt. on L. S.
N. 45° W	4 ½	Ms. to a pt. on L. S. passd a Island & Sand bar (3)
N. 66 W	3 ½	Ms. to a pt. on S. S.
N. 8 W.	2	Ms. to a pt. on L. S. leaving a Sand Island on which we camped to the left, on this Island I lost my notes, in a Storm.
	20 ½	

[Clark]   *July 13th Friday* 1804

Set out at Sun rise, and prosd. on under a gentle Breeze, at two miles passed the mouth of a Small river on the S. S. Called by the Indians *Tar-ki-o*, a Channel running out of the river three miles above (which is now filled up with Sand) runs into this Creek & and formed a Island Called *St.*

Josephs Several Sand bars parralel to each other above— In the first bend to the left is Situated a Butifull & extensive plain, Cover'd with Grass resembling Timothy except the Seed which resembles *Flax* Seed, this plain also abounds in Grapes of defferent Kinds Some nearly ripe. I Killed two Goslings nearly Grown, Several others Killed and cought on Shore, also one old Goose, with pin fethers, She Could not fly— at about 12 miles passd. a Island Situated in a bend on the S. S. above this Island is a large Sand bar Covered with willows. The wind from the South, Camped on a large Sand Bar makeing out from the L. P. opposit a high hanson *Prarie*, the *hills* about 4 or 5 miles on S. S. this plain appeard extensive, the Clouds appear to geather ⟨fro⟩ to the N. W. a most agreeable Breeze from the South (I walked on Shore on the S. S. the lands are low Subject to overflow)

Last night at about 10 oClock a violent Storm of wind from the N. N. E. which lasted with Great violence for about one hour, at which time a Shower of rain Succeeded.

Course Distance & Reffrs. July 13th

N. 8° E	1	me. to pt. on S. S. psd ⟨the⟩ Sd. Isld.
N. 28° E	3 ½	Ms. to pt. on L. S. psd. Riv & Isd. (1)
S 70° W	3	ms. to pt. on S. S. opsd. a prarie (2)
N. 46° W.	1 ½	me. on S. S. opsd. the Prarie & a Hill
N. 30° W.	1 ½	ms. to a pt. on L. S.
N. 45° W.	4 ½	Ms. to a pt. on L. S. psd. an Isd. (3)
N. 66° W.	3 ½	Ms. to a pt. on S. S.
N. 8° W.	2	Ms. to a pt. on L. S. a Sand Isd.
	20 ½	Miles

The men on Shore did not join us this after noon—[7] The river nearly on a Stand— the high lands on the S. S. has only been Seen at a Distance ⟨on th⟩ above the Nordaway River, those on the S. L. aproaching the river at every bend, on the Side next to the river well timbered, the opsd. Side open & the Commencmt. of Plains.

1. Biddle's notation at the upper left-hand corner of this sheet of the Field Notes (document 31) reads, "14 July to 18."

2. Ordway also refers to Clark's difficulties in making up his lost notes. This strongly indicates that there was no daily journal by Lewis for the period to which he could refer. Also, Clark must have been delaying at least a day or two in copying his Field Notes into his notebook journal Codex A. See Introduction to this volume.

3. The Tarkio River, otherwise Big Tarkio Creek, reaches the Missouri River in Holt County, Missouri. It seems likely that in 1804 and for the rest of the century, the mouth was some miles farther down the Missouri than it is now. MRC map 19; MRR maps 54, 55.

4. Using the present course of the Missouri River, we would place this camp in eastern Richardson County, Nebraska.

5. "John Orway FG" is written beside the courses and distances for July 13. "FG" may be "Sg," perhaps for "Sergeant." Over the above is written, "Appere. from Camp," which may be in Clark's hand and unrelated to the rest, which appears to be in Ordway's hand. The subsequent lines are upside down between the courses and distances and the main entry, partially under the latter. They may refer to the return of Auguste or Pierre Chouteau at River Dubois from the Osages on April 22, 1804 (see above).

6. What appears to be "Day" and one or two illegible letters are written vertically directly above the numeral "(1)," at right angles to the courses and distances. The connection with the rest of the material is not apparent.

7. According to Ordway, one of the men was Reubin Field, who was in charge of the horses. Another, noted on July 14 by Clark, was Goodrich.

[Clark]

Course Distance and Reffurrence July 14th 1804[1]

N 70° W.	2	ms. to a pt. on S. S. pass an Isld. Small on S. S. (1) a violent Storm from N. E
N. 20° W.	2	ms. to a pt. on L. S. wind from N. W. by N.
N. 30° W	1	me. on the L. S.
N. 50° W	2 ½	ms. to the Lower point of an Island
N. 87 W.	1 ½ / 9	to a second point of same Island on Lad. side of the same ⟨below⟩ a little above the lower point of this island a creek falls in on the Stard. called by the *Maha* Neesh-nah-ba-to-na— this is a considerable creek is as large as the mine river, and runs parallel with the Missouri through much the greater portion of it's course[2]

July the 14th Satturday   Some hard Shours of rain accompaned with Some wind detained us untill about 7 oClock, we then Set out and proceeded on about a mile a[nd] th atmispeir became Suddenly darkened by a blak & dismal looking Cloud, we wer in a Situation, near the upper point of a Sd. Isd. & the opsd Shore falling in   in this Situation a Violent Storm of Wint from the N, E   (passing over an Open plain, Struck the boat nearly ⟨broad Side⟩ Starboard, quatering, & blowing down the Current)   the exerssions of all our Men who were out in an instant, aded to a Strong Cable and Anchor was Scrcely Sufficent to Keep the boat from being thrown up on the Sand Island, and dashed to peices   the Waves dasthed over on the Side next to the wind   the lockers which was covered with Tarpoling prevented the[m] coming into the boat untill the Boat was Creaned [careened] on the Side from the Wind[3]   in this Situation we continued about 40 minits, the two perogues about a quater of a mile above, one of them in a Similer Situation with the Boat, the other under the charge of George Gibson in a much better position, with her Ster[n] faceing the wind, this Storm Suddenly Seased, & 1 minit the river was as Smoth as glass, the wind Shifted to the S. E and we Set Sail, and proceeded on   passed (1) a Small Island on the S. S. and Dined—   R: Fields who has charge of the horses &c. on Shore did not join us last night—.   passed a old fort where Mr. Bennet[4] of St Louis winttered 2 years & traded with the Otteaus & Panies   on the S. S. 1 me. abov the little Island, I went out on the L. S. and observed two Elk on a Iand in the river, in attempting to get near those elk obseved one near us   I Shot one.   continued on Shore & thro the bottom which was extensive, Some Small Praries, and a peponce [preponderance] of high rich & well timbered bottom, in the Glades I saw wild Timothy, Lams quarter Cuckle bur[5] & rich weed, on the edges Plumbs of different kinds Grapes, and Goose berries, Camped on the L. S.[6]   Ruben Fields and Gulrich [Goodrich] joined the Party   two men unwell, one a *Felin* on his finger, river fall

[Clark]   *July 14th, Satturday* 1804

Some hard Showers of rain this morning prevented our Setting out untill 7 oClock, at half past Seven, the atmispr. became Sudenly darkened by a black and dismal looking Cloud, at the time we were in a Situation (not to be bettered) near the upper point of the Sand Island, on which we lay, and the opposit Shore, the bank was falling in and lined with Snags as far as we could See down,—.   in this Situation The Storm which passd over an open Plain from the N. E. Struck the our boat on the Starbd. quarter, and would have thrown her up on the Sand Island dashed to peces in an Instant, had not the party leeped out on the Leward Side and kept her off with the assistance of the ancker & Cable, untill the *Storm* was over, the waves Dashed over her windward Side and She must have filled with water if the Lockers which is covered with Tarpoling & ⟨prevented⟩ Threw of the water & prevented any quantity Getting into Bilge of the Boat

In this Situation we continued about 40 Minits. when the Storm Sudenly Seased and the river become Instancetaniously as Smoth as Glass.

The two *perogus* dureing this Storm was in a Similar Situation with the boat about half a mile above—   The wind Shifted to the S. E & We Saled up   passed a Small (1) Isld. Situated on the S. S. and Dined & Continud two hours, men examine their arms—   about a Mile above this Island, passed a Small Tradeing fort on the S. S. where, Mr. Bennet of St. Louis Traded with the Otteaus & Panies two years. I went on Shore to Shoot Some Elk on a Sand bar to the L. S. I fired at one but did not get him, went out into a large extensive bottom the greater part of which over-flows, the part that dose not overflow, is rich and well timbered, Some Small open Praries near the hills, the Boat passed the lower part of a large Island Situated on the S. S.   above the Lower point of this Island on the S. S. a (2) large Creek coms into the river Called by the *Maha's* [NB: *Mahar*] Indians *Neesh-nah-ba-to-na* 50 yds [NB: *Neĕsh-năh bă tē na*] [7]   this is a consid-erable Creek nearly as large as the Mine River, and runs parrelel with the Missouri, the Greater part of its Course. In those Small Praries or glades I saw wild Timothey, lambs-quarter, Cuckle burs; & rich weed.   on the edges Grows Sumr. Grapes,[8] Plum's, & Gooseberries. I Joined the boat which had Came to and Camped in a bend opposd. the large Island before mentioned on the L. S.   Several men unwell with *Boils*, *Felns*, &c.   The river falls a little.

Course Distance & Reffers *July* 14th

N. 70° W.	2	ms. to a point on S. S. a Sml. Isd. S. S. (1)
N. 20° W	2	Ms. to a pt. L. S. wind Shift N. W. by N.
N. 30° W.	1	me. on the L. S.
N. 50 W	2 ½	Ms. to Low pt. of an Isd. S. S.
N. 87 W	1 ½	Ms. to a pt. on S. Side of Isd. psd. a Creek (2)
	9	

1. Clark here places his courses and distances ahead of the main entry for July 14 in the Field Notes, and he does so intermittently from here on. This edition follows his changing practice.

2. This last course and distance notation appears to be largely in Lewis's hand.

3. Evidently the boat was tilted on the beach so that the lower hull was toward the wind, preventing the waves from coming into the hull.

4. Probably François M. Benoit, who had engaged in the trade with the Osages for several years before the Louisiana Purchase, or possibly a relative. Benoit was a partner of Manuel Lisa, and like Lisa, had somehow antagonized Lewis during the winter before the expedition set out, causing the captain to write, "Damn Manuel and triply Damn Mr. B." The post was in northwest Holt County, Missouri. Osgood (FN), 62 n. 8; Nasatir (BLC), 2:677–80; Lewis to Clark, May 6, 1804, Jackson (LLC), 1:180 and n. 2; MRC map 20.

5. "Lams quarter" is *Chenopodium album* L., lamb's quarters, and "cuckle bur" is *Xanthium strumarium* L., cocklebur. Steyermark, 611–12; Gilmore, 26; Fernald, 1473.

6. The camp would be on the Nebraska side, near the Nemaha-Richardson county line. On the opposite shore the same line divides Atchison and Holt counties, Missouri. MRC map 20; MRR map 56.

7. According to Thomas Say, "nish-na-bot-ona" (today's Nishnabotna) is an Oto Indian name signifying "canoe making river." Evidently its mouth in 1804 was many miles farther down the Missouri River than at present. The party probably passed the mouth near the present Atchison-Holt county line. Thwaites (EWT), 27:300; Nicollet (MMR), 379; MRC map 20; MRR maps 56, 58.

8. Summer grape is probably *Vitis aestivalis* Michx., summer grape, pigeon grape. The specification of "summer" grape instead of other *Vitis* species is noteworthy. Summer grape is distinguished from other grape species by the white to silver underside of the leaves. It may be confused with *V. cinerea* Engelm., grayback grape, which also has lighter undersides of leaves and also occurs in the area. Fernald, 997; Steyermark, 1036–37; Barkley, 219.

[Clark]

Course Distance and refferrnnces July 15th 1804[1]

N. 30° W.	3 ½	ms. to a pt. of a willow Isld. on the L. S. psd. the Isld. on S. S. (1)
S. 75 W.	¼	mile to a Lard point of the same Island— the boat passed to Lard of Isld. the hill here projects to the river—
N. 89 W.	¼	to a lard pt. on the same island— the hills here leave the river—
N. 88 W.	¼	to a point on Lard main shore opposite a sand bar, took merd. Altd. ⊙s L L.
Due W.	1 ¼	mile to a pt. ⟨Lard⟩ Stard. oposite which the hills again touch the river.

N. 45 W.	1 ½	mile to the mouth of Little *Ni ma-haw* on the Lard. in a bend oposite the lower point of a large sand bar—
N. 30 E	1 ½	to a point on Lard. a deep bend to the right below this point
N. 30 W.	½	to pt. Lard.
N. 15	¾	to a pt. of an Island. due E. from this about three miles is a large Pond

July 15th Sunday 1804.   a heavy fog this morning which Detained us untill 7 oClock, put Drewyer Sgt. Floyd on Shore, at 9 I took two Men[2] and went on Shore, with a view to Kill Some elk, passed thro open plains, and barroney lands [barrens]   Crossed three butifull Small Streams of water,[3] Saw great quantity of Cherres Plums, Grapes & Berries of Difft. Kinds, the lands Generally of a good quallity, on the Streams the wood ⟨Grases⟩ escapes the fire, at about 7 miles I Struck the river at the mouth *Ne ma har* Creek about 40 yds wide,[4] near this Creek on a high part of the Prarie I had a extensive View of the river & Countrey on both Sides.   on S. a contnuation of the plain as far as I could See, on the N. a bottom Prarie of about 5 ms. wide & 18 or 20 long, hills back of this Plain. I Swam across the Creek and waited for the Boat about three miles above, we camped opsd. an Island.[5]

[Clark]

July 15th, Sunday   a heavy Fog this morning prevented our Setting out before 7 oClock, at nine I took two men and walked on the L. S.   I crossed ⟨two⟩ three butifull Streems of runnig water heading in the Praries   on those Streem the lands verry fine covered with pea Vine & rich weed[6]   the high Praries are also good land Covered with Grass entirely void of timber except what grows on the water,[7] I proceeded on thro those praries Several miles to the mouth of a large Creek on the L. S. called (2) [*NB: Little*] *Ne ma har*   this is a Small river, about 100 yds. above the mouth it is 40 yards wide, at the mouth (as all other Creeks & rivers falling into the Missourie are) much narrower than a little distance up.   after continueing at the mouth of this Creek about an hour, I Swam across and proceeded on about 3 miles and halted to wate for the boat, which was Some distance below—   In all this days march thro woods & Praries, I only Saw three Deer & 3 fawns—   I had at one part of the Prarie a verry extensive view of all the Countrey around up and down the river a Considerable distance, on the Larbd. Sd. one Continul Plain, on the S. S. Some timber on the bank of the river, for a Short distance back of this timber is a bottom Plain of four or five miles back to the hills and under the hills between them & the river   this plain appeared to extend 20 or 30 miles, those Hills have but little timber, and the Plain appears to Continu back of them—   I Saw Great quantities of Grapes, Plums, or 2 Kinds wild Cherries of 2 Kinds, Hazelnuts, and Goosberries.

we Camped in a point of woods on the Larboard S. opsd. a large Island.

Course Dists. and refrs. July 15th 1804

N 30° W	3 ½	ms. to a pt. on a willow Isd. on the L. S. passed the head of the large Isd. on S. S. (1)
N 70° W	¼	of a Me. to L pt. on Sd. Isd. the boat passed to the L. S. Hills projects to river
N 89 W.	¼	of a Me. to a pt. of Sd. Isld. the Hills here leave the river.
N 88° W.	¼	of a mile to a pt. on main Shore L. S. opposit a Sand bar took Medn. altd. ⊙ L L
West	1 ¼	ms. to a pt. on S. S. opposit to which the hills again touch the river.
N 45° W.	1 ½	ms. to the mouth of *Ne-ma-haw* Creek in a bend to L. S. (2) opsd. Low pt. of Sd. bar
N. 30° E	2	ms. to a pt. on L. S. a Deep bend to the right below the pt.
N 15 E.	¾	me. to the lower pt. of a Isd. east of this Isd. is Said to be a Pond.
	9 ¾	

(*Point of observation No. 20.*)

[Lewis]   *Sunday July 15th*[8]

On the upper point of an Island[9] mentioned in the 2ed & 3rd course of this day.

Observed meridian Altd. of ⊙ L. L. with Octant by back observatn.   42′ 11′ —″

Latitude deduced from this observatn.   40° 8′ 31.8″

This evening I discovered that my Chronometer had stoped, nor can I assign any cause for this accedent; she had been wound up the preceding noon as usual. This is the third instance in which this instrument has stopt in a similar manner since she has been in my possession, tho' the fi[r]st only since our departure from the River Dubois. in the two pre-ceding cases when she was again set in motion, and her rate of going de-termined by a series of equal altitudes of the ☉ taken for that purpose, it was found to be the same precisely as that mentioned in the preliminary remarks [*i.e., July 22, 1804, below*] to these observations, or 15 s & 5 tenths too slow in 24 h—as her *rate of going* after stoping, and begin again set in motion has in two instances proved to be the same, I have concluded, that whatever this impediment may procede from, it is not caused by any material injury which her works have sustained, and that when she is in motion, her error on *mean time* above stated, may be depended on as ac-curate. In consequence of the chronometer's having thus accidentally stoped, I determined to come too at the first convenient place and make such observations as were necessary to ascertain her error, establish the Latitude & Longitude, and determine the variation of the nedle, in order to fix a *second point of departure*. accordingly on [*see Lewis's observation for July 16 below, where this note continues*]

1. The first course is in Clark's hand; the remainder of these July 15 courses and dis-tances are by Lewis. This is probably because Clark was ashore much of the day. The sec-ond entry, S. 75 W., disagrees with the Codex A course, given as N 70° W. There are also other variations.

2. One of them was Ordway.

3. In southeastern Nemaha County, Nebraska. Two of the streams were probably later Beadow and Deroin creeks. MRC map 20; MRR map 56.

4. The Little Nemaha reaches the Missouri River in Nemaha County, a little below the present town of Nemaha. MRC map 20; MRR map 56.

5. This last sentence is written at right angles to the rest of the entry, over the rest, but appears to be part of the entry. Clark ran out of space at the bottom of the page. The camp, according to the present course of the Missouri, would be in Nemaha County, somewhat above the present town of Nemaha. Opposite is Atchison County, Missouri. MRC map 20; MRR map 56.

6. The "pea Vine" may refer to *Amphicarpa bracteata* (L.) Fern., hog peanut, which is a common species with a vining habit typically found in the area described. "Rich weed" is observed correctly in its appropriate moist, shaded streamside habitat. Steyermark, 953.

7. They were now seeing the eastern margin of the Great Plains; the characteristic tree-lessness was new to them and worthy of comment. The area along the Missouri is more wooded today because prairie fires have been controlled.

8. Lewis's observation from Codex O.

9. Probably later Morgan Island. MRC map 20; MRR map 56.

[Clark][1]

July 16 1804 Monday   Set out verry early and proceeded on the Side of a Prarie   passd the head of the Island opsd. which we Camped last night, (1) passed a Small willow Island off the L. point, hills make near the river   (2) passed a large Island nearest the L. S. below the pt. a Small willow Isd.   also one on the Side.   this large Island is called *fair Sun*[2] the wind favourable from the South. Boat run ⟨a Sho⟩ on a Sawyer, (4) pass a place on the L. S. where the hill abt. 20 acres has Sliped into the river lately   Just above passed under a clift of Sand Stone[3] L. S.   a number of Burds Nests in the holes & crevises of this rock which Continus 2 miles,[4] (5) passed a willow Island in a Deep bend to the S. S.   river 2 mile wide at this place, not[e] Deed [dead?] Snags across, passed the Lower point of a Island called Isle *Chauvin* Situated on the L. Point opposit an extensive Prarie on the S. S., This prarie I call *Ball pated*[5] Prarie from the range ball [bald] hills, at from 3 to 6 miles from the river as far as my Sight will extend, we camped in a point of woods opsd. the Isd. on S. S. in a bend.[6]

Course Distance & reffurrences July 16th 1804.

1	N. 70° W	½	me. to a point on the Left of the Island, opsd. to which we Camped last N[ight]
2.	N 35° W	1 ½	ms. to a Bend to the L. S. in a prarie opsd. the head of the Island
3.	N 30 E	1	Ms. to the lower point of a willow Isld. opps L. Pt (1)
4	N. 40 W	¼	me. up the Sd. Willow Island— The high lands near the river L. S.
5.	N 30 W.	2	Ms. to a pt. Sd. of Sm. Isd—on S. S. psd. a pt. on the L. S at ¾ psd. the Small Isd.—
7.	N 35 W	½	me. to a L. S. of a Small Willow Island, in the pt. of the large Isd. psd. a Small Willow Isd. (3)[7]
6.	N 15 E	1 ½	me. to the lower pt. of a Isd. Called *Good Sun* psd. a Small Isd. at the Lowr Point (2)
8.	N 15° W	¾	to a pt. of on the ⟨Sd. Small Island⟩ L. S., high lands ¾ of a me. on L. S. land open
9.	N. 38 W.	¾	To a pt. ⟨of the Isd.⟩ on the left side of the Isd. psd. over a Sml. Sd. Isd. on L. S.

10. N. 54 W.	¾	To Lower pt. of a Sml. Will. Isld. on the Side of the large Isd.
11. N. 38 W	¾	To a pt on L. S. [*one word illegible*] is the Sand Island took altd. of ☉ L. L. *40° 20′ 12″ N.*
N. 52 W	½	To a pt. of the Island high land below or near the riv
13. N. 50° W	1 ¼	miles To a pt. on L. S. above the head of the Island high land at this point— (4)
N. 58° W.	2	Miles To a pt. on the S. S. North on the S. Point ¼ me. Wind from S. purpn. [*one word illegible*] ⁸ Clift of Sand Stone on L. S
15 N 40° E	6 / 20	miles to a upr Pt. of wood on the bend on the Stbd. ⟨L.⟩ Side ⟨opsd.⟩ Some high Ball hills at about 4 miles from the river on the S. S. passd. a Sand bar, from the S. Sd. (5) a willow Island in S. bend, 4 Praries on L. Side & camped in upper point of wood, in a prow. river fall 3 Inches ⁹

[Clark]   *July 16th Monday* 1804

Set out this morning verry early and proceeded on under a gentle breeze from the S   passed the upper point of the Island an extensive Prarie on the L. S.   passed a large (1) Island Called Fair Sun Isd. a Small willow Isld. at the lower point on the L. S.   the boat passd on the L. S. of those Islands   Several Small Sand Islands in the Channel, the Boat run on the point of a Snag, (2) passed a place above the Island L. S. where about 20 acres of the hill has latterly Sliped into the river above a clift of Sand Stone for about two miles, the resort of burds of Different Kinds to reare their young. (5) Passed a willow Island in a Deep Bend to the S. S. opposit the river is about two miles wide, and not verry Deep as the Snag may be Seen across, Scattering, passed the Lower point of an Island called by F[rench] ⟨Chauvin's⟩ [*NB: Chauve Island*] ¹⁰ Situated off the L. Point opposit an extensive Prarie on the S. S. This Prarie I call *Ball pated Prarie*, from a range of Ball Hills parrelel to the river & at from 3 to 6 miles distant from it, and extends as far up & Down as I Can See, we Camped in a point of woods on the L. S. above the Lower point of the Island.   river falling.

Course Distance & refr. July 16th

N. 70° W.	½	a Me. to a pt. on the left of the Isd. opposd.
N. 35 W.	1 ½	ms. to a bend L. S. in Prarie opsd. hd. of Isd.
N 30° E	1	me. to to the Lowr. pt. of wil: Isd off L pt. (1)
N. 40° W	¼	me. to pt. ⟨Island psd. pt. L. S. Sm Isd.⟩
N. 30° W.	2	me. to a pt. S. of a Sm: Isd on S. S. psd. pt. L. S.
N. 15° E	1 ½	me. to pt. of Good Sun Isd. psd. w Isd. (2)
N 35° W.	½	me. to L. S. Sm: W: Isd. psd. a Sm. W: Isd. (3)
N 15° W	¾	me. on L. S. High Land Mn Shore
N. 38° W.	¾	me. to pt. Left of Isd. psd. Sm W: Isd. L. S.
N. 54° W	¾	me. to pt. of Sm: W: Isd. on the Sd. of the Isd.
N. 38° W.	¾	me. to pt. L. S. took Mdn. altd. Latd 40° 20′ 12″.
N. 52° W	½	me. to pt. of the Isd. opsd. High Land.
N. 50° W.	1 ¼	ms. to pt. on L. S. above hd. of Isd. (4)
N. 58° W.	2	ms. to pt. on S. S. psd. Sand Stone Clifts
North	¼	me. on the S. point
N 40° E	6	ms. to the upr. pt. of a wood in the bend to the S. S. above
	20 ¼	the Lowr. Point of a Isld. L. S. a prarie above & Som ball Hills at abt. 4 ms. (I calld Ball Hill Prarie)

[Lewis][11]

Monday 16th   we set out at an early hour; the morning was cloudy; could find no convenient situation for observation; proceeded untill a little before noon when we came too—

(*Point of observation No. 21.*)

On the Lard. Shore opposite to the center of good Island where I observed the meridian altitude of ☉'s L. L. with Octant by the back observation, wich gave me the Latitude—   40° 20′ 12″ N.

I now set the Chronometer as near noon as this observation would enable me, and proceeded untill evening, when we came too on the Stard. shore opposite the *lower point* of the *Island of the Bald prarie* where we encamped.

1. Biddle's notation at the head of this sheet of the Field Notes (document 32) reads "July 16 to 19."

2. Named for a St. Louis fur trader who once wintered there, Eugene Pouree *dit* Beausoleil, from whom it became Beausoleil (fair, or good, sun) Island. It was later Sun Island, and perhaps Sonora Island, a few miles upstream from present Brownville, Nemaha County, Nebraska. The island has apparently disappeared. McDermott (WCS), 141; MRC map 20; MRR maps 57, 58.

3. Rocks exposed along this reach of the Missouri River are mapped as basal Permian Admire Group, the lowermost unit of which is the cliff forming Indian Cave sandstone. Burchett et al.; Condra & Reed.

4. One naturalist has supposed the birds to be bank swallows, *Riparia riparia* [AOU, 616]. Swenk, 122.

5. "Chauvin" was Bald Island in the middle of the nineteenth century, later probably splitting into McKissock and Hogthief islands. See McDermott (WCS), 149–50, on possible French name. Bald-pated prairie lies on the Missouri-Iowa state line, and much of it is probably within present Waubonsie State Park, Fremont County, Iowa, appearing much as it did in 1804. The term bald-pated refers to the open prairies that exist on the steep loess bluffs that parallel the Missouri river above this point. Those are also referred to as the loess hills and have a unique, drought-tolerant prairie vegetation that occupies the steep southwest facing slopes that intercept the dry prevailing northwest winds for much of the year. Prior, Halberg, & Bettis; Warren map 2; MRC map 21; MRR maps 58, 58-L, 59, 59-L.

6. In this area the Missouri has shifted considerably to the west since 1804. A large portion of Nemaha County, Nebraska, is now on the east side of the Missouri River, and the camp may have lain within that loop, in what is now called the McKissock Island area. More likely, it would have been in Atchison County, Missouri, a few miles northeast of Peru, Nebraska. MRC map 21; MRR map 58. Some words crossed out at the end of this sentence may be "pardon a moi," in Clark's hand.

7. Note that this course and the next were apparently transposed, which is probably why Clark numbered them. He corrected the error in his notebook journal Codex A.

8. This word could be interpreted as "Delr." or "Dilr.," which could be associated with the previous word for an abbreviation for "perpendicular."

9. The following courses, immediately under the regular course column, were both circled and crossed out: N. 40 E, N. 28 W, N. 25 W.

10. Biddle apparently crossed out Clark's word and substituted his own.

11. Lewis's observation from Codex O.

[Clark]

July 17th Tuesday, we concluded to ⟨Stay⟩ lay by to day to fix the Longitude, and get the Cronometer right, (She run down Day before yesterday), Several men out hunting to day Capt. Lewis rode out to *Neesh-nahba-to na* Creek[1] which passes thro. the Prarie (on which there is Some few

trees) within [*blank*] Mile of the Missoureis, wind from the S E.   Several
of the party have tumers of different Kinds Some of which is verry troublesom and dificuilty to cure. I took a meridian *altitude* (43° 27°) which made
the Lattitude of this place 40° 27′ 6″ ⁴/₁₀ North.— (The Ball Hills ⟨run⟩)
bear N 25° W for 30 mes. The bend on L. S. passing the Isd. on the right
Side is N. 28° W. 4 ms.) Took equal altitudes

Took Suns Azmuth Comps Sextnt. & time
obsd. ☽ moon an Spica ★ Star West

Time			Distance		
H					
8	53	11	41°	50	00
″	59	0	41	53	15
9	2	58	41	54	0
″	5	49	41	55	0
″	8	2	41	56	0
″	15	24	41	57	0
″	21	10	41	58	0
″	25	18	42	0	0

		h	m	s
Took equal atitudes	1st	5	53	10

altitude		28° 51′ 45″
Azmuth		N 85° W

		H	m	″
Time	2d	5	59	20
altitude		26	35	30
Comps. azh			N. 84° W.	

h	m						
7	50	8	⎫	4	4	38	⎫
″	15	28	⎬ A M	″	6	3	⎬ P M
″	52	55	⎭	″	7	24	⎭

Altd. 69° 36″ 00″

Tried a part of the comn pt. [common point?] of the Current in 40 Seconds   the water run 50 fathem   30″ & 20″ in places

Cap Lewers returned, Saw Some hand Som Countrey, the Creek near
the high land is rapid and nearly as muddy as the river, & rising   Gutrich

[Goodrich] caught two verry fat Cat fish   G Drewyer Kill'ed 3 Deer, & R Fields one, a puff of wind brought Swarms of Misquitors, which disapeared in two hours, blown off by a Continuation of the Same brees.

[Clark]

Bald Pated Prarie   July 17th, Tuesday 1804   We Concluded lay by at this place to day to fix the Lattitude & Longitude of this place to Correct the cromometer run down Sunday)   Several men out by day light hunting Capt. Lewis Concld. to ride out to *Neesh-nah-ba-to-na* Creek which passes under the ball hills near this place and at one place a little above this Camp is within 300 ⟨miles⟩ yards of the Missouris   on this Creek grows Some few trees of oake walnut & mulberry. I took Meridian altitude of ☉ L. L. (43° 27′) which made the Lattitude 40° 27′ 5″ ⁴/₁₀ North—   wind from the South E.   Several of the party much aflicted with *tumers* of different Kinds, Som of which is verry troublesom and dificuelt to cure. Capt. Louis returned in the evening.   he Saw Som hand Some Countrey & Says that the aforesaid Creek is rapid muddey and running—   [NB: *running*]   This Creek which is at 10 or 12 [NB: *where he saw it*] from its mouth, within 300 yds of the river [NB: *Missi*] is at least 16 foot Lower than the river—   The high Lands from our Camp in this *Bald Pated* Prarie bears N 25° W. up the R.

Took equal altitudes

	h	m	s			h	m	s
A M	7	50	8	P M		4	4	38
″		15	28	″			6	3
″		52	55	″			72	4

Altitude   69° 36′ 00″
Took Suns Azmath with Comps & Sextent & Time

			1st Sets altid:			Time		
Comps.			h	m	s	h	m	s
N.	85°	W.	28°	51′	45″	5	53	10
				2d Set				
N.	84°	W.	26°	35′	30″	5	59	20

Observed the moon ☽ & Spica ★ Star West
Made

Time			distance		
8	53	11	41°	50′	00″
″	59	0	″	53	15.
9	25	8	″	54	0
″	5	49	″	55	″
″	8	2	″	56	″
″	15	24	″	57	
″	21	10	″	58	″
″	25	28	42	0	0

The Common Current taken with a Log runs 50 fathen in 40″— Some places much Swifter in 30″ and even 20 Seconds of time— five Deer killed to day

(Point of Observation No. 22 & of departure No. 2.)

Camp at the lower point of the Island of the bald Prarie

[Lewis]   *Tuesday July 17th*[2]

Observed Equal Altitudes of the ☉ with Sextant.

	h	m	s		h	m	s
A. M.	7	50	8	P. M.	4	4	38
	″	51	28		″	6	3
	″	52	55		″	7	24

Altd. by Sextant at the time of observtn.   69° 36° —°

Observed Meridian Alt. of ☉'s L. L. with Octant by back observation   43° 27′ —″

Latitude deduced from this observtn.   40° 27′ 6.4″

From Equal Altitudes of ☉'s center found that ☉'s Center was truly on the Meridian

	h	m	s
M. T. P. M. Chronometer at	11	58	51

		m	s
Chronometer too slow M. T.	6	51.6	
☉'s Magnetic azimuth by Cirumfertr.		N. 85° W.	

	h	m	s
Time by Chronometer P. M.	5	53	10
Altd. of ☉'s L. L. by Sextant	28°	51′	45″

		h	m	s
Time by Chronometer P. M.		5	59	20
Altd. by Sextant of ☉'s L. L.		26°	35′	30″

Observed time and distance of ☉ and Spica ♍ ★ West.

		Time				*Distance*		
		h	m	s				
P. M.	8	53	11		41°	51°	—″	
	″	59	—		″	53	15	
	9	2	58		″	54	—	
	″	5	49		″	55	—	
	″	8	2		″	56	—	
	″	15	24		″	57	45	
	″	21	10		″	58	30	
	″	25	18		″	42	—	

Observed Altitude of pole Star with Sextant   81°   9′   15″

		h	m	s
Time by Chronometer P. M.		10	23	18

1. The Nishnabotna River now enters the Missouri in this vicinity, roughly opposite Peru, Nebraska, following part of the 1804 bed of the Missouri; then, as Clark notes, it ran parallel to the larger stream in western Atchison County, Missouri, mouthing near the Atchison-Holt county line. MRC maps 20, 21; MRR map 58.

2. Lewis's observation from Codex O.

[Clark][1]

altd. North Star[2]
Time   10 23 m 18   81° 9′ 15″ July 17
Cronometer too Slow 6 Mts   51 s ⁶/₁₀ to Day

July 18th Wednesday   a fair morning   the river falling fast, Set out at Sunrise under a gentle Breeze from S. E by S.   at 3 miles passed the head of the Island on L. S. called by the French Chauve or bald pate (1) opsd. the middle of this Island the Creek on L. S. is within 300 yds. of the river.   back of this Island the lower point of (2) another Island in the bend to the L. S.   passed large Sand bar making out from each point with many channels passing through them, "Current runs 50 fathm. in 41 Seconds" but little timber on either Side of the river, except the Isds. &

points which are low wet & Covered with lofty trees, Cotton wood Mulberry Elm &c. &c. passed the head of a long Island in high water at this time no water passes thro: the Channel (3) opposit the Lower point of a Island on the L. S. pass the Island and opsd. the point (4) above & on the L. S. the hills come to the river, This Hill has Sliped into the river for about ¾ of a mile, and leaves a Bluff of considerable hight back of it this Hill is about 200 foot high compsd. of Sand Stone inter mingled with Iron ore of an inferior quallity on a bed of Soft Slate Stone.[3]

Course Distance & Rifferes July 18th, 1804

N. 28° W.	3 ¾	ms. to Curve in the bend to the L. S. passing Bend of the Island on L. S. Several Sand bars on Left the Creek Nea[r] (1)
S 28° W.	3 ¾	ms. to a pt. on the S. S psd. the head of the Island on the L. S. one behind this (2)
S 32° W.	½	me. on S. pt. passed a Sand bar, a long Island on the L. S. in high water
S 88 W.	¼	me. on Do. a Sand bar to the left wind from the S. W. hard
N 55 W.	¼	me. on do do do do—
N. 48 W.	2 ½	ms. to a pt. on L. S. psd. a Sand bar L. S.
N. 64 W.	2 ½	ms. to a pt. on S. S. passed the ⟨head⟩ Place where water runs out to form the Isd of the Island (2) and lower pt. of a Isd. S. S. (3)
N 50 W	3	Ms. to a pt. on S. S. opsd. a red bank on L. S. Iron ore (4)
N. 8° E	1 ½	ms. to a pt on L. S. opsd a Small Island in the middle of the river Camped (5)
	18	

We passed a verry bad Sand bar (4) a little above the hill and incmpd [*hole*] on the L. S. opposit a Small Island in the river,[4] Saw a Dog this evening appeared to be nearly Starved to death, he must have been left by Some party of Hunters we gave him Some meet, he would not come near, G Drewrer brought in 2 Deer this evening

[Clark]   *July 18th Wednesday 1804*

a fair morning the river falling fast Set out this morning at Sun rise under a Gentle Breeze from the *S. E. by S.* passing over the Prarie, at about 3 Miles we passed the head of the Island L. S. Called by the French *Chaube* or *Bald pate* opposit the middle of (1) This Island the Creek on the S. S. is nearest the river, In high water an Island is formed in the bind above the last (2)— Measured the Current and found that in forty one Seconds it run 50 fathoms but little timber is to be Seen except in the Low points on Islands & on Creeks, the Groth of timber is generally cotton Mulberry Elm Sycomore &c &c. passed a Island on the 2d point to the S. S. opposite the water (3) whin high passes out in the Plain oppsid this Island on the L. S. the hills jut to the river (4) this Hill has Sliped from the top which forms a Bluff above & 200 foot above the water, about ¾ of a mile in length & about 200 feet in Depth has Sliped into the river it is Composed of Sand Stone intermixed with an indiffert. Iron ore near the bottom or next to the water is a Soft Slate Stone, Som pebble is also intermixt, we passed a verry bad Sand bar and incamped on the L. S. at the lower point of the oven Islands & opposit the Prarie Calld. ⟨by the french Four le Tourtue⟩ [*NB: Baker's oven*][5] Saw a Dog nearly Starved on the bank, gave him Som meet, he would not follow, our hunters killed 2 Deer to day

Course distance & reffers. July 18th

N. 28° W	3 ¾	ms. to a Curve in the bank passed a bend of the Isd. & Several Sand bars (1)
S. 28° W	3 ¾	ms. to pt. on S. S. psd. the head of the Isd. on L. S. one back in bend (2)
S. 32° W	½	me. on S. pt. psd. a Sand bar
S. 88° W	¼	me. on S. S. wind S. W.
N 55° W	¼	me. on S. S.
N. 48° W	2 ½	mes. to a pt. on L. S. psd. a Sand bar L. S.
N 64° W	2 ½	ms. to a pt. on S. S. low banks on L. S. (2) an Isd. S. S. (3)
N 50° W	3	ms. to a pt. on S. S. opsd. a red bank on L. S. Some Iron (4)
N. 8° E	1 ½	mes. to pt. on L. S. opsd. a Small Isld. in the river on above (5)
	18	

The Cremimoter too Slow *6* minits *51* seconds & ⁶⁄10

altitude of the north Star ★ last night at

h	m	S		d	′	″
10	23	18	*was*	81	9	15

1. Under this and the following entry in the Field Notes are the following, in Lewis's hand, indicating the sheet's use as an envelope during the winter at River Dubois: Capt. William Clark   River Dubois   pr. Sergt. Floyd   Note—   send your letter down if possible by Monday evening—. There are also some calculations:

85	:	33		[*illegible*]	11½ = 12
9		25			
76		8		12	

12
20
35
2 | 79
38
29   due
as party to
[*words unclear*]

55   due
3   dollars
20   for Clo:
75

[29?] Pay
32   Clo:
61

2. This line and the following two could go with the July 17 entry. Clark chose to place it with July 18 in his Codex A entry, and I have followed his order.

3. Rocks along the bluffs of the Missouri River near Nebraska City have been mapped as Pennsylvanian Wabaunsee Group. The lower part of the Otoe shale is a red shale, which has stained the very thin limestone beneath it and may have been mistaken for "Iron ore of an inferior quallity." A sandstone bed overlies the Otoe, and it is underlain by a bluish gray shale. Condra & Reed.

4. Probably in present Otoe County, Nebraska, a little below Nebraska City and above the Missouri-Iowa boundary on the opposite shore. MRC map 21; MRR map 59.

5. Nicollet shows Lower and Upper Oven islands; opposite the former, on the bluffs in Fremont County, Iowa, he indicates a feature labeled "Terrien's Oven." Apparently the name persisted for some years after 1804, but it does not appear on MRC map 21 of the

1890s or on later maps. The actual location is in the vicinity of present Nebraska City, Otoe County, Nebraska. Coues (HLC), 1 : 48–49 n. 110; Nicollet (MMR), 382–83; MRR map 59. Biddle apparently crossed out "by the french Four le Tourtue" and substituted "Baker's oven."

[Clark]

of no consequence 3 [1] July 19th   afte[r] breakfast which was on a rosted Ribs of a Deer a little and a little Coffee I walked on Shore intending only to Keep up with the Boat, Soon after I got on Shore, Saw Some fresh elk Sign, which I was induced to prosue those animals by their track to the hills   after assending and passing thro a narrow Strip of wood Land, Came Suddenly into an open and bound less Prarie, I Say bound less because I could not See the extent of the plain in any Derection, the timber appeared to be confined to the River Creeks & Small branches, this Prarie was Covered with grass about 18 Inches or 2 feat high and contained little of any thing else, except as before mentioned on the River Creeks &c, This prospect was So Sudden & entertaining that I forgot the object of my prosute and turned my attention to the Variety which presented themselves to my view   after continueing on this rise for Some minits, I deturmined to make my course to a line of woods to S: E.   I found in this wood a butifull Streem of running water, in prosuing it down Several others Joined it and at 3 miles fell into the river between 2 clifts,[2] I went up & under one clift of dark rich Clay for ½ me.   above this a Clay bank which had Sliped in   her[e] I found Sand Stone Containing Iron ore, this ore appears to be inbeded under the Clay just above the water[3]

[Clark][4]

Course Distance & reffers.

North	¼	me. to the Lower pt. of a Isd on L. S. called Bakers oven (1)
N 10° W	1 ¼	ms. to a pt on the L. S. bad Sand bars psd. the 2 Isds. (1)
N 45° W	1	me. on the L. Side Sand bar on S. S.
N. 85° W	2	me. S. S. opsd. high land (2)— a Sand bar on the S. Side in a bend
N 82 W.	¾	Me. to the mouth of a Creek in a bend on L. side Above a Clift

N. 13 W	2 ½	me. to Pt. L. S. psd. a Sliped in bank (3) a Isd. on the S. S. a run L. S.
N. 54° W	3 10 ¾	ms. to pt. on S. S. opsd. Some Clifts, passed a willow Isld. in midl. a Deep bend to the L. S. a large Sand bar on L. S. (4)

July 19th Thursday 1804

Set out early   pass between 2 Islands one in mid: & the other L. S. opsd. wher Prarie aproaches the river S. S. This place is called the Bakers oven or in french Four le Tour tere   passd. Some high lands 4 ½ ms. above the Isds. on the L. S. forming a Clift to the river of yellow earth, on the top a Prarie, passd. many a bad Sand bar in this distance, & the river wide & Shallow, above this Clift 2 Small butiffull runs Come from the Plains & fall into the river, a Deer lick on the first, above those two Creeks, I found in my walk on Shore Some ore in a bank which had Sliped in to the river ¾ me. above the Creeks, I took a cerequite around & found that those two runs mentioned contained a good proposion of wood Surrounded by a plain, with grass about 18 Inchs. high, [(]Capt Lewis walked on Shore after Dinner)   in the first bind to the right above those Runs passed a Small Island opsd. is a Sand bar   I call this Island Butter Island, as at this place we mad use of the last of our butter, as we approach this Great River *Platt* the Sand bars are much more noumerous than they were, and the quick & roleing Sands much more danjerous, where the Praries aproach the river it is verry wide, the banks of those Plains being much easier to undermine and fall than the wood land   passed (4) a willow Island Situated near the middle of the river, a Sand bar on the S. S. and a Deep bend to the L S.   camped on the right Side of the Willow Island—[5]   W. Bratten hunting on the L. S Swam to the Island. Hunters Drewyer killed 2 Deer, Saw great numbers of young gees. The river Still falling a little   Sand bars thick   always in view.

[Clark]   *July 19th, Thursday 1804*

Set out early   passed between two Small Islands, one in the middle of the river, the other Close on the L S. opposit a prarie S. S. Called (1) by the french *Four le tourtre*,[6] The Bakers oven Islands, passed (2) Some high Clift 4 ½ miles above the Islands on the L. S. ⟨forming⟩ of yellow earth   passed Several ⟨bad⟩ Sand bars that were wide and at one place verry Shallow (two Small butifull runs falls into the river near each other at this Clift, a Deer Lick 200 yards up the Lowest of those runs[)][7]   Those runs head at no great distance in the plains and pass thro: [*NB: Skirts*] of timber to the river. In my walk on Shore I found Some ore in the bank above those runs which I take to be Iron ore (3)   at this place the Side of the hill has Sliped about half way into the river for ¾ of a Mile forming a Clift from the top of the hill above. In the first bend to the right passed a Small Island a Sand bar opposit,—   worthey of remark as we approach this great River Plate the Sand bars much more numerous and the quick or moveing Sands much worst than they were below   at the places where Praries approach the river it is verry wide those places being much easier to wash & under Mine than the wood Land's.   (4) passed a Willow Isd. Situated near the Middle of the river and a large Sand makeing out from the S. S.   a Deep bend to the L S.   we Camped at the head of this Island on the Starboard Side of it, Hunters Killed Two Deer. Saw great numbers of young Gees   River falling a little.

Course Distance & refrs. July 19th

North	¼	of a me. to Lowr. pt. of a Isd. L. S. (1)
N 10° W	1 ¼	ms. to pt. on L. S. Sand bar psd. Isd. (1)
N. 45° W	1	me. on the L. S. a Sand bar on S. S.
N. 85° W.	2	ms. to pt. on S. S. opsd. High land (2)
N. 82° W.	¾	me. to the Mo: of a run in bend L. S. (3)
N 13° W.	2 ½	ms. to pt. L. S. psd. Sliped bank (3) a Island on S. S. a run L. S.
N. 54° W.	3	ms. to a pt. on S. S. opsd. Some Clifts passd.
	10 ¾	a Will. Isd. in midl. a Deep bend on the L. S. a Sand bar S. S. (4)

(*Point of observation No. 23.*)

[Lewis]   *Thursday July 19th*[8]

Under a bold Bluff on Lard. shore, opposite to the Stard. point terminateing the 4th course of this day.—

Observed Meridian Altd. of ☉'s L. L. with Octant by back observation   44° 15' —

Latitude deduced from this obsert.   40° 29′ 50″

1. These words occur immediately in front of the date in the Field Notes (document 32). There is no apparent connection to the July 18 entry above or to anything else. Since there is a second, separate Field Notes entry for this date, Clark may have intended to indicate that there was nothing important in this first one. There is a course overwritten to one side of this entry: N 54° W.

2. In his Codex A entry and the second Field Notes entry, below, Clark indicates that there were two creeks. They are probably North Table Creek and South Table Creek, which reach the Missouri River at Nebraska City, Otoe County, Nebraska. MRC map 21; MRR maps 59, 60.

3. See July 18, 1804, n. 3.

4. This is a second entry for July 19, or a continuation of the first, on a separate sheet (document 33) of the Field Notes. Biddle's notation at the top of this sheet reads, "July 19 to 21." Clark divided the text around the course material. Here the text is brought together for ease of reading.

5. Probably in Fremont County, Iowa, two to three miles upstream and opposite present Nebraska City. MRC map 21; MRR map 60.

6. Biddle apparently placed brackets around the phrase "by the french Four le tourtre" and then crossed it out, all in red ink.

7. South Table Creek.

8. Lewis's observation from Codex O.

[Clark][1]

July 20th Friday 1804, a fog this morning and verry Cool   George Drewyer Sick   proceed on over a Sand bar, Bratten Swam the river to get his gun & Clothes left last night   psd a large willow Isd. on the L. S.   (1) passed the mouth of *l'Eau que pleure* the English of which is *the water which Cry's*[2]   this Creek is about 20 yards wide   falls into the river above a Clift of brown Clay[3] L. S. opposit a willow Island, at this Creek I went on Shore[4] took R Fields with me and went up this Creek Several miles & crossed thro: the plains to the river above with the view of finding Elk, we walked all day through those praries without Seeing any, I killed an emence large yellow Wolf—[5]   The Countrey throu which we walked after leaveing the Creek was good land covered with Grass interspersed with Groves & Scattering timber near and about the heads of Branches

Course Distance & Reffrs. July 20th 1804

N. 18° E   3   me to a Pt. L. S.   psd. a Willow Island on S. S.   a Creek
                        on L S.—(1)

⟨N. 48 W.	2 ½	m. to pt. Lard. oposite to a deep bend and prarie *on the Stard. oposite this* pt. to the right of it is the upper point of a small Is. with a large sand bar below it the Is. is sepe-rated by a narrow chal. from L. S.⟩[6]
N. 48 E.	2 ½	m. to a pt. on Std. side of an Island. oposite the upper pt. of a 2nd. Island which is devided from it by a narrow Channel— a deep bend to Sd. side of this small Is-land—
N. 5 W	3	m. to Lard point of an Isd.
Due N.	6	m, to the point of an Isld. on Lard. side of the same.
N. 18 W	<u>3 ½</u> 18⟨½⟩	ms. to a Point on the L. S. high land psd. the hd. of Isld. a large Sand bar on the L. S. on Which there was two Swans Capt Lewis tried to kill[7]
⟨N. 22 W.	3	ms. to a pt L. S. opsd. a pt. of high Land psd. Pigeon C. S. S.
N. 28° W		ms. to a pt Starboard S passed. [*blank*] & over a Willow pt. on the L. S. and a pt. of high land L S (1) [*Several words illegible*]⟩

one of them without Suckcess, Camped above the bar on the L. S.[8]   a verry agreeable Breeze all night   Serjt. Pryor & Jo: Fields brought in two Deer   river Still falling.   a large Spring ¾ me. below camp[9]

[Clark]   *July 20th, Friday* 1804

a cool morning   passed a large willow Island (1) on the S. S. and the mouth of Creek about 25 yds. wide on the L. S. Called by the french l'*Eue-que pleure* [*NB: L'Eau qui pleure*],[10] or the the *Water Which Cry's* [*NB: Weeping water*]   this Creek falls into the river above a Clift of brown Clay opposit the Willow Island, I went out above the mouth of this Creek and walked the greater part of the day thro: Plains interspesed with Small Groves of Timber on the branches and Some Scattering trees about the heads of the runs, I Killed a Verry large yellow wolf, The Soil of Those Praries appears rich but much Parched with the frequent fires—[11]   after I returned to the Boat we proceeded around a large Sand bar makeing out from the L. S. opsd. a fountain of water comeing out of a hill L. S. and affording water Suffient to turn a mill

The Praries as far as I was out appeared to be well watered, with Small

Streems of running water   Serjt. Pryor & Jo: Fields brought in two Deer
this evening— a verry Pleasent Breeze from the N. W. all night— river
falling a little, It is wothey of observation to mention that our party has
been much healthier on the ⟨Trip⟩ Voyage than parties of the Same Number is in any other Situation   Tumers have been troublesom to them all

Course Distance & refrs. July 20th

N 18° E	3	ms. to a pt. on L. S. psd. a wil: Isd. on S. S. a Creek on L. S. (1)
N. 48° E	2 ½	ms. to a pt. on S. S. of an Isld. opsd. the upr. pt. on 2d Isd. which is divided from it by a narrow Chanl. a Deep bend to S. S.
N. 5° W	3	ms. to a Lbd. pt. of an Island
North	6	ms. to the pt. of an Isd. on L. S. of Sam[e]
N. 18° W	3 ½	ms. to a pt. on L. S. high Land psd. the head of an Isd. above is a large Sand bar on L. S. (2)
	18	

From this evenings incampment a man may walk to the ⟨Pane⟩ [*NB:
Pawnee*] Village on the S ⟨East⟩ bank of the Platt River in two days, and to
the *Otteaus* in one day [12]   all those Indians are Situated on the South bank
of the Plate River, as those Indians are now out in the praries following &
Hunting the buffalow, I fear we will not See them.

1. The July 20 entry and courses and distances are on one sheet (document 33) of
the Field Notes, but they are in disordered fragments. Here they have been arranged
closer to what was evidently the intended sequence. Under the July 20 entry is the following address in an unknown hand: "Jeffersonville   May 4th   1804   25   Captain William
Clark   Kahokia or Mail some-where on the Missoria's   Captain W C."

2. Weeping Water Creek, in Otoe County, Nebraska. Apparently the original Omaha
and Oto name was more nearly "murmuring water." Stewart (APN), 528; MRC maps 21,
22; MRR map 60.

3. Outcrops here have been mapped as the lower part of Pennsylvanian Wabaunsee
Group. Burchett et al.

4. The remainder of this portion of the entry was written above the first part, with
asterisks used to connect them.

5. The gray wolf, probably *Canis lupus nubilus*, perhaps a Lewis and Clark discovery
and now extinct; a yellow color is noted by Jones, 215. Burroughs, 84–88; Cutright
(LCPN), 87, 440.

6. This crossed-out course and the following three, not crossed out, are in Lewis's
hand.

7. This sentence continues below the crossed-out courses, "N. 22 W. 3" and "No 28° W," which are for the next day, with the words "one of them." Pigeon Creek, not mentioned on July 21, was probably later Wabonsie Creek, Fremont County, Iowa. MRR map 61.

8. If the river has not shifted significantly, this camp would be in Cass County, Nebraska, a little above Spring Creek. On the opposite shore is Fremont County, Iowa. MRC map 22; MRR map 61.

9. Probably the source of Spring Creek in Cass County, Nebraska. MRR map 61.

10. Biddle apparently crossed out "l'*Eue-que pleure*" in red ink.

11. The frequency and occasionally the magnitude of prairie fires was noted by the Corps of Discovery as they entered the Great Plains. The fires were ecologically important wherever grass growth was abundant to prevent secondary growth. They were set by lightning or accidentally by humans, or often Indians set fires purposely for signaling or for improving grazing. The party noted those different types of fires and understood their purposes. See entries at August 17 and 25, September 16, 1804, and particularly March 6, 1805. Pyne; White, 184–86, 374–75 n. 17; Moore.

12. The Pawnee village appears to be the Linwood site, occupied by the Chawis (Grand Pawnees) at this time. It is on the east bank of Skull Creek, about three miles south of the Platte River near the modern town of Linwood, Butler County, Nebraska. The identification of the Oto village is less sure but it may be the Yutan site, about two miles east of Yutan, Saunders County, Nebraska. Wedel (PA), 29–31; Grange, 19.

[Lewis]   [*July 21, 1804*][1]

by a boiling motion or ebolition of it's [the Platte's] waters occasioned no doubt by the roling and irregular motion of the sand of which its bed is entirely composed.   the particles of this sand ⟨is driven in large bodies⟩ being remarkably small and light it is easily boied up ⟨and by the water⟩ and is hurried ⟨in large⟩ by this impetuous ⟨current in⟩ torrent ⟨sometimes⟩ in large masses from place to place in with irristable forse, collecting and forming sandbars in the course of a few hours which as suddenly disapated to form others and give place perhaps to the deepest channel of the river.   where it [the Platte] enters the Missouri it's superior force ⟨drives the⟩ changes and directs the courant of that river against it's northern bank where it is compressed within a channel less than one third of the width it had just before occupyed.   it dose not furnish the missouri with it's colouring matter as has been asserted by some, but it throws into it immence quantities of sand and gives a celerity to it's courant of which it abates but little untill it's junction with the Mississippy.   the water of this river is turbid at all seasons of the year but is by no means as much so as that of the Missourie.   The sediment it deposits, consists of very fine particles of white sand while that of the Missoury is composed principally of a dark rich loam—in much greater quantity[2]

21st July ⟨we made some many experiments to determin the velocity of the courant of the Missour in different parts⟩ from the experiments and observations we were enabled to make with rispect to the comparative velocities of the courants of the rivers Mississippi Missouri and Plat it results that a vessel will float in the Mississippi ⟨about⟩ below the entrance of the Missouri at the rate of four miles an hour.   in the Missouri from it's junction with the Mississsippi to the entrance of the Osage river from 5½ to 6   from thence to the mouth of the Kanzas from 6½ to 7.   from thence to the Platte 5½ while the Plat is at least 8.—   The Missouri above the junction of the river plat is equal to about 3½ miles an hour as far as the mouth of the Chyenne[3] where its courant still abates ⟨to about 3 miles an hour⟩ and becomes equal to about three miles an hour   from information it dose not increase it's volocity for [*sentence incomplete*]

[Clark][4]

July 21st Satturday, Set out verry early and a Gentle Breeze from the S. E   proceeded on very well, passed a (1) Willow Island L. S. opsd. a bad Sand bar   passed Some high land covered with Timber, in this Hill is Semented rock & Limestone[5]   the water runs out and forms Several little Islands in (2) high water on the S. S.   a large Sand bar on the S. S. above and opposit the wooded High Land, at about 7 oClock the wind Seased and it Commenced raining   passed many Sand bars opposit or in the Mouth of the Great River Plate[6]   this river which is much more rapid than the Missourie ha[s] thrown out imence quantities of Sand forming large Sand Banks at its mouth and forced the Missourie Close under the S. S.   the Sands of this river Comes roleing down with the Current which is Crowded with Sand bars and not 5 feet water at any place across its mouth, the Rapidity of the Current of this river which is greater than that of the Missourie, its width at the Mouth across the bars is about ¾ of a mile, higher up I am told by one of the bowmen[7] that he was 2 winters on this river above and that it does not rise ⟨four⟩ 7 feet, but Spreds over 3 miles at Some places, Capt Lewis & my Self went up Some Distance & Crossed   found it Shallow. This river does not rise over 6 or 7 feet

Course Distance & Reffurences July 21st 1804

N. 22° W.	3 ½	ms. to pt. S. S. opposit a point of high land on the L. S.
N. 28° W.	6 ½	ms. to a pt. on S. S. psd a pt of willows a Willow Isd (1) on L. S & a high pt. on the L. S. passed ⟨Sand bar in the river on a Island large on⟩ the L. S. Sm. cr. Small Channel (2)
N. 39° W.	3⟨½⟩	miles to a pt. on S. S. ⟨just Below opposit⟩ the R.
	13⟨½⟩	Plate. psd. a pt. High Land Covd. with wood L. S. a Sand bar near the S. S. a large Sand bar
N. 8° W	2	ms. to a point L. S. the Junction of the Missr. & Platt Rivers a Verry extensive View of the river pass many Sand bars in every direction thrown out by the Plate R which *runs East*
	15	
N. 10° W.[8]	4	The Same Course Continud up the Missourie to a Pt. L S [blank] Miles passed a Sand bar on the S. S. wind N.
	19	

Proceeded on   passed the mouth of Papillion or Butter fly Creek[9] 3 miles on the L. S. a large Sand bar opposit on that Side   Camped above this bar on L. S.[10]   a great number of wolves about us all night   R. Fields killed a Deer   hard wind N. W.   cold

[Clark]   *July 21st, Satturday 1804*

Set out early under a gentle breeze from the S. E.   proceeded on verry well, passed (1) a willow Island on the L. S. opposit a bad Sand bar, Some high lands covered with timber L. S   in this hill is limestone & Seminted rock of Shels &c. (2)[11]   in high water the opposit Side is cut thro: by Several Small Channels, forming Small Islands, a large Sand bar opposit the Hill   at 7 oClock the wind luled and it Commnc'd raining, arrived at the lower Mouth of the Great River *Platt* at 10 oClock (about 3 ms. above the Hill of wood land, the Same range of High land Continus within ¾ of a mile of the mouth below[)]   This Great river being much more rapid than the Missourie forces its current against the opposit Shore, The Current of This river Comes with great Velocity roleing its Sands into the Missouri, filling up its Bend & Compelling it to incroach on the ⟨S⟩ [NB: North] Shore—   we found great dificuelty in passing around the Sand at the mouth of this River   Capt Lewis and My Self with 6 men in a perogue went up this Great river Plate about ⟨2⟩ 1 [NB: one] miles, found

the Current verry rapid roleing over Sands, passing through different
Channels none of them more than five or Six feet deep, about ⟨900⟩ 600
yards Wide at the mouth— I am told by one of our Party who wintered
two winters on This river that "it is much wider above, and does not rise
more than five or Six feet" Spreds verry [*NB?: wide with many Small islands
Scattered thro' it*] and from its rapidity & roleing Sands Cannot be nava-
gated ⟨by⟩ with Boats or Perogues— The Indians pass this river in Skin
Boats which is flat and will not turn over. The Otteaus a Small nation
reside on the South Side 10 Leagues up, the Panies on the Same Side 5
Leagus higher up— about 10 Leagus up this river on the S. Side a Small
river Comes into the Platt Called Salt River,[12] "The waters So brackish
that it Can't be Drank at Some Seasons["] above this river & on the North
Side a Small river falls into the Platt Called *Elk* [*NB: Horn*] *River*[13] This
river runs Parralal withe the Missouri— at 3 miles passed a Small river
on the L. S. Called *Papillion* or Butterfly C: 18 yds. wide a large Sand bar
off the mouth, we proceeded on to get to a good place to Camp and Delay
a fiew days, passed around this Sand bar and Came to for the night on the
L. S. a verry hard wind from the N. W. I went on Shore S. S. and proceeded up one mile thro: high Bottom land open a Great number of
wolves about us this evening

Course Distance & Refrs. July 21st:

N. 22° W.	3 ½	ms. to a pt. S. S. opposit a pt. of High lands on the L. S.
N. 28° W.	6 ½	ms. to a pt. on S. S. psd a naked pt. & wilr. Isl'd (1) on the L. S. & a high pt. on L. S. (2)
N. 39° W.	3	ms. to a pt. on S. S. just below the Platt river passd. a pt. of High Land Covd. with wood L. S. a Sd. bar near the S. S.
N. 8° W	2	ms. to a point in the junction of the Platt & Missouri verry extensive up the Platt West & Missourie North Passed many Sand bars in the Mouth Platt river

15 ms. to Platt

1. This fragment in Lewis's hand is on one side of document 35 of the Field Notes. The
date "21st July" is written in the left margin. It is obviously a draft for his "Summary View
of Rivers and Creeks" which was copied into Codex O. It is unclear whether he wrote it on
July 21 or later at Fort Mandan. The reverse of this sheet carries lunar calculations from

February 23, 1805, made at the fort. The notes invite the question of lost journals by Lewis for this period of the expedition (May 14, 1804 to April 6, 1805) which is discussed in the Introduction to this volume. Osgood (FN), 85 n. 3. Lewis's "Summary" will appear in a later volume; it may be found for comparison in Thwaites (LC), 6:38–40.

2. The sediment of the Platte River is dominated by sand derived in large part from the Rocky Mountains and the sand-rich sediments it passes through in western and central Nebraska. The Missouri, on the other hand, flows through South Dakota along the glacial boundary and between loess bluffs on the Nebraska and Iowa borders. A large part of its sediment load, as a result, is silt and clay from those sources.

3. Presumably the portion about the current above the mouth of the Platte was added after they reached the Cheyenne River in South Dakota on October 1, 1804, unless the whole was written at that time.

4. Biddle's notation at the head of this sheet of the Field Notes (document 34) reads, "July 21 to 22."

5. The basal part of the bluffs along the Missouri River here are the Plattsmouth and Spring Branch limestones of middle Pennsylvanian age (Shawnee Group). Condra & Reed; Wayne.

6. The French name Platte, meaning "flat," is a more or less exact rendering of the Omaha and Oto names *nibtháçka* or *nįbráska*, "flat river," which gave Nebraska its name. It enters the Missouri between Cass and Sarpy counties. Fletcher & La Flesche, 90; Fitzpatrick, 13; MRC map 22; MRR map 63.

7. Either Labiche or Cruzatte; the latter, in particular, seems to have spent considerable time in eastern Nebraska trading with the Indians. Both were half Omaha and were very likely born in the region, sons of French traders. See Appendix A, this volume.

8. This final course material is not found in the Codex A entry.

9. Papillion, or Big Papillion, Creek reaches the Missouri in Sarpy County, within a mile or so north of the mouth of the Platte. MRC map 22; MRR map 63.

10. In Sarpy County, a little above the mouth of Papillion Creek. The river's course was probably farther west in 1804 than in later times, close to where the creek emerges from the bluffs. Nicollet (MMR), 385; MRC map 22; MRR map 63.

11. Probably King Hill, a high bluff and conspicuous point of timbered land in Cass County, about three miles below the mouth of the Platte. The party is now reaching a region where large areas of timbered land are noteworthy. MRR map 62.

12. Modern Salt Creek, which runs northeastward to meet the Platte in Saunders County, Nebraska.

13. The Elkhorn River of northeast Nebraska reaches the Platte in northwest Sarpy County.

[Clark][1]

July 22nd Sunday   Set out verry early with a view of getting Some timbered land & a good Situation to take equil altitudes in time   proceeded on nearly a North 15° W ⟨*Course*⟩ 7 ms. to a pt. S. S. opposit Some high

Lands on L. S. above the upper point of a long willow Island in the middle of the river   6 Deer killed to Day   we deturmined to Stay here 4 or 5 days to take & make obsvts. & refresh our men   also to Send Despatches back to govement—[2]   Wind hard N. W.   Cold

Cours & Distance Above the Platt

N. 15° W.   10   miles to a point on Sarboard Side, where we
                                    Campd to delay a few days—

W Clark[3]

The distance assending the Missourie from the mouth each Day &c &c[4]

miles

21	from the mouth to *St. Charles*
3 ¼	
18	
9	
10	
10	
18	
15 ½	
104 ¾	To the Gascennade river ⟨N⟩ S. S.
4	
17	} 34
13	
138 ¾	Great Osarge River South S.
5	
17 ½	
12	} 63 ½
14	
14	
201 ¾	To the Mine River S. S.
12	} 25
13	
226 ¾	To the two Rivers of Charlton N S
10	} 19
9	
245 ¾	old Missourie Village N. Side
9	
254 ¼	To the Grand River North Side

8
12
10
17 ½
6 ¾
7 ½ } 110 Miles from Grd. R. to. kansas
10 ½
3 ½
11 ½
13
9 ¾

364 ¼   To the Kansa's River South Side

7
10
12
11 ½ } 67
11 ¼
15

431 [or 433]   To the 2d old Village of the *Kansas*

433
10
12 } 48
14
12 ¼

479   To the Nordaway   R: N S.

14
10 } 30
6

510⟨¼⟩   To Grd. Ne Ma har R. S. S.

20 ½
9 ½ } 0½
9 ¾
20 ¼

570⟨¾⟩   Bald pated Prarie N. S.

18
10⟨¾⟩
18
14⟨½⟩

630   T: the Great River Platt South Side

2	635
4	
6	
6<u>42</u>	To the Camp of Observation above the R. Platt on the right Side

A. M.			P M		
			h	m	"
8	0	40	3	51	56
"	2	9	"	52	14
"	3	38	"	53	45
			altd. 72	49	00

The Lattitude of River Debous 38° 55′ 19″ 6/10 N. and Longtd. 89° 57′ 45″ W of *Greenich*[5]

The do—of the gasconade River 38° 44′ 35″ N. & Longtd about 91° 16′ 00′ W.

The do of the Great Osage River 38° 31′ 6″ N. & Longtd. about 91° 38′ W.

The do of th mouth of Kansez 39° 5′ 25″ North

The do of Nordaway river— 39 55 56 do

The do of the Bald pated Prarie 40 27 6 do

The do of Camp above River Plate— 41 3 19 N.

22nd of July 1804 Completlly arranged our Camp, posted two Sentinals So as to Completely guard the Camp, formd bowers for the min &c. &. Course from R *Plate N 15° W. 10 Ms.*

[Clark]   *July 22nd, Sunday 1804*

Set out verry early with a view of Getting to Some Situation above in time to take equal altitudes and take Observations, as well as one Calculated to make our party Comfortabl in a Situation where they Could recive the benifit of a Shade— passed a large Sand bar opposit a Small river on the L. S. at 3 miles above Plate Called Papillion or Butterfly Creek[6] a Sand bar & an Willow Island opposit a Creek 9 ms. above the Plate on the S. S. Called *Mosquitos* Creek[7] Prarie on both Sides of the river. Came too and formed a Camp on the S. S. above a Small Willow Island, and opposit the first Hill which aproach the river on the L. S. and covered with timbers of Oake Walnut Elm &c. &. This being a good Situation and much nearer the Otteaus town than the Mouth of the Platt, we concluded to delay at this place a fiew days and Send for Some of the Chiefs of that nation to let them Know of the Change of Government, The wishes of our Government to Cultivate friendship with them, the Objects of our journy and ⟨the⟩ to present them with a flag and Some Small presents

Some of our Provisions in the French Perogue being wet it became necessary to Dry them a fiew days— Wind hard from N W. five Deer Killed to day— The river rise a little

The Course & Distance from the Plate river to Camp

N. 15° W.   10 miles, psd. 3 pts. L. S. & 2 pts. S. S.

⟨Courses⟩ Distances of the Missouri and each days assinding—from the mouth to St Charles

Miles	21 miles	
	3 ¼	
	18	
	9	
83	10	
	10	
	18	
	15 ½	
	104 ¾	To the *Gasconnade* River S. S
	4	
34	17	
	13	
	138 ¾	Great *Osarge* River S. S.
	5	
	17 ½	
63 ½	12	
	14	
	14	
	201 ¼	*Mine* River South Side
25	12	
	13	
	226 ¼	the two Rivers of *Charlton* N. S
19	10	
	9	
	245 ¼	Old *Missouri* Village N. S.

<u>9</u>	<u>9</u>	
	254 ¼	*Grand* River North Side
	8	
	12	
	10	
	17 ½	
110	6 ¾	
	7 ½	
	10 ½	
	3 ½	
	11 ½	
	<u>13</u>	
	364 ¼	To the *Kanzas* River South Sd.
	7	
	10	
67	12	
	11 ½	
	11 ¼	
	<u>15</u>	
	431	To upper or 2nd old Village of the *Kanzas* S. S
	10 ¾	
49	12	
	14	
	<u>12</u> ¼	
	480	To the *Nordaway* River N. S.
	14	
30	10	
	<u>6</u>	
	510	To the Grand *Ne Ma haw* River S. S.
	20 ½	
60	9 ½	
	9 ¾	
	<u>20</u> ¼	
	570	*Bald pated Prarie* North Side
	18	
60	10	
	18	
	<u>14</u>	
	630	Miles = 210 Leagues to the Great *River Plate* on the South Side—
<u>12</u>	<u>12</u>	
	642	*To Camp*

409

(*Point of Observation No. 24.*)

[Lewis]   *Sunday July 22ed*[8]

on the Starboard shore above the River Platte, the mouth of which bore S. 15° E. distant 10 miles.—

Observed Equal Altitudes of the ☉ with Sext.

	h	m	s			h	m	s
A. M.	8	53	53		P. M.	2	58	37
	"	55	20			3	—	—
	"	56	48			"	1	28

Altd. by Sextant at the time of observation   92° 37′ —″

Observed Meridian altd. of ☉'s L. L. with Octant by the back Obsetn.   46° 31′ —″

Latitude deduced from this obsertn.   41° 3′ 19.4″

Observed time and distance of ☽ and Antares ★ West, with Sextant.—

	Time			*Distance*		
	h	m	s			
P. M.	10	23	20	58	42	—
	"	28	3	"	43	30
	"	32	7	"	44	—
	"	35	4	"	45	7
	"	38	15	"	47	—
	"	41	34	"	48	15

Camp 10 miles above the mouth of the river Platte.

[Lewis]   July 22nd 1804.[9]

A summary discription of the apparatus employed in the following observations; containing also some remarks on the manner in which they have been employed, and the method observed in recording the observations made with them.—

1st— a brass Sextant of 10 Inches radius, graduated to 15′ which by the assistance of the nonius was devisible to 15″; and half of this sum by means of the micrometer could readily be distinguished, therefore—7.5″ of an angle was perceptible with this instrument: she was also furnished with three eye-pieces, consisting of a hollow tube and two telescopes one of which last reversed the images of observed objects. finding on experiment that the reversing telescope when employed as the eye-piece gave me a more full and perfect image than either of the others, I have most generally imployed it in all the observations made with this instrument; when thus prepared I found from a series of observations that the quantity of her *index error* was 8′ 45″—; this sum is therefore considered as the standing error of the instrument unless otherwise expressly mentioned. *the altitudes* of all objects, observed as well with this instrument as with the Octant were by means of a reflecting surface; and those stated to have been taken with the sextant are the degrees, minutes, &c shewn by the graduated limb of the instrument at the time of observation and are of course the double altitudes of the objects observed.

2ed— A common Octant of 14 Inches radius, graduated to 20′, which by means of the nonius[10] was devisbile to 1′, half of this sum, or 30″ was perceptible by means of a micrometer. this instrument was prepared for both the *fore* and *back* observation; her *error* in the fore observation is 2° +, & and in the *back observtion* 2° 11′ 40.3″ +

at the time of our departure from the River Dubois untill the present moment, the sun's altitude at noon has been too great to be reached with my sextant, for this purpose I have therefore employed the Octant by the *back* observation. the degrees ′ & ″, recorded for the sun's altitude by the back observation express only the angle given by the graduated limb of the instrument at the time of observation, and are the complyment of the *double Altitude* of the sun's observed limb; if therefore the angle recorded be taken from 180° the remainder will be the *double altitude* of the observed object, or that which would be given by the fore observation with a reflecting surface.

3rd— An Artificial Horizon on the construction recommended and practiced by Mr. Andrw. Ellicott of Lancaster, Pensyla., in which water is used as the reflecting surface; believing this artificial Horizon liable to less error than any other in my possession, I have uniformly used it when the object observed was sufficiently bright to reflect a distinct immage; but as much light is lost by reflection from water I found it inconvenient in most cases to take the altitude of the moon with this horizon, and that of a star impracticable with any degree of accuracy.

4th— An Artificial Horizon constructed in the manner recommended by Mr. Patterson of Philadelphia; glass is here used as the reflecting surface. this horizon consists of a glass plane with a single reflecting surface, cemented to the flat side of the larger segment of a wooden ball; adjusted by means of a sperit-level and a triangular stand with a triangular mortice cut through it's center sufficiently large to admit of the wooden ball partially; the stand rests on three screws inserted near it's angles, which serve as feet for it to rest on while they assist also in the adjustment. this horizon I have employed in taking the altitude of the sun when his image he has been reather too dull for a perfect reflection from water; I have used it generally in taking the altitude of the moon, and in some cases of the stars also; it gives the moon's image very perfectly, and when carefully adjusted I consider it as liable to but little error.—

5th— An Artificial Horizon formed of the index specula[11] of a Sextant cemented to a flat board; adjusted by means of a sperit level and the triangular stand before discribed. as this glass reflects from both surfaces it gives the images of all objects much more bright than either of the other horizons; I have therefore most generally employed it in observing the altitudes of stars—

6th— A Chronometer; her ballance-wheel and [e]scapement were on the most improved construction. she rested on her back, in a small case prepared for her, suspended by an universal joint. she was carefully wound up every day at twelve oclock. Her rate of going as asscertained by a series of observations made by myself for that purpose was found to be 15 Seconds and a 5 tenths of a second too slow in twenty four howers on *Mean Solar time*. This is nearly the same result as that found by Mr. Andrew Ellicott who was so obliging as to examine her rate of going for the space of fourteen days, in the summer 1803. her rate of going as ascertained by that gentleman was 15.6 s too slow M. T. in 24 h. and that she went from 3 to 4 s. slower the last 12 h, than she did the first 12 h. after being wound up.—

at 12 OCk. on the 14th day of may 1804 (being the day on which the detachment left the mouth of the River Dubois) the Chronometer was too fast M. T. 6 m. 32 s. & ²⁄₁₀.— This time-piece was regulated on *mean time*, and the time entered in the following observations is that shewn by her at the place of observation. the day is recconed on Civil time, (i e) commencing at midnight.

7th— A Circumferentor, circle 6 Inches diameter, on the common construction; by means of this instrument adjusted with the sperit level, I have taken the magnetic azimuth of the sun and pole Star. It has also been employed in taking the traverse of the river:— from the courses thus obtained, together with the distances estimated from point to point, the chart of the Missouri has been formed which now accompanys these observations. the several points of observation are marked with a cross of red ink, and numbered in such manner as to correspond with the celestial observations made at those points respectively.

1. This July 22 entry is written over this address: Genl. W. Johnston P M Vincennes Capt. William Clark   Saint Louis   Attention of Jno. Hay Esqr. Post Mastr. Cahokia IT.

2. This site, which they called Camp White Catfish, was on the Iowa side, near the Mills-Pottawattamie county line, using the present river course. On the high land on the opposite side is present Bellevue, Sarpy County, Nebraska. This is the first specific mention of plans to send back a party with dispatches for President Jefferson—an intention not actually carried out until April 1805. See Introduction to this volume. MRC map 23; MRR map 64.

3. This calculation is just below Clark's signature: $3 \mid 632$
$$210—\tfrac{2}{3}$$

4. Mileage tables, evidently made at Camp White Catfish, are at right angles to the July 22 entry on this sheet of the Field Notes (document 34). These calculations are overwritten by the mileage table:

$$
\begin{array}{ccc}
53 & 642 & 12 \\
 & \underline{53} & \\
 & 112 & \\
 & \underline{106} & \\
 & 6 &
\end{array}
$$

5. These positions, presumably written at Camp White Catfish, are above a second entry for July 22, 1804, in the Field Notes, on a different sheet (document 36) from the previous entry.

6. Biddle apparently placed brackets around the phrase "a large Sand bar . . . Butterfly Creek" and drew a line through it, all in red ink.

7. In Pottawattamie County, Iowa; still called Mosquito Creek. In 1804 its mouth was probably a few miles farther south, in present Mills County, below Bellevue. Warren map 4; MRC map 23

8. Lewis's observation from Codex O.

9. Lewis's description of astronomical instruments from Codex O.

10. A nonius is a method for dividing the arc of a circle into a given number of parts. Bedini (TT), 475.

11. The index specula is simply the mirror from a sextant. Bedini (SILC), 62.

Chapter Five

From the Platte to Vermillion River

July 23–August 24, 1804

[Clark]   *Camp 10 Ms. above the river Plate Monday July the 23rd—*
a fair morning— Sent out a party of 5 men to look to timber for Ores
two other parties to hunt at 11 oClock Sent, G. Drewyer & Peter Crusett
½ Indn. to the Otteaus Village about 18 ms. West of our Camp, to invite
the Chiefs & principal men of that nation to come & talk with us &. &.,
also the *panis* if they Should meet with any of that nation (also on the
S. Side of the Plate 30 ms. higher up) (at this Season of the year all the
Indians in this quater are in the Plains hunting the Buffalow from Some
Signs Seen by our hunter and the Praries being on fire in the derection of
the Village induce a belief that the Nation have returned to get green
Corn) raised a flag Staff put out Some provisions which got wet in the
french Perogue to Sun & Dry— I commenced Coppying my map of the
river to Send to the Presdt. of U S. by the Return of a pty of Soldiers,
from Illinois[1] five Deer Killed— one man a bad riseing on his left
breast.[2] Wind from the N. W.

Equal altitudes taken at this place the two following days Viz:

	h	m	S		h	m	S
July the 22nd Sunday A M	8	53	53	P M	2	58	37
	"	55	20		3	0	0
		56	48		3	1	28

Given altitude 92° 37 0

		h	m	s			h	m	s
July 26th	A M	7	33	32	P M	4	15	21
			34	35		"	16	51
			36	22		"	18	14

[Clark]

Equal altitudes July 23rd 1804
Cromtr. [two?]

		h	m	s			Time		
							h	m	s
	A M	8	0	49		P M	3	51	56
	"		2	9		"		52	14
	"		3	38		"		53	45

Altitude 72° 49′ 00″

Camp *White Catfish* ⟨Nine⟩ 10 Miles above the Platt River Monday the 23rd of July 1804—

A fair morning   Set a party to look for timber for Ores, two parties to hunt.   at 11 oClock Sent off George Drewyer & *Peter Crousett* with Some tobacco to invite the Otteaus if at their town and Panies if they Saw them to Come and talk with us at our Camp &c. &c.   (at this Season the Indians on this river are in the Praries Hunting the Buffalow but from Some Signs of hunters near this place & the Plains being on fire near their towns induce a belief that they this nation have returned to get Some Green Corn or rosting Ears)   raised a flag Staff Sund & Dryed our provisions &c.   I commence Coppying a map of the river below to Send to the P. [president] [*blank*] U S   five Deer Killed to day   one man with a tumer on his breast, Prepared our Camp   the men put their arms in order

Wind hard this afternoon from the N. W.

Equal altitudes taken at the White Catfish Camp, 10 miles above the river Platt—[3]

July the 22nd Sunday 1804

		h	m	S			h	m	
	A M	8	53	53		P M	2	58	37
	"		55	20			3	00	00
	"		56	48		"		1	28

Given Altitude   92° 37′ 00″

July 25th Wednesday

	h	m	s		h	m	s	
A M	8	5	20	P M	3	44	38	
"		6	42	"	—	—		lost
"		8	7½	"		47	27	

Altd Given   74° 19′ 30″

July 26th Thursday

	h	m	s		h	m	s
A m	7	33	32	P. M.	4	15	22
"		34	55	"		16	51
"		36	22	"		18	14

Altitude Given not put down

[Lewis]   *Monday July 23rd* [3]

Observed Equal Altitudes of the ☉ with Sext.

	h	m	s		h	m	s
A. M.	8	—	49	P. M.	3	51	56
"		2	9	"		52	14
"		3	38	"		53	45

Altitude by Sextant at the time of Obstn.   72° 49′ —″

Observed Meridian Altd. of ☉'s L. L. with Octant by the back observt.   46° 55′ —″

Latitude deduced from this Obstn. [*blank*]

1. There are no extant Clark route maps of the Missouri to Camp White Catfish, except for a few sketch maps in the Field Notes (figs. 6, 9, 10, 14, and 15). It seems likely that there were twelve maps of the river that are now lost. See *Atlas*, 7. The map Clark was working on was not sent back at this time, since a return party was not dispatched. The soldiers for the intended return party were of Corporal Richard Warfington's squad, consisting at this time of Frazer, Boley, Dame, Tuttle, and White (see above, May 26, 1804). They were "from Illinois" in the sense that their unit, Captain Amos Stoddard's artillery company, was stationed in the "Illinois country." See Appendix A, this volume.

2. A boil or abscess.

3. Lewis's observation from Codex O.

[Clark] [1]

White Catfish Camp 24th of July Tuesday.   a fair morning   the wind rose with the Sun & blows hard from the S.   thos Southerley Breezes are dry Cool & refreshing. the Northerley Breezes which is more frequent is much Cooler, and moist, I continue my Drawing. Cap Lewis also ingaged prepareing Som paper to Send back,[2] one of the men cought a *white Catfish*, the eyes Small, & Tale resembling that of a Dolfin.[3]

[Clark]   *White Catfish Camp* 10 *Ms. above Platt*

24th, of July 1804   Tuesday   a fair day   the wind blows hard from the South, the Breezes which are verry frequent on this part of the *Missouri* is cool and refreshing. Several hunters out to day; but as the game of all Kinds are Scarce only two Deer were brought in—   I am much engaged drawing off a map, Capt. Lewis also much engaged in prepareing Papers to Send back by a pirogue—   Which we intended to Send back from the river Plate—   observations at this place makes the *Lattitude* 41° 3′ 19″ North[4]

This evening Guthrege [Goodrich] Cought a *white Catfish*, its eyes Small & tale much like that of a *Dolfin*

[Lewis]   *Tuesday July 24th*[5]

☉'s Magnetic Azimuth by Circumftr.   S 85° E.

	h	m	s
Time by Chronometer A. M.	8	8	8
Altd. of ☉'s U. L. by Sextant	75° 5′ 15″		

1. Biddle's note at the head of this sheet of the Field Notes (reverse of document 36) reads, "July 22 to 27."

2. If Lewis wrote any dispatches to Jefferson at this time, they have not been found. Some of the material he was preparing may be in the specialized journals (see Introduction and Appendix C, this volume). In any case, no dispatches were sent from Camp White Catfish.

3. Perhaps the channel catfish, and if so, the captains can be credited with discovering the species. Cutright (LCPN), 74, 425.

4. This latitude is a few minutes too far south. MRC map 23.

5. Lewis's observation from Codex O.

[Clark]

White Catfish Camp 25th of *July Wednesday*.   Several hunters Sent out. at 2 oClock the Two men Sent to the Otteaz Village returned and informed that no Indians were at the *Town*   they Saw Some fresh Sign near that place which they persued, but Could not find them, they having taken

precausions to Conceal the rout which they went out from the Village—
the Inds. of the Missouries being at war with one & the other or other
Indians, move in large bodies and Sometimes the whole nation Continue
to Camp together on their hunting pls.   Those men inform that they
passed thro a open Plain all the way to the Town a feiw Trees excepted on
the water courses— they Cross the *papillion* or the Butterfly Creek within
a feiw miles of Camp and near the Village a handsm. river of 100 yards
Wide Called the *Corne de chearf* [Corne du Cerf] or the Elkhorn, which
mouths below the Town in the Plate N. Side.[1] Wind from the S. E.   2 Dee[r]
& a Turkey Killed to Day   Several Grous Seen in the Prarie

[Clark]   *White Catfish Camp*

   25th of *July Wednesday*   a fair morning Several hunters out today   at 2
oClock *Drewyer* & *Peter* [Cruzatte] returned from the *Otteaus* Village; and
informs that no Indians were at their towns, They Saw Some fresh Signs
of a Small party but Could not find them.   in their rout to the Towns
(Which is about 18 miles West) they passed thro a open Prarie Crossed
papillion or Butterfly Creek and a Small butifull river which run into the
Platt a little below the Town Called *Corne* de *charf* [*NB: Corne de Cerf*] or
Elk Horn river   this river is about 100 yards wide with Clear water & a
gravely Channel.— wind from the S. E   two Deer Killed to day   1 Turkey   Several Grous Seen to day.[2]

[Lewis]   *Wednesday July 25th*[3]
   Observed Equal Altds. of the ☉ with Sextant.

	h	m	s		h	m	s
A. M.	8	5	20		3	44	38
	"	6	42		☉ obscured by cloud		
	"	8	7.5		3	47	27

Altd. by Sextant at the time of Observtn.   74° 19′ 30″

   1. Apparently they had traveled through Sarpy County, Nebraska, in a general westerly direction, crossing the Elkhorn River near where it meets the Platte. The village is
evidently the Oto site noted on July 20.
   2. Probably the ruffed grouse, with which the captains were already familiar. Cutright
(LCPN), 15.
   3. Lewis's observation from Codex O.

[Clark]

Whit Cat fish Camp 26th of July Thursday.   the wind blew Verry hard all
Day from the South with Clouds of Sand which incomoded me verry much
in my tent, and as I could not Draw in the Boat was obliged Combat with
the Misqutr. under a Shade in the woods—.   I opened the Breast of a
man   the discharge gave him ease &c.[1]   5 beaver Caught near Camp—[2]
only 1 Deer Killed to day.   The Countrey back from Camp on the S. S. is
a bottom of about 5 ms. wide   one half the Distn. timber, the other high
bottom Prarie, the opsd. Side a high Hill about 170 foot rock foundatio.
Timbered back & below.   a Prarie[3]

[Clark]   *Catfish* which is *White Camp*

26th of July Thursday 1804   the wind blustering and hard from the
South all day which blowed the Clouds of Sand in Such a manner that I
could not complete my pan [*X: plan*] in the tent, the Boat roled in Such a
manner that I could do nothing in that, I was Compessed to go to the
woods and Combat with the Musqutors, I opened the Tumer of a man on
the left breast, which discharged half a point. [pint?]

five Beever Cough[t] near this Camp the flesh of which we made use
of—   This evening we found verry pleasent—   only one Deer Killed
to day. The Countrey back from Camp on the S. S. is a bottom of about
five mile wide, one half the distance wood & the ball. [balance?] plain
high & Dry.   the opposed Side a high Hill about 170 foot ⟨rock founda-
tion⟩ [*NB: rock foundation*], Covd. with timber, back & below is a Plain.

[Lewis]   *Thursday July 26th*[4]
Observed Equal Altitudes of ☉ with Sextant.

	h	m	s		h	m	s
A. M.	7	33	32	P. M.	4	15	24
	"	34	55		"	16	51
	"	36	22		"	18	14

Altitude by Sextant at the time of Obst.   62° 18′ 15″

1. He opened the boil or abscess on the man's chest to let it drain.
2. The American beaver, *Castor canadensis*, was already a familiar species. Hall, 2 : 601 – 5.
3. The note, "(27)" comes at the end of this entry, perhaps as a guide to the next date.
4. Lewis's observation from Codex O.

[Clark]¹

Course Distance and reffurence July 27th

North	1 ½	miles to a willow point on the L. S.
West	2	do to Sand pt. on S. S. opsd. a pond L. S.
N. 10° E	3	do to a point of ⟨high Land on⟩ the L. S. passd. a large Sand bar in the river
N. 8 W	4	do to a Pt. on S. S. opposit a high part of the Prarie
N. 54 E	4 ½	miles to a coops of wood in a bend to the L. S. passed
	<u>15</u>	a Pt. on S. S. opposit the Commencement of this Course I went out on the L. S. at Some riseing land, and found about 200 acres of Land immediately on the river Covered with Mouns of Dift hight's & Shapes a pond back & low land, all round— a Beyau above

white Catfish

Camp July 27th Friday,   Charged the Boat and Perogue after a Small Shower of rain, Completed our ores & poles, Crossed over the two horses, with a View of their going on the S W. Side of the Missouri and Set out at Half past 1 oClock   proceeded on Verry well under a gentle Breeze. passed a high Island of high wood land on the L. Side just above Camp, this Island is formed by a *pond* Supplied by a great number of Springs from this hill, this Pond has 2 out lets, & when the river is high the water passes thro the pond, passed a Sand Island in the 2nd bend to the right. Camped in a bend to the ⟨right⟩ L. S. in Some wood,² I took R. Fields & walked on Shore & Killed a Deer, and did not get to the Boat untile after night   a butifull Breeze from the N W. this evening which would have been verry agreeable, had the Misquiters been tolerably Pacifick, but thy were rageing all night, Some about the Sise of house flais [flies]

[Clark]   *White Cat fish Camp* 10 ms above *Platt*

27th of July Friday, a Small Shower of rain this morning, at 10 oClock Commence Loading the Boat & perogue; had all the Ores Completely fixed; Swam over the two remaining horses to the L. S. with the view of the Hunters going on that Side, after Getting everry thing Complete, we Set Sale under a gentle breeze from the South and proceeded on, passed a Island (formd by a Pond fed by Springs) on the L. S. of high ⟨wooded⟩

Land Covered with timber, in the 2nd bend to the right a large Sand Island in the river a high Prarie on the S. S.—. as we were Setting out to day one man Killed a Buck & another Cut his Knee verry bad[3] Camped in a Bend to the L. Side in a [*NB: copse*] Coops of Trees, a verry agreeable Breeze from the N W. this evening. I Killed a Deer in the Prarie and found the Misquitors So thick & troublesom that it was disagreeable and painfull to Continue a moment Still.

Course & Distance. refrs. July the 27th.

North	1 ½	ms. to a willow pt. on the L. S.
West	2	ms. to Sand pt. on S. S. opsd. a pond L. S
N. 10° E.	3	ms. to pt. of W. L. S. psd. a large Sd. bar in the middle of the river
N. 8° W.	4	ms. to a pt. on S. S. opsd. Some mounds (Ottos Village) on the L. S. psd Bluff L S N.
N. 54° E	4 ½	Ms. old Ayauwars V. to a pt. of wood land in a bend on L. S. psd. a pt. S. S.
	15	

I took one man R. Fields and walked on Shore with a View of examoning Som mounds on the L. S. of the river— those mounds I found to be of Deffirent hight Shape & Size, Some Composed of Sand Some earth & Sand, the highest next to the river all of which covered about 200 acres of land, in a circular form on the Side from the river a low bottom & Small Pond. The Otteaus formerly lived here[4] I did not get to the boat untile after night.

[Lewis]   *Friday July 27th*[5]

Observed time and distance of ☽ and α Aquilae, ★ West *with Sextant*

	Time			*Distance*		
	h	m	s			
A. M.	2	47	6	64°	48'	15"
	"	55	9	"	50	30
	"	59	39	"	51	30
	3	2	12	"	52	—
	"	4	42	"	52	45
	"	6	31	"	53	—

I wished to have taken one or two sets more with moon and Aquilae, but the clouds obscured the star. I was also anxious to have taken some sets with Aldeberan, then in reach of observation and East of the moon, but was prevented by the intervention of the clouds, which soon became so general as to obscure the whole horizon.—

Observed meridian Altitude of ⊙'s L. L. with Octant by the back obs. 48° 44′
Latitude deduced from this obstn. 41° 5′ 35.2″

1. Biddle's notation at the head of this sheet of the Field Notes (document 37) reads "27 July to 30." The words "5 beaver" appear in the upper right corner, perhaps referring to the previous day's catch. The word "cajaux" appears to one side at the end of the entry.

2. Within the area covered by the Clark-Maximilian maps (*Atlas* map 13), in the vicinity or north of the present Douglas Street Bridge (Interstate 480). The course of the river may then have approximated the later Carter Lake. Nicollet (MMR), 386; Warren map 5; MRC map 23; MRR map 65.

3. Ordway says that Shannon killed the deer. It was Whitehouse who cut his knee, as he himself revealed.

4. The "mounds" Clark describes are on a floodplain and are shown in an area generally inhabited by the Oto Indians. Such settings were rarely used for permanent Indian villages, although winter encampments and temporary camps were sometimes built there. The description of the varying composition of these mounds, especially the presence of sand, suggests the mounds may be of natural origin, like the "fortifications" Clark notices on September 2. In any event, the area today is downtown Omaha. Wedel (PHH), 48.

5. Lewis's observation from Codex O.

[Clark]

July 28th Satturday   Set out this morning early, the wind blou from the N. W. by N.   a Dark Smokey Morning, Some rain   at 1 me. passed a Bluff on the S. S. it being the first high land approachig the river above the Nodaway, a Island and Creek S. S.   just abov this creek I call ⟨Bald⟩ Indian Knob[1]   G. Drewyer Came with a Dee[r] & informs he heard fireing to the S. W.   I walked on Shore on the S. S.   found some good Prarie out from the S. pt. The High Lands approach the river 1st bend to left   The party on Shore brought in a *Missouri* Indian who resides with the Otteauz, this Indian & 2 others were Hunting in the Prarie   their Camp is about 4 miles off. This Indian informs that his nation[2] is in the Plains hunting the Buffalow, the party with which he is encamped is about 20 familey Hunting the Elk, we landed on S. S. below an Island[3]

Course Distance & reffurence's the 28th of July 1804 Satturday

S 82° E	1	Mile on the L. Side to pt. of a Sand bar L. S
N. 10° W	½	me. on the L. S. the high land approaches the river on S. S. this is the first place the high land has touched the river above the *nordaway.* nearest 3 Ms.
N. 30° W.	½	m on L. S.
N. 77° W	3	m to a point on the L. S. passed a Island & creek on S. S abov Bluffs
N. 60 W	3	ms. to a pt. on S. S. psd. the Isd. S. S. ⟨& opsd. the old Otteaus village⟩ L. S
N. " "	¾	m. the same course continued—4
N. 63 E.	2	m. to a pt. Lard. opposite to a small ⟨willow⟩ island from which it is divided by a cannel of [*blank*] yards in width
	10 ¾	

[Clark]   *July the 28th, Satturday 1804*

Set out this morning early, the wind from the N W. by N.   a Dark Smokey morning   Some rain   passed at 1 me. a Bluff on the S. S. the first high land above the Nodaway aproaching the river on that Side   a Island and Creek 15 yds. wide on the S. S. above this Bluff, as this Creek has no name call it Indian Knob Creek   our party on Shore Came to the river and informs that they heard fireing to the S W.   below this High Land on the S. S. the Aiawuay [Iowa] Indians formerly lived,[5] ⟨below this old village about ⟨7⟩ 5 miles passed Some monds on the L S. in a bend Where the *Otteauze* Indians formerly lived, This Situation I examined found it well situated for Defence   about 2 or 300 acres of Land Covered with mounds⟩[6]   The flank came in & informed they heard two Guns to the S. W.   the high land approaches in the 1st bend to the left, we camped on the S. S. below the point of an Island, G Drewyer brought in a *Missourie Indian* which he met with hunting in the Prarie   This Indian is one of the fiew remaining of that nation, & lives with the Otteauz, his Camp about 4 miles from the river, he informs that the 'great gangue' of the nation were hunting the Buffalow in the Plains.   h[i]s party was Small Consisting only of about 20 Lodges, [*blank*] miles furthr a nother Camp where there was a french man, who lived in the nation, This Indian appeard spritely, and appeared to make use of the Same pronouncation of the Osarge, Calling a Chief *Inca*[7]

Cours. Distance & reffers. July 28

S. 82° E.	1	me. on the L. Side to pt. of a Sand bar L. S
N. 10 W.	½	me. on the L. S. a High Bluff on the Stabd. S. above the Old Village of the *Aiaawaz* this High Land the lst abov *Nordaway* which approaches the S. S.
N. 30° W.	½	on the L. Side
N. 77 W.	3	ms. to a pt. on the L. S. psd. an Isd. & Indian Knob Creek S. S.
N. 60 W.	3	ms. to a pt. on the S. S. passed The aforesaid Island S. S.
N. 60 W.	¾	on the S. S.
N. 63 E	2	ms. to a point L. S. opsd. a Island in the M. river
	10 ¾	

1. Apparently Pigeon Creek, in Pottawattamie County, Iowa, north of Council Bluffs. *Atlas* map 13; MRC map 23; MRR map 66.

2. The Field Notes entry continues after a break for the course material.

3. In Pottawattamie County, somewhat north of Council Bluffs. *Atlas* map 13; MRC maps 23, 24; MRR map 66.

4. This course and the next one are in Lewis's hand.

5. Shown on *Atlas* map 13, just north of present Council Bluffs. MRC map 23; MRR map 65. Archaeological evidence for this site is unknown.

6. These are the mounds mentioned July 27.

7. The Osage and Missouri languages are both of the Siouan language family, though of different divisions within that family, the first in the Dhegiha, the second in the Chiwere division. "Inca" has no connection with the Incas of South America. Robert L. Rankin (personal communication) identifies the word as *hа́ka*, the Osage word signifying "sacred being" or "chief"; La Flesche gives it as *Ho^n-ga*. Din & Nasatir, 4; La Flesche, 65.

[Clark]

1st course the 29th July[1]

North	¾	of a mile on L. S Isld (1)
N. 80° W	½	ms. to a Pt. on L. S opsd. Bowyer Rivr (2)

⟨N. 85 W	2	ms. to a wood⟩ in a bend L. S. High Land
⟨North	¾⟩	to pt. on S. S.
		The 4 courses of the 29th to come in here
N. 11° E.	3 ½	miles to an object in the bend Stard. Shore. (4)
N. 70° W.	2 ½	miles to a point of timber on the L. S. below a Clean High Prarie
⟨S. 8	<u>1⟩</u>	proceeded on ½ a mile & camped on the S. S.—
	12	

July 29th Sunday   We Sent one frenchman *le Liberty*[2] & the Indian to the Camp to envite the party to meet us at the next bend of High Land on the L. S.   a Dark morning   wind from the W. N. W.   rained all last night— Set out at 5 oClock &, proceeded on   passed the Island, opposit this Island on the S. S. the Creek called Indian Knob Creek which mouths Several miles on a Direct line below, is within 20 feet of the Missouri & about 5 feet higher

Cought three large Cat fish to day verry fat   one of them nearly white those Cat are So plenty that they may be Cought in any part of this river but fiew fish of any other Kind.—

(4) at the commencement of this course passed much fallen timber apparently the ravages of a dreadful haricane which had passed obliquely across the river from N. W. to S. E. about twelve months since.   many trees were broken off near the ground the trunks of which were sound and four feet in diameter.[3]

Willard lost his gun in Bowyers R.   R. Fields Dive & brought it up[4]

All the Wood Land on this part of the Missouries Appear to be Confined to the Points & Islands.

Boyers River is provably [probably] 25 yds. Wide, Willard near loseing his Gun in this river, two men Sick & Sevral with Boils, a Cold Day   Wind from the N W.   Som rain the fore part of the Day.[5]

[Clark]   July 29th Sunday 1804

Sent a french man *la Liberty* with the Indian to Otteaze Camp to invite the Indians to meet us on the river above—   a Dark rainey morning   wind from the W. N. W.—   rained all the last night—   Set out at 5 oClock   opposit the (1) Island, ⟨in⟩ the bend to the right or S. S. is within 20 feet of Indian Knob Creek, the water of this Creek is 5 feet higher than that of the River.   passed the Isld.   we Stoped to Dine under Some high Trees near the high land on the L. S.   in a fiew minits Cought three verry large *Catfish* (3) one nearly white, Those fish are in great plenty on the Sides of the river and verry fat, a quart of Oile Came out of the Surpolous fat of one of these fish   (4) above this high land & on the S. S. passed much falling timber apparently the ravages of a Dreadfull harican which had passed obliquely across the river from N. W. to S E about twelve months Since, many trees were broken off near the ground the trunks of which were Sound and four feet in Diameter, (2) about ¾ of a Me. above the Island on the S. S. a Creek coms in Called Boyers R.   this Creek is 25 yards wide,   one man in attempting to Cross this Creek on a log let his gun fall in, R. Fields Dived & brought it up   proceeded on to a Point on the S. S. and Camped.[6]

Course Distanc & Refrs. July 29th

North	¾	of a Mile on the L. S. an Island on the right of the Course (1)
N. 80° W.	½	me. to a pt. on the L. Side passed Bowyers Creek S S (2)
N. 85° W.	2	ms. to a wood in a bend on the L. S. below a Hill
North	¾	me. on the S. S. (3)
N. 11° E.	3 ½	Ms. to a tree in the bend S. S. passed a Harican (4)
N. 70° W.	2	to a point of wood on the S. S. Camped S. S.
	10	

1. The courses and distances for this entry in the Field Notes (document 37) are divided in the original but are here brought together for ease of reading. Clark identified the match-up with asterisks. There are variations between the courses and distances here and those in Codex A. Lewis appears to have written the course that begins N. 11° E.

2. The first mention, at least by this name, of this man, evidently a French *engagé*. Presumably one or both of the "La bartees" listed by Clark on July 4, 1804 refer to him. For the problems associated with his identity, see Appendix A, this volume. Because he was not a soldier, he did not desert, in the precise legal sense, but only quit the expedition.

3. This paragraph appears to be in Lewis's hand. The "hurricane" was probably a tornado.

4. July 29 was not Willard's day: he lost his rifle while returning to the previous camp to retrieve his forgotten tomahawk. Boyer River, or Creek, reaches the Missouri River in northwest Pottawattamie County, Iowa. *Atlas* map 13; MRC map 24; MRR maps 66, 67; Petersen, 270–71.

5. These calculations are under the July 29 entry:

10	10
15	15
10	10
1	12
36	47 ¾
32	32
688	80

6. Apparently in Pottawattamie County, Iowa, somewhat above the Washington-Douglas county line, Nebraska, on the opposite shore. *Atlas* map 13; MRC map 24; MRR map 66.

[Clark] [1]

July the 30th Monday   Set out early & proceeded on *West 3¾ mes. passd. one pt. to the L. S and one to the S. S.* to a Clear open Prarie on the L. S. which is on a rise of about 70 feet higher than the bottom which is also a prarie covered with high grass Plumbs Grape Vine & Hezel—both forming a Bluff to the River, the Lower Prarie is above high water mark at the foot of the riseing ground & below the High Bluff   we came to in a grove of timber and formed a Camp [2]   raised a flag Pole, and deturmind to waite for the Ottu Indians—   The white Horse which ⟨I⟩ we found below Died last night, after posting out the Guards &c. &. Sent out 4 men to hunt   I am ingaged in [*blank*] and Drawing off my courses to accompany the map Drawn at *White Catfish* Camp, Capt. Lewis and my Self walked in the Prarie on the top of the Bluff and observed the most butifull prospects imagionable, this Prarie is Covered with grass about 10 or 12 Inch high, (Land rich)   rises about ½ a mile back Something higher and is a Plain as fur as Can be Seen, under those high Lands next the river is butifull Bottom interspersed with Groves of timber, the River may be Seen for a great Distance both above & below meandering thro: the plains between two ranges of High land which appear to be from 4 to 20 ms. apart, each bend of the river forming a point which Contains tall timber, principally Willow Cotton wood some Mulberry elm Sycamore & ash.   the groves Contain walnit coffeenut[3] & Oake in addition & Hickory & Lynn [linden][4]   Jo. Fields Killed *Brarow* or as the Ponie [Pawnee] call it *Cho car tooch*,[5] this animale burrows in the ground & feeds on Bugs and flesh principally the little Dogs of the Prarie, also Something of Vegetable Kind   his Shape & Size is like that of a *Beever*, his head Mouth &c. is like a Dog with its ears Cut off, his tale and hair like that of a Ground *hog*   Something longer and lighter, his interals like a Hogs, his Skin thick & loose, white & hair Short under its belly, of the Species of the *Bear*, and it has a white Streake from its nose to its Sholders, the Toe *nails* of its fore feet which is large is 1 Inch and ¾ qtr. long and those of his hind feet which is much Smaller is ¾ long. We have this animale Skined and Stuffed. Short legs, raseing himself just above the ground when in motion   Jo & R. fields Killed Som Deer at a Distance and Came in for a horse to bring them in, they have not returned this evening, a gred number of Swans in a pond above L. S. ⟨N. W. from   our opposit⟩ to our Camp.   Serjt. Floyd verry unwell a bad Cold &c.[6]   Several men with Boils, great qts. of Catfish   G. D. [George Drouillard] Cought one Small Beever alive. Som Turkey & Gees Killed to day.   arms & all things in order.   a fair evining, and Cool.

[Clark]   *July 30th Monday* 1804

Set out this morning early   proceeded on to a Clear open Prarie on the L. S. on a rise of about 70 feet higher than the bottom which is also a Prarie both forming Bluffs to the river of High Grass & Plumb bush Grapes &c. and Situated above high water is a Small Grove of timber at the foot of the Riseing Ground between those two priraries, and below the Bluffs of the high Prarie we Came too and formed a Camp, intending to waite the return of the french man & Indians—   the white horse which we found near the Kanzeis River, Died Last night

Course Distanc &c. July 30th

S 82° W.	2	Mes. to a point of wood on the L. S. above a pt. on the L. S. and opsd. one on S. S.
West	1 ¼	ms. to the lower part of a Bluff & High Prarie on L. S. came too.
	3 ¼	

posted out our guard and Sent out 4 men, Captn. Lewis & went up the Bank and walked a Short Distance in the high Prarie.   this Prarie is Covered with Grass of 10 or 12 inches in hight. Soil of good quallity &, Still further back at the Distance of about a mile the Countrey rises about 80 or 90 feet higher, and is one Continual Plain as fur as Can be Seen, from the *Bluff* on the 2d rise imediately above our Camp the most butifull prospect of the River up & Down and the Countrey opsd. prosented it Self which I ever beheld; The River meandering the open and butifull Plains, interspursed with Groves of timber, and each point Covered with Tall timber, Such as willow Cotton Sun [*NB: Some*] Mulberry, Elm, Sucamore, Lynn & ash (The Groves Contain Hickory, Walnut, Coffeenut & Oake in addition)—

Two ranges of High Land parrelel to each other and from 4 to 10 miles Distant between which the river & its bottoms are Contained. (from 70 to 300 feet high)

Joseph Fields Killed and brought in an Anamale Called by the French *Brárow*, and by the Ponies *Cho car tooch* this Anamale Burrows in the Ground and feeds on Flesh, (Prarie Dogs), Bugs, & vigatables— "His Shape & Size is like that of a Beaver, his head mouth &c. is like a Dogs with Short Ears, his Tail and Hair like that of a Ground Hog, and longer, and lighter. his Interals like the interals of a *Hog*,["]

his Skin thick and loose, his Belly is White and the Hair Short— a *white* Streek from his nose to his Sholders.

The toe nails of his fore feet is one Inch & ¾ long, & feet large; the nails of his hind feet ¾ of an Inch long, the hind feet Small and toes Crooked, his legs are Short and when he Moves Just Suffcent to raise his body above the Ground ⟨he⟩ He is of the Bear Species. we hav his Skin Stuffed—

Jo. & R. Fields did not return this evening, Several men with Verry bad *Boils*— Cat fish is Cought in any part of the river Turkeys Gees & a Beaver Killed & Cought every thing in prime order men in high Spirits. a fair Still evening Great no. misquitors this evening

[Lewis]   July the 30th[7]

this day Joseph Fields killed a *Braro* [*EC: Badger Taxidea americana*] as it is called by the French *engáges*. this is a singular anamal not common to any part of the United States. it's weight is sixteen pounds.— it is a carniverous anamal. on both ⟨of the⟩ sides of the upper jaw is fexed ⟨two⟩ one long and sharp canine tooth.— it's eye are small black and piercing.

1. Biddle's notation at the head of this sheet of the Field Notes (document 38) reads "July 30 to Aug. 1st."

2. In Washington County, Nebraska, near the present town of Fort Calhoun, about fifteen miles north of Omaha. This bluff became known as the Council Bluff (or, with adjacent bluffs, as the Council Bluffs) from the meeting the captains held there with the Indians during the next few days. The city of Council Bluffs, Iowa, although it is downstream and on the opposite bank, takes its name from these bluffs. The camp was in the river bottom immediately below the bluffs; the river, which now runs well to the east of the bluffs, then came nearly to their foot at this point. The bluffs today are the site of Fort Atkinson State Historical Park. *Atlas* map 13; Nicollet (MMR), 387; MRC map 24; MRR map 67; Appleman (LC), 336–37.

3. Kentucky coffee tree, *Gymnocladus dioica* (L.) K. Koch. Barkley, 157; Gilmore, 37.

4. This description of Lewis and Clark's Council Bluff and neighboring bluffs typifies the central Missouri River vegetation and the topography of the bluff forests and upland prairies. The entry accurately lists the original trees that occupied the elevations above the river. The trees typical of the floodplain are distinguished from those of the first and second bluffs, and the species listed provide an early comparison with the current vegetation. Weaver, 37–54; Aikman, 38, 59.

5. The badger was probably the first zoological specimen preserved by Lewis on the expedition. Lewis skinned and stuffed it to send back to Jefferson. In early 1806 the president noted the specimen, saying that the species was "not before known out of Europe," although in fact, the animal had been described from Canadian specimens in 1778. Clark noted one killed at River Dubois on February 6, 1804, with no indication that it was new to him. Lewis gives a more detailed and scientific description on February 26, 1806. "Brarow" is from the French *blaireau* and the Pawnee word is *cuhkatus*. Jefferson to C. F. C. Volney, February 11, 1806, Jackson (LLC), 1:291; Cutright (LCPN), 70. See Lewis's zoological note this same day.

6. The first indication in the journals of the illness that would result in Floyd's death in less than a month.

7. Here begin Lewis's natural history notes as entered in Codex Q (see Appendix C). These notes, written irregularly until December 1805 in this notebook, are normally placed after the regular daily entries in this edition. Occasionally there are exchanges among journalists and between this journal and regular journals, but it is unclear which journalist is the original writer or into which notebook the records went first. Elliott Coues has randomly added scientific names for species on the pages here placed convenient to the subject and identified as his emendations. See above, n. 5, for the badger.

[Clark]

July 31st Tuesday   a fair Day   3 hunters out this morning   G. Drewyer Killed a verry fat Buck   one Inch fat on the ribs   Merdn. altd Latd. is *41° 18′ 0″ ⁵⁄₁₀*—North.   R & Jo: Fields returned at 10 oClock   the[y] Killed 3 Deer, and lost the horses, Cought a Small Beever which is already taim, Several men out hunting the horses without Sukcess, The

Ottoes not yet arrived, I complete the Copy of the Courses &c. &c.   Mus-
queters verry troubleson

[Clark]

July 31st, Tuesday   a fair Day three Hunters out, Took meridian altitude   made the Lattd. *41° 18' 1" 5/10 N*.   R. & Jo: Fields returned to Camp
They Killed 3 Deer.—   The Horses Strayed off last night. Drewyer Killed
a Buck   one inch of fat on the ribs, R. & Jo: Fields returned without any
meet haveing been in persuit of the horses—   The Indians not yet arrived. Cought a young Beever alive which is already quit tame—.   Cought
a Buffalow fish—[1]   The evening verry Cool, The Musqutors are yet
troublesom.—

(Point of observation No. 25.)

[Lewis]   Tuesday July 31st[2]

Camp at Council Bluffs, Larboard shore.—

Observed Meridian Altd. of ☉'s L. L. with Octant by the back observtn.   51°
4' 30
Latitude deduced from this obsertn.   41° 18' 1.5"

1. This could be one of several varieties of buffalo fish: *Ictiobus cyprinellus*, bigmouth; *I.
bubalus*, smallmouth; or *I. niger*, black. Lee et al., 404–6.
2. Lewis's observation from Codex O.

[Lewis and Clark]   [*Weather, July 1804*][1]

July   saw some geese with their young, caught several they are not yet
        feathered nor can they fly   the old geese are in the same situation
        at this season.

4th   a great number of young geese and swan in a lake oposit to the
        mouth of the 4th of July Creek, in this lake are also abundances of
        fish of various species.   the pike [hap?] catt, sunfish &c &c perch
        Carp, *or buffaloe fish,*—[2]

12   the deer and bear begin to get scarce and the Elk begin to appear—

23rd   Cat fish is verry Common and easy taken in any part of this river.
        Some are nearly white perticilary above the Platte River.

1. These July remarks, placed at the end of the month, are Lewis's in the Weather Diary and Clark's in Codex C; they are nearly identical, but Lewis has no entry for July 23. Weather observations apparently ceased entirely after July 23 until September 19, as far as known records indicate, except for casual observations in Clark's daily journals.

2. The words "*or buffaloe fish*" after "carp" appear only in Lewis's Weather Diary. The pike is probably northern pike. The "catt" is either channel cat or *Ictalurus melas*, black bullhead. The perch could be *Stizostedion canadense*, sauger; *S. vitreum*, walleye; or *Perca flavescens*, yellow perch. The carp is perhaps *Carpiodes carpio*, river carpsucker; the carp was not introduced into the United States until 1877. Clark lists "Sun perch" instead of "sunfish." American sunfish belong to the family *Centrarchidae*. Lee et al., 133, 446, 441, 745, 747, 713, 367, 152, 577–614.

[Clark]

August the *1st 1804*   a fair morning, Sent out two men after the horses & one back to examine if the Indians have been there,[1] [*blank*] Beever Cought last night, the air is Cool and pleasing

Equal altitudes & magnetic Azmoth

azmth	altd.	Time	m	s		h.	m	s.
Comp. N. 86° E.	68° 47′ 15″	= A. M.	7	52	55	P. M.	3	50	42
			"	54	20		"	52	3
			"	55	47		"	53	31

Prepared the Pipe of Peace verry flashey.   wind rose at 10 oClock and blowed from the W. S. W.   very pleasent all day   Several men geathering grapes &c.   two men after the horses which Strayed the night before last.   those Praries produce the Blue Current Common in the U. S.   the Goose Berry Common in the U. S, two Kind of Honeysuckle, the Bush which I have Seen in Kentucky, with a paile Pink flower, also one which grow in Clusters about 4 or 5 feet high bearing a Short flour in clusters of the like Colour.   the leaves Single.[2]   3 Deer & an Elk Killed to day. This being my birth day I order'd a Saddle of fat Vennison, an Elk fleece & a Bevertail to be cooked and a Desert of Cheries, Plumbs, Raspberries Currents and grapes of a Supr. quallity.[3]   The Indians not yet arrived.   a Cool fine eveninge   Musquetors verry troublesom, the Praries Contain Cheres, Apple, Grapes, Currents, Rasp burry, Gooseberris Hastlenuts and a great Variety of Plants & flours not Common to the U S. What a field for a Botents [botanist] and a natirless [naturalist]

[Clark]

August the 1st 1804   a fair morning   Despatched two men after the horses lost yesterday, one man back to the place from which the messinger was Sent for the Ottoes to See if any Indians was or had been there Since our deptr.   he return'd and informed that no person had been there Sence we left it. The Prarie which is Situated below our Camp is above the high water leavel and rich Covered with Grass from 5 to 8 feet high intersperced with Copse of Hazel, Plumbs, Currents (like those of the U.S.) Rasberries & Grapes of Dift. Kinds.   also produceing a Variety of Plants and flowers not Common in the United States, two Kind of *honey Suckle* one which grows to a kind of a Srub. Common about Harrods burgh in Kentucky[4]   the other are not So large or tall and bears a flow[er] in Clusters Short and of a light Pink Colour, the leaves differ from any of the othe Kind in as much as the Lieves are Distinkd & does not Surround the Stalk as all the other Kind does[5]

one Elk and three Deer Killed to day also two Beever Cought

The wind rose at 10 oClock from the W. S. W. and blew a Steedy and agreeable Breeze all Day.

The Musqutors verry troublesom this evening in the bottoms.

Took equal altitudes to day and the azmuth with the Commencement of the A. M.

Time of alt'd

		h	m	s			h	m	s
N. 86° E	A M	7	52	55		P M	3	50	42
	"	7	54	20		"	3	52	3
	"	7	55	47		"	3	53	31

The Altitude given 68° 47′ 15″

The Indians not yet arrived   we fear Something amiss with our Messinger or them.

[Lewis]   *Wednesday August 1st*[6]

Observed meridian Altd. of ☉'s L. L. with Octant by the back observtn.   51° 29′ 30″

Observed Equal Altitudes of the ☉ with Sextant.

	h	m	s			h	m	s
A. M.	7	52	55	P. M.	3	50	42
"		54	20	"		52	3
"		55	47	"		53	31

Altitude given by Sextant at the time of this observation 68° 47′ 15″

⊙'s Magnetic azimuth by Circumferenter N. 86° E.

			h	m	s
Time by Chronometer	A. M.		7	52	55
Altitude by Sextant of ⊙'s U. L.			68°	47′	15″

Latitude of place deduced from two
observtns. of ⊙'s Merdn. altd. being as
mean of the same 41° 17′ 0.2″

---

1. Whitehouse records that Drouillard and Colter went after the horses, while Gibson went to look for the Otos and La Liberté.

2. The Blue Current is *Ribes americanum* Mill., wild black currant, which has an eastern United States distribution as Clark mentions. Fernald, 751; Barkley, 134. The two kinds of "honeysuckle" are not true honeysuckle species, since no native *Lonicera* fits the description here. They are likely *Symphoricarpos occidentalis* Hook., wolfberry, western snowberry, which was new to Clark, and *S. orbiculatus* Moench, coralberry, Indian-currant, buck-brush, with which Clark was familiar in Kentucky. Fernald, 1336; Barkley, 328–29.

3. Clark interlined this entire sentence later. It was his thirty-fourth birthday.

4. Harrodsburg, in Mercer County in central Kentucky, was named for James Harrod, an early settler. Stewart (APN), 198.

5. Biddle apparently has drawn a red line through the passage beginning "also produc-ing" to here.

6. Lewis's observation from Codex O.

[Clark]

August 2nd 1804   wind from the S E   G: Drewery returned with the horses & one Doe Elk   the countrey thro which he passed is like what we See from the Bluff above Camp   three men out Hunting   one Beaver caught this morning.

at Sunset 6 chiefs and their warries [warriors] of the Ottos,[1] and Missoures, with a french man by the name of *Far fonge*,[2] we ⟨Spoke⟩ Shook hands and gave them Some Tobacco & Provisions, they Sent us Water Millions[3]   Three verry large & fat Bucks Killed to day   the wind Continue hard from the S. E.—   the 4 qtr. of one Buck weigh'd 147 wt   1½ Inch fat on the ribs

[Clark]   *August 2nd Thursday* 1804

A verry pleasent Breeze from the S. E.   The Two men Drewyer & Colter returned with the horses loaded with Elk, those horses they found about 12 miles in a Southerly Derection from Camp.

The Countrey thro which they passed is Similar to what we See from Camp.   one Beaver & a foot of Beaver caught in trap Cought this morning—

at Sunset Mr. *Fairfong* [*NB: Ottoe interpreter resident with them*] and a pt. of Otteau & Missourie Nation Came to Camp, among those Indians 6 were Chiefs, the principal Chiefs   Capt. Lewis & myself met those Indians & informed them we were glad to See them, and would Speak to them tomorrow, Sent them Som rosted meat Pork flour & meal, in return they Sent us Water millions.   [every?] man on his Guard & ready for any thing

Three fat Bucks Killed this evening   the 4 qtrs. of one weighed 147 lbs.

[Lewis]   *August 2ed* 1804.[4]

This day one of our Hunters brought me a *white Heron* [*EC: Herodias egretta*].   this bird as an inhabitant of ponds and Marasses, and feeds upon tadpoles, frogs, small fish &c—   they are common to the Mississipi and the lower part of the *ohio* River, (ie) as high as the falls of that river.—

this bird weighed two lbs.—   it's plumage is perfectly white and very thin—

	F	I.
from extremity of beak to the extremity of toe	4	7 ¼
from tipp to tip of wing on the back	4	11

it's beak is yellow pointed, flated crosswise and 5 Inches in length from the upper region of the bill to the eye is one inch in length, covered with a smoth yellow skin   the plumage of the head projecting towards the upper bill and coming to a point a[t] an Inch beyond the eyes on the center of the upper bill. The mouth opens to distance of the eyes—   The eye is full and projecting reather, it is ⟨7/10 of an Inch⟩ 7/10 of half an inch.   four joints in the wing—

	Inches
1st joint from body in length	6
2ed Do.	8 ¼

3rd Do.		3 ½	
4th Do.		1	
1st Joint Number of feathers	7	Length of	3
2nd	18	⟨from⟩ 6 ⟨to⟩	
3	6	from 10 to 12	
4th	5	12	

it's legs are black— the neck and beak occupy ½ it's length. it has four toes on a foot— the ⟨left⟩ outer toe on the right foot is from the joining of the leg to extremity of toe nale 4 Inch & ¼ has four joints exclusive of the nail joint— the next is 4¾ inches has three joints exclusive of the nale joint. the next is 3¾ and has two joints, the heel toe has one joint only and is 3 Inches in length. the nails are long sharp and black— the eye is of a deep seagreen colour, with a circle of of pale yellow around the sight forming a border to the outer part of the eye of about half ⟨it's⟩ the width of the whole eye. the tale has 12 feathers of six inches in length.— the wings when folded are the same length with the tale.—

has 2 remarkable tufts of long feathers on each side joining the body at the upper joint of the wing. these cover the feathers of the 1st joint of the wings when they are over extended

1. The Otos were always a small tribe, having no more than one village at any one time. During the late seventeenth and the eighteenth century, they moved westward from the Mississippi River across Iowa and lived with or near the Iowa Indians. About 1798 the Otos were joined by the Missouris, and the two were subsequently regarded as one tribe. Both were horticulturalists and hunters, and both, like the Iowas, spoke a Siouan language of the Chiwere group. The Oto town, in Lewis and Clark's time, was apparently in Saunders County, Nebraska, on the Platte a little above the mouth of the Elkhorn. Jackson (LCO); Chapman (OM); Whitman; Hodge, 2:164–66.

2. This man was apparently living with the Oto tribe as a trader. It has been suggested that he was Charles Courtin (see entry for September 15, 1804), but that would require a misspelling remarkable even for Clark. He may have been the trader who carried back the information about the party's progress that Jefferson had received by November 1804. He is also "Faufon," "Far-fong," "Faufonn," and other variations in the journals; he remains unknown. Osgood (FN), 95–96 and n. 3; Jackson (LLC), 1:216–17 n. 1, 219 n. 1, 2:513, 741.

3. The familiar watermelon, *Citrullus vulgaris* Schrad, is an African species. Gilmore, who documents the cultivation of watermelons by the American Indians from as early as the seventeenth century, argues for the existence of an undescribed native species of *Cit-*

rullus, but his view is challenged by those who believe watermelons to have been introduced by Europeans. Gilmore, 68–77; Cutright (LCPN), 67 n. 14.

4. Lewis's natural history notes from Codex Q. This bird is the great egret.

[Clark]

August 3rd Friday   prepare a Small preas[en]t for those Indians and hold a Councul[1]   Delivered a Speech & made 8 6 chief [*hole*]   gave a fiew preasents and, a Smoke a Dram, Some Powder & Ball—[*hole*]   the man [La Liberté] we ⟨left⟩ Sent not yet come up, Those people express great Satisfa[ct]ion at the Speech Delivered   they are no Oreters, big [beg?], open Counternances, ottoes large   Missor [Missouris] Small

at 4 oClock Set out under a gentle Breeze from the S. E   proceeded on N. 5° E 5 Ms.   Passed a Pt. on the S. S. and round a large Sand bar on the L. S. and Camped above,[2] below a great number of Snags quit [quite?] across the river, The Musquitors more numerous than I ever Saw them, all in Spirrits, we had Some rough Convasation G. Dr. [Drouillard?]—about boys.

The Osage & Kansies are the Same language[3]

the Ottoes & Mahars Speek many words of the Osarge language

The Ottos, Aiaways [Iowas], & Missouries Speake the Same language

the Panies & Recreries [Arikaras] Speak the Same language also the Loups [Skiris] & repub. [Republican Pawnees, or Kitkahahki]

the Mahar, & Poncarar [Poncas] the Same Language

The Cheaun [Cheyennes], Mandin & Grovanter [Gros Ventres, or Hidatsas] the Same

The Probibility is that those defferant tribes have once formed ⟨one⟩ 3 great nats.   Viz: the Missouries, Osarge, Kanzes, Ottoes, Mahars, & Poncaras & Aiauaies [Iowas] one nation.

The Panies, Loups, Republican, Recrerees the 2nd

The Mandans Cheeons, & Grovanters the 3rd

T[h]e tribes of the Soux all retain the name 4th

It is possible that the ⟨Mandain⟩, Mahar & Poncarear may have been a Distinct nation, as they only Speek Some words of the osage which have the Same Signification[4]

25 Days to St Ta fee   S. of W. Cross the heads of Arkansies around the head of Kanzies River[5]

after Delivering a Speech informing thos Children of ours of the Change which had taken place,[6] the wishes of our government to Cultivate friendship & good understanding, the method of have good advice & Some Directions, we made ⟨8⟩ 1 Great Chief to the[7] who was not present, to whom we adresed the Speech & Sent Some presents or Meadels[8] & *flag*, we made 2 Second Chiefs one for the Missouris & another for the Ottos (those two tribes are nearly equal 170 each) and 4 principal men, to thos principal men to thos we gave a Small Comtn. [commission][9] to each man to whom w[e] gave authority, a preasn of *Br. Clt.* [breech clout] Gart.[erin]g. Paint & a med. or Contn a Small Coms. was delivered for the whole

each Chief & principal man delivered a Speech acknowledging ther approbation to what they had heard and promised to prosue the good advice and Caustion, they were happy w[ith?] ⟨Ther⟩ new fathers who gave good advice & to be Depended on all Concluded by asking a little Powder & a Drop of Milk [whiskey].

I answered those Speeches gave them 50 balls one Canister of Powder & a Dram— after Cap Lewis Shot his air gun a few times which astonished the nativs, we Set Sail. recved from thos people water millions &—

The Cheifs & Principal men of the Ottoes & Missouris made by M L. & W C the 3rd August 1804[10]

Viz.	Indian Names	Tribe	English Signifiation
1.	We-ar-ruge-nor	Ottoe	Little Thief
2.	Shingo-ton go	Otto	Big horse
	We tha a	Missourie	Hospatallity
3	Wau-pe-ur	Miss:	
	Au-ho-ning ga	M	
	Ba Za con ja	Ottoe	
	Au-ho-ne-ga	Miss.	

from this place I am told by Mr. *Faufong* the interpeter that it will take a man 25 Days to go to St. a fee pass, the heads of Arkansas, round the Kansas head, across Some mountains from the top of which the City may be Seen the Spaniards have envited those Indians & the Panies to trade with them & Some french & a few indians are gorn from the Panias to that City this Summer—

The Situation of this place which we Call *Council Bluff* which is hand-som ellevated   a Spot well Calculated for a Tradeing establishment,[11] the Bank high & leavel on top well Calculated for a fort to Command the Countrey and river   the low bottom above high water & well Situated under the Command of the Hill for Houses to trade with the Natives   a butifull Plain both abov and below   at no other bend on either Side does the High land touch the river for Some distance up, as I am told.

those Bluffs afford good Clay for Brick, a great quantity on the 3 points one Opsd. one abov & one below.—   the Situation I am informed is, within 1 Days march of the Ottoes, 1 ½ of the Panias, 2 of the Mahars, & 2 ½ of the Loups Villages, also Convenient to the roveing Bands of Soux, Those people are now at war with each other, an establishment here would bring about peace and be the means of Keeping of it.[12]

Augt. 3d[13]   Camped on the upper point of a large Sand bar L. S.   Mis-quters verry bad. Some place near Conncill Bluff will be the most proper place for a tradeing establishment, for maney of the nations, the distance is to the Ottoes one Days, Ponies [Pawnees] 1 ½ days, to the Mahar, 2 days, to Loups[14] 2 Days & a half 16 or 1800 men—and convenient for Some ⟨The Republicans are also⟩ bands of the Sues,

⟨Your letter of the 7th of Feby I recved With great pleasure⟩[15]

[Clark]   *August 3rd, Friday* 1804

mad[e] up a Small preasent for those people in perpotion to their Con-siqunce.   also a package with a meadile to accompany a Speech for the Grand Chief ⟨which we intend to send to him⟩   after Brackfast we Col-lected those Indians under an orning of our Main Sail, in presence of our Party paraded & Delivered a long Speech to them expressive of our jour-ney the wirkes of our Government, Some advice to them and Directions how They were to Conduct themselves, ⟨made one⟩ the princapal Chief for the nation ⟨to whom⟩ being absente we sent him the Speech *flag* Meadel & Some Cloathes.   after hering what they had to say Delivered ⟨two of⟩ a medal of Second Grade to one for the Ottos & and one for the Missourie ⟨part of the nation⟩ present and 4 medals of a third Grade to the inferior Chief   two for each tribe. Those two parts of nations, Ottos & Missouries now ⟨forming one of⟩ residing together is about 250 men are ⟨nearly equal in number⟩ the Ottoes Composeing ⅔d and Missourie ⅓ part[16]

The names of the Chiefs we acknowledged Made this day are as follows Viz[17]

	Indian name	English signftn.		
1st	*We ár ruge nor*	Ottoe *Called Little Theif*		
2	⎰ Shōn gŏ tōn gŏ	"	"	Big Horse
	⎱ We the a	*Miss:*	"	Hospatality
	Shon Guss Còn	*Ottoe*	"	White horse
	Wau pe ùh	M.		
	Āh hŏ nīng gă	M.		
	Baza cou jà	Ottoe		
	Āh hŏ nē gă	M.		

Those ⟨people⟩ Chiefs all Delivered a Speech acknowledgeing Their approbation to the Speech and promissing to prosue the advice & Derictions given them   that they wer happy to find that they had fathers which might be depended on &c.

We gave them a Cannister of Powder and a Bottle of whiskey and delivered a few presents to the whole after giveing a *Br: Cth:* [breech cloth] Some Paint guartering & a Meadele to those we *made* Cheifs   after Capt Lewis's Shooting the air gun a feiw Shots (which astonished those nativs) we Set out and proceeded on five miles on a Direct line passed a point on the S. S. & round a large Sand bar on the L. S. & Camped on the upper point. The Misquitors excessively troublesom this evening   Great appearance of wind and rain to the N. W.   we prepare to rec've it—   The man *Liberty* whome we Sent for the Ottoes has not Come up   he left the Ottoes Town one Day before the Indians. This man has eithered tired his horse or, lost himself in the Plains   Some Indians are to hunt for him,

The Situation [*WC: 25 Days from this to Santafee*] of our last Camp *Councill Bluff* or Handssom Prarie appears to be a verry proper place for a Tradeing establishment & fortification   The Soil of the Bluff well adapted for Brick, Great deel of timbers abov in the two Points.   many other advantages of a Small nature.   and I am told Senteral to Several nations   Viz. one Days march from the Ottoe Town, one Day & a half from the great Pania village,[18] 2 days from the Mahar Towns, two ¼ Days from the *Loups* Village, & Convenient to the Countrey thro: which Bands of the Soux [*NB: rove &*] hunt. perhaps no other Situation is as well Calculated for a Tradeing establishment. The air is pure and helthy So far as we can Judge.—

Course of Augt. 3rd

N. 5° E   5   ms. to a pt. on L. S.   psd. a pt. on the S. S. & a Sand bar L S

1. This council is discussed in Ronda, 17–23.

2. The campsite, depending on shifts of the river, could be in either Harrison County, Iowa, or Washington County, Nebraska, some miles south of the present town of Blair, Nebraska. MRC map 24; MRR map 67.

3. These notes on the conference with the Otos and Missouris and the country around the Council Bluff are on both sides of document 39 of the Field Notes. They are placed here because of the date August 3, given at one point in the document, and their general relation to the day's events.

4. Clark is attempting to analyze information he has gathered from his own observation and that of traders on the languages and relationships of the western tribes. The Omaha, Osage, Ponca, and Kansa languages are of the Dhegiha group of the Siouan language family, so similarities in vocabulary are not surprising. The Iowa, Oto, and Missouri languages are of the Chiwere division of the Siouan family. The Mandan and Hidatsa (Gros Ventre) tongues form separate groups within the Siouan family. The Pawnees and Arikaras spoke related languages of the Caddoan language family. Clark's "Loups" are the Skiri Pawnees, and the "Republicans" are the Kitkahahki Pawnees, both of them speaking dialects of the Pawnee language, which belongs to the Caddoan linquistic family. The Cheyennes spoke an Algonquian language unrelated to any of the others mentioned; probably they were little known to Clark's trader informants, hence the misinformation. Hollow & Parks.

5. At this time, Europeans outside the Spanish Empire had only a vague idea of even the geographical location of Santa Fe, a city nearly two hundred years old, and knew little of the geography of the Southwest. The Spanish government preferred that this ignorance continue. In 1792 Pedro Vial, a Frenchman serving Spain, and two New Mexicans crossed from Santa Fe to the Missouri and St. Louis. Vial estimated that he could have made the trip in twenty-five days, except for difficulties with Indians. Vial's estimate may have been the original source of Clark's information, which came from "Faufong." Jefferson had instructed Lewis to gather information about the possibility of trade with Santa Fe, and Lewis actually contemplated a reconnaissance up the Kansas River in the winter of 1803–4 to examine part of the route, before Jefferson vetoed the idea. The mountains "from the top of which the City may be Seen," mentioned later, are probably the Sangre de Cristo Range in Colorado and New Mexico. DeVoto, 186–87; Allen, 74–75; Loomis & Nasatir, 28–73; Nasatir (BR), 86–106; Albert Gallatin to Jefferson, March 14, 1803, Jefferson to Gallatin, March 20, 1803, Jefferson's Instructions to Lewis [June 20, 1803],

Lewis to Jefferson, October 3, 1803, Jefferson to Lewis, November 16, 1803, Jackson (LLC), 1:27–28, 31–32, 63, 131, 137.

6. The figures are upside down under this entry:

186	64
1434	5
108	
1728	69

7. Apparently Clark left the sentence incomplete; he may have intended it to mean: "we made 1 Great Chief to the [*Otos, Little Thief*]." They would meet him later, on August 19, 1804. In the spring of 1805, Little Thief, with two other Otos, a Missouri, and three Republican Pawnees (Kitkahahkis) journeyed down the Missouri to St. Louis, intending to visit Washington. Circumstances forced a long delay in St. Louis, during which Little Thief became ill. He insisted on returning home but died a few miles up the Missouri. Jackson (LCO), 247–48.

8. The custom of presenting medals bearing the reigning sovereign's image to Indian chiefs was one long followed by European powers. United States medals bore the portrait of the current president. Jefferson medals came in three sizes with the same basic design; 105 mm (the largest ever issued), 76 mm, and 55 mm. Prucha, xiii–xiv, 92–93.

9. These commissions were simply certificates issued to prominent Indians of lesser rank than chief in lieu of medals. See Ronda, 6.

10. Linguistic analysis of these Oto and Missouri personal names by Robert L. Rankin, Kenneth Miner, and John E. Koontz shows some discrepancies in the translations by Clark. "We-ar-ruge-nor" does not signify "Little Thief," although its actual meaning cannot be determined. *Šǫ́ge tháka* literally means "Big Horse." *Widá'e* signifies "He Pities them," which may be a reasonable equivalent to "Hospitality." In the second entry for August 3, Clark adds the name "White Horse," which is more correctly *Šǫ́ge ska*.

11. In 1819, the army established Fort Atkinson on the Council Bluff just east of present Fort Calhoun, Washington County, Nebraska. Several hundred troops were stationed there, and it was the army's most westerly outpost until abandoned in 1827 because it was considered too remote from white settlements to serve any useful purpose. Ney.

12. On the left margin of this sheet (reverse of document 39) are these figures:

1.64	36	64
	72	36

The entire page is written over what was apparently a draft for a pay roll, with headings as follows (upside down to main text and with part of the left edge of the page cut off):

Terms of Service Charged Months Days	Pay per Month Dols. Cts.	Amount of pay Dollars Cents	Bounty resd.	Cash receiv'd in Lieu of Clothing & Provisions Dols. Cts.	Total Amount Received Dols. Cts.	Remarks

13. This August 3 entry is on a sheet of the Field Notes (document 40) separate from the preceding material.

14. The Skiri Pawnees, called Loup ("wolf") Pawnees by the French. The Loup River in Nebraska derives its name from them. If Clark's "Republicans" were the Republican (Kitkahahki) Pawnees, he was badly misinformed about their having any connection with the Sioux, their bitter enemies through most of nineteenth century. Since he crossed out this line later, he probably received more nearly correct information. Hodge, 2:589–91. The Loup villages are the Palmer site. Grange, 18, 21. See also July 20 and 27, 1804. The Pawnee (Chawi) village is the Linwood site. See Grange, 18–19. See Wedel (PHH), 49–60, for the Oto village site.

15. This line, which is heavily crossed out, was apparently a first draft for a letter. Biddle's notation on this sheet of the Field Notes (document 40) comes after the August 3, 1804, entry and reads "Aug. 3 to 6."

16. Someone has apparently crossed through the lines from "the princapal Chef" on. The text, originally quite disordered here, has been arranged as accurately as possible.

17. Biddle apparently added some of these diacritical marks in red ink.

18. Clark may refer to the village of the Grand (Chawi) and Republican (Kitkahahki) Pawnees. *Atlas* map 126.

[Clark]

Course Disstance & Reffurance August 4th Satturday, 1804

S. 80° W.	1 ½	Me. to an old Tradeing house on the L. S. passed a Sand pt. Makeing from S. pt (1) bad ps.
N. 25 W.	2 ¼	mes. to a Willow pt. on the L. S. passed a large Sand bar (2) psd. a Creek on L. S. (3)
S. 70 W.	1 ¾	ms. to a Willow point on S. S. passed maney Snags. opsd a Crēek of the Ponds L. S.
N. 24 W.	2 ½	ms. to a Willow point on L. S. passed a Sand from S. Point
N. 24 W	3 ½	ms. to a Copse of willows in a bend L. S. willow pt. on the S. S. opsd. a ⟨Smooth Plain,⟩ river verry wide & Shallow
S. 84 E.	3 ½ ——— 15	Mes. to a point Lard side passing a ⟨Stard⟩ pot. on Stard Side. Wind E. due[1] The high land is Some distanc from the river on both Sides and at this place is ⟨not within 20 miles of⟩ apt. [approximately?] 10 or 12 Miles apart, the tops of the high land on the S. S. appiair to contain ⟨more timber that that on the Larboard Side, the willow is low & not So plenty as below.⟩[2]

August 4th   at 7 oClock the heavens darkened and a violent wind from the N W. Succceeded which lasted about ⟨half⟩ an hour, with a little rain.

Set out this morning early thro a narrow part of the [channel], the whole Channel Confined in Some parts between the (1) Sand on one Side & the bank on the other (which is washing in) within 200 yards, this Chanl. Crouded with Snags.   at 1½ m: passed an old tradeing house L. S. where one of our Crew passed 2 years *P. C* [Pierre Cruzatte] tradeing with the Mahar; & Ponies—[3]   above 1 me. a (3) Creek[4] Coms in opsd. a large bad (2) Sand bar   this (3) Creek is the outlett of 3 ponds, which recved ther water from the Smaller Streams running from the hills on the L. S, Great qts. of Gees, passed in the next bend L. S. an out let to the Pond, Butifull bottom Prarie on both Sides of the river, Pumey [pumice] Stone is found on the Sides of the river of various Sizes.[5] Wind a head. Reed the man who went back to the Camp of last night for his Knife has not Come up this evening—[6]   we Camped at a pt. on the L. S. at a Beaver house.[7]   1 Buck Killed to daye.[8]

[Clark]   *August 4th Satturdaye*

   Set out early—   (at 7 oClock last night we had a Violent wind from the N W   Som little rain Succeeded, the wind lasted with violence for one hour   after the wind it was clear Sereen and Cool all night.)   proceeded on   passed thro betwen Snags which was quit across the Rivr   the Channel Confined within 200 yards one Side a Sand pt. S S. the other a Bend, the Banks washing away & trees falling in constantly for 1 mile, abov this place is the remains of an old Tradeing establishment L. S. where Petr. Crusett one of our hands Stayed two years & traded with the *Mahars*   a Short distance above is a Creek (3) the out let of Three Ponds comunicateing with each other, those Ponds or rether Lakes are fed by Springs & Small runs from the hills.   (2) a large Sand Island opposit this Creek makeing out from the L. Point, from the Camp of last night to this Creek, the river has latterly Changed its bed incroaching on the L. Side, in this Sand bar I Saw great Nos. of wild gees—   passed a Small Creek on the L. S about 3 miles above the last   both of those Creek's are out lets from the Small Lake which reive their water from the Small Streems running from the high land—   great ma[n]y *Pamey* Stones on the Shore of various Sises   the wind blew hard—   *Reed* a man who went back to Camp for his knife has not joined us.   we camped at a Beaver house on the L. S.— one Buck Killed to day—

Course Distance & refs. 4th August 1804

S. 80° W.	1 ½	ms. to an old Tradeing House on the L. S. passed a S pt. from S. S. (1)
N. 25° W.	2 ¼	ms. to a willow pt. on the L. S. pass a large Sand Isd. & Creek on the L. pt (3)
N. 70° W.	1 ¾	ms to a willow pt on the S. S. psd a Sm: Creek L. S. & many Snags
N. 24° W.	3 ½	ms. to a willow pt. on the L. S. passed a Sand from a S. pt.
S. 84° E	3 ½ 15	ms. to a pt. on the L. S. passed a pt. on the S. S. here the high Lands is Some Distance from the river on both Sides, and at the this place the High lands are at least 12 or 15 miles apart, the range of high land on the S. S. appear to Contain Some timber— that on the L. S. appear to be intireley Clear of any thing but what is Common in an open Plain, Some Scattering timber or wood is to be Seen in the riveens and where the Creeks pass into the Hill— the points and wet lands Contain tall timber back of the willows which is generally Situated back of a large Sand bar from the Points.

(*Point of observation No. 26.*)

[Lewis]   *Saturday August 4th 1804*[9]

On the Starboard shore, opposite to the mouth of *pond inlet.*—

Observed meridian altd. of ☉'s L. L. with Octant by the back observatn.   53° 20′ 30″

Latitude deduced from this obsertn.   41° 25′ 3.8″

note—the ☉'s disk was frequently obscured in the course of this observation, it is therefore probable that it is not accurate by 2 or 3 minutes of Latitude, and I believe it too much by that sum.

1. It appears that Lewis wrote this line of the course material.

2. This column of figures is in a blank space beneath the courses and distances of this entry: ½, 3 ¼, 4 ½, 1 ¼, 2 ¼, with a total of 12.

3. Perhaps the post established by Mackay in the fall of 1795, somewhere in the vicinity of the Oto villages, before he went on upriver to establish Fort Charles. Perhaps on Mill Creek, south of Blair, Washington County, Nebraska. *Atlas* map 14; Warren map 6; MRC map 24; MRR map 67; Osgood (FN), 99 n. 7; Nasatir (BLC), 1 : 97–98.

4. Probably Fish Creek, Blair. *Atlas* map 14; MRC map 24.

5. Several exposures of volcanic ash (pumice), long called the Pearlette Ash, have been observed along the Missouri River bluffs north of Omaha, and one near the mouth of

Ponca Creek, south of Blair, was recorded by Miller. Although they were long considered to represent a single ash fall, recent studies have shown that there are at least three in eastern Nebraska and western Iowa, with ages between .6 and 2.0 million years. At present (1984) no ash beds exposed in this reach of the river have been dated. Miller; Reed & Dreeszen; Boellstorff; Izett. The pumicestone could also be one of several varieties of rock produced by burning of coal beds in North Dakota and carried to this point by floods. The rocks are not volcanic. Information of Robert N. Bergantino, Montana Bureau of Mines and Geology.

6. Reed had, in fact, deserted.

7. Owing to shifts in the Missouri River, the campsite may be in either Washington County, Nebraska, or Harrison County, Iowa, northeast of Blair, Nebraska. *Atlas* map 14; Warren map 6; MRC map 24.

8. Four illegible words are written at right angles to this entry, in a column. The last three appear to be only initial letters followed by dots. The initial letters appear to be: W, W, T [or F], and [R?].

9. Lewis's observation from Codex O.

[Clark]

August 5th   Set out early   wind from N E.   Great appearance of Wind & rain, (I have remarked that I have not heard much thunder in this Countrey) ⟨Lightning is Common as in other Countries⟩ a verry large Snake was Killed to day called the Bull Snake, his Colour Some thing like a rattle Snake Something lighter—[1]   the bends of the river to day is washing away the banks, haveing nothing to oppose the turbelance of the [river] when Confined by large hard Sand Points, forceing this Current against the bends—   the Soil of the entire bottom between the high land, being the mud or *Ooze* of the river of Some former period mixed with Sand & Clay easely melts and Slips, or washies into the river   the mud mixes with the water & the Sand collects on the points[2]   Camped on the S. S.—[3]   I went on[4] Shore S. S. this evening   Saw Some turkeys and in persueing them Struck the river 12 miles below the place by water I went out, I think the Peninsuly is about 370 yards across Subjuct to overflow; & washes into numerous Channels, Great quantities of Graps ripe & of three Defferent Kind   Some large & fine. I Killed a Turkey, and made Camp in the Night, Musqutors verry troubleson—   Reed the man who went back for his Knife has not yet joined us

Courses & Distance of Aug 5th Sunday

S. 60° E.	1 ½	across a large Sand bar to a point on M Stbd. Shore below a large willow Island on S. Bend

447

N. 20 W.	¾	Ms. to a pt. above a Sand bar on the opsd. the upper pt. of the Island, (much Beaver Sign)
N. 34 W	3 ¼	Ms. to a pt on the L. S. passed one on the S. S.
North	¾	m. to a pt. on the right of a Sand Island making from the L. Pt.
S. 45 W.	2 ¼	Ms. to 3 Small trees in a Bend L. S. passi'g over a Sand point S. S.
N. 45 W	4 ½	Ms. to a point on S. S. the High land Grat Distanc from the R
North	1 ¼	on the S. S. to a pt. of Sand bar—opsd. a falling in bank river narrow
N. 70 E.	¼	on the S. Sand bar
S. 30 E.	2	Ms. to the Pt. of a Sand bar makeing out from the L. point the Same continued ½ miles psd. a Sand in the md.
N. 45 E	2 ½ ——— 20 ½	to the ⟨mouth⟩ lower point of an Island close to Stard Shore it behind this Island on the Stard side that the Soldier's river disimbogues itself [5]

[Clark]   5th of August Sunday 1804

Set out early   great appearance of wind and rain   (I have observed that Thundor & lightning is not as common in this Countrey as it is in the atlantic States)   Snakes are not plenty, one was killed to day large and resembling the rattle Snake only Something lighter—.   I walked on Shore this evening S. S.   in Pursueing Some Turkeys I [s]truck the river twelve miles below within 370 yards, the high water passes thro this Peninsulia; and agreeable to the Customary Changes of the river I Concld. [*NB: Should Calculate*] that in two years the main Current of the river will pass through. In every bend the banks are falling in from the Current being thrown against those bends by the Sand points which inlarges and the Soil I believe from unquestionable appearns. of the entire bottom from one hill to the other being the mud or ooze of the River at Some former Period mixed with Sand and Clay easily melts and Slips into the River, and the mud mixes with the water & the Sand is washed down and lodges on the points—   Great quantites of Grapes on the banks, I observe three different Kinds at this time ripe, one Of the no. is large & has the flaver of the Purple grape.[6]   camped on the S. S.   the Musquitors verry troubleson. The man who went back after his Knife has not yet come up, we have Some reasons to believe he has Deserted

Course Distance & Refrs. August 5th

S. 60° E	1 ½	ms. crossgn. a large Sd. bar to a pt. on mn. S. Sd. bel[ow]: a willow Isd. in St. Bend
N. 20 W.	¾	ms. to a pt. above a Sad. bar opsd. the upper pt. of the Sd. Island Beaver
N. 34 W.	3 ¼	ms. to a pt. on the L. S. passed one on the Starboard Side
North	¾	Me. to a pt. on the right of a Sand Isd. makeing from the L. pt.
S. 45° W.	3 ¼	mes. to 3 Small trees in Prarie & bend to the L. S. passed a Sand pt. S. S.
N. 45° W.	4 ½	Ms. to a pt. on S. S.
North	1 ¼	Ms. on the S. S. to the pt. of a Sand bar river narrow
N. 70° E	¼	Ms. on the Sand bar S. S.
S. 30 E	2	ms. to the pt. of a Sand bar making out from the L. pt. psd. a Sand.
S. 30 E	½	Me. on the point
N. 45° E	2 ½	mes. to the lower point of an Island Close to S. S. ⟨at⟩ behind this Island on S. S. the *Soldiers* river disimboques itself.
	20 ½	

[Lewis]   August 5th 1804[7]

Killed a serpent [*EC: Pituophis melanol*] on the bank of the river adjoining a large prarie.

	F	Inch
Length from nose to tail	5	2
Circumpherence in largest part—		4 ½
Number of scuta on belly— 221		
Do. on Tale— 53		

No pison teeth therefore think him perfectly inocent— eyes, center black with a border of pale brown yellow Colour of skin on head yellowish green with black specks on the extremity of the scuta which are pointed or triangular   colour of back, transverse stripes of black and dark brown of an inch in width, succeeded by a yellowish brown of half ⟨colour of belly & scuta⟩ that width—

the end of the tale hard and pointed like a cock's spur—

the sides are speckled with yellowish brown and black.— two roes of black spots on a lite yellow ground pass throughout his whole length on the upper points of the scuta of the belly and tale ½ Inch apart   this snake is vulgarly called the cow or bull snake from a bellowing nois which it is said sometimes to make resembling that anamal, tho' as to this fact I am unable to attest it never having heard them make that or any other noise myself.—

I have frequently observed an acquatic bird [*EC: sterna antillarum*] in the cours of asscending this river but have never been able to procure one before today, this day I was so fortunate as to kill two of them, they are here more plenty than on the river below.   they lay their eggs on the sand bars without shelter or nest, and produce their young from the 15th to the last of June, the young ones of which we caught several are covered with down of a yellowish white colour and on the back some small specks of a dark brown.   they bear a great resemblance to the young quale of ten days oald, and apear like them to be able to runabout and peck their food as soon as they are hatched— this bird, lives on small fish, worms and bugs which it takes on the virge of the water   it is seldom seen to light on trees an qu[i]te as seldom do they lite in the water and swim tho' the foot would indicate that they did it's being webbed   I believe them to be a native of this country and probly a constant resident.—

the weight of the male bird is one ounce and a half, it[s] [l]ength from b[e]ak to toe 7½ inches   from tip to tip of wing across the back one foot seven inches and a half   [the beak] is one ⅛ inch lonong, large where it joins the head flated on the sides and tapering to a sharp point, a little declining and curvated, a fine yellow, with a shade of black on the extremity of upper beak; the eye is prominent, black and on a angular scale of ½ Inc; occupyse 3⅓ in width.   the upper part of the head is black from the beak as low as the middle of the eye and a little below the joining of the neck except however some white which joins the upper part of the beak ⟨and extends⟩ which forks and passing over the sides of the forehead terminate above each eye— the under part of the bird, that is the thr[o]at and cheeks as high as the eye, the neck brest belly and under part of the wings and tail are of a fine white, the upper part of the neck, back, and wings are of a fine, quaker colour, or bright dove colour with reather more of a bluish tint—except however the three first or larger feathers in the wing which on upper side are of a deep black. the wing has four joints—

No. Joint	Length of joint	No. of feathers	Length of do.
1	1½	a Clump of feathers not strong but loosly connect with the flesh of the wing	1½
2	2	16	2
3	1½	7	from 2½ to 4½
4	¾	3	5½

the tail has eleven feathers the outer of which are an inch longer than those in the center gradually tapering inwards which gives the tale a forked appearance like that of the swally [swallow]   the largest or outer feathe[r] is 2¾ that of the shortest 1¾—   the leg and thye are three inches long the leg occupying one half this length   the thye is covered with feathers except about ¼ of an inch above the knee   the leg is of a bright yellow and nails long sharp and black   the foot is webbed and has three toes forward; the heel or back toe is fixed to the leg above the palm of the foot, and is unconnected by a web to the other toes, it has no nail.   the wings when foalded lap like those of the swallow and extend at least an inch and a half beyond the tale.   this bird is very noysey when flying which is dose exttreemly swift   the motion of the wing is much like that of *kildee*   it has two notes one like the squaking of a small pig only on reather a high kee, and the other kit'-tee'- kit'-tee'- as near as letters can express the sound—   the beak of the female is black and the black and quaker colour of the male in her is yellow[i]s[h] brown mixed with dove colour

(Point of Observation No. 27.)

[Lewis]   *Sunday August 5th*[8]

On the Larboard shore of main channel, and on the starboard side of the Sand Island.—

Observed meridian Altd. of ☉'s L. L. with Octant by the back observtn.   54°
3′ —″

Latitude deduced from this observation   41° 30′ 6.7″

1. The bullsnake is *Pituophis melanoleucus sayi*. See Lewis's description from Codex Q, below, on this date. Burroughs, 275–76; Benson, 89.

2. Records of wells drilled through the floodplain sediments of the Missouri River in this region generally show that thirty to more than fifty feet of "blue" or gray clay, post-Pleistocene alluvium, overlie the sand and gravel that fill the lower part of the valley.

3. In Harrison County, Iowa, near the Burt-Washington county line, Nebraska on the opposite shore. Shifts of the Missouri River and of the lower course of the Soldier River over the years have evidently been substantial. *Atlas* map 14; Warren map 6; MRC maps 24, 25; MRR maps 68, 69.

4. Clark continued the narrative from here following the courses and distances. It is rearranged for ease of reading.

5. This last course appears in Lewis's hand, as are also the words "the same continued ½ miles" in the previous line.

6. The three grape species are probably *Vitis aestivalis* Michx., summer grape, pigeon grape; *V. riparia* Michx., river-bank grape; and *V. vulpina* L., winter grape. The larger grape (*V. riparia*) tasted like the "Purple grape," which may be the cultivated concord grape, *V. labrusca* L. Barkley, 219–20; Fernald, 997–98.

7. Lewis's natural history notes from Codex Q. See n. 1 this date for the snake. The "acquatic bird" is the least tern, *Sterna antillarum* [AOU, 74]. The bird used for comparison is the killdeer, *Charadrius vociferus* [AOU, 273]. Burroughs, 231–32.

8. Lewis's observation from Codex O.

[Clark][1]

August 6th Monday 1804   at 12 oClock last night a Violent Storm of wind & rain from the N. W.   one perogue (*Bapteest Le Joness* [La Jeunesse] *Patroon*)[2] lost her Colours   Set out early & proceeded on   passed a large Island on the S. S.   back of this Island *Rivie de Soldiert*[3] Come in on the S. S.—   the Solder's River is about the Sise of Nodaway 20 yd. wide at the mouth, passed two remarkable places, where the River had once ⟨river⟩ Passed—   We have every reason to belive that one man has *Deserted Moses B: Reed*   he has been absent three Days and one french man we Sent to the Indian Camps has not joined us, we have reasons to beleve he lost himself in attempting to join us at the *Council Bluff*—   we are deturmind to Send back 4 men to take *reede* Dead or alive, also hunt *La Liberty* and to meet us at the Mahar nation as Soon as the order is executed.

Course Distance reffurence. 6th Augt. Monday 1804

N. 30° E	1	me. to a pt on the L. S. the Island opposit and about opsd. Soldier's River
N. 15 E	3 ½	Mes. to pt. in a bend S S below a chanl. of the river lately filled up passed a Sand bar below making from pt. below the upr. Pt of R. (1) This Island is Seperated from the S. S by a Chanl. of 40 yds. Swift Crt.
West	1	mile to a pt. of woods above a large Sand bar Makeing out from the L. point.
West	1 ½	ms to a pt on L. S. Willows
S. 55 W.	3 ½	Ms. to a pt. of Willows on the S. S. the land naked & within 3 Ms of the R. Ld
N. 10 W.	½	on the S. pt. a Sand bar in the Middle
N. 18 E	3	mile passing over a Sand bar on L. S. to a pt. on the Same Side.
North	1 ½	me. to a pt. on the S. S
N. 18 W	½	on the Sand bar from the pt.
East	3⟨½⟩	to a Pt. Willows making from the L. point psd. a place of Snags
N 16 E	1 ½	ms. to a pt. on the S. S. an old bed of the River S. S. but fiew ⟨no⟩ Snakes on this part of the river[4]
	20 ½	

[Clark]   6th August, Monday 1804

At 12 oClock last nigh a violent Storm of wind from the N W.   Some rain   one pr. of Colours lost in the Storm from the bige Perogue. Set out early and proceeded on   passed a large Island on the S. S.   back of this Isd. Soldiers River mouths, I am told by one of the men that this river is about the Size of Nadawa river *40* yards wide at the mouth. Reed has not yet come up.   neither has La Liberty the frenchman whome we Sent to the Indian Camps a fiew miles below the *Council Bluffs.*

Course Destance &. August 6th

| N. 30° E. | 1 | me: to a pt. on L. S. opposit the mouth of Soldiers River S. S. |

N. 15° E.	3 ½	Ms to a pt. in a bend to the S. S. below a chanl. of the river laterly filled up passed a Sand bar from the L. pt.
West	2 ½	Ms to a willow point on the L. S passed a Sand bar makeing out from the L. pt.
S. 55° W.	3 ½	Ms. to a pt. of willows on the S. S. the high land within 3 miles of the river on the L. S.
N. 10° W.	½	me. on the S. pt. a Sand bar in R.
N. 18° E.	3	ms. passing over a Sand bar on the L. S. to a pt. on the Same Side of the Missourie.
North	1 ½	Ms. to a pt. on the S. S.
N. 18 W.	½	me. on the Sand from the pt.
East	3	me. to a pt. of willows on L. pt. passed a place where the Snags were thick.
N. 16° E	<u>1 ½</u>	ms. to a pt. on the S. S. and a place where the river formerly run leaving Ponds in its old Channel S S.
	20 ½	

1. Under the August 6 entry is written the following:

Leav

[Zages?]   60 = 150

[Salem?] 110 = <u>300</u>

450

And at right angles to the rest of the page is this address revealing that the sheet had earlier served as an envelope: Jeffersonville I. T.   Feb. 9th 25   Captain William Clark   near Cahokia   By Mail.

2. The only reference to La Jeunesse as "patroon," that is, foreman of the French boatmen. Clark may have intended to refer to Baptiste Deschamps, the actual patroon, or he may only have meant that La Jeunesse was in charge of the one pirogue at this time. See Appendix A, this volume.

3. The mouth of Soldier River, in Harrison County, Iowa, has apparently moved about considerably over the years, just as the Missouri has changed course. See *Atlas* map 14. It is questionable that there were any white soldiers on this stream before Lewis and Clark. The name probably derives from the French trader's term *soldier* for members of Indian warrior societies, who often kept order in camp and protected traders. Petersen, 464–65; Hodge, 2:614–15; Nicollet (MMR), 388; Warren map 6; MRC maps 24, 25; MRR maps 68, 69.

4. The courses and distances give the only information on this day's camp, other than that on *Atlas* map 14. It was apparently on the starboard side, in Harrison County, Iowa, roughly halfway between the Soldier and Little Sioux rivers. MRC map 24; MRR maps 69, 70.

[Clark]

August 7th Tuesday   last night about 8 oClock a Storm of wind from the N. W. which lasted ¾ of an hour   mosquitors more troublesom last night than I ever Saw them, Set out late this morning   wind N.

Course		Dis	
North	2		ms to a Pt. of Willows on the L. S. opposit, Saw 10 Pelicans flying
N. 25 W.	½		me. on the L point
N. 45 W.	½		me. on the L. point of a Sand bar
N 45 W.	1		me. to the point of a Sand bar makeing out from the L pt.
S 12 E	2 ½		me. to the do— do from the St. Point Win fair—
S. 70 E.	½		me to the willows on the S. S. G. Drewyer, R. Fields, W. Bratten & Wm Labiese [Labiche],[1] sent after Reed Deserted, La Liberty absent & a Speech to the ottoes with a view to get a fiew of their Chief to the Mahars to make a peace between them, Sent Some Tobacco, Wampon, and Speech als[o] gave pointed orders to the party in writeing[2]
N. 36 W.	2 ½		ms. to a pt. of Willows on the L S. a large Sand makeing out from it—
N. 73 W.	3		ms. to a pt. of willows S. S. I went out and discovered that two Bayoues run thro the point & Cutit [cut it] into Island, which I call Detachment Islands[3] as from this bend We detached Drewyr R. Fields Bratten & Labiecue no Game of any Kind
N. 83° E	2 ½		Ms. to a pt. of Cotton wood, passing over a Sand bar from the Said point
N. 32 W.	1 ½		ms. to a Sand point makeing out from the S. point
N. 12 E	½		m to the willows on the S. S. and camped
	18		

[Clark]   7th *August Tuesday 1804*

last night at 8 oClock a Storm from the N W. lasted ¾ of an hour   let out late this morning   wind from the North— at 1 oClock dispatched George Drewyer, R. Fields, Wm. Bratten & Wm. Labieche back after the Deserter reid with order if he did not give up Peaceibly to put him to

Death[4] &c. to go to the Ottoes Village & enquire for La Liberty and bring him to the Mahars Village, also with a Speech on the occasion to the Ottoes & Missouries— and directing a few of their Chiefs to come to the Mahars, & we would make a peace between them & the Mahar and *Souex*, a String of wompom & a Carrot of Tobacco. proceeded on and Camped on the S. S.[5]

Course Dist. & remarks Augt. 7th 1804

North	2	ms. to a pt. of willows on the L. S.
N. 25° W.	½	Me. on the L. point
N 45° W.	1 ½	me. on the L. pt. of a Sd. bar
S. 12° E.	2 ½	ms. do do.
S. 70° E.	½	me. to the willows on the S. S.
N. 36° W.	2 ½	Ms. to a pt. of willows on the L. S. a large Sand makein out
N. 73° W.	3	ms. to a pt. of willows on the S. S. I went thro to the next bend up a Beayoue S. S. form'g two Isds I call Detachment Isd.
N. 83° E.	2 ½	Ms. to a pt. of Cotton wood L. S Psd. a Sand bar from L. pt.
N. 32 W.	1 ½	ms. to a Sand pt. from the S. pt.
N. 12° E.	½	me: to the willows on the S. S.
	17	

1. Almost certainly François Labiche. He is referred to again as "William" on August 18 and 19, 1804.

2. These must have been clear and specific orders to take Reed dead or alive, made a matter of record so that the responsibility would fall on the captains, not on the men sent out.

3. This situation, in Harrison County, Iowa, was still present in altered form about 1890 but has since disappeared. *Atlas* map 14; MRC map 25; MRR maps 69, 70.

4. Biddle apparently crossed out two lines of this entry in red, covering the words from "reid" to "Death." In his *History*, Biddle did not mention that the detachment had orders to kill Reed if they could not take him alive. Probably the passage was crossed out because either Clark or Biddle did not care to mention this aspect of the affair. Coues (HLC), 1 : 69.

5. Probably in northwest Harrison County, a few miles below the mouth of the Little Sioux River. *Atlas* map 14; MRC map 25; MRR map 70.

[Clark]

Course Distance & reffurenc August the 8th Wednsday 1804

N. 20° E	2	miles to the pt. of a Sand Isld. from the S S. the river narrow & choked up with Snags (1)
S. 50 E	2	mls. to a pt. of Willows on the L. S. Dame Killed a Pelican
East—	½	mile on the Side of Sand Island from the L. pt
North	1 ½	ms. to the mouth of little Rivers De ⟨Peux⟩ Cueoux [Sioux] S. S. (2)
N. 70° W	2	ms. to the Lower point of an Island on the [*blank*] no water, (3)
N. 20 W	1	me. to a pt. on the right Side of the Island
N. 52 W.	7	ms. to a pt. of high wood in a bend to the L. S. passed the Isd. at ¼ of a me. on the point of which was great numbers of Peli[c]an river wide & Shoal, ⟨Cap Lewis took medn. altd⟩
	16	

Half altitude of ⊙s below Little S. river S. S.

h   m
8   26   59
8   28   29
8   30   8

altitude   80° 14 m 15″   1 ½ Ms. below *Little R. de Sous*

I walked on Shore with one man Collins,—the bottoms Covered with very [*sentence incomplete*]   Collin Killed an elk, I fired 4 times at one & have reasons to think I Kiled him but could not find him, The Misqutors were So troublesom and Misqutors thick in the Plains that I could not Keep them out of my eyes, with a bush.   in my absens Capt Lewis Killed a Pelican on Pelicans Island, at which place maney Hundreds had Collected, they left 3 fish which was fresh and very good, we camped on the S. S. in a Streght part of the river—[1]

August the 8th 1804[2]   Set out this morning at the usial time   at about 2 miles (1) passed a part of the river So choked up with Snags that we found a little dificult to get thro' with Safty, the wind as usial from the N W.   one of the Soldiers Killed a Pilican on the Sand Isd.   passed the mouth of Little (2) *River de Cueoux*[3] on the S. S.   this river is about 80 yards wide & navagable for Pirogus Some distance & runs parrelel to the Missourie   it coms in from the River from the N E, it contains great Quantitys of fish Common to the Countrey.   two Miles above is (3) an Island   the Channel formerly run on the right ⟨but that side is now nearly filled up⟩ with Sand.—   the Current runs to the left.   many hundreds of Pelicans on [the Shore of?] this Island—   we call it Pelican Isld.   Cap Lewis Killed one   This river Soux Called by the *Sueoux Eá-Neah Wau-de-pon* i'e *Stone R*[4] heads in three Leagues of the river Demoin, and passes thro a Lake about 20 Legues in Sircfs. [circumference] which is also within 5 Leagus of the Demoin, this lake at one place is confined by two rocks within a narrow Space—⟨also⟩ this lake of Different widths, with many Small Islands, from the Lake to the Mahars about ⟨60 or 70 miles⟩ ⟨F[rench] Leagus⟩ distant 4 Days march to the Dog Plains [Prairie du Chien] 90 Leagues, one Principal branch of the Demoin is calld. Cat river, the Lake which this river Litt Souex heads in is Called *Despree* [d'Esprit][5]

Cap Lewis took merdn. altitude and made the Lattitude.   *41° 42′ 34³/₁₀* North.   altd. of *Sun* ☉—   *56° 9′ 00″*—

[Clark]   8th August Wednesday 1804

Set out this morning at the usial time   at two miles passed (1) a bend to L. S. Choaked up with Snags   our boat run on two in ⟨twisting⟩ turning to pass through, we got through with Safty   the wind from N W.   (2) passed the mouth of a River on the S. Side Called by the *Soux Indians Eă-neăh Wáu de pón* (or Stone river)   the French call this river *Petite Rivre de Cuouex* [*NB: riviere des Sioux*]   it is about 80 yards wide and as (Mr. Durion Says whos been on the heads of it and the Country abt) is navagable for Perogues Som Distance   runs Parrelel to the Missourie Some Distance, then falls down from N E thro a roleing Countrey open, the head of this river is 9 miles from the R Demon [*NB: Des moines*] at which place the *Demoin* is 80 yd wide, this Little Cuouex passes thro a lake called ⟨Despree⟩ [*NB: D'Esprits*] which is within 5 Leagues of the *Deemoin*   the Said Lake is about 20 Leagues in Circumfrance and is divided into 2 by two rocks approaching Verry Near each other, this Lake is of various width, Containing many Islands—   from this Lake to the Maha 4 days march, as is Said to be near the Dog Plains   one princpal branch of the Demoin is Called Cat River   The Demoin is Sholey

Capt. Lewis took Medn. Altitude of the Sun   made it 56° 9′ 00″   Lat 41° 42′ 34″ and I took one man and went on Shore   the man Killed an Elk   I fired 4 times at one & did not Kill him, my ball being Small I think was the reason,[6]   the misqutors So bad in the Praries that with the assistance of a bush I could not Keep them out of my eyes, the boat turned Several tims to day on Sand bars—   in my absenc the boat passed a Island 2 miles above the litte Scouex R   on the upper point of the Isld Some hundreds of Pelicans were Collected, they left 3 fish on the Sand which was verry fine, Capt Lewis Killed one & took his dimentions, I joined the boat and we Camped on the S S.

worthe of remark that *Snakes* are not plenty in this part of the Missourie

Course Diste. & rffr. 8th Augt.

N. 20° E	2	ms. to the pt. of a Sd. Isd. from the S S.
N. 50 E	2	ms. to a pt. of wils. on the L. S.
East	½	me. on the right of a Sand Island
North	1 ½	me. to the mouth of Little River desioux Calld. by *Soux Ea neah-wau de pon*) Stone River
N. 70° W	2	mes. to the Lower pt. of Pelican Isd. (3)
N. 20 W	1	me. to a right Hand pt. of Sd. Isd.
N. 52 W.	7	ms. to a Pt. of High woods in a bend to L. S. haveing passed the Pelican Isd.[7]
	16	

one & a half miles South of Littl Riv. de Cuouex took half altitude with Sextn.

Time		
h	m	s
8	26	59
8	28	29	altd. 80° 15′ 15″
8	30	3

[Lewis]   August 8th 1804[8]

we had seen but a few aquatic fouls of any kind on the river since we commenced our journey up the Missouri, a few geese accompanied by their young, the wood duck which is common to every part of this country & crains of several kinds which will be discribed in their respective places— this day after we had passed the *river* Souix as called by Mr. MacKay (or as is more properly called the stone river,[)] I saw a great number of feathers floating down the river those feathers had a very extraordinary appearance as they appeared in such quantities as to cover pretty generally sixty or seventy yards of the breadth of the river. for three miles after I saw those feathers continuing to run in that manner, we did not percieve from whence they came, at length we were surprised by the appearance of a flock of Pillican [*EC: Pelecanus erythrorhynchus*] at rest on a large sand bar attatched to a small Island the number of which would if estimated appear almost in credible; they apeared to cover several acres of ground, and were no doubt engaged in procuring their ordinary food; *which is fish*, on our approach they flew and left behind them several small fish of about eight inches in length, none of which I had seen before— the Pellican rested again on a sand bar above the Island which we called after them from the number we saw on it. we now approached them within about three hundred yards before they ⟨attemted to fly⟩ flew; I then fired at random among the flock with my rifle and brought one down; the discription of this bird is as follows.—

Habits

They are a *bird* of *clime* remain on the coast of Floriday and the borders of the Gulph of mexico & even the lower portion of the Mississippi during the *winter* and in the Spring (see for date my *thermometrical observations at the river Dubois.—*) [*April 6, 1804*] visit this country and that fa[r]ther north for the purpose of raising their young— this duty seems now to have been accomplished from the appearance of a young Pilacon which was killed by one of our men [Dame] this morning, and they are now in large flocks on their return to their winter quarters. they lay usually two eggs only and chuise for a nest a couple of logs of drift wood near the water's edge and with out any other preperation but the thraught [throat] formed by the proximity of those two logs which form a trough they set and hatch their young which after nurture with fish their common food

Measure

	F	I
F[r]om beak to toe	5	8
Tip to tip of wing	9	4

Beak Length		1	3
Do. Width	from		2 to 1 ½
Neck Length		1	1 1
lst Joint of wing		1	1
2ed Do.		1	4 ½
3rd Do.		—	7
4th do.		—	2 ¾
Length of leg including foot			1 0
Do. of thy			1 1

Discription of Colour &c

The beak is a whiteish yellow the under part connected to a bladder like pouch, this pounch is connected to both sides of the lower beak and extends down on the under side of the neck and terminates in the stom-ach— this pouch is uncovered with feathers, and is formed [of] two skins the one on the inner and the other on the center side   a small quan-tity of flesh and strings of which the anamal has at pleasure the power of moving or drawing in such manner as to contract it at pleasure.   in the present subject I measured this pouch and found it's contents 5 gallons of water—

The feet are webbed large and of a yellow colour, it has four toes   the hinder toe is longer than in most aquatic fouls, the nails are black, not sharp and ½ an inch in length

The plumage generally is white, the feathers are thin compared with the swan goose or most aquatick fouls and has but little or no down on the body.   the upper part of the head is covered with black f[e]athe[r]s short, as far as the back part of the head—   the yellow skin unfeathered ex-tends back from the upper beak and opening of the mouth and comes to a point just behind the eye

The large f[e]athers of the wings are of a deep black colour—   the 1st & 2nd joint of [the wings] from the body above the same is covered with a second layer of white feathers which extend quite half the length of those large feathers of the wing—   the thye is covered with feathers within a quarter of an inch of the knee.

				Inch	
1st Joint of wing has feather[s]	No. 21		Length	9	Black
2ed Do.		No. 17	Length	13	Inch

461

3rd Do.	No. 5	Length 18 Inch
4th Do.	No. 3	Length 19 Inch

it has a curious frothy subs[t]ance which seems to devide its feathers from the flesh of the body and seems to be composes of globles of air and perfectly imbraces the part of the feather which extends through the skin.— the wind pipe terminates in the center of the lower part of the upper and unf[e]athered part of the pouch and is secured by an elastic valve commanded at pleasure.—

The green insect known in the U' States by the name of the *sawyer* or [*EC: Katydid*] *chittediddle*, was first heard to cry on the 27th of July, we were then in latitude 41° some minutes.

The *prarie hen* or *grouse*, was seen in the praries between the Missouri and the river platte

(Point of observation No. 28.)

[Lewis]   *Wednesday August 8*[9]

On the Starboard shore, the mouth of the river E-a-nearh'war-da-pon or Stone river bearing Due N. distant one ½ miles, made the following observations with Sextant.

Altitude of—			Time by Chronometer			
				h	m	s
⊙'s U. L.	80°	14′	15″	A. M.	8	26	59
⊙'s Center	"	"	"		"	28	29
⊙'s L. L.	"	"	"		"	30	3

(Point of observation No. 29.)

On the Larboard Shore, the mouth of Stone river bearing due E. one mile dist.

Observed meridian Altitude of ⊙'s L. L. with octant by the back observatn. 56° 9′ —″

Latitude deduced from this observt.   41° 42′ 34.3″

1. Probably in southwest Monona County, Iowa, not far above the Harrison County line. It is possible, however, that river shifts have placed the site in Burt County, Nebraska. *Atlas* map 15; Nicollet (MMR), 390; MRC map 25; MRR map 71.

2. This Field Notes entry for August 8 immediately follows the one above. Clark may have regarded the above paragraph as an appendage to the courses and distances.

3. The Little Sioux River reaches the Missouri in northwest Harrison County, Iowa, near the present town of Little Sioux. Nicollet notes that the Sioux name implies a rock somewhere along its length. (See note 4 below.) Pelican Island, above its mouth, is Wood Island on Warren's 1855 map; it seems to have joined the Iowa shore by the end of the century. Nicollet (RIIM), 27; *Atlas* map 15; Warren map 6; MRC map 25; MRR map 70.

4. Douglas R. Parks gives the Sioux word as *Iŋyaŋ yaŋke watpa*, or "Rock River."

5. Spirit Lake in Dickinson County, Iowa, a source of one of the main branches of the Little Sioux River. The Little Sioux River heads in Jackson County, Minnesota. Concerning Cat River, either Clark was misinformed, or the name of this tributary of the Des Moines has been changed. It does not appear on his 1805 or 1810 maps (*Atlas* maps 32a, 32b, 32c, 125). Petersen, 252–55, passim.

6. Evidently Clark was carrying his small rifle, which seems to have been a long-barreled "Kentucky" of relatively small caliber, of the sort often called a squirrel gun. Killing a large mammal like an elk with such a weapon would call for great accuracy. Russell (GEF), 38.

7. Some words here in red ink, apparently written and crossed out by Biddle, part of which are: "North side" and "Ordway."

8. Lewis's natural history notes from Codex Q. The bird, as Coues notes in his interlineation, is the American white pelican, first noticed in weather remarks for April 6, 1804. The "green insect" is the common katydid, which seemed familiar to Lewis. It could be any of a number of varieties. The "prarie hen" is probably the greater prairie chicken (see November 16, 1803). The notes on the katydid and greater prairie chicken may have been added later.

9. Lewis's observation from Codex O.

[Clark]

Course distance & reffuren the 9th of August Thursday

N. 30° E	2 ½	ms. to the pt. of a Sand bar on the L. Side Wind fair
N. 32 W.	1	me. to the pt. of High woods on the L. Side
N. 22° W.	2 ½	Ms. to a Pt. of high woods on S. S.— a large Sand bar makeing out from it
N. 15° W.	2	Ms. to a pt. of High land, L. S opsd. to which the River latterly run, & a Circut of 5 Leagues has been cut off. the old Channel is Ponds & Isds.
*N 15 W.	⟨2	m. across a large Sand bar to a point of woods⟩ on Lard. Shore, this is opposite to the cut point. 6 leagues arround[1]
N. 46 W.	1 ½	m. to willow point on stard Side.

N. 35° W	2	m. S S. the river now came gradually arround to the E. of north no point apearing
N. 60° E.	2 ½	miles, to a willow point on Sard side—
N. 44 W.	3 ½	miles to point Stard. Shore
	17 ½ [2]	

9th Augt Thursday 1804[3]   The fog of this morning detained us untill ½ passed 7 oClock at which time we left our moreing and proceeded on under a gentle Breeze from the S. E, I went on Shore   found the Land the Same as yesterday   Killed a Turkey and Camped on the L. S.[4]   great deel of Beaver Sign to day   one Beaver Cought   Musquetors worse this evening than ever I have Seen them.

[Clark]   9th August Thursday 1804

The fog being thick detained us untile half pasd. 7 oClock at which time we Set out and proceeded on under Gentle Breeze from the S E   I walked on Shore, Saw an Elk, crossed a Istmust [isthmus] of ¾ of a mile to the river,[5] & returned to the boat   Camped on the L. S. above a Beaver Den.   Musqutors verry troubleson.

Course Distance & reffn Augt 9th

N. 30° E	2 ½	ms. to a Point of a Sand bar on the L. S.
N. 32° W.	1	ms. to a pt. of high wood on L. S.
N. 22 W.	2 ½	ms. to a pt. of high wood on the S. S. a large Sand bar from it
N. 15 W.	2	ms. to a pt. of high Land L. S. opsd. to which the river latterly cut thro Saveing 6 Leagues S. S.
N. 46° W.	1 ½	ms. to a willow pt. on the S. S.
N. 35 W.	2	ms. to the S. S. the river comeing gradually arround to the Rigt.
N. 60° E	2 ½	ms. to a willow pt. on the L. S.
N. 44 W.	3 ½	to a point on S. S.
	17 ½	

1. This and the remaining courses and distances are in Lewis's hand.

2. Below the course and distance table at the bottom of document 41 is a line in Clark's

hand: "⟨N. 60 W 1¾ to a pt of⟩ Sand L. S;" apparently the first course of August 10. Also a column of figures: 2½, 3½, 5, subtotal 11, 1½, and a total of 12½.

3. Biddle's notation at the top of the reverse of this sheet of the Field Notes (document 41) reads, "Aug 9th to 12."

4. Because of shifts in the Missouri River, the campsite is now in Harrison County, Iowa, a mile or two south of present Onawa, on the west side of present Guard Lake, which seems to approximate the 1804 course of the river as shown on *Atlas* map 15. Warren map 7; MRC map 26; MRR map 72.

5. See *Atlas* map 15.

[Clark]   *August 10th*[1]

Course Distance and remarks 10th of August 1804 Friday.

N. 60° W.	2	ms. to a pt. of Sand makeing from the L. point
S. 80° W.	½	me. on the to a Drift wood. This place is called Coupe a Jarcke[2] a place where the river cut through and shortend the River Sevl. mls.
South 18° E,	2½	ms. to Som Snags near some Willows on the S. S. passd. the High ⟨land⟩ wood on L. S. in this Co's at 1 me
S. 20° W.	2½	ms. to a ⟨Black⟩ Burnt Stump on the Bank in the bend to L. S. at which place I was yesterday at this place within ¾ of a mile & round the bends 13 ms.
West	3½	ms. to two Cotton wood trees at the Mouth of a Small Creek in a bend to the L. S. near the high land a ⟨Bluff⟩ clift &c 1 me. above.
N. 40° W.	1½	ms. to a Clift of yellow Sant Stone[3] on the L. S. this is the first high land which touches the river above Councel Bluff, (this Clift is one mile only[)]
N. 52° W.	1½	ms. to the pt. of a Saand barr from the S. point passed the Clift. on L. S.
N. 79° E	3	ms. to a pt. of Small willows on the L. S. passing the high timber on S S. at 1 me wind hard from the S. W.
N. 29 E	½	of a mile on the L. point, the boat run on a log & detained us 10 minits
North	1½	me. to the Pt. of a Sand bar makeing out from the L. point

N 68° W.	¾	mes. on the L. point a Sand bar making out from this Course.
N. 85° W.	2 ½ 22 ¼	Ms. to the Lower point of a willow Island off the S. point— *Black bird* the late King of the *Mahars* Toom or inclosed grave on the top of a high round Hill of about 300 feet in the Prarie L. S. bore west about 4 miles.[4] (Musquters bad)

[Clark]   10th *August Friday* 1804

Set out early this morning. Course

N. 60° W. about 2		miles to a Sand makeing out from the Larboard point.
S. 80 W.	½	me. to a Drift log on the Sand This place is Called *Coupee as Jacke* the river laterly Cut through Saveing Sevl. mes
S. 18° E	2 ½	ms. to a burnt Stump in a bend to the L. S. this place I was at yesterday.
S. 20° W.	2 ½	ms to a ⟨Black⟩ Burnt Stump on the Bank in the bend to L. S. at which place I was yesterday at this place within ¾ of a mile & round the bends 13 ms
West	3 ½	ms. to 2 Cotton wood trees at the mouth of a run on the L. S. near the high land & below a Bluff.
N. 40° W.	1 ½	to a clift of yellow Sand Stone the first high land touching the river above the Council Bluff.
N. 52° W.	1 ½	ms. to the pt. of a Sand bar from the Starboard pt. passed the Clift L. S.
N. 79° E.	3	ms. to a pt. of willows on the L. S.
N. 29 E.	½	me. on the L. pt.
North	1 ½	ms. to a Sand bar from the L. pt.
N. 68 W.	¾	mes. on the Sand bar from L. Pt.
N. 85 W.	2 ½ 22 ¼	ms. to the lower pt. of a willow island near the S. point from this Island the high hill which the Late King of the Mahars was buried on is high and bears West 4 miles— we camped on this Island.[5] Misquitors verry trouble some. much Elk & Beaver Sign

1. The courses and distances appear to be the only entry for August 10, 1804, in the Field Notes. The similar brevity of the Codex A entry for this day suggests that Clark had

little time or energy left at the end of the day. A figure near the course heading appears to be 19¾.

2. Coupée à Jacques means simply "Jacques's Cut." Part of it apparently forms present Blue Lake, at Lewis and Clark State Park, Monona County, Iowa. *Atlas* map 15; McDermott (WCS), 150; Osgood (FN), 103 n. 8; MRC map 26; MRR map 72.

3. Two quarries along the valley and bluffs near Fort Calhoun, Nebraska, have been excavated in limestones of Pennsylvanian age, but no sandstone is reported in them. The Dakota sandstone (Cretaceous) has not been reported in this area. The hill is immediately north of Decatur, Burt County, Nebraska, and appears prominently in Nicollet. *Atlas* map 15; Nicollet (MMR), 391; MRC map 26; MRR map 72.

4. See *Atlas* map 15. They visited this landmark the next day.

5. In Monona County, considerably east of the Missouri River's present course and, as Clark indicates, east or southeast of Blackbird Hill. *Atlas* map 15; MRC map 26; MRR map 72.

[Clark]

August 11th Satturday 1804 about day this morning a hard wind from the N. W. followed by rain, we landed at the foot of the hill on which Black Bird[1] The late King of the mahar who Died 4 years ago & 400 of his nation with the Small pox was buried (1) and went up and fixed a white flag bound with Blue white & read[2] on the Grave which was about 12 foot Base & circueller, on the top of a Penical about 300 foot above the water of the river, from the top of this hill may be Seen the bends or meanderings of the river for 60 or 70 miles round & all the County around the base of this high land is a Soft Sand Stone[3] Bluff of about 40 or 150 foot, the Crooked, passed a Creek Called *Wau-Con di peche* C or *Bad God* Creek of bad Spirits on the L. S[4] above the Bluff on this Creek the Mahars had the Small pox ⟨& 400 of them Died⟩ 4 years ago, *Lattitude 42° 1′ 3″ 8/10* taken on the Point above the Creek. the river is verry Crooked, we are now within ¾ of a mile of the river at a place we Shall not get around to untill tomorrow noon— We er [are] 3 Legues from the Mahars by land and the great deel of Beaver sign induce a belief that those people do not hunt much.

Course & Dis. Augt 11th

S. 52° W.	½	me. on the Sand point S. S of the Sand Island Wind N. W
N. 25 W.	2	ms. to a pt. of low willows from a L. pt. passing over a Sand bar from the Sd. pt. psd. the Isd.
N 72 W.	2 ¼	ms. to a pt. on the S. S. Willows opposit the high pt of land which the Maha King was bured Cap Louis and my

		Self went up, & fixed a whit Flag on the grave a wind & rain Strike in from S
N. 24 W.	½	Me. on the Side of the willows S. S. a Sand bar passed a Creek on the (1) L. S. called *Wau con di Peeche Great* Spirrit is bad
S. 81 E	2 ¾	ms. to the begining of a pt. of willows on the L. S. at the comencement of this Course is a Small channel passing about half way thro a Prarie from a bend to the L. S. within ¾ a mile and [*blank*] miles round the point *The Flag* bore S. 12° E.
N. 84° E.	6	ms. to the high wood above, a Prarie in the bend on S. S the river wide & Shallow. the wood is opsd. a pt
N. 22° E	1 ¼	ms. to a pt. of willows on the L. S.
North.	1 ¾	ms. to a Cotton tree in a bind to the S. S. haveing passd. a Sand pt. from the L. Side & camped on the L. S.[5] Cap Lewis Killed a Duck.
N 45 W	1 ½	me. to a Sand Pt. on the L. Side. a number of Blue crains flying over
	17 ½	

I have observed a number of places where the river has Changd its Bead at different times

Time & Dist. the Moon & Sun

H	m	s			
1	13	45	73°	6′	45″
″	16	48	73	6	0
″	18	39	73	6	0
″	20	55	73	7	45
″	22	25	73	8	30
″	24	24	73	9	30
″	25	45	73	9	30
″	27	43	73	10	45
″	29	33	73	11	30
″	31	30	73	12	0

[Clark]   11th August Satturday 1804.

about day light this Morning a hard wind from the N W. with Some rain   proceeded on arround the right of the Isld.

S. 52° W.	½	a mile on the Sand pt.
N. 25 W.	2	Ms. to a pt. of low willows from the L. S. passd. the Isd. & a Sand bar makeing from the S. point.
N. 72 W.	2 ¼	ms. to a pt. on the S. S.

a hard wind accompanied with rain from the S. E.   after the rain was over Capt. Lewis myself & 10 men[6] assended the Hill on the L. S. under which there was Some fine Springs to the top of a high point where the *Mahars King Black* Bird was burried 4 years ago.   a mound of earth about 12 Diamuter at the base & 6 feet high is raised over him turfed, and a pole 8 feet high in the Center   on this pole we fixed a white flage bound with red Blue & white; this hill about 300 feet above the water forming a ⟨Clift⟩ Bluff between that & the Water of Various hight from 40 to 150 feet in hight yellow Soft Sand Stone   [*WC: Died of Smallpox*][7] ⟨we return⟩ from the tops of this Nole the river may be Seen Meandering for 60 or 70 Miles, we Decended & Set out N. 24 to W. ½ me. passing over a Sand bar on the S. pt. along the Willows.   to the river opposit a Small Beyeau on the L. S. which is the Conveyance of the high water from a bend which appears near in a northerly direction, haveing passed a Creek in a Deep bend to the L. S. Called by the *Mahars Wau can di Peeche* (Great Spirrit is bad) on this Creek & Hills near it about 400 of the Mahar Died with the Small Pox—   Took Medn. *Altitude* & made the Latd.   *42° 1′ 3″ 8/10 N.   also the Moons Distanc from the Sun*

	Time				Distance		
	H	m	S		d.	m.	S
P M	1	13	45		73	6	45
	"	16	48		73	6	0
	"	18	39		"	6	0
	"	20	55		"	7	45
	"	22	25		"	8	30
	"	24	24		"	9	30
	"	25	45		"	9	30
	"	27	45		"	10	45
	"	29	33		"	11	30
	"	31	30		"	12	00

S 81° E	2 ¾	Miles to the beginning of a point of willows on the L. Side

N. 84° E.	6	miles to a high wood above a Prarie on the S. S. opposit a Sand point
N. 22° E.	1 ¼	to a pt. of willows on the L. S.
North	1 ¾	to a Cotton tree in a bend to the Starboard Side passed a
miles 17		Sand bar on the L. S. & Camped the Musqutors Verry troublesom Great nos of Herrons this evening[8]

I have observed a number of places where the River has onced run and now filled or filling up & growing with willows & cottonwood

(Point of observation No. 30.)

[Lewis]

Saterday August 11th[9]

On the starboard shore one mile above the mouth of the *Creek of Evil Sperits.*

Observed Meridian Altd. of ⊙'s L. L. with Octant by the back observatn.   58° 31' —"

Latitude deduced from this observtn.   42° 1' 3.8"

Observed time and distance of ⊙'s and ☽'s nearest limbs; the West.—   with Sextant.

	h	m	s				
P. M.	1	13	45		73°	6'	45"
"		16	48		"	6	—
"		18	39		"	7	15
"		20	55		"	7	45
"		22	25		"	8	30
"		24	24		"	9	30
"		25	45		"	10	45
"		27	43		"	11	30
"		31	30		"	12	—

1. Blackbird (*Wazhiⁿ gaçabe*) was a notorious character along the Missouri, noted for his friendship with white traders and his strong rule over his own people. Under his leadership the Omahas rose to prominence on the eastern plains. Reports of his war deeds are mixed, but he seems to have had great authority because of his sorcery, especially in the deaths of the enemies who were likely killed by his use of poisons obtained from traders. Legend has it that he was buried seated on the back of his horse, on the hilltop where he used to watch for the coming of his friends the traders. Nasatir (BLC), 1:282–94; Appleman (LC), 334–35; Thwaites (EWT), 14:317–20, 22:277; Fletcher & La Flesche, 1:82–83, 173; *Atlas* map 15; MRC map 26; MRR map 72.

2. Clark used an asterisk as a reference to the remainder of the daily narrative, which followed the courses and distances and astronomical observations. The material is brought together for ease of reading.

3. The Dakota sandstone, basal Cretaceous, is exposed along streams and the Missouri River bluffs.

4. Blackbird Creek in Thurston County, Nebraska, southeast of present Macy. The Omaha name may be *wako*ⁿ*dagi pezhi te*; Robert L. Rankin (personal communication) gives it as *wakkáda ppéži* or "bad spirit." Fletcher & La Flesche, 1:91; *Atlas* map 15; MRC map 26; MRR map 73.

5. The extreme bend of the Missouri River, at whose eastern extremity they camped, has long since been cut off. Indeed, pencil marks on *Atlas* map 15, probably by Prince Maximilian, indicate that it was already cut off when he passed that way in 1833. The campsite, therefore, is some miles east of the present course of the river, in Monona County, Iowa, in the vicinity of present Badger Lake, apparently the river's old course. MRC map 26; MRR map 73.

6. None of the enlisted journal-keepers indicate clearly that they were with this party, although Gass says that "we" raised the flag on the hill.

7. These words were squeezed in at the bottom of the page in Codex A.

8. Clark changes the designations from "crains" to "Herrons" between entries. It is the great blue heron, first mentioned in weather remarks for February 13, 1804. Swenk, 120. This is probably the correct course for the day. Clark's last entry in the Field Notes for August 11 probably belongs with his August 12 entry (as carried there) and the total should be 17.

9. Lewis's observation from Codex O.

[Clark]¹

12th August Sunday 1804   a South wind   We Set out early   the river wider than usial, and Shallow, at 12 we halted in a bend to the left to take the Meridian altitude, & Dine, & Sent one man across where we took Dinner yesterday to Step off the Distance across *Isthmus*, he made it 974 yards, and the bend around is 18¾ miles above this bend about 4 miles, a yellow & Brown Bluff Comnuces and Continus 3 or 4 miles on the L. S.   this Bluff has Some Sand Stone, Some rich Black mole [mold] mixed with yellow Clay,² a fiew Red Ceeder³ on the tope, which is ⟨about⟩, from 20 to 150 foot high   the hill Still riseing back, I think may be estemated at 200 foot   on the top is timber, the wind for a few hours this evening was hard and from the S. E.   In the evening about 5 oClock Cap L. & My Self wen on Shore to Shoot a Prarie wolf⁴ which was barking at us as we passed⁵ This Prarie Wolf barked like a large fest [feist] and is not much larger, the Beaver is verry plenty, not with Standing we are almost in Sight of the

Mahar Town— Cought a verry Large Catfish this morniong, prepared the Indian present which we intend given to the *Mahars*. P. Wiser apt. Cook to Serjt: Floyds Squad from to day[6]

Course Distance August 12th & reffurences

N. 45° W.	1 ½	to a Pt. of willows on the L. Side
S. 42 W.	½	me. on the pooint of a Sand bar from the L. S. the river is wide here
S. 22 E.	2 ¼	ms. to the pt. makeing out from the L. S. passed the timber on the L. S. at ½ m.
N. 78 W.	3 ½	ms. to the pt. of willows on the L. S. wind favourable from the South[7]
S 68 W.	2 ½	ms. to the upper pt of Some Cotton trees in the bend to L. S. at this place the Isthums is only 973 yd wide or from one bed to the other & 18¾ miles around, the Mahar Kings grave is S. 18° E about 2 ½ miles Took medn. altd. 59° 8′ 0″—
N 49° W.	4 ½	ms. to a pt. on the S. S. opposit a Bluff, haveing passed a Sand point makeig out on S. S. at 1 me. & one from the L. S. at 2 ½ mes.—
N. 12 W.	3	ms. to a pt. on the S. S. a Red Ceeder Bluff of about 200 feet high on the L. S.
N. 46 E.	2 ¾	to a pt. of ⟨willows⟩ Sand Island on the L. S. a ⟨Sand bar makeing out⟩ and Camped on the Sand Island,[8] the Misquitors verry troublesom, both Cap Lewis & myself are much ingaged ⟨we⟩ preparing despatches to Send back by the Perogue which will return as Soon as those despatches are ready.[9] (Broke a faverate De[c]anter)
N. 2	20 ¼	

[Clark]   12th *August Sunday 1804*

Set out early under a gentle Breeze from the South   the river wider than usial and Shallow   (1) at 12 oClock we halted to take a meridian altd. of the *Sun* & Sent a man *back* or I may Say across to the Bind of the river where Capt. Lewis took the Mdn. altitude yesterday, to Step off the distance, he made it 974 yards across, the Distance arround the bend is 18¾ miles— about 4 miles above the bend on the L. S. is the Commencement of a Bluff which is about 4 miles extending on the river, of yellow

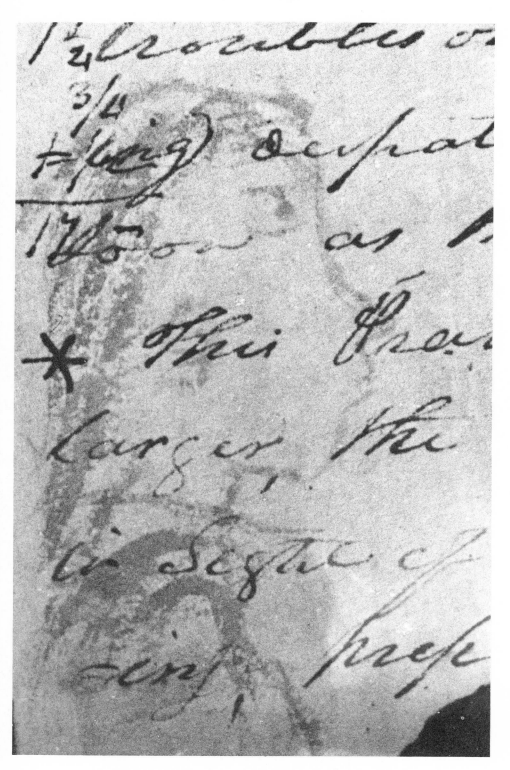

16. Profile of a Boy, August 12, 1804, Field Notes, document 42

and brown Clay   in Some parts in it near the river a Soft Sand Stone is inbeded on the top (which is from 20 to 150 feet above the water, & rises back) is Covered with timber, a fiew red Ceider is on this Bluff, the wind Comes round to the S. E.   a *Prarie Wolf* Come near the bank and Barked at us this evening, we made an attempt but could not git him, this Animale Barkes like a large *feste* Dog. Beever is verry Plenty on this part of the river. I prepare Some presents for to give the Indians of the *Mahars* nation. Wiser apt. Cook & Supentdt. of the Provisions of Sergt. Floyds Squad.   we Camped on a Sand Island in a bend to the S. S.   Musquitors verry troublesom untile the wind rose.   at one or 2 oClock

Course Distance &c. August 12th

N. 45° W.	1 ½	ms. to a pt. of willows on the L. S.
S. 42 W.	½	Me. to a Sand on the L. point
S. 22 E	2 ¼	to a pt. makeing out from the Larbd S. passed the Timber L. S.
N. 78 W	3	ms. to a pt. of willows on the L. S.
S. 68 W.	2 ½	ms. to a Grove of Cotton Trees in the bend L. S. (1)
N. 49 W.	4 ½	ms. to a pt. on the S. Side opsd. a Bluff passed a pt. at 1 Ms. on S. S. & one at 2 ½ on L. S.
N. 12° W	3	ms. to a pt. on L. S. opsd. a Bluff
N. 46 E.	2 ¾	ms. to a Sand Island in the Bend to S. S. (Camped)
	20 ¾	

(*Point of observation No. 31.*)

[Lewis]   *Sunday August 12th*[10]

On the Larboard shore in the center of a bend, being North, and measurement 974 yards from the Lard. Shore opposite to the point of observation of yesterday.

Observed Meridian altitude of ☉'s L. L. with Octant by the back obstn.   59° 8' —"

Latitude deduced from this observatn.   42° 1' 47.6"

1. Biddle's notation at the head of this sheet of the Field Notes (document 42) reads, "Aug. 12 to 14."

2. The "stone" exposed below the mouth of the Little Sioux consists of shales and some limestone of Cretaceous age.

3. Eastern red cedar.

4. A coyote, *Canis latrans*, one of the most characteristic western animals, then little known to science. Apparently they did not actually get a specimen until September 18, 1804. Cutright (LCPN), 85; Hall, 2:924–28.

5. Clark used an asterisk as a reference to a continuation of the narrative after the courses and distances. The material is brought together for ease of reading.

6. John B. Thompson had previously held this position in Floyd's squad (see above, July 8, 1804). Apparently he had proved unsatisfactory.

7. Clark wrote this course and description in red ink or chalk. There are also some numbers (40, 8, and No. 12) in red and the profile of a boy under the text (fig. 16).

8. In either Monona or Woodbury County, Iowa, near the county line. *Atlas* map 15; MRC map 27; MRR maps 73, 74.

9. Another indication that they still intended to send back Corporal Warfington's squad in the near future. In fact, they did not do so until April 7, 1805. There are some figures to the side of the course material and the text that follows it:

$$
\begin{array}{ll}
\underline{|\ 50} & 6 \\
283 & 1\,\tfrac{1}{4} \\
19:\tfrac{3}{4} & \tfrac{3}{4} \\
\underline{8} & \underline{1\,\tfrac{1}{2}} \\
28 & 17 — \\
2 &
\end{array}
$$

10. Lewis's observation from Codex O.

[Clark]

13th of August Munday 1804.   Set out this morning at Day light the usial time and proceeded on under a gentle Breeze from the S. E.   passed the Island.

N. 66° W.	2 ¾	mls. to pt. of low willows on the S. S. a Sand bar make-ing out from it &
N. 11 W.	5 ¼	ms. to a pt. of Cotton wood on the ⟨L. S.⟩ bend to the S. S. passing over ⟨1 ½ Ms to⟩ the pt. of a Sand bar from the S. S. & one from the L. Side, Wind fair
S 44° W,	2 ½	Mes. to a point on the S. S.
West	¾	to a Willow Isd on S. point and opsd. to which Mr. Mackey had a Small fort in which he traded withe the Mahars the winter 95 & 96 & call the place *Fort Charles*[1]

N. 50 W.	1⟨¾⟩	Mes. to a Point of high woods below the Mo. of a beayuw from a Pond in a Bend to the L. S.
N. 20 E	2 ¼	me. to a pt. of Willows on the L. S. passed a Creek on which the Mahar village² is Situated at 1½ me. a Sand bar on the S. S. & one on the L. S. Passed the Willow Island on the S. S. *Wind hard*
North	¼	of a me. on the Sand bar L. S.
N. 69 W.	2 ½ ———— 17	ms. to the upper pt. of Cotton wood in a Bend in the L. S. opsd. a lge Island, he[re] We Came too formed a Camp on the Sand L. S.³ & Dispatched Sgt. Oddeway Peter Crousett & 3 men to the Village of the Mahars, 1 League for the nation to Come and talk with us on tormorrow, the S. E. wind Continues high, we take Some Lune [lunar] observations and go—

From this *Fish Camp* the River is N 55° West as far as Can be Seen, the Sand bar only changeing the Derection of the Current   the Hills leave the river on the L. Side

[Clark]   *August 13th Monday 1804*

Set out this morning at Light the usial time and proceeded on under a gentle Breeze from the S E

N. 66° W.	2 ¾	ms. to a pt. of Low willows on the S. S. a bar makeing out. passed the Sd.
N. 11° W.	5 ¼	to a pt. of Cotton wood. ⟨L. S.⟩ in a Bend to the S. S. passed over the pt. of a Sand bar from L. S.
S. 44° W	2 ½	to a pt. on the S. S. opposit to the place Mr. Ja: McKey had a tradeing house in 95 & 96 & named it Fort Charles
West	¾	of a Mile to the Pt. of willow Isd. on the L. point
N. 50° W.	1	me. to a point of high wood below the mouth of a Beayoue Communicating with a Pond L. S.
N. 20° E.	2 ¼	mes. to a pt. of willows on the L. S. passed a Creek at 1½ mes. on which the Mahar Village is Situated a Sand bar on S. S. & one on L. S haveing passed the willow Isd.
North	¼	me. on the Sand bar L. S.
N. 69 W.	2 12 ———— 17 ¼	ms. to the upper Point of Some Cottonwood trees in a Bend to the L. S. opposit the lower pt. of a large Island

476

Situated on the S. S. we formed a Camp on a Sand bar on the L. S. & Detached Sergt. Ordeway Peter Crusatt, Geroge Shannon Werner & Carrn.[4] to the Mahar Village with a flag & Some Tobacco to invite the Nation to See & talke with us on tormorrow— we took Some Luner obsivations this evening. the air Pleasent

(*Point of observation No. 32.*)

[Lewis]

Monday, August 13th[5]

On the Laboard shore about three miles East of the Maha vilage.

Observed time and distance of ⊙'s & ☽'s nearest Limbs.—with Sexant.

		Time			*Distance*	
	h	m	s			
P. M.	3	57	9	95°	56′	15″
	4	1	32	"	58	—
	"	4	45	"	59	30
	"	6	51	96	—	—
	"	7	57	"	—	30
	"	9	17	"	—	45
	"	11	52	"	1	7.5
	"	13	—	"	2	—
	h	m	s			
P. M.	4	51	9	96°	12′	30″
	"	52	33	"	13	—
	"	54	5	"	13	30
	"	55	26	"	14	—
	"	56	22	"	14	15
	"	57	36	"	14	30
	h	m	s			
P. M.	4	33	18	96°	7′	45
	"	34	44	"	8	30
	"	35	7	"	8	37.5
	"	37	22	"	9	15
	"	38	24	"	9	45
	"	39	22	"	9	45
	h	m	s			
P. M.	5	7	59	96°	17′	45″

″	10	56	″	18	30
″	12	33	″	19	45
″	15	5	″	20	15
″	16	6	″	20	15
″	17	1	″	20	45
″	18	5	″	21	—
″	19	1	″	21	22.5

1. Mackay established this post, named for the reigning king of Spain, Charles IV, in November 1795, and wintered there. From here his companion, Evans, made his journey up the Missouri to the Mandan villages. The site was in Dakota County, Nebraska, southeast of Homer and south of Omaha Creek, but has not been discovered by researchers. Nasatir (BLC), 1:98–108; *Atlas* maps 7 and 16; MRC map 27; MRR maps 74, 75.

2. This is perhaps the best-known Omaha village. It was called "Big Village," or Tonwontonga. Fletcher & La Flesche, 86, 99; Champe; Steinacher & Carlson, 29–36. It is in Dakota County, about one mile north of present Homer and six and a half miles south of Dakota City, on or near U.S. Highway 77. Appleman (LC), 335; *Atlas* map 16; MRC map 27; MRR map 75.

3. In either Dakota County, Nebraska, or Woodbury County, Iowa, and a few miles south of present Dakota City. *Atlas* map 16; MRC 27; MRR map 75.

4. One of the few references to "Carrn.," who is otherwise "E. Cann" and "Cane" (see July 4 and August 25, 1804). Presumably he was one of the French *engagés*, although he is not mentioned under that name in the list of boatmen of May 26, 1804. See Appendix A, this volume.

5. Lewis's observation from Codex O.

[Clark][1]

14th of August   at 12 oClock the Party Sent yesterday to the Towns returned, and informed that they Could not find any Indians, they had not returned from hunting the Buffalow in the Praries, wind Shifted to the N W.   Our party Sent after the Deserter and to the Otteau towns, have not Came up as yet

The Situation of this Village, now in ruins Siround by enunbl. [innumerable] hosts of grave[s]   the ravages of the Small Pox (4 years ago)   they follow the Buf: and tend no Corn[2]

[Clark]   *14th August Tuesday* 1804

a fine morning wind from the S E   The men Sent to the Mahar Town last evening has not returned   we Conclude to Send a Spye to Know the cause of Their delay   at about 12 oClock the Party returned and informed. us that they Could not find the Indians nor any fresh Sign, those people have not returned from their Buffalow hunt, Those people haveing no houses no Corn or any thing more than the graves of their ancesters to attach them to the old Village, Continue in pursuite of the Buffalow longer than others who had greater attachments to their native Village—the ravages of the Small Pox [*NB: about 4 years ago*] (which Swept off 400 men & women & Children in perpoposion) has reduced this Nation not exceeding 300 men and left them to the insults of their weaker neighbours which before was glad to be on friendly turms with them—   I am told whin this fatal malady was among them they Carried ther franzey to verry extroadinary length, not only of burning their Village, but they put their *wives* & Children to *D[e]ath* with a view of their all going together to Some better Countrey—   They burry their Dead on the tops of high hills and rais mounds on the top of them,—   The cause or way those people took the Small Pox is uncertain, the most Probable from Some other Nation by means of a warparty

1 River Dubois { Latd—		38°	55′	19	⁶⁄₁₀
Longtd.—		89	57	45	
2 Gasconade Lattitude		38	44	35	
3 Great Osarge River Latd.		38	31	6	9
4 Kancez River Latd.		39°	5	25	7
On L. S. 1½ ms. above Dimond Island is Lattitude		39°	9′	38″	6
3 ms. below the 2d old Village of the Kancez L. S. Latd.		39°	25′	42″	5
on L. S. below the lower Point of Nordaway Island Latd.		39°	39′	22″	⁴⁄₁₀
L. S. opposit the Center of Good Island Latd.		40°	20′	12″	
opsd. a Island mentiond in the 2d & ed, course of the 15th of July on L. S Latd.		40°	8′	31″	8
Bald pated Prarie Latd		40°	27′	6″	4
Pt. opposit to a [point?] of an Island being the extremety of the 4th course of July the 19th on L. S Latd.		40	29	50	

White Catfish Camp above the River Platt Latd.	41°	3'	19"	4/10
Council Bluff Camp fifty miles above Platt Latd	41	17	0	
St. Chalres No. 1 Latd.	38	54	39	
1 ½ Mile below Split rock Creek	⟨37	6⟩		
Great Ne-ma-haw River L.	39	55	56	
on the S. S. opsd. pond Inlet August 4th N 26 Latd.	41	25	3	
On the Side of a Sand Island August 5th No. 27 Lat	41	30	6	
on the L. S. Little Rive Souix	41	42	34	3/10
on the pt. S. S. above the Hill on which the Mahar King was burid No. 30	42	1	3	8
Three Ms. N.E of the Mahars Village Camp *Fish* aug 14th	42	13	41	
Mo. of Grand River—	38	47	54	
Mo. of Charliton Rivers				

Observed Time and Distance of the Sun & Moon the Moon East the 13th of August Monday 1804.   three Miles NE of the Mahars old village at Fish Camp—

		Time			Distance		
		h	m	s			
	P M	3	57	9	95°	56'	15"
		4	1	32	"	58	"
		"	4	45	"	59	30
		"	6	51	96	0	0
1st		"	7	57	"	0	30
		"	9	17	"	0	45
		"	11	52	"	1	7½
		1	13	0	"	2	0
		4	33	18	96	7	45
		"	35	7	"	8	37½
2nd		"	37	22	"	9	15
		"	38	24	"	9	45
		"	39	22	"	9	45
		4	51	9	96	12	30
		"	52	30	"	13	0
		"	54	5	"	13	30

3rd						
	"	55	26	"	14	0
	"	56	22	"	14	15
	"	57	36	"	14	30

	h	m	s			
	5	7	59	96	17	45
	"	10	56	"	18	30
	"	12	33	"	19	45
4th	"	15	5	"	20	15
	"	16	6	"	20	15
	"	17	1	"	20	45
	"	18	5	"	21	"
	"	19	1	"	21	22½

August 14th 1804

Took the Mametter Azmath of the Sun this morning at

Time			Diste.			[Needle?]
h	m	s				
7	3	4	59	19′	15″	N. 87° E
h	m	s		2nd		
7	41	19	62	0′	0″	N. 88° E

Equal Altitudes 14th Augt

	h	m	s		h	m	
A M	7	45	16	P M	3	45	15
	"	46	43		"	46	47
	"	48	12		"	"	"	lost

Altd. produced 63° 26′ 45″

Cho car tooch or *Brarow*[3]

[Lewis]   *Tuesday August 14th*[4]

⊙'s magnetic azimuth by Circumferenter   N. 87 E.

		h	m	s
Time by Chronomerter A. M.		7	3	4
Altitude by Sextant of ⊙'s U. L.		59°	19′	15″

⊙'s magnetic azimuth by Circumferenter   N. 88 E.

		h	m	s
Time by Chronomerter A. M.		7	41	19

Altd. of ⊙'s U. L. by Sextant   62°   —′   —″

Observed Equal Altitudes of the ⊙ with Sextant.

	h	m	s			h	m	s	
A. M.	7	45	16		P. M.	3	45	15	
	″	46	43			″	46	17	not certain
	″	48	12			″	Lost by clouds		

Altd. given by Sextant at the time of obstn.   63° 26′ 45″

Observed Meridian altitude of ⊙'s L. L. with Octant by the back observatn. 42° 12′ 10.9″

1. The following address in Clark's hand is under the entries (August 13, 14, and 15) on this sheet of the Field Notes (document 42), at right angles to the rest of the writing. The last sentence is upside-down to the address. Presumably Clark used this sheet as an envelope to send a letter to Lewis at St. Louis during the winter at River Dubois: "Capt. Meriwether Lewis, S. Louis, pr. Mons Vansee Gutaru, I will thank you to send the letter directed to [prukhon? prudhom?] and Smiley to the post office to go by the next mail." Considering Clark's usual difficulty with French names, the bearer of the letter may have been Vincent Guitard, a resident and landowner in the St. Louis area for some years. Houck, 2:55, 101.

2. The Omahas were at one time closely related to the Poncas; both spoke dialects of the same language of the Dhegiha group of the Siouan linguistic family, and both were horticulturists and hunters. The Omahas may have settled in Nebraska by 1700 or even a little earlier. By 1750 they were generally in Nebraska, although they hunted and camped on both sides of the Missouri River in the region. In the last decade of the eighteenth century, they made much trouble for the French traders who wished to ascend the Missouri River beyond the Omaha village to trade with the Arikaras and Mandans. During the winter of 1799–1800 they experienced a catastrophic smallpox epidemic that is supposed to have reduced their numbers to about 900-1500 people, which would be close to Clark's estimate of "300 men," counting three to five persons per adult male. (Personal communication of John Ludwickson.) Thereafter they did not appear as an obstacle to white expansion. Clark's statement that they had no corn is hard to understand, for they regarded corn as one of their most important food sources. He may mean that they planted corn but then went buffalo hunting and so did not stay home to tend their crop, which would be consistent with Plains Indian horticultural practices. His statement in Codex A that they had no houses may be explained by the remark here that the village was in ruins; ordinarily at least the more industrious families had permanent earth lodges. The condition of the place may have resulted from the burning of the village during the smallpox epidemic, which may have left their society in disarray for some time, delaying their efforts to rebuild. Ordway says that they had about three hundred "cabins," meaning perhaps that he saw their burned remains. If the wooden frame of an earth lodge was burned, the lodge would collapse. Hodge, 2:119–21; Fletcher & La Flesche, 1:96–98, 261–70, passim; Smith (OI); Nasatir (BLC), 1:280ff.

3. Here ends the notebook journal Codex A, except for an astronomical observation of June 23, 1804, placed with that date. The words "Cho car tooch or *Brarow*" are on a page by themselves, and were probably jotted down as a note when Clark first heard the information. See entries at February 6 and July 30, 1804.

4. Lewis's observation from Codex O.

[Clark]

August 15th Wendesday   I took ten men[1] & went out to Beaver Dam across a Creek about a mile S W from Camp,[2] and with a Brush Drag[3] caught 308 fish, of the following kind (i'e) Pike, Samon, Bass, Pirch, Red horse, Small Cat, & a kind of Perch Called on the Ohio *Silverfish*[4]   I also Caught the Srimp[5] which is Common to the Lower part of the Mississippi, in this Creek & in the Beaver Pond is emince beads of Mustles[6] Verry large & fat—   in my absence Capt Lewis Send the Souex interpr [Dorion] & a party to a Smoke which appeared to rise at no great distance to the north with a view to find Some Band of that nation, they returned and informed that the [fires] had been made Some time by Some Small party, and the hard wind of to day had set the Prarie on fire from Some high trees, which was left burning   all well, Party from Ottoes not come up.

Camp three Miles N. E of the Mahar Village

[Clark]   August 15th Wednesday 1804[7]

I went with ten men to a Creek Damed by the Beavers about half way to the Village, with Some Small willow & Bark we mad a Drag and haulted up the Creek, and Cought 318 fish of different kind i'e' Peke, Bass, Salmon, perch, red horse, Small Cat, and a kind of perch Called Silverfish, on the Ohio.—   I cought a Srimp prosisely of Shape Size & flavour of those about N. Orleans & the lower party of the Mississippi   in this Creek which is only the pass or Streight from Beaver Pond to another, is Crouded with large Mustles Verry fat, Ducks, Pliver of different Kinds are on those Ponds as well as on the river[8]   in My absence Capt. Lewis Sent Mr. Durioue the Souix interpeter & three men to examine a fire which threw up an emence Smoke from the Praries on the N. E. Side of the River and at no great distance from Camp—   the Object of this party was to find Some Bands of Seouex which the inptr. thought was near the Smoke and get them to Come in—   in the evening this Party returned and infoermed, that the fire arrose from Some trees which had been left burning by a Small party of Seoux whom had passed [*NB?: by that place*] Several Days— the wind Setting from that point, blew the Smoke from that pt. over our Camp. our party all in health and Sperrits the men Sent to the Ottoes & in pursute of the Deserter *Reed* has not yet returned or joined our party.

[Lewis]   *Wednesday August 15th*[9]

Observed Equal Altitudes of ☉, with Sextant

	h	m	s			h	m	s
A. M.	8	0	29		P. M.	3	28	42
	"	1	52			"	30	11
	"	3	28			"	31	38

Altd. by Sextant at the time of this observt.   68° 45′ 45″

Observed meridian Altd. of ☉'s L. L. with Octant by the back observatn.   61° 27″ —

Latitude deduced from this observt.   42° 15′ 13.4″

1. Floyd says he was with this party.

2. The courses of the creeks through the river bottom in this area have been altered, forcing them into man-made ditches; identifying this stream is therefore difficult. Possibly it was present Pigeon Creek, in Thurston County, Nebraska. The fishing spot was presumably northeast of present Macy. *Atlas* map 16; MRC map 27; MRR map 75.

3. Some sort of net or barrier, made of brush, probably reaching entirely across the creek.

4. Since no species of salmon are native to the Great Plains, although there is a possibility that *Salvelinus fontinalis*, brook trout, once was, Clark's "samon" may be *Hiodon tergisus*, mooneye, or *H. alosoides*, goldeye; the bass may be either smallmouth bass or largemouth bass; the red horse is probably *Moxostoma macrolepidotum*, shorthead red horse; the "small cat" may be the channel catfish, or *Noturus flavus*, stonecat; the silverfish may be *Aplodinotus grunniens*, freshwater drum—as early as 1780 this was called the white perch in present Ohio. Lee et al., 74–75, 605, 608, 427, 446, 455; Trautman, 698–99.

5. Probably a crayfish, of the genus *Cambarus*. Coues (HLC), 1:76 n. 41.

6. These mussels may be in the family of *Margaritanidae* or *Unionidae*. Pennak, 704–10.

7. With this entry begins Clark's notebook journal Codex B, which runs through October 3, 1804. See Appendix C. The words "Oake Cha ha har the Corvuss bird," are on a page by themselves at the beginning of this notebook, probably written when he first received the information. The Sioux word attempted by Clark is *uŋkcek'iħa*. The bird is the black-billed magpie, *Pica pica* [AOU, 475], of which they obtained a specimen on September 16, 1804. Cutright (LCPN), 84–85.

8. The "Ducks, Pliver" and the like are not identifiable, but one naturalist speculates

that the former was the wood duck, and the latter either the lesser golden-plover, *Pluvialis dominica* [AOU, 272], or black-bellied plover, *P. squatarola* [AOU, 270] or "some other species of plover or plover-like shore bird." Swenk, 121–22.

   9. Lewis's observation from Codex O.

[Clark][1]

Ottoes returned to the Village 4th of August, the Panies the 15th of August.

Lake Daespere Mad Lake [Lake d'Esprit] *the head of the Little Souix* River

$$
\begin{array}{ccc}
42 & 15 & 13 \\
42 & 12 & 10 \quad - \\
\hline
\lfloor 3 & 3 \\
\hline
1 & 31 \\
\hline
42 & 13 & 41
\end{array}
$$

From the Mahars to the White River	80 Leagus	
to the Chion [Cheyenne] R.	150 "	
to the Richarees [Arikara]—	250 "	
then to the Mandins	10	
thence to the Wattesoons[2]	3 — to Muneturs[3]	3

Louisiana ⟨Lark [*other words crossed out*]⟩

Fish Camp on a Sand bar 3 Ms. N. E of the Mahars Town

Aug. 16th 1804

a Verry cool morning   the winds as usial from the N W. Capt Lewis with [12?] men[4] went out to the Creek & Pond & Caught about 800 fine fish with a Bush Drag of the following kind i'e' 79 Pike, 8 Salmon, 1 Rock, 1 flat Back, 127 Buffalow & readHorse, 4 Bass & 490 Cat, with many Small & large Silver fish,—[5]   I had a mast made & fixed to day   The Party Sent to the Ottoes not yet arrived.   the wind Shifted around to the S E.   the night's are Cool & a Breeze rises after generally; Sometimes before night which Blows off the Musquitors cools the atmospere.[6]

$$
\begin{array}{cc}
28 & 49 \\
13 & 41 \\
\hline
15 & 8
\end{array}
\qquad
\begin{array}{ccc}
[7?] & 70 & 15 \\
& & 70 \\
\hline
& 1050 \\
& 173
\end{array}
\qquad
\begin{array}{c}
70 \\
5 \\
\hline
350 \\
6
\end{array}
$$

[Clark]   *16th* August Thursday 1804

Fishing Camp 3 ms. N. E. of the *Mahars.*   a verry cool morning the wind as usial from the N W.

Capt Lewis took 12 men & went to the Pond & Crek between Camp and the old Village and Cought upwards of 800 fine fish, 79 Pike, [*WC: resembling Trout 8 fish resembg Salmon Trout*][7] 8 Salmon, 1 Rock, 1 flat Back, 127 Buffalow & red horse 4 Bass & 490 Catt. with many Small Silver fish [*WC: & Scrimp*]   I had a Mast made & fixed to the Boat to day, the Party Sent to the Ottoes not yet joined us—   the wind Shifted arround to the S. E.   everry evening a Breeze rises which blows off the Musquitors & Cools the atmispeire.

1. A collection of miscellaneous material probably written at various times is squeezed in above the August 16, 1804, entry in the Field Notes (document 43). Some of it clearly belongs to the period at the "Fishing Camp."

2. The "Wattesoons," a group of many names, were the Awaxawi, a division of the Minitari, or Hidatsa, people (see October 27, 1804).

3. The spelling of the original is by no means clear, but the location of this tribe relative to the Mandans and "Wattesoons" leaves no doubt that Clark meant some variation of "Minitari" (Hidatsa).

4. Gass may have been with this party, though his reference is unclear.

5. The "Rock" may be the white or rock bass, *Morone chrysops.* It is difficult to identify Clark's "flat Back." Criswell suggests it was sometimes a synomym for a sucker (family *Catostomidae*), but this does not seem likely; perhaps *Pylodictis olivaris*, flathead catfish. The silverfish may the same as those mentioned on August 15 or they may be minnows. Lee et al., 574, 742; Criswell, 39, 83.

6. The figures below come immediately after the August 16 entry in the Field Notes.

7. In Codex B, the first two words of the interlined passage and the words "8 Salmon" were later crossed out, perhaps by Biddle in 1810.

[Clark]

17th August 1804.   a fine morning   Wind from the S. E.   I will here annex the Latds & Distances of the Different notable placies from the River Dubois or Mouth up:

miles by water

To St Charles *Village* on the N. side	21	in Latitude	38°	54′	39″	North
" the mouth of the Gasconade S. do	104	" do	38	44	35	"
" the mouth of the Great Osarge S. "	138	" do	38	31	6	"
" mo. of *Mine* River S. "	201					

" the mo. of the 2 Charltons R: N. "	226				
" the mo. of Grand River on the N. side					
" just above the old Missouries Village	254	in Lattitude 38° 47 54 North			
" the mo: of the Kanzies River S. Sd.	366	" do	39	5	25	"
" the [Pt?]: above the Dimont Island—		" do	39	9	38	"
" Creek Independance below the place where the Kanzes had their 2d Village S. S.	433	" do	39	25	42	"
" the Mo. of Nodawa River N. S.—	481	" do	39	39	22	"
" the mo: of Grand *Ne ma har* R. S. S.	511	" do	39	55	56	"
" Isd. opsd. the Bald Pated Prarie N. S.	570	" do	40	25	7	"
" the Mo: of River *Platt* S. S.	632				
" the White Catfish Camp 10 Ms. abov—	642	" do	41	3	19	"
" Council Bluff (with the Ottoes) S. S.	682	" do	41	17	—	"
" Mo. of the Little *Siouex* River N. S.	766	" do	41	42	34	"
" Camp Opsd. the *Mahars* Village S. S.	864	" do	42	13	41	"

The Longitudes are not yet Calculated, We must be at this time about 99° 45′ 00″ West of Greenwich—[1]   I Collected a grass much resembling wheet with a grain like Rye, much fuller of grain, one like Rye & one like Barley Grass Small, a Grass like Timothey except the Seed which is on branches from the main Stalk—[2]

Late this evening one of the party Sent after the deserters returned & joined us, he left the party 3 miles back, they cought both Deserters, one of them *La liberty*, got away from them, the Great Chief & 2nd Chief of the ottoes accompaned the Party with a view to bring about a Peice between themselves & the Mahar   a great missfortune that the Mahars have not returned from the hunt—   Sent & fiered the Prarie near Camp to bring in the Mahars & Souex if any are near.   a Cool evening, 2 Beever Cought

[Clark]   17th August ⟨Thursday⟩ Friday 1804.

a fine Morning   the wind from the S. E.   I collected a grass much resembling wheat in its grouth the grain like Rye, als[o] Some resembling Rye & Barly.   a kind of Timothey, the Seed of which branches from the main Stalk & is more like flax Seed than that of a Timothey—

at 6 oClock this evening *Labieche* one of the Party Sent to the Ottoes joined, and informed that the Party was behind with one of the Deserters M B. Reed and the 3 principal Chiefs of the Nations—   La Liberty they cought but he decived them and got away— the object of those Chiefs comeing forward is to make a peace with the Mahars thro: us—. as the Mahars are not at home this great object cannot be accomplished at this time Set the Praries on fire to bring the Mahars & ⟨Missouries⟩ Soues if any were near, this being the usial Signal.

a Cool evining two Beaver Cought to day.

1. The "Fish Camp" was just north of 42° 21′ N., so their calculated position is a little too far south. The longitude, more difficult to calculate to start with, is further off. The camp was near 96° 25′ W. MRC map 27; MRR map 75.

2. Canada wildrye, first noticed July 10, 1804.

[Clark]

18th August 1804   a fine morning, despatched Jo. Fields for the Party from the Ottoes, whom did not Come up last night   Wind from the S. E. [(]*Panies ⟨arived⟩ returned from their hunt, the 12th of August)[1]   in the after Part of the Day the Party arrived, we had a Short talk after which we gave them Provisions to eate & proceeded to the trial of Reed, he confessed, & we Sentenced him only to run the Ganelet four times thro: the Detachment & party, and not to be considered in the future as one of the Permonant Party, after the Punihment of about [500?] Lashes,[2] at night we had Some talk with the Chiefs about the Cause of War between them and the Mahars.   posponed the further consultation untill tomorrow. had a Dance which lasted untile 11 oClock, the Close of Cap Lewis Birthday.[3]   a fine evening   wind S. E

Day & year of[4]

⟨N. 5   N. 52 W. 7   Miles to a point of highwoods on Stard. and having passed the lower point of Pellican Island ¼ of a mile, to which the last course was taken⟩

36	⟨Children⟩	1 Frenchman
45	⟨Ottoes & Missouries⟩	2 Great Chiefs of the Ottoes—
45	⟨you do Somethig⟩	2 Second Chifs of the Missouries—
126		5 Wariors, accompanied the Party

Sent to the Towns, i e Reiubin Fields Will: Brattin G. Drewyer & W Labieche. [*Ed: this was on August 7*].

My Father, I am Sorry that the first man I brought:—

[Clark]   18th August ⟨Friday⟩ Satday 1804

a fine morning.   Wind from the S. E. in the after part of the Day   the Party with the Indians arrivd.   we meet them under a Shade near the Boat and after a Short talk we gave them Provisions to eat & proceeded to the trail of Reed, he Confessed that he "Deserted & Stold a public Rifle Shot-pouch Powder & Bals" and requested we would be as favourable with him as we Could consistantly with our Oathes—which we were and only Sentenced him to run the Gantlet four times through the Party & that each man with 9 Swichies Should punish him and for him not to be considered in future as one of the Party—

The three principal Chiefs petitioned for Pardin for this man

After we explained the injurey Such men could doe them by false representation, & explang. the Customs of our Countrey they were all Satisfied with the propriety of the Sentence & was witness to the punishment.[5] after which we had Some talk with the Chiefs about the orrigan of the war between them & the Mahars &c. &c.—   it commenced in this way i'e' in two of the Missouries Tribe resideing with the Ottoes went to the Mahars to Steel horses, they Killed them both which was a cause of revenge on the part of the Missouris & Ottoes, they also brought war on themselves [*WC: Cap L. Birth day*][6]   Nearly in the Same way with the Panea Loups [Skiri Pawnees] and they are greatly in fear of a just revenge from the Panies for takeing their Corn from the Pania Towns in their absence hunting this Summer.

the evening was Closed with an extra Gill of Whiskey & a Dance untill 11 oClock.

[Lewis]   *Saturday, August 18th*[7]

Observed meridian altd. of ⊙'s L. L. with Octant by the back observt.   63° 23' —"

Latitude deduced from this obsetn.   [*blank*]

Observed Equal altitudes of the ⊙ with Sextant

	h	m	s		h	m	s
A. M.	7	38	1	P. M.	3	46	48
	"	39	28		"	48	13
	"	40	58		"	49	42

Altd. by Sextant at the Time of Obstn.   60° 8' —"

1. The sentence between parentheses is an interjection in the main narrative.

2. The official record of this trial does not appear in the Orderly Book or elsewhere. See n. 5, below.

3. August 18 was Lewis's thirtieth birthday.

4. Various miscellaneous undated material, much of it crossed out, is written in the middle of the August 18 entry at the top of the sheet of the Field Notes (document 43). The course and description are in Lewis's hand, the remaining material is in Clark's. Some of the material seems to be tentative beginnings for speeches, made to or by the Indian chiefs. Material dealing with this council on document 43 is written in different directions on the sheet and has been sorted out as well as can be done.

5. In this Codex B entry the sentences relating to Reed's trial and punishment are crossed out. No account of the episode appears in the narrative of the day in Biddle's *History*, although he notes Reed's apprehension among the events of August 17. Coues (HLC), 1:77–78.

6. This interlineation is at the top of a page in Codex B, probably inserted there because space was available.

7. Lewis's observation from Codex O.

[Clark]

19th of August Sunday 1804   a fine morning   wind from the S. E   I prepd. a present from the Chiefs & Warriers, the main Chief Brack fast with us naked; & beged for a Sun glass.—[1]   at 10 oClock we assembled the Cheifs & Warriers under an Orning and delivered a Speech, explanitary of the One Sent to this Nation from the *Council Bluff,* &c. &c.—[2]

Children   When we Sent the 4 men to your towns, we expected to See & Speake with the Mahas by the time you would arrive and to ⟨make⟩ lay the foundation of a peace between you and them

The Speech of Petieit Villeu Little Thief, If you think right and Can waite untill all our Warriers Come from the Buffalows hunt, we Can then tell you who is our men of Consequnce—   My fathers always lived with the father of the B together & we always live with the Big hose—[3]   all the men here are the Suns of Chief and will be glad to get Something from the hands of their fathers.—   My father always directed me to be friendly with the white people, I have always done So and went often to the french, give my party pieces of Paper [commissions] & we will be glad—   The names[4]

a Meddel to *Car ka pá há* or *Crow's head*

a Comsi or Cfte. *Sar ná no ne* or Iron Eyes[5]   a *Ottoe* approves & says he is [a] Brave[6]

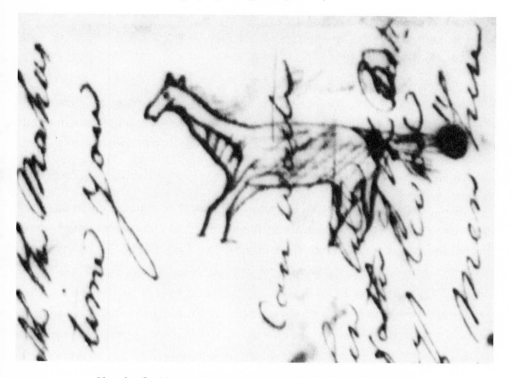

17. Sketch of a Horse, August 19, 1804, Field Notes, document 43

"	*Nee Swor un ja* Big ax	a Ottoe approves.
"	*Star gra hun ja* Big blue Eyes	a Ottoe ⟨approves⟩ Delivers up his comtn. [commission]
"	*Ne ca sa wa*—Black Cat	a Missouris approves the Council & he wants paper for his men at home, he after wards came & petitioned for his Paper
"	*War-sar sha co—Brave Man*	*aproves*

The Speach of the Big Horse I went to the hunt Buffalow I heard your word and I returned, I and all my men with me will attend to your words— you want to make peace with all, I want to make peace also, the young me[n] when they want to go to war where is the goods you give me to Keep them at home, if you give me Some Whisky to give a Drop to my men at home.

I came here naked and must return home naked. if I have Something to give the young men I can prevent their going to war. You want to make peace with all, It is good we want Something to give my men at home. I am a pore man, and cant quiet without means, a Spoon ful of your milk [whiskey] will qui[e]t all.

2nd Speech of the *Little Thief*[7]   I want Mr. Faufon & Mr. La bieche to make a piece with the Panies Loups [Skiri Pawnees]. I want William to go & make a piece with the Loups, he can Speake english & will doe will [well] to go.—[8]   refused that William LaBiech shall accompany *Faufon*[9]

[*Ed: Clark now returns to his narrative*][10]

Those people were not well Satisfied with the Presents given them, they were much Surprised at the air gun and Several curiosities which were Shown them none more than the magnet, those people became extreemly troublesom to us begging Whisky & little articles. Sergt. Floyd was taken violently bad with the Beliose Cholick and is dangerously ill   we attempt in Vain to releive him, I am much concerned for his Situation—   we could get nothing to Stay on his Stomach a moment   nature appear exosting fast in him   every man is attentive to him ⟨york prlly⟩ [York principally?]

[Clark]   19th August ⟨Satturday⟩ Sunday 1804

a find morning wind from the S. E.   prepared a Small Present for the Cheifs and warriers present.   the main Cheif Brackfast with us, & beged for a Sun glass, those People are all naked, Covered only with Breech Clouts Blankits or Buffalow Roabes, ⟨of⟩ the flesh Side Painted of Differant Colours & figures. At 10 oClock we assembled the Chiefs & warriers 9 in number under an orning, and ⟨Cap Lewis⟩ we explained the Speech Sent to the nation from the Council Bluffs by Mr. Faufon. The ⟨two⟩ 3 Chiefs and all the men or warriers made Short Speeches approveing the advice & Council their great father had Sent them, and Concluded by giveing themselves Some Credit for their acts.

We then brought out the presents and exchanged the *Big horses* Meadel & gave him one equal to the one Sent to the Little Thief[11] & gave all Some Small articls & 8 Carrots of Tobacco,[12]

we gave one Small Meadel to one of the Cheifs & a Sertificate to the others of their good intentions.

Names

The Little Theif   Grd. Cheif I have mentioned before
The Big horse

> *Crows Head* (or) *Kar Ka paha* — Missory
> *Black Cat* (or) *Ne ma Sa wa* — do
> *Iron Eyes* (or) *Sar na no no* — Ottoe
> *Big ax* (or) *Nee Swar Un ja* — do
> *Big Blue Eyes* — Star gea Hun Ja — do
> *Brave Man* (or) *War Sar Sha co*

One of those Indians after reciving his Certificate delivd. it again to me the *Big blue eyes* the Chief petitioned for the Ctft. again, we would not give the Certft. but rebuked them verry roughly for haveing in object goods and not peace with their neighbours— this language they did not like at first, but at length all petitioned for us to give back the Certificate to the Big blu eyes he came forward and made a plausible excuse, I then gave the Certificate the Great Cheif to bestow it to the most Worthey, they gave it to him, we then gave them a Dram & broke up the Council, the Chiefs requested we would not leave them this evening. we deturmed to Set out early in the morning we Showed them many Curiosities and the air gun which they were much asstonished at. those people beged much for wishey— Serjeant Floyd is taken verry bad all at onc with a Beliose Chorlick we attempt to relieve him without Success as yet, he gets wordse and we are muc allarmed at his Situation, all attention to him.

1. Probably a "burning glass," that is, a lens for focusing the sun's rays to start a fire, an item the Indians would find both useful and intriguing. Lewis had purchased eight dozen of them for presents in Philadelphia in 1803. Lewis's Summary of Purchases [June 1803], Jackson (LLC), 1:93.

2. The remainder of the material on this page of the Field Notes (document 43) is upside-down to the foregoing. Three words (*"Roloje," "Francis,"* and *"Durwain"*) appear above the Indian speeches at the edge of the page. For Roloje Creek, see below, August 22, 1804. "Durwain" is likely a variation of Dorion. It may be, then, that Francis (or François) Dorion is the name of the son of old Pierre Dorion, the Sioux interpreter; the date when this younger Dorion joined the party is not clear. See below, August 29, 1804. Authorities generally give young Dorion's name as Pierre. Jackson (LLC), 2:414. "Francis" may refer to someone else.

3. The drawing of the horse at this point in the Field Notes (fig. 17) may be only a doodle, but it suggests that the chief Big Horse may have been carrying his shield or some other object bearing his personal symbol which Clark copied here.

4. Linguistic analysis by Robert L. Rankin, Kenneth Miner, and John E. Koontz yields the following: *Kháxe paha* signifies "Crow head"; "Sar ná no ne" does not mean "Iron Eyes," but no definite translation is possible; *Įswe xáje* signifies "Big Ax"; *Ištá graxaje* means "Very Big Eyes," without reference to the color blue; *Mįkhe sewe* apparently means

"Black Raccoon," perhaps Clark's word "cat"; and *Wašóšegǫ* may be translated as "Like [a] Brave." *Waphíya* may be translated as "He does [what is] Good."

5. In 1811, traveler H. M. Brackenridge noted a Nebraska bluff, south of the mouth of the Platte, called *L'oeil aufer* (Iron Eye), "from an Indian chief who was scaffolded here some years ago." Maximilian, in 1833, heard the Oto name as "Ischta Maso." Since this was Oto territory, it is not unlikely that the chief interred there was the one met by the captains. The hill, which Nicollet labeled both "L'oeil de fer" and "Iron eye hill," is the later Rock Bluff Point, in Cass County, Nebraska, south of Plattsmouth. Nicollet (MMR), 384; MRC map 22; Thwaites (EWT), 6:76 and n. 26, 22:265 and n. 219.

6. "Brave" implies a specific social status gained through war exploits (and perhaps vision power and membership in warrior societies). Such a status among the related Omahas has been confirmed. Research also suggests that the Oto organization of warfare was like that of the rest of the Plains Indians. Dorsey, 217; Whitman, 10–12.

7. This paragraph is upside-down following the August 21 entry in the Field Notes (document 43) but clearly belongs here.

8. The third reference to François Labiche as "William" (see above, July 4 and August 7, 1804). The special desire of the Otos for his services suggests that they knew him previously, probably from earlier trading ventures. See Appendix A, this volume.

9. Under this paragraph, upside-down to the writing, appear these figures: 3, 3, 10, and a total of 16.

10. Biddle's notation at the head of this portion of the Field Notes (reverse of document 43) reads, "Augt. 17 to 25."

11. Apparently the captains had originally (August 3) given Big Horse a second-class medal (diameter 76 mm) and now gave him one of the large (105 mm) medals. Since a certain spiritual power was associated with such gifts, more was involved than mere jealousy. Prucha, 92–93; Ronda, 22.

12. Tobacco was transported in the form of twisted rolls called "carrots" because of their shape. Criswell, 22.

[Clark]

20th *August* Monday   after gieving faufon Some goods the Indians a Canister of whiskey, we Set out under a jentle Breeze from the S. E Shields went with the horses—   I am Dull & heavy   been up the greater Part of last night with Serjt. Floyd, who is a[s] bad as he can be to live   the [motion?] of his bowels having changed &c. &c. is the Cause of his violent attack &c. &c.

Course

N. 56° W.	3	mes. to a pt. of Willows on the Island S. S
North	¾	of a mile on the left of the Said Island—
N 72° E	2 ½	mes. to the upper pt. of the Island

N 18° E.	2 ½	miles to the lower point of an Island on the S. S. passed Some Sand bars in the river
North	3 ½	miles to a Bluf on the S. S. and the first above the old Ayauwa Village on the S. S.

we Came to [to] make a warm bath for Sergt. Floyd hopeing it would brace him a little, before we could get him in to this bath he expired, with a great deel of composure, haveing Said to me before his death that he was going away and wished me to write a letter—[1]   we ⟨took⟩ Buried him to the top of a high round hill over looking the river & Countrey for a great distance   Situated just below a Small river without a name to which we name & call Floyds river, the Bluffs Sergts. Floyds Bluff—[2]   we buried him with all the honors of War, and fixed a Ceeder post at his head with his name title & Day of the month and year   Capt Lewis read the funeral Service over him   after paying everry respect to the Body of this desceased man (who had at All times given us proofs of his impatiality Sincurity to ourselves and good will to Serve his Countrey)   we returned to the Boat & proceeded to the Mouth of the little river 30 yd. wide & Camped[3]   a butifull evening

[Clark]   20th August Monday 1804

Sergeant Floyd much weaker and no better. Made Mr. Fauforn the in-terpter a fiew presents, and the Indians a Canister of whisky   we Set out under a gentle breeze from the S. E. and proceeded on verry well—   Ser-jeant Floyd as bad as he can be   no pulse & nothing will Stay a moment on his Stomach or bowels—

Passed two Islands on the S. S. and at first Bluff on the S S. Serj.' Floyd Died with a great deel of Composure, before his death he Said to me, "I am going away"   ["]I want you to write me a letter"—   We buried him on the top of the bluff ½ Miles below a Small river to which we Gave his name, he was buried with the Honors of War much lamented; a Seeder post with the (1) Name Sergt. C. Floyd died here 20th of August 1804 was fixed at the head of his grave—   This Man at all times gave us proofs of his firmness and Deturmined resolution to doe Service to his Countrey and honor to himself   after paying all the honor to our Decesed brother we Camped in the mouth of *floyds* river about 30 yards wide, a butifull evening.—

495

Course Dists. & reffn. 20th Augt.

N. 56° W.	3	ms. to pt. of a willow Isd. S. S.
North	¾	Me. on the left of the Island
N. 72 E.	2 ¼	Me. to the upr. pt. of the Isd.
N. 18 E	2 ½	ms. to the lower pt. of an Isd. on the S. S. passed Sand bars
North	3 ½	ms. to Sjt. Floyds Bluff on S. S. the lst above Aiaways Village a fiew miles above Platt R.
	1 ⅛	To the mo: of Floyds River on S. S. & camped
	13	

1. The probability is that Floyd died of a ruptured appendix and consequent perito-nitis. The ailment was not even recognized by medical science until twenty years after the expedition, and the first successful surgical treatment came in 1884. Probably no physi-cian of the time could have done much more for Floyd than the captains did. A purgative like Rush's pills, their usual remedy for digestive disorders, could only have hastened Floyd's death, but this is probably what Dr. Benjamin Rush himself would have prescribed if he had been present—along with bleeding, which would have accomplished nothing. The place of Floyd's death is near Sergeant Bluff on the Iowa side of the river, near the present town of Sergeant Bluff, Woodbury County, Iowa. Chuinard, 238–39; Coues (HLC), 1 : 79–80 n. 44; *Iowa Guide*, 426; *Atlas* map 16; MRC map 27; MRR map 76.

2. Within present Sioux City, Woodbury County; later travelers often remarked on the site, and George Catlin painted it in 1832. By 1857 the Missouri had undercut the bluff and the grave was opened and some of the bones lost. Citizens of Sioux City moved the bones to a new burial site. In 1895 the bones were again examined, and a concrete slab and a one-hundred-foot monument was erected in 1901. The Floyd River still bears his name. Appleman, (LC), 285–87; *Atlas* map 16; MRC map 27: MRR map 76.

3. Just above the mouth of the Floyd River in modern Sioux City, Woodbury County. *Atlas* map 16 has an error in this day's course that may have resulted from faulty course readings. There is an extreme curve to the northeast above the previous camp, which would send the Missouri River off in the direction of Minnesota. Clark must have realized his mistake and corrected it on the Fort Mandan (*Atlas* maps 32a, 32b, 32c) and later maps. MRC map 27; MRR map 76. I am indebted to V. Strode Hinds of Sioux City, for pointing out this discrepancy.

[Clark]

21st August Tuesday   we Set out verry early this morning under a Gentle Breeze from the S. E   Course S. 82° E 3 mes to the upper pt. of a Bluff on the S. S.   passed Willow Creek[1] and Some ⟨Stone⟩ rock ⟨above⟩ below the mouth of the Seouex river[2] on the Starboard Side   those Clifts are about 170 fee[t] high, this river heads with the St. peters[3] and is navagable 75 Leagues (by the act. of Mr. Durien [Dorion]) to a fall of near 200 for [from], 2 large & Som Small Pitchs[4]   below the falls on the ⟨left⟩ right a Creek coms in on which ⟨all⟩ the red pipe Stone is percured, & in the praries about, a place of Peace with all nations.[5]

South	1 ¼	Miles to the lower pt of a Sand & willow Island in the Middle of the river
S. 48 W.	1 ¾	Miles to the head of the Said Island, passing Sand bars thro which the water passes the whole Course River Shalow & wide *Wind blow's hard*
West	2	mes. to a high wood on the L S., passed a large Sand bar from S. S. *river wide*
N. 36° W.	4	ms. to a Beyau above wher the Mahars had a village in the bend to the L. S. a Sand bar on S. S. & one in the middle a large Island on the S. S. on which we Saw 4 wolves, on mat [one man] out Hunting *Shannon*
N. 18 E	2	ms. to a Pt. of willows on the L. S. Wind verry hard from the S. E. Latd. 42° 28′ 49″ ⁶/₁₀ North. this Countrey has a great Sameness but little timber
N. 22° W.	¾	on the L. S. opsd. to which the R. *Sieuix* is within 2 miles on the S. S.—
S 50° W.	¼	me. on L. S.
S 28 W.	2	me. to willow pt. on the S. S.
S 78 W.	1 ½	on the Sand bar to the L. S.
N. 12 W.	2	ms. to a Willow Pt. the L. Side pass Sand bars
S. 60 W	1 ¾	mes. to on the Sand bar on the L. S. exme. & Give Sjt. Pryor Sg Floyds things except shot p[ouch]. & Tomhk. [tomahawk]
South	2 ½	ms. to a low willows on S. S. *and incamped* on the
	22 ¾	L. S. one man out 2 with the Horses.

[Clark]   21st August Tuesday 1804

We Set out verry early this morning and proceeded on under a gentle Breeze from the S. E.   passed willow creek Small on the S. S. below a Bluff of about 170 feet high and one ½ mes. above Floyds river   at 1 ½ miles higher & above the Bluff passed the *Soues River* S. S.   this River is about the Size of Grand river and as Mr. *Durrien* our Soues intptr. says "navagable to the falls 70 or 80 Leagues and above these falls Still further, those falls are 200 feet or there abouts & has two princapal pitches, and heads with the St. *peters* passing the head of the Demoien, on the right below the falls a Creek Coms in which passes thro Clifts of red rock which the Indians make pipes of, and when the different nations Meet at [*X: a Sort of asylum for all nations, no fightg there*] those queries all is piece, passed a place in a Prarie on the L. S. where the Mahars had a Village formerly.[6] the Countrey above the Platt R has a great Similarity.   Campd. on the L. Side.[7]   Clouds appear to rise in the west & threten wind. I found a verry excellent froot resembling the read Current, the Scrub on which it grows resembles *Privey* & about the Common hight of a wild plumb—[8]

Course Distanc & refrs. 21st Augt.

S. 82° E.	3	mes. to the upper part of a Bluff below the Souex river on S. S. passed willow Creek at 1 ½ Ms. S. S.
South	1 ¼	mes. to Lower pt. of a willow Island in the Midle of the river one on S. S. opsd.—
S. 48 W.	1 ¾	mes. to the head of the Isld passed Several Sand bars disiding the Current, wind hard
West	2	ms. to a high wood on the L. S. passed a large Sand bar from the S. S. *River wide*
N. 36 W.	4	mes. to a Beyau is a bend to the L. S. above where the Mahars once had a Village a Sand bar in the Middle of S. S.
N. 18 E.	2	mes. to a pt. of Willows on the L. S. wind hard from S E
N. 22° W.	¾	mes. on the L. S. opsd. to which the Soues river is within 2 miles on the S. S
S. 50 W.	¼	me. on the L. S.
S. 28 W.	2	mes. to the willow pt. on the S. S.
S. 78 W.	1 ½	mes. to the Sand bar on S. S.
N. 12 W	2	mes. to a willow pt. on the L. S. passed a Sand bar.
S. 60 W	1 ¾	mes. on the Sand bar on the L. Side
South	2 ½	miles to Some low willows on the S. S.
	24 ¾	

The two men Sent with the horses has not joined us as yet[9]

(*Point of Observation No. 33.*)

[Lewis]   *Tuesday, August 21st*[10]

On a large sand bar Stard., 4 miles above the mouth of the river Souix.

Observed meridn. Altd. of ☉'s L. L. with Octant by the back observation   65°
47′ —

Latitude deduced from this observatn.   42° 28′ 29″

1. Perry Creek, which meets the Missouri at Sioux City, Woodbury County, Iowa. *Atlas* map 16; MRC map 27; MRR map 76.

2. The Big Sioux River reaches the Missouri after skirting the western edge of Sioux City. It forms the South Dakota–Iowa boundary, Union County, South Dakota lying to the west. *Atlas* maps 16 and 17; MRC map 27; MRR map 76.

3. The St. Peters River is the present Minnesota River. The source of the Big Sioux in northeast South Dakota is fairly close to that of the Minnesota River on the Minnesota–South Dakota border, in the area called Coteau des Prairies. Petersen, 230–33.

4. "Pitch" is frequently used by the captains in reference to a waterfall. The term was used in Virginia for a slope or descent. McJimsey, 103.

5. The red stone is catlinite, named for the artist George Catlin, who brought it to the attention of mineralogists. It is found at the quarries along Pipestone Creek, Pipestone County, in southwestern Minnesota. The area is now a national monument and only Indians are allowed to extract the stone. Tradition holds that the quarries were neutral ground where all tribes met in peace. Hodge, 1:217–19; Catlin, 2:164–71; Woolworth.

6. The Omahas are said to have had a village here before founding Tonwontonga; it was called *Ti tañga jiñga*. Dorsey notes that the lodges here were made of wood, that is, they were bark-covered "wig-wams," not earth lodges or tipis. Dorsey, 213. This village was probably located several miles west of present Dakota City, Dakota County, Nebraska, on the west side of the Missouri River. *Atlas* map 16; MRC map 27; MRR maps 76, 78.

7. In Union County, south of present Jefferson, and probably on the north side of Lake Goodenough, which appears to have been the 1804 bed of the Missouri. *Atlas* map 17; MRC map 28; MRR map 78.

8. *Shepherdia argentea* (Pursh) Nutt., buffaloberry, was then new to science. The privey, or privet, used for comparison is *Ligustrum vulgare* L., a native of Europe. Barkley, 203.

9. Reubin Field was with the horses on August 23, but it is not clear that he was one of the two mentioned here.

10. Lewis's observation from Codex O.

[Clark]

22nd of August ⟨Friday⟩ Wendesday 1804   Set out early   wind from the South. G Shannon joined the Boat last night. Course this morning is S 47° W. *1¼* on the S. point   West 1¼ me. to the Commencement of a Bluff on the L. S.   the High land near the river for Some distance below. This Bluff contain Pyrites alum, Copperass & a Kind Markesites also a clear Soft Substance which ⟨will mold and become pliant like wax⟩ Capt lewis was near being Poisened by the Smell in pounding this Substance I belv to be *arsenic* or Cabalt. I observe great Quantity of Cops. ans [copperas] and almin [alum] pure & Straters of white & brown earth of 6 Inch thick.[1]   a Creek Coms in above the Bluffs on which there is great quantities of those minerals, This Creek I call *Roloje* a ⟨name given me last night in my Sleep,⟩[2] at those Allom banks Shields joined in with two Deer—

Course

N. 18° W.	2 ½	ms. to a point High wood on the L. S. passed the Creek & a Sand bar
N. 56° E.	5 ½	ms. to a ⟨Bluff⟩ Clift on the L. S. opsd. a pt on the S. S. passed Sand bars on both Sides of the river (2)
N. 54° E	2	mes. to a pt. of Sand on the L. S. opsd. to which the Souix R. is near the Missou and 3 or 4 ms. east at which place this river Comes out of the high Countrey.
N 48 W.	6 ½ / 19	to a Single tree in a butiful large Prarie [*one word illegible*] Pt. on the S. S. passed a Pt. of Sand on the S. S. 2 sand bars in the River wide this Said Course continued to the upper tree of Some Woods

Camped on the S. S.[3]   a Great Deel of Elk Sign fresh   Capt. Lewis took a Dost of Salts this evening to carry off the effects of (arsenec) or cobalt which he was trying to find out the real quallity[4]   (2) passed a Clift of Rock much impregnated with alum, Containing also a great quantity of Cabalt—

ordered a Vote of the men for a Sergeant of the three highest numbers a choice to be made [*two words illegible, crossed out*] Gass Bratton & Gibson—   Gass[5]   is worth remark, that my Ink after Standing in the pot 3 or four days Soaks up & becons thick

[Clark]   22nd August Friday 1804

Set out early wind from the South   at three miles we landed at a Bluff where the two men Sent with the horses were waiting with two Deer, by examonation of this (1) Bluff Contained alum, Copperas, Cobalt, Pyrites; a alum rock Soft & Sand Stone.   Capt. Lewis in proveing the quality of those minerals was near poisoning himself by the fumes & tast of the *Cabalt* which had the appearance of Soft Isonglass—   Copperas & alum is verry pure, Above this Bluff a Small Creek Coms in from the L. S. passing under the Clifts for Several miles, this Creek I Call Roloje a name I learned last night in m[y] S[leep].   (2) ⟨Eight⟩ Seven miles above is a Clift of Allom Stone of a Dark Brown Colr. Containing also in crusted in the Crevices & Shelves of the rock great qts. of Cabalt, Semented Shels & a red earth.   from this the (3) river bends to the East and is within 3 or 4 miles of the River Soues at the place where that river Coms from the high land into the Low Prarie & passes under the foot of those Hills to its mouth.[6]

Capt Lewis took a Dost of Salts to work off the effects of the Arsenic, we Camped on the S. S.   Sailed the greater part of this day with a hard wind from the S. E.   great deel of Elk Sign, and great appearance of wind from the N. W.

Course Distance & refr. 22nd Augt

S 47° W.	1 ¼	mes. on the S. point.
West	1 ¼	mes. to the lower point of a Bluff on the L. S. (1)
N. 18 W.	2 ½	ms. to a pt. of high wood on the L. S. passed. a Creek (2)
N. 56 W.	5 ½	Ms. to a ⟨Blu⟩ Clift on the L. S. opsd. a pt. passd a Sand bar on both Sides of the river (3)
N. 54 E.	2	mes. to a pt. of Sand on the L. S. opsds. the R Souis is near the Missouries. (4)
N. 48 W.	6 ½	Ms. to a Tree in the Prarie on the S. S. psd a pt. of Sand on the S. S. 2 Sand bars in the middle of the river—
	19	

ordered a vote for a Serjeant to chuse one of three which may be the highest number   the highest numbers are P. Gass had 19 Votes, Bratten & Gibson

1. Pyrite and marcasite are both ferrous sulfide minerals, although they have different crystal forms. Copperas is one name for the mineral melanterite, a hydrous ferrous sulfate that results from the weathering of pyrite and marcasite. Clark's reference to Lewis's being poisoned by substances in this area is unclear, and the mineral is indeterminable. The bluff begins above present Jackson, Dakota County, Nebraska. *Atlas* maps 16 and 17; MRC map 28; MRR map 76.

2. Clark crossed out the words giving the source of the name and cut short his mention of it in his Codex B entry. The creek is probably the present Aowa, or Ayoway, Creek which reaches the Missouri in Dixon County, Nebraska, near present Ponca. The name derives from the Omaha, *Maxúde waa i te*, "where the Iowa farmed." The Iowas moved from this village down to the one noted July 28. Fletcher & La Flesche, 91; *Atlas* map 17; Osgood (FN), 112 n. 6.

3. Probably in Union County, South Dakota, somewhat south of the present community of Elk Point. MRC map 28; MRR map 79.

4. The purging of the body by a laxative was a favorite method of removing harmful substances. Chuinard, 230–31.

5. See the Detachment Order for August 26, 1804.

6. *Atlas* map 17.

[Clark]

23rd August ⟨Satturday⟩ Thursday 1804   Set out this morning verry early, the two men R. Fields & Shannon did not Come up last night, I went out and Killed a fine Buck, J. Fields Killed a Buffalow, 2 Elk Swam by the boat whilst I was out and was not Killed, many guns fired at it   R. Fields Came up with the horses & brought two Deer, Collins Killed a Small doe, Several Prarie wolves Seen   Course West 4 Mls. to the mouth of a Small run between two Bluffs of yellow Clay   North 3¼ miles to the upper Pt. of Some timber in the bend to S. S. near where R. fields Killed the Buffalow[1]   passed the pt. of High Land on S. S at ¼ of a mile, Capt. Lewis went out with 8 men & brought the buffalow to the river at this bend, C. Lewis Killed a Goose, wind blew hard ⟨I am obliged to make the next Corses Short on ackount⟩ of the flying Sands which rasies like a Cloud of Smoke from the Bars when the wind ⟨rise⟩ Blows, the Sand being fine and containing a breat [great] perpotion of earth and when it lights it Sticks to every thing it touches   at this time the grass is white   S 48°   3 miles to a point of willows on the S. S. haveing passed the Sand Island L. S   Camped on the L S above the Island[2]   Saw an elk Standing on a Sand bar. Shields Shot it thro' the neck   10¼ [Ed: the day's mileage accumulation]

[Clark]   23rd *August Thursday* 1804

Set out this morning verry early   the two men with the horses did not
Come up last night   I walked on Shore & Killed a fat Buck— J: Fields
Sent out to hunt   Came to the Boat and informed that he had Killed a
Buffalow in the plain a head   Cap Lewis took 12 men and had the buf-
falow brought to the boat in the next bend to the S S.   2 Elk Swam the
river, and was fired at from the boat   R. Fields came up with the Horses
and brought two Deer   one Deer Killed from the Boat. Several Prarie
Wolves Seen to day   Saw Elk Standing on the Sand bar

The Wind blew hard West and raised the Sands off the bar in Such
Clouds that we Could Scercely See   this Sand being fine and verry light
Stuck to every thing it touched, and in the Plain for a half a mile the dis-
tance I was out every Spire of Grass was covered with the Sand or Dust   We
Camped on the L. S. above a Sand Island   one Beaver Cought

Course Distance & refrs. Augt. 23rd

West	4	mes: to a Small run betwen two Blufts of yellow & Blue earth
North	3 ¼	mes. to Some timber in a bend to the S. S. passed a willow Island, a Sand Isd. opsd. psd. a pt. of High Land S S. at ¼ of Me.
S. 48° W.	3	mes. to a pt. of willows on the S. S. haveing passd. the Sand bar on the L. point.
	10 ¼	

1. The Field Notes state "J. Field" at one point and "R. Field" at another, whereas the
Codex B entry indicates that Joseph, not Reubin, Field killed the buffalo; Whitehouse
confirms that it was Joseph. This was the first buffalo, or bison, killed by a member of the
party. Burroughs, 147.

2. In either Dixon County, Nebraska, or Clay County, South Dakota. The Missouri
River has shifted considerably in this vicinity since 1804, and the mouth of the Vermillion
River (Clark's "White Stone River," August 24, 1804), above the camp in 1804, now reaches
the Missouri below the campsite. The site would be a mile or so to the southeast of present
Vermillion, South Dakota. *Atlas* map 17; Nicollet (MMR), 398–99; Warren map 10; MRC
map 28; MRR map 80.

[Clark]

24th August ⟨Sunday⟩ Friday 1804. Some rain last night & this morning, we Set out at the usial time and proceeded on the Same Course of last

night   Continued S. 48° W. 2¼ mes. to the Commencement of a Blue Clay Bliff on L S. about 180 or 190 feet high   West under rugged Bluffs 1¾ ms. passing Several Small Dreens [drains], falling into the river   those Bluffs has been lately on fire and is yet verry Hott,[1] Great appearance of Coal, & imence quantities of Cabalt in Side of that part of[2] the Bluff which Sliped in, on the Sides of the hill great quanities of a kind of Current or froot resembling the Current in appearance much richer and finer flavd.   grows on a Scrub resembling a Damsen and is now fine and makes a Delightfull Tart[3]   above this Bluff I took my Servent and a french boy I have and walked on Shore   I killed a Deer which york Packed on his back   In the evening I Killed two Buck Elk and wounded two others which I could not pursue by the Blood as my ball was So Small ⟨I⟩ to bleed them well, my boys each Shot an elk—[4]   it was late and I Crossed a Point Struck the river above and halted the boat and 12 men went out brought in the meat   all the after part of the day it rained   we are all wet. Capt Lewis and my Self Concluded to visit a High Hill Situated in an emence Plain three Leagues N. 20° W. from the mouth of White Stone river, this hill appear to be of a Conic form and by all the different Nations in this quater is Supposed to be a place of Deavels or[5] that they are in human form with remarkable large heads and about 18 inches high; that they ⟨remarkably⟩ are very watchfull and ar armed with Sharp arrows with which they can kill at a great distance; they are said to kill all persons who are so hardy as to attemp to approach the hill; they ⟨have a⟩ state that tradition informs them that ma[n]y indians have suffered by these little people and among others that three Maha men fell a sacrefice to their murceyless fury not meany years since—   so much do the Mahas Souix Ottoes and other neibhbouring nations believe this fable that no consideration is sufficient to induce them to approach this hill.[6]

Due N.[7]	2	m. from a willow point at the upper part of a bluff lard. to a willow point on the same side, the river leaves the Lard Bluff at the commencement of this course
S [82?] W	4[8]	
N. 15 E.	1 ¼	m. to a point on Stard.
N. 10 E	¼	m. to an object in the bend Stard. extensive sand bar on the Lard. side

N. 45 W.	1 ½	to the lower point of small willow Island.
W.	1 ¼	m. to the upper point of a sandbar connected with the Island (1)
S. 40 W	2 ½	to a willow point Stard shore
	11 ½⁹	

[Clark]   24th *August Friday* 1804

Some rain last night, a Continuation this morning; we Set out at the usial time and proceeded on the Course of last night to the (1) Commencement of a blue Clay Bluff of 180 or 190 feet high on the L. S. Those Bluffs appear to have been laterly on fire, and at this time is too hot for a man to bear his hand in the earth at any debth, gret appearance of Coal. An emence quantity of *Cabalt* or a Cristolised Substance which answers its discription is on the face of the Bluff— Great quantities of a kind of berry resembling a Current except double the Sise and Grows on a bush like a Privey, and the Size of a Damsen deliciously flavoured & makes delitefull Tarts, this froot is now ripe, I took my Servent and a french boy and Walked on Shore Killed Two Buck Elks and a faun, and intersepted the Boat and had all the meat butchered and in by Sun Set at which time it began to rain and rained hard, Cap Lewis & my Self walk out & got Verry wet, a Cloudey rainey night,— In my absence the Boat Passed a Small (2) River Called by the Indians White Stone River.¹⁰ this river is about 30 yards wide and runs thro: a Plain & Prarie in its whole Course In a northerley direction from the mouth of this Creek in an imence Plain a high Hill is Situated, and appears of a Conic form and by the different nations of Indians in this quarter is Suppose to be the residence of Deavels. that they are in human form with remarkable large heads and about 18 Inches high, that they are Very watchfull, and are arm'd with Sharp arrows with which they Can Kill at a great distance; they are Said to Kill all persons who are So hardy as to attempt to approach the hill; they State that tradition informs them that many Indians have Suffered by those little people and among others three *Mahar* men fell a Sacrefise to their murceyless fury not many years Since— So much do the Maha, Souis, Ottoes and other neighbouring nations believe this fable that no Consideration is Suffecient to induce them to apporach the hill

Course Distanc & Refrs. 24 Augt

S. 48° W.	2 ½	Mes. to the Commencement of a Blue Clay Bluff of 180 or 190 feet high on the L. S
West	1 ¾	mes. under the Bluff passd. two Small runs from the Bluff, those Bluffs have been latterly on fire & is yet verry hot (1)
North	2	mes. to a point on S. S.
N. 10° E.	¼	me. to an object in the bend on S S an extensive Sand bar on the L. S.
N. 45° W.	1 ½	me. to the lower point of a small willow Island.
West	1 ¼	Mes. to the upper point of a Sand bar connected with the Island passed the Creek (2)
S. 40 W.	2 ½	Mes to a willow pt. on the S. S.[11]
	10 ½	

[Lewis]   *Friday, August 24th*[12]

This day the Chronometer stoped again just after being wound up; I know not the cause, but fear it procedes from some defect which it is not in my power to remedy.—

1. As late as 1877, some scientists believed that the bluff was a true volcano caused to erupt when the flooding Missouri River poured water onto molten rock in subterranean caverns. By 1900, investigations proved that the eruptions were due to the heat of oxidation of damp pyritiferous and carbonaceous Carlile shale on fresh exposures provided by the rapid erosion of the river bluffs. Threet; Barbour, 231–32. This bluff was later called the "Ionia volcano," after the now defunct town of Ionia, Dixon County, Nebraska. Coues (HLC), 1:84 n. 52; *Nebraska Guide*, 395; *Atlas* map 17; MRC map 29; MRR map 80.

2. The narrative for August 24 continues on the next sheet of the Field Notes (document 44), indicated by an elaborate asterisk. Biddle's note at the top of document 44 reads "Aug. 25th," but in fact this side of the sheet continues the August 24 entry. The August 25 entry begins on the reverse. The number ten, circled, also appears at the top of the page and may be keyed to a second August 25 entry on document 47 which has a similar circled ten. The circled ten should probably be on the reverse of document 44, which has the first August 25 entry.

3. The buffaloberry; see August 21, 1804. The damson plum mentioned for comparison is *Prunus insititia* L. Barkley, 203; Fernald, 876.

4. The first of several indications that York, in spite of his status as a slave, carried a gun.

5. The entry of August 24, 1804, in the Field Notes continues on document 45; the circled number two and an asterisk are used as references from one sheet to the next. The remaining portion is in Lewis's handwriting.

6. The supernatural associations linger in the present name of Spirit Mound, in Clay County, South Dakota, about eight miles north of Vermillion. Coues (HLC), 1 : 86 n. 1; Appleman (LC), 353; *South Dakota Guide*, 405; *Atlas* map 17; MRR map 82-L.

7. These courses and distances appear to be in Lewis's hand and are at the end of document 43. There are discrepancies between them and the courses and distances in the Codex B entry.

8. This line probably does not belong here.

9. These figures follow the courses and distances in the lower right corner or document 43:

$$
\begin{array}{r}
881 - \\
21 \\
\hline
902\ ^{3}/_{4} \\
12\ ^{1}/_{4} \\
\hline
915
\end{array}
$$

10. The present Vermillion River, reaching the Missouri in Clay County, southeast of the town of Vermillion. The mouth has probably shifted farther down the Missouri since 1804. The present name presumably alludes to a reddish color in the water and the banks; Indians obtained both red and white earth paints from the river valley, the latter perhaps accounting for Clark's calling it "White Stone River." *Atlas* map 17; Nicollet (MMR), 398–99; Warren map 10; Fletcher & La Flesche, 92; MRC map 9; MRR map 80.

11. *Atlas* map 17 seems to place this camp on the larboard side of the Missouri. Because of subsequent shifting of the river, the site is probably in Clay County, south and a little west of the town of Vermillion. MRC map 29; MRR map 80.

12. Lewis's observation from Codex O.

[Clark]   [*undated, ca. August 24, 1804*][1]

(1) About the center of this Sand Island the river of white Stone (as Called by Mr. Evins Kenvill R.[)][2] falls in on the Stard. Side   it appear to be about 25 or 30 yards Wide; at the mouth of this river 10 Indians had latterly cross Supposed be be Soues, the part of a band which are at war with the *Mahars*, This Soues nation are divided into bands Som 100 to 500 men in a band   at peace with eath other, ther Interest & prejudices different, for instance one band the most envetterate enimy of the mahars, all the other Bands in the greatest harmony with that nation and even go with thim to War, those Soues, follow the Buffalow, & Kill them on foot, they pack their Dogs, which carry ther Bedn. [burden?]

1. This undated entry forms one side of document 45 of the Field Notes. It deals with matters that place it close to this date. The page has a large *x* across it.

2. See Evans's map 1 (*Atlas* map 7) and Introduction to *Atlas*. Besides White stone, it has also been called the Washisha, the White Earth, the Smoky Earth, and the Redstone (by Clark on the return trip). It is now the Vermillion.

Appendix A

Members of the
Expedition

Illustrators charged with making a picture to represent "The Lewis and Clark Expedition" have usually produced variations on a familiar theme: the two captains, slightly differentiated by dress, gaze off into the western distance; Sacagawea stands nearby with her infant, sometimes pointing the way. Clark's black servant, York, is usually prominent, especially in recent years, and Toussaint Charbonneau and Lewis's dog, Scannon (or Seaman), are frequently present. In the background an anonymous collection of buckskin-clad figures representing the rest of the party follow their leaders' gaze toward the horizon or go about their labors. This familiar picture represents the popular conception of the expedition; unfortunately, it also represents fairly accurately the actual state of knowledge about the men who went with the captains on their great trek.[1]

About the captains there is abundant information; most of the Corps of Discovery, however, lived obscure lives before and after their season of glory. For many there exists the scantiest record, or none at all, about their lives before 1803 and after 1806. The records of the expedition themselves provide, in most cases, only the barest hints about their personalities, virtues, and weaknesses. William Clark seems to have thought of the permanent party as his "Band of Brothers," in some sense; he had some interest in their later careers, but even he apparently lost track of several of them. Some twenty years after the return to St. Louis, he drew up a list of thirty-four; eighteen, including Lewis, he knew or believed to be dead—six of them, in testimony to the hazards of frontier life, listed as "killed"—and for five he apparently had no information. One of those he thought dead, Patrick Gass, not only was alive but would outlive Clark and every other expedition member.[2]

Sacagawea has attracted much attention in this century from historians and writers of fiction, but the amount written about her far exceeds the actual information about her life and personality. York is a natural symbol of black participation in the westward movement, but even less is known of him as a man. John

Colter acquired fame in his own right as an explorer through his travels and adventures in the Rockies after the expedition. Toussaint and Jean Baptiste Charbonneau have shared some of Sacagawea's glory. For most of the rest, even such journal keepers as John Ordway and Joseph Whitehouse, we can give at best a brief sketch of their lives. For some, we cannot even be sure of the correct spelling of their names.

The captains drew their men from three principal sources: Anglo-American frontiersmen from the Ohio Valley, U.S. Army enlisted men, and the French settlers of Illinois and Missouri. In the letter offering Clark the chance to second him on the expedition, Lewis wrote that his friend should recruit some young men in Kentucky and Indiana. Clark was instructed to pick backwoodsmen, skilled in hunting and outdoor life and used to hardship, rather than "young gentlemen." Clark had several recruits gathered at Clarksville, Indiana Territory, when Lewis picked him up in October 1803; those have become known as the "Nine Young Men from Kentucky," although two of the men listed under that head, George Shannon and John Colter, may have joined Lewis on his journey down the Ohio by the time he reached Cincinnati.[3]

Most of the remaining men evidently joined the expedition during the winter at River Dubois. Many were enlisted men from four companies of the U.S. Army stationed at small posts in the West: Captain Daniel Bissell's company of the First Infantry Regiment, stationed at Fort Massac, Illinois; Captain Russell Bissell's company of the same regiment, stationed at Fort Kaskaskia, Illinois; Captain John Campbell's company of the Second Infantry Regiment, stationed in Tennessee; and Captain Amos Stoddard's company of artillerists, stationed at Fort Kaskaskia. Clark seems to have suspected that the men sent from Tennessee, at least, were picked on the time-honored principle of getting rid of those who could best be spared by their original unit (see Clark's entry, December 22, 1803). Some backwoodsmen from the Illinois and Missouri settlements may have joined during the winter, but for a number of men there is no indication of when and where they first joined or whether they were already in the army. All those not already in the military service who were chosen for the permanent party enlisted as soldiers, except York, Clark's slave, and George Drouillard, the civilian interpreter and hunter. Two French boatmen with experience in the Indian trade on the Missouri, François Labiche and Pierre Cruzatte, enlisted for the permanent party.[4]

It would appear that the captains decided during the winter of 1803–4 that they would send back a party of men from somewhere up the Missouri during the first year of the expedition. Such a party could carry back dispatches, maps, completed journals, and plant, animal, mineral, and anthropological specimens to President Jefferson, giving him a progress report and sparing the expedition the labor of carrying such objects for the entire journey. The thought that something would be saved if they themselves failed to return must have been in their minds. Clark's Dubois Journal contains several lists of names, marked and annotated, showing that he was evaluating the men and trying to determine, on the basis of character and ability, who should be in the permanent and return parties. By April 1, 1804, as indicated by a detachment order, the captains had determined the constitution of the two parties, so far as the enlisted soldiers were concerned, and for the most part they adhered to that plan. Certain changes became necessary because of subsequent events, a possibility they had no doubt anticipated from the start. For instance, the two enlisted French boatmen, François Labiche and Pierre Cruzatte, joined the ranks of the permanent party. Moses B. Reed and John Newman were expelled from the permanent party, the first for desertion, the other for insubordination. Sergeant Charles Floyd died, and Patrick Gass, another member of the permanent party, assumed his rank. To make up the losses in the permanent party, the captains transferred Robert Frazer from the original return party and enlisted Jean Baptiste Lepage, a French trapper encountered at the Mandan villages.

As matters developed, the return party did not set out during the summer or fall of 1804, as originally planned. On April 7, 1805, when the captains and the permanent party left Fort Mandan headed up the Missouri, they were able to send back this return group in the keelboat and one canoe. An exact list exists for the group bound for the Pacific, but for the returning body there remain some mysteries. Corporal Richard Warfington was in charge of the party, and the captains both say that he had with him in the keelboat six soldiers and two Frenchmen, with two more Frenchmen in the canoe.

Among the six soldiers were Reed and Newman, expelled from the permanent party. Four other soldiers were intended from the first for the return party, probably Privates John Boley, John Dame, Ebenezer Tuttle, and Isaac White. It seems possible, if unlikely, that the mysterious John Robertson, or Robinson, was one of them, instead of either Tuttle or White (see the sketch of Robertson).[5]

Most of the returning Frenchmen were certainly *engagés*—hired boatmen—who had been with the expedition from the start. It is quite clear from the records that the captains regarded their status to be entirely different from that of the enlisted men. They were not soldiers and did not require the same care in record keeping as that demanded by the army. Clark's usual difficulties in spelling were compounded with French names, and Lewis's spelling of French names was not much better.

Another factor complicating the records was the custom of the Mississippi valley French of giving *dit* names, nicknames by which a man might be better known than by his surname. Unlike English nicknames, these might be passed on from father to son and were considered significant enough to be used in official records. Commonly they referred either to a personal characteristic or to a place of origin or residence. Thus we have Louis Blanchette, *dit le Chasseur* (the hunter), founder of St. Charles, Missouri, and Jacques Chauvin, *dit Charleville*, probably after the city in France. Hence, French names in expedition records may be either surnames or *dit* names, and this may account for some of the inconsistencies in the lists.[6]

There are two principal lists of *engagés*, which were evidently intended to be complete, one in a detachment order of May 26, 1804, the other in Clark's Field Notes under July 4, 1804. They are inconsistent in both names and numbers, and there is no certainty whether the inconsistencies represent additions or discharges, use of surnames or *dit* names, or simple forgetfulness. There is also a record of men paid off in St. Louis after their return from Fort Mandan in 1805, but it is obviously incomplete. Some of the men may not appear there because they were discharged at the Arikara or Mandan villages in the fall of 1804 and received their pay in cash. It is at least possible that men were added or discharged along the Missouri, recruited from St. Louis-bound trading parties or leaving the expedition and joining such a party. The captains' lack of attention to the Frenchmen may have extended to failure to note such changes among the *engagés*.[7]

The purpose of this appendix is to give brief sketches of those known to be associated with the expedition up to August 24, 1804. Individuals are listed alphabetically within groups: the leaders; sergeants; privates, corporal, interpreter, and servant; and *engagés*. Sketches of Sacagawea, Toussaint Charbonneau, Jean-Baptiste Charbonneau, and Jean Baptiste Lepage, all of whom joined during the winter of 1804–5 at Fort Mandan, will appear in the next volume. For the two captains only a brief biography is necessary. For most of the others it is possible to include most of the principal facts, with an indication of the sources for further study. In most cases there is no new, previously unpublished information, but an effort has been made to draw together the work of previous researchers in the field. In a few cases, doubts and unresolved questions about some men, such as John Robertson and La Liberté, have necessitated disproportionately long sketches of men whose actual importance to the expedition was minor.

Captain Meriwether Lewis (1774–1809). Born in Virginia, he joined the army in 1794 and served in the Ohio Valley and the Old Northwest Territory, where he became friends with Clark. He became Jefferson's private secretary in 1801, while retaining his military rank, and in 1803 the president assigned him the task of conducting the expedition. After the expedition he became governor of Louisiana Territory, where he encountered difficulties that caused him severe emotional problems. He died by his own hand on the Natchez Trace in Tennessee. Dillon; Bakeless (LCPD).

Second Lieutenant William Clark (1770–1838). The younger brother of George Rogers Clark, he moved from Virginia, where he was born, to Kentucky with his family at the age of fourteen. Joining the army in 1792, he participated in the campaigns of General Anthony Wayne in the Northwest, rising to the rank of captain; Lewis was under his command for a time. He left the army in 1796 to attend to family business, but he kept in touch with Lewis and was apparently the other's first choice to share command of the expedition. Because of army red tape, he received only a second lieutenant's rank, but he and Lewis concealed this from the men, and he was always referred to as Captain Clark. After the expedition he had a distinguished political career, including the governorship of Missouri Territory, but for much of the time until his death he was in charge of relations with the Indians west of the Mississipi, with his headquarters in St. Louis. The Indians knew that city simply as "Red Head's Town," after him, and he strove to maintain some degree of justice and equity in the relations between Indian and white. Loos; Bakeless (LCPD); Steffen.

Sergeant Charles Floyd (1782–1804). Born in Kentucky, he was one of the nine young men from that state on the expedition. Lewis regarded him as "a young man of much merit," and he was made a sergeant before the start of the expedition. He is remembered principally as the only member lost on the voyage; he died on August 20, 1804, near present Sioux City, Iowa, perhaps of a ruptured appendix. He kept his journal until a few days before his death. He may have been a distant relative of William Clark. Floyd's (or Floyd) River in Iowa was named for him. Lewis to Henry Dearborn, January 15, 1807, Jackson (LLC), 1 : 366, 370 n. 3; Clarke (MLCE), 39; Garver.

Sergeant Patrick Gass (1771–1870). Born in Pennsylvania, of Irish ancestry, he belonged to Captain Russell Bissell's company of the First Infantry, having joined the army in 1799 after service in a volunteer Ranger unit. He was promoted from private to sergeant after Floyd's death in August of 1804, having officially joined the expedition on January 1, 1804. His skill as a carpenter was of great value to the expedition. His journal, published in 1807 after considerable alteration, was the first journal from the expedition to see publication. He stayed on in the army and served in the War of 1812, losing an eye in an accident, which caused his discharge. Marrying at the age of sixty, he eventually settled in Wellsburg, West Virginia, and died there in 1870, the last known survivor of the expedition. Clarke (MLCE), 39–40; Jacob; Forrest; Smith (SSPG); McGirr.

Sergeant John Ordway (ca. 1775–ca. 1817). One of the journalists of the expedition, he was born and apparently grew up in New Hampshire. He joined from

Captain Russell Bissell's company of the First Infantry and was placed on the expedition roll on January 1, 1804, but he was already at Camp Dubois some time before that. He was the only one of the original sergeants to come from the regular army, and probably for that reason he often took care of the paperwork and was in charge of the camp when the captains were both absent. Ordway kept his journal faithfully throughout the expedition. He seldom appears in the journals except in carrying out some duty, attesting to his reliability. After the expedition he acompanied Lewis and a party of Indians to Washington, D.C., then returned to New Hampshire, having taken his discharge. In 1809 he settled in Missouri, became prosperous, and married. He and his wife had died by 1817. Clarke (MLCE), 40–41.

Sergeant Nathaniel Hale Pryor (1772–1831). He was born in Virginia and was a cousin of Charles Floyd, also with the expedition. He moved to Kentucky with his parents in 1783 and joined the expedition on October 20, 1803, at Clarksville, Indiana, as one of the nine young men from Kentucky. He was one of the few members already married, having taken a wife in 1798. He may have kept a journal, like the other sergeants, but none has been found. The captains considered him "a man of character and ability" and after the expedition helped him secure an officer's commission in the army. In 1807 he was in charge of the expedition to return the Mandan chief Sheheke to his tribe, but he was forced to turn back by the Arikaras. He resigned from the army in 1810 and entered the Indian trade on the Mississippi; he rejoined the army in 1813 and rose to captain, serving in the Battle of New Orleans. After the War of 1812 he became a trader among the Osages on the Arkansas River, married an Osage woman, and remained with the tribe until his death. He served briefly as government agent for the Osages in 1830–31. Pryor, Oklahoma, and the Pryor Mountains and town of Pryor, both in Montana, bear his name. Clarke (MLCE), 41–42; Settle.

Private John Boley (dates unknown). Boley, sometimes "Boleye" in the records, was probably born in Pittsburgh, Pennsylvania, and was living in Kaskaskia when he joined the army in 1803. He came from Captain Russell Bissell's company of the First Infantry Regiment. He had some disciplinary trouble at River Dubois and was designated for the return party. After returning from Fort Mandan in 1805 he accompanied Zebulon M. Pike's expedition to the upper Mississippi in that year, and in 1806 he went with Pike to the southwest and the Rockies. Part of that group, including Boley, returned east down the Arkansas River before Pike and the rest were captured by the Spanish. After his discharge he settled in Missouri and reportedly accompanied a civilian party to the Rockies. In 1823, he and his wife were living in Carondelet, near St. Louis. Jackson (LLC), 1:237 n. 7; Clarke (MLCE), 60.

Private William E. Bratton (1778–1841). Often "Bratten" in the journals, he was born in Virginia and moved to Kentucky with his family in about 1790. He enlisted with the expedition on October 20, 1803, as one of the nine young men from Kentucky. Bratton was useful to the expedition as a hunter and blacksmith. During the spring of 1806 he was incapacitated for some weeks by a mysterious back ailment, perhaps the longest spell of serious illness experienced by any member of the expedition, finally being cured by an Indian sweat bath. After the expedition he lived in Kentucky and Missouri, served in the War of 1812, married in 1819, and lived in Ohio and Indiana. He died and was buried at Waynetown, Indiana. Clarke (MLCE), 43–45; Chuinard, 348–76; Lange (WB).

Private John Collins (?–1823). Born in Maryland, Collins officially joined the expedition on January 1, 1804, although he was probably at the River Dubois camp before that; he may have transferred from Captain Russell Bissell's company of the First Infantry. Collins was involved in disciplinary troubles as often as any other man in the expedition, leading Clark to call him a "black gard"; at River Dubois he stole a local farmer's hog and was frequently drunk and disobedient. On the first summer of the voyage he was court-martialed for stealing whiskey from the official supply while detailed to guard it. Nonetheless, he was from the first a member of the permanent party, presumably because of redeeming qualities perceived by the captains. He may have settled in Missouri after the expedition. Later he was with William Ashley's trapping venture to the upper Missouri and was killed in Ashley's battle with the Arikaras in 1823. Clarke (MLCE), 45.

Private John Colter (ca. 1775–1813). Colter, probably the only member of the Corps whose fame does not rest primarily on his service with the expedition, was born in Virginia. As a youth, he and his family moved to Maysville, Kentucky, where he intercepted Lewis on the captain's voyage down the Ohio, becoming one of the nine young men from Kentucky. His enlistment dates from October 15, 1803. After some disciplinary difficulties during the winter at River Dubois, he proved useful to the expedition as a hunter. On the return journey he received permission to leave the party at the Mandan villages to join a small trapping expedition headed back up the Missouri. He spent an additional four years in the mountains as an independent trapper and working for Manuel Lisa's Missouri Fur Company. In his wanderings he was apparently the first white man to see the region of present Yellowstone Park, and his tales of hot springs and geysers led to derisive jokes about "Colter's Hell." His escape, naked, from the Blackfeet near the Three Forks of the Missouri has become a western legend. On his return to civilization in 1810 he was able to add information to Clark's great map of the West. Settling in Missouri, Colter married; he died in 1813 of jaundice. Clarke (MLCE), 46–48; Haines; Vinton; Harris.

Private Pierre Cruzatte (dates unknown). Often referred to as "Peter Cruzat" and other variations in the journals, he was half French and half Omaha. His official enlistment date was May 16, 1804, at St. Charles, Missouri, but he may have been recruited earlier. He was an experienced Missouri River boatman who had already participated in the Indian trade as far as Nebraska and was hired for his skill and experience. Unlike the other French boatmen, he and François Labiche were enlisted as members of the permanent party. He was one-eyed and nearsighted, and his fiddle playing often entertained the party. At times he also acted as an interpreter. Lewis paid tribute during the expedition to his skill and experience as a riverman and to his integrity, but in the postexpedition list of members he receives no special recommendation; this is perhaps because the myopic Cruzatte had accidentally wounded Lewis while the two were hunting in August 1806. Speculation places him with John McClellan's expedition to the Rockies in 1807. Clark lists him as "killed" by 1825–28. Clarke (MLCE), 62–63; Jackson (LLC), 1:371 n. 8; Clark's List of Expedition Members [ca. 1825–28], ibid., 2:638; Majors, 573.

Private John Dame (1784–?). Dame, born in New Hampshire, joined the army in 1801; he was assigned to the expedition from Captain Amos Stoddard's artillery company and designated for the return party. He is mentioned once in the journals, August 8, 1804, for killing a pelican. Jackson (LLC), 1:237 n. 7; Clarke (MLCE), 60.

Interpreter George Drouillard (?–1810). Generally "Drewyer" or some variant in the journals, he was probably born in Canada, the son of a French-Canadian father and a Shawnee mother, and migrated as a youth to the Cape Girardeau district of Missouri with his mother's people. He met Lewis at Fort Massac, Illinois, in November 1803, possibly while employed by the army there, and agreed to serve the expedition as an interpreter. He was apparently considered a civilian employee, not an enlisted man, during the expedition. His skill with the Indian sign language was of great value to the captains, and he was also one of the Corps's best hunters; whenever one of the captains set out to scout ahead of the party, Drouillard was likely to be chosen to accompany him, because of those abilities and his general skill as a scout and wilderness man. After the expedition's return he became a partner in Manuel Lisa's fur trading ventures on the upper Missouri and the Yellowstone. On a return trip to St. Louis he was able to contribute information to Clark's map of the West. Drouillard was with the party of Lisa's men who established a fur post at the Three Forks of the Missouri in 1810, and near there in that year he died at the hands of the Blackfeet. Clarke (MLCE), 40; Skarsten (GD) and (GDLC); Lewis to Henry Dearborn, January 15, 1807, Jackson (LLC), 1:368–69; Lange (GD).

Privates Joseph Field (ca. 1772–1807) and Reubin Field (ca. 1771–1823?). The two brothers, called "Field" or "Fields" at various times in the journals, were born in Virginia and came to Kentucky at an early age; they were among the nine young men from Kentucky, and their official enlistment date was August 1, 1803, indicating that they were among the first men recruited by Clark in the neighborhood of his home. Reubin had some disciplinary difficulties at River Dubois, but both were chosen for the permanent party. They were among the best shots and hunters in the Corps of Discovery and with George Drouillard were often chosen to accompany the captains on special reconnaissances; both were with Lewis in his fight with the Blackfeet on July 17, 1806. Lewis wrote, "It was their peculiar fate to have been engaged in all the most dangerous and difficult scenes of the voyage, in which they uniformly acquited themselves with much honor." Joseph apparently died less than a year after the return of the expedition; Clark listed him as "killed," as distinguished from those who died a natural death. One theory suggests that he was with the mysterious expedition of John McClellan to the Rockies when his death occurred, but in that case it hardly seems that word of his death could have reached Kentucky by October 1807, when it was officially recorded. Reubin settled in Kentucky, married, and died by early 1823. Lewis to Henry Dearborn, January 15, 1807, Jackson (LLC), 1:367; Clark's List of Expedition Members [ca. 1825–28], ibid, 2:638; Clarke (MLCE), 48–49; Appleman (JRF); Majors, 573; Lange (EB).

Private Robert Frazer (?–1837). "Frazer" is the accepted form of his name, but in the journals he is often "Frazier," "Frasure," and other forms that probably indicate how his comrades pronounced his name. Accounts saying that he was born in Vermont and was once a fencing master are apparently in error; he was probably born in Virginia. There is no information on when he joined or if he had previously been in the army. Frazer was not at first part of the permanent party but was transferred from the intended return party on October 8, 1804, to replace Moses Reed after the latter's expulsion. Frazer kept a journal and received special permission from the captains to publish it, but the publication never took place and the journal is apparently lost. His map of the expedition, far below the standard set by Clark, has survived (*Atlas* map 124). He accompanied Lewis to Washington, D.C., after the expedition, then returned to Missouri and settled there. He died in Franklin County, Missouri. Clarke (MLCE), 61; Cutright (HLCJ), 20 and n. 4.

Private George Gibson (?–1809). Born in Pennsylvania, he was one of the nine young men from Kentucky. He was a good hunter and played the fiddle for the party on occasion. He served as an interpreter, probably through the medium of sign language. He may have been with Nathaniel Pryor's party attempting to return the Mandan chief Sheheke to his home in 1807 and was perhaps wounded then. He died in St. Louis. Clarke (MLCE), 49.

Private Silas Goodrich (dates unknown). Goodrich, sometimes "Guterage" or some variation in the journals, was born in Massachusetts. The time and place of his joining the Corps are unknown, although he was officially enrolled in January 1, 1804; possibly he was then a resident of Missouri, and he may already have been in the army. He was one of the expedition's best fishermen. He reenlisted in the army after the expedition. Clark lists him as dead by 1825–28. Clark's List of Expedition Members [ca. 1825–28], Jackson (LLC), 2:638; Clarke (MLCE), 50.

Private Hugh Hall (ca. 1772–?). Hall was born in Massachusetts, joined the army in 1798, and was transferred to the expedition from Captain John Campbell's company of the Second Infantry Regiment in November 1803. Clark notes that he drank. He and John Collins were court-martialed in June 1804 for tapping the offical ration whiskey and getting drunk, Collins having been detailed to guard the supply. Hall was in the St. Louis area in 1809, when he borrowed money from Lewis; Clark apparently had no information to record about him in 1825–28. Jackson (LLC), 1:371 n. 15; Clark's List of Expedition Members [ca. 1825–28], ibid., 2:638; Clarke (MLCE), 50.

Private Thomas Proctor Howard (1779–?). Howard was born and reared in Massachusetts and joined the army in 1801; he was assigned to the expedition from Captain John Campbell's company of the Second Infantry Regiment, officially enrolling on January 1, 1804. Clark noted at River Dubois that Howard "never Drinks water." On February 9, 1805, returning to Fort Mandan from the Indian villages after the gate was closed, he climbed over the wall. The next day he was tried for setting a "pernicious example" to the Indians by showing them that the wall was easily scaled. The sentence was fifty lashes, remitted on the recommendation of the court. This was the last recorded court-martial of the expedition. A Thomas Howard was again serving in the army in 1808. Clark had no information to record on him in 1825–28. Jackson (LLC), 1:371 n. 14; Clark's List of Expedition Members [ca. 1825–28], ibid., 2:638; Clarke (MLCE), 50.

Private François Labiche (dates unknown). He is referred to as "La Buish," "Leebice," and other spellings in the journals. Though traditionally regarded as half French and half Omaha, he may be the "mulatto" mentioned by Charles Mackenzie as interpreting French for the captains at Fort Mandan. (The only other possible mulatto would have been York, who surely spoke no French). Labiche was apparently recruited at Kaskaskia, though the official date of his enlistment is May 16, 1804, at St. Charles, Missouri. Like Cruzatte he was an enlisted member of the permanent party, not a hired boatman, undoubtedly chosen for his experience as a boatman and Indian trader. Lewis took special note of his services as an interpreter, recommending that he receive a bonus; he went with Lewis to Washington, D.C., after the expedition to interpret for the Indian chiefs. He may be the François Labuche who lived in or near St. Louis and baptized seven children there between 1811 and 1834. It is possible that "Labiche" may have been a nickname, the family name being Milhomme. Clark listed him as living in St. Louis in 1825–28. Lewis to Henry Dearborn, January 15, 1807, Jackson (LLC), 1:367, 371 n. 16; Clark's List of Expedition Members [ca. 1825–28], ibid., 2:638; Masson, 1:336–37; Clarke (MLCE), 64.

Private Hugh McNeal (dates unknown). He was born and reared in Pennsylvania and may have been in the army before joining the expedition. A man of that name was on the army rolls as late as 1811. Clark lists him as dead by 1825–28. Jackson (LLC), 1:371 n. 17; Clark's List of Expedition Members [ca. 1825–28], ibid., 2:639.

Private John Newman (ca. 1785–1838). Newman was born in Pennsylvania and joined the expedition from Captain Daniel Bissell's company of the First Infantry Regiment. He avoided the disciplinary troubles of some of the others at River Dubois, and his record was apparently good until October 1804, when he was confined for "having uttered repeated expressions of a highly criminal and mutinous nature." Tried by court-martial, he received seventy-five lashes and was expelled from the party. His offense may have consisted of angry, defiant words uttered in a moment of bad temper, or he may have been involved in something more serious in collusion with Moses Reed. Since he could not be abandoned in the wilderness, he accompanied the party to Fort Mandan, doing hard labor, then went back with the return party in April 1805. During the intervening months he worked hard to redeem himself, in the hope of being restored to the permanent party, but although the captains were pleased with his conduct, they did not deem it wise to alter their verdict. After the expedition Lewis suggested that Congress allow Newman the pay for his period of service up to his expulsion. He did receive some pay and a land warrant as a member of the expedition, and he may have settled in Missouri. He married at least once but had no children of record. In the 1830s he trapped on the Missouri in the Dakotas for some years and was killed by the Yankton Sioux in the summer of 1838. Clark included him in his list of 1825–28, indicating some interest in Newman's welfare, although he had no information to record. Lewis to Henry Dearborn, January 15, 1807, Jackson (LLC), 1:365–66, 372 endnote; Clark's List of Expedition Members [ca. 1825–28], ibid., 2:639; Clarke (JN); Clarke (MLCE), 51.

Private John Potts (1776–1808?). Potts was born in Germany and had been a miller; he joined the U S. Army in 1800. He was with Captain Robert Purdy's company in Tennessee when ordered to join the expedition in November 1803. In 1807 he joined Manuel Lisa's fur-trading venture to the upper Missouri. He was with his old comrade John Colter when the two were ambushed by Blackfeet near the Three Forks of the Missouri; Potts was killed and Colter narrowly escaped. Jackson (LLC), 1:371 n. 20; Clarke (MLCE), 51; Harris, 133–34.

Private Moses B. Reed (dates unknown). Reed's antecedents and the point at which he joined the expedition are unknown. He was a member of the permanent party as it was originally constituted, but in August 1804 he attempted to desert; apprehended, he was tried, convicted, and expelled from the party. He remained with the expedition doing hard labor until sent back with the return party in April 1805. Ordway records that Reed was confined on October 12, 1804, at the same time that John Newman was arrested for "mutinous expression." This is the only indication that Reed may have been involved in Newman's offense, but if so, then Newman may have been guilty of something more than a fit of bad-tempered insubordination. Conceivably the two were in collusion to defy the captains' authority in some way, or perhaps Reed tried to induce some other men to support Newman's defiance. There is no other record of Reed's confinement at this time or of his being punished; since he had been dishonorably discharged, the captains may have doubted their legal authority to punish him. After his return to St. Louis, he dropped out of sight. When Clark made up his list of party members in 1825–28, he included Newman but not Reed, evidence of his total lack of interest in the latter's fate. Clarke (MLCE), 52; Clark's List of Expedition Members [ca. 1825–28], Jackson (LLC), 2:638–39.

Private John Robertson (ca. 1780–?). Also "Roberson" in the journals, he is thought to be the Corporal John Robinson, born in New Hampshire, who was serving with Captain Amos Stoddard's artillery company at the time of the expedition. Clark refers to him as a corporal on December 26, 1803, but in subsequent references where rank is given he is a private; apparently he was demoted for some reason. Perhaps he was the unnamed corporal Clark criticized on January 4, 1804, for having "no authority" over his men; this is even more likely because the captains were so completely satisfied with Corporal Richard Warfington, the only other corporal with the expedition. Robertson had some difficulties involving drinking during the River Dubois winter. In an undated list in Clark's Field Notes (placed under April 12, 1804) he is designated for the return party. The last dated mention of his name is in the Orderly Book for April 1, 1804, where he is also designated as one of those to return from somewhere up the Missouri. There is no subsequent dated reference to his name, and he is not in the detachment order of May 26, 1804, concerning the organization of squads. On June 12, 1804, Joseph Whitehouse wrote that a man from Captain Stoddard's company was sent back to St. Louis with a trading party encountered coming down the river; no one else bothered to record the incident, and Whitehouse gives no name and no reason for his return. If Robertson was with the expedition until June 12, it is peculiar that he is not mentioned in the May 26 detachment order. If he was not the man from Stoddard's company sent back, then there are only two men known to have been from this company who are not mentioned in the journals after June 12, and if one of them was sent back, and Robertson had left some time earlier, then there exist problems in accounting for the six soldiers who were with the return party from Fort Mandan under Corporal Warfington in 1805. No reason is anywhere indicated why Robertson would be taken along yet not included in the detachment order of May 26. A purely speculative possibility may be mentioned. The detachment order of May 26 specifically exempts Thomas P. Howard from duty with the pirogues without giving any reason, such as a special assignment. It could be that Howard, designated for the permanent party, was temporarily incapacitated by some illness or injury but was expected to recover in a short time. Robertson might then have been taken along to replace Howard, the preferred man, if the latter did not recover as quickly as anticipated. Howard having improved as hoped, the less desirable Robertson was sent home. Difficulties with this hypothesis are that no such illness of Howard's is mentioned, and the party with which the unnamed man returned was not the first one met coming down the river. Presumably Robertson returned to his original unit, but there is no further record of him. Clarke (MLCE), 61–62; Jackson (LLC), 1:373 endnote.

Private George Shannon (1785–1836). The youngest member of the party, Shannon was born in Pennsylvania and moved to Ohio with his family in 1800. He joined Lewis at Maysville, Kentucky, with an official enlistment date of October 19, 1803, and is usually listed with the nine young men from Kentucky. In the fall of 1804 he was lost for over two weeks and nearly starved; some sources state that he was continually getting lost, which is unjust, since the only other time he was separated from the party for a few days, on the headwaters of the Missouri in 1805, was hardly his fault. In 1807 he was with Nathaniel Pryor's party in the attempt to return the Mandan chief Sheheke to his people and was wounded in the encounter with the Arikaras; the wound cost him his leg. Eventually he received a government pension for his injury. In 1810 he assisted Nicholas Biddle in the preparation of his history of the expedition. Clark offered him an opportunity to join him in the fur trade, but Shannon chose to study law, and by 1818, after university training, he was practicing in Lexington, Kentucky. He pursued the legal and political career common on the frontier in his day, eventually serving as senator from Missouri. He died and was buried in Palmyra, Missouri. Clarke (MLCE), 52–53; Lange (PGS).

Private John Shields (1769–1809). Born in Virginia, Shields emigrated with his family to Tennessee in 1784; in 1790 he married and was thus one of the few married men with the expedition. He enlisted on October 19, 1803, and is usually listed as one of the nine young men from Kentucky; in fact, he was the oldest member of the permanent party whose age is known, with the exception of Toussaint Charbonneau. Shields was involved in a virtual mutiny against Sergeant Ordway's authority at River Dubois, greatly disappointing the captains, who evidently expected him as the oldest to display a greater sense of responsibility. During the expedition, however, his skills as a blacksmith, gunsmith, and carpenter were invaluable. "Nothing was more peculiarly useful to us, in various situations," wrote Lewis, "than the skill and ingenuity of this man as an artist, in repairing our guns, accoutrements, &c." Lewis recommended that Congress give Shields a bonus for his services. After the expedition Shields trapped in Missouri for a time with Daniel Boone, a kinsman, then settled in Indiana, where he died and was buried. Clarke (MLCE), 53–54; Lewis to Henry Dearborn, January 15, 1807, Jackson (LLC), 1:367; Lange (JS).

Private John B. Thompson (dates unknown). His place of birth and date of joining the expedition are unknown, but he may have lived in Indiana. He seems to have had some experience as a surveyor. Clark refers to him during the expedition as "a valuable member of our party." His postexpedition career is equally obscure; Clark listed him in 1825–28 as "killed." Speculation places him with John McClellan's expedition in the Rockies in 1807. Clarke (MLCE), 354; Majors, 573; Clark's List of Expedition Members [ca. 1825–28], Jackson (LLC), 2:639.

Private Ebenezer Tuttle (1773–?). Tuttle was born in Connecticut and joined the army in 1803. He was a member of Captain Amos Stoddard's artillery company. The only mention of him in the journals is in a detachment order of May 26, 1804. Possibly he was the unnamed man from Stoddard's company sent back on June 12, 1804; otherwise he was with the return party from Fort Mandan in 1805, as originally planned. Jackson (LLC), 1:237 n. 7; Clarke (MLCE), 62.

Corporal Richard Warfington (1777–?). In the journals his name appears as "Warpenton," "Worthington," "Wortheyton," and other versions. He was born in North Carolina, joined the army in 1799, and was transferred to the Corps of Discovery from Captain John Campbell's company of the Second Infantry Regiment on November 24, 1803, holding the rank of corporal. The captains apparently found him reliable and efficient and decided to put him in charge of the party they intended to send back from some point on the Missouri. That party was not dispatched nearly as soon as originally intended, and on August 4, 1804, Warfington's enlistment expired. Believing that he was the only one of the intended return party who was really trustworthy, the captains asked Warfington not to take his official discharge at that time, so that he could retain his rank and authority over the return group and ensure the safety of the dispatches, journals, and specimens sent back. Warfington remained with the group at Fort Mandan, conducted the return party to St. Louis in 1805, and carried out his command of that body to the captains' complete satisfaction; he even managed to keep alive a prairie dog and four magpies Lewis sent to Jefferson. Lewis recommended that Warfington receive a bonus beyond his regular pay. Clark apparently had no information about him in 1825–28. Clarke (MLCE), 59–60; Lewis to Henry Dearborn, January 15, 1807, Jackson (LLC), 1:364–65, 372 endnote; Clark's List of Expedition Members [ca. 1825–28], ibid., 2:639; Cutright (LCPN), 377.

Private Peter M. Weiser (1781–?). Weiser, descended from the noted frontier diplomat Conrad Weiser, was born and apparently reared in Pennsylvania. He was probably a member of Captain Russell Bissell's company of the First Infantry Regiment, stationed at Kaskaskia, before joining the expedition. In spite of some minor disciplinary trouble at River Dubois he was made a member of the permanent party. In 1807 he joined Manuel Lisa's fur-trading venture up the Missouri, and for the next few years he was on the Yellowstone and the Missouri headwaters with Lisa's men, including some old comrades from the expedition. It has been conjectured that he also crossed the Continental Divide to the Snake River valley in Idaho; at any rate, Clark's map of the West (*Atlas* map 126), published in 1814, shows "Wiser's R." as a tributary of the Snake in western Idaho, in country not visited by the expedition. It is not known whether Clark received the information from Weiser himself or from one of his associates, such as Drouillard or Colter. The river, with the correct spelling, and an Idaho town, still bear his name. Clark listed him in 1825–28 as "killed"; he may have been one of those killed by the Blackfeet while operating out of Lisa's post at the Three Forks of the Missouri in 1810, or perhaps he fell in some later fur-trade skirmish. Clarke (PW); Clarke (MLCE), 59; Clark's List of Expedition Members [ca. 1825–28], Jackson (LLC), 2:639.

Private William Werner (dates unknown). Often "Warner" in the journals, he may have been born in Kentucky and may have been in the army before joining the Corps; his actual date of joining is uncertain. He fought with John Potts during the River Dubois winter, and he was convicted of being absent without leave at St. Charles, Missouri, at the outset of the expedition. Otherwise his service was apparently satisfactory but unremarkable. He appears briefly in the records after the expedition, having been advanced some money in 1807 by Lewis and allowed the use of a government horse. In 1825–28 Clark understood him to be living in Virginia. Clarke (MLCE), 54; Clark's List of Expedition Members [ca. 1825–28], Jackson (LLC), 2:639.

Private Isaac White (ca. 1774–?). White was born in Massachusetts and joined the army in 1801. He was a member of Captain Amos Stoddard's artillery company. The only mention of him in the journals is in a detachment order of May 26, 1804. Possibly he was the man of Stoddard's company sent back on June 12, 1804; otherwise he was with the return party from Fort Mandan in 1805. Jackson (LLC), 1:237 n. 7; Clarke (MLCE), 62.

Private Joseph Whitehouse (ca. 1775–?). An expedition journalist, Whitehouse was probably born in Virginia and went to Kentucky with his family in about 1784. He enlisted officially on January 1, 1804, transferring from Captain Daniel Bissell's company of the First Infantry Regiment, stationed at Kaskaskia. He was in some sort of disciplinary difficulty during the winter at River Dubois but was allowed to remain with the expedition. During the expedition he often acted as a tailor for the other men. In 1807 in Missouri he was ordered arrested for debt. He later rejoined the army, served in the War of 1812, and deserted in 1817. Clark apparently had no information about him in 1825–28. Clarke (MLCE), 55–56; Clark's List of Expedition Members [ca. 1825–28], Jackson (LLC), 2: 639; Cutright (HLCJ), 242–64.

Private Alexander Hamilton Willard (1778–1865). Born in New Hampshire, he was living in Kentucky when he enlisted in Captain Amos Stoddard's artillery company in 1800. He was tried and convicted on July 12, 1804, of sleeping while on sentry duty; the offense, under the military regimen of the Corps, was punishable by death, but instead he was given one hundred lashes. He was a blacksmith and apparently assisted John Shields in this work during the expedition. Lewis hired him as government blacksmith for the Sauk and Fox Indians in 1808, and the next year he held the same position with the Delawares and Shawnees. He served in the War of 1812 and lived in Missouri and Wisconsin. His marriage in 1807 produced twelve children. In 1852 he emigrated with his family to California and there died and was buried near Sacramento. There is some suggestion that he kept a journal on the expedition, but if so, it is lost. Jackson (LLC), 1:372 n. 26; Clarke (MLCE), 56.

Private Richard Windsor (dates unknown). Often "Winser" or Winsor" in the journals, he may have come from Captain Russell Bissell's company of the First

Infantry Regiment. Like many of the other soldiers detailed to the expedition, he officially enlisted for the expedition on January 1, 1804. During the trip he was often assigned as a hunter. He settled in Missouri after the expedition but rejoined the army and served until 1819. In 1825–28 Clark listed him as living on the Sangamon River in Illinois. Clarke (MLCE), 59; Clark's List of Expedition Members [ca. 1825–28], Jackson (LLC), 2:638.

York (ca. 1770–?). York is the only name given for Clark's slave in the journals or any primary document. He seems to have been about the same age as Clark, or a few years younger, and to have been Clark's companion from childhood, in the fashion of the slaveholding South. Clark legally inherited York from his father in 1799. The journals and other primary sources indicate that he was large and strong and perhaps overweight. He seems to have carried a gun and to have performed his full share of the duties with other members of the party; a body servant who could neither defend himself nor carry his share of the load would have been an unacceptable luxury on the expedition. Tales of his sexual prowess among Indian women or of his being the expedition's buffoon rest largely on the racial bias of later historians, not on evidence in the journals. York received his freedom sometime after 1811 and then operated a wagon freight business in Tennessee and Kentucky. By Clark's account, the business failed, and York then decided to rejoin his old master in St. Louis but died of cholera on the way, sometime before 1832. An alternative account has it that he made his way west to the Rockies and was living with the Crows in the 1830s; the tale is unlikely but not wholly impossible. Betts (SY); Clarke (MLCE), 38.

Engagé E. Cann (dates unknown). He appears in Clark's list of *engagés* under July 4, 1804. Elsewhere in the journals the name appears in versions that have been deciphered as "Carr," "Cane," and "Carn"; some of the variation may be due to Clark's handwriting, not his spelling. Cann was presumably with the return party of 1805. He has been identified as Alexander Carson (ca. 1775–1836), a relative of Christopher "Kit" Carson, on the basis of a second-hand account stating that Carson claimed to have come to the mountains with Lewis and Clark; there is no more direct evidence. Cann was perhaps born in Mississippi and wintered with the Arikaras in 1809–10. In 1811 he joined the overland Astorians led by Wilson Price Hunt, crossing the Rockies with them, and spent a number of years trapping in the mountains and on the Columbia, working for the North West Company and the Hudson's Bay Company. In 1833 he settled permanently in the Willamette Valley in Oregon and was killed by Indians in 1836. Clarke (MLCE), 68–69; Jackson (LLC), 1:373 endnote; Stoller.

Engagé Charles Caugee (dates unknown). He is mentioned in a list of *engagés* under July 4, 1804, and may have been with the return party from Fort Mandan in 1805. Nothing else is known of him. Clarke (MLCE), 68.

Engagé Joseph Collin (dates unknown). He should not be confused with John Collins, an enlisted man with the permanent party. Collin is listed as an *engagé* on May 26, 1804, and in no other list. Because there is no record of his being paid, he may have been paid in cash when discharged in the fall of 1804, at either the Arikara or Mandan villages. He may also be the man picked up at the Arikara villages on the expedition's return in 1806. A Joseph Collin from the Montreal area in Canada was married at Portage des Sioux, Missouri, in 1818. See also the sketch of La Liberté, below. Clarke (MLCE), 69–70.

Engagé Jean Baptiste Deschamps (dates unknown). He was the "patroon"—foreman—of the French boatmen, presumably because of his experience and maturity. Virtually nothing is known of him, though he may have been residing with his wife at St. Charles, Missouri, in 1792. Clarke (MLCE), 63.

Engagé Charles Hebert (dates unknown). He is listed as an *engagé* on May 26, 1804, and nowhere else. Possibly he is the "Charlo" of Clark's list of July 4, 1804. He has been identified as a Canadian who married in St. Louis in 1792 and may have lived near St. Charles or Portage des Sioux, Missouri. Since there is no record of his being paid, he may have been discharged at the Mandan villages in the fall of 1804 and paid in cash. Perhaps he returned with the return party of 1805, having wintered with the expedition at Fort Mandan. Clarke (MLCE), 69.

Engagé Jean Baptiste La Jeunesse (?–1806?). He is also "La Guness" and, apparently, "Lasones," in the journals. He was probably from St. Rose, Quebec, Canada. In 1797 in St. Louis he married the sister of Etienne Malboeuf, another expedition *engagé*. La Jeunesse was discharged, and presumably paid off, at the Mandan villages in the fall of 1804 and set off with Paul Primeau downriver in a canoe on November 6. He may have stopped off at the Arikara villages or elsewhere for the winter. He was apparently dead by September 1807, when his wife remarried. Clarke (MLCE), 64–65.

Engagé La Liberté (dates unknown). An *engagé* of this name was sent on July 29, 1804, to the Oto Indians in northeastern Nebraska to invite them to confer with the captains. He took the opportunity to quit the expedition, and though a party was sent to apprehend him, he escaped and appears no more in the expedition record. Attempts to identify him further have mired in confusion about his actual name. La Liberté seems to have been a common name among the French Canadians and Mississippi Valley French involved in the fur trade and river travel at the time. Thus, a La Liberté was working for the North West Company in Canada in 1799 and might be the same man. The *engagé* who left the party spoke the Oto language to some extent, so he must have lived among them for a while. His singularly appropriate name may be only a *dit* name, not a formal surname. He does not appear under that name in the list of *engagés* in the detachment order of May 26, 1804; this could mean that he was hired later, perhaps picked up from some party of traders headed down the Missouri. However, he may only be concealed on the May 26 list under another name, especially if La Liberté is only a *dit* name. The list of July 4, 1804, in Clark's Field Notes gives "Joseph La bartee," and also "J. Le bartee"; each time the name has an asterisk beside it. On the first occurrence, "Le bartee" is assigned to a pirogue, the second time to the large keelboat. Did Clark err and list the same man twice, or were there two men with the same surname or *dit* name? Did the asterisk indicate the error, or refer to the similarity of names? Ordway refers to the deserter first on July 29, 1804; Quaife gives the name as "Jo Barter," but Ordway's manuscript version can as readily be interpreted as "Bartee." At any rate, Ordway later calls him "La Liberty," confirming that he is one of the possible two "Le bartees." Donald Jackson has uncovered, in an 1819 Illinois legal document, a reference to "Joseph Callin *dit* La Liberty of portage des Scioux." This could easily be the *engagé* Joseph Collin of the expedition, especially since he is not mentioned by the name Collin in the Field Notes list of July 4. This could explain how La Liberté became "Joseph Le bartee" in that list.

The question remains, however, whether there were two men with this *dit* name or only one, and whether, if there were two, Collin was the deserter. (Technically, he was not a deserter in the military sense because he was a hired boatman rather than an enlisted man.) There is no record of Collin's having been paid, which would have been the case if he had deserted, but it could also mean that, like some other *engagés*, he was discharged at the Arikara or Mandan villages and paid in cash. A man picked up at the Arikaras in 1806, who had perhaps been with the expedition in 1804, could have been Collin; this man, in any case, could hardly have been the deserter, since he would have avoided the expedition, and they would not have given him a ride home. Thus it is quite possible that Joseph Collin bore the *dit* name La Liberté and is referred to as "Joseph Le bartee" by Clark because of this. It is also possible, however, that there was another *engagé* with that same *dit* name, and if so, either might have been the deserter. Since he was a civilian employee, not an enlisted soldier, his desertion was not quite so serious as that of Moses Reed, which occurred at about the same time, although La Liberté did take a "public horse" with him when he was sent to the Otos. A Joseph La Liberté was married in St. Louis in 1835, and a La Liberté, aged 60, was buried there in 1837.

If there are two La Libertés, and Collin is one of them, which other *engagé* is concealed under this name? One is clearly named Joseph, while the initial of the other appears to be "J." Besides Collin there is no other "Joseph" among the known *engagés*. The only other whose initial might be "J." is Baptiste La Jeunesse, whose actual given name was presumably Jean-Baptiste. However, he apparently appears as "Lasones" in the same July 4 list as the two Le bartees. The discrepancies in both name and number between the principal lists of *engagés* do not allow any certainty on this matter. Quaife (MLJO), 102; Clarke (MLCE), 63–64, 69–70; Jackson, "La Liberté Identified," typescript.

Engagé Etienne Malboeuf (ca. 1775–?). He was from Lac de Sable, Canada, and his mother may have been an Indian; he was baptized in St. Charles, Missouri, in 1792. In 1804, he was residing in Kaskaskia, Illinois. Like most of the other *engagés*, he returned from Fort Mandan in 1805. Clarke (MLCE), 65.

Engagé Peter Pinaut (ca. 1776–?). Undoubtedly Pierre to his fellow Frenchmen, he is presumably the "Charles pineau" of Lewis's financial accounts. He may also be the "Charlo" mentioned in one list in Clark's Field Notes. Pinaut was the illegitimate son of a French father and a Missouri Indian mother, and was baptized in St. Louis in 1790, suggesting that he grew up in the Indian country on the Missouri. The only mention of him in the journals is in the detachment order of May 26, 1804. Lewis's Account [August 5, 1807], Jackson (LLC), 2:422; Clarke (MLCE), 65–66.

Engagé Paul Primeau (dates unknown). He is variously "Primaut," "Preemau," and "Premor" in the journals. He came from Chateauguay, Canada, and was married in St. Louis in 1799. He was discharged, and presumably paid off, at the Mandan villages in the fall of 1804, and on November 6, with Jean-Baptiste La Jeunesse, set out downriver in a canoe for St. Louis. He may have wintered with the Arikaras or elsewhere. In 1807 he was probably in Missouri. Clarke (MLCE), 66.

Engagé François Rivet (ca. 1757–1852). Born at Montreal, Rivet, also referred to as "Reevey" and such variations, came to the Mississippi Valley at an early age and engaged in hunting and trading in Louisiana. He may have left the return party of 1805 at the Arikara villages. He soon headed up the Missouri again, perhaps with Manuel Lisa's trading company, for about 1809 he was in the Flathead country of northwest Montana, where he married and fathered two sons. In 1813 he was employed by the North West Company among the Flatheads, and was still there in 1824, working as both trapper and interpreter. In 1829 he transferred to Fort Colville on the upper Columbia, and in 1832, at the age of seventy-five, he was placed in charge of the post by the Hudson's Bay Company. After retiring in 1838 he settled in the Willamette Valley in Oregon. Clarke (MLCE), 66–67; Munnick (FR).

Engagé Peter Roi (dates unknown). There were many early settlers in the "Illinois country" with the surname Roi or Roy, descended from pioneers of French and Indian blood who were there even before the founding of St. Louis, having come from Canada. Pierre Roy, born in 1786 at Ste. Genevieve, Missouri, may be the man, but there is no evidence. Clark also gives the name as "Roie." On August 21, 1806, at the Arikara villages in South Dakota, the returning expedition encountered one of their former *engagés*, whom Clark identifies as "Rokey"; he had probably stayed behind when the return party of 1805 went down to St. Louis and now returned to Missouri with the expedition. It has been suggested that his name was Rocque, a name that appears on no expedition roster. John Ordway also refers to this man by name, and in Quaife's edition the name is given as "Ross." Examination of the manuscript shows that Ordway's letters can easily be interpreted as "Roie" or even "Roei." "Rokey" was therefore probably Peter Roi, and there is no need to search for Rocque or Ross. This interpretation is strengthened by the fact that Roi was not among the expedition *engagés* who received their pay in St. Louis in 1805. Clarke (MLCE), 67, 70; Quaife (MLJO), 392; Jackson (LLC), 1 : 237 n. 7.

Notes

1. Cutright (HLCJ), 237–38.

2. Clark's List of Expedition Members [ca. 1825–28], Jackson (LLC), 2 : 638–39.

3. Lewis to Clark, June 19, 1803, and August 3, 1803, Clark to Lewis, August 21, 1803, Lewis to Henry Dearborn, January 15, 1807, ibid., 1 : 57–60, 115–17, 117–18, 369–73 nn. The remaining seven of the nine are: Floyd; Pryor; Bratton; the Field brothers, Joseph and Reubin; Gibson; and Shields.

4. Ibid., 369–73 nn.; Appleman (LC), 62–64, 366 n. 54. No muster roll for Russell Bissell's company has been found; such a document would clarify some of the doubts about several men.

5. The question of the composition of the return party will be considered at greater length under April 7, 1805, in the appropriate volume of this edition.

6. McDermott (FS), 28–30; Clarke (MLCE), 21–22, 63 n. 23.

7. Jackson (LLC), 1 : 237 n. 7, 2 : 422.

Appendix B

Provenance and Description of the Journals

Lewis's and Clark's Journals

From 1806 to 1814 Jefferson strove to have the expedition's history published, but the appearance of Biddle's work in the latter year by no means ended the usefulness of the manuscript journals in the eyes of the originator of the enterprise. Fully appreciating the value of the documents, the former president began a campaign to bring the material together under safe management. "The right to these papers is in the government," Jefferson declared, and he wished to reclaim them for the nation.[1] There was, however, no adequate national repository at the time, so Jefferson decided on the American Philosophical Society, with which he had been associated for so long, as the most reliable custodian for such items. As president of the society he was sure that the documents would receive proper care under that institution's stewardship. In fact, Jefferson was the first to obtain any materials from the expedition for inclusion in the society's archives, from the estate of Philadelphia naturalist Benjamin Smith Barton.

As noted in the Introduction, Lewis had discussed the intended publication of the history of the expedition with Barton in 1807 and may then have commissioned Barton to prepare the scientific portions of the work. Clark arranged for Barton to carry out this task in 1810, and in order to give both Biddle and Barton access to the journals, Clark decided to have the natural history portions of the daily journals copied into other notebooks for the naturalist's use. In many of the journals, passages are scored out and the words "copy for Dr. Barton" interlined or written in the margin. Biddle carried three such notebooks, Codices P, Q, and R (under Coues's system), from Fincastle to be turned over to Barton. Barton failed to carry out his assignment, but the three notebooks remained in his possession until his death in 1815 and were not used by Biddle for his edition. Biddle had access to the same material as Barton, since he had the regular journals from which the copies were made, but he did not utilize the scored passages in his volumes, and relatively little on natural history appears in the 1814 edition. Some years later, Biddle recalled his delivery to Barton: "My impression however is that the packet for Dr. Barton consisted of small notebooks and some papers. The books were chiefly extracts relative to natural history taken from the original journals."[2]

After Barton's death, José Corrèa da Serra, Portuguese diplomat and friend of Jefferson, recovered the three notebooks for Jefferson. Corrèa da Serra obtained one notebook from Barton's widow in March 1816 and sent it to Jefferson by way of the president's granddaughter, Ellen Wayles Randolph, who had been visiting Philadelphia. In June, Corrèa da Serra obtained three other notebooks from Barton's estate but discovered that one was not an item from the Lewis and Clark expedition and returned it to the widow. Jefferson deposited the three natural history journals with the society in November 1817.[3]

Lewis had entrusted the plant specimens from the expedition to the botanist Frederick Pursh, who carried a number of them off to Europe. He described many of them and applied Latin binomials, giving appropriate credit to Lewis and Clark. While some of the specimens disappeared, others eventually returned to America; all are now in the Academy of Natural Sciences of Philadelphia. Many of the zoological and ethnological specimens went to the artist and naturalist Charles Willson Peale, to be displayed in his Philadelphia museum, then the only public natural history museum in the country. After Peale's death they were scattered and virtually all are lost.[4] The botanical specimens at the academy will form a separate volume of this edition, and an introduction to that work will discuss the nature and provenance of that collection.

With Barton's material secure in the American Philosophical Society, Jefferson worked to get the remaining journals—those in Biddle's hands—into the society's vaults also. In fact, in September of 1816, at the same time he was working to recover the journals in Barton's estate, Jefferson began a correspondence to regain the "travelling pocket journals" for the government. Clark quickly authorized Biddle to deliver all the papers from the expedition to Jefferson but left Biddle the best judge of which papers to release. Clark also added certain stipulations concerning the documents: that John Ordway's journal be returned to him since the captains had personally purchased it from the sergeant; and that Clark, his heirs, or agents should have access to the papers at all times.[5]

In April 1818, Biddle supposedly turned over to the society all the materials he had in hand, with the exception of Ordway's journal, which he was supposed to return to Clark. Along with the materials, Biddle submitted a list of the items he was delivering to the society. That list and society accession records stand as the first small survey of Lewis and Clark documents.[6] The deposit included the following:

> Fourteen volumes of the Pocket Journal
> of Messrs. Lewis & Clark.

A volume of astronomical observations
and other matter by Captain Lewis.

A small copy book containing some notes
by Captain Lewis.

A rough draft of his letter to the
President from St. Louis announcing his return.

Two statistical tables of the Indian tribes
west of the Mississippi river made by
Governor Clark.[7]

After their deposition in 1818, the journals remained in the vaults of the American Philosophical Society, obscure and almost unused, until their discovery by Elliott Coues in 1892. Late in that year Coues obtained permission to take them to his home in Washington, D.C., and there he set to work to classify, collate, describe, and arrange in chronological order those important documents. Working tirelessly throughout the Christmas season, Coues by mid-January 1893 had completed his survey of the journals deposited by Jefferson and Biddle and presented a report of his findings to the society. Coues explained that he had discovered "18 bound note books, and 12 small parcels of other Mss., making in all 30 codices . . . something like 2,000 written pages." Coues found thirteen volumes bound in red morocco, the so-called red books, which he designated as Codices D through P; four notebooks bound in marble-covered boards, which he labeled Codices A, B, Q, and R; a single journal bound in brown leather, which he called Codex C; and twelve loose parcels (many containing sheets torn from the red and marble-covered books), which he covered and interspersed with the other codices and which he arranged as Codices Aa, Ba, Fa, Fb, Fc, Fd, Fe, Ia, La, Lb, S and T. He designated those fragments according to the notebook journal to which each was closest in time. Thus, Lewis's Codex Aa contains entries for two days in the same period of some three months covered by Clark's Codex A. In his report Coues also gave descriptions of each codex that until this day have stood as the definitive survey of the journals.[8]

Coues was not the first to codify the journals. Clark had numbered some of the journals during the expedition and used the numbers in cross-references. Codices A, B, and C he called numbers 1, 2, and 3; Voorhis No. 1 (to be discussed below) was his number 4; and Codex G was number 5. Although his cross-references are not so direct, Clark seems to have used the numbers 6, 7, and 8 to designate Codices H and I and Voorhis No. 2. Later, Biddle imposed his own numbering system, and present Codices A–N became notebooks 1–14. Clark apparently adopted Biddle's numbering system when the men worked on the journals together at Fincastle. Several of the double-lettered codices (like Codex Fb) are cross-referenced to Clark's regular journals using Biddle's numbers rather than the captain's own system from the expedition. This edition will use Coues's system.[9]

Lewis and Clark made their daily entries in journals that Coues called Codices A–N, and the loose sheets he arranged as double-lettered codices. Codices A–N were the "fourteen volumes of the Pocket Journal of Messrs. Lewis & Clark" deposited by Biddle. Biddle would not have listed the double-lettered items separately. In his time they were not individually bound documents but were probably separated or loosely inserted into the regular notebooks when Coues discovered them. The contents of the remaining six notebooks and covered sheets that Coues designated as Codices O, P, Q, R, S, and T are quite dissimilar to the other journals. Lewis and Clark apparently reserved them for noting miscellaneous observations and events, and for that reason they are here called the specialized journals.[10]

While in the East after the expedition in 1807, Lewis made arrangements with other persons besides Barton to aid him in publishing the results of the transcontinental trip. He turned to Ferdinand Rudolph Hassler, a Swiss mathematician at West Point, for help with the astronomical observations that he and Clark had so carefully taken on the trip. When in 1810 Clark began to collect the papers left in Lewis's estate, he noticed that the book of astronomical observations was missing and queried Hassler on its whereabouts. We must assume that Lewis left such a notebook with Hassler. Strong evidence suggests that Hassler had one of the red books from the journey, an item Biddle listed as a "volume of astronomical observations and other matter by Captain Lewis." This is the notebook that Coues labeled Codex O.[11]

Codex O is actually in two parts and is completely in Lewis's hand. The first part is filled with astronomical observations from May 18, 1804, to March 30, 1805; the second part is a summary of the principal affluents of the Missouri River from Camp Dubois to Fort Mandan, with information about streams higher up gleaned from Indian testimony. The notebook was prepared at Fort Mandan based on the captains' field notes, their on-the-spot astronomical observations, and their discussions with Indians and traders. It is generally believed that this notebook was sent to Jefferson in April 1805, as the permanent party of the Corps of Discovery started out of Fort Mandan and as another group returned to St. Louis carrying a boatload of artifacts, papers, and specimens to be forwarded to the president. Codex O would have been among the papers sent to Jefferson. If so, then Lewis would have regained the journal from the president in early 1807 and probably turned it over to Hassler at that time.[12]

As far as can be determined, Hassler made only one mention of the journal in his possession. Calling it "a fair copy, which I see has many faults in writing," Hassler wrote that "my journal in hands goes till Fort Mandan [point of observation] No. 51." Codex O is the only notebook that answers the description. Daily entries in the regular journals often carried the longitude and latitude readings within the text, but the reading for point of observation No. 51 is found only in Codex O. By 1810 Hassler was asking to see the original diaries so he could examine all the astronomical observations made during the expedition, but Biddle was unwilling to let them go. Thus, Hassler may have been hampered in his work, and he later complained that he could have finished the work in 1807 if he had received all the material then.[13] Nothing is known of Codex O again until 1817 when Jefferson was attempting to bring all the journals together, at which time it was reported that Hassler had "given up the calculations in despair." It is unknown when Hassler relinquished the journal in his possession, but it was among the papers that Biddle delivered to the society in April 1818.[14]

Codices P, Q, and R already had some specialized material in them and also contained many blank pages. As such, they were ideal for another purpose; those three notebooks were used for transferring the natural history material from the regular journals, so that both Biddle and Barton could have access to expedition documents at the same time. Lewis, the naturalist of the expedition, apparently placed some miscellaneous observations of plants and animals in the notebooks. Codex Q had Lewis's zoological notes from July 30, 1804, to about January 1806. Codex R contained Lewis's botanical notes from May 10 to November 17, 1804, and a zoological note on "a bird of the Corvus genus" (blackheaded jay). Codex P had only a few pages of weather information and only a couple of lines of daily entry writing, which are overwritten and barely readable. Biddle or Clark apparently tore the pages of daily entry material out of the notebook to use the blank pages on either side for copying purposes. Coues found the daily entry pages (Lewis's remarks for September 9–11, 1805) as loose sheets, which he covered and labeled Codex Fc. Coues failed to note, however, that the loose pages came from Codex P and that the entry for September 10 in Codex Fc stops abruptly in midsentence. It connects very nicely with words in Lewis's hand upside down from the main text on p. 80 of Codex P.

Clark started copying the natural history material into Codex P, following some of Lewis's writing in the first pages of the notebook. He began with April 9, 1805, immediately after the group left Fort Mandan and where the first natural history material occurs at that time. Several lines into the copied entry another hand takes up the copying. In fact, there appear to be two hands at work on copying besides Clark, who wrote only a few lines here and there in Codex P. Biddle does not seem to have done any of the copying in any of the three Codices, P, Q, and R, and it may be that the copying was completed before Biddle arrived at Fincastle. The identity of the copyist or the copyists remains a mystery. It may be that Clark hired a clerk from Fincastle or someone earlier at St. Louis, or perhaps a family member did the work. The copyist made a number of errors. For instance, incorrect dates appear for some entries and several entries may be combined under a single date. Also, some of the material designated "copy for Dr. Barton" was overlooked, such as an entry for September 20, 1805, in Codex Fd. Biddle may have noticed this oversight later, for a note by Biddle in the codex calls attention to this passage.[15]

The copying in Codex P ends with an entry for February 17, 1806, and the few remaining pages of the journal are filled with Lewis's weather data—placed there during the trip or immediately thereafter. During the period of this copied material (April 9, 1805, through February 17, 1806) there exists a large gap in Lewis's regular journal-keeping. The hiatus is roughly from August 26, 1805, to January 1, 1806, with only a few scattered entries of daily events (such as the material in Codex Fc) but with no natural history notes. It is noteworthy that the copied entries in Codex P fall off dramatically during this same period. There are only two notebook pages of natural history notes for seven days (October 17, 23, November 19, 29, December 9, 27, and 31, 1805). The entries are fewer and shorter for this period than for those either preceding or following it. All the material comes from Clark's journals at the society, which Coues labeled Codices H and I. Perhaps Lewis kept no regular journal during this time; at least, it is apparent that neither Clark nor Biddle had access to additional Lewis items for copying into the notebook.

After filling up the available space in Codex P, the copyist began to enter material into Codex R. The first entry takes up where Codex P left off, February 18, 1806, and the copying continues until March 11, 1806, when the notebook is filled. Again an unknown writer is at work on the copying; the copyist appears to be the second person who was working on Codex P. Clark apparently did no copying in this codex or in Codex Q, but he may have written directions for Barton here and there in both books. The copyist finally turned to Codex Q to enter the remaining natural history material, and it appears that the same person completed both Codices R and Q. Codex Q carries the natural history matter from March 11 to August 10, 1806, about when Lewis stopped his journal writing. There were several blank pages left in the journal after the final copied entry so the copyist placed additional specialized material on those pages in order to fill out the notebook. The final few pages were copied from Clark's journals and include entries that precede the initial date of April 9, 1805, in Codex P (i.e., February 12, 27, 1805, and August 22, 24, September 1, 17, 1804).[16]

Codex S is the least complex of the specialized journals, and its circumstances have been fairly well known since Coues's time. It was the item Biddle called "a rough draft of his [Lewis's] letter to the President announcing his return." It consists of two letters by Lewis on letter paper rather than on notebook paper torn from the journals. The first, dated September 23, 1806, was written to Jefferson and is probably a draft or a retained copy. Jefferson's copy, in his papers at the Library of Congress, contains many small variations from the codex but no substantial differences. The second letter was dated September 21, 1806, and ends in midsentence at the bottom of a page indicating that additional pages are missing. The letter has no addressee, but Coues thought it was intended for the president; Thwaites conjectured that it may have been a draft of a letter that Lewis promised Jefferson in his letter of September 23. If so, however, why the confusion of dates? Donald Jackson believed from the poor penmanship of the letters that they were written on the boats before the men reached St. Louis on September 23. Moreover, it appeared to him that the date "23" had been added some time after the letter was originally written. Thus, the dates on the letters may not be a true indication of the order or time of their execution. After September 23, the captains' opportunity for writing diminished greatly as they were feted and honored everywhere.[17]

The provenance of Codex T was not apparent to Coues and Thwaites because material unknown to either of them had to come into the archives of the society before the codex could be matched to its missing pages. Moreover, it does not appear on Biddle's list or in the society's accession records. It must have come with the Biddle deposit, but because it was a loose sheet, it went unrecorded until Coues's time—as did the double-lettered codices. In 1913, Charles and Edward Biddle deposited in the Library of Congress thousands of papers accumulated by their grandfather, Nicholas Biddle. In examining the papers prior to their delivery, one grandson discovered manuscripts associated with the Lewis and Clark expedition. These important documents were in time donated to the society and will be discussed below. One item, however, is necessary to understanding the contents of Codex T.[18]

Among the papers of the Biddle family deposit was a small notebook of forty-eight pages covered with loose boards. The sheets appear to be letter paper cut to a size of about six inches by four inches and used by Clark as a field notebook in place of the regular notebooks. The little field book contains mainly miscellaneous items and is almost exclusively in Clark's hand but with occasional notes by Lewis. Most important perhaps is Clark's field draft of his notes for January 6–10, 1806 (misdated 1805 in the notebook), when he and a small party visited the whale site on the Pacific coast near their winter camp at Fort Clatsop in present Oregon. As might be expected for a field notebook, the entries are irregularly placed and in many instances are nearly illegible.[19]

Near the end of the notebook is a section in which Clark seems to be correcting some of his earlier estimates of courses and distances of the outbound journey. There are also passages that lay out the most advantageous route across portions of the trip with listings of various geographic points along the way. This material was probably written near the end of the expedition since Clark's route on the Yellowstone River in July and August 1806 is mentioned. The very last material seems to be a summing up of the party's trip from Fort Mandan in April 1805, to Fort Clatsop on the Pacific coast, and the return. The writing ends in midsentence on the last page where the Corps has reached the western slope of the Rocky Mountains in May and June 1806. It is here that the text of Codex T matches that of the field notebook and continues the narrative of the return journey until Clark reached the confluence of the Yellowstone and Missouri rivers. In fact, several words from the text of the field notebook are repeated on the first line of Codex T. The one problem with linking the two conclusively is that the paper differs considerably. Codex T is one sheet, apparently of letter paper, measuring about seven and one-fourth inches by four and one-half inches. Clark may have filled his little notebook and turned to a convenient scrap of paper to finish his writing. Later the scrap piece and notebook became separated while in Biddle's possession and arrived at the society in different accessions: Codex T in 1818 and the field notebook a century later. So exactly do the texts match that they will be combined in the new edition.[20]

Coues apparently overlooked two items listed in Biddle's 1818 deposit and did not include them in his description of materials in the American Philosophical Society. The first was "a small copy book containing some notes by Captain Lewis." This notebook has no resemblance to the red or marble-covered journals and is apparently a book that Lewis used some years before the expedition without filling. Into this notebook he placed some botanical notes from the expedition, but for the most part the pages are filled with weather data. For this reason it is here called the Weather Diary. The weather entries are in the hands of both Lewis and Clark, but Lewis has done a greater share of the writing. The notes cover the period from January 1, 1804, to April 9, 1805, but entries fall off sharply after May 14, 1804, as the expedition got underway from Camp Dubois. Indeed, there are only nine entries between May 14 and September 19, when consistent entries resume, and these nine entries are concerned with natural history observations rather than meteorological matter. This notebook could have returned with the boatload of items destined for Jefferson in April 1805, it could have crossed the continent with the captains, or it may have been buried in one of the caches established by the Corps. Since weather data was also kept in the regular journals, it is not clear whether Biddle used this notebook or the daily-entry journals for the weather tables appended to his work.[21]

Biddle's other item of deposit undetected by Coues was "two statistical tables of the Indian tribes west of the Mississippi river made by Governor Clark." The first of the two tables was the "Estimate of Eastern Indians," originally executed by Clark at Fort Mandan. At least two copies were made—one sent to the secretary of war in April 1805, which is now lost, and a second copy, which is now at the society. Jefferson prepared his own *Message from the President . . .* (1806), in which he included a "Statistical View of Indian Nations," from the secretary's copy. There are differences between Jefferson's printed version and the manuscript at the society, to be noted when the material appears in this edition. The other table, now called "Estimate of Western Indians," Clark probably prepared at Fort Clatsop. Clark's "Western Indians" were those west of the Rocky Mountains. The estimate in this statistical table may have come from notes already written into Codex I, with revisions of tribal numbers and changes from the original codex draft from place to place. Variations with the codex will be noted in this edition.[22]

Other journals from the expedition reemerged in 1903, items that Clark had retained after the return of the Corps of Discovery. In August of that year Thwaites discovered a wealth of journals, maps, letters, and other material in the New York home of Julia Clark Voorhis and her daughter Eleanor Glasgow Voorhis. Julia had obtained the material from the estate of her father, George Rogers Hancock Clark, the fourth child of William Clark. The Voorhis manuscripts were a golden find of hitherto unknown materials and are now deposited as the Voorhis Collection in the Missouri Historical Society, St. Louis.[23] The letters relating to the expedition have appeared in Jackson's work, while the maps are printed in the *Atlas* of the present edition and are for the most part at Yale University. Some of the miscellaneous material will appear in this and subsequent volumes of this edition or will be useful in annotating journal items.

The principal items of the Voorhis journals consist of five notebooks—four like the red books at the American Philosophical Society and one a field book bound in rough elkskin. The first three red books are standard daily-entry journals in Clark's hand and cover the periods of April 7–July 3, 1805 (Voorhis No. 1), January 30–April 3, 1806 (Voorhis No. 2), and April 4–June 6, 1806 (Voorhis No. 3). The fourth red book, also by Clark, has no daily-entry material but rather carries miscellaneous material including weather data, distance estimates, botanical and zoological notes, statistics on Indians, a few longitudinal and latitudinal readings, and additional notes from later periods. The Elkskin-bound Journal covers the period from September 11 to December 31, 1805, and is clearly a notebook that Clark kept in the field; the material is repeated in Clark's Codices G, H, and I at Philadelphia.[24] There is an additional red book in the Voorhis Collection, but it is filled with memoranda unrelated to the expedition. On the outside front cover that notebook carries the words, "9 to 12 Augt. 1806" but has no entries for that period. As noted in the Introduction, Codex Lb at Philadelphia covers those very dates in Lewis's hand and must originally have been pages from that notebook.

The Voorhis Collection also includes an unbound Orderly Book that was once a part of one of the marble-covered books. The orders cover the period from April 1, 1804, to January 1, 1806, and occur once or twice a month from February to August 1804; then come two orders for October 1804, and a final one for January 1806. The orders are in the handwriting of Lewis, Clark, and Ordway, in about equal proportions. Two earlier orders by Lewis (February 20 and March 3, 1804) are on letter paper and are not repeated in the Orderly Book; one fragment of letter paper carries part of an order by Clark (April 7, 1804) which appears in full in the book in Ordway's hand. It may be that Lewis and Clark were writing the orders separately and then transferring them to the Orderly Book.

Two other items from the Voorhis Collection appear to be field notes kept by Clark. One is an apparent first draft of daily-entry notes from April 16 to 21, 1806, that is repeated by Clark in Voorhis No. 3. The other field draft covers the dates July 13–19 and July 24–August 3, 1806, while Clark was on the Yellowstone River. Thwaites did not print this latter material, probably because he thought it too repetitious of existing entries in Clark's Codex M; it will be printed in this edition. The writing is almost exclusively course and distance notes but much more extensive than that written in the regular journals. The gap in the journal-writing occurs because the Yellowstone party camped for several days in July in order to build canoes to float the remainder of the river, so no course and distance record was needed.[25]

Why did Clark not leave the materials with Biddle after their visit at Fincastle in 1810 or else turn them over to the American Philosophical Society in 1817 when Jefferson was attempting to bring all the expedition materials together in a safe depository? It is certain that Biddle at least saw the Voorhis journals, because in one (Voorhis No. 4) he has jotted some queries and requests to Clark. Probably he viewed the journals at Fincastle, scribbled in the notes, but left Clark to take them back to St. Louis. Thwaites's answer to the question of Clark's reason for keeping the journals was that much of the material was repetitious of other journals and that some items may have been deemed of less historical significance. Clark probably reasoned that Biddle had the same coverage in Lewis's notebooks and thus his own were superfluous. This would have been particularly true of Voorhis No. 2, which was written during a period when Clark was largely copying Lewis's notes verbatim. Of course, the Elkskin-bound Journal material was also repeated for Biddle, and in a neater, more legible format, in some red books.[26]

In 1913, besides the small notebook that fits with Codex T, Biddle's grandsons discovered other expedition items among their grandfather's papers. The heirs recovered all the items associated with the expedition from the Library of Congress where they had been placed and deposited them with the American Philosophical Society between 1915 and 1917.[27] One of the more important pieces was the journal kept by Lewis, and later Clark, of the preliminary trip from Pittsburgh to Camp Dubois, from August 30 to December 12, 1803, here called the Eastern Journal. In spite of a two-month gap, the entries cover a period of which little had previously been known. Besides the important information about this portion of the expedition, the notebook also contains extensive notes by Biddle, probably made during his visit with Clark in April 1810. The ninety-three pages of notes, rather than the daily entries in the Eastern Journal, might explain why Biddle retained the notebook. Actually, these notes are only the latter portion of the notes he made at Fincastle; the remainder are in a notebook like the marble-covered books, which forms another item of the Biddle family deposit. A great number of pages are missing from the front of that book and it is quite possible that the Orderly Book at St. Louis was once under the covers. Perhaps Biddle tore the orderly pages from the book at Fincastle to utilize the remaining blank pages, gave the orders to Clark, and when he had filled the unused pages simply continued his writing on blank pages of the Eastern Journal.[28]

After editor Quaife had completed his work of publishing the Eastern Journal and Ordway's journal, the Biddle family presented more expedition items to the society, but none were as exciting as Ordway's or the Eastern Journal. One group of manuscripts in that deposit, called the "three memo books," includes the Biddle notebook in which were written points of discussion with Clark at Fincastle in 1810 (the companion to the notes in the Eastern Journal), Clark's notebook with the first draft for January 6–10, 1806 (discussed above in connection with Codex T), and a journal kept by Clark on a trip to make a treaty with the Osages in 1808.[29]

The final manuscripts in the Biddle family's donation are called the "seven manuscript items." Five of those items—all in Clark's hand and never before published—will be included in this edition at appropriate spots: (1) "The Countrey and Rivers in advance or above the Mandans"; (2) and (4) "A Slight view of the Missouri River"; (3) "A Summary Statement of the Rivers & Creeks which fall into the Missouri"; and (5) "[A statistical?] view of the Indian Nations inhabiting the territory of Louisiana and the countries adjacent to its nothern and western boundaries." The first and third items are very similar to material in Lewis's Codex O and may have been preliminary notes for that codex. Items two and four appear to have once been a single document and will be combined when printed. The last item may have been a preliminary version of the tabular statement on the Eastern Indians. Of the two items that are not included in this edition, one (6) is labeled "Extracts from Capt. Mackay's Journal." It is printed elsewhere and is discussed in the introduction to this edition's *Atlas*. The final item (7) is a sheet that may have served as a wrapper for the other six pieces and is marked on one side in Clark's hand "For Mr Biddle." On the reverse it has some jottings by Clark in answer to queries by Biddle. The jottings may have been a draft for Clark's letter to Biddle of December 7, 1810, and the "seven manuscript items" were probably enclosures with that letter. Those items for the most part, then, were probably copied into Codex O and the Estimate of Eastern Indians during the stay at Fort Mandan.[30]

Why did Biddle retain the "seven manuscript items" instead of turning it over to the American Philosophical Society with the other expedition manuscripts in 1818? Recall that Clark had left Biddle "the best judge of the papers to be delivered" to the society. Biddle probably viewed the items as drafts that were duplicated in the notebooks that he gave to the society. Moreover, he may have considered them as Clark's personal papers since they came to him later and were not a part of the materials he received at Fincastle. Biddle probably did not return them to Clark through some oversight, similar to his keeping of Ordway's journal and the Eastern Journal. When Biddle placed expedition materials with the society in 1818, he noted that he was depositing the manuscripts that he had received from Clark in the spring of 1810—"the papers & documents deemed necessary for the publication of the Travels." Thus it seems that Biddle had separated the two groups of documents in his own mind as he had also separated them before his deposit.[31]

The history of the Clark Field Notes, as indicated in the Introduction to this volume, is both simple and mysterious. There seems no reason to doubt that those sixty-seven sheets, aptly described as "rough" notes, were written by Clark at Camp Dubois and on the journey up the Missouri on the dates given, as preliminary notes for his notebook journals. As explained in the Introduction, it seems likely though not certain that Clark sent the River Journal to Jefferson from Fort Mandan in April 1805, at the same time sending the Dubois Journal to his brother Jonathan Clark for safekeeping. Apparently he retrieved the River Journal from Jefferson on his return in 1807; at any rate, he evidently put the Dubois and River journals together at some time, for they were found in one bundle. Biddle evidently saw the River Journal in 1810, since he made notations of the dates on most of the sheets, but he either did not take them with him after visiting Fincastle that year or returned them to Clark later. How they made their way from Clark's possession to General Hammond's desk in St. Paul is unknown.[32]

The federal government sought to gain possession of the Field Notes after their discovery in 1953 on the ground that the expedition had been a government enterprise and all documents produced on the journey were public property. This doctrine, once established, could have applied equally well to the expedition documents at the American Philosophical Society and the Missouri Historical Society. Jefferson might have agreed, considering his statement that "the right to these papers is the government," but the federal courts did not sustain this view. The Field Notes are now in the keeping of the Beinecke Library at Yale University, along with most of the original maps.[33]

A final journal, here called Lewis's Astronomy Notebook, is a relatively new discovery that has never before been printed. This is apparently a child's copybook that Lewis used before the expedition when he visited Philadelphia and trained with Robert Patterson in taking astronomical observations. Patterson placed instructions and examples in the book, and it is filled with tables, charts, and explanations for celestial sightings in both men's hands. It even contains actual observations from May 20 and 21, 1805. It also includes a map by Lewis given him by Yellept, principal chief of the Wallas Wallas, about April 27, 1806, during the party's final days on the Columbia River. The map and observations will appear at appropriate places in this edition. The book's provenance before 1928 is a mystery. It was purchased in that year by the State Historical Society of Missouri, Columbia, from the heirs of William Clark Breckenridge (no relation to the captain), a noted St. Louis collector of Missouriana. It was first discovered by John Logan Allen, and the map was printed in his *Passage through the Garden*.[34]

Enlisted Men's Journals

Another of the large remaining questions concerning the journals of the Lewis and Clark expedition is whether the presently known records of the enlisted men are complete. Faced with a knowledge of repeated discoveries of expedition manuscripts over the years, no one would state unequivocally that we now have the total literary records of the expedition. Moreover, it is well known that there are great gaps in the subordinates' writings, as there are in the captains', and often in such a haphazard arrangement as to imply the existence of additional notes. The known journals of the enlisted men can be quickly but not definitively explained. Sergeant Patrick Gass's original journal is missing, and all that remains of his writing is the severely edited version done by McKeehan, which is discussed in the Introduction.

The journal of Sergeant Charles Floyd, at the State Historical Society of Wisconsin, is brief because the author died early in the trip (August 20, 1804) near present Sioux City, Iowa. Floyd's journal was probably sent to his relatives in Kentucky in April 1805 with the returning crew. Thwaites discovered Floyd's journal in 1893 among the papers of Lyman Draper, former head of the State Historical Society of Wisconsin, but it is not now clear how Draper came to have the journal. Draper received a large collection of Clark materials from John Croghan, Clark's nephew, and the Floyd journal may have been among those items. Draper also corresponded with Mary Lee Walton, a sister of Floyd, and she may have been the source for the journal, although nothing in their correspondence indicates it. Or, Draper may have gotten the journal from some unknown person at an unknown date. His records of acquisition are practically nonexistent, and the journal's provenance has long been lost.[35]

Private Joseph Whitehouse's journal is in two versions, both now at the Newberry Library, Chicago. The first version is the private's original manuscript and is in three parts bound under a single cover of animal hide, perhaps elkskin. The journal covers the period from May 14, 1804, to November 6, 1805. When Thwaites discovered the journal in 1903, it was in the hands of Gertrude Haley, whose acquisition of the notebook is somewhat obscure. Thwaites learned that about the time of his death (date unknown), Whitehouse gave the journal to Canon de Vivaldi, an Italian priest. In about 1860, Vivaldi deposited it with the New-York Historical Society where it remained until 1893, when he gave Mrs. Haley and her husband an order for it because the couple had advanced him some money. Thwaites became aware of its existence when Mrs. Haley attempted to sell it to the Library of Congress. He persuaded his publisher, Dodd, Mead, and Company, to make the purchase. After Thwaites completed his editing, the journal was sold to Edward Everett Ayer, a Chicago collector of rare books, who eventually donated it to the Newberry Library. The journal is largely in Whitehouse's handwriting, but Clark and at least two other persons have also written in the notebook. The journal contains a number of gaps, most notably from January 21 through April 30, 1805.[36]

In 1966 a paraphrased version of Whitehouse's journal was discovered in Philadelphia. That year, George W. White, a professor of geology from the University of Illinois, Urbana, was visiting Sessler's bookstore in the city and was shown the paraphrase. He informed Donald Jackson, a colleague at Illinois, of his find. Jackson had edited the *Letters of the Lewis and Clark Expedition* in 1962 and immediately realized the journal's significance. He reported the find to the Newberry Library and that institution soon purchased it. The paraphrased version is important for a number of reasons: it fills the gaps in Whitehouse's original piece; it extends the journal-keeping to April 2, 1806; and it reveals that the private probably kept a journal for the remainder of the expedition. This revelation is apparent from a notation preceding the entry of March 23, 1806, which reads, "Volume 2nd." The paraphrased notebook did not allow space for further entries after April 2, which may have been entered in another book now lost.[37]

The provenance of the paraphrased version is even more obscure than that of the original. The original cover of the notebook had a label that read, "Journal of Captains Lewis and Clark's Expedition. Written by Joseph Whitehouse. Property of E. Clarence Lighthall Mustin A.M. 5851." Before the words "Property of . . ." the words "Formerly the" have been added by another hand and then below

"5851" the phrase "Presented to George S. Mustin A.D. 1850." Jackson did a considerable amount of editing work on this journal but eventually decided that there was too little that was new to warrant its publication. It will appear in this edition. During his work Jackson attempted to discover more about Whitehouse and the Mustins but was largely unsuccessful. He also had little success in tracing the journal back beyond Sessler's bookstore because the previous owner of the journal had died. Perhaps someday more information will be discovered, or the remainder of the paraphrased version may be found, or even the whole of the original.[38]

An examination of Biddle's papers by his grandsons in 1913 led to the discovery of important expedition documents that Biddle, for some reason, had not turned over to the American Philosophical Society. The finding of one volume of the journal of Sergeant John Ordway, for which Thwaites had searched in vain, led to a further search, which turned up not only the rest of the Ordway journal but the Eastern Journal and other papers. Ordway's journal, covering every day of the expedition in three notebooks and written by one of the more literate enlisted men, provides a useful supplement to the captains' accounts. One notebook is a marble-covered piece like Codices A, B, Q, and R, while the others are bound with loose boards or left unbound. Biddle had use of the sergeant's journal while preparing the 1814 *History*, and a few words scribbled here and there in the books may be his writing. Clark had requested that Biddle return the three volumes to him after using them, because they had been purchased by Clark from the sergeant. Biddle failed to comply, perhaps through an oversight, and the books remained among his papers for a century.[39]

Lewis had directed all the sergeants to keep diaries, so we should assume that Sergeant Nathaniel Pryor—besides Gass, Floyd, and Ordway—kept a journal, but one has never been found, if it ever existed. Importantly, Clark had specifically directed Pryor to keep a journal when the men separated in July 1806, for Pryor to travel on a special mission to the Mandan Indian villages. Pryor's mission failed prematurely. When he reunited with Clark he discovered that he had left his saddlebags behind, which contained his "papers," but he was able to retrieve the bags before the day was out. Those "papers" may have been journals, but we have no journals by Pryor today. There is one other journal known to be missing—that of Private Robert Frazer—for which a prospectus was published in 1806, but no book ever appeared.

In all, we can count a total of six journals by enlisted men, yet Lewis wrote from Fort Mandan that seven of the men were keeping journals. Lewis may have been excluding Floyd since he had died earlier, leaving us to locate two other journalists. George Shannon has traditionally been thought to have kept a journal, but that seems doubtful. Shannon personally assisted Biddle at Philadelphia during work on the 1814 paraphrase, and although he praised the young man's intelligence and help, the editor never referred to a diary by Shannon, but he did allude to those of Ordway and Gass (the latter probably being the printed version rather than the original). There is some evidence that Private Alexander Willard kept a journal and that it was accidentally destroyed. It could be that Lewis was including Floyd in his count and thus only one other journalist has to be found, and that would be Willard. Lewis's seven journalists, then, would include: Gass, Ordway, Frazer, Pryor, Whitehouse, and perhaps Floyd and Willard.[40]

Notes

1. Jefferson to Corrèa da Serra, January 1, 1816, Jackson (LLC), 2:608.

2. Clark to Barton, May 22, 1810, Biddle to William Tilghman, April 6, 1818, ibid., 548–49, 636.

3. Jefferson to Corrèa da Serra, January 1 and July 20, 1816, Corrèa da Serra to Jefferson, March 29 and June 16, 1816, Jefferson to Clark, September 8, 1816, Jefferson to Peter S. Du Ponceau, November 7, 1817, ibid., 607–9, 615, 618–19, 631–33; APS (MCHL), November 19, 1817 [abstracted in Thwaites (LC), 7:405–6]. After Barton's death, Biddle also tried to recover the natural history journals. Biddle to Clark, May 29, 1816, Jackson (LLC), 2:614. The journals Barton used (Codices P, Q, and R) will be discussed in more detail below.

4. Cutright (LCPN), 349–92.

5. Jefferson to Clark, September 8, 1816, Clark to Biddle and Clark to Jefferson, October 10, 1816, Clark to Biddle, October 17, 1816, and January 27, 1818, Jackson (LLC), 2:619, 623–26, 634–35; Cutright (HLCJ), 68–70.

6. Biddle to William Tilghman, April 6, 1818, John Vaughan to Biddle, April 8, 1818, Jackson (LLC), 2:635–37; APS (MCHL), April 8, 1818 [also in Thwaites (LC), 7:406–7].

7. Vaughan to Biddle, April 8, 1818, Jackson (LLC), 2:637.

8. The quote is from Cutright and Brodhead, 345. The report of his finding is from Coues (DOMJ), 18–19. Codices P, Q, and R were Jefferson's deposit of 1817, the remaining journals were deposited by Biddle in 1818. Coues's description also lists six items associated with the period of Biddle's deposit. One is a letter from Biddle to William Tilghman, April 6, 1818, Jackson (LLC), 2:635–37. Two pieces are memoranda of the deposits by Jefferson and Biddle, apparently in John Vaughan's hand. Another is Biddle's notes on intended illustrations in his work. A final paper, again apparently in Vaughan's hand, appears to be an abstract of Jefferson's recollection in 1816 of the Lewis and Clark manuscripts. The final item is an engraved copperplate of "The Fisher," which Coues thought had no connection with Lewis and Clark. Coues (DOMJ), 31–32.

9. Clark's cross-references from the expedition included entries for May 14 (Field Notes), September 16 (Field Notes), and October 2, 1804, and May 10, 1805. References in Codices Fb, Fd, La, and Lb by Clark all use Biddle's numbers to explain where those journals fit into the regular notebooks.

10. The regular daily journals designated Codices A–N and the double-lettered items have been discussed in the Introduction, under the journal-keeping methods of Lewis and Clark. The specialized journals are discussed in Moulton, 194–201.

11. Lewis and Clark Account, May 3, 1807 (to Hassler), Clark to Hassler, January 26, 1810, Biddle to Tilghman, April 6, 1818, Jackson (LLC), 2:462, 463 n. 4, 491–92, 636; Coues (DOMJ), 28–29.

12. Coues and Thwaites believed that Codex O was sent to Jefferson in April 1805. Coues (DOMJ), 28–29; Thwaites (LC), 6:263.

13. Hassler to [Robert Patterson?], August 12, 1818, Biddle to [Vaughan?], [ca. October 13, 1818], Jackson (LLC), 2:557, 560–61.

14. Jefferson's efforts are revealed in his correspondence of November and December 1817 in ibid., and in APS (MCHL), November and December 1817. The quote about Hassler is from APS (MCHL), November 19, 1817 [also in Thwaites (LC), 7:405]. Biddle to William Tilghman, April 6, 1818, John Vaughan to Biddle, April 8, 1818, Jackson (LLC), 2:635–37; APS (MCHL), April 8, 1818 [also in Thwaites (LC), 7:406–407]. Coues called Codex O an "unknown deposit" and "not deposited by Biddle; perhaps by Jefferson." He failed to notice in Biddle's list of his deposit and in the society's accession records one notebook that was listed as a "volume of astronomical observations & other matter by Captain Lewis." This was Codex O and was acknowledged as such by Thwaites in his annotation of the reprint of Coues's description. Coues (DOMJ), 20, 28; Thwaites (LC), 7:414 n. 1.

15. Coues did not seem to realize this shift in the person of the copyist; at least he named Clark as the author of the codex in his "Description." However, someone (probably Coues) has scratched out the word "Clark" on the note attached to the codex and has written: "another hand." Thwaites believed that the handwriting was Clark's "at a much later period [since] the handwriting corresponds to his later habit." No significant difference has been discovered between Clark's writing of 1806 and 1810 and Clark's hand clearly stands out at those places where he has written. Coues (DOMJ), 29; Thwaites (LC), 6:136. Biddle's recollection in later years about the notebooks given to Barton was "not as accurate as it would have been had they fallen more immediately under [his] examination." His words seem to indicate that he had nothing to do with the copying. Biddle to William Tilghman, April 6, 1818, Jackson (LLC), 2:635–36.

16. Coues credited Clark as the author for both Codices Q and R. Although Thwaites realized that the codices were copies of existing notes, he, like Coues, failed to notice the new handwriting and he, too, called Clark the author. Coues (DOMJ), 30; Thwaites (LC), 6:135, 141.

17. The letters are in Thwaites (LC), 7:331–37, and Jackson (LLC), 1:317–25. Jackson's discussion of the letters was of considerable help in this interpretation of Codex S. Coues (DOMJ), 30–31.

18. Quaife (MLJO), 26.

19. This field notebook appears to have come into the American Philosophical Society after Quaife's publication. Clark's journal-writing of January 6–10, 1806, is repeated in Codex I.

20. Coues called Codex T "a mere excerpt, without proper beginning or end, speaking

of geographical and other matters of no special consequence." He thought it in Clark's hand but was troubled that the text speaks of Clark in the third person, but Clark spoke of himself in the third person throughout the final portion of the notebook. Thwaites, also without access to the field notebook, printed Codex T as an individual piece in his miscellaneous volume. He noted that the single sheet had been inserted into its cover by the wrong edge and that one has to begin reading on the second page for it to make sense. For unknown reasons, Thwaites divided Codex T into two widely separated pieces and neglected to identify the second piece as coming from this codex. Coues (DOMJ), 31; Thwaites (LC), 6:78–79, 268.

21. Coues (HLC), 3:1264–98; Thwaites (LC), 6:165–87. Thwaites combined the two versions in his edition.

22. Thwaites (LC), 6:80–120. The Weather Diary and the estimates were discovered by I. M. Hays of the society; he alerted Thwaites to their existence and the diary was included in Thwaites's edition. Cutright (HLCJ), 111–12.

23. Cutright (HLCJ), 117–18; Thwaites (LC), 1:l–li.

24. Cutright (HLCJ), 118–19; Thwaites (LC), 1:li–liii. The Elkskin-bound Journal is also discussed in the Introduction.

25. The material for April is printed in Thwaites (LC), 4:288–311. Although Thwaites did not print the July–August material in full, he did substitute certain items from it for the codex material. See ibid., 5:263 n. 1, 303 n. 1, 311 n. 1. He also printed a map from the fragment without identifying its source (ibid., 270). There are a number of other miscellaneous items in the Voorhis Collection, some published by Thwaites and others that will be published for the first time in this edition. They are listed in Appendix C under "Miscellaneous Documents of Lewis and Clark."

26. Ibid., 1:liii–lv. Biddle's notes in Voorhis No. 4 are printed in Jackson (LLC), 2:555. In 1826, in what may have been Clark's last word on the journals, he wrote, "neither do I recollect any copies [of journals] retained by me at Saint Louis, except the Original Map [*Atlas* map 125]." Clark to Albert Gallatin, March 31, 1826, Jackson (LLC), 2:643–45. Perhaps he simply forgot his notebooks that have become the Voorhis Collection.

27. Society records show that the Biddle family items were deposited between 1915 and 1917 and for a short time in 1917 were recalled by the family. In 1949 the entire lot was formally presented to the society. The family also donated the six copper plates that were the originals used to print the maps in Biddle's 1814 edition. APS (MCL), February 16 and August 19, 1915, February 24, May 15, and November 1, 1917; APS (YB), 87, 94.

28. Cutright (HLCJ), 131, 137–43. The Eastern Journal is identical in physical appearance to Codex C. Jackson was the person who discovered Biddle's use of the Eastern Journal and the companion notebook for taking notes. He printed Biddle's notes and they will not be repeated in this work. Jackson (LLC), 2:497–545.

29. Clark's Osage diary is printed in Gregg.

30. Quaife (ECMJ), 186–210; Clark to Biddle, December 7, 1810, January 24, 1811, Jackson (LLC), 2:562–66.

31. Clark to Biddle, October 17, 1816, Biddle to Tilghman, April 6, 1818, Jackson (LLC), 2:626, 635.

32. Cutright (HLCJ), 145–52; Osgood (FN), xxix. See Introduction, this volume, on the discovery of the Dubois and River journals at St. Paul, Minnesota, in 1953.

33. Cutright (HLCJ), 152–63; Tomkins, passim.

34. Information of the State Historical Society of Missouri, July 31, 1983. The map is in Allen, 340. The Astronomy Notebook may be the "statistical table" that Patterson refers to in Patterson to Jefferson, June 18, 1803, Jackson (LLC), 1:56.

35. Cutright (HLCJ), 90–91, 104–27; Butler, 225–52; Walton to Draper, October 5, 1872, William D. Meriwether to Draper, October 3, 1872, Draper Collection, State Historical Society of Wisconsin, Madison; Josephine Harper, interview with the editor, State Historical Society of Wisconsin, July 16, 1982.

36. Cutright (HLCJ), 113–15.

37. Ibid., 242–64. Cutright has here written an excellent essay on the paraphrase and compares it to the original in an extensive discussion.

38. Ibid., 242–48; Jackson to editor, December 9, 1982 (with enclosures detailing his efforts). The Newberry Library has replaced the original cover on the paraphrase, but it is pictured in Jackson (LLC), vol. 2, after p. 566. The cryptic "A.M. 5851" probably stands for *anno mundi*, which, using Bishop Ussher's system of dating creation at 4004 B.C., would make the date 1847 A.D.

39. Thwaites (LC) 1:l; Quaife (MLJO), 26; Cutright (HLCJ), 128–33; APS (MCL). Within one volume of Ordway's journal were found two separate sheets of paper. One is a list of "Comercial Posts" in Lewis's hand, probably a postexpeditionary piece on which Lewis speculated about possible posts after 1806. The other item is a torn sheet of letter paper on which a small portion of the "Multonomah" (Willamette) River is shown and notes by Clark and Lewis that are nearly the same as some notes Clark made on a map in Codex M. A comparison between the two versions of notes will be made at the appropriate place in this edition.

40. Lewis's Orderly Book entry, May 26, 1804; Thwaites (LC), 1:xxxiv, xxxix–xl, liv–lv; Lewis to Jefferson, April 7, 1805, Jackson (LLC), 1:232; Clark's entries, July 23 and August 8, 1806; Frazer's Prospectus, [October 1806], Jackson (LLC), 1:345–46; Cutright (HLCJ), 9, 60, 242 n. 3; Biddle to Clark, July 7, 1810, July 8, 1811, Jackson (LLC), 2:551, 569. On Willard's possible journal, see Wheeler, 1:124 and Betts (WE), 7–8, 8 n. 34. Betts has an interesting discussion of the subordinates' journals and disagrees with the assumption that Floyd was counted as one of the seven. However, he does not speculate on the identity of the missing diarist.

Appendix C

Calendar of Journals
and Manuscripts

This calendar does not account for the many scattered entries in the journals and manuscripts that are not in proper sequence. Such misplaced entries will be noted at the point of their placement in the edition. The heading for each item dates the journals according to major writings; significant contents are then noted sequentially. The material is arranged by the final dated entry, thus some beginning dates will appear to be out of order. Exceptions to this arrangement will include material that is a first or rough draft, which will precede the regular journal. Thus, Clark's Field Notes will precede the finished journals (i.e., Codices A and B) that cover early portions of the time period; and the Elkskin-bound Journal will come before Codices G, H, and I. Coues's arrangement of the journal fragments (Codices Aa, Ba, Fa, Fb, Fc, Fd, Fe, Ia, La, and Lb) has been maintained, although such ordering does not fit this scheme. Other journals (such as Codices O, P, Q, and R) do not follow Coues's ordering, while Codex S (drafts of letters) has been dropped because it is not journal material. Codex T is not listed here separately but is included with other materials with which it belongs (see First Draft, January 6–10, 1806). Undated tabulated and collated material (e.g. Estimate of Eastern Indians) was probably put together by the captains at stopping places like Fort Mandan and Fort Clatsop and such undated items will follow regular journals covering those periods.

The size given for the documents is the page or paper size, with the larger dimension always given first. The covers of notebooks are usually one-eighth to one-quarter inch larger. The total given for notebook pages occasionally varies from Coues's count due to his numbering of flyleaves on which the captains had written and his counting of missing sheets when they were apparent. The enlisted men's journals are listed in the order in which they will appear in this edition.

ABSTRACT OF LEWIS'S AND CLARK'S DAILY JOURNALS

Lewis	*Clark*

Eastern Journal
August 30–September 18, 1803
November 11–28, 1803

Eastern Journal
November 28–December 12, 1803

Field Notes (Dubois Journal)
December 13, 1803–February 9, 1804
March 21–May 14, 1804

Field Notes (River Journal)
May 14, 1804–April 3, 1805

Codex A
May 13–August 14, 1804

Codex Aa
May 15 and 20, 1804

Codex B
August 15–October 3, 1804

Codex Ba
September 16–17, 1804

Codex C
October 1, 1804–April 7, 1805

Codex D
April 7–May 23, 1805

Voorhis No. 1
April 7–July 3, 1805

Codex E
May 24–July 16, 1805

Codex F
July 17–August 22, 1805

Codex Fa
August 1–4, 1805

Codex Fb
August 23–26, 1805

Codex Fc
September 9–10, 1805

Codex Fd
September 18–22, 1805

Lewis	*Clark*

Elkskin-bound Journal
September 11–December 31, 1805

Codex G
July 1–October 10, 1805

Codex H
October 11–November 19, 1805

First Draft
January 6–10, 1806

Codex I
November 19, 1805–January 29, 1806

Codex Ia
November 29–December 1, 1805

Codex J
January 1–March 20, 1806

Voorhis No. 2
January 30–April 3, 1806

Codex K
March 21–May 23, 1806

First Draft
April 16–21, 1806

Voorhis No. 3
April 4–June 6, 1806

Codex L
May 24–July 4, 1806
July 15–August 8, 1806

Codex La
July 3–15, 1806

Codex Lb
August 9–12, 1806

First Draft
July 13–19, 1806
July 24–August 3, 1806

Codex M
June 7–August 14, 1806

Codex N
August 15–September 26, 1806

LIST OF ABBREVIATIONS

CtY   Frederick W. and Carrie S. Beinecke Collection of Western Americana, or William Robertson Coe Collection, Yale University, New Haven, Connecticut

DNA   Record Group 64 (Planning and Control Case File), National Archives and Records Service, Washington, D.C.

ICN   Edward Everett Ayer Collection, Newberry Library, Chicago, Illinois

MoHi   James M. Breckenridge Collection, State Historical Society of Missouri, Columbia

MoSHi   Eleanor Glasgow Voorhis Memorial Collection, Missouri Historical Society, St. Louis

PPAmP   American Philosophical Society, Philadelphia, Pennsylvania

ViU   Lewis-Marks Papers, Alderman Library, University of Virginia, Charlottesville

WHi   Lyman Draper Collection, State Historical Society of Wisconsin, Madison

CALENDAR OF JOURNALS AND MANUSCRIPTS

Major Documents of Lewis and Clark

Eastern Journal, August 30–December 12, 1803, Lewis, Clark, and Biddle
  PPAmP; Quaife (MLJO), 31–76; Biddle family's deposit; brown, leather-covered book, 256 pages (10 sheets apparently cut out; unpaged); 8″ × 4¾″; includes Lewis's journalizing, August 30–September 18, 1803, about 30 pages left blank by Lewis that were filled with notes by Biddle in 1810, Lewis's journalizing November 11–28, 1803, Clark's journalizing, November 28–December 12, 1803, and Biddle's notes for the remainder of the notebook; for Biddle's notes, see Jackson (LLC), 2:497–545; illustrations of sandbars.

Field Notes (Dubois Journal), December 13, 1803–May 14, 1804, Clark
  CtY; Osgood (FN), 3–38; Beinecke's deposit; 12 individual sheets of letter paper of various sizes; only journal account of winter at Camp Dubois; gap from February 10 to March 20, 1804, while Clark away from camp; illustrations of keel boat and pirogue; maps of confluence of Ohio and Mississippi rivers and confluence of Mississippi and Missouri rivers.

Field Notes (River Journal), May 14, 1804–April 3, 1805, Clark (and occasionally
    Lewis)
  CtY; Osgood (FN), 41–188; Beinecke's deposit; 55 individual sheets of letter paper of various sizes; from November 6, 1804, to April 3, 1805 the entries are less frequent and somewhat briefer; illustrations of manitou, manitou-buffalo-Indian together, boy's profile, horse, and man with a pipe; maps of area about Little Osage Women's Creek, area about Osage River, from Osage River to the two Charitons, area about Kansas River with conjectural extensions, area of Bonhomme Island, area near present Fort Randall dam, Big Bend of Missouri River, and area below Cannonball River with country to the east to the Red River.

Codex A, May 13–August 14, 1804, Clark
  PPAmP; Thwaites (LC), 1:3, 7, 16–110, 6:3–5; Biddle's deposit No. 1; Clark's journal No. 1; marble-covered book, 184 pages; 6½″ × 3¾″; includes Clark's table of distances from the mouth of the Missouri to "Big Sioux River" (front flyleaf), Clark's note on country about mouth of Missouri River (pp. 2–3), Clark's journalizing, May 13–August 14, 1804 (pp. 3–179), some latitude readings (pp. 180–81), and astronomical observations (pp. 182–83); illustration of a manitou (p. 34).

Codex Aa, May 20 and 15, 1804, Lewis

PPAmP; Thwaites (LC), 1:17, 22–25; Biddle's deposit; no number; 8 pages from one of the red books; 7⅞″ × 4⅛″; "Part of No. 1 [*i.e., Codex A*]" (p. 8) in unknown handwriting (perhaps Clark).

Codex B, August 15–October 3, 1804, Clark

PPAmP; Thwaites (LC), 1:110–78, 6:136; Biddle's deposit No. 2; Clark's journal No. 2; marble-covered book, 180 pages; 6½″ × 3¾″; brief note on Corvus bird (p. 2) and money due party members, September 4, 1804 (inside back cover).

Codex Ba, September 16 and 17, 1804, Lewis

PPAmP; Thwaites (LC), 1:150–51, 152–54; Biddle's deposit, no number; 8 pages from one of the red books; 7⅞″ × 4⅞″; "This a part of No. 2 [*i.e., Codex B*]" (p. 8) in unknown handwriting (perhaps Clark).

Codex R, May 10–November 17, 1804, Lewis

PPAmP; Thwaites (LC), 6:135–36, 141–51, 164; Jefferson's deposit from Barton's estate); marble-covered book, 164 pages; 6½″ × 3¾″; includes Lewis's botanical register, May 10–November 17, 1804 (pp. 4–49), Lewis's zoological note, December 18, 1805 (pp. 50–53), copies of natural history material by an unknown person from other journals, February 18–March 11, 1806 (pp. 59–162), and Lewis's note on "Lava," September 20, 1804 (p. 163); illustration of "convolvalist" leaf (p. 37).

Codex C, October 1, 1804–April 7, 1805, Clark (and occasionally Lewis)

PPAmP; Thwaites (LC), 1:4, 7, 176–286, 6:56–60, 165–88, 268, 269, 270–79; Biddle's deposit No. 3; Clark's journal No. 3; brown, leather-covered notebook, 276 pages (total varies from page numbers); 8″ × 4¾″; includes Clark's journalizing, October 1, 1804–February 2, 1805 (pp. 2–160), Lewis's journalizing, February 3–13, 1805, while Clark was absent (pp. 160–74), Clark's journalizing, February 3–March 21, 1805 (pp. 174–98), Lewis's entry for March 16, 1805 (pp. 199–202), Clark's journalizing, March 22–April 7, 1805 (pp. 202–14), Clark's weather diary, January 1, 1804–April 7, 1805 (gap from May 15 to September 19, 1804) (pp. 216–46, reading backward), Clark's "The Distances of Sunday places with the Latiduds anexed" (p. 247), Clark's "A Summary Statement of the Rivers, Creeks and most remarkable places . . . in the year 1804 . . . [with additional names from Indian information, 1804–1805]" (pp. 248–53, reading backward), "Baling Invoice of Sundries for Indian Presents," in unknown handwriting (pp. 256–74, reading backward), and Clark's "The names of the Forts or British Trading Establishments on the Ossiniboine" (inside back cover); illustrations of war hatchet (p. 158) and battle ax (p. 165); map of Mississippi, Minnesota, and Red rivers (p. 255).

Weather Diary, January 1, 1804–April 9, 1805, Lewis and Clark

PPAmP; Thwaites (LC), 6:137–40, 165–87; Biddle's deposit, no number; red, blue, and yellow (marbled) paper-covered notebook, 60 pages (unpaged); 7¾" × 6¼"; notebook that Lewis had used some years earlier without filling; includes some botanical notes, undated (ca. 1803–1804), Lewis's accounts as a paymaster in 1800, Lewis's travel notes in 1800 and 1801, and Lewis and Clark's weather diary, January 1, 1804–April 9, 1805 (gap from May 15 to September 19, 1804).

Codex O, Astronomical Observations, May 18, 1804–March 30, 1805, and "A Summary view of the Rivers and Creeks, which discharge thems[elves] into the Missouri . . ." undated (ca. April 1805), Lewis

PPAmP; Thwaites (LC), 6:230–62, 29–55; Biddle's deposit (from Hassler), no number; one of the red books, 122 pages (total varies from page numbers); 7⅞" × 4⅞"; probably sent to Jefferson in April 1805; includes Lewis's description of astronomical instruments, July 22, 1804 (pp. 1–6), Lewis's observations, May 18, 1804–March 30, 1805 (pp. 6–52), and Lewis's "A Summary view . . ." (pp. 69–128).

Estimate of Eastern Indians, undated (ca. April 1805), Clark

PPAmP; Thwaites (LC), 6:80–113; Biddle's deposit, no number; 7 sheets or pieces of letter paper pasted together to form one large sheet; 35" × 28" (size varies slightly); probably a copy of a similar estimate (now lost) sent to Jefferson in April 1805, and which appeared in his *Message from the President . . .* (1806) in a section entitled "A Statistical View of Indian Nations inhabiting the Territory of Louisiana and the Countries adjacent to its northern and Western boundaries."

Codex D, April 7–May 23, 1805, Lewis

PPAmP; Thwaites (LC), 1:283–373, 2:3–65, 6:192–93; Biddle's deposit No. 4; one of the red books, 140 pages; 7⅞" × 4⅞"; includes Lewis's journalizing, April 7–May 23, 1805 (pp. 3–139) and Lewis's weather remarks for June 1805 (p. 140) which page goes with Codex Fe.

Voorhis No. 1, April 7–July 3, 1805, Clark (and occasionally Lewis)

MoSHi; Thwaites (LC), 1:287–374, 2:5–209, 6:5–8; Voorhis's deposit; Clark's journal No. 4; one of the red books, 172 pages (unpaged; perhaps 10 sheets added: at May 25 and 31, after June 17, and second May 31 entry at end of book); 7⅞" × 4⅞"; includes Lewis's notes on Indians, undated (front flyleaf), Clark's journalizing, April 7–June 17, 1805, "The mule Deer Described in Book No. 8 [*i.e, Voorhis No.* 2]" apparently in Clark's hand, Lewis's entry for part of May 14, 1805, Clark's courses around the Great Falls of the Missouri River, June 17–19, 1805, "rest Continues 10 pages back [*i.e., rest of June 20 entry*]" in unknown handwriting (perhaps Clark), Clark's journalizing, June 17–July 3, 1805,

Clark's second entry for May 31, 1805, and Clark's notes on "Portage No. 1" (end flyleaf); illustration of bighorn; maps of Falls and Portage of Missouri, Great Falls of Missouri, "Handsom" Falls of Missouri, and Upper Falls of Missouri.

Codex E, May 24–July 16, 1805, Lewis

PPAmP; Thwaites (LC), 2:67–235, 6:5–8; Biddle's deposit No. 5; one of the red books, 156 pages (2 sheets added, pp. 131–34); 7⅞″ × 4⅞″; includes Lewis's copies of Clark's notes from Voorhis No. 1 for periods when the two were separated, June 4–8 (pp. 50–53), June 11–16 (pp. 84–92), June 17–20 (pp. 98–103), and Clark's survey notes of Great Falls of Missouri by Lewis (pp. 103–6); map of "Draught of the Falls and Portage" (pp. 132–33).

Codex F, July 17–August 22, 1805, Lewis

PPAmP; Thwaites (LC), 2:238–385, 3:3–16; Biddle's deposit No. 5; one of the red books, 152 pages (total varies from page numbers); 7⅞″ × 4⅞″; "This part to come in on the 20th, related to Capt. C thro the interpreter" (p. 104) apparently in Clark's handwriting; illustrations of Indian smoking-pipe (p. 99) and fish weir (p. 147).

Codex Fa, August 1–4, 1805, Lewis

PPAmP; Thwaites (LC), 2:292–307; Biddle's deposit, no number; 8 pages from one of the red books; 7⅞″ × 4⅞″; Lewis's journalizing, August 1–4, 1805 and the date "August 5th 1805" without additional writing.

Codex Fb, August 23–26, 1805, Lewis

PPAmP; Thwaites (LC), 3:17–43; Biddle's deposit, no number; 26 pages from one of the red books; 7⅞″ × 4⅞″; "this Comes into No. 7 [i.e., Codex G] between the 23d and 26 August 1805" and "This has been Copied from W. C. Journal and Coms in as above in No. 7" (p. 26) both apparently in Clark's handwriting.

Codex Fc, September 9 and 10, 1805, Lewis

PPAmP; Thwaites (LC), 3:57–61; Biddle's deposit, no number; 4 pages from one of the red books; 7⅞″ × 4⅞″; these pages were torn from Codex P and match with words in Lewis's hand on p. 80 of that codex, which continue the writing for the entry of September 10.

Codex Fd, September 18–22, 1805, Lewis

PPAmP; Thwaites (LC), 3:71–83; Biddle's deposit, no number; 8 pages from one of the red books; 7⅞″ × 4⅞″; "(This is a part of Book No. 7 [i.e., Codex G] to be referred to and examined after the 9th Sept. 1805.—[)]" (p. 8) apparently in Clark's handwriting and "look forward 4 leaves" (p. 8) apparently in Biddle's handwriting; the latter note in Biddle's hand is upside down to the other writing on the page and may refer to a note by Biddle on p. 3 or one on p. 5, both of which read "copy for Dr Barton."

Codex Fe, April–September 1805, Lewis (and occasionally Clark)

PPAmP; Thwaites (LC), 6:185–98; Biddle's deposit, no number; two fragments from the red books; 7⅞″ × 4⅞″; one fragment of 10 pages comes from Codex D and is weather diary, April 1–June 30, 1805 (the weather remarks for June are found in Codex D, p. 140); the other fragment of 6 pages is from another red book and is weather diary, July 1–September 30, 1805 (Clark wrote the separate "remarks" for July and August entries, the rest is in Lewis's handwriting).

Codex P, July–September 1805, Lewis (and occasionally Clark)

PPAmP; Thwaites (LC), 6:136, 169–71, 193–98, 269–70; Jefferson's deposit (from Barton's estate); one of the red books, 124 pages (total varies from page numbers); 7⅞″ × 4⅞″; includes Lewis's weather notes, February–March 1804 (flyleaf and p. 1), copies of natural history material from other journals (partially by Clark but largely by an unknown person), April 9, 1805–February 17, 1806 (pp. 13–124), notes upside down by Lewis that continue writing for September 10, 1805, in Codex Fc (p. 80), two sheets cut out that become Codex Fc, Lewis's weather diary, July 1–September 30, 1805, which Clark apparently wrote for September 21–30 (pp. 125–31, reading backward), Lewis's miscellaneous memorandum, undated (ca. January–May 1804) (p. 133), and Lewis's financial memoranda, December 1803–March 1804 (end flyleaf); illustration of an Indian digging instrument (p. 92), which was probably copied from Codex I, p. 135.

Elkskin-bound Journal, September 11–December 31, 1805, Clark

MoSHi; Thwaites (LC), 3:62–300, 6:22–23; Voorhis's deposit; only such journal of its kind, handsewn, and bound in rough elkskin, 224 pages (unpaged); 6¼″ × 4¼″; Lewis seems to have made only one notation in the notebook, when he wrote some course and distance matter for November 5, 1805; "Presented to J. J. Audubon at St. Louis April 19th 1843—by D. D. Mitchell—Supt. Indian Affairs" (last page) in unknown handwriting (perhaps Mitchell); illustrations of shape of a hut door, flounder, and native hat; 19 maps that show short stretches of travel from Travelers' Rest and along the Lolo Trail to the confluence of the Columbia and Snake rivers, then to the confluence of the Columbia and Deschutes rivers (maps also show the area around Fort Clatsop and other nearby areas).

Codex G, July 1–October 10, 1805, Clark

PPAmP; Thwaites (LC), 2:203–386, 3:9–106, 6:9–21; Biddle's deposit No. 7; Clark's journal No. 5; one of the red books, 152 pages; 7⅞″ × 4⅞″; includes some distance and latitude notations by Clark (flyleaf and p. 1, reading backward) and Clark's journalizing, July 1–October 10, 1805.

Codex H, October 11–November 19, 1805, Clark

PPAmP; Thwaites (LC), 3:108–235, 6:263–64; Biddle's deposit No. 8; perhaps Clark's journal No. 6; one of the red books, 152 pages; 7⅞″ × 4⅞″; includes Clark's journalizing, October 11–November 19, 1805 (pp. 5–152), Clark's "The Course's Distances and Remarks Decending the Lewis's river from the mouth of Koskoskia . . ." (pp. 15–22), and Clark's "Course Distance & Remarks Decending the Columbia River from the Lewis's River . . . to the Great Pacific Ocean—" (pp. 132–48); "See another book [*i.e., Codex I*] for perticulars" (p. 152) probably Clark's handwriting; illustration of shape of a hut door (p. 63); maps of Great Falls of the Columbia (flyleaf and p. 1), Long and Short Narrows of the Columbia (pp. 2–3), Great Rapids of the Columbia (p. 4), and confluence of Columbia and Snake rivers (p. 33).

Codex Q, July 30, 1804–ca. December 18, 1805, Lewis

PPAmP; Thwaites (LC), 6:122–35; Jefferson's deposit (from Barton's estate); marble-covered book, 184 pages; 6½″ × 3¾″; includes Lewis's zoological notes, August 2, 1804–ca. December 18, 1805 (pp. 4–56) and copies of natural history material by an unknown person from other journals, March 11–August 10, 1806, with additional material from August and September 1804, and February 1805 (pp. 57–181); illustrations of iron scimitar (p. 88) and bone fishhook (p. 111), both probably copies from regular journals (Codex K, pp. 14 and 83 or Voorhis No. 2 and No. 3).

Detachment Orders, February 20, 1804–January 1, 1806, Lewis, Clark, and Ordway

MoSHi; Thwaites (LC), 1:7–193, 3:302–4; Voorhis's deposit; 70 pages from one of the marble-covered books; 6½″ × 3¾″; two orders by Lewis (February 20 and March 3, 1804) on letter paper are not included in the notebook; one fragment of letter paper carries part of an order by Clark (April 7, 1804) that is given in full in the notebook; orders for April 7, 21, May 4, 16, and 17, 1804, are in Ordway's handwriting, orders for May 26, July 8, August 26, 28, 1804, and January 1, 1806, are in Lewis's handwriting, orders for June 29 and October 8, 1804, are in Clark's handwriting, and orders for July 12 and October 13, 1804, are partly written by Lewis and partly by Clark.

First Draft, January 6–10, 1806, Clark (and occasionally Lewis)

PPAmP; unpublished; Biddle family's deposit; sheets are letter paper cut to size, 48 pages (unpaged); 6″ × 4″ (size varies slightly); includes Clark's "Distances of the mouthes of Rivers Creeks and Most remarkable places from Fort Mandan & Lattiduds in 1805," cf. Thwaites (LC), 6:61–70, Clark's journalizing, January 6–10, 1806 (given as 1805), Clark's "Distances" continued, which includes "along the Seacost to the N. W. by N," cf. Thwaites (LC), 6:70, "From the Warciacum upper village . . . ," cf. Thwaites (LC), 6:69, and "along the coast [S. S. E.]," cf. Thwaites (LC), 6:71, Clark's astronomical observation, January 31, 1806 (with some notes by Lewis), Clark's course and distance calculations, undated (ca. January 1806), Clark's summary of party's route across the continent and return (here Codex T comes in at the end), undated (ca. August 1806); illustration of "skaite"; map of Clark's route to whale site on Pacific coast.

Codex I, November 19, 1805–January 29, 1806, Clark (and occasionally Lewis)
    PPAmP; Thwaites (LC), 3:235–363, 4:4–23, 6:61–72, 113–20, 185–205; Biddle's deposit No. 9; perhaps Clark's journal No. 7; one of the red books, 156 pages (perhaps 2 sheets added, pp. 153–56); 7⅞" × 4⅞"; includes Clark's "Estimated Distances . . . [from Fort Mandan to Pacific Coast]" (pp. 2–12), Clark's weather diary, April 1, 1805–January 31, 1806 (pp. 13–33), Clark's journalizing, November 19, 1805–January 29, 1806 (pp. 34–144), "See Book No. 8 [*i.e.,* *Voorhis No.* 2]" (p. 145) probably Clark's handwriting, Clark's extra entries for January 1–3, 1806 (pp. 145–46, reading backward), Clark's "Estimate of Western Indians" (pp. 147, 150–51, 153–55, reading backward), Lewis's "Estimate of Western Indians" (pp. 148–49, reading backward), and Clark's "A List of the names as given by the Indians of the Traders . . ." (p. 156); illustrations of native hat (p. 80), barb (p. 119), bone fishhook and line (p. 122), digging instrument (p. 135), native hat (p. 144), and knife (p. 144); maps of Point William (p. 11) and mouth of Columbia River (p. 152).

Codex Ia, November 29–December 1, 1805, Lewis
    PPAmP; Thwaites (LC), 3:255–62; Biddle's deposit, no number; 10 pages perhaps from one of the marble-covered books; 6½" × 3⅝"; includes Lewis's journalizing, November 29–December 1, 1805 (pp. 1–6, 8–9) and "Capt. Lewis rough notes when he left Capt. Clark near the mouth of Columbia for a few days to examine the S. W. side" (p. 10) apparently in Clark's handwriting; map of Point Adams (p. 7).

Codex J, January 1–March 20, 1806, Lewis
    PPAmP; Thwaites (LC), 3:301–62, 4:3–193, 6:202–11; Biddle's deposit No. 10; one of the red books, 152 pages; 7⅞" × 4⅞"; includes Lewis's journalizing, January 1–March 20, 1806 (pp. 3–145) and Lewis's weather diary, January 1–March 31, 1806 (pp. 145–52, reading backward); 21 illustrations showing the material culture of coastal Indians and local flora and fauna; 6 illustrations stand out for their artistic worth (cf. Voorhis No. 2): head of a vulture (p. 80), eulachon (p. 93), head of a cock of the plains (p. 107), head of a white gull (p. 115), head of a brant (p. 131), and salmon trout (p. 133).

Estimate of Western Indians, undated (ca. March 1806), Clark

PPAmP; Thwaites (LC), 6:113–20; Biddle's deposit, no number; 4 sheets of letter paper; 13½″ × 9½″; map of area of Bonhomme Island.

Voorhis No. 2, January 30–April 3, 1806, Clark

MoSHi; Thwaites (LC), 4:25–242, 6:205–11; Voorhis's deposit; Clark's journal No. 8; one of the red books, 152 pages (unpaged); 7⅞″ × 4⅞″; includes Clark's journalizing, January 30–April 3, 1806, Clark's weather diary, February 1–March 31, 1806, and Clark's table of "Longitude to each Degree of Latitude from the Equator to the pole" (end flyleaf); 23 illustrations showing the material culture of coastal Indians and local flora and fauna; one illustration stands out for its ethnological interest: Clark's illustration of Clatsop head-flattening techniques and results (front flyleaf); 6 illustrations stand out for their artistic worth (cf. Codex J): head of a vulture, eulachon, cock of the plains, head of a white gull, head of a brant, and salmon trout; map of area about confluence of Willamette and Columbia rivers.

Codex K, March 21–May 23, 1806, Lewis

PPAmP; Thwaites (LC), 4:194–369, 5:3–59, 6:212–18; Biddle's deposit No. 11; one of the red books, 152 pages; 7⅞″ × 4⅞″; includes Lewis's journalizing, March 21–May 23, 1806 (pp. 1–147) and Lewis's weather diary, April 1–May 31, 1806 (pp. 147–52, reading backward); illustrations of iron scimitar (p. 14), two views of a canoe (p. 33), ground plan of a native house (p. 39), bone fishhook (p. 83), and "scooping" fish net (p. 139); map of area about confluence of Willamette and Columbia rivers (pp. 28–29).

First Draft, April 16–21, 1806, Clark

MoSHi; Thwaites (LC), 4:288–311; Voorhis's deposit; sheets are letter paper cut to size, 16 pages (unpaged); 5″ × 4¼″ (size varies slightly); illustration of bone used in Indian game.

Voorhis No. 3, April 4–June 6, 1806, Clark

MoSHi; Thwaites (LC), 4:244–372, 5:8–113, 6:212, 215–18; Voorhis's deposit; one of the red books, 152 pages (unpaged); 7⅞″ × 4⅞″; includes Clark's journalizing, April 4–June 6, 1806, Clark's weather diary, April 1–May 31, 1806 (reading backward), and Clark's list of Chopunnish names for prominent rivers (end flyleaf); illustrations of bone fishhook, fish weir, and "scooping" fish net; maps of trails through the Rocky Mountains to the Missouri and Yellowstone rivers (front flyleaf and first page) and Indian sketch of area of confluence of Columbia and Snake rivers and extensions of each (last page).

Codex L, May 24–August 8, 1806, Lewis

PPAmP; Thwaites (LC), 5:60–238, 6:23–24, 218–23, 265; Biddle's deposit No. 12; one of the red books, 150 pages; 7⅞″ × 4⅞″; includes Lewis's journalizing, May 24–July 4, 1806 (pp. 1–81), "a Suplemnt [*i.e., Codex La*] to Come in here inclosed" (p. 81) probably Clark's handwriting, gap from July 5–14, 1806, with some pages left blank (pp. 82–98), Lewis's journalizing, July 15–August 8, 1806 (pp. 99–144), "a Suplt. [*i.e., Codex Lb*] to Come in here" (p. 144) probably Clark's handwriting, and Lewis's weather diary, June 1–August 12, 1806 (pp. 145–49, partially reading backward); Lewis's note on Joseph Dickson and Forrest Hancock (end flyleaf).

Codex La, July 3–15, 1806, Lewis

PPAmP; Thwaites (LC), 5:183–202; Biddle's deposit, no number; sheets are letter paper cut to size, 18 pages; 8″ × 5″ (size varies slightly); "a part of M. L. notes to Come into the book No. 12 [*i.e., Codex L*]—after the 4' July," (p. 18) probably Clark's handwriting and "where ten blank leaves were left by M. L. for the insertion of this matter. Dec. 10, 1892. Coues" (p. 18) in Coues's handwriting; map of a portion of Lewis's route on Big Blackfoot River (p. 4).

Codex Lb, August 9–12, 1806, Lewis

PPAmP; Thwaites (LC), 5:239–44; Biddle's deposit, no number; 8 pages from one of the red books; 7⅞″ × 4⅞″; this fragment probably comes from a red book at MoSHi that has notation on its cover, "9 to 12 Augt. 1806" but with no such entries or any expeditionary material; the notebook appears to have several pages missing from the front; "To be anexed to Book No. 12 [*i.e., Codex L*] at the last" (p. 7) probably Clark's handwriting and "Aug. 9–12 1806" (p. 7) probably Coues's handwriting.

First Draft, July 13–19 and July 24–August 3, 1806, Clark

MoSHi; selectively published; Thwaites (LC), 5:263, 303, 311; Voorhis's deposit; sheets are letter paper cut to size, 38 pages (unpaged); 6¼″ × 4¼″ (size varies slightly); covered with torn letter paper with following words on outside: "Journal Papers Relative to memorandoms Maps &c." and "Papers relating to Journey to Pacific" both in unknown handwriting; contains largely "course and distance" information; map of a portion of Clark's route on Yellowstone River.

Codex M, June 7–August 14, 1806, Clark (and occasionally Lewis)

PPAmP; Thwaites (LC), 5:115–82, 245–339, 6:218–20, 223–28; Biddle's deposit No. 13; one of the red books, 152 pages (total varies from page numbers); 7⅞″ × 4⅞″; includes Clark's journalizing, June 7–August 3, 1806 (pp. 3–122), Lewis's journalizing, undated (written on or after August 12, 1806) (pp. 122–24), Clark's journalizing, August 4–14, 1806 (pp. 125–46), Clark's weather diary, June 1–August 31, 1806 (pp. 146–52, reading backward), and Clark's "Memorandum" of things to do, undated (ca. August 1806) (p. 154); map from Indian information showing drainage and trails east and west from Bitterroot Mountains (pp. 1–2).

Codex N, August 15–September 26, 1806, Clark

PPAmP; Thwaites (LC), 5:339–95, 6:24–28, 56–59, 61–78, 121–22, 140–41, 228–29, 266–68, 276–80; Biddle's deposit No. 14; one of the red books, 152 pages (total varies from page numbers); 7⅞" × 4⅞"; includes Clark's memorandum of goods (pp. 1–2), Clark's journalizing, August 15–September 26, 1806 (pp. 3–78), Clark's notes on sketches (pp. 83–85), miscellaneous notes apparently by Clark and an unknown person (pp. 122–27, reading backward), "refur to Book No. 9 [*i.e., Codex I*]—from the 19 Nov to 29 of January 1806 for a Statement of the River Rochejhone & that part of our rout from the Falls of Missouri across the mountains on our outward bound journey all of which is estimate" (p. 128) probably Clark's handwriting, Clark's (and partially Lewis's) "A Summary Statement of the Rivers Creeks and most remarkable places . . . [from Camp Dubois to Pacific Coast and return]" (pp. 128–42, reading backward), Clark's "Courses and Compiled Distances from the Enterance of Travellers rest Creek into Clarks River to the Falls of Missouri" (pp. 144–48, reading backward), Clark's weather diary, September 1806 (pp. 151–52, reading backward), and Clark's natural history notes (pp. 153–54, reading backward); maps of area of Bonhomme Island (2 sketches, pp. 81 and 82) and Lewis's route from Travelers' Rest to White Bear Islands (pp. 149–50).

Voorhis No. 4, Miscellaneous Notebook, Clark

MoSHi; Thwaites (LC), 6:56–71, 114–20, 121–22, 140–41, 166–67, 179–82, 198–201; Voorhis's deposit; one of the red books, 154 pages (unpaged); 7⅞" × 4⅞"; includes Clark's weather diary, January and December 1804, and January, October, November, and December 1805, Clark's "Estimated Distances . . . [from Fort Mandan to Pacific Coast]," Clark's "Estimate of Western Indians," Clark's botanical and zoological notes (cf. Codex N, pp. 153–54), Biddle's queries and Clark's notes for Biddle, Clark's "A Summary Statement of Rivers Creeks and most remarkable places . . . [from Camp Dubois to Pacific Coast], "Clark's longitudinal and latitudinal readings, Clark's postexpeditionary notes (ca. 1808); maps of confluence of Columbia and Snake rivers and adjacent areas, Great Falls of Columbia, Long and Short Narrows of Columbia, and Great Rapids of Columbia.

Miscellaneous Documents of Lewis and Clark

Miscellaneous memorandum, undated (ca. 1804), Clark

CtY; Thwaites (LC), 1:15–16; Coe Collection of maps; one sheet of letter paper folded to size; 12⅛" × 8⅛"; reverse of *Atlas* map 3a on which Clark has written "A Memorandom of Articles in readiness for the Voyage."

Miscellaneous memoranda, undated (ca. 1804), Lewis and Clark

MoSHi; Thwaites (LC), 1:4–6; Voorhis's deposit; one sheet of letter paper folded to size; 12″ × 6⅞″; memoranda from Camp Dubois and Fort Mandan; includes Lewis's "Information of Mr. John Hay, commencing at the discharge of the Ottertail Lake, which forms the source of the Red River, to his winter station on the Assineboin River" and Clark's "The Course from the Fort Mandan to the *Fort Chaboillez's* on the Assinna Boin is North 150 Miles" (ca. November 1804).

Indian Speeches, October and November 1804, Clark

MoSHi; Thwaites (LC), 7:303–6; Voorhis's deposit; two sheets of letter paper folded to size; 15″ × 9½″; includes the following in Clark's handwriting: Speech of Kakawissassa (or Lighting Crow), October 11, 1804, Speech of Posecopsahe (or Black Cat), undated (October 31, 1804), Speech of Sheheke (or Big White), November 1, 1804, Speech of Kagarnemoghge or Cargarnomokshe (or Raven Man), October 30, 1804, Speech of Principal Chief of "Wautesoon" (i.e., Amahami or Awaxawi), October 30, 1804, miscellaneous ethnographic notes, Speech of 2d Chief of Arikaras (Pocasse or Hay), undated (ca. October 12, 1804), and Speech of 3d Chief of Arikaras (Piaheto or Eagles Feather), undated (ca. October 12, 1804); one separate sheet of letter paper, badly torn; 8½″ × 7″; "Speech of the Cherry" (or Caltarcata) in Clark's handwriting, undated (ca. October 29, 1804).

Donation Book, 1804 and 1805, Vaughan and Seybert (and occasionally Lewis)

PPAmP; Thwaites (LC), 6:151–57, 157–58, 159–64; red, blue, and yellow (marbled) paper-covered notebook into which Vaughan and Seybert copied Lewis's natural history and other notes, 72 pages (unpaged); 12⅝″ × 7⅞″; the data was gathered on way to and during stay at Fort Mandan; under Vaughan's heading "Donations November 16, 1805 from Meriwether Lewis Dried Plants &c put into Dr B. S Bartons hands for Examination" are included the following: copy of Lewis's botanical specimens, May 10–October 18, 1804 (9 pages), copy of Lewis's mineralogical specimens, May 30, 1804–February 13, 1805 (8 pages), and copy of a letter from Lewis to Jefferson, March 5, 1805, begun by Vaughan and completed by Lewis (for letter and additional information, see Jackson (LLC), 1:220–21).

Miscellaneous geographic memoranda, 1804–5, Clark

MoSHi; unpublished; Voorhis's deposit; one sheet of letter paper folded to size; 14⅜″ × 9″; apparently this data was gathered on way to and during stay at Fort Mandan; includes Clark's "A Summary Statement of Rivers, Creeks & most remarkable places, their Distances &c. &c. from the mouth of the Missouri, as high up that River as was explored in the year 1804," Clark's "The upper part of the River Missouri &c. is from Indians information taken at Fort Mandan in the winter 1804.5," Clark's "The names of Rivers, Creeks and the most remarkable places on the Kansaws River, from Information," Clark's "The names of Rivers, Creeks and the most Remarkable places on the Platt River, from Information," and Clark's "The names of Rivers Creeks & mountains on the Yellowstone River, from Indian information"; also 5 sheets of letter paper folded to size; 14¼″ × 9″; Clark's "The Courses and estimated distances of the Missouri from its mouth to the Mandan Nation as taken assending in the year 1804"; and one other sheet of letter paper folded to size; 12″ × 8⅜″; includes Clark's "Names of remarkable places Rivers Creeks Empping into the Missouri" and Clark's list of streams along the Yellowstone River based on Indian information.

Miscellaneous ethnographic memoranda, undated (ca. 1804–5), Clark

MoSHi; unpublished; Voorhis's deposit; two separate sheets of letter paper folded to size; 16¼″ × 12″; preliminary notes on Indian tribes probably made at Fort Mandan (cf. Estimate of Eastern Indians above); one sheet labeled "Nations of Indians inhabiting the country to the North of New Mexico & West of Mississippi . . . in 1805"; another sheet labeled "the Names of Nations & tribes which is thought to be advantageous Situations for Establishments—Some Estimations of their production."

Miscellaneous memoranda, undated (ca. 1804–5), Clark

PPAmP; unpublished; Biddle family's deposit; individual sheets of letter paper of various sizes; apparently this data was gathered on way to and during stay at Fort Mandan and probably sent to Jefferson in April 1805; includes Clark's "The Countrey and Rivers in advance or above the Mandans is from Indian information only 1805" (2 pages, cf. Codex O, pp. 117–22, Lewis's "A Summary view . . ."), Clark's "A Slight view of the Missouri River" (4 pages), Clark's "A Summary Statement of the Rivers & Creeks which fall into the Missouri . . ." (12 pages, cf. Codex O, pp. 69–117, Lewis's "A Summary view . . ."), Clark's description of the Indian nations (4 pages), and Clark's "[A statistical?] view of the Indian Nations inhabitating the territory of Louisiana and the countries adjacent to its nothern and western boundaries" (1 page, cf. Estimate of Eastern Indians above).

"Latitudes of certain points or places from Fort Mandan to Fort Clatsop," April–August 1805, Lewis

MoSHi; unpublished; Voorhis's deposit; unidentified sheet of paper partially torn; 6″ × 4¼″; gives latitude readings for Lewis's points of observations (nos. 1, 2, 7, 17, 19, 24, 30, and 42).

Astronomy Notebook, 1803, 1805, and 1806, Patterson and Lewis

MoHi; unpublished; Breckenridge Collection; apparently a child's copybook used by Patterson for instructing Lewis in astronomical observations and giving models for such calculations, 30 pages (unpaged); 7½″ × 6⅝″; includes Patterson's examples, forms, and tables, Lewis's "Statistical Table," Lewis's "Explanations and notes on the foregoing table," and Lewis's "Point of observation No. 21," May 20, 1805, and "Point of observation No. 22," May 21, 1805; map by Lewis, "Sketch given us by Yellept the principal Chief of the Wollahwollah Nation" (ca. April 27, 1806).

Speech for Yellowstone River Indians, 1806, Clark
  MoSHi; Thwaites (LC), 5:299–301; Voorhis's deposit; two sheets of letter paper folded to size; 14½″ × 9½″.

Miscellaneous ethnographic memoranda, undated (ca. 1806), Clark
  MoSHi; unpublished Voorhis's deposit; three sheets of letter paper folded to size; 12″ × 8¼″; preliminary list of names of Indian tribes probably made at Fort Clatsop (cf. Estimate of Western Indians above); includes Clark's "Indian Names" and "A List of the nations and tribs of Indians residing west of the Rocky Mountains &c."

"A summary Statement of Rivers Creeks and most remarkable places . . . to the falls of sd. River [Missouri] . . . 1804.5 & 6 by Captains Lewis & Clark," undated (ca. 1806), Clark
  ViU and DNA; unpublished; microfilm and photostatic copies made in the mid-1950s from a private collection; the original of the document is not now available; this is probably a copy of one of the many such summary statements written by Lewis and Clark.

Documents of Enlisted Men

Journal of Charles Floyd, May 14–August 18, 1804 (occasionally Clark's writing)
  WHi; Thwaites (LC), 7:3–26; Draper deposit; notebook of marble boards, 56 numbered pages and 18 unnumbered blank pages; 7½″ × 5⅞″; includes Floyd's due bills and entry for March 13, 1804 (p. 1), Floyd's journalizing, May 14–August 18, 1804 (pp. 2–54), Clark's occasional writing, June 22–25, 1804 (pp. 22–25) and Floyd's miscellaneous notes (pp. 55–56).

Journal of John Ordway, May 14, 1804–September 23, 1806 (occasionally Clark's writing)
  PPAmP; Quaife (MLJO), 79–402; Biddle family's deposit (3 notebooks); *notebook 1:* handstitched sheets covered with loose boards, 322 pages (erratically paged); divided into 4 parts; *pt. 1* (7¾″ × 6¼″) includes notation "Detachment Orders, Camp River Dubois" and latitude readings (1 unnumbered page), Ordway's journalizing, May 14–October 10, 1804 (pp. 1–90), and several unnumbered pages of Ordway's latitudes from St. Charles to Fort Mandan (1 page), Ordway's estimated distances "as taken by Capt. William Clark" from mouth of

Missouri to Fort Mandan (2 pages, reading backward), and notation "Orderly Book For the Detachment kept by Sergt. Ordway—Commenceing on the 1st day of April 1804" (1 unnumbered page); *pt. 2* (8¼″ × 6½″, size varies slightly) includes Ordway's journalizing, October 10, 1804–March 1, 1805 (pp. 91–145) and notation "A Journal continued from 90th page" (p. 91); *pt. 3* (8⅛″ × 6½″) includes notation "A journal continued from page (145)" (p. 147) and Ordway's journalizing, March 1–April 2, 1805 (pp. 147–53); *pt. 4* (8½″ × 6½″, size varies slightly) includes notation "continued" (p. 1), Ordway's journalizing, April 1–May 28, 1805 (pp. 1–50), "From this not consulted mem." apparently in Biddle's handwriting (p. 10); notation "Journal continued" (p. 41), Ordway's journalizing May 28–September 30, 1805 (108 unnumbered pages), and Ordway's mileage table (2 unnumbered pages); *notebook 2:* marble-covered book, 184 pages (unpaged); 6½″ × 3¾″; includes notation "Sergt. Ordway's Journal Commencing the first Oct. 1805 . . . ," Ordway's journalizing, October 1, 1805–May 15, 1806, Ordway's "Estimated Distance in miles ascending the Missourie, Crossing the Rockey Mountains and descending the Kooskookes, Lewises river and the Columbia River of all remarkable places & Latidudes &c." (10 pages, reading backward), and Ordway's list of personnel, dated "Fort Clatsop 22nd March 1806" (3 pages, reading backward); and *notebook 3:* no cover, 120 pages (unpaged); 7½″ × 4⅛″; includes notes on wildlife March–August 1806 (2 pages), Ordway's journalizing, May 16–September 23, 1806, about 7 sheets torn from the journal but no apparent break in journal, Ordway's mileage table from Fort Mandan to mouth of Missouri (4 pages, reading backward), and Ordway's notes on Indian trade items (2 pages, reading backward).

Journal of Patrick Gass, May 14, 1804–September 23, 1806

Manuscript lost; Gass; some gaps in journalizing; published first at Pittsburgh in 1807 by David McKeehan and printed by Zadoc Cramer, 262 pages; numerous reprints since that time.

Journal of Joseph Whitehouse, May 14, 1804–November 6, 1805 (original, with some writing by Clark and unknown persons) and May 14, 1804–April 2, 1806 (paraphrase)

ICN; Thwaites (LC), 7:29–190; original; paraphrase unpublished; Ayer's deposit (original); institutional purchase (paraphrase); the original journal is bound in animal skin and is in three parts, 292 pages (unpaged); *pt. 1* (7⅜″ × 6″) entries May 14, 1804–May 27, 1805; *pt. 2* (8¼″ × 6″, larger size varies slightly) entries May 28–August 31, 1805; *pt. 3* (8¼″ × 6″) entries September 1–November 6, 1805; original journal includes Whitehouse's journalizing, May 14, 1804–May 27, 1805 (with occasional writing by Clark and unknown persons), Whitehouse's "Latudes of the Diffrent remarkable places on the Missouri river," Whitehouse's distance chart from Camp Dubois to Big Bend of Missouri River, White-house's "Remarks [*latitudes*] of Different places," and Whitehouse's journalizing, May 28–November 6, 1805 (with several gaps in journalizing); the paraphrase is in a notebook of bound boards (not the original cover), 368 pages (i–ix, 1–351, and 1–8); 12¾″ × 7¾″; includes title page, preface, list of members of expedition party, Whitehouse's paraphrased journalizing, May 14, 1804–March 23, 1806 (pp. 1–351), *"End of first Volume"* (p. 351), *"Volume 2nd"* (p. 1, pagination renumbered), and Whitehouse's paraphrased journalizing, March 23 (second entry)–April 2, 1806 (pp. 1–8).

Sources Cited

Abel
: Abel, Annie Heloise, ed. *Tabeau's Narrative of Loisel's Expedition to the Upper Missouri.* Norman: University of Oklahoma Press, 1939.

Aikman
: Aikman, John M. *Distribution and Structure of the Forests of Eastern Nebraska.* University of Nebraska Studies, no. 26, 3–75. Lincoln, 1926.

Allen
: Allen, John Logan. *Passage through the Garden: Lewis and Clark and the Image of the American Northwest.* Urbana: University of Illinois Press, 1975.

Alvord
: Alvord, Clarence Walworth. *The Illinois Country, 1673–1818.* Chicago: A. C. McClurg, 1922.

Anderson
: Anderson, Bern. *Surveyor of the Sea: The Life and Voyages of Captain George Vancouver.* Seattle: University of Washington Press, 1960.

Anson
: Anson, Bert. *The Miami Indians.* Norman: University of Oklahoma Press, 1970.

AOU
: American Ornithologists' Union. *Check-list of North American Birds.* 6th ed. Baltimore, Md.: American Ornithologists' Union, 1983. [AOU] in brackets with numbers refers to a species item number in the book.

Appleman (JRF)
: Appleman, Roy E. "Joseph and Reubin Field, Kentucky Frontiersmen of the Lewis and Clark Expedition and Their Father, Abraham." *Filson Club Historical Quarterly* 49 (January 1975): 5–36.

Appleman (LC)
: ——. *Lewis and Clark: Historic Places Associated with Their Transcontinental Exploration (1804–1806).* Washington, D.C.: United States Department of the Interior, National Park Service, 1975.

APS (Arch)
: American Philosophical Society. Archives.

APS (CS)
: ——. Communications to the Society.

APS (EP) ———. *Early Proceedings of the American Philosophical Society . . . 1744–1828*. Philadelphia: McCalla and Stavely, 1884.

APS (JCS) ———. Journal of Corresponding Secretary.

APS (MCHL) ———. Minutes of the Committee of History and Literature, 1817.

APS (MCL) ———. Minutes of the Committee on Library, 1915–17.

APS (YB) ———. *Year Book, 1949*. Philadelphia: American Philosophical Society, 1950.

Atlas Moulton, Gary E., ed. *Atlas of the Lewis and Clark Expedition*. Lincoln: University of Nebraska Press, 1983.

Augur Augur, Helen. *Passage to Glory: John Ledyard's America*. New York: Doubleday, 1946.

Austin Austin, Aleine. *Matthew Lyon: "New Man" of the Democratic Revolution, 1749–1822*. University Park: Pennsylvania State University Press, 1981.

Baily Baily, Francis. *Journal of a Tour in Unsettled Parts of North America in 1796 and 1797*. 1856. Reprint. Edited by Jack D. L. Holmes. Carbondale: Southern Illinois University Press, 1969.

Bakeless (DB) Bakeless, John. *Daniel Boone: Master of the Wilderness*. New York: William Morrow, 1939.

Bakeless (LCPD) ———. *Lewis and Clark, Partners in Discovery*. New York: William Morrow, 1947.

Bakeless (LCBE) ———. "Lewis and Clark's Background for Exploration." *Journal of the Washington Academy of Sciences* 44 (November 1954): 333–38.

Baldwin (KA) Baldwin, Leland D. *The Keelboat Age on Western Waters*. Pittsburgh: University of Pittsburgh Press, 1941.

Baldwin (WR) ———. *Whiskey Rebels: The Story of a Frontier Uprising*. 2d ed. Pittsburgh: University of Pittsburgh Press, 1968.

Barbour Barbour, Erwin H. *Nebraska Geological Survey, Report of the State Geologist*. Lincoln: Nebraska State Geological Survey, 1903.

Bareis & Porter Bareis, Charles J., and James W. Porter, eds. *American Bottom Archaeology: A Summary of the*

FAI-270 Project Contribution to the Culture History of the Mississippi Valley. Urbana: University of Illinois Press, 1984.

Barkley   Barkley, T. M., ed. *Atlas of the Flora of the Great Plains*. Ames: Iowa State University Press, 1977.

Barry   Barry, Louise. *The Beginning of the West: Annals of the Kansas Gateway to the American West, 1540– 1854*. Topeka: Kansas State Historical Society, 1972.

Bedini (EASI)   Bedini, Silvio A. *Early American Scientific Instruments and Their Makers*. Washington, D.C.: Smithsonian Institution Press, 1964.

Bedini (SILC)   ——. "The Scientific Instruments of the Lewis and Clark Expedition." *Great Plains Quarterly* 4 (Winter 1984): 54–69.

Bedini (TT)   ——. *Thinkers and Tinkers: Early American Men of Science*. New York: Charles Scribner's Sons, 1975.

Belting   Belting, Natalia Maree. *Kaskaskia under the French Regime*. Urbana: University of Illinois Press, 1948.

Benson   Benson, Keith R. "Herpetology on the Lewis and Clark Expedition: 1804–1806." *Herpetological Review* 3 (1978): 87–91.

Betts (SY)   Betts, Robert B. *In Search of York: The Slave Who Went to the Pacific with Lewis and Clark*. Boulder: Colorado Associated University Press, 1985.

Betts (WCW)   ——. " 'We commenced wrighting &c.'—A Salute to the Ingenious Spelling and Grammar of William Clark." *We Proceeded On* 6 (November 1980): 10–12.

Betts (WE)   ——. " 'The writingest explorers of their time': New Estimates of the Number of Words in the Published Journals of the Lewis and Clark Expedition." *We Proceeded On* 7 (August 1981): 4–9.

Billups   Billups, A. C. "Fossil Land Shells of the Old Forest Bed of the Ohio River." *Nautilus* 16 (May 1902–April 1903): 50–52.

Blaine   Blaine, Martha Royce. *The Ioway Indians*. Norman: University of Oklahoma Press, 1979.

Boellstorff   Boellstorff, John D. "Chronology of Some Late Cenozoic Deposits from the Central United States and the Ice Age." *Transactions of the Nebraska Academy of Sciences* 6 (1978): 35–49.

Bragg & Tatschl   Bragg, Thomas B., and Annehara K. Tatschl. "Changes in Flood-Plain Vegetation and Land Use along the Missouri River from 1826 to 1972." *Environmental Management* 1 (1977): 343–48.

Braun   Braun, E. Lucy. *Deciduous Forests of Eastern North America*. 1950. Fac. ed. New York: Hafner Publishing Co., 1967.

Bray (ETG)   Bray, Robert T. "European Trade Goods from the Utz Site, and the Search for Fort Orleans." *Missouri Archaeologist* 39 (December 1978): 1–87.

Bray (MIT)   ——. "The Missouri Indian Tribe in Archaeology and History." *Missouri Historical Review* 55 (1960–61): 213–25.

Brobst & Pratt   Brobst, Donald A., and Walden P. Pratt. *United States Mineral Resources*. United States Geological Survey Professional Paper 820. Washington, D.C.: United States Department of Interior, 1973.

Brown   Brown, Lloyd A. *The Story of Maps*. Boston: Little, Brown, 1949.

Buck & Buck   Buck, Solon J., and Elizabeth Hawthorn Buck. *The Planting of Civilization in Western Pennsylvania*. Pittsburgh: University of Pittsburgh Press, 1939.

Burchett et al.   Burchett, R. R., V. H. Dreeszen, E. C. Reed, and G. E. Pritchard. "Bedrock Geologic Map Showing Thickness of Overlying Quaternary Deposits, Lincoln Quadrangle and Part of Nebraska City Quadrangle, Nebraska and Kansas." United States Geological Survey, Miscellaneous Geologic Investigations (map I–729), 1972.

Burroughs   Burroughs, Raymond Darwin. *The Natural History of the Lewis and Clark Expedition*. East Lansing: Michigan State University Press, 1961.

Butler   Butler, James Davie. "The New Found Journal of Charles Floyd, a Sergeant under Captains Lewis and Clark." *Proceedings of the American Antiquarian Society,* n.s., 9 (April 1894): 225–52.

Butterfield   Butterfield, Consul W. *History of the Girtys.* 1890. Reprint. Columbus, Ohio: Long's College Book Co., 1950.

Callahan   Callahan, James Morton. *Semi-Centennial History of West Virginia.* [Charleston]: Semi-Centennial Commission of West Virginia, 1913.

Callender (Fox)   Callender, Charles. "Fox." In Trigger, 15: 636–47.

Callender (Sauk)   ——. "Sauk." In Trigger, 15:648–55.

Callender (Shaw)   ——. "Shawnee." In Trigger, 15:622–35.

Callender, Pope, & Pope   Callender, Charles, Richard K. Pope, and Susan M. Pope. "Kickapoo." In Trigger, 15:656–67.

Catlin   Catlin, George. *Letters and Notes on the Manners, Customs, and Condition of the North American Indians. . . .* 2 vols. London: privately published, 1841.

Champe   Champe, John L. "A Report for the Laboratory of Anthropology, University of Nebraska." In *Proceedings of the Fifth Plains Conference for Archeology,* Notebook 1, edited by John L. Champe, 14–17. Lincoln: Laboratory of Anthropology, University of Nebraska, 1949.

Chapman (OM)   Chapman, Berlin B. *The Otoe and Missourias: A Study of Indian Removal and the Legal Aftermath.* Oklahoma City: Times Journal Publishing Co., 1965.

Chapman (AM)   Chapman, Carl H. *The Archaeology of Missouri.* 2 vols. Columbia: University of Missouri Press, 1975–80.

Chapman (IO)   ——. "The Indomitable Osage in Spanish Illinois (Upper Louisiana) 1763–1804." In McDermott (SMV), 287–313.

Chapman (LOM)   ——. "The Little Osage and Missouri Indian Village Sites, ca. 1727–1777 A.D." *Missouri Archaeologist* 21 (December 1959): 1–67.

Chapman (OOIT)	——. *The Origin of the Osage Indian Tribe*. Vol. 3 of *Osage Indians*. Edited by David Agee Horr. 3 vols. New York: Garland Publishing, 1974.
Chatters	Chatters, Roy M. "The Not-So-Enigmatic Lewis and Clark Airgun." *We Proceeded On* 3 (May 1977): 4–6.
Chuinard	Chuinard, Eldon G. *Only One Man Died: The Medical Aspects of the Lewis and Clark Expedition*. Glendale, Calif.: Arthur H. Clark, 1979.
Clarke (JN)	Clarke, Charles G. "John Newman." In Hafen, 9:299–304.
Clarke (MLCE)	——. *The Men of the Lewis and Clark Expedition: A Biographical Roster of the Fifty-one Members and a Composite Diary of Their Activities from All Known Sources*. Glendale, Calif.: Arthur H. Clark, 1970.
Clarke (PW)	——. "Peter M. Weiser." In Hafen, 9:385–91.
Clifton	Clifton, James A. "Potawatomi." In Trigger 15: 725–42.
Condra & Reed	Condra, G. E., and E. C. Reed. "The Geological Section of Nebraska." *Nebraska Geological Survey Bulletin* 14 A. Lincoln: Nebraska Geological Survey, 1959.
Cook	Cook, Warren L. *Flood Tide of Empire: Spain and the Pacific Northwest, 1543–1819*. New Haven: Yale University Press, 1973.
Cote, Reinertsen, & Killey	Cote, William, David Reinertsen, and Myna Killey. Illinois State Geological Survey, *Guide Leaflet*. Geological Science Field Trip, Thebes Area, Alexander County, Jonesboro and Thebes Quadrangles. Urbana: Illinois Department of Registration and Education, 1968.
Coues (DOMJ)	Coues, Elliott. "Description of the Original Manuscript Journals and Field Notebooks of Lewis and Clark, on which was based Biddle's History of the Expedition of 1804–1806; and which are now in the possession of the American Philosophical Society in Philadelphia." *Proceedings of the American Philosophical Society* 31 (January 1893): 17–33.
Coues (HLC)	——, ed. *History of the Expedition under the Com-*

mand of Lewis and Clark. . . . 1893. Reprint. 3 vols. New York: Dover Publications, 1965.

Coues (NLEH)   ——, ed. *New Light on the Early History of the Greater Northwest.* 3 vols. New York: Harper, 1897.

Cramer (5th)   Cramer, Zadok. *The Navigator; or, The Traders' Useful Guide in Navigating the Monongahela, Allegheny, Ohio and Mississippi Rivers. . . .* 5th ed. Pittsburgh: Zadok Cramer, 1806.

Cramer (6th)   ——. *The Navigator; Containing Directions for Navigating the Monongahela, Allegheny, Ohio and Mississippi Rivers. . . .* 6th ed. Pittsburgh: Cramer and Spear, 1808.

Criswell   Criswell, Elijah Harry. *Lewis and Clark: Linguistic Pioneers.* University of Missouri Studies, vol. 15, no. 2. Columbia: University of Missouri Press, 1940.

Cumings   Cumings, Samuel. *The Western Navigator; Containing Directions for the Navigation of the Ohio and the Mississippi. . . .* Philadelphia: E. Littell, 1822.

Cutright (HLCJ)   Cutright, Paul Russell. *A History of the Lewis and Clark Journals.* Norman: University of Oklahoma Press, 1976.

Cutright (IGHB)   ——. "I gave him barks and saltpeter. . . ." *American Heritage* 15 (December 1963): 59–61, 94–101.

Cutright (LCD)   ——. "Lewis and Clark and DuPratz." *Bulletin of the Missouri Historical Society* 21 (October 1964): 31–35.

Cutright (LCPN)   ——. *Lewis and Clark: Pioneering Naturalists.* Urbana: University of Illinois Press, 1969.

Cutright (ML)   ——. "Meriwether Lewis Prepares for a Trip West." *Bulletin of the Missouri Historical Society* 23 (October 1966): 3–20.

Cutright & Brodhead   Cutright, Paul Russell, and Michael J. Brodhead. *Elliott Coues: Naturalist and Frontier Historian.* Urbana: University of Illinois Press, 1981.

Davidson   Davidson, Gordon Charles. *The North West Company.* Berkeley: University of California Press, 1918.

DeConde   DeConde, Alexander. *This Affair of Louisiana.* New York: Charles Scribner's Sons, 1976.

DeVoto	DeVoto, Bernard. *The Course of Empire*. Boston: Houghton Mifflin, 1952.
Diller (JMJ)	Diller, Aubrey. "James Mackay's Journey in Nebraska in 1796." *Nebraska History* 36 (June 1955): 123–28.
Diller (NM)	——. "A New Map of the Missouri River Drawn in 1795." *Imago Mundi* 12 (1955): 175–80.
Dillon	Dillon, Richard. *Meriwether Lewis: A Biography*. New York: Coward-McCann, 1965.
Din & Nasatir	Din, Gilbert C., and A. P. Nasatir. *The Imperial Osages: Spanish-Indian Diplomacy in the Mississippi Valley*. Norman: University of Oklahoma Press, 1983.
Dorsey	Dorsey, J. Owen. "Omaha Sociology." Bureau of American Ethnology, Third Annual Report, 205–308. Washington, D.C.: Government Printing Office, 1884.
Dunlay	Dunlay, Thomas W. "'Battery of Venus': A Clue to the Journal-Keeping Methods of Lewis and Clark." *We Proceeded On* 9 (August 1983): 6–8.
Edmunds	Edmunds, R. David. *The Potawatomis: Keepers of the Fire*. Norman: University of Oklahoma Press, 1978.
Espenshade	Espenshade, A. Howry. *Pennsylvania Place Names*. State College: Pennsylvania State College, 1925.
Fenton	Fenton, William N. "Northern Iroquoian Culture Patterns." In Trigger, 15:296–321.
Fernald	Fernald, Merritt Lyndon. *Gray's Manual of Botany*. 8th ed. New York: D. Van Nostrand, 1970.
Fitzpatrick	Fitzpatrick, Lillian Linder. *Nebraska Place-Names: Including Selections from the Origin of the Place-Names of Nebraska, by J. T. Link*. Edited by G. Thomas Fairclough. Lincoln: University of Nebraska Press, 1960.
Fletcher & La Flesche	Fletcher, Alice C., and Francis La Flesche. *The Omaha Tribe*. 1911. Reprint. 2 vols. Lincoln: University of Nebraska Press, 1972.
Foley & Rice	Foley, William E., and C. David Rice. *The First Chouteaus: River Barons of Early St. Louis*. Urbana: University of Illinois Press, 1983.
Forrest	Forrest, Earle R. *Patrick Gass: Lewis and Clark's Last*

	Man. Independence, Pa.: privately published, 1950.
Fortier	Fortier, John B. "New Light on Fort Massac." In McDermott (FFW), 57–71.
Fowke	Fowke, Gerard. *Antiquities of Central and Southeastern Missouri.* Bureau of American Ethnology, Bulletin 37. Washington, D.C.: Government Printing Office, 1910.
Garver	Garver, Frank Harmon. "The Story of Sergeant Charles Floyd." *Mississippi Valley Historical Association Proceedings* 2 (1908–9): 76–92.
Gass	Gass, Patrick. *A Journal of the Voyages and Travels of a Corps of Discovery. . . .* Pittsburgh: Zadok Cramer, 1807.
Gibson	Gibson, Arrell Morgan. *The Kickapoos: Lords of the Middle Border.* Norman: University of Oklahoma Press, 1963.
Gilmore	Gilmore, Melvin R. *Uses of Plants by the Indians of the Missouri River Region.* 1919. Reprint. Lincoln: University of Nebraska Press, 1977.
Gleason & Cronquist	Gleason, Henry A., and Arthur Cronquist. *Manual of Vascular Plants of Northeastern United States and Adjacent Canada.* New York: D. Van Nostrand, 1963.
Glover	Glover, Richard, ed. *David Thompson's Narrative, 1784–1812.* Toronto: Champlain Society, 1962.
Goddard	Goddard, Ives. "Delaware." In Trigger, 15:213–39.
Grange	Grange, Roger T. *Pawnee and Lower Loup Pottery.* Nebraska State Historical Society, Publications in Anthropology, no. 3. Lincoln: Nebraska State Historical Society, 1968.
Greenwood	Greenwood, David. *Mapping.* 1944. Reprint. Chicago: University of Chicago Press, 1964.
Gregg	Gregg, Kate L., ed. *Westward with Dragoons: The Journal of William Clark.* Fulton, Mo.: Ovid Bell Press, 1937.
Hafen	Hafen, LeRoy R., ed. *The Mountain Men and the Fur Trade of the Far West.* 10 vols. Glendale, Calif.: Arthur H. Clark, 1965.

Hagan   Hagan, William T. *The Sac and Fox Indians.* Norman: University of Oklahoma Press, 1958.

Haines   Haines, Aubrey L. "John Colter." In Hafen, 8: 73–85.

Hall   Hall, E. Raymond. *The Mammals of North America.* 2d ed. 2 vols. New York: John Wiley and Sons, 1981.

Halsey   Halsey, Ashley, Jr. "The Air Gun of Lewis and Clark." *American Rifleman,* August 1984, 36–37, 80–82.

Hamilton   Hamilton, William Baskerville. *Anglo-American Law on the Frontier: Thomas Rodney and His Territorial Cases.* Durham, N.C.: Duke University Press, 1953.

Harris   Harris, Burton. *John Colter: His Years in the Rockies.* New York: Charles Scribner's Sons, 1952.

Heitman   Heitman, Francis B. *Historical Register of the United States Army, from Its Organization, September 29, 1789, to September 29, 1889.* Washington, D.C.: National Tribune, 1890.

Hill & Wedel   Hill, A. T., and Waldo R. Wedel. "Excavations at the Leary Indian Village and Burial Site, Richardson County, Nebraska." *Nebraska History* 17 (January–March 1936): 3–73.

Hinds   Hinds, Henry. *The Coal Deposits of Missouri.* Jefferson City: Missouri Bureau of Geology and Mines, 1912.

Hodge   Hodge, Frederick Webb, ed. *Handbook of American Indians North of Mexico.* 1912. Reprint. 2 vols. St. Clair Shores, Mich.: Scholarly Press, 1968.

Hoffhaus   Hoffhaus, Charles E. "Fort de Cavagnial: Imperial France in Kansas, 1744–1764." *Kansas Historical Quarterly* 30 (Winter 1964): 425–54.

Hollow & Parks   Hollow, Robert C., and Douglas R. Parks. "Studies in Plains Linguistics: A Review." In *Anthropology on the Great Plains,* edited by W. Raymond Wood and Margot Liberty, 68–97. Lincoln: University of Nebraska Press, 1980.

Holmgren   Holmgren, Virginia C. "A Glossary of Bird Names Cited by Lewis and Clark." *We Proceeded On* 10 (May 1984): 28–34.

Houck   Houck, Louis. *A History of Missouri from the Earliest Explorations and Settlements until the Admission of the State into the Union.* 3 vols. Chicago: R. R. Donnelley and Sons, 1908.

Howard   Howard, Robert P. *Illinois: A History of the Prairie State.* Grand Rapids, Mich.: William B. Erdmans Publishing Co., 1972.

Howe & Koenig   Howe, W. B., and J. W. Koenig. *The Stratigraphic Succession in Missouri.* Rolla, Mo.: Division of Geological Survey and Water Resources, 1961.

Hult   Hult, Ruby El. *Guns of the Lewis and Clark Expedition.* Tacoma: Washington State Historical Society, 1960.

Illinois Guide   *Illinois: A Descriptive and Historical Guide.* Compiled and written by the Federal Writers' Project of the Work Projects Adminstration. American Guide Series. 2d ed. Chicago: A. C. McClurg, 1947.

Innis   Innis, Harold A. *The Fur Trade in Canada: An Introduction to Canadian Economic History.* 1930. Reprint. Toronto: University of Toronto Press, 1970.

Iowa Guide   *Iowa: A Guide to the Hawkeye State.* Compiled and written by the Federal Writers' Project of the Works Progress Administration. American Guide Series. New York: Viking Press, 1938.

Irving (IS)   Irving, John Treat. *Indian Sketches.* Edited by John F. McDermott. Norman: University of Oklahoma Press, 1955.

Irving (Astor)   Irving, Washington. *Astoria.* 1836. Reprint. Portland, Oreg.: Binfords and Mort, 1967.

Izett   Izett, Glen A. "Volcanic Ash Beds: Records of Upper Cenozoic Silicic Pyroclastic Volcanism in the Western States." *Journal of Geophysical Research* 86 (1981): 10200–10222.

Jackson (DS)   Jackson, Donald. "Call Him a Good Old Dog, But Don't Call Him Scannon." *We Proceeded On* 11 (August 1985): 5–8.

Jackson (LCO)   ———. "Lewis and Clark among the Oto." *Nebraska History* 41 (September 1960): 237–48.

Jackson (SBLC)	———. "Some Books Carried by Lewis and Clark." *Bulletin of the Missouri Historical Society* 16 (October 1959): 3–13.
Jackson (TJ)	———. *Thomas Jefferson and the Stony Mountains: Exploring the West from Monticello*. Urbana: University of Illinois Press, 1981.
Jackson (LLC)	———, ed. *Letters of the Lewis and Clark Expedition with Related Documents, 1783–1854*. 2d ed. 2 vols. Urbana: University of Illinois Press, 1978.
Jacob	Jacob, John G. *The Life and Times of Patrick Gass*. Wellsburg, Va.: Jacob and Smith, 1859.
Johnsgard	Johnsgard, Paul A. *Grouse and Quails of North America*. Lincoln: University of Nebraska Press, 1973.
Jones	Jones, J. Knox, Jr. *Distribution and Taxonomy of Mammals of Nebraska*. Lawrence: University of Kansas, 1964.
Kastner	Kastner, Joseph. *A Species of Eternity*. New York: Knopf, 1977.
Knight	Knight, J. B. "The Location and Areal Extent of the Saint Louis Pennsylvanian Outlier." *American Journal of Science*, 5th ser., 25 (January 1933): 25–48, 166–78.
Kortright	Kortright, Francis H. *The Ducks, Geese and Swans of North America: A Vade Mecum for the Naturalist and the Sportsman*. Washington, D.C.: American Wildlife Institute, 1942.
La Flesche	La Flesche, Francis. *A Dictionary of the Osage Language*. Bureau of American Ethnology, Bulletin 109. Washington, D.C.: Government Printing Office, 1932.
Lange (EB)	Lange, Robert E. "The Expedition's Brothers— Joseph and Reuben Field." *We Proceeded On* 4 (July 1978): 15–16.
Lange (GD)	———. "George Drouillard (Drewyer)—One of the Two or Three Most Valuable Men on the Expedition." *We Proceeded On* 5 (May 1979): 14–16.
Lange (JS)	———. "John Shields: Lewis and Clark's Handyman: Gunsmith—Blacksmith—General Mechanic— for the Expedition." *We Proceeded On* 5 (July 1979): 14–16.

Lange (PGS)	———. "Private George Shannon: The Expedition's Youngest Member—1785 or 1787–1836." *We Proceeded On* 8 (July 1982): 10–15.
Lange (WB)	———. "William Bratton—One of Lewis and Clark's Men." *We Proceeded On* 7 (February 1981): 8–11.
Larocque	Larocque, François-Antoine. *Journal of Larocque from the Assiniboine to the Yellowstone in 1805.* Edited by L. J. Burpee. Ottawa: Government Printing Bureau, 1910.
Lee et al.	Lee, David S., Carter R. Gilbert, Charles H. Hocutt, Robert E. Jenkins, Don E. McAllister, and Jay R. Stauffer, Jr. *Atlas of North American Freshwater Fishes.* Raleigh: North Carolina State Museum of Natural History, 1980.
Little	Little, Elbert L., Jr. *Atlas of United States Trees.* Vol. 1, *Conifers and Important Hardwoods.* Washington, D.C.: United States Department of Agriculture, Forest Service, 1971.
Loomis & Nasatir	Loomis, Noel M., and Abraham P. Nasatir. *Pedro Vial and the Roads to Santa Fe.* Norman: University of Oklahoma Press, 1967.
Loos	Loos, John Louis. "A Biography of William Clark, 1770–1813." Ph.D. diss., Washington University, 1953.
McDermott (FS)	McDermott, John Francis. "French Surnames in the Mississippi Valley." *American Speech* 9 (February 1934): 28–30.
McDermott (GMVF)	———. *A Glossary of Mississippi Valley French, 1673–1850.* St. Louis: Washington University, 1941.
McDermott (MIG)	———. "The Myth of the 'Imbecile Governor'—Captain Fernando de Leyba and the Defense of St. Louis in 1780." In McDermott (SMV), 314–91.
McDermott (WCS)	———. "William Clark's Struggle with Place Names in Upper Louisiana." *Bulletin of the Missouri Historical Society* 34 (April 1978): 140–50.
McDermott (FFW)	———, ed. *Frenchmen and French Ways in the Mississippi Valley.* Urbana: University of Illinois, 1969.
McDermott (OC)	———, ed. *Old Cahokia: A Narrative and Documents Illustrating the First Century of Its History.* St.

Louis: St. Louis Historical Documents Foundation, 1949.

McDermott (SMV)   ——, ed. *The Spanish in the Mississippi Valley, 1762–1804*. Urbana: University of Illinois Press, 1974.

McGirr   McGirr, Newman F. "Patrick Gass and His Journal of the Lewis and Clark Expedition." *West Virginia History* 3 (April 1942): 205–12.

McJimsey   McJimsey, George Davis. *Topographic Terms in Virginia*. New York: Columbia University Press, 1940.

MacKay   MacKay, Douglas. *The Honourable Company: A History of the Hudson's Bay Company*. New York: Tudor Publishing Co., 1938.

Madison   *History of Madison County*. 1882. Reprint. Edwardsville, Ill.: W. R. Brink, 1972.

Majors   Majors, Harry M. "John McClellan in the Montana Rockies, 1807: The First Americans after Lewis and Clark." *Northwest Discovery* 2 (November–December 1981): 554–630.

Masson   Masson, L. R., ed. *Les Bourgeois de la Compagnie du Nord-ouest*. . . . 1889–90. Reprint. 2 vols. New York: Antiquarian Press, 1960.

Mathews   Mathews, John Joseph. *The Osages: Children of the Middle Waters*. Norman: University of Oklahoma Press, 1961.

Miller   Miller, Robert D. "Geology of the Omaha-Council Bluffs Area, Nebraska-Iowa." U.S. Geological Survey Professional Paper 472. Washington, D.C.: U.S. Government Printing Office, 1964.

Missouri Guide   *Missouri: A Guide to the "Show Me" State*. Compiled by Workers of the Writers' Program of the Work Projects Administration. American Guide Series. Rev. ed. New York: Hastings House, 1954.

Moore   Moore, Conrad T. "Man and Fire in the Central North American Grassland, 1535–1890: A Documentary Historical Geography." Ph.D. diss., University of California, Los Angeles, 1972.

Moulton   Moulton, Gary E. "The Specialized Journals of Lewis and Clark." *Proceedings of the Ameri-*

	can Philosophical Society 127 (June 16, 1983): 194–201.
MRC	Missouri River Commission. *Map of the Missouri River from Its Mouth to Three Forks, Montana, in Eighty-four Sheets.* Washington, D.C.: Missouri River Commission, 1892–95.
MRM	*Missouri River: Mouth to Rulo.* Kansas City, Mo.: Corps of Engineers, 1947–49.
MRR	*Missouri River: Rulo, Nebraska, to Yankton, South Dakota.* Omaha, Nebr.: Corps of Engineers, 1947–49.
Munnick (FR)	Munnick, Harriet D. "François Rivet." In Hafen, 7:237–43.
Munnick (PD)	——. "Pierre Dorion." In Hafen, 8:107–12.
Nasatir (BR)	Nasatir, Abraham P. *Borderland in Retreat: From Spanish Louisiana to the Far Southwest.* Albuquerque: University of New Mexico Press, 1976.
Nasatir (JM)	——. "James Mackay." In Hafen, 4:185–206.
Nasatir (SWV)	——. *Spanish War Vessels on the Mississippi, 1792–1796.* New Haven: Yale University Press, 1968.
Nasatir (BLC)	——, ed. *Before Lewis and Clark: Documents Illustrating the History of the Missouri, 1785–1804.* 2 vols. St. Louis: St. Louis Historical Documents Foundation, 1952.
Nebraska Guide	*Nebraska: A Guide to the Cornhusker State.* Compiled and written by the Federal Writers' Project of the Works Progress Administration. American Guide Series. New York: Viking Press, 1939.
Neiburger, Edinger, & Bonner	Neiburger, Morris, James G. Edinger, and William D. Bonner. *Understanding Our Atmospheric Environment.* 2d ed. San Francisco: W. H. Freeman, 1982.
Ney	Ney, Virgil. *Fort on the Prairie: Fort Atkinson on the Council Bluff, 1819–1827.* Washington, D.C.: Command Publications, 1978.
Nichols	Nichols, William. "Lewis and Clark Probe the Heart of Darkness." *American Scholar* 49 (Winter 1979–80): 94–101.
Nicollet (MMR)	Nicollet, Joseph N. Maps of the Missouri River, Joseph N. Nicollet Papers, vol. 2, pt. 2, Manu-

scripts Division, Library of Congress, Washington, D.C.

Nicollet (RIIM) ——. *Report Intended to Illustrate a Map of the Hydrographical Basin of the Upper Mississippi River. . . .* Washington, D.C.: Blair and Rives, 1843.

Nute Nute, Grace Lee. *The Voyageur.* 1931. Reprint. St. Paul: Minnesota Historical Society, 1955.

Oglesby Oglesby, Richard Edward. *Manuel Lisa and the Opening of the Missouri Fur Trade.* Norman: University of Oklahoma Press, 1963.

Ohio Guide *The Ohio Guide.* Compiled by workers of the Writers' Program of the Work Projects Administration. American Guide Series. New York: Oxford University Press, 1940.

Olson Olson, Kirk. "A Lewis and Clark Rifle?" *American Rifleman*, May 1985, 23–25, 66–68.

Osgood (ODS) Osgood, Ernest S. "Our Dog Scannon—Partner in Discovery." *Montana, the Magazine of Western History* 26 (July 1976): 8–17.

Osgood (FN) ——, ed. *The Field Notes of Captain William Clark, 1803–1805.* New Haven: Yale University Press, 1964.

Parks Parks, Douglas R. "Bands and Villages of the Arikara and Pawnee." *Nebraska History* 60 (Summer 1979): 214–39.

Pennak Pennak, Robert W. *Fresh-water Invertebrates of the United States.* New York: Ronald Press, 1953.

Petersen Petersen, William J. *Iowa: The Rivers of Her Valleys.* Iowa City: State Historical Society of Iowa, 1941.

Prior, Halberg, & Bettis Prior, Jean G., George R. Halberg, and E. Arthur Bettis III. "Loess Hills Geology." *Iowa Conservationist* 43 (April 1984): 3–5.

Prucha Prucha, Francis Paul. *Indian Peace Medals in American History.* Lincoln: University of Nebraska Press, 1971.

Pryor & Ross Pryor, W. A., and C. A. Ross. *Geology of the Illinois Parts of the Cairo, La Center, and Thebes Quadrangles.* Illinois State Geological Survey Circular 332. Urbana: Illinois Department of Registration and Education, 1962.

Pyne	Pyne, Stephen J. "Indian Fires." *Natural History* 92 (February 1983): 6–11.
Quaife (ECMJ)	Quaife, Milo Milton, ed. "Extracts from Capt. McKay's Journal—and Others." *Wisconsin Historical Society Proceedings* 63 (1915): 186–210.
Quaife (MLJO)	——, ed. *The Journals of Captain Meriwether Lewis and Sergeant John Ordway Kept on the Expedition of Western Exploration, 1803–1806.* Madison: State Historical Society of Wisconsin, 1916.
Ray	Ray, Louis L. "Geomorphology and Quaternary Geology of the Owensboro Quadrangle, Indiana and Kentucky." *Geological Survey.* Professional Paper 488. Washington D.C.: U.S. Department of the Interior, 1965.
Ray & Lurie	Ray, Verne F., and Nancy Oestreich Lurie. "The Contributions of Lewis and Clark to Ethnography." *Journal of the Washington Academy of Sciences* 44 (November 1954): 358–70.
Raynolds & Simpson	Raynolds, W. F., and James H. Simpson. *Map of the Mississippi River between the Mouth of the Illinois and the Mouth of the Ohio Rivers.* St. Louis: Corps of Engineers, 1878.
Reed & Dreeszen	Reed, E. C., and V. H. Dreeszen. "Revision of the Classification of the Pleistocene Deposits of Nebraska." Nebraska Geological Survey Bulletin no. 23. Lincoln: Conservation and Survey Division, University of Nebraska, 1965.
Rice	Rice, Otis K. *The Allegheny Frontier: West Virginia Beginnings, 1730–1830.* Lexington: University Press of Kentucky, 1970.
Ronda	Ronda, James P. *Lewis and Clark among the Indians.* Lincoln: University of Nebraska Press, 1984.
Roseboom & Weisenburger	Roseboom, Eugene Holloway, and Francis Phelps Weisenburger. *A History of Ohio.* New York: Prentice-Hall, 1934.
Russell (FTT)	Russell, Carl P. *Firearms, Traps, and Tools of the Mountain Men.* New York: Knopf, 1967.
Russell (GEF)	——. *Guns on the Early Frontiers: A History of Firearms from Colonial Times through the Years of the Western Fur Trade.* Berkeley: University of California Press, 1962.

Saindon   Saindon, Bob. "The Lost Vocabularies of the Lewis and Clark Expedition." *We Proceeded On* 3 (July 1977): 4–6.

Saucier & Seineke   Saucier, Walter J., and Kathrine Wagner Seineke. "François Saucier, Engineer of Fort de Chartres, Illinois." In McDermott (FFW), 199–229.

Sellers   Sellers, Charles Coleman. *Charles Willson Peale.* New York: Charles Scribner's Sons, 1969.

Settle   Settle, Raymond W. "Nathaniel Pryor." In Hafen, 2:277–84.

Skarsten (GD)   Skarsten, M. O. "George Drouillard." In Hafen, 9:69–82.

Skarsten (GDLC)   ——. *George Drouillard, Hunter and Interpreter for Lewis and Clark and Fur Trader, 1807–1810.* Glendale, Calif.: Arthur H. Clark, 1964.

Smith (OI)   Smith, G. Hubert. *Omaha Indians: Ethnohistorical Report on the Omaha People.* New York: Garland, 1974.

Smith (EOI)   Smith, Huron H. *Ethnobotany of the Ojibwe Indians.* Bulletin of the Public Museum of the City of Milwaukee, vol. 4. Milwaukee, Wis.: Public Museum, 1932.

Smith (SSPG)   Smith, James S., and Kathryn. "Sedulous Sergeant, Patrick Gass." *Montana, the Magazine of Western History* 5 (July 1955): 20–27.

South Dakota Guide   *South Dakota: A Guide to the State.* Compiled by the Federal Writers' Project of the Works Progress Administration. American Guide Series. 2d ed. New York: Hastings House, 1952.

Speck   Speck, Gordon. *Breeds and Half-Breeds.* New York: Clarkson N. Potter, 1969.

Steffen   Steffen, Jerome O. *William Clark: Jeffersonian Man on the Frontier.* Norman: University of Oklahoma Press, 1977.

Steinacher & Carlson   Steinacher, Terry L., and Gayle F. Carlson. *Nebraska Highway Archaeological and Historical Salvage Investigations, 1969–1975.* Nebraska State Historical Society, Publications in Anthropology, no. 10. Lincoln: Nebraska State Historical Society, 1983.

Stephens   Stephens, H. A. *Woody Plants of the North Central*

	Plains. Lawrence: University Press of Kansas, 1973.
Stewart (APN)	Stewart, George R. *American Place-Names: A Concise and Selective Dictionary for the Continental United States of America*. New York: Oxford University Press, 1970.
Stewart (AAGS)	Stewart, Henry, Jr. "The American Air Gun School of 1800 (with Corollary Verification of the Lewis and Clark Air Rifle Maker)." *Monthly Bugle*, February 1977, 2–7.
Steyermark	Steyermark, Julian A. *Flora of Missouri*. Ames: Iowa State University Press, 1963.
Stoller	Stoller, Ruth. "Alexander Carson." In Hafen, 9:43–52.
Swanton	Swanton, John R. *The Indian Tribes of North America*. Bureau of American Ethnology, Bulletin 145. Washington, D.C.: Government Printing Office, 1952.
Swenk	Swenk, Myron H. "A History of Nebraska Ornithology: III. Period of the Explorations of the Early Nineteenth Century (1804–1854)." *Nebraska Bird Review* 3 (July 1935): 115–25.
Swetnam & Smith	Swetnam, George, and Helene Smith. *A Guidebook to Historic Western Pennsylvania*. Pittsburgh: University of Pittsburgh Press, 1976.
Taylor	Taylor, E. G. R. *The Haven-Finding Art: A History of Navigation from Odysseus to Captain Cook*. London: Hollis and Carter, 1958.
Threet	Threet, Richard L. "The 'Ionia Volcano' in Dixon County, Nebraska." Abstracted in *Proceedings of the Sixty-fifth Annual Meeting*. Lincoln: Nebraska Academy of Sciences, 1955.
Thwaites (EWT)	Thwaites, Reuben Gold, ed. *Early Western Travels*. 32 vols. Cleveland: Arthur H. Clark, 1904–7.
Thwaites (JR)	——, ed. *The Jesuit Relations and Allied Documents*. 73 vols. Cleveland: Burrows Brothers, 1896–1901.
Thwaites (LC)	——, ed. *Original Journals of the Lewis and Clark Expedition, 1804–1806*. 8 vols. New York: Dodd, Mead, 1904–5.

Tomkins	Tomkins, Calvin. "Annals of Law: The Lewis and Clark Case." *New Yorker*, October 29, 1966.
Trautman	Trautman, Milton B. *The Fishes of Ohio.* Rev. ed. Columbus: Ohio State University Press, 1981.
Trigger	Trigger, Bruce G., ed. *Handbook of North American Indians.* Vol. 15, *Northeast.* Washington, D.C.: Smithsonian Institution Press, 1978.
Tucker	Tucker, Sara Jones, comp. *Indian Villages of the Illinois Country.* Springfield: Illinois State Museum, 1942.
Tyrrell	Tyrrell, Joseph B., ed. *David Thompson's Narrative of His Explorations in Western America, 1784–1812.* Toronto: Champlain Society, 1916.
Unrau	Unrau, William E. *The Kansa Indians: A History of the Wind People, 1673–1873.* Norman: University of Oklahoma Press, 1971.
Vinton	Vinton, Stallo. *John Colter, Discoverer of Yellowstone Park: An Account of His Exploration in 1807 and of His Further Adventures as Hunter, Trapper, Indian Fighter, Pathfinder and Member of the Lewis and Clark Expedition.* New York: Edward Eberstadt, 1926.
Voorhis	Voorhis, Ernest. *Historic Forts and Trading Posts of the French Regime and the English Fur Trading Companies.* Ottawa: Department of the Interior, 1930.
Walker	Walker, Charles M. *History of Athens County, Ohio, and Incidentally of the Ohio Land Company and the First Settlement of the State at Marietta.* . . . Cincinnati: Robert Clarke, 1869.
Wallace	Wallace, W. Stewart, ed. *Documents Relating to the North West Company.* Toronto: Champlain Society, 1934.
Warren	Warren, Gouverneur K. "Original Sketches of a Reconnoissance of the Missouri River from the Northern Boundary of Kansas to a point sixty two miles above Fort Union made during the Summers of 1855 and 1856." Manuscript Map in 39 sheets, Record Group 77, National Archives, Washington, D.C.

Watrous   Watrous, Stephen D., ed. *John Ledyard's Journey
               through Russia and Siberia, 1787–1788: The Jour-
               nal and Selected Letters.* Madison: University of
               Wisconsin Press, 1966.

Wayne   Wayne, W. J. *Guidebook for Field Trip on Urban Geol-
               ogy in Eastern Nebraska.* Lincoln: Nebraska Geo-
               logical Survey, 1971.

Weaver   Weaver, J. E. "Flood Plain Vegetation of the Cen-
               tral Missouri Valley and Contacts of Woodland
               with Prairie." *Ecological Monographs* 30 (Janu-
               ary 1960): 37–64.

Wedel (PHH)   Wedel, Mildred Mott. "The Prehistoric and His-
               toric Habitat of the Missouri and Oto Indians."
               In *Oto and Missouri Indians,* 25–76. New York:
               Garland Publishing, 1974.

Wedel (KA)   Wedel, Waldo R. *An Introduction to Kansas Archeol-
               ogy.* Bureau of American Ethnology, Bulletin
               174. Washington, D.C.: Government Printing
               Office, 1959.

Wedel (PA)   ——. *An Introduction to Pawnee Archeology.* Bureau
               of American Ethnology, Bulletin 112. Washing-
               ton, D.C.: Government Printing Office, 1936.

Wentworth   Wentworth, Edward N. "Dried Meat—Early Man's
               Travel Ration." *Agricultural History* 30 (January
               1956): 2–10.

Weslager   Weslager, C. A. *The Delaware Indians, A History.*
               New Brunswick, N.J.: Rutgers University Press,
               1972.

West Virginia Guide   *West Virginia: A Guide to the Mountain State.* Com-
               piled by workers of the Writers' Program of the
               Work Projects Administration. American Guide
               Series. New York: Oxford University Press,
               1941.

Wheeler   Wheeler, Olin D. *The Trail of Lewis and Clark,
               1804–1806.* 2 vols. New York: G. P. Putnam's
               Sons, 1904.

White   White, Richard. *The Roots of Dependency: Subsis-
               tence, Environment, and Social Change among the
               Choctaws, Pawnees, and Navajos.* Lincoln: Univer-
               sity of Nebraska Press, 1983.

Whitman	Whitman, William. *The Oto.* Columbia University Contributions in Anthropology, vol. 28. New York: Columbia University Press, 1937.
Wilford	Wilford, John Noble. *The Mapmakers.* New York: Knopf, 1981.
Williams	Williams, David. "John Evans' Strange Journey." *American Historical Review* 54 (January 1949): 277–95, and (April 1949): 508–29.
Willman et al.	Willman, H. B., Elwood Atherton, T. C. Buschbach, Charles Collinson, John C. Frye, M. E. Hopkins, Jerry A. Lineback, and Jack A. Simon. *Handbook of Illinois Stratigraphy.* Illinois State Geological Survey Bulletin 95. Urbana: Department of Registration and Education, 1975.
Wittke	Wittke, Carl, ed. *The History of the State of Ohio.* 6 vols. Columbus: Ohio State Archaeological and Historical Society, 1941–44.
Wolff	Wolff, Eldon G. *Air Guns.* Milwaukee, Wis.: Milwaukee Public Museum, 1958.
Wood	Wood, W. Raymond. "William Clark's Mapping in Missouri, 1803–1804." *Missouri Historical Review* 76 (April 1982): 241–52.
Woolworth	Woolworth, Alan R., comp. "The Red Pipestone Quarry of Minnesota." *Minnesota Archaeologist* 42 (1983): 1–137.
Wylie	Wylie, Paul E. *The Essentials of Modern Navigation.* New York: Harper and Brothers, 1941.

Index

This index will serve as an aid to the reader, without being exhaustive. Lewis's and Clark's variant spellings of personal names, place names, names of Indian tribes, and everyday words have compounded the usual problems of indexing a work such as this, which deals with a myriad of subjects. The basic principles are as follows. Correct spellings are used in the index, often without reference to Lewis's and Clark's variants, since a gloss or textual note usually corrects the misspelling. Usual but understandable variants appear in parentheses after the correct word. Distinctive and repeated misspellings (such as Drewyer for Drouillard) are given as cross-references to the correct word. This is particularly the case with names of members of the party and Indian tribes. The notes are indexed more thoroughly here than in most works. This is essential for locating the party by modern place names and identifying species by their current popular and scientific names. Those place names that locate campsites or that give information on geographic situations associated with the expedition are of primary concern. Incidental place names in the notes do not appear in the index. The expedition's camps are listed by state and county.